Colombo

Madras

Bombay

Karachi

Calcutta
New Delhi

Kabul

Tashkent

Tehran

Abadan

Baku

Aden

Addis Ababa

Riyadh

Khartoum

Cairo

Ankara

Novosibirsk

Moscow

Belgrade

Rome

Tunis

Tripoli

Lourenço Marques

Johannesburg

Capetown

Mombasa

Elizabethville

Nova Lisboa

A F R I C A

Fort Lamy

Lagos

Novy Port

Leningrad

EUROPE

Warsaw

Algiers

Dickson I.

Mur-
mansk

Berlin

Oslo

Paris

Casablanca

Monrovia

Nordvik

London

Madrid

Lisbon

Dakar

SVALBARD

ARCTIC OCEAN

+
North
Pole

Reykjavik

AZORES

O C E A N

Thule

Pt. Barrow

Godthab

Anchorage

Gander

Goose Bay

Natal

NORTH

Edmonton

Ottawa

Limestone

New York

A T L A N T I C

Vancouver

Seattle

Chicago

Washington

San Francisco

Los Angeles

Miami

Habana

TRINIDAD

Caracas

Manaus

Rio de Janeiro

AMERICA

Mexico City

Panama

Bogotá

SOUTH

AMERICA

Quito

La Paz

Lima

Buenos Aires

INTERNATIONAL POLITICS

THE MACMILLAN COMPANY
NEW YORK · CHICAGO
DALLAS · ATLANTA · SAN FRANCISCO
LONDON · MANILA

THE MACMILLAN COMPANY
OF CANADA, LIMITED
TORONTO

INTERNATIONAL POLITICS

Foundations of International Relations

Norman J. Padelford

MASSACHUSETTS INSTITUTE OF TECHNOLOGY

George A. Lincoln

UNITED STATES MILITARY ACADEMY

NEW YORK   THE MACMILLAN COMPANY

PREFACE

FRANCIS BACON once spoke of Science as the "endless frontier." Today, the peoples of this country and other free nations are being increasingly impressed with the fact that international politics is a realm of endless frontier. Problems of vast complexity, some filled with the portent of great dangers, arise in seemingly endless succession, and in some instances defy solution. Directly and materially the effects of the contemporary international scene come home to touch the life of every citizen. They affect our tax burdens. They place a large proportion of our young manhood in the armed forces. And our very security depends upon the outcome of the conflicts among the ideological systems contending for the mind of man and the struggles among powers armed with nuclear weapons.

In a democracy such as ours, with its extensive privileges of citizen participation in the conduct of public affairs, a large responsibility rests upon all to be informed of the interests, the objectives, and the course of events affecting our nation. The policies and actions of the government must accord in the long run with the will and the wish of the citizenry as a whole.

Elihu Root, one of America's most eminent statesmen, writing in 1922 on the bearing of democracy upon United States participation in foreign affairs, trenchantly observed that if the diplomacy of a popular democracy were to be a success it would be subject to one "inevitable condition." This, said Mr. Root, is that the people "must acquire a knowledge of the fundamental and essential facts and principles upon which the relations of nations depend. Without such knowledge there can be no intelligent discussion and consideration of foreign policy and diplomatic conduct. Misrepresentation will have a clear field and ignorance and error will make wild work with foreign relations." [1] Writing three decades later in 1954, Walter Lippmann remarked that "We have suddenly acquired responsibilities for which we were not prepared—for which we are not now prepared—for which, I am very much afraid, we are not now preparing ourselves" adequately. [2]

[1] Elihu Root, "A Requisite for the Success of Popular Diplomacy," *Foreign Affairs,* Oct., 1922.
[2] Walter Lippmann, "The Shortage of Education," *The Atlantic,* May, 1954.

v

The authors believe that only as the citizens of free nations acquire a knowledge of the "fundamental and essential facts and principles" of international affairs can they prepare themselves to exercise fully their high responsibility. Our objective has been to stress those fundamental elements and foundational principles which we believe underlie the policies and actions of nations generally. We hope that the facts, principles, and trends which we have described and discussed will give the reader a basis of understanding which materially assists him in comprehending the issues and problems facing this nation.

In writing a book of modest length upon a subject having almost infinite ramifications, we recognize that there are many aspects of international relations which we have had to pass by or mention briefly. Many important matters often a subject of complete books, or the lifework of distinguished scholars and statesmen, have had to be dealt with in single pages or even a paragraph. We regret the necessity for such concision and offer the numerous references in the footnotes for those who would pursue some subjects further. We also acknowledge that there may be differences of opinion on the selection of topics and the emphasis to be given various subjects, and can only trust that our presentation may add one more way of viewing the field of foreign affairs. We have tried to state the pros and cons on obscure or controversial questions and to present the thread of world affairs fairly as we have seen it.

The authors are indebted to a large circle of colleagues and friends for helpful suggestions and constructive criticism in the preparation of this volume. Among those who have reviewed and assisted in revisions of drafts of the manuscript have been Dr. Joseph E. Johnson, President of the Carnegie Endowment for International Peace; Professors Leland Goodrich, Oliver J. Lissitzyn, and John H. Wuorinen of Columbia University; Professors Gordon Allport, Merle Fainsod, William Langer, Arthur Smithies, and Derwent Whittlesey of Harvard University; Professor Stephen B. Jones of Yale University; Colonel Andrew J. Goodpaster of SHAPE; Professor John Masland of Dartmouth College; Professor Michael J. Flack of Vassar College; Dean Robert B. Stewart of the Fletcher School of Law and Diplomacy; Dean John E. Burchard of the Massachusetts Institute of Technology; and Dr. Raymond Dennett of the Scandinavian-American Foundation.

We express our appreciation to members of our departments. Through long and repeated deliberations with us, through contributions of fact and substance, through reading the manuscript, and by unceasing encouragement they have helped us to complete this task. Especial thanks are due in this connection to Professors James E. Boyce, Roy Olton, and Harris Proctor, Mr. John Rawlinson, Mr. Robert Humphrey, Mrs. Eleanor Kearns Bluhm, Miss Barbara Conner and Miss Sarah Louise Kriner at MIT. Among those at the United States Military Academy to whom we are particularly indebted are Colonel Herman Beukema; Lt. Colonels C. A. Cannon, William Clark, and James Holland; and Captains R. W. Coonrod, A. A. Jordan, R. J. Klemmer, T. H. McLendon, W. W. Posvar, and W. H. Griffith. We also express our gratitude to Miss Beatrice Rogers, editorial assistant of the Department of Economics at MIT, who kindly typed our final manuscript.

Because the picture is often worth a thousand words we have included many maps and charts. Mr. Lucas Manditch of *The New York Times* assisted us in obtaining permission to use the copyrighted maps originally appearing in that newspaper. Many of the MIT Series of maps (some of which are published separately by the Denoyer-Geppert Company of Chicago) were drawn by Mr. Robert C. Forget of Boston.

Many others in educational institutions and within government have aided us with comments, and with the assemblage and correction of facts. We thank them all for their constructive effort in our behalf. We of course absolve them from all errors both as to fact and to judgment.

It should be emphasized that the authors are writing altogether as private citizens and are not undertaking to present the policy view of the United States Government or any agency thereof.

This book has been prepared on a line-by-line collaborative basis. We here record our respective appreciation not only for our colleague's labors but also of the give and take through which the final manuscript was achieved. Finally, we wish to acknowledge the debt which is owing to our wives and families for the encouragement they have given us along the way and for the many sacrifices they have endured while we have pursued the tasks of authorship.

NORMAN J. PADELFORD
GEORGE A. LINCOLN

July, 1954

CONTENTS

V. ORGANIZING THE INTERNATIONAL COMMUNITY: THE SEARCH FOR COLLECTIVE SECURITY

LIST OF ILLUSTRATIONS

PART I

Introduction

CHAPTER I

The Focus of World Politics

INTRODUCTION

The relations between the principal states of the world are increasingly becoming one of the most important aspects of contemporary life. Hardly a day passes when the newspapers and radio broadcasts do not report some event affecting the national security, well-being, and peace of millions of people. This may be some political or military action in Europe, Asia, or the Middle East. It may be the emergence of an economic or political crisis in some vitally situated country. It may be a clash among the Great Powers in a meeting of the United Nations. It may be the development of a new scientific or techno-logical device that increases the industrial and military strength of one group of states and thus heightens the fear of their opponents. Owing to many com-plex causes mankind has reached a point where events and forces originating at any place on the globe are apt to affect the lives of men and the policies of states everywhere.

However true it may be, because of modern means of communication and transportation and because of the growing interdependence of people every-where, that man is now living in what Wendell Willkie once called "One World," the fact remains that politically mankind is divided into some seventy sovereign states. Each of these states exercises complete authority over a defi-nite part of the Earth's surface. The contacts and associations between the governments of these states form the basis and the substance of international relations and of world politics.

THE FIELD OF INTERNATIONAL RELATIONS

In the broadest sense, the field of international relations comprises myriads of contacts among individuals, business organizations, cultural institutions, and political personalities of many different countries.

Whenever people travel abroad, or whenever a business concern exports its

3

manufactures or seeks a concession to develop some natural resource overseas, international relations are established. The same occurs when a religious body sends missionaries to work in another land, or a humanitarian agency such as the Red Cross sends relief to a country suffering from disaster.

Private activities such as these often far outnumber the official dealings between governments. They are an important part of the fabric of modern civilization to which we owe much of our knowledge of the world. Our standards of living have been raised by the flow of commodities which private international trade makes possible. Our progress in science and technology has been aided by interchange of knowledge among scientists which private international contacts have facilitated. And in times of crisis the friendship of other peoples has often been a valuable asset to security and welfare.

When people speak of "international relations," however, they are usually thinking of the relationships between states as such. This is to be expected in view of the fact that it is states which make the vital decisions affecting peace and war, and that it is their governments which have the authority to regulate business, travel, commerce, use of resources, political ideas, territorial jurisdiction, nationality, communications, employment of armed forces, and other aspects of international affairs.

INTERNATIONAL POLITICS

The relationships between states we describe as "international politics," that is, the interaction of state policies. This is the core of contemporary international relations. It is to this primarily that we shall direct our attention.

What is the province of international politics? Briefly, it deals with "those forces which mold the foreign policies of national states, the manner in which they are exercised, and the influences which limit their effectiveness." [1] This is a complex segment of human affairs.

The forces which shape the actions and relationships of states spring in the first instance from the roots of human behavior—individual and group desires, social consciousness, and human suspicions and fears. They are conditioned by the geographical facts of each state. They are influenced by the characteristics of the population, the institutions of government, the status of the national economy, the qualities of leadership which happen to prevail at any given time, the ideologies that capture men's minds and emotions, and perhaps most of all in our times, by the force of nationalism. Over and above these basic factors, which have many nuances and subtle connections, the international politics of states are affected, as are local and national politics, by the

[1] Grayson Kirk, *The Study of International Relations in American Colleges and Universities* (New York, 1947), p. 10.

experiences of national history warning men of what is safe and what is to be feared, what is desirable and what is to be avoided.

We may say that four tendencies, generally shared among states, exercise varying influences upon international politics. These are (1) a tendency of some peoples to seek jurisdiction over territory and other peoples; (2) a desire for communication with other countries; (3) a striving for improved standards of living and for an expanding economy; and (4) a search for strength and for national security.

These tendencies, added to the differing interests of states, inevitably bring the states into contact with one another and lead them to take actions necessitating adjustment of their relationships with one another.

Difficulties Involved. The conduct of international relations is often fraught with difficulties due to barriers of language, differing cultures, and variations of race. Current relationships are influenced by suspicions growing out of past competitions and conflicts. Differences of viewpoint are frequently nurtured by nationalistic sentiments or magnified by propaganda. Domestic political interests may tie the hands of governments, or commit them to momentary actions seriously affecting long-term national interests and objectives. And behind the foreign policy of aggressively minded states may stand a military organization prepared to support the political arm by force if called upon, thereby endangering the peace and security of other states.

Another complicating factor of world politics in a world composed of over seventy sovereign states [2] is that a major move in international politics now entails negotiations and adjustments among a large number of governments. This is not an insignificant fact. For, although the industrial and technical revolutions have introduced profound changes in the physical bases of international relationships, the mechanics of international politics still revolve about the procedures of negotiation, treaty-making, international conferences, and the advancement of security through alliances, blocs, and international organization. These often require laborious effort. They may consume precious time when peace and security are at stake in the face of aggression. They may be productive of satisfactory agreements. However, the history of international relations has been strewn with many treaties and agreements that have gone unfulfilled or have been denounced and abrogated because they did not satisfy national interests.

Struggle for Power. The possession of power, in the broad sense, is a *sine qua non* in any society for the advancement of group interests and for the maintenance of law and order. In an international society where there is no

[2] The United States in 1953 had diplomatic relations with seventy-five countries. Ninety-one political entities were members of the Universal Postal Union.

over-all government to regulate the conduct of states, or to protect national rights and interests, states must seek for themselves the strength to achieve and to safeguard these ends.

Spurred on by need and by national feelings, states continually seek to improve their positions economically and politically. To attain these objectives they adopt and pursue internal policies aimed at strengthening their national economies, enlarging their industrial capacity, building up their armed forces, expanding their national domain, increasing their population, and promoting their national unity. And to supplement their efforts at home, states externally seek new markets abroad, added sources of raw materials, preferential trade arrangements, positions of influence in international gatherings and organizations, friends and allies, and diplomatic and military victories. The competitions which arise among states in the pursuit of these policies readily lead to struggles for influence and power.

Dynamic Character. Since states are generally seeking to increase their influence, the relationships among them are never static. Their relative strengths do not remain fixed for any length of time. Instead, as the patterns of power change, readjustments in national policies inevitably follow.

Policies may change as governments come and go. States that were friendly under one set of circumstances may drift apart or come into conflict under another. Ideologies rise and wane and in doing so may alter the motivations and alignments of nations. Developments in science and technology constantly affect the relationships between states. The spread of industrialization and of nationalism to hitherto underdeveloped lands is releasing new economic and social forces altering existing relationships among many countries.

The essence of international politics is the continual interplay of state policies within these kaleidoscopic patterns. And among the Great Powers in particular the course of politics is in large measure governed by a struggle for some balance favorable to their own national interest.[3]

One legacy of this incessant struggle is that suspicions, jealousies, and rivalries permeate interstate relationships and make permanent harmonious relations difficult. Because of this, as well as because of the widespread belief in the nation-state as a supreme value, states naturally prefer to remain independent rather than submit to a universal dominion whereby any one state or political system would dominate all.

THE COMMUNITY OF STATES

The relations between states do not take place in a vacuum. They occur in what men have called the society or community of states. This is not the

3 See G. L. Schwarzenberger, "Towards the Climax," *World Affairs*, Oct., 1950, pp. 385–400.

"world" in a vague, indefinite sense. It is the total of politically mutually interacting sovereign states existing at a particular time. In a juridical sense, international relations take place between the states which recognize one another as such, which engage in diplomatic relations with each other, and which agree to be bound by the principles of international law.[4]

The idea of a society of states can be traced back to the ancient Stoic philosophers. The society as it exists today embraces a group of sovereign states, unequal in power, but equal juridically in status. Each independent state claims the right to exercise an exclusive jurisdiction within defined territorial limits.[5]

Nature of Community. The society of states is not a community in the same sense as a nation-state. The "community" has no constitution. It has no formal structure or government. There are few values universally shared. There may be a consensus among states at times, but the community as such has no corporate will that makes itself consistently felt independently of the sovereign states. And there has been to date little social consciousness of a world community as a whole. Some states have shared goals, but these do not as yet extend to the creation of a world or regional government that would supersede national sovereignty and possess authority to bind states regardless of their national interests or without their consent.

In the same way as the struggle for power is perhaps the major dynamic force of international politics, so national sovereignty, the legal expression of national feeling, may be said to be the dominant feature of the society of states.

Composition and Membership. Originally the "legal" community was restricted to the European, Christian states.[6] Russia was not admitted until the end of the seventeenth century. The recognition of the United States in 1783 and of the Latin American Republics in the nineteenth century extended the community beyond Europe. After the admission of Turkey in 1856, the circle was widened to include non-Western and non-Christian countries until it became truly global after World War I. Today the community contains some seventy recognized states of the most varying cultural backgrounds, political systems, religious faiths, and economic development. Sixty of these states are

[4] For analysis of the society of states concept see especially Percy C. Corbett, *Law and Society in the Relations of States* (New York, 1951), chs. 2–4; Edwin D. Dickinson, *Law and Peace* (Philadelphia, 1951), ch. 1; Sir Alfred Zimmern, "International Law and Social Consciousness," *Grotius Society Transactions* (London, 1935), vol. xx, pp. 25–44.

[5] T. A. Walker, *A History of the Law of Nations* (Cambridge, 1899), p. 148. On the Congress of Westphalia and its significance see D. J. Hill, *A History of Diplomacy in the International Development of Europe* (New York, 1924), vol. II, pp. 592–607; L. Gross, "The Peace of Westphalia, 1648–1948," *Am. J. Int. Law,* Jan., 1948.

[6] E. Gibbon says in his *Decline and Fall of the Roman Empire* (London, 1781), ch. 38, that the original society was made up of "twelve powerful, though unequal kingdoms, three respectable commonwealths and a variety of smaller though independent states."

now Members of the United Nations. It cannot be said that this organization is as yet wholly representative of the society of states. Should the fourteen political entities now applicants for membership be admitted, however, it would embrace virtually the entire political community.

Not every entity that proclaims itself to be a state is automatically accepted into the society of states. Acceptance, and accordance of the rights and privileges of coequal status, depend upon "recognition" by the greater part of the existing states.[7] This must be gained through establishing independence and sovereignty as a fact to the satisfaction of others, then winning friends and supporters among the states, and finally gaining recognition by these states either individually or collectively.

Not all countries succeed in obtaining recognition. Japan's puppet Manchukuo, for example, was never able to secure general recognition from its inception in 1933 to its downfall in 1945.[8]

Participation in the international community carries with it no positive assurance that a state once recognized will forever enjoy full territorial integrity, political independence, diplomatic relations, or juridical personality. Political existence has been precarious for many. Numerous countries have disappeared through conquest, merger, or disintegration. Korea, for instance, ceased to be an independent state from 1910 to 1945. Poland lost its existence as a sovereign state during the nineteenth century when its territories were partitioned among Prussia, Russia, and Austria-Hungary. Thus the society has a changing composition, and among its members continual variations occur in relative strength and influence.

THE INTERNATIONAL POLITICAL PROCESS

The various means by which states endeavor to protect their national interests, to adjust their relationships with one another, and to settle international differences constitute the international political process. Generally speaking, there are two broad classifications of procedures: (1) routine, peaceful measures and (2) measures of pressure or violence.

Peaceful Procedures. Most relations between states are handled, as are private and national affairs, by discussion, negotiation, and agreement. These procedures involve diplomatic exchanges, conferences, the negotiation and conclusion of treaties and agreements, establishment of trade and economic

7 On existence and recognition see J. L. Brierly, *The Law of Nations* (4th ed., Oxford, 1949), pp. 122–141; H. W. Briggs, *The Law of Nations* (2nd ed., New York, 1952), pp. 99–132; H. Lauterpacht, *Recognition in International Law* (Cambridge, 1947); P. C. Jessup, *Modern Law of Nations* (New York, 1948), ch. 2.

8 The so-called Mongolian Peoples Republic has not been accepted outside of the Soviet orbit.

arrangements, and political collaboration of many kinds. These affairs may be disposed of directly between two or more states through the ordinary channels of diplomacy, that is, through the established contacts of Foreign Offices and diplomatic representatives, or they may be handled through some international organization such as the United Nations or the Organization of American States.

Assertions of national position, demands, and clashes of policy inevitably accompany the international political process. These are to be expected from states which represent large bodies of people and powerful interests. As a consequence, economic, political, and moral pressures are frequently brought to bear by one government upon another in this process in order to obtain various advantages.

Differences and disputes sometimes become so acute that mediation, conciliation, or arbitration provide the only means of peaceful adjustment. At times clashes of national policy become so serious that one of the parties, or some third state, may appeal to an international organization or world tribunal in an effort to resolve a crisis or to maintain international peace and security.

Because international disputes make headline news, the public is often more conscious of these situations than it is of the run-of-the-mill grist of foreign affairs. As a result, popular opinion is inclined to view world politics as a sequence of crises. For the most part, foreign relations are unobtrusively transacted through routine diplomatic procedures in which governments endeavor to find bases of agreement that will not only satisfy their own national interests but will at the same time produce international accord. These agreements constitute a web of commitments by which states voluntarily make certain pledges to one another and establish mutual links.

Competition and Conflict. Throughout the history of international relations, states have competed over territory and national jurisdiction, over access to raw materials and markets, and over relative positions in the international community. This is to be expected in a world situation where there are limited resources, rising populations, and pressing economic needs, and where national interest is accepted as the supreme criterion of national policies. As long as this situation continues, competition and conflict between states must be anticipated.

The competing character of relations among states does not, of course, always result in war. Rivalry, struggle, and war have, however, been an almost incessant accompaniment of international politics.[9] These have resulted partly from the ambitions of leaders and peoples, and partly from deep-seated na-

[9] Walter Lippmann, "The Rivalry of Nations," *The Atlantic Monthly*, Feb., 1948. See Quincy Wright, *A Study of War* (Chicago, 1942); and ch. 10 below.

tional, social, economic, and religious differences.[10] The lack of strong, cohesive forces within the community of states, the power of nationalist ideology and the absence of an international organization powerful enough to minimize conflicts within peaceful limits have permitted a large number of disputes among states to result in violent conflicts. As one writer has said, "There is a tendency for conflict to become total and absolute, and to split the community of nations into halves which would destroy one another in absolute war." [11]

Alexander Hamilton, writing in *The Federalist* papers more than a century and a half ago, put his finger on the roots of these conflicts. "To presume a want of motives [for violent contests between disunited political bodies]," he wrote, "would be to forget that men are ambitious, vindictive and rapacious. To look for a continuation of harmony between a number of independent unconnected sovereignties, situated in the same neighborhood [now the entire globe], would be to disregard the uniform course of human events, and to set at defiance the accumulated experience of ages."

"The causes of hostility among nations are innumerable," observed Hamilton. "There are some which have a general and almost constant operation upon the collective bodies of society. Of this description are the love of power, or the desire of pre-eminence and dominion—the jealousy of power, or the desire of equality and safety. There are others which are more circumscribed . . . within their spheres: such are the rivalships and competitions of commerce between commercial nations. And there are others, not less numerous than either of the former, which take their origin entirely in private passions; in the attachments, enmities, interests, hopes and fears, of leading individuals in the communities of which they are members." [12]

The resolution of differences between states is difficult because of the complex factors, powerful organizations, and often heightened emotions which become involved. When tensions do not become too great, or when some acceptable recourse for adjustment other than the use of force appears, peace may be maintained. In this circumstance the conflict may either be "settled" in a peaceful manner, or it may drift into a more quiescent condition and ultimately cease to be a dangerous problem for international relations.

Tensions Affecting International Relations. Tensions continually beset national and international relationships, so much so that some psychologists say that we live in a "climate of tensions and hostility." [13] These tensions stem in part from man's nature, and in other respects from the conditions surrounding modern social life.

---

10 Quincy Wright "The Nature of Conflict," *Western Pol. Quar.*, June, 1951, pp. 193–209.
11 *Ibid.*, p. 208.
12 *The Federalist*, No. VI.
13 George W. Kisker (ed.), *World Tension, The Psychopathology of International Relations* (New York, 1951), p. 297.

The industrial and technological revolutions characterizing the nineteenth and twentieth centuries, by disrupting established cultures and institutions, have contributed to this situation through the social processes of urbanization, mass production, economic fluctuation, and the destructiveness of modern war which have imparted a widespread feeling of insecurity. Moreover, the liberal democratic ideas associated with the development of Europe in the last three hundred years have been given a tremendous impetus by the political and industrial revolutions that have followed in their train. Working together or combating one another, these various influences have given rise to insecurity and to ideological cleavages.

Whether these tensions develop into conflicts and wars depends in the final analysis upon the policies and decisions of the governments involved. In many situations tensions can be controlled. But at times, when conflicts become too continuous or strike at the heart of national security or pride, they become difficult to arrest.

Pressure Politics and Violence. When tensions and conflicts reach a certain point, states tend to exert pressure upon their opponents in order to bring about, in accordance with their own self-interest, a change in the policies or attitudes of the other party. War is the ultimate manifestation of this effort. But there are many less violent ways in which states can attempt to exercise pressure or coercion upon others.

Propaganda campaigns may be waged to undermine the position or the morale of an opposing state or to obtain other political advantage. Economic pressures may be applied by manipulating credits, instituting embargoes or trade wars, seizing foreign assets, or terminating treaties. Appeals may be made to international bodies for support or for condemnation of the policy of an opposing state. Alliances may be formed against a state or group of states. Armed forces may be mobilized and moved to the vicinity of another state (the "show of force") to put pressure upon its government. Force may be handled in other ways so to create a "war of nerves" to induce the other party to change its policy. Diplomatic relations may be severed. Finally, war itself may be resorted to as an instrument of national policy. All of these techniques have been employed in modern times.

The possibility of a resort to threats or to the use of armed force always looms in the background of international politics. In a large share of the relations between states these are not employed. Between friendly states the armed forces possessed by each, or potentially available to it, play little part in daily political dealings. But in situations where irreconcilable vital interests come into serious clash, the size and readiness of forces can become a determining factor. States generally regard the use of force as legitimate for the defense or protection of their national interests, while some states have regarded the aggressive use of armed force as a justifiable means of advancing their national interests abroad.

The Place of War. War has occupied a prominent place throughout the history of world politics. This is amply indicated by the fact that since 1500 there have been some 278 international wars, including at least 15 general wars involving all or most of the strongest states.[14]

To the leaders of states, war has, in the past, often been viewed as a political instrument—"a continuation of political transactions by different means."[15] As President Eisenhower once put it, war is "an extension of political policy to the field of force." Through resort to war, whether taken up offensively or defensively, states endeavor to impose their will upon one another.

Arnold Toynbee, scanning the horizon of history, challenges the institution of war. Acknowledging that the only justification for war is peace, he finds that peace has never dependably followed from war. Peace arrangements have seldom prevented the recurrence of war between nations.[16] Fortunately, perhaps, the use of armed force for total war has now become "too ponderous and costly a weapon to use except when the stakes are so high that national existence demands it."[17]

The costly wars that states have fought, and the cataclysmic devastation that could result from a total atomic war, are sobering realities of international politics. Happily, most states are satisfied to seek their objectives by peaceful rather than by forceful means. The majority of them have joined the United Nations for the express purpose, as the Charter states, of saving "succeeding generations from the scourge of war" (Preamble). And they have committed themselves to "settle their international disputes by peaceful means in such a manner that international peace and security, and justice are not endangered," and "to refrain from the threat or use of force against the territorial integrity or political independence of any State, or in any other manner inconsistent with the Purposes of the United Nations" (Article 2).

Whether this resolve will be any more effective in keeping international political action within peaceful bounds than previous treaty proclamations have been can be demonstrated only with the passage of time. The number of states subscribing to these principles may be notable, but numbers alone are

---

14 Quincy Wright, *Study of War*, vol. I, appendix xx.

15 Karl von Clausewitz, *On War* (Trans. by J. J. Graham; new rev. ed., London, 1918), vol. I, xxiii. See essay on Clausewitz's theories in E. M. Earle (ed.), *Makers of Modern Strategy* (Princeton, 1944), ch. 5.

16 Arnold Toynbee's *War and Civilization* (ed. by Albert V. Fowler, New York, 1950), presents a detailed analysis of his views on war.

17 Grayson Kirk, *The Study of International Relations in American Colleges and Universities* (New York, 1947), p. 13.

no sure guide. States remain sovereign; they are all subject to the influence of political and social forces. Points of view change as circumstances alter. There is little doubt that world opinion has become increasingly opposed to the arbitrary use of force and coercion in international affairs. Nevertheless, the United Nations Charter recognizes the right of each state to retain national armed forces with "the inherent right of individual or collective self-defense" (Article 51), and it bases the process of maintaining and enforcing international peace and security upon the supply of "armed forces, assistance, and facilities" by the Member states.[18] The best hope of dissuading a potential aggressor from using violence within the community of states will continue to reside in those states that wish to preserve peace and still maintain sufficient armed strength and unity of purpose to make it clear to the government of an aggressor that resort to war will lead to a costly fight and probable or certain defeat.

THE PROBLEM OF CHANGE

The achievement of a satisfactory adjustment between dynamic and static elements within the state system has always been one of the chief problems in international politics.

This problem becomes acute when some ruler or government adopts a policy of aggrandizement at the expense of others, or when a previously defeated state undertakes to change peace treaty arrangements or to win back territories taken from it. Revolutionary political forces and ideologies also give rise to the problem, for these forces are seldom willing to compromise in their drive to win additional adherents.

The Limitations of Diplomacy. The function of diplomacy is to carry out the policies of a nation in the most effective manner. When differences arise between states, diplomacy is available to help them to find ways and means of reconciling their differences. Diplomacy cannot always succeed in this mission, however, when nations are unwilling to alter irreconcilable positions. Stalemates can and do develop. In such situations relationships easily become taut. Tensions rise and a crisis develops in which both sides are prone to consider the possibility of using force. Once this point is reached it is not easy for either side to retreat from its position. The negotiating process becomes frozen by mutual suspicions. Nations resort to armaments in the hope of so changing the balance of power that some modification can be brought about, either peacefully or, if need be, by the use of force. Competitive arming is frequently accompanied by a competitive race for allies and strategic positions. From these steps a new cycle of tensions arises in which each side

[18] Articles 43–49.

becomes increasingly suspicious of every move of the other. Arrangement of a mutually acceptable change may then become impossible. In the end, war may seem a more desirable choice than unending tension and fear.

This was the course of international politics from 1931 to World War II after Japan had embarked upon its imperialistic venture in the Far East and Hitler had set Germany on the path of changing the territorial arrangements and balance of power established by the Treaty of Versailles. There are ominous elements of a similar trend in Great Power relationships since 1945.

At one time changes could be composed within Europe by adjusting the balance of power among the European states. But since the first decade of the present century, the European states alone have been unable to balance the power of such states as Germany and the Soviet Union without bringing extra-European powers into the balancing process, and this in itself has produced new problems of world change.

Psychological Approaches. Another approach to the problem is that of trying to get at and to adjust the psychological causes of war. This is expressed in the philosophy that "since wars begin in the minds of men, it is in the minds of men that the defenses of peace must be constructed." [19] Following this conception an eminent group of scientists recently attempted a preliminary analysis of the tensions affecting international understanding. In conclusion they observed that "the problem of peace is the problem of keeping group and national tensions and aggressions within manageable proportions, and of directing them toward ends that are at the same time personally and socially constructive." [20] Although *The New Yorker* may jibe that "to date, apparently, no distinguished generals or admirals or parliamentarians anywhere have troubled to read" this report, it is conceivable that studies of this nature may ultimately throw some useful light on ways of reducing tensions in international politics.

INCREASING EMPLOYMENT OF INTERNATIONAL ORGANIZATION

One hundred years ago there was no regularly organized body that could deal with the world's political problems; there was no international administrative agency; there was no world court. There was only one international technical commission—the Rhine River Commission. Today the international community has the United Nations with its General Assembly, Security Council, Economic and Social Council, Trusteeship Council, International Court of Justice, ten affiliated Specialized Agencies, and fifteen more or less permanent

19 Constitution of the United Nations Educational, Scientific and Cultural Organization.
20 Hadley Cantril (ed.), *Tensions That Cause Wars* (Urbana, 1950), p. 18. See also Otto Klineberg, *Tensions Affecting International Understanding, A Survey of Research,* Social Science Research Council Bulletin 62 (New York, 1950).

International Commissions. In addition, there is the Permanent Court of Arbitration at The Hague, numerous technical organizations not directly connected with the United Nations, and a series of regional bodies.

These provide according to their charters a set of mechanisms designed to deal with virtually "any question" or "situation" of international relations "not essentially within the domestic jurisdiction of any state."

Many of these agencies, including the United Nations Security Council and the General Assembly, have been organized so that they may be able to function continuously. The agendas of some of these bodies require months of diplomatic meetings. Their debates range over practically the entire spectrum of international affairs. Preparation for meetings of these organizations, servicing the delegations attending them, and implementing the resolutions passed by them have become some of the major aspects of foreign affairs. Contests for position within the organizations and over their agendas and resolutions are today one of the most prominent features of international politics. Seventy-five years ago the United States was not appropriating a dollar for international organization. In 1951 the budget of the United Nations—not including the specialized agencies—was $47,798,600. To this the United States was contributing 38.92 per cent.

Usefulness of Organizations. States have turned to increasing use of international organizations because they afford a convenient means of getting representatives of many states together periodically to discuss questions of common concern. They provide an institutionalized setting within which situations of stress and change may be discussed in the presence of a broader participation than that of conflicting parties alone, and through which the interests and efforts of a large number of states can be concerted. More than this, the public nature of the meetings of the various international organizations responds to the belief in the merits of "open diplomacy" which Western democratic peoples have held.

The creation of these multipartite organizations constitutes a step in the direction of bringing the world community more closely together politically and of conducting its business upon an orderly community-wide basis. Their existence provides a means of focusing international "opinion" on crucial issues, as well as a medium for bringing about joint action against states refusing to recognize the rights of others or attempting to change the *status quo* by violence.

Being composed of representatives of sovereign states, the international organizations now in existence can proceed in any instance only as far as the instructions to the various delegations from their home governments permit. In many cases these bodies have been useful in elucidating issues and finding formulae of agreement. When grave crises arise, an organization of sovereign states always faces the possibility that the participants will be reluctant to approve measures that may expose them to the necessity of using their own armed forces to prevent or stop aggression. This was the stumbling block of the League of Nations when Japan, Italy, and Germany committed the aggressions that led to World War II. It is a latent possibility always before the United Nations. Insistence on peaceful international procedures makes the handling of aggressive political forces difficult when the community has no wholly dependable basis for the enforcement of its collective opinion or will.

Search for Further Guarantees. The limitations inherent in diplomacy and in the contemporary international organizations have led to recurrent searches for more effective guarantees of peace and security. At San Francisco in 1945 a conscientious effort was made by the states represented there to build a United Nations stronger and more universal than the League of Nations. In some ways the statesmen succeeded in this effort; in other ways they produced a mechanism with serious shortcomings, as we shall see in a later chapter.

Since 1945 there has been a stream of proposals to "strengthen" world organization. Some would lay greater stress upon the General Assembly of the United Nations, thereby seeking to by-pass the veto in the Security Council. Some would build up stronger regional bodies along the patterns of the North Atlantic Treaty and the Organization of American States. Some favor limiting national sovereignty along the lines blueprinted by the Acheson-Lilienthal-Baruch proposals for the international control of atomic energy. Others would strike out toward some federation of the democracies, or toward world government merging national sovereignty into a supranational body, even though such extreme measures might open a Pandora's box of world domination by one power or political force.

THE INTANGIBLE ELEMENTS

In the final analysis, progress in international relations depends upon the intangibles of life: the willingness of statesmen, politicians, and peoples to cooperate with other nations in pursuance of mutual advantages; the amount of knowledge, good will, and friendliness, or of suspicion and hostility, that prevail; the relative strength and determination of the forces of right, justice, mercy, and tolerance throughout the world; the strength of aggressive elements bent on satisfaction of narrow passions and hatreds.

These intangible factors cannot be measured. They cannot be produced or eliminated by any neat formula of organization or supranational government. But they are a very real part of the setting of international relations. They can and do exercise powerful, though often unseen, influences. And in so far as possible they must be considered in the calculations of national policy and of international relationships.

It is not easy to distinguish in the history of international relations a steady upward curve of peace or constructive achievement. Instead there have been a series of ups and downs—periods of international accord and periods of conflict and destruction. In all, one can sense some rhythmic movement, as in the vastness of the ocean. By triangulating the crests with some of the bench marks of human history there are evidences that in its international relations mankind is being borne forward toward some ultimate destiny. From an age of complete anarchy we are moving through an era of unprecedented organizational activity. The end could be an atomic war in which the human race would obliterate itself. Or it could be a gradual progression toward some more perfect balancing of international order and human freedom.

The challenge this presents, to private individuals as well as to statesmen, is one which will be constantly in the background as we study the fundamentals and problems of international relations.

In the chapters that follow we shall first seek to explore some of the factors that affect a country's external position and condition the policies which it adopts. Following this we shall consider how national policies are made and applied, familiarizing ourselves with some of the interrelationships of domestic and international politics. Finally, we shall examine the international political process and some of the principal problems besetting contemporary international affairs.

SUGGESTED READINGS

Edward H. Carr, *Twenty Years Crisis, 1919–1939* (London, 1940).

W. Friedman, *An Introduction to World Politics* (Toronto, 1951).

Norman Hill, *Contemporary World Politics* (New York, 1954).

Thorsten V. Kalijarvi and Associates, *Modern World Politics* (3d ed., New York, 1953).

Grayson Kirk, *The Study of International Relations* (New York, 1947).

Salvador De Madariaga, *Theory and Practice in International Relations* (Philadelphia, 1937).

Hans J. Morgenthau, *Politics Among Nations* (2nd ed., New York, 1954).

Norman D. Palmer and Howard C. Perkins, *International Relations* (Boston, 1953).

Frederick B. Schuman, *International Politics* (5th ed., New York, 1953).

Georg Schwarzenberger, *Power Politics* (New York, 1952).

Harold and Margaret Sprout, *Foundations of National Power* (Princeton, 1952).

Robert Strausz-Hupé and Stefan T. Possony, *International Relations* (New York, 1950).

A. Zimmern, *The Study of International Relations* (New York, 1931).

PART II

*Basic Factors Affecting National
Policy and International Politics*

CHAPTER II

Geography and International Politics

THE FACTS of physical geography and their bearing upon men and states are among the most fundamental influences upon world affairs. Location, climate, topography, size, shape, the nature of the soil, the possession or lack of raw materials, and sources of irrigation have a vital bearing upon the conditions and relations of states. National security, economic well-being, and the relative national power which a state can bring to bear in world affairs are intrinsically connected with them. An understanding of international affairs begins with these facts and their influences.[1]

The "community of nations" today is very largely the product of the growth of the so-called state system which first evolved in Europe and then spread throughout the world by the expanding influence and power of Europe. The manner in which Europe initially developed was largely affected by the geography of the so-called continent, in reality a large peninsula of the Eurasian land mass. Then, as the course of international relations began to involve the peoples, the continents, and the seas beyond the confines of Europe, these relations became closely bound to the facts of geography in those other areas as well.[2]

LOCATION AND CLIMATE

The location which a nation occupies on the face of the globe gives it a certain climate which the natural forces of the universe tend to fix into a fairly definable pattern. This climate has effects upon the activities and the attitudes of the peoples that inhabit the area.[3]

Climate, as defined by Webster, is "the average condition of the weather at

---

[1] General writings on geography having particular relevance to the study of international relations include James Fairgrieve, *Geography and World Power* (8th ed., London, 1941); Derwent Whittlesey, *The Earth and the State* (New York, 1939); H. R. Fifield and G. E. Pearcy, *World Political Geography* (New York, 1948).

[2] See H. K. Smith, *The State of Europe* (New York, 1951), pp. 3–15.

[3] A classic study on the influence of climate is Ellsworth Huntington, *Civilization and Climate* (New Haven, 1924).

a place, over a period of years, as shown by temperature, wind velocity, rains, etc." We know that the climate of an area affects the health and temperament of people. As was suggested by Aristotle long ago, modern biological research has shown that the climates of the middle latitudes react on human beings in a manner highly favorable to rapid economic and technological progress. This is not to say that man cannot adapt himself to extremes of heat and cold. We know that he can. To what extent it will pay him to do so is a pertinent question, for there are also to be considered such related matters as soil qualities, diseases, insects, and weed growth.

Climate and Human Energy. Extreme, continuous heat has generally retarded the economic and industrial development of peoples situated in the equatorial belt. Similarly, we may note that the regions which are excessively cold and dry have also been slow in developing their latent resources. Observe on a world map that it is in the middle latitudes, where there are frequent changes in weather and a stimulating climate, that all the so-called Great Powers of modern times have been cradled. The enervating heat and humidity of the equatorial regions can now be compensated for, at least to an extent, by adaptation and the devices of modern air conditioning. The polar climates, by contrast, which absorb so much bodily energy in the production of heat merely to keep people alive that little energy is left for productive purposes, do not lend themselves to ameliorative devices in the same degree.

Climate and Productivity. Climate is closely related to a nation's productivity. Climatic conditions have much to do with both the formation and the use of soils as well as the kinds and qualities of vegetable and animal products that they can produce. Extreme cold or dryness precludes agricultural or pastoral production in large enough quantities to sustain large populations. This helps to explain why no modern Great Power has a political center above the Arctic Circle nor in such an arid location as the Sahara or Gobi desert. In the heat and rainfall of the equatorial regions, vegetable and animal life flourish, making these regions large suppliers of certain resources such as rubber, spices, drugs, and tropical foods. Large-scale industrial activity, particularly in the extraction of minerals and the production of raw materials, is carried on in the tropical and subtropical regions of Africa, South America, Malaysia, and India. But as yet no first-rank industrial or military power has arisen in modern times with its principal center of life and power situated in these regions.

Economic and military activity now going on in the American and Siberian far north demonstrates that man can adapt himself and his machines even to the rigors of climate in these spaces. Not only can he extract from them riches in minerals, metals, and timber, but he can gain the strategic advantages which geographical placement at the top of the world astride the short communication routes between the land masses of America and Eurasia confers.[4]

Within the middle latitudes there are many variations in climate stemming from the influences of oceanic and continental masses. These variations may contribute to a nation's productive capacity. The location of a state in relation to some of these climatic influences may be quite important in world affairs. Consider the case of England which is actually in the same latitude as Labrador, Kamchatka, and Northern Sakhalin. How different would have been the history of the British Isles and the probable influence of London on world affairs if the English ports had been ice-locked throughout half the year, as are those of these other regions. The fortunate flow of the warm North Atlantic drift (or Gulf Stream as it is popularly called) by England has made a significant difference.

THE FACTOR OF POSITION

A state's participation in international affairs is largely affected by its location with respect to neighboring countries and to the Great Powers.

Position Relative to Centers of Power. A state located remotely from the center of world politics and away from the main friction zones of power politics may be able to pursue its own national life as it sees fit without much outside interference. It may also be able because of its position to follow an isolationist policy. The geographic positions of such countries as New Zealand, Costa Rica, Ethiopia, and the United States have had more than a little to do with the histories and policies of these countries in the past.

By the opposite logic, of course, states situated close to the "epicenter" of world politics, or located in regions where the interests and ambitions of the Great Powers tend to cross, are more likely to become involved in the interplay of power politics. The territories of the European countries, especially of the smaller lands in Central and Eastern Europe, the "shatter zone," have been the scene of repeated conflict and war.

If the people of a particular state wish to live in isolation, a location which places them in the natural axis of Great Power politics will be viewed as "unfavorable." If, on the other hand, they wish to influence world affairs, a location close to some of the strategic areas will tend to augment their influence, other things being equal. In the words of the late Nicholas J. Spykman, "power is local."[5]

4 H. W. Weigert, V. Stefansson, and others, *New Compass of the World* (New York, 1949) contains informative discussions of significant developments taking place in the Arctic regions.
5 N. J. Spykman's two works, *America's Strategy in World Politics* (New York, 1942) and *Geography of the Peace* (New York, 1944), are instructive reading on the relationships between factors of geography, national power, and strategy.

England's position close to the continent of Europe, astride the sea lanes leading to and from it, has naturally produced not only a large interest in continental affairs, but also given the British a position of enormous influence in international relations. Similarly, Japan was destined to acquire large power in the Orient when the power and efficiency of its armed forces were increased to exceed those of its continental and oceanic neighbors. By the same token, a strong Germany situated in the heart of Europe inevitably gave it international advantages with its interior lines of communication within the Continent. Likewise, the Soviet Union's position, touching Europe, the Middle East, and the Far East, is bound to make it a factor in the politics of each of those areas. Technological developments and the economic interdependence of nations can affect, of course, the relative qualities inherent in different positions and therefore necessitate new policies and attitudes. The English Channel once conferred great protective advantages upon the British Isles. But the development of long-range planes and guided missiles has qualified the security of its insularity off the coast of Europe. Oceanic space no longer confers the same degree of isolation and protection which it did two generations ago. In other words, "position" can no longer be viewed as a permanent datum of ecological location. It must be interpreted as location multiplied by technology.

Position in Relation to Oceans. Landlocked states such as Austria, Hungary, Czechoslovakia, and Switzerland tend to be at a disadvantage compared with states having outlets to the sea. In foreign commerce they must depend upon the friendship of neighboring states for the safe passage of persons and goods bound to and from overseas. Unless they enjoy the advantage of an unenviable terrain, or redoubtable mountain frontiers, as does Switzerland, they are likely to suffer pressures from their surrounding neighbors and offer aggressors a tempting objective. In an age when sea power swayed the course of history, location adjacent to one of the major oceans was an essential to Great Power status.[6] It may not be so vital in an era in which air and atomic power are playing a large role in world politics. But until planes are able to carry vast quantities of men and materials across the longest oceanic spaces as efficiently as vessels, a position adjacent to the high seas and the possession of large sea power will remain valuable assets to Great Power influence.

Position and World Politics. One can find many illustrations in history of the connection between strategic locations and world politics. World politics might have been different, for example, if Russia had possessed unobstructed, ice-free ports fronting directly on the great seas. Its lack of warm-water ports and its historic belief and determination that Russia should possess such out-

---

6 See Alfred T. Mahan, *The Influence of Seapower in History, 1660–1783* (Boston, 1890), *passim.*

lets have contributed to crises in international relations on a number of occasions. During the past century Britain shielded its own imperial routes and interests by upholding the Turkish Empire in order to prevent Russia's seizing the Turkish Straits. Since World War II the United States has expended millions of dollars in military aid to the Republic of Turkey in order to buttress the territorial integrity and political independence of this state which guards what have become the arteries and interests of the free nations as a whole.

A look at the map will quickly reveal what a different strategic situation would prevail in the Mediterranean area if Russia were to establish itself there. Native ambitions and imperial interests have impelled Russian rulers to seek outlets to the Mediterranean and the Persian Gulf. Equally natural interests impel Britain and the United States to "contain" Russia in order to safeguard the Suez Canal route, to protect the rich oil resources of the Middle East, to prevent Western Europe from being outflanked in the south, and to prevent Asia from being cut off from Europe.

The location of the Balkans and of the Middle East, destines these areas to be focal points in power politics. The positions of Greece, Iran, and Yugoslavia readily reveal why the East-West conflict over them has become so bitter. Korea is likewise a focal point in world politics, owing to its strategic position between the Asiatic mainland and Japan.

Belgium provides another example of a state forced into the international arena, although its people have desired neutrality in international conflicts. Because of its location, Belgium has found itself overrun by invaders twice during the first half of the twentieth century. In a different way, the location of Belgium at the mouth of the Scheldt River opposite Britain has led that country to interest itself closely in Belgium's foreign affairs in order that no other Great Power might control that strategic location and so threaten British security. In fact, Britain's Lord Palmerston was influential in obtaining the Great Power protocol in 1830 which recognized Belgium as a "perpetual neutral."

Position and Widening Defense Concepts. The position which a state occupies has a decided influence on the defense policy which it may adopt. Being territorially adjacent to Germany and with a history of German invasion, France has in the past mounted a defense along its borders to give the minimum of security. But nothing France can do can give a degree of security comparable to that which Canada and the United States enjoy with over 3,000 miles of ocean separating them from Germany. France may arm itself "to the teeth." Help may be sought from allies and refuge sought in a Maginot line of defense, but the hard fact remains that across a few hundred yards of Rhine River, or even directly across a post-marked land line, German forces and guns have in the past been able to prepare massed assaults upon French territory. This history is one reason, relative population is another, and the marked differential in industrial production is a third, why France has been so outspoken in its demands for "collective security."

In recent years, with the developments in transportation, communications, and technology, even the states in the Americas have begun to realize that the area which must be defended in the interests of national security extends far beyond their immediate land borders and the three-mile limit on the high seas. Specific recognition of this may be seen in the Inter-American Treaty of Reciprocal Assistance signed at Rio de Janeiro in 1947. This pact sets forth the principle of collective security for the entire "American hemisphere," extending from pole to pole, and embraces a sea area in the Atlantic and Pacific stretching in most places more than 300 miles from the coastline. An even broader application is found in the North Atlantic Pact, whereby the United States and Canada join with countries on the rimland of Europe, from which they are separated by ocean, in a military defense "to promote stability and well-being in the North Atlantic area." The entry of Greece and Turkey into the NATO complex reveals the tremendous extent of national security interests.[7]

LAND FORM

Before considering the part which topography has played in the formation of individual states, let us first examine how it has affected the development of whole continents. The first thing one observes is the great contrast which exists in the physical features of the continents. Some land masses such as Europe and the eastern part of the United States have a depressed coast which, because of the large number of drowned river valleys, provides many good harbors and an easy means of access to the interior. Others, such as the western coast of South America where the Andes barrier extends almost to the sea, have few harbors and river systems so that penetration into the country directly from the sea is difficult or impossible. When one compares the coasts of Europe and Africa, one notes the contrast between the much-indented coastline of Europe and the almost smooth coastline of Africa. With the Sahara to the north and the limited number of openings to the interior, it is not difficult to understand why the exploration and settlement of Africa was historically far behind that of other areas of the world. External barriers like the deserts of China and Egypt long served as a source of protection to those nations. Numerous other examples can be found of a correlation between topography and the pattern of discovery, exploration, and world settlement of many areas of the world.

[7] See ch. xxi for discussion of the Inter-American and North Atlantic Treaties.

Relation to Climate. Topography has an important influence on the climate of an area. High coastal barriers of large continents affect the amount of rainfall which can reach the interior. Coastal mountain ranges account largely for the arid conditions of northwestern Africa, the western deserts of the United States, and the dry interior of Central Asia. Tibet is very dry, for example, because the sea winds cannot carry their moisture over the Himalayas. Instead, this moisture is dropped in tropical rainfalls on the southern approaches to the Himalayas where the heaviest precipitation on the globe is recorded.

Similarly, the combined barrier provided by the Swiss Alps and the narrow Strait of Gibraltar keeps out the cold winds and waters of the Atlantic from the Mediterranean region, making it warmer than Northwestern and Central Europe.

Bearing on Political Development. A third way in which topography has affected the development of countries is its influence upon the formation of political units. When a country has been protected from external aggression by natural barriers, and when its internal physical situation has been favorable, national unification and the consequent development of political power has tended to occur more quickly than when the opposite has been true. One can see illustrations of this in the histories of Rome, England, and Japan. In vast continental regions like Africa and South America, which are not interlaced by natural lines of communication criss-crossing the land in various directions, political unification has had geographical barriers, as well as other difficulties, to surmount.

In Central America, for example, topography has been ascribed by historians as the main reason for failure to achieve some kind of political unity. Upon a quick glance at a map, Central America appears to be a natural geographic unit; it seems absurd that it should be divided into six small countries. The Central American Confederation which was formed at the time of the Spanish American Revolution lasted only about fifteen years, and numerous attempts since to forge another union of the countries in that narrow portion of land connecting the two large American continents have met with failure. Why should a people who are linked linguistically be divided as to national loyalty? Differences in early Indian cultures, the mountains which break into several ranges in that region, plus climate, diseases, soil conditions drawing the centers of population into disconnected highlands, and the absence of other natural, unifying means of communication, as well as the divergent interests of ambitious national leaders, provide some clues to the answer to this question.

Relation to European Expansion. Topography conspired with the restless, vigorous nature of Western European man to induce the overseas expansion and colonialism of the Western European states. Fronting upon the Mediterranean or the Atlantic, and, in many instances, having navigable inland waterways leading to these high seas, European mariners and adventurers were quite naturally beckoned to explore the far seas and ultimately the lands which they found and claimed for their sovereigns. Quite different was the case of Eastern Europe and Russia—cut off from direct or easy all-year access to the Atlantic, and separated from the Pacific by the inhospitable tracts of Siberia. Russia, by its land connection with Asia, was led to expand eastward, even establishing outposts in Alaska and on the present Pacific coast of the United States until forced to retire in the nineteenth century.

Topography and Defense. Topography naturally plays a crucial hand in the military defense of nations, and so affects their international relations.

Notice on a map of Europe how the great North European plain merges with the Low Countries to form a corridor between the North Sea and the upland masses of Eastern France, the Saar, Luxembourg, South Germany, and Czechoslovakia. It is no surprise that this has been a historic route of march and battleground of European armies. Through this corridor wheeled the Nazi hordes in 1940, violating the neutrality and integrity of the Netherlands and Belgium to outflank the French armies entrenched in the Maginot Line forts guarding the passes by Verdun, Metz, Strasbourg, and Belfort. Once the German armies were able to get by the water barriers in the Netherlands and the Belgian forts guarding the approaches to Brussels, Antwerp, and Sedan, there was little to stop their powerfully armored columns from cutting the less mobile French and British forces to pieces and racing to the Channel ports. Looking to the east, the eastward portion of the North German Plain is now a potential corridor for the movement of Soviet forces.

Valuable as topographic features still remain in the defense of every country, it must be stressed that the developments in air power, in long-range guided missiles, and in nuclear weapons are rapidly changing the equations of offense and defense. The methods of mass bombing practiced against Germany in 1944–1945 demonstrated that an enemy's cities, centers of production, and lines of communication could be destroyed far behind the battle lines.

SIZE

Another factor, almost too obvious to merit mention, which has an effect on a country's development and on its role in international affairs is its size. While a relatively large area is not in itself necessarily a means to prosperity or power, states generally find spaciousness an asset sooner or later and in one way or another.

It is quite apparent that the large diversified territories of the United States and the Soviet Union, for example, are valuable assets to each of these countries. They could not support their people without them. Without such areas at their command and the resources located within these areas, their hope for the future could not be what it is. Moreover, where once the vast, unoccupied spaces of Canada, Australia, and China appeared as holdings of dubious worth, explorations and scientific activity are demonstrating that they contain valuable riches and usable space.

Smallness of size, however, does not necessarily prevent a people from attaining a high standard of living, as the Swiss and the Danes in particular have shown. So long as their people remain as ingenious as they are in the use of available resources, and are able to pursue an active international trade, the size of their national domain need cause them little economic concern. But it remains an obvious fact that their restricted territories cannot possibly provide the material resources or sustain populations comparable to those of France or Germany.

Large expanse may be advantageous in providing a variety of climates, soils, and minerals, and space within which to develop. Ambitious, expanding peoples living within narrow confines have often sought improvement in their well-being and in their international position through territorial expansion in their own neighborhood or overseas. Britain, Belgium, the Netherlands, Portugal, Japan are examples. Spatial extent may also be an asset to a state in providing room for maneuver and a cushion against an initial assault in case of war.

From the point of view of national power, size alone provides only one element in a complex equation. Great Power status is achieved and determined by size and population plus resources, industrial development and technological skill, favorable climate, a certain cultural level, and political leadership.[8]

RAW MATERIALS

The economic life of a state is primarily conditioned by its possession, or lack thereof, of natural resources. These resources—soil and its products, water and its products, minerals—have a major and often overriding influence on a state's economic pattern and on its policies in international dealings. Lacking an adequate supply of natural resources, a state can rarely hope to achieve a high standard of living for its people or a strong posture in international affairs. National strength seems impossible of attainment today without industrialization. Industrialization, in turn, is very dependent on availability of raw materials, particularly minerals.

[8] *Foundations of National Power,* by Harold and Margaret Sprout (rev. ed., New York, 1951), contains a systematic treatment of the subject of national power.

The location of raw materials affects population and industrial patterns. It is also a major factor influencing the foreign trade pattern of each state and of the entire world. As a simple example, all the world uses tin and all the free world at least looks to Malaya and Bolivia for tin. As another example, the soil of Denmark produces agricultural products in abundance but no coal. Hence, the distribution of natural resources tends to make Denmark a non-industrialized agricultural state with a major requirement for imports of fuels and other minerals.

Raw Materials and Foreign Policy. If a state is substantially self-sufficient in raw materials, they are not likely to be of primary concern in its international relations. But no state, with the possible exception of the USSR, possesses raw materials, in variety and quantity sufficient to support a fully industrialized economy. Even the USSR has deficiencies in a few materials. Hence, materials are a primary concern in the international affairs of nearly every state. Even those with a primarily agricultural economy have increasing ambitions toward industrialization, and therefore an increasing interest in materials, some of which must come from abroad. This increasing dependence on economic foreign relations for the maintenance of a standard of economic prosperity is a fact of modern international life. The dependence is of two types. We have discussed, thus far, the need for imports. But certain states are also dependent on exports.

The United States economy might, at first, be considered as comparatively free from dependence on exports of raw materials. This is true as far as minerals are concerned. But our wheat, cotton, and tobacco industries have long owed a substantial part of their prosperity to foreign exports. The more striking examples, however, are those states which acquire most of their foreign exchange—their ability to pay for imports—from the export of one or two materials. Chile (copper), Brazil (coffee), Bolivia (tin), Malaya (tin), and Iran and Saudi Arabia (oil) are examples of such one-commodity export economies. Traditionally raw materials have tended to fluctuate widely in demand and in price on the international market. Even as the countries with a deficiency face a hazard in having a supply of a key commodity cut off, so do some producing countries face a danger of economic disruption (and perhaps a consequent political crisis) if there is a reduction in world import requirements.

Distribution of Natural Resources. The states of the world are certainly not equally endowed with natural resources. Even for the well-known resources of soil and water, some states are far ahead of others. The three principal minerals, coal, iron, and petroleum, are most unequally distributed. These three minerals are the basis of industry, and a state must either possess them or acquire them through international arrangements if it is to be strong economically, and particularly if it is to be strong militarily.

But the point most frequently overlooked until recent years is the number and diversity of materials, particularly minerals, required to support a modern industrialized economy. The need for, and use of, most of these has developed since the beginning of this century. For instance, the industrial (and military) use of titanium (jet engines), germanium (transistors), and uranium (nuclear weapons and power) has developed in the lifetime of those reading this book.

A general grasp of the number and distribution of materials is a prerequisite to sound thinking on international affairs.[9] The accompanying map indicates the countries which produce 10 per cent or more of the total world production of some of the more essential raw materials. This map does not, of course, give a key to the requirements of the various states. The United States, with approximately 40 per cent of the industrial production of the world, is by far the greatest single consumer.

Significance of Resource Situation. What do you deduce from this tabulation? Here are some of the things which stand out. First, no country contains a sufficiency of all essential raw materials. Second, natural resources are very unevenly distributed throughout the world. The United States and the USSR [10] are richly endowed; Australia, Greece, and Italy are poorly supplied. There is a question about China's resources.

What is the variation in raw material supplies likely to lead to in international relations? Does it not point to rivalry, competition, and struggle among states for what they regard as sufficient quantities of those materials in which they are lacking? It has been an inducement to colonialism and imperialism. On the other hand, the development of freer trade policies and collective security agreements can reduce the tension growing out of the search for raw materials.

Factors to Be Borne in Mind in Policy Consideration. In facing a situation in which a nation, whether the United States or any other, is lacking adequate

[9] On raw materials and their implications see George A. Lincoln and associates, *The Economics of National Security* (2nd ed., New York, 1954); C. K. Leith, J. W. Furniss and C. Lewis, *World Minerals and World Peace* (Washington, 1943); Eugene Staley, *Raw Materials in Peace and War* (New York, 1937); W. Van Royen and O. Bowles, *The Mineral Resources of the World* (New York, 1952), being vol. II of the *Atlas of the World's Resources*. The most authoritative and complete study on the U. S. raw materials situation is the *President's Materials Policy Commission Report* (Washington, 1952).

[10] On Soviet resources see S. S. Balzak, V. F. Vasyutin, Y. G. Feigin (eds.) *Economic Geography of the USSR*, Am. Edition edited by Chauncy D. Harris (New York, 1949); George Cressey, *The Basis of Soviet Strength* (New York, 1949); Harry Schwarz, *Russia's Soviet Economy* (New York, 1950); Dimitri Shimkin, *Minerals a Key to Soviet Power* (Cambridge, 1953).

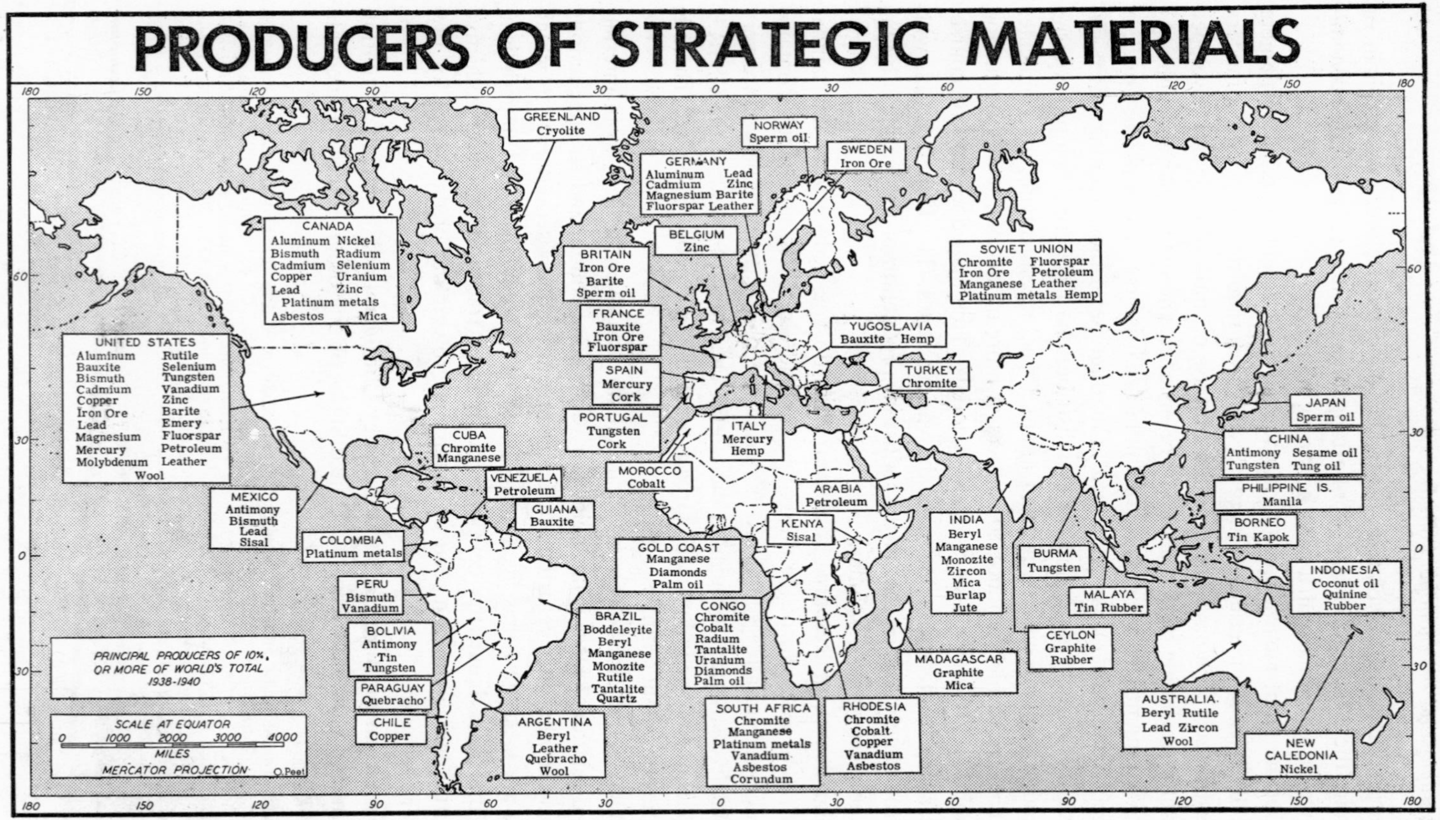

PRODUCERS OF STRATEGIC MATERIALS

FIGURE II:1

supplies or reserves of essential raw materials, four considerations must be borne in mind: namely, the elements of time, distance, mass, and political action required for satisfaction of national needs.

Overcoming raw materials shortages requires time. New sources cannot be found, explored, opened up, and brought into production overnight. Years of effort may be expended in this, as they have been for example in the discovery and preparation of the new iron ore fields in Ontario, Quebec-Labrador, and Venezuela. The time factor must also be weighed not only in terms of the immediate future but of the probable requirements needed in order to cope with the demands occasioned by the rising world population and, even more important, by increased industrialization.

The element of distance separating the location of additional sources of supply from the industrial centers in which they are processed must also be weighed by policy makers, for added transportation distances usually mean increased costs, as when for instance materials must be brought from Africa instead of being found within the United States. And the policy maker cannot afford to overlook the potential danger to which long supply lines are exposed in time of war. Hence, his consideration must extend to thinking about the ways and means of protecting those supply lines in time of emergency.

The mass of raw material tonnage that must be moved to satisfy national requirements must also be taken into account. Industrialization and advances in technology demand constantly increasing masses of materials. Obtaining and maintaining the necessary transportation equipment to move these supplies is an essential part of the forward-thinking which has to be put into dealing with the long-run aspects of actual and potential shortages in the raw material situation. This, like the other aspects of the problem which we have just mentioned, strikes immediately into the whole question of national economic policy, financing, and caring for a costly merchant marine.

The foreign policy of every state sooner or later, and in one degree or another, is concerned with raw materials. States that are comparatively richly endowed, as is the United States, can lean heavily on the initiative of private enterprisers to fill the deficiencies. States which are very dependent on imports tend to pay more formal attention to assuring access to sources and an uninterrupted flow of supply from foreign areas. There is a "materials diplomacy" which is an important component of international affairs.

United States Raw-Materials Situation. A summary account of the United States raw-materials situation will indicate the importance and the complexities of "raw materials" diplomacy. In the early 1950's over seventy materials were classified as "strategic and critical," a term given by the Congressional Act providing for stockpiling of those necessary materials essential to national defense which the United States must import in substantial proportions. A comparison with the corresponding list in 1940 which contained only fifteen materials indicates the rapid expansion of types of materials essential to industry and also the depletion of national reserves.

The strategic and critical materials include not only minerals but many organic products such as coconut oil, shellac, wool, and pepper. The United States is now a net importer of all metals except two (magnesium and molybdenum). Of the strategic and critical materials mentioned above, over forty are not produced in the United States in sufficient quantities to mention; of those produced in this country in any significant amounts, only eight are available to meet one-half of our peace-time requirements. Thirteen are not available in the entire Western Hemisphere! The map on the opposite page with the graphs which appear with it depict the need for an extremely close relationship between foreign policy and certain strategic raw materials, especially with respect to those minerals which are critical and for which the nation is materially dependent on foreign sources.[11]

Specific Measures for United States Policy. Having the United States raw materials and international political positions in mind, in particular, let us ask what measures are needed to insure an adequate supply of vital materials not presently obtainable within the United States in the foreseeable future. This is the issue with which the President's Materials Policy Commission was confronted when it drew its report in 1952. Since total self-sufficiency is impracticable and impossible, the Commission recognized that a solution depends upon a combination of technological, diplomatic, and political measures involving:

1. Stockpiling, principally with imports from the free world, for use in a military emergency.
2. Arrangements with foreign sources assuring a steady flow of imports.
3. Conservation, regulation, and more efficient utilization of present and potential domestic resources.
4. Development of synthetics and substitutes.

The United States stockpiling program, geared to the estimated requirements for major war, has been moving forward, but the arrangements with foreign sources are replete with difficulties. In 1948, for instance, the USSR abruptly cut off the flow of manganese and chromite to the United States, forcing the latter to seek those vital ferroalloys from other sources. In 1951 Bolivia

11 See The President's Materials Policy Commission Report, *Resources for Freedom, vol. I* (Washington, 1952), p. 157. See also John E. Orchard "Strategic Materials: Procurement and Allocation" *Proceedings Acad. of Pol. Sci.,* May, 1951 pp. 305–326.

FREE WORLD LIFELINES ARE LONG AND EXPOSED

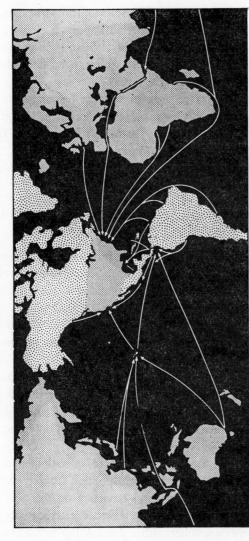

MINERAL IMPORTS VITAL TO U. S. SECURITY

FOREIGN SOURCES OF 29 PRINCIPAL INDUSTRIAL MINERALS IN 1951

FROM WESTERN HEMISPHERE   FROM EASTERN HEMISPHERE   DOMESTIC

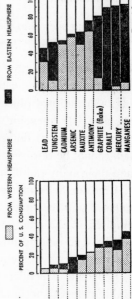

Source: U. S. Bureau of Mines

President's Materials Policy Commission Report

FIGURE II:2

and Malaya raised the price of tin so high (135 per cent) that the United States chose temporarily to cease purchases for the stockpile.

Since most (75 per cent) of the materials in the stockpile list come from the underdeveloped regions of the earth, financial and technical assistance to these areas for development of raw materials is now an important element of national policy. Materials may shift from the critical and strategic category due to development of synthetics and substitutes and to improved technology making practical and commercial use of low grade ores.

While the United States dependence on foreign sources for materials is serious, similar dependence of every other nation except the Soviet Union is much more serious. Even the USSR is short of natural rubber and a few minerals. The key conclusion of the President's Materials Policy Commission with reference to the United States is even more forcefully applicable to all other nations:

There is no such thing as a purely domestic policy toward materials that all the world must have; there are only world policies that have domestic aspects.

Dealing with the raw materials problem in a realistic fashion involves thinking about a complex network of complicated and often delicate matters involving: (a) national objectives, (b) research and development, (c) emergency supplies, (d) financing, both public and private, (e) foreign trade policy, (f) price control, (g) domestic politics, and (h) international politics. The problem cannot be resolved, for any country, without keeping all of these questions and their many ramifications in mind at all times.

Urge for Self-Sufficiency. Nearly all powers at one time or another have pursued policies aimed at greater self-sufficiency, in their home territories or empires, in the more essential natural resources. The fear and frequency of war have stimulated this, although providing for defense needs is only one of the reasons why nations desire self-sufficiency.

Economic dependence reduces the freedom of action of a nation, and in reality reduces and dilutes the nation's power in world politics. Consequently, we find in modern international politics a general tendency on the part of states which are lacking in some critical raw materials to exert pressures to improve their position in one way or another, either through the procurement of special concessions or preferential trading arrangements abroad or through the acquisition of territories possessing supplies of these materials. Germany's feeling of insufficiency played a large part in the German drive for expansion in both World Wars I and II. A lack of adequate supplies of many essential raw materials in the Japanese home islands was one element prompting the Japanese leaders to engage in their imperialist adventure from 1932 to 1945.

Problems in Seeking Self-Sufficiency. Since complete self-sufficiency is an impossible achievement for a modern nation, each country is faced with the difficult problem of evolving a balanced economic program of independence in some economic items while making arrangements to provide the remainder through foreign trade. A country such as Great Britain which cannot hope to maintain any large degree of self-sufficiency in its home land logically turns to foreign trade, the possession of colonies, and the cementing of close political relations with other friendly nations which may assist in assuring its national well-being. The diverse situations of nations make for conflicting policies since, if the powers more nearly self-sufficient progress further along that line, they may reduce the trade essential to the survival of the less self-sufficient countries.

The economic health and power of the various countries turn in varying degrees (depending on the order of their self-sufficiency) on their foreign trade and their ability to finance that trade by exports in goods or by some other medium of exchange. The problems which arise in this connection are discussed in Chapter IV. Suffice it to say here that the problems of providing adequate foreign exchange to finance the purchase of raw materials abroad, as well as the assurance of access to needed supplies, have become vital questions for many nations. The efforts of foreign aid and technical assistance programs to assist in the development of production in underdeveloped lands have been useful steps in helping to meet the rising world needs.

SOME SPECIAL RESOURCE SITUATIONS

Let us now turn for a moment to a few specific resource situations affecting international relations.

Food and Agricultural Products. Food and agricultural products are the joint products of soil, climate, man, and food and agricultural techniques. The most important product is food. The areas of the world deficient in food have a critical weakness which may require the most complicated remedial actions. Britain's increasing deficiency during the last 100 years logically promoted a strong navy to guard the sea lanes, a large merchant marine to carry foodstuffs, industries to support exports, overseas investments, and an intensive interest in world affairs. Japan, in much the same situation, turned to a militant imperialism as well as to expedients such as far-ranging fishing fleets. Most of Eastern and Southern Asia, together with Western Europe, are food-deficient areas. Russia, Central Europe, Australia, and the Americas are, in general, food-surplus areas.

After food, the most important agricultural products are probably cotton and wool. These are localized to a considerable extent in their production.

Perhaps the most localized of the more critical products of the soil is rubber, grown in quantity only in Malaya and Indonesia.

Sources of Energy. Adequate sources of energy (power) are one of the most important foundations of national strength and of a high standard of living. Modern technology and industry are dependent upon them. The sources cf energy that come out of the ground in the form of coal and petroleum are essential to the production and operation of machines and to heavy transport which is capable of adjusting geographical deficiencies and local surpluses. These energy sources also make possible agricultural production above a subsistence level. Water power contributes only a small proportion of the total work energy harnessed by man. Industrial utilization of atomic energy is on the way, with intensive experimentation going on in England, the United States, and Russia. Sooner or later the energy derivable from this source may become important in quantity. The relative insufficiency in some advanced industrialized countries of immediately consumable supplies of petroleum and uranium has made these sources of energy an object of Great Power politics.

Petroleum. Petroleum products have become vital necessities to the prosperity and security of industrial nations. They provide versatile, easily transported and stored fuels; they are used in a wide range of products from plastics to medicines. No suitable substitute has yet been found for them in the field of lubricants. The demand for petroleum will undoubtedly increase steadily with the further expansion of automotive transport and aviation, and would increase enormously should there be another war.

The United States has long led the world in oil production and consumption, using and producing over half of the world's total. Though the United States reserves are large and production high, the demand for crude petroleum has become greater in peacetime than at present can be supplied domestically. The nation faces the prospect of increasing dependence on foreign sources as reserves dwindle and demand continues to rise.

Some of these foreign sources are in the Western Hemisphere, as in Venezuela, the world's second largest producer. The Middle East, now credited with over half of the world's proved reserves, is bulking larger and larger in petroleum production. At present the United States can buy from the Middle East; whether or not this trade could continue in the event of war would depend upon circumstances of the time.

The United States must, then, look for alternate and safe sources of liquid fuel. Possibilities lie in conservation measures, encouragement of Latin American drilling and production, exploitation of off-shore fields, full prospecting of all of North America, particularly of Canada, and unimpeded imports from abroad while this is still possible in order to lessen the drain on Western Hemisphere reserves. Further, within the United States are tremendous reserves of oil-bearing shale, and oil can be produced from coal. Full use of these potential sources awaits further research. The outlook is that the United States can secure for its use, even in time of emergency, adequate liquid fuel to last for many years to come.

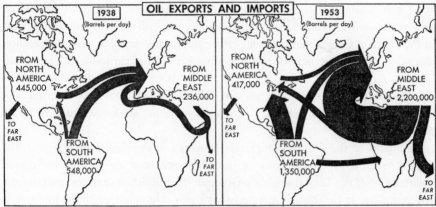

President's Materials Policy Commission Report

FIGURE II:3

The Soviet Union probably possesses some of the world's largest oil reserves. The Baku oil field adjoining the Caspian Sea has long been one of the most notable producing areas. Oil deposits may extend for distances under this sea and along its surrounding shores. In recent times a "second Baku" has been opened on the western slopes of the Ural Mountains. Oil formations extend from the Caspian to the Arctic Ocean shores. Oil is also found in Sakhalin Island off Eastern Siberia. The Soviet's chief problems are, as in many other aspects of its economy, long-distance transportation and adequate technology. In addition to its own supplies, the Soviet Union now enjoys the use of the rich Rumanian deposits. And it is of course in close proximity to the vast Middle Eastern fields.[12]

Uranium. The conventional concept of energy resources was profoundly affected in the latter stages of World War II by developments in the field of nuclear science, for the employment of the atomic bomb by the United States heralded the utilization of fissionable elements as a source of energy. Since

12 On oil resources and strategy see Wallace E. Pratt and Dorothy Good, *World Geography of Petroleum* (Princeton, 1950); Halford L. Hoskins, "Middle East Oil in United States Foreign Policy," Public Affairs Bulletin No. 89 (Washington, 1950); Report of President's Materials Policy Commission, *Resources for Freedom*, vol. III, pp. 2–14, June, 1952; R. R. Sharp, "America's Stake in World Petroleum," *Harvard Bus. Rev.*, Sept., 1950, reproduced in Padelford (ed.), *Cont. Int. Rels. Readings,* 1950–1951, pp. 239–252.

other major powers have subsequently solved the techniques of atomic production processes, the availability of necessary raw materials assumes tremendous importance.

The most widely publicized sources of atomic energy are uranium and plutonium which is derived from uranium. Although at least 100 minerals are thought to contain uranium, only two—pitchblende and carnotite—contain enough for commercial extraction at the present time. The most important known deposits of pitchblende, the major ore mineral of uranium, are located in the Belgian Congo and Canada. Other important deposits exist in Czechoslovakia and East German Silesia. Uranium is found in carnotite in Utah, New Mexico, Arizona, and Colorado. Uranium has been mined in England, Portugal, Australia, Soviet Turkestan, and Siberia. These locations are not all-inclusive, for workable deposits of uranium minerals are known to exist in all the continents.

Estimates of the known commercial reserves of uranium have varied from 30,000 to 500,000 tons; however, detailed estimates by various individual countries have not been disclosed. Although the published data on reserves are not complete, it has been estimated that there is enough uranium to furnish atomic energy for a substantial part of future world energy requirements providing technology finds a way to utilize these sources commercially.

Another important source of energy from fissionable elements is thorium, obtained from monazite which is found in beach sands, dunes, and stream gravels. The largest known deposits of suitable sands are located along the coasts of India and Brazil. Supplies also have been secured in Australia, Ceylon, and the United States. Swedish shales also contain large potential stores of uranium ore.

From the limited information available, it appears that quantities of materials essential to atomic development are controlled by states on both sides of the Iron Curtain. It must be noted, however, that accessibility depends to a certain extent on alliances and friendly trade relations within the non-Communist areas and on satellite arrangements within the Communist orbit. Any political realignment on either side and any further developments creating new resource requirements for progress in nuclear science could have profound effects in the field of international relations.[13]

13 For discussions of uranium sources see N. J. Padelford (ed.), *Cont. Int. Rels. Readings,* 1949–1950 (Cambridge, 1949), pp. 31–37; John B. DeMille, *Strategic Minerals* (New York, 1947), p. 546; William Van Royen and Oliver Bowles, *The Mineral Resources of the World* (New York, 1952), pp. 137–139

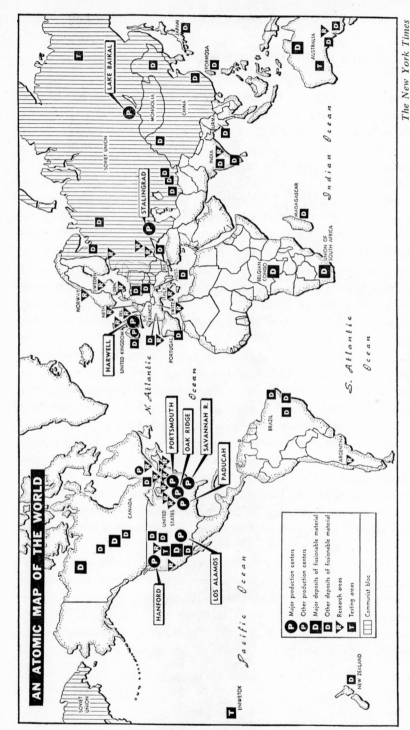

AN ATOMIC MAP OF THE WORLD

HANFORD
LOS ALAMOS
PADUCAH
PORTSMOUTH
OAK RIDGE
SAVANNAH R.
HARWELL
STALINGRAD
LAKE BAIKAL
ENIWETOK
NEW ZEALAND

Major production centers
Other production centers
Major deposits of fissionable material
Other deposits of fissionable material
Research areas
Testing areas
Communist bloc

The New York Times

FIGURE II:4

41

OTHER STRATEGIC AND ECONOMIC FACTORS
RELATIVE TO RESOURCE SITUATION

Depleted Supplies. One of the salient facts of the world mineral situation is that Nature did not endow any nation with complete self-sufficiency in raw materials, and that all nations except the USSR have numerous major deficiencies. Even the United States, as we have seen, is heavily dependent upon foreign sources now for important minerals.

A second significant fact is that mineral, soil, and water resources are being rapidly depleted in many parts of the world by man's voracious demands, inventiveness, and waste. One of the most sobering truths confronting the United States is that many of its own mineral resources are no longer adequate to support another world war effort comparable to the last one. Minerals, once gone, do not reappear. Synthetics, substitutions, and supplies from abroad may suffice. However, foreign supplies are of no value unless there is assurance that a flow of them can be channeled to the United States in sufficient quantities, whenever needed, to sustain whatever demands may have to be placed upon them.

Foreign policy must be calculated on the bed-rock reality that *within the United States proper* reserves of many minerals are not adequate to national defense or even peace-time industrial requirements at a time when America's most likely enemy, the Soviet Union, is still in the early stages of exploiting the resources located within its immense empire. United States foreign policy must be predicated upon obtaining necessary supplies from dependable foreign sources. The strategy of raw materials is one of the most vital phases of foreign-policy planning.[14]

Britain, Germany, and the United States demonstrated during the last war that extraordinary things can be done under emergency circumstances. Nevertheless, no nation can shrug off mineral shortages today with a Micawber-like attitude that something will "turn up."

Exhaustion of soil is a matter which is manageable within reasonable limits. Improved scientific methods have done a great deal to improve worn-out soil and to prolong its fertility. Modern irrigation has greatly increased agricultural production in many parts of the world. However, the question of the world's future food supply and the startlingly lowering water table in many regions are provoking serious thought on the part of scientists today. The potential

14 See W. B. Fairchild, "Renewable Resources," *Geographical Rev.*, Jan., 1949; "Some Aspects of the United States Mineral Self-Sufficiency," by E. W. Miller in N. J. Padelford (ed.) *Cont. Int. Rels. Readings,* 1949–1950, pp. 22–30; and "Strategic Materials: Procurement and Allocation," by John E. Orchard in *Proceedings Acad. Pol. Sci.,* May, 1951, pp. 305–326, will be found valuable supplementary readings.

population increases in many areas, for example, Japan and India, far exceed any probable improvements in soil productivity.[15]

Location of Resources. The totality of resources which a country possesses in relation to others is not the only aspect of the raw-material situation which is of interest to governments and to students of international affairs.

1. PROXIMITY TO FRONTIER. The geographic location of the various resources within the domain of each state is important; if vital supplies of critical raw materials are located close to the international boundaries of a state—particularly near the boundary with a potential enemy—obviously more thought must be given for their protection than if they are located in a remote area not likely to be invaded by an enemy.

A few illustrations will suffice to point up the problem. The principal French deposits of iron ore are located in Lorraine, which lies adjacent to German territory. Given the relative national power of France and Germany, it is apparent that France was particularly vulnerable in its steel requirements during the rising tension prior to World War II. Russia's principal coal, iron, manganese, and nickel resources, as well as its major heavy industries, were located before World War II in the Ukraine and Donbas. The Nazis demonstrated that these could be quickly overrun and turned against Russia in World War II. Now the Soviet Union is concentrating upon building up additional sources and industries behind the protective wall of the Ural Mountains in Siberia. In another conflict Soviet strength would be greater not only because industrial capacity has been increased, but because the nation would be relatively less dependent than heretofore upon raw materials located in the more exposed western regions.

The United States has been in a particularly fortunate position in the past two wars, inasmuch as its own raw-material supplies and industries have been separated from the striking power of its enemies by the entire distance of the Atlantic and Pacific Oceans, plus the continental mileage of the United States itself. With the development of guided missiles and transcontinental bombers, the United States becomes more vulnerable than in the past to destructive attack. Yet even with the large concentrations of key industries along the Atlantic and Pacific seaboards, the United States still enjoys—thanks to geography—the greatest security of all the Great Powers with respect to the location of stores of raw materials and war industries.

2. DISTANCE TO UTILIZATION SITES. Another important question of geography with regard to the location of a nation's raw materials is where they are located with respect to complementary materials and to manufacturing cen-

[15] See William Vogt, *Road to Survival* (New York, 1948); Fairfield Osborn, *Our Plundered Planet* (Boston, 1948) and *The Limits of the Earth* (New York, 1953).

44

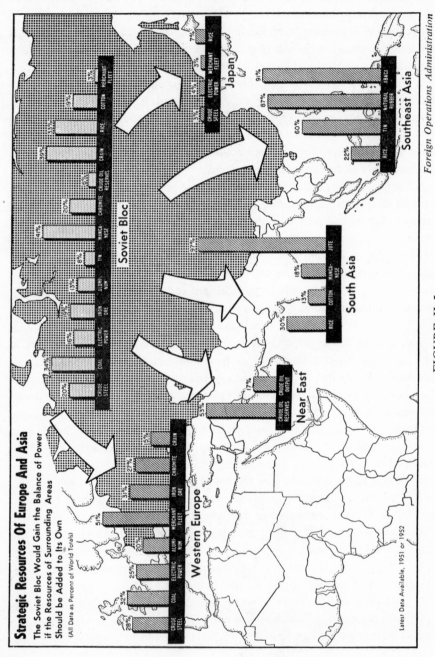

FIGURE II:5

Foreign Operations Administration

ters. Between two nations having approximately the same resources and industrial capacity, the country whose raw materials are most efficiently located with respect to other needful resources and established manufacturing centers will have an economic advantage over the other, assuming all other factors to be equal.

A comparison of carriage distances involved in the United States and Soviet coal-iron-steel manufacturing complexes will throw considerable light on the industrial efficiency of the two nations. American carriage of Lake Superior iron ore to the Pittsburgh–Youngstown steel mills involves a journey of 900 miles, most of it by relatively cheap water transport. Ample coal is less than 100 miles distant. In the Soviet Union, by contrast, coal is transported to the Ural steel furnaces from the Karaganda field 600 miles away, or from the Kuzbass district 1,417 miles away. And quantities of iron ore are reported to have been transported, also by rail, from Krivoi Rog in the Ukraine 1,600 miles distant. Comparing the economic effort required to make coal and iron in the United States and in the Ural region of the USSR, it is clear that the United States has had a comparative advantage. The combination of coal and iron present in the Soviet Ukraine has made this region a much more efficient and natural production unit than the Ural steel industry.

As the United States must now look farther afield for substantial stores of high-grade iron ore to replace the nearly exhausted Mesabi Range in Minnesota, the comparative advantage may lessen—although developing techniques for using lower-grade ores may result in continuing much the same transportation pattern. Vast new ore fields are now being developed across the Canadian border at Steep Rock Lake, Ontario, on the Quebec-Labrador border, and in the Venezuelan hinterland near the Orinoco River. Utilization of most of these ores necessitates longer hauls, but the advantage of water transportation is still available, even though in the case of the Venezuelan ores it may become hazardous in time of war.[16]

BOUNDARIES

One of the characteristics of a state is the possession of political control over a specific area of the earth's surface. That area has boundaries which abut on areas under the political control of other sovereign states or on international waters. The Geographer of the United States Department of State estimated, before World War II, that there were more than 100,000 miles of boundaries—20,000 miles in Europe alone. The area of Europe west of the Soviet Union now has over seven miles of boundary for every thousand square miles of area. The rise of the new states along the rimland of Asia since World

[16] See T. W. Lippert, "Cerro Bolivar—Saga of an Iron Ore Crisis Averted," in Padelford (ed.), *Cont. Int. Rels. Readings,* 1950–1951, pp. 261–270.

War II has added further to the total length of the world's boundaries and also to the existent and potential disputes over them.

Boundaries have increased in importance with the increase in representative government and the rise of nationalism. Boundaries have been a critical element in European affairs for a long while. They are only now becoming critical in the Middle East and Asia as a whole. Governments and peoples who once thought of their boundary as a general area rather than a clearly demarcated line are now becoming nationalistically sensitive about its exact location.[17]

Types of Boundaries. There are two general types of boundaries—natural and artificial. The former are marked by nature, for example, mountains, rivers, and shore lines. The latter have to be marked by man to be distinguishable to local inhabitants. They may follow parallels of latitude or longitude, the median line of a lake, or be determined by other means.

One can also categorize boundaries from the standpoint of the reasons for their location: security, imperialism, economic or ethnic factors, historical reasons, or some combination of these. The boundary between India and Pakistan, for example, was determined primarily by considerations of religion. In the case of the present boundary between Italy and Yugoslavia, the line established by the Peace Treaty of 1947 was based in principle upon ethnic distribution, although in the final analysis political factors were the determining criterion.

Although ethnic boundaries may conform to the principle of "self-determination," which played a large part in the boundary-making of 1919, it is often difficult to determine where the ethnic boundaries lie since different peoples may be intermingled; for example, the villages may be principally one people and the countryside another. Moreover, ethnic boundaries are not always consistent with economic and security considerations. The area of Trieste is an example of the contradictions encountered. The city is over two-thirds Italian; the surrounding countryside is predominantly Yugoslav. For historical and prestige reasons, Italians have strong attachments to Trieste. As a port it is perhaps needed more by Yugoslavia and Austria than by Italy. The city is so located as to be susceptible to a coup unless considerable adjoining territory is owned by the state possessing Trieste.[18]

The boundaries established during and after World War II were based much

---

17 For treatment of boundaries see S. W. Boggs, *International Boundaries* (New York, 1940); Norman Hill, *Claims to Territory in International Law and Relations* (New York, 1945); Stephen B. Jones, *Boundary Making* (Washington, 1945); Roderick Peattie, *Look to the Frontiers* (New York, 1944). See also Isaiah Bowman, "The Strategy of Territorial Decisions," *Foreign Affairs,* Jan., 1946; Jean Gottman, "Geography and International Relations," *World Politics,* Jan., 1951.
18 See A. E. Moodie, *The Italo-Yugoslav Boundary* (London, 1945).

less on ethnic factors than those established after World War I, and were principally determined by security and political factors. The ethnic problem was solved by the Soviet Union (and Czechoslovakia) through the simple expedient of removing the alien peoples. Poles were moved from what had been

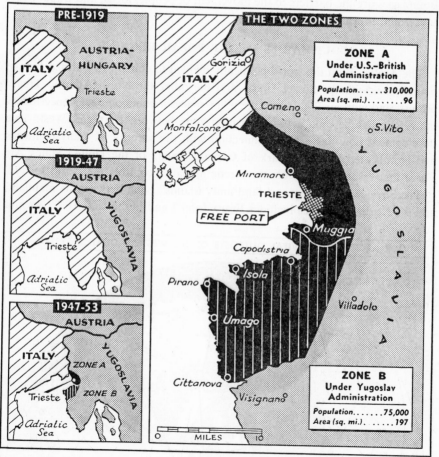

FIGURE II:6

The New York Times

Eastern Poland to lands once occupied by Germans. Approximately 8,000,000 Germans were forced from East Germany and the Sudetenland into Germany west of the Oder. When the lines of the new Israeli state emerged from the fighting in Palestine they became fixed, by and large, where hostilities were terminated by truce agreements, regardless of ethnic considerations.

The Function of Boundaries. In addition to defining the limit of political control of a government, boundaries are the checkpoints, and sometimes the barriers, for innumerable administrative and economic matters. The "Iron Curtain" and "Bamboo Curtain" are colorful terms for particular boundary lines where passage is gravely restricted or entirely denied. There are emigration, immigration, and customs checks incident to all boundary crossing. Boundaries are the barriers to the movement of people, ideas, and trade which is essential to a more unified world.

BOUNDARIES IN THE POLAR REGIONS

The Arctic. With the world politically divided to contain two armed camps, one aligned with the Soviet Union and the other the North Atlantic Treaty powers, and with air flights into the polar spaces a common occurrence today, the Arctic has become a vast transition zone between East and West. This development now has a vital connection with the security of many countries and is indicated by the remark of General Spaatz of the United States Air Force that "whoever controls the Arctic air lanes controls the world today."

The Soviet Union claims all land and "islands" lying between its mainland and the North Pole. This includes Franz Josef Land in the west (82° N) and

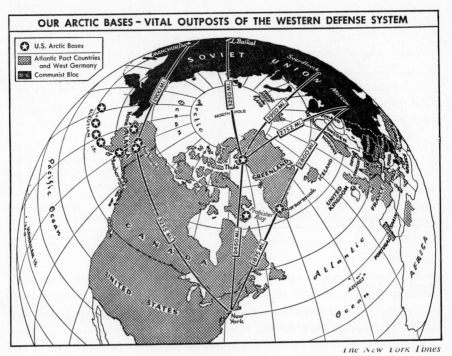

The New York Times

FIGURE II:7

Wrangel Island in the east. Among the countries on the American side of the Pole there is no boundary dispute in the Arctic; on the contrary, cooperative relationships prevail for mutual defense in the Far North where United States territory comprises Alaska, and Canadian jurisdiction extends from the Alaska-Canadian boundary on the west to the northern tip of Ellesmere Island (83° N) in the northeast. Since the Permanent Court of International Justice ruled against Norway's claim to Eastern Greenland, the whole of that land has been recognized as Danish sovereignty.

Polar Ice Spaces. Application of the "sector" principle of jurisdiction from the extremities of the mainland to the Pole may lead to serious disputes if planes of either of the Great Powers fly deeply into the space on the farther side of the Pole, or utilize ice islands as bases as the United States has done successfully. The Soviet Government has not openly asserted exclusive jurisdiction over all ice and air space on its side of the Pole, but Soviet jurists have done so, and the Government has demonstrated, in shooting down an unarmed American plane over the Baltic and over the Japan Sea, that it does not hesitate to use armed force to exclude foreign planes from what it considers its sphere. Although not claiming Arctic rights on a "sector" basis, the American, Canadian, and Danish governments have not excluded use of the principle if needed for defense purposes. For the time being no government has taken an extreme position. A serious crisis between East and West could readily convert the Arctic Ocean, however, into a most sensitive boundary area.[19] In another world war it could become a strategic center.

The Antarctic. The Antarctic has drawn increasing attention in recent years. Numerous expeditions have visited it, and competing territorial claims have been made within the continent and adjoining ocean spaces.

Nine nations hold claims to territory in the Antarctic. Australia, Argentina, Chile, and New Zealand claim ownership, on the "sector" principle, of territories lying between the outer limits of their homeland and the South Pole. Other claims are rested upon historic or recent explorations, the establishment of outposts, or the dropping of flags. The United States has never formally staked a claim for itself, and has not recognized the claims of others. Lands have, however, been claimed for the United States by Lincoln Ellsworth and Admiral Byrd, of which Washington has kept a careful record. Overlapping claims, as shown on the accompanying map, have led to several incidents, indicating that clarification must some day be obtained. Should radioactive

---

[19] See E. Plischke, "Trans-Polar Aviation and Jurisdiction Over Arctic Air Space," *Am. Pol. Sci. Rev.,* Dec., 1943; G. Smedal, *Acquisition of Sovereignty Over Polar Areas* (Oslo, 1931); T. A. Taracouzio, *Soviets In the Arctic* (New York, 1938).

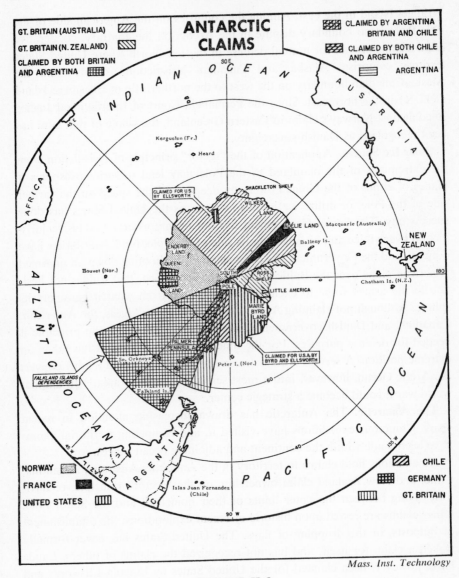

Mass. Inst. Technology

FIGURE II:8

materials be discovered in quantity, or the Antarctic become drawn into the Great Power struggle, boundaries and jurisdiction in this region might quickly assume a good deal of international importance. It is an area to watch.[20]

20 R. E. Byrd, "Our Navy Explores Antarctica," *United Nations World*, Sept., 1949; H. R. Lillie, "Antarctica in World Affairs," *Canadian Geographical Journal*, June, 1948; Brian Roberts, "The Exploration of Antarctica," *Nature Magazine*, March 22, 1947.

STABILITY OF BOUNDARIES AND PROBLEMS OF CHANGE

A quick look at history shows that a great many boundaries have been unstable. Europe from the Rhine area to the plains of Russia has been the scene of continual boundary shifts. The Middle East, and now the rimland of Asia, have many unstable areas, for example, the Israeli boundary, Kashmir, and the boundary between North and South Korea. Natural boundaries are not necessarily a satisfactory answer. Rivers and mountains may split natural economic units and peoples of the same ethnic make-up. On the other hand, artificial boundaries may prove to be quite stable; witness the United States-Canadian boundary and the 400-year stability of the Swiss boundary.

The rise of nationalism has made increasingly difficult the shifting of boundaries without use of force. The relinquishment of the smallest bit of territory becomes a national loss and a political issue of tremendous importance. The plebiscite (used in the Saar in 1935 and recommended for the Kashmir dispute) is a partial but incomplete answer.

Some states have entered into conventions defining the methods for dealing with boundary disputes. But these usually apply only to minor matters such as the changes incident to a shift in a river channel. The Charter of the United Nations and the Statute of the Court of International Justice afford means for reference of boundary disputes to the world organization. But there is no clear formula for dealing with the desire of one state for a major readjustment (such as Hitler desired) when the states affected oppose that readjustment. Boundary disputes are still a threat to world peace.

OVERCOMING GEOGRAPHIC FACTS

In the preceding pages we have seen some of the ways in which states are affected by geographic factors. These factors play an important role in the development of countries. They interact upon standards of living and relative national power. They affect foreign relations in a multitude of ways. Geographic facts are not the only forces, however, which influence the conditions and relations of nations. We shall see that other fundamental factors are capable of exerting powerful effects as well. Moreover, we must note that man has shown an increasing technical skill in overcoming geographic barriers which stand in his way.

By digging the Suez Canal, man altered basic facts of geography through creating a new short water route between Europe and the Far East, eliminating the necessity of circumnavigating Africa. In the same way, the Americans who moved mountains in Panama to cut the isthmian canal between the Atlantic and the Pacific not only greatly shortened the water distance between New

York and California but enabled the industries situated in Eastern North America to trade cheaply in the Pacific region. The canal also permitted the American fleet to shuttle quickly between the Atlantic and Pacific Oceans, with important military and political consequences.[21] Once the St. Lawrence Seaway becomes a reality, the Quebec-Labrador ores are assured a more secure route to American blast furnaces.

By learning how best to adapt himself and the knowledge of science and technology to the circumstances of environment, modern man has been progressively advancing productivity and ameliorating living conditions in the diverse areas of the world. Technological advances in rain-making may some day make it possible to influence climatic and productive conditions in arid regions, and the practical use of solar energy is by no means inconceivable. One can only surmise the possibilities latent in the development of atomic energy for changing stubborn geographic facts and, within limits, their relevance for mankind.

POLITICAL GEOGRAPHY AND GEOPOLITICS

The Science of Political Geography. In the preceding pages we have been considering some of the relationships between earth conditions and man's political institutions and the policies of states. The science of these relationships is known as political geography.[22] As one geographer has said, "Every political unit describes an areal pattern of nuclear core, constituent or administrative regions, problem areas, vulnerable zones, capitals, strategic spots, and boundaries—all affecting its success even if not vital to its persistence. These features take form with respect to specific conditions of the natural environment." [23]

Geopolitics—Applied Political Geography. The close connection which exists between the facts of geography and the conditions and activities of states has inevitably led men to study the details of these relationships in terms of their application to national policies and international politics. This application of the knowledge of political geography to the problems of statecraft is frequently referred to as geopolitics. Broadly interpreted and properly speaking, geopolitics is the study of geography as it may condition foreign policy and political phenomena.

The word *geopolitik* was first conceived by the Swedish geographer, Rudolf

21 See Miles P. Du Val, *And the Mountains Will Move* (Stanford, 1947); N. J. Padelford, *The Panama Canal in Peace and War* (New York, 1942).
22 See R. Hartshorne, "Recent Developments in Political Geography," *Am. Pol. Sci. Rev.*, Oct., Dec., 1935, pp. 785–804, 943–966.
23 Derwent Whittlesey, *The Earth and the State* (New York, 1944), p. 585. This is the best general text on political geography. See also H. R. Fifield and G. E. Pearcy, *World Political Geography* (New York, 1948). On the human side of geography see especially C. L. White and G. T. Renner, *Human Geography: Ecological Study of Society* (New York, 1948).

Kjellen, in 1916 in his study of the *State As A'Form of Life.* Drawing heavily upon the earlier writings of the German geographer, Friedrich Ratzel (1844–1904), Kjellen emphasized that the life and the power of the state depend upon its territory, soil, rivers, roads, raw materials, and food, as well as upon its people, government, economy, and culture.

Concepts of geopolitics also stem from the writings of the British geographer, Sir Halford Mackinder (1861–1947). Mackinder considered the organization of the earth's land space in relation to the balance of power and warned of the dangers of the great land mass of Eurasia uniting politically and militarily to the disadvantage of the marginal rimland states that depended upon sea power. A group of German geographers under the leadership of Karl Haushofer (1869–1946) distorted the thesis of the relationships between earth and state into what was called *Geopolitik* to support German imperialist ambitions, the theory being that to have a healthy life a state must be nourished by acquiring new lands or what Haushofer called "Lebensraum." In the United States, Admiral Alfred T. Mahan and the late Professor Nicholas Spykman (1893–1943) are notable for their writings on geopolitics; the former for his interpretations of the influence of sea power, and the latter for his exposition of an essentially American interpretation of power forces. We shall note in particular the theories of Mackinder, Mahan, and Spykman.[24]

Mackinder's Ideas. Let us first consider Sir Halford Mackinder's ideas, which have made a deep impression upon geopolitical thinking throughout the world. Mackinder's theories were first set forth in a paper entitled "The Geographical Pivot of History," presented to the Royal Geographic Society in London in 1904.[25]

Studying the global features of the earth, Mackinder observed that three-fourths of the earth is water, while only one-fourth is land. The formation of the land masses led Mackinder to speak of the joint continent of Europe, Asia, and Africa as the *World Island,* and to suggest that the reason seamen did not long ago use the term *World Island* was that they could not make the voyage around it, since the Arctic ice-cap, two thousand miles wide, prevented this.

---

[24] For readings on geopolitics see Isaiah Bowman, "Geography Versus Geopolitics," *The Geographical Review* Oct., 1942; A. Dorpalen, *The World of General Haushofer* (New York, 1942); Andrew Gyorgy, *Geopolitics: The New German Science* (Berkeley, 1944); Johannes Mattern, *Geopolitics* (New York, 1942); articles in Padelford (ed.), *Cont. Int. Rels. Readings 1949–1950,* pp. 2–13; *ibid.,* 1950–1951, pp. 23–37; Sprout, *op. cit.,* ch. 5; Robert Strausz-Hupé, *Geopolitics: The Struggle for Space and Power* (New York, 1942); H. W. Weigert, *Generals and Geographers* (Oxford, 1942); H. W. Weigert and V. Stefansson, *Compass of the World* (New York, 1944), chs. 12, 13, 18, 25; D. Whittlesey in E. M. Earle, *Makers of Modern Strategy* (Princeton, 1944), ch. 16, "Haushofer: The Geopolitician."

Some geopolitical writings reflect the influence of Darwinism on European thinking, as, for example, the theories of Ratzel, Kjellen, and to some extent Haushofer. Others stem more from a study of developments of technology and extrapolations from British and continental experience.

[25] Mackinder's principal work is his *Democratic Ideals and Reality* (London, 1919; reprinted, New York, 1942).

From this viewpoint Mackinder then proceeded to determine the *pivot area* or *Heartland* of the *World Island*. As described in his *Democratic Ideals and Reality,* published in 1919, the Heartland is the northern part and interior of Eurasia. It extends, according to his analysis, from East Europe into Siberia, being the region of Arctic or interior drainage.

Three dominant features of environment characterize the Heartland. First, there lies within this area the widest plain and plateau in the world. Secondly, across this plain flow a number of great rivers. Some of these flow into inland bodies of water which have no outlet to the ocean; others flow northward to the Arctic Ocean, but these are virtually inaccessible to the outside world because of the ice of the Arctic Ocean. The third feature of the Heartland region is a grassland zone. This zone traverses the breadth of the plain eastward and westward but does not cover its entire surface.

Mackinder, in his later years, revised somewhat his conception of the Heartland in an attempt to see how his theories of geopolitical regions corresponded to the territory of the Soviet Union. In 1943 he excluded from the Heartland a region east of the Yenisei River which he called *Lenaland Russia.*[26] This is a rugged country of mountains, plateaus, and valleys, covered almost completely by coniferous forests. In contrast, Mackinder then referred to the territory west of the Yenisei as *Heartland Russia.* The dramatic development of air power in World War II made no great change in Mackinder's thinking.

It was Mackinder's belief that the Heartland contains elements of potential strength sufficient for controlling the whole world. His classic warning was:

> Who rules East Europe
> commands the Heartland;
> Who rules the Heartland
> commands the World Island;
> Who rules the World Island
> commands the World.

Let us now see into what geopolitical regions Mackinder divides the rest of the world. Bordering on the Heartland he sees an *Inner* or *Marginal Crescent,* an area which includes the countries of Germany, Austria, Turkey, India, and China. All these regions are, in Mackinder's opinion, vulnerable to penetration by land forces from the Heartland. The remaining countries—Great Britain, South Africa, Australia, the United States, Canada, and Japan—are denoted as lands of the *Outer* or *Insular Crescent.*[27]

26 "The Round World and the Winning of the Peace," *Foreign Affairs,* July, 1943.
27 Other geopolitical writers differ somewhat on terminology. The late Nicholas Spykman of Yale spoke of Heartland and *Rimlands,* meaning by the latter essentially the Eurasian lands open to maritime access which are virtually the same as those included in Mackinder's Inner Crescent.

In the 1943 article mentioned above, Sir Halford called attention to a mantle of deserts which seems to be hung around the north temperate regions. Proceeding eastward from the Sahara Desert, it includes the deserts of Arabia, Iran, Tibet, and Mongolia, and then extends by way of the wilderness of Lena-land, Alaska, and the Laurentian Shield of Canada to the subarid belt of the United States. This belt of wilderness covers about one-fourth of the land on the globe but contains only about one-seventieth of the world's population.

GEOPOLITICAL CONCEPT OF WORLD

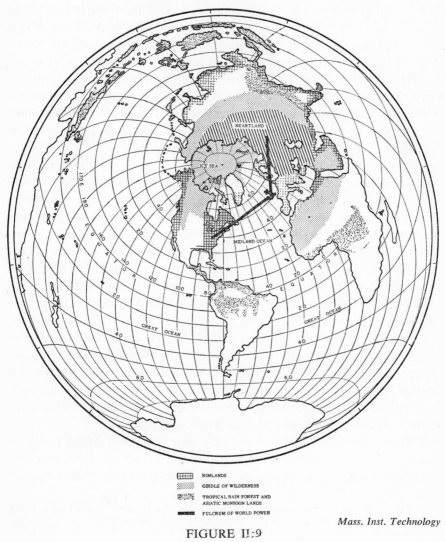

RIMLANDS
GIRDLE OF WILDERNESS
TROPICAL RAIN FOREST AND ASIATIC MONSOON LANDS
FULCRUM OF WORLD POWER

Mass. Inst. Technology

FIGURE II:9

Within this belt lie the significant Heartland and the basin of the *Midland Ocean* (North Atlantic) with its various subsidiary seas (the Mediterranean, Baltic, and Caribbean). This region between the Missouri and Yenisei Rivers, containing about a thousand million people, he considered to be the *fulcrum of world power.*

Outside these areas lie the *Great Ocean* (Pacific, Indian, and South Atlantic) and the lands which drain to it (Asiatic Monsoon lands, Australia, South America, Africa south of the Sahara, and the west coast of North America). Mackinder saw among these lands of the *Outer World* two regions which hold promise of development in the future. One is the tropical rain forests which border either side of the South Atlantic in South America and Africa. He foresaw the possibility of these lands sustaining a thousand million people, if they are devoted to agriculture and if technical and medical progress can somehow render the tropics as productive of human energy as the temperate zones. Finally, Mackinder noted the thousand million people who inhabit the *Monsoon Lands of India and China,* and expressed the hope that they might soon increase in prosperity corresponding to the other thousand million who will be living between the Missouri and Yenisei Rivers.

In appraising the theories of geopolitics of any author, the circumstances and time of their writing must be taken into consideration. Mackinder's book, *Democratic Ideals and Realities,* appeared in 1919 while representatives to the Peace Conference were meeting at Versailles. His later ideas on geopolitics were published in 1943, during World War II. At both times the most important question of the day was how to prevent the resurgence of a strong Germany. Mackinder sought to stress to the peacemakers what he considered the danger of allowing Germany to obtain a position where it could control the Heartland—and thus the world. We cannot know how Mackinder might have revised his ideas today in the light of the rise of the Soviet Union as one of the two major World Powers. But it is probable that he would see in the fact of Soviet power extending into middle Germany a substantiation of his theories about the control of the Heartland, and he would very probably advise his country and the rest of the Western world to regard very seriously the combination of Soviet Communist power with China and the possible combination of the power of the Heartland and the Monsoon lands.

Mahan's Theory. Let us now turn to the ideas of Admiral Alfred T. Mahan as expounded in his book, *The Influence of Sea Power,* which has had considerable influence, particularly on the national policy of the United States.[28]

---

[28] Alfred T. Mahan, *The Influence of Sea Power on History, 1660–1783* (Boston, 1890). See also Allan Westcott (ed.), *Mahan on Naval Warfare, Selections from the Writing of Rear-Admiral Alfred T. Mahan* (Boston, 1942); R. J. Kerner, *The Urge to the Sea* (Berkeley, 1942)

Mahan, who wrote at the close of the nineteenth century, thought of the sea as a vast plain, unbroken by obstacles, crossed by many unmarked but heavily traveled highways. He recognized the fact that the courses which vessels can pursue are limited to some extent by conditions such as wind, current, and depth of water; but he was convinced that overland transportation could never compete, either commercially or strategically, with movement by sea. He envisioned the sea as an efficient and facile means of communication, the great bond of nations.

Proof of the importance of control of the seas was seen by Mahan in the rise and exploits of British naval power. Mahan doubted, however, that Great Britain could permanently retain its exclusive position as mistress of the seas; and he looked to a time when Britain would be succeeded by the United States as the leading maritime power. Since Mahan was convinced that the result of a Great Power war would ultimately be determined at sea, he urged the United States to build a large navy capable of fighting a war *away* from home. His reasoning supported the thesis that the United States should have both an Atlantic and a Pacific fleet, including the largest capital ships.

Mahan's ideas were based on the proposition that no continental power of Europe or Asia could challenge successfully the maritime leadership of the English or American peoples. He believed that no nation with strong neighbors across its land frontiers, as, for example, France, Germany, and Russia, could control the seas. In his opinion the cost of maintaining sufficient land armaments to protect even one exposed frontier virtually eliminated the possibility of competing with a nation which, having no land frontier to defend, as in the case of Britain and the United States, could concentrate its defense activities in building up a large navy. Mahan, of course, wrote before the invention of the airplane and atomic weapons. These have fundamentally changed the ability of many states to fight a war completely away from home, as Germany and Japan discovered in World War II.

Mahan persisted in these ideas until his death in 1914, although by that time the rise of Germany as the strongest land power and the second strongest sea power (exceeding at that time the United States) was beginning seriously to challenge his theories. Germany made a powerful bid in the years 1914–1918 to achieve victory on land in France and Russia, and at the same time to cut the jugular vein of Britain by submarine warfare. But British and American seapower outbuilt and defeated the German attempt to control the seas, to starve Britain, and to isolate the European battlefield. Troopships poured American soldiers into Europe to help turn the tide of battle in 1918.

In the years 1940–1945 the destruction of the twin threats of Germany and Japan to the free nations of the world showed again that the possession and exercise of dominant sea power was indispensable to the attainment and preservation of British and American security. This need for dominant power seems, however, to be so evident as to make the assertion of its necessity an obvious truism. But this must be correlated with an analysis of the sum total of other needs to assure national security in the last half of the twentieth century, including particularly an integrated defense establishment, a far-sighted raw-material policy, and wise consideration of commitments with others.[29]

Spykman's Views. From the viewpoint of the United States at the mid-twentieth century, the writings of the late Professor Nicholas J. Spykman of Yale are especially noteworthy. Spykman was particularly concerned with the relationship of world geographic and political factors to the United States position and to its foreign policy. Although his views were propounded before the full import of strategic air power and the strategic position of the Arctic were generally appreciated, and before the potentialities of nuclear science were known, they have relevance today.[30]

Spykman stressed the importance of geography as the "most fundamentally conditioning factor" in the formulation of foreign policy because it is the most permanent. But he warned against adoption of the idea that geography could explain all phenomena in international affairs and he recognized the effects of psychology of peoples, emotions, and morality. "The geographical determinism," he wrote, which seeks to explain "by geography all things from the fourth symphony to the fourth dimension paints as distorted a picture as does an explanation of policy with no reference to geography." Continuing this theme he added: "Unfortunately for the political scientist with a fondness for simplification, but fortunately for the statesman striving to overcome the geographic handicaps of his country, neither does the entire foreign policy of a country lie in geography, nor does any part of that policy lie in geography. The factors that *condition* the policy of states are many; they are permanent and temporary, obvious and hidden; they include, apart from the geographical factor, population density, the economic structure of the country, the ethnic composition of the people, the form of government, and the complexes and pet prejudices of foreign ministers; and it is their simultaneous action and interaction that create the complex phenomena known as 'foreign policy.' "[31]

29 See Herbert Rosinski, "Mahan and the Present War," *Brassey's Naval Annual*, 1941; Rosinski, "The Role of Sea Power in Global Warfare of the Future," *Brassey's Naval Annual*, 1946, pp. 102–166; M. T. Sprout in Earle (ed.), *op. cit.*, ch. 17 entitled, "Mahan: Evangelist of Sea Power."

30 Professor Spykman's most notable work was his *America's Strategy in World Politics* (New York, 1942). See also his *The Geography of the Peace* (New York, 1944).

31 "Geography and Foreign Policy," by permission of *Am. Pol. Sci. Rev.*, Feb., 1938, pp. 28, 29, 30. Copyright 1938 by the American Political Science Association. A second installment of his discussion on geography appears in the April, 1938, issue. See further Nicholas J. Spykman and Abbie A. Rollins, "Geographic Objectives in Foreign Policy, I and II," *ibid.*, June and August, 1939.

In his principal work he emphasized what is now more generally under-stood, that the relative power of states "depends not only on military forces but on many other factors—size of territory, nature of frontiers, size of popu-lation, absence or presence of raw materials, economic and technical devel-opment, financial strength, ethnic homogeneity, effective social integration, political stability, and national spirit." [32]

At a time when many Americans still retained vestiges of isolationist think-ing, Spykman was pointing out that the Old World (Mackinder's World Island) might become so organized as to encircle the New World unless the United States employed its capability, in cooperation with Britain, to create a world balance of power. Although he doubted the ability of Mackinder's Heartland to dominate the world immediately—because of its climatic limita-tions, uneven dispersal of essential resources, and the physical-strategic bounds created by its northern, eastern, and southern borders—he neverthe-less visualized a possible evolution of the world political situation by which the United States and the Americas might become globally surrounded by powers controlling the continents of Eurasia, Africa, and Australia, and be cut off from them by the Atlantic and Pacific Oceans. He foresaw China's becoming dangerously powerful in Asia.

Adopting exclusively neither the sea power nor the land mass thesis of world power, Spykman considered that America's true policy should be to prevent dominant power from being established in the continental rimlands of Europe, the Middle East and South Asia, and the Far East. Should a united imperialist power develop in these areas, he foresaw a threat to America, Britain, and the Soviet Union. Leagued with Britain, and possessing large sea power, Spykman considered it possible that control could be established over the Eurasian rimland and that "who controls the Rimland rules Eurasia; who rules Eurasia controls the destinies of the world." But Spykman was not plead-ing for American domination of the world. He essentially desired to see the establishment of a world at peace with a balance of power within Eurasia itself and world security resting upon some form of arrangement between the United States, Britain, and the Soviet Union. History has borne out the impli-cation of many of his thoughts.[33]

IMPACT OF TECHNOLOGY ON INFLUENCE OF GEOGRAPHY

The technological developments in recent years particularly in airpower and in the weapons of mass destruction have introduced new factors, or at least new dimensions, into the relationships of geography, power, and policy.

[32] *America's Strategy in World Politics*, p. 19.
[33] For a provocative review of Spykman's thoughts see Edgar S. Furniss, Jr., "Contributions of Nicholas John Spykman to the Study of International Politics," *World Politics*, April, 1952.

Although sea power is capable of reaching most coastal areas of the globe and of assisting the projection of power inland therefrom, it is foreclosed from the Arctic shores of most of the USSR and North America the greater part of every year. Moreover, the vital centers of both land masses are located far from these shores. Air power, however, is now capable of traversing and penetrating all parts of the globe. There is no important political or industrial center beyond its reach. The importance of the short-cut air space across "the roof of the world" is demonstrated by the growth of air bases on both sides of the Arctic and by the large amount of air activity over the Arctic Ocean. The shorelands of the *Icy Sea* are no longer an impenetrable rimland.[34]

These thoughts do not imply, however, that geography is not still important in the military power equation. Distance combined with technology can be utilized to develop defenses. In fact, the huge concentrations of destructive power which technology now makes it possible to launch in a short time have made distance and space more important than ever in the strategy of defense. This consideration in itself will press nations toward coalitions which give geographic depth to a defense plan as well as providing the resources necessary both for defense and for the attainment of higher standards of living.

The facts of geography and of politics indicate that nowadays no nation can live wholly unto itself. No nation, large or small, can expect to obtain absolute military security; certainly there is no security to be found in the concept, perhaps once sound, of isolation.

Man's political world exists, and his national policies must function, within the facts of his natural environment. These provide certain fixed points of reference. The resources of his world taken in combination with his own energy and his ability to exploit them wisely can be made to serve his well-being and his defense. They are a beginning point in calculating the national power of states. A study of these assets and points of reference is essential to any sound thinking on international politics. But although the facts of geography remain fixed we must keep in mind that the realities of modern technology have altered their significance and probably will continue to do so in the future.

SUGGESTED READINGS

Samuel W. Boggs, *International Boundaries* (New York, 1940).
Andrew Gyorgy, *Geopolitics, The New German Science* (Berkeley, 1944).
Stephen B. Jones, *Boundary Making* (Washington, 1945).

34 See Lt. Col. Harry A. Sachaklian, "Air Power and the Heartland," *Air Quar. Rev.,* Summer, 1950. See also S. C. Cooper, *The Right to Fly* (New York, 1947); E. Huntington, "Geography and Aviation," *Air Affairs,* Vol. II (1947), pp. 46–60; Stefan T. Possony, *Strategic Air Power: The Pattern of Dynamic Security* (Washington, 1949).

George A. Lincoln and associates, *Economics of National Security* (rev. ed., New York, 1954).

Fairfield Osborn, *The Limits of the Earth* (New York, 1953).

G. E. Pearcy, R. H. Fifield, and associates, *World Political Geography* (New York, 1948).

President's Materials Policy Commission Report, *Resources for Freedom* (Washington, 1952).

Nicholas J. Spykman, *America's Strategy in World Politics* (New York, 1942).

L. Dudley Stamp, *Land for Tomorrow* (New York, 1952).

G. Taylor, *Geography in the Twentieth Century* (New York, 1951).

W. Van Royen and O. Bowles, *Mineral Resources of the World* (New York, 1952).

H. W. Weigert, V. Stefansson, and others, *New Compass of the World* (New York, 1949).

Derwent Whittlesey, *The Earth and the State* (New York, 1939).

E. W. Zimmerman, *World Resources and Industries* (rev. ed., New York, 1950).

CHAPTER III

Population and World Politics

IN THE preceding chapter we discussed the relationship of geographical factors to a nation's position in world politics. Let us now consider the human element.

IMPORTANCE OF UNDERSTANDING POPULATION CONDITIONS

Population is one of the basic ingredients of statehood. It is one of the fundamental factors in the economic and cultural life of each nation and of the world. The size and characteristics of a nation's population are among the principal determinants of the role which it can occupy in international relations. Population pressures in certain countries have led to policies of national expansion, imperialism, and wars of conquest. The desire of peoples to migrate to countries with higher standards of living, or to lands where freedom reigns in place of political terror, has produced a succession of international problems. Scientists have become alarmed over the implications of the continually mounting world population and the shrinking stores of irreplaceable natural resources. One population expert has said that every long-term economic problem has a population problem at its roots. In short, the factor of world population is one of the key aspects of international relations.

DISTRIBUTION OF WORLD POPULATION

Let us take a look at the world population situation. On page 64 is a diagram entitled *Relative Population By Countries* and on page 63 a tabulation of principal populations in continental groupings. Examine these carefully. What deductions can you draw from them?

The most critical fact brought out by these figures is the very uneven distribution of the more than 2,400,000,000 total world population. It is packed into Europe, with massive blocks in Asia; but it has low percentages per land area in Africa, the Americas, and Australasia.

COMPARATIVE AREAS AND POPULATION [1]

CONTINENT	PER CENT OF WORLD'S AREA	1952 ESTIMATED POPULATION	PER CENT OF WORLD'S POPULATION
Africa	22.3	200,000,000	8.2
Americas	31.0	336,000,000	13.8
Asia (ex. USSR)	19.95	1,295,000,000	53.1
Europe (ex. USSR)	3.63	396,000,000	16.25
USSR	16.4	193,000,000 [a]	7.93
Oceania	6.32	13,300,000	.55

[a] Last available estimate of USSR, 1946. Statements from USSR sources are to the effect that population is increasing at a rate of about 3 million a year.

Population Situation in Asia. A glance at the schematic diagram may suggest that there is room in Asia to accommodate the large numbers there. But now look at a physical map of Asia. The enormous wastelands of the Gobi Desert, the Himalaya Mountain belt, the recesses of Sinkiang, the rugged areas of interior China, and the vast frigid tracts of Siberia afford little attraction. Asia has room, but a good deal of it is room in which modern man does not readily choose to live. A demographic map will quickly show that a large part of Asia's population lives compressed together along the coastlines, river valleys, and fertile plains of China, India, Java, and Japan. The population is congested in these areas and sparse in the upland, mountainous, and jungle regions. In parts of remote Sinkiang there are less than two persons per square mile. On the other hand, in some of the rice-producing regions of south China there are as many as 4,000 per square mile. The Province of Kiangsu, for instance, in which Shanghai is situated, has almost 36.4 million people living in an area of 41,818 square miles—approximately the area of the state of Ohio. This is six times as many people as live in Ohio, and nearly three times the population of New York State. Kiangsu is said to be the most densely inhabited political unit in the world.

It has been estimated that over one billion persons living in China, India, Indonesia, and Japan—one half of the world's total population—actually live within roughly 8 per cent of the world's land area if the localities of principal habitation are considered.[2] It is little wonder that there is unrest in Asia, that Indians have wanted to migrate to Africa, and that Chinese and Japanese have pressed outward toward the Americas, Australasia, and southeast Asia. This suggests an issue for international relations that may well trouble statesmen in the years to come, especially when it is realized that some of these other regions not only have much lower densities but lower birth rates and more ample resources. This issue has already produced friction as a result of

[1] Computed from *United Nations Statistical Yearbook, 1952* (New York, 1952), Table 1A.
[2] See G. E. Pearcy, R. H. Fifield, and associates. *World Political Geography* (New York, 1948), p. 530.

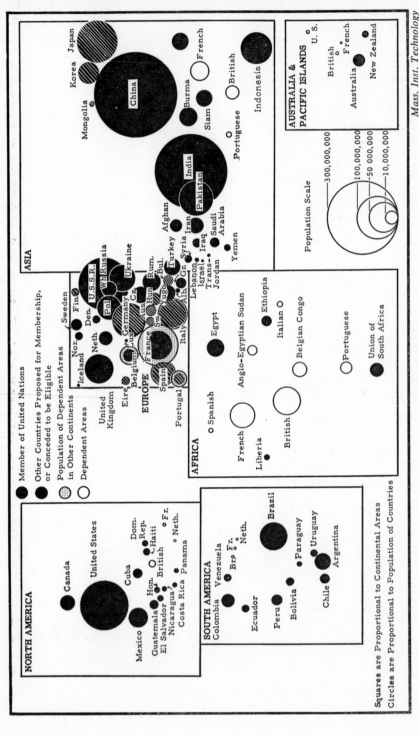

RELATIVE POPULATION BY COUNTRIES

FIGURE III:1

Mass. Inst. Technology

the "White Australia" policy which denies admission of Asiatics to that island continent. Similarly, the 1924 Immigration Law of the United States, which until 1945 barred all East Asiatics from any annual quota of immigration into this country, stirred strong protests among Japanese and Chinese.[3]

Land Population and Politics in Africa. The diagram may also suggest that Africa is capable of sustaining a vastly greater population. But look again at a topographic and a climatological map of Africa. The Sahara Desert and the tropical rain forests of equatorial Africa occupy a sizable part of the continent. These areas are not inviting to large populations. Some of the peripheral areas can support considerably larger populations, provided the water table which is already dropping does not lower too rapidly. In the north in the Nile Valley there already exists one of the densest population centers in the world. The figures for the inhabited areas of Egypt show a population density of 1,426 per square mile.

African space is large compared to the continent's present population. As industrialization, transportation facilities, and economic development increase in response to world demands for Africa's goods and markets, large growth may well occur in its population, if experience in other parts of the world holds true. In the meantime one of the principal questions confronting the black and colored peoples in certain sections of East and South Africa is their freedom and right to inhabit fertile and desirable areas in view of restriction measures adopted or being considered with respect to them. For some time to come Africa's population problems may be more concerned with issues of racial discrimination and segregation than with the pressure of numbers.[4]

Compression of Population in Europe. The diagram on *Relative Population By Countries* emphasizes the great density of population in Europe. With the smallest of the continental areas, Europe's twenty-six states (excluding the USSR, the Ukraine, and White Russia, but including Turkey) contain a population of nearly 400 million. If the peoples of European Russia are added to Europe, as the diagram portrays, Europe's proportion of the world's population rises to nearly one-fourth of the total. The number of states, combined with the press of population, tell part of the story why Europe has so many crises and wars. There is no room within Europe for territorial or for population expansion except by conflict. Pressures build up demands for economic and political policies which are bound to create friction.

Some measure of Europe's population situation is indicated by the estimate reached at an international conference in 1951 that Europe has over five mil-

---

[3] Asia's population problems are analyzed in W. S. Thompson, *Population and Peace in the Pacific* (Chicago, 1946). For discussion of migration, see p. 82 below.
[4] See W. M. Macmillan, *Africa Emergent* (Penguin Books, 1949).

lion more people than its economy can support save by a "debased" standard of living, unemployment, food insufficiencies, and inequitable tax levies. Italy alone has been estimated to have a "surplus" manpower of three million.[5] Conditions such as these afford opportunities for revolution, dictatorship, and war unless they are alleviated.

The already existing pressures of population upon available land spaces, coupled with the difficulty of building up expanding economies to raise standards of living beyond their present levels, explain why some of the European nations have become increasingly concerned with the post-war trend of events in Asia and other parts of the world which have closed these areas to major emigration. More extensive applications of technology to industry may help boost Europe's economic productivity. But fundamentally the continent faces a situation in which pressures are likely to become no lighter in the foreseeable future. The resistance of foreign countries, including the United States, to admit large numbers of immigrants indicates that by and large Europe must live with its population problem. Hence the rest of the international community must be prepared for problems which may stem from this.

The Americas. Of all the continental regions the Americas have the most evenly balanced ratio between area, resources, and population. Neither North nor South America as a whole suffers from excessive population. In some localities there are pressures, and in some of the Central American lands in particular there are extraordinarily high birth rates.[6] In spite of this, both continents have spaces capable of accommodating many more people, even without pressing into the marginal waste lands. But it may well be that each has what may be called an "optimum population," [7] considering resources available, standards of living, and relative absence of political tensions.

Australasia and Oceania. This is the least heavily populated space area in the inhabited part of the world. If percentage of the world's land area is divided by the percentage of world's population possessed by a continental area, Oceania will be found to have a ratio of 14–1. By comparison the ratio for the Americas is 2¾–1; for Africa, 3–1. This suggests great space for peopling. The Chinese and Japanese have for decades been cognizant of the islands of Oceania and the sparsely inhabited regions of Australia and New Zealand as outlets for their teeming populations. But one must remember that Australia

---

[5] *The New York Times*, Oct. 21, 1951, iv, p. 4. On the possible future of European population see F. W. Notestein, *The Future Population of Europe and the Soviet Union, 1940–1970* (Geneva, 1944).

[6] See p. 78 below.

[7] See M. Gottlieb, "Optimum Population, Foreign Trade and World Economy," *Population Studies*, Sept., 1949, pp. 151–169.

has a vast heartland of desert which will remain largely uninhabitable until new means of irrigation can be found, while in the Pacific islands local economic conditions will not support much larger populations. Eventually ways may be found whereby the continent of Australia may prove capable of supporting larger numbers of people. But for the present there are distinct limits to the numbers it can support with present standards of living which the Australians naturally wish to maintain and improve.[8]

HIGH AND LOW PRESSURE AREAS

World Density Pattern. In nearly any atlas you will find a world map showing the density of population. Such a map is worth careful examination. It reveals a certain fairly definable pattern which bears a close relation to geographical factors. Notice that the heaviest populations tend to be situated along coastlines, river valleys, lake rims, and rich alluvial deposits. Moderate population densities generally prevail in the continental interiors. The scarcest populations live in the Arctic, sub-Arctic, desert, mountainous, and inaccessible tropical regions.

The following table, based upon statistics available through the United Nations, indicates the comparative densities of a few countries.[9]

HIGH PRESSURE COUNTRIES	INHABITANTS PER SQUARE MILE	LOW PRESSURE COUNTRIES	INHABITANTS PER SQUARE MILE
Java	1010	United States	47
Netherlands	739	Soviet Union	23
Japan	544	Brazil	14
United Kingdom	526	Canada	3
Germany	490	Australia	2
India	460		
Italy	390		

With population densities such as those possessed by the Western European states, industrialization and an active foreign trade have been a requisite to the attainment of a high standard of living. The same has been true of Japan. The eagerness with which India is pressing toward industrialization reveals an awareness in its case also of the urgency of raising productivity if starvation and want are to be alleviated in the midst of a rising birth rate and population density.[10]

[8] See H. L. Wilkenson, *The World's Population Problems and a White Australia* (Melbourne, 1930).

[9] Computed from data in *Statistical Yearbook of the United Nations, 1948* (New York, 1949).

[10] See F. W. Notestein, "Problems of Policy in Relation to Areas of Heavy Population Pressure," in *Demographic Studies of Selected Areas of Rapid Growth (Milbank Memorial Fund Quar.,* 1944).

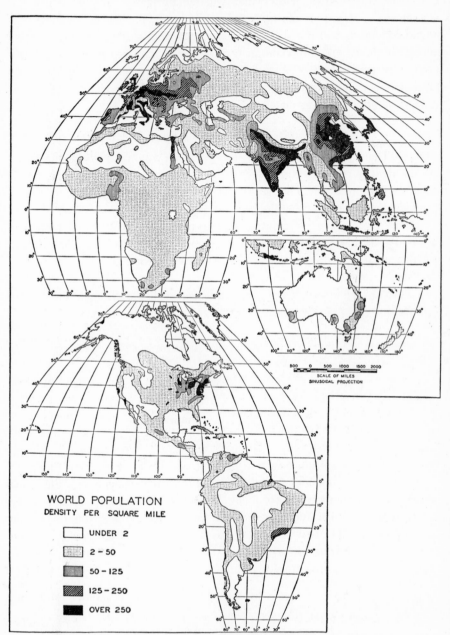

WORLD POPULATION
DENSITY PER SQUARE MILE

UNDER 2

2 – 50

50 – 125

125 – 250

OVER 250

D. H. Davis, The Earth and Man, *Rev. Edn. Copyright 1948 by The Macmillan Company*

FIGURE III:2

Easement Problems. The pressure problem is probably greatest in the Nile Valley of Egypt, the Ganges Valley of India, in some of the rice-raising lands of Southeast China, and in Java. The economies of these regions are essentially agricultural. To get above the bare subsistence level, more fertile land per person is needed in a predominantly agricultural economy than in an industrial state having a variegated economy and able to engage in foreign trade to supplement what cannot be grown or produced within its own limits.

The difficulties facing the leaders in these highest pressure countries are two-fold: (1) to find an outlet where some of their people may emigrate, and where they would be willing and able to go; and (2) to obtain the capital necessary to introduce industrialization on a scale large enough to ease the pressure upon the land. The first of these courses does not hold much hope of a solution, since a high birth rate can easily outstrip emigration arrangements. Moreover, countries with a severe population pressure have had relatively poor success in inducing their people to emigrate to colonial or underdeveloped areas in significant numbers. The more attractive lands for settlement have interposed immigration barriers to protect their own domestic economies and national composition. And often peoples have preferred to stay with their own kin rather than migrate to pioneer lands. Of a different order but no less serious are the questions of finding capital for industrialization and markets for manufactured goods in a world economy of increasing competition. This was a serious issue before World War II; it remains an urgent one today. One of the key issues facing the United States and the nations of the free world generally is how to assist the peoples of the high-pressure areas, and especially the friendly peoples of South and East Asia, to cope with the economic and political problems to which their population situations and their economic aspirations give rise. For this is closely related to the global struggle with the force of communism.[11]

With the unclaimed land of the world gone, and with trade competition increasing, easement of population conditions is bound to be a slow and arduous process. The territorially large, low-pressure countries such as Australia, Brazil, and Canada naturally tend to appear attractive as outlets for the compressed populations of Europe and Asia. Statistics make them appear this way. A glance at physiographic and climate maps will quickly show that there are large areas in each of these countries which are not conducive to settlement. In Australia there is the great arid desert. In Brazil there are the equatorial jungles. In Canada there are the frigid northlands. Man will no doubt

[11] A thought-provoking analysis of the international dangers stemming from population pressure will be found in Warren S. Thompson, *Danger Spots in World Population* (New York, 1930). See also A. M. Carr-Saunders, "Crowded Countries and Empty Spaces," *Foreign Affairs*, April, 1950.

conquer these barriers with the aid of time and technology. But progress toward a solution will require provision of development capital—a major problem in itself. For the present these regions do not provide an international solution to the world's population problem. It would appear that the era of great migrations is closed.

We shall consider in Chapter V the policies which have been adopted by the United States and others to make capital and technical assistance available for the development of the so-called underdeveloped lands.

Expansion of Low-Pressure Countries. High-pressure countries are by no means the only ones whose peoples seek foreign lands. The Soviet Union, with a great land area and vast resources, continues to seek control over a larger domain. In this instance the reason appears to lie in political motivations. Historical national ambitions, security considerations, the urge to influence the flow of raw materials or the character of markets, a sense of mission to develop other lands, and a lust for power have been generally more influential in leading nations to territorial expansion than has high population pressure.

It may also be noted that emigration sometimes occurs from low-pressure areas to higher-pressure localities. Thus, ever since 1849 the Irish have been leaving Erin for the crowded cities of the United States. In this case economic and cultural considerations have been a predominant factor.

Migration movements may also be caused or stimulated by political factors quite apart from demographic considerations, as in the case of thousands who have fled from nazism and communism in Europe, the Moslems who fled from Hindu rule in India, and the Arabs who were forced from Palestine when the State of Israel was established. Population pressure is but one of the motivations underlying mass movements of peoples.

POPULATION GROWTH SINCE 1800

Scarce data are available to show with accuracy what the population of the world was before the beginning of the nineteenth century. By 1800 it had probably reached the neighborhood of 906 million.[12] Since that time, however, it has more than doubled to attain the present approximate 2.4 billion.

Europe's population, excluding the Soviet Union, has increased more than threefold since 1800, from 100 million to 400 million. If European Russia is included, it can be reckoned that the population of the European continent has more than quadrupled. This increase has occurred notwithstanding the succession of wars in the past century and a half, and the fact that more than 50

---

[12] *Population Bulletin,* June, 1951.

million of Europe's people have migrated to other continents. The English-speaking white peoples alone have increased tenfold in the past century and a half.[13]

There are three principal explanations of the amazing increase in world population since 1800.

Decline in Death Rates. A first and principal cause of the large increase in world population has been a marked decline in death rates. This is illustrated in what has happened to infant mortality. It has been recorded that in France in the middle of the eighteenth century out of every 1,000 babies not more than 540 lived to be five years of age. In Germany until the latter part of the nineteenth century as many as 300 babies died during the first year. Today the rate has been reduced to 43 per 1,000 in England. In the United States there are now no more than 32 deaths per 1,000 in the first year. In Germany infant mortality has been reduced to 64. Great variations exist in mortality rates to-day. Sweden and New Zealand have the lowest rate, with 25 deaths per 1,000 births. On the other hand, Chile, Roumania, Burma, and India have a rate in excess of 160.

The reductions in death rates which have occurred in many parts of the world have resulted from advances in medical science, public health, sanitary engineering, and popular education. These have blazed the trail for dramatic changes, and the end is not yet.[14] Should medical science succeed in reducing the infant death rate in India, for instance, to a point comparable to that prevailing in some of the Western countries, while the birth rate remained at its present high level, India would be faced with a food problem which would surpass anything the world now knows. Malnutrition, starvation, and disease now account for vast numbers of deaths of infants as well as adults. If medical science succeeds in improving birth and general sanitary conditions in Oriental countries, there will need to be a major change in the production and the distribution of world food supplies. Otherwise we can expect the effects will include international trouble.

Coupled with the decreasing death rate owing to scientific progress, there

[13] For study of past population trends see A. M. Carr-Saunders, *World Populations, Past Growth and Present Trends* (Oxford, 1936), and R. R. Kuczynski, *Population Movements* (London, 1936). Some authorities have figured that the world population increased about 500 million from 1650 to 1800, while from 1800 to 1950 it increased nearly a billion and a half. It has been figured that the English-speaking peoples alone increased from something like 5.5 million in 1600 to 200 million in 1940. R. P. Vance, "Malthus and the Principle of Population," *Foreign Affairs,* July, 1948, p. 682; C. B. Fawcett, "The Numbers and Distribution of Mankind," *Scientific Monthly,* vol. 64, (1947), pp. 389–396.

[14] For data on death rates see Warren S. Thompson, *Population Problems* (New York, 1942) and R. R. Kuczynski, *The Balance of Births and Deaths* (New York, 1928). For current figures see latest *Statistical Yearbook of the United Nations.*

has been a decline in the practices of abortion and infanticide which used to be common in some Asiatic countries. This has contributed somewhat to the increases in population—how much it is hard to say.

Rise in Birth Rates. A second cause of the world population growth has been a marked increase in birth rates throughout the world. In Japan, for example, the birth rate increased from 25 per 1,000 people in 1872, when modernization and urbanization started, to 34.9 in 1925. As a result, Japan's population may triple itself in a century. This jump has been attributed to a variety of causes, including prohibition of abortion, government propaganda for large families, increase in food supply and in opportunities for gainful employment, and improvements in medical care and sanitation. As one student of Japanese affairs has said, the industrial revolution in Japan produced in a period of two generations changes comparable to what took a century in the West.[15] General increases in birth rates have also been noted in other parts of the world during this same period of time. In each of these instances, increased economic opportunities also appear to have played an important part.

Some idea of the increase which is going on even now in the world can be gained from a moment's survey of the table of Crude Birth Rates found in the *United Nations Statistical Yearbook*. Several countries have an insistent rate of more than 40 births per 1,000 population year after year. The pressure problem has by no means attained its peak.

Lengthening Life Span. A third cause of increased population has been a lengthening of the span of human life. This has kept pace with the declining death rate of infants, and has resulted in progressively larger net populations at given times. In 1800 the average life span in Europe was 30 years. It was slightly over 35 years in the United States at that time. Today the life expectation of the average inhabitant of the United States, the Western European countries, and the British Commonwealth has risen to 60 years or more.[16]

Studies made by the United Nations show that there are "great contrasts between different regions." For example, "the mean expectation of life at birth" in 1921–1931 for India (including Burma and Pakistan) was "about 27 years for both sexes. As a contrast, the New Zealand life table of 1934–1938 shows a mean expectation of life at birth of 65.5 years for men and 68.4 years for women." Stated in another way, the United Nations has found that today 81 per cent of the New Zealand people can expect to live to be 50 years

---

[15] A. E. Hindmarsh, *The Basis of Japanese Foreign Policy* (Cambridge, 1936), pp. 30–55; see also E. F. Penrose, *Population Theories and Their Application with Special Reference to Japan* (Stanford, 1934). For the Orient in general see Warren Thompson, *Population and Peace in the Pacific* (Chicago, 1946).

[16] The life expectancy in the United States is figured to be 61.6 years for men and 65.89 for women. *Statistical Abstract of the United States, 1952* (Washington, 1952).

of age, but only 15 per cent in India can now hope to survive to this age.[17]

Owing to the inadequacy of demographic statistics in many countries, only an approximation can be given of the present-day world life expectancy figure. It may be in the neighborhood of 35 years. Whatever it may be precisely, there is an unmistakable trend toward greater longevity.

The lengthening life span can be attributed in part to improved sanitation, better care for the infirm and aging, and general medical progress. It is also due in large measure, directly and indirectly, to the industrial revolution which has made possible in some areas of the world better housing, better and more food, more gainful and health-minded employment, and more capital goods.

PRESENT POPULATION TRENDS

In view of the tremendous increase in world population during the past 150 years, it becomes pertinent to ask if present trends point to an indefinite continuance of this growth. If this rise is to continue, it is clear that, if peace and security are to prevail, the nations must face realistically, on a far bolder basis than has been done thus far, the related problems of food supply, dwindling water levels, the distribution of natural resources and goods, employment, and international migration.

Statistical Difficulties. In trying to visualize what trend there may be in world population, it must be realized that statistics for reasonably accurate plotting of changes exist only for about one-fourth of today's world population. No accurate figures are available for China, Africa, the East Indies, the Soviet Union, and parts of Latin America. Indeed, demographic investigations have shown that for a large number of geographical areas estimated to contain 40 per cent of the world population, size and trends can only be "guesstimated." It is quite possible that errors of computation may run over 100 million in the present 2.4 billion world figure.

General World Picture. Using available information, the United Nations Secretariat has tentatively concluded that for the world as a whole a natural increase of 1 per cent a year was taking place just before World War II. Allowing for error, it is possible that pressure upon the world's living space and its productive resources may be growing by something like 23 to 25 million lives per year.[18] This means that every morning in the year there are at least 65,000 more persons to be fed than on the previous day.

Position of the United States. Among the Western Powers the United States is in one of the most favored positions regarding population growth. As re-

---

[17] The data on present age spans are from the United Nations Department of Social Affairs, *World Population Trends, 1920–1947* (New York, 1949), pp. 12–13.

[18] United Nations, *World Population Trends, 1920–1947* (New York, 1949), pp. 3, 11.

cently as 1943 it was estimated that by 1953 it would have no more than 144,000,000. In fact, the figure was just over 160,000,000. This is a result of the war boom in marriages and births. Admitting that variations in the rate of growth may occur—as, for example, continuance of the higher birth rate, authorization of large-scale immigration, or, in the opposite direction, a devastating atomic war or epidemic—estimates have suggested that in 1975 the population will exceed 190,000,000. Actually, the present trend points to something near 225,000,000. It is hard for Americans to realize that since 1947 the crude birth rate in the United States has practically equaled that of India, and that, as a British geographer has observed, the high rates of population increase are not in India and China or in crowded Europe, but in the Americas.[19]

Nevertheless, in the coming years the United States will be far exceeded in gross population by China and India. The Soviet Union will undoubtedly continue to have a substantial margin of population. To retain its position of leadership in world affairs, the United States, under these circumstances, must further strengthen its efforts in science and technology; it must extend the relative percentage of highly skilled and educated persons in the populace; it must search out new means of power; and it must continue to have moral and political strength.

Studying population trends, some experts have classified countries in three categories: (1) those facing "incipient decline"; (2) countries of "transitional growth"; and (3) regions of "high potential growth." Let us look at these briefly.

1. COUNTRIES OF INCIPIENT DECLINE. These are countries which have passed through a period of rapid growth, where death rates have been cut, and where birth rates have on the whole tended to decline. They therefore have populations which have an inclination toward remaining within fairly narrow bounds unless an unforeseen reversal occurs. Included in this category are the nations of Central and Western Europe, Australia, and New Zealand.

In Western Europe and North America, birth rates were high and families large in the early stages of the industrial and agricultural revolutions in the nineteenth century. As time wore on, after peoples had become habituated to higher standards of living, an attitude became prevalent to have fewer children, thereby reducing expenses and having greater means for material possessions. Coupled with this undoubtedly was apprehension regarding economic security due to fluctuations in the business cycle in an increasingly urbanized and industrialized society.

A few figures will illustrate this trend. In France, for example, the rate of

[19] L. D. Stamp, *Land for Tomorrow* (Bloomington and New York, 1952), p. 212.

births was 31.4 in 1808. In 1933 this was down to 16.2. In the United Kingdom the drop during the century preceding World War II was equally precipitous, from 31 to a low of 14.9 in 1933. In many of the Western states birth rates have risen remarkably since World War II. In 1947 the rate was 21 in France; 20.8 in the United Kingdom; 24 in Australia. The United States has startled all observers by jumping from a rate of 17 before the war to 25.8 in 1947.[20] No one knows whether such rates will be sustained.

France is probably in the most serious position of the Western Powers as far as population outlook is concerned. Before World War II France had more deaths than births. This trend has stopped, but the margin is still a slim one. From a manpower point of view France has not yet recovered from World War I. Compared to Germany in the years ahead, its outlook is dark; for it is estimated that by 1971 a reunited Germany may expect 26 per cent more men between the ages of 15 and 34 than it had in 1946.[21] Even in 1951 the population of all Germany was 65,417,000 as compared to 42,239,000 for France.

2. COUNTRIES OF TRANSITIONAL GROWTH. Countries in this category are in the mid-stages of industrialization. Economic and political conditions are such that peoples live in some doubt of their future. Birth rates on the whole are high, but after a further increase in the next quarter century it is expected that their populations will reach a point of stability or begin to decline. Among the countries now in this group may be included Japan,[22] some of the Central European states, and the Soviet Union.

The Soviet Union. The inclusion of the Soviet Union in any trend-line picture is difficult because of the lack of authentic statistics. Working with fragmentary figures, and relying heavily on the pre-war trends (which may or may not exist now), population experts have placed the population in 1950 at about 200,000,000, and they have tentatively estimated the USSR population by 1970 at 250,000,000. This does not include the satellite states. If this growth materializes, it will be an increase of 30 per cent within one generation, and will in itself more than equal the present populations of either the United Kingdom, Brazil, Italy, or France. It is possible, of course, that social or other factors may retard such a growth.

20 For a general résumé of population trends see L. D. Stamp, *Land for Tomorrow* (Bloomington and New York, 1952), ch. ii. For studies of European population trends see A. M. Carr-Saunders, *Population* (London, 1931); F. W. Notestein *et al., The Future Population of Europe and the Soviet Union* (Geneva, 1944); G. Frumkin, *Population Changes in Europe Since 1939* (New York, 1951).

21 "The Demography of War: Germany," *Population Index,* October, 1948, pp. 291–308.

22 On the prospects of Japan's population see W. S. Thompson, *Population and Peace in the Pacific,* pp. 98–99; I. B. Taeuber and E. G. Beal, "The Dynamics of Population in Japan," *The Milbank Memorial Fund Quart.,* July, 1944. Some estimates have placed Japan's probable population in 1970 between 93,000,000 and 105,000,000.

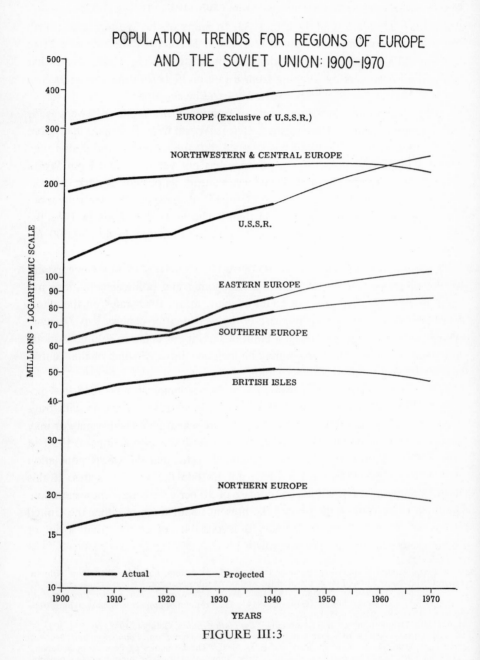

POPULATION TRENDS FOR REGIONS OF EUROPE AND THE SOVIET UNION: 1900-1970

EUROPE (Exclusive of U.S.S.R.)

NORTHWESTERN & CENTRAL EUROPE

U.S.S.R.

EASTERN EUROPE

SOUTHERN EUROPE

BRITISH ISLES

NORTHERN EUROPE

MILLIONS - LOGARITHMIC SCALE

YEARS

Actual   Projected

FIGURE III:3

Once past the 1970–1990 peak, the Soviet population may respond to the effects of industrialization and education, and begin to taper off. Whatever happens, the fact will remain that if the USSR reaches such a peak, its people will then outnumber the combined populations of the United Kingdom, France, Germany, and Italy by about 40,000,000. This is a contingency the economic, political, and military implications of which cannot be overlooked.[23]

3. REGIONS OF HIGH POTENTIAL GROWTH. Countries within this category are those which have yet to be fully industrialized. They are what are now being spoken of as "underdeveloped areas." Included in this group are China, South and Southeast Asia, the Middle East, Latin America, and parts of Africa. These areas are only on the threshold of economic expansion compared with the Western Powers, Japan, and even the Soviet Union. If the process of industrialization, with its resultant increase in per capita income and consumption, takes place in these areas and the general pattern of population increase follows as it has elsewhere, the entire picture of world affairs may be altered.

In China, with an estimated population of 460,000,000, we must bear in mind that even a normal growth adds a tremendous number of individuals every year. In the face of such numbers it is easy to underestimate potential growth. If China should have twenty-five years of relative tranquillity and economic growth, an increase of more than 100 million people by 1970 would not be inconceivable. It is, of course, possible that the "sorrows" of China—famine, flood, pestilence, and war—will continue unabated for a long time to come, checking the natural increase of China's population.

India has experienced "high growth" for the past two decades. Between 1931–1941 there was an increase of over 50,000,000 people, and another 24,000,000 were added in the next decade. Professor Thompson says that if India increases at the rate prevailing during the past decade and a half it will have a population of 680,000,000 in 1981. How likely this may be depends upon its developments in agriculture, industry, and medicine. "A natural increase of 15 per cent a decade is so common," he says, "that it is safe to say that it will be the pressure of India's population on its food supply and its ability to control disease which will determine its growth."[24] Such possibilities in India and China do not encourage expectations for a material increase in the standard of living.

[23] On Soviet population trends see Frank Lorimer, "Population Prospects in the Soviet Union," in H. W. Weigert, V. Stefansson, and R. E. Harrison (ed.), *New Compass of the World* (New York, 1949), pp. 162–181. For an earlier analysis see Notestein *et al.*, *op. cit.*
[24] On Chinese and Indian population trends see Thompson, *Population and Peace in the Pacific*, pp. 182–183, 225–226; K. Davis, "Demographic Fact and Policy in India," *The Milbank Memorial Fund Quart.*, July, 1944; K. Davis, *The Population of India and Pakistan* (Princeton, 1951).

Latin America has some of the highest birth rates in the world. In Mexico, Costa Rica, El Salvador, Ecuador, and Puerto Rico, rates fluctuate around 40 per 1,000. Latin America as a whole is experiencing a natural rate of increase of about 2 per cent per year.

FUTURE POPULATION

The magnitude of the population problem facing mankind is indicated when it is realized that at least half of the world's present population lives in the regions of high potential growth, of which India and China are typical. This means that large additions to the total world population are to be expected in the next fifty years, barring exceptional contingencies.

Possible World Total in Year 2000. One estimate made by the Office of Population Research at Princeton University suggests that in the year 2000 the total population of the world may number 3,300,000,000. United Nations statisticians have made a "calculated guess" that the present population may possibly double in the next seventy years.[25] Professor Kingsley Davis has gone so far as to suggest that "if the present geometric pace were to last until the year 2240 the earth would hold 21,000,000,000 people." Professor L. Dudley Stamp has calculated that if the estimated rate of world increase between 1920–1947 of 1.15 per cent—which is less than that of the United States, South America, or India today—were to be maintained, there might be 1,266,000,000,000 people by the year 2500.[26] But let us now suggest the smaller figure; that is high enough. Abstract reasoning on future populations in a distant future with conjectural rates of increase does not necessarily describe what *will* happen.

Owing to the high natural increases taking place in Asia and its outlying islands, these lands seem destined eventually to become the center of gravity of world population, with Asia alone possibly accounting for as many as 2 billion in the year 2000.

Effects upon International Relations. Population increases, whatever they may be, are bound to have an effect upon future international relations. The peoples in the high concentration areas are certain to claim a larger voice in world affairs. Their influence will be felt in international politics much more than it is today. Should Asia become industrialized to the extent of Europe and, with industry, amass mechanized military forces, the power position of the Western states in the world community might well be altered. Should China remain linked with the Soviet Union, and should India, together with other heavily populated parts of Asia, become assimilated to the Soviet orbit, world

[25] *United Nations Bulletin,* Feb. 1, 1953, p. 107. See also *The New York Times,* May 3, 1954.
[26] See table on possible future populations calculated at differing rates of increase in Stamp, *op. cit.,* p. 30.

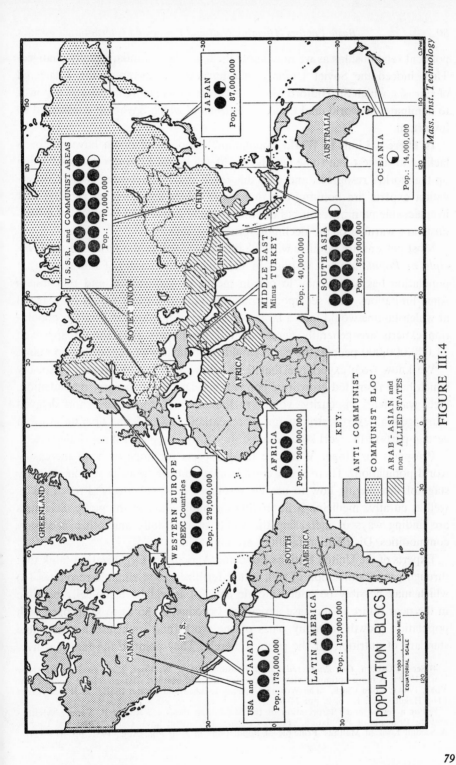

POPULATION BLOCS

FIGURE III:4

Mass. Inst. Technology

political relationships as we now know them would be fundamentally changed. Then indeed the Soviet Union might have within its grasp the *Heartland* of Eurasia, which Sir Halford Mackinder foresaw as giving its possessor power to dominate the world, and the Asiatic *Rimland* which Spykman considered so important.

Is There a Limit to World Population? Prophets of doom have not been lacking to suggest that some day the world will become "overpopulated," using up the world's resources, and with this reach some cataclysmic crisis. Conservation experts are pointing out that water tables are lowering rapidly; that irreplaceable natural resources are approaching exhaustion in places. Agronomists are warning of the declining fertility of soils.[27]

Most persons are familiar with the theme set forth in the *Essay on the Principle of Population* by Malthus in the eighteenth century. He warned that population has a tendency to outrun means of subsistence, and that unless some limitations were set upon population growth a point would be reached at which famine would face a large percentage of mankind.[28] Modern population experts are generally agreed that if the human race should approach 21,000,000,000 people, the earth would be incapable of supporting so many.

We know from experience that there are various limiting forces in society which have restricted growth of populations. Disease, exposure, malnutrition, vice, war, fear, insecurity, voluntary limitation of conception, and delayed marriage—all exert restraints upon population growth. Some operate more in certain parts of the world than others. But all told they have a restricting effect.

Prospects for Hope. What are the prospects for hope with an increasing world population? There are a considerable number. Man is still in an early stage of discovering how to use his resources most effectively. Preventive as well as curative medicine is improving the habitability of the globe. Scientists are finding ways of increasing the yields of foodstuffs and other necessary commodities. Distribution facilities are improving.

Experts of the United Nations Food and Agriculture Organization think that through proper utilization of soil, water, fertilizers, and climatic resources (to which may possibly be added atomic energy) it will be technically possible in the near future to increase agricultural production so as to keep pace with population growth in many parts of the world and to insure a reasonable standard of nutrition for the peoples therein. They point to the fact that live-

27 See F. Osborn, *Our Plundered Planet* (Boston, 1948); W. Vogt, *Road to Survival* (New York, 1948). A more optimistic view is expressed in K. F. Mather, *Enough and to Spare* (New York, 1944); Colin Clark, "The World's Capacity to Feed and Clothe Itself," in *World Ahead* (The Hague), vol. I, no. 2, pp. 74–88.

28 For a review and interpretation of the Malthusian thesis see Rupert P. Vance, "Malthus and the Principle of Population," *Foreign Affairs*, July, 1948; S. A. Cain, "Food and People: A Second Look at Malthus' Principle of Population" in *J. of Pol.*, Aug., 1951, pp. 315–324.

stock production in the United States has increased 50 per cent per breeding unit in the past thirty years; that meat and milk production have increased enormously in Western Europe in the last two hundred years; that optimum use of fertilizers could raise "crop yields by 30 per cent as an average around the world." [29]

There are certain conditioning factors associated with such a prospect. In the first place, the amount of cultivable and productive land in the world is limited. More land can be brought into productive use, and considerable land now in use can be made to yield more, but there are limits.[30] In the second place, if an increasing population is to enjoy an adequate nutritional standard and if existent want and suffering are to be alleviated, the profligate, destructive practices applied to natural resources so extensively employed, particularly within the New World in the last century, must be checked. Conservation must be practiced in the nonrenewable resources, and scientific cultivation habits must be developed in respect to the renewable resources. In the third place, sufficient food can be produced for a rising world population only if a greater percentage of the total world population engaged in individual agricultural production can increase its output beyond the subsistence level, especially in many of the so-called "underdeveloped" areas. Possibly more can be done to correlate the needs of food-deficient areas with existent surpluses.

On the whole it is fair to say that we are still a long way from an "over-populated" globe. Standards of living are slowly rising in many parts of the world, along with increases in population. In time the present increasing rates of population growth may be retarded through humane and educational methods before they reach unmanageable proportions. The community of states as a whole is becoming more concerned with the problems of world population and world resources, which is a prerequisite to international co-operation in solving them. Food and commodity surpluses are being shared more than ever with those in want. Steps are being taken to correlate agriculture and industry for an efficient use of the world's resources.[31] The problem area has only barely been touched, however, and if mankind is to avoid grave perils it must receive ever-increasing attention.

[29] Report of study team in *The New York Times*, May 21, 1953.

[30] C. B. Fawcett, "The Extent of Cultivatable Land," *Geographical J.*, vol. 76 (1930), pp. 504–509.

[31] The lectures by L. Dudley Stamp cited above discuss some of these points. See also P. H. Hatt (ed.), *World Population and Future Resources* (New York, 1952); F. L. Clark, *Feeding the Human Family* (London, 1947); J. de Castro, *The Geography of Hunger* (Boston, 1952). Colin Clark, Australian economist, figures that by increasing agricultural output 1½ to 2 per cent per annum the world can feed a population increase of 1 per cent per annum and have a margin left over for rising standards of consumption. ("The World Will Save Money in the 1950's," *Fortune*, July, 1950, p. 90.) Scientists have reported that certain chemicals added to foods may be able to retard population growth without affecting human fertility. *The New York Times*, Oct. 20, 1951.

MIGRATION

Migration Movements. Man is a restless animal. His movements have covered the face of the globe. There is not an area which he has not sought to explore. There are no lands capable of supporting life which he has not endeavored to people. Great migration movements have at times taken place as men have sought better living conditions, more abundant or fertile land, freedom from persecution or tyranny, and freedom of worship. Such migrations accompanied and followed the colonization of the Americas, Africa, and

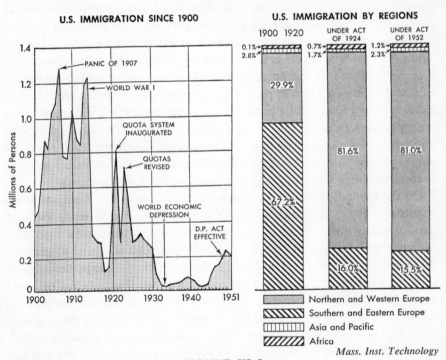

FIGURE III:5

Australasia. It is estimated that during the nineteenth century and up to World War I more than 60,000,000 peoples migrated from Europe, some 38,000,000 alone coming to the United States. Following World War II another large migration occurred as peoples hating communism fled from Eastern Europe and war-weary Europeans migrated to Africa, the Antipodes, and the New World.[32]

32 See Kingsley Davis, "World Population in Transition," *Annals*, Oct., 1945; H. Maurer, "The Right to Move," *Fortune*, Oct., 1947; J. B. Schechtman, *Population Transfers in Asia* (New York, 1949).

Restriction Measures. In recent decades the freedom of man to move readily from one country or continent to another has been extensively curtailed. The United States began as early as 1882 to restrict free immigration by setting up classes of excluded immigrants. By 1917 as many as thirty grounds of exclusion were defined by law, and all immigration was shut off from a "barred zone" of Southeast Asia. In 1924 additional barriers were raised by the adoption of the quota system both for individual countries and for Europe as a whole, permitting a total of 150,000 European immigrants a year. By the same act all aliens not eligible for naturalization were excluded. This applied principally to Asian peoples. Beginning in 1943 the United States progressively removed the stigma of exclusion for peoples of Asian countries, placing them on a quota basis, although the 1952 Immigration Act, redefining United States policy, retained and even increased other restrictions upon immigration. In 1948, 1950, and again in 1953, Congress authorized the admission of a limited number of displaced persons and other refugees in excess of the quotas to ease conditions resulting from the war and the spread of communist dictatorship.[33]

Other countries which have received large numbers of immigrants in the past have also adopted measures designed to restrict further mass migration into their territories. One of the most notable of these measures was the "White Australia" policy adopted by Australia beginning in 1855, by means of which Oriental immigrants are excluded. Canada, New Zealand, and South Africa have also passed laws or made administrative arrangements restricting or barring Oriental immigration, in addition to regulating immigration generally. Restrictions upon immigration are also applied by many European and Latin American countries to hold down selectively the numbers of foreigners who may come into their lands in any one year.[34]

Dealing with the Problem. The curtailment of migration opportunities creates serious difficulties with population pressures existing in Europe and with rising pressures in Asia clamoring for better living conditions. Alleviation of the existent population pressure in these areas might temporarily, at least, ease economic and political conditions there. The desire of peoples inhabiting the uncrowded countries to retain their own standard of living and political stability is equally understandable. Only as prosperity and high standards of productivity are maintained in these areas can there be hope of extending pros-

[33] For review of United States policy see W. S. Bernard, *American Immigration Policy—A Reappraisal* (New York, 1950). The 1952 McCarran-Walters Act is Public Law 414, 82nd Cong., 2nd Sess. See also F. L. Auerbach, *The Admission and Resettlement of Displaced Persons in the United States* (rev. ed., New York, 1950).

[34] On migration regulations see M. R. Davie, *World Immigration* (New York, 1936); J. Isaac, *Economics of Migration* (London, 1947).

perity and raising standards of living elsewhere. These low-pressure countries justifiably wish to assure themselves that the acceptance of additional people will provide a net per capita increase, not a decrease, in the supply of food and productive goods, that it will not result in an unacceptable change in the composition of the nation or a disturbance of its political equilibrium.

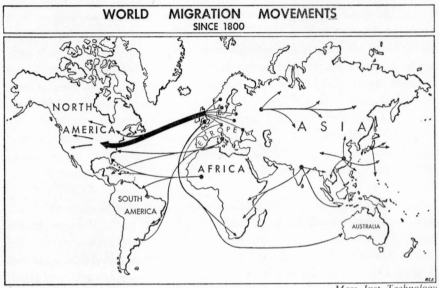

WORLD   MIGRATION   MOVEMENTS
SINCE 1800

Mass. Inst. Technology

FIGURE III:6

Since there are no longer any large, easily habitable, unclaimed, empty spaces capable of accommodating vast numbers of immigrants, any alleviation of the world population situation through migration can be accomplished peacefully only with a large measure of patience, good will, and cooperation. At best, the contribution of migration is likely to be minor on a world-wide basis and to be confined to favorable areas such as the possible lessening of population pressure in Italy through emigration. But it seems unreasonable to envisage an emigration from India of the order of population increase in the decade from 1943 to 1953 (24 million) or a yearly emigration of even a considerable fraction of the current increase in high-pressure population areas (perhaps 10 to 15 million). Aspects of the migration problem are being tackled through the International Labor Organization, intergovernmental discussions and private endeavor. In the final analysis each state must decide for itself what its own circumstances permit.[35]

35 See W. Friedmann, "Migration and World Politics," *International J.,* Summer, 1952.

ECONOMIC DEVELOPMENT AND POPULATION CHANGE

There has been much discussion in recent years about the "development of backward areas." Plans, both of a governmental and private nature, have been drawn up and launched for the granting of technical assistance and other aid to some of the heavily populated "underdeveloped lands" to promote economic development. Participating in this have been the United States Government, the United Nations, the International Bank for Reconstruction and Development, the Commonwealth Colombo Plan, and an increasing amount of private enterprise. Carried to fruition as planned, many of these projects should be of distinct benefit to the peoples of the countries lacking modern productive methods and equipment, although their effects will be visible only in a decade or so.

Questions arise, nevertheless, whether the sequel to attempts at economic and social advancement will be heavy increases in the population areas receiving assistance, thereby increasing their food production but not their per capita consumption. Should this prove to be the case, the query then poses itself whether either the locality or the world will be better off.

The problem is as much psychological and educational as it is economic.[36] Given the urge for the improvement of standards of welfare and consumption now shared by many peoples, the desirability of knitting up more closely the productive forces of the world, the international stabilization which may be gained through assisting the development of countries suffering from malnutrition and underproduction, and the self-interest of the powers in gaining access to sources of strategic and critical raw materials, it is not likely that "Point Four" type assistance will be withheld because of the possibility that greater populations may arise. This is not to say, however, that the larger problem will not have to be tackled as scientifically as possible.

POPULATION AND NATIONAL POWER

One of the most important aspects of population is, of course, the close relationship of this demographic factor to national power. Any nation that aspires to be a Great Power must obviously have a sufficiently large population. Numbers are essential to the armed forces which a Great Power must be able to bring into being to support its foreign policies and its world political position in time of tension or war. Numbers are equally vital to the large diversified production which a Great Power must have in industry, agriculture,

[36] On relation of "Point Four" type assistance to world population problems see especially the works of Stamp and Hatt, cited above. See also "Aiding Underdeveloped Areas Abroad," H. L. Hoskins (ed.), *The Annals*, March, 1950; and J. de Castro, *The Geography of Hunger* (Boston, 1952).

engineering, and science to provide it with the sinews of economic and industrial strength necessary to obtain and hold a leading position in world affairs.

Gross Population. National defense being one of the foremost things with which the modern state must concern itself, the total number of persons which any given state can put into uniform and support, in comparison with other states, is a subject of constant examination. In recognition of this fact, pre-war Nazi Germany and Fascist Italy made concerted efforts to bring about an increase in their national populations. The Soviet Union has also adopted pronatalist policies. The Fascist Government in Italy imposed a special tax on all bachelors. At the same time taxes were cut for the heads of large families and prizes were awarded for large families. The reasons of state behind such inducements were made obvious by Mussolini when he said: "Prolific nations have a right to Empire . . . nations with empty cradles cannot conquer or keep empires." [37]

But armed forces are not the only measure of population power. The size, quality, and adaptability of a country's labor supply is quite as important as the number of men that can be put under arms. In 1940 the total available labor force in the United States—including those currently unemployed—amounted to approximately 55,000,000 persons. In 1944, at the peak of the war effort, with 12,000,000 under arms, the average labor force totaled 64,-000,000 (including the armed forces).[38] The ability thus to expand the American labor force by addition of women, retired, and young people, plus the added productivity of American industry, were vital factors in bringing about Allied victory. The Germans, on the other hand, depended materially on slave labor for the increase in their labor force.

The human factor in national power must be viewed both from the standpoint of quantity of the population, and also their skills, morale, and health. Let us examine this point in some detail.

Large and Small Populations. Total population gives some index of relative national power. Each of the countries ranking as Great Powers has populations numbering more than 40,000,000 in their metropolitan homelands. But we can note that there are several states with populations in excess of this number which have not been ranked as "Great Powers"—including Brazil, India, Pakistan, and the United States of Indonesia.

What figures indicate, then, is that size of population enters into the classification of a state as a Great Power, but it is not the sole determinant. At the

---

37 On the German pronatalist policy see F. H. Hankins, "German Policies for Increasing Births," *Am. J. Sociology*, March, 1937. The USSR laws are described in Alex Inkeles, "Family and Church in the Post-War USSR," *Annals*, May, 1949.

38 J. F. Dewhurst and Associates, *America's Needs and Resources* (New York, 1947), pp. 554–565.

same time we can observe that some states with relatively small populations play an important role in international relations. Note, for example, the important place which countries like Australia, Belgium, Canada, Egypt, and Saudi Arabia have occupied in world affairs from time to time. A state which has a small population may compensate *to some extent* for smaller numbers through the leadership qualities of its representatives, the importance of its strategic location, its ability to supply certain critical raw materials, and particularly its political association with one or more of the Great Powers.

A small country facing a Great Power alone in battle may be at a disadvantage due, among other things, to population differential, although this does not always hold true. Japan had a much smaller population than China. Yet she successfully employed her greater industrial and military efficiency to strip Manchuria from China in 1932 and then to invade large sections of China from 1937 to 1945 as well as to wage war with the United States and the British Empire.

Population Size and National Efficiency. More people might make Australia a greater power, but not necessarily. On the other hand, fewer people to support might be of advantage to a country like India because the standard of living could be higher, thereby making more production available above the subsistence level to give economic and political stability to provide means for furthering national policies. In economically underdeveloped lands a high percentage of population must work solely for their own food. Little margin is left for producing export goods or expanding the nation's influence. In the United States economy, on the other hand, only a relatively small percentage of the working population (about 12 per cent) is required for the production of food, leaving a high percentage for industry, service, and professional activity.

The proposition can be put this way: taking states of relatively comparable size and population, the lower the relative percentage of a nation's gross population which must expend its energies in satisfying the minimum requirements of domestic consumption, the greater the influence which the nation can bring to bear upon international relations. Compare, for example, England and Brazil. Their populations are approximately equal. But their world power positions have up to now been vastly different. Compare also the relative influence in international affairs generally of Belgium, the Netherlands, and Sweden on the one hand, and countries of comparable size in Latin America and Asia. These small countries, as well as such countries as France and Italy, which might otherwise be classed merely as Middle Powers, have counted heavily in international affairs because they have developed national industries to a relatively high degree of efficiency and are large participants in world trade.

Utilization Coefficient. The most significant aspect of population in relation to national power is the way in which a given people develop and utilize their natural resources and strategic position, their qualities of morale, leadership, and political unity. Where elements of industrialization and national cohesion are lacking, a large population can be a liability rather than a source of strength, as has been demonstrated in the history of China.

The Soviet Union has a population exceeding that of the United States by about 50 millions. It has a labor force (excluding women on farms, which compose a considerable percentage of the total labor force) exceeding that of the United States by possibly 15 to 20 million workers. But there is no doubt about the present productive superiority of American industry and technology. In economic and industrial competition the United States surpasses the Soviet Union several fold in most items. Why? The reasons include capital plant and power (energy) supplementing the efforts of the average worker. They also include a difference in number of skilled workers, of which the United States has many more, although the USSR was leading in the actual number of graduates from engineering and technical schools in 1953. The net result is that the productivity per man-hour of American workers is several times that in the Soviet Union.

Gross population is a very important quotient in world affairs. In the testing furnace of war it may be decisive. But mathematical equivalents are by no means the only or the final measure of position or even of security. Genius can compensate for some lack of numbers or size. Essential, of course, to the success of the less congested country is a suitable store of resources within the country or accessible to it.[39] At the same time let us not overlook the accomplishments of the Swiss. Having virtually no natural resources save attractive mountain scenery and an energetic populace deeply imbued with the principles of freedom, Switzerland's people have boosted the productive capacity and economic importance of their country far beyond a natural expectancy point because of their technical skill, efficient manufacturing, and trading ingenuity.

Age and Sex Distribution. The age and sex distribution patterns of populations are important items in considering the national power of various states. It will be obvious, other things being equal, that if States X and Y have approximately the same gross populations, but X has 50 per cent more men of military age (15–34) than Y, then X has a significant power advantage over Y. Such states have a larger proportion of young, vigorous manpower in the

---

39 An argument for the gross population position will be found in R. Strausz-Hupé and S. Possony, *International Relations in the Age of Conflict between Democracy and Dictatorship* (New York, 1950), chs. 4–5.

labor force and proportionately fewer old people to support. States with "young populations," that is, with a high percentage of people of military and child-bearing ages, tend to be more expansionist than countries with low birth rates, fewer males than females, and a high percentage of peoples in the aging brackets.

Dispersed or Centralized Populations. Another way of considering the relation of population to national power is to examine the percentage of a nation's total population which is located in the home land. The population of metropolitan France is 41,000,000; the French Union reckons 61,000,000 more. But the power of France which wins or loses in Europe and in world politics is primarily that of the French home land, plus the North African manpower. The sum total of peoples subject to the French flag has outnumbered Germany roughly 10–6. Yet the 60,000,000 German people focused in the heart of Europe have twice since 1914 made deep invasions into France from which Germany has been expelled only by virtue of a large part of the Western world coming to the military aid of France. Thus it may be seen that in time of war, centrality of population is of great advantage to a nation, since it increases the ease with which a country can assemble its maximum available manpower and enables its military leaders to operate from interior lines of communication and transportation. In time of peace it is a boon to a nation's industrial production. It decreases costs of distribution and hence facilitates rising standards of living.

The Minority Problem. The problem of the states in Central Europe which have large minority groups living within their borders is not unlike that of some of the past great empires. The pre-war Republic of Czechoslovakia, for example, was constantly in a dangerous position owing to the large numbers of Germans living in the Sudetenland, the disaffected Poles in the Teschen area, the Slovaks, and the Hungarians inhabiting the southern borders of the country. National policies had to reflect compromises among the interests of these people. When the Munich crisis brewed in 1938, the Sudeten Germans demanded cession of their land to Germany, the Slovaks insisted upon autonomy, the Hungarians clamored for Hungarian rule of their lands. The result was internal weakness. This helps explain why the Czechs expelled the Sudeten Germans when their country was reconstituted in 1945. The Czechs' pre-war trouble was the same reef upon which the Austro-Hungarian Empire foundered in 1918.

The national ambitions of Europe's minority peoples are very tenacious. Oftentimes these minority groups find it difficult to work together harmoniously either with the majority or with other minority groups. Countries with such divided populations are consequently never as strong relatively as their total numerical population figures would seem to indicate. The fears which these fractured populations harbor as a result of past persecutions and separations are one of the deepest-seated facts of European politics.

Organizability. Another population characteristic which is vital in considering the national power of states is the extent to which the people of any given country or countries are inherently united or easily brought together for great national tasks.

Given two nations having populations of about the same size and approximate equality in other factors of national power, it is obvious that a nation whose peoples are politically united behind their government and who can be readily mobilized into an organized national effort has an advantage over a state whose peoples are divided among themselves, who resist orders and instructions from their government, or who are imbued with such a strong provincialism that they will act only when their locality is threatened.

In the war between Japan and China from 1937 to 1945, the Japanese had a distinct advantage over their adversary because the Chinese people were unwilling to concert as a whole body against their foe. Likewise the Germans had an edge over the French in 1940 because the French people were divided among themselves and reluctant to throw their entire weight into a united war effort. In 1940 Hitler as well as the Japanese leaders thought they need not worry about America entering the war because of the strong isolationist sentiment and political differences which had been prevailing within the United States. But they underrated the ability of the American people to close their ranks when they felt their security threatened.

Morale and Strength. A further quality which enters into the determination of a nation's world position is the ability of its people to endure hardships and to turn them into increased strength. How well can a given people withstand the rigors of war? Will they hold tenaciously to their objectives, or will they let them slip away because of preference for an easier way of life? How do they meet long-continued privations? These traits are not easily evaluated; by some they are called "imponderables." Nevertheless, they weigh in the scales of destiny when nations are on the anvil of war with all its devastation. And they count heavily when pestilence, famine, or depression stalks abroad.

The Chinese Army was no match for the military efficiency of Japanese arms following 1937, but large numbers of the Chinese people displayed heroic qualities of endurance which enabled a portion of the nation to hold out for freedom until the allied forces came to their assistance.

Churchill's epic call to the British after Dunkirk revealed a quality of national morale very different from that exhibited by the French in 1940. Said Churchill when all allies were gone on the continent of Europe and the

United Kingdom stood alone facing the Nazi aggressors: "I have nothing to offer you but blood, tears, toil, and sweat . . . Our aim? It is victory. Victory at all costs—victory in spite of all terrors—victory, however long and hard the road may be, for without victory there is no survival."

Similarly, one must in fairness credit the fortitude shown by the Russian people in meeting the Nazi holocaust which reached to the doors of Leningrad, Moscow, and Stalingrad, and then was slowly fought back to Berlin itself.

These attributes of fortitude cannot be computed with scientific accuracy in comparable figures between different peoples. It may be true that the attributes are more a product of fortunate leadership than they are characteristics of particular nations. There can be no denial, however, that they were factors of power which played historic roles in the Armageddon of World War II. They cannot be ignored by any who wish to grapple with the realities of world politics.

We should not overlook the importance of morale, ideals, and ideology as energizing elements in the lives of peoples. The belief in the values of freedom and democracy held by the American people has been a powerful force in bringing this nation to its present stature and in enabling it to attain a position of world leadership. The maintenance of these ideals and the moral sources from which they spring is of utmost moment to America in the present struggle with communism.

POPULATION POLICY FOR THE UNITED STATES

From the facts at our disposal it is apparent that the United States and other freedom-loving nations face a long-term power struggle with the forces of communism. War may not be inevitable. But a contest for the mind of man, for a way of life, and for a realigned world relationship is in full swing.

In view of its global responsibilities and role of world leadership, the large population of the United States is a distinct asset. In peace the United States must have a population skilled in all the arts of production sufficient to provide for not only its own wants but also, if need be, to strengthen the life, the economies, and the morale of friendly nations determined like America to press back forces of oppression and terror. If hostilities occur, the United States must have a population sufficient to supply the necessary means of production, the requisite number of fighting forces, and the essential direction of civilian defense.

Given the present world outlook, the question properly occurs whether population matters in the United States should be allowed to take their own course without additional governmental action or propaganda, or whether the government should encourage a more rapid increase in the national population by admitting larger numbers of immigrants or otherwise. Raising such a question leads in turn to the related one of what effect a large increase in population might have upon standards of living and the American way of life.

These are serious and perplexing questions. They merit diligent thought by all who are interested in preserving peace and security and in advancing human well-being.

SUGGESTED READINGS

J. de Castro, *The Geography of Hunger* (Boston, 1952).

Robert C. Cook, *Human Fertility, the Modern Dilemma* (New York, 1951).

W. D. Forsythe, *The Myth of Open Spaces* (Melbourne, 1942).

G. Frumkin, *Population Changes in Europe Since 1939* (New York, 1951).

P. K. Hatt (ed.), *World Population and Future Resources* (New York, 1952).

R. Mukerjee, *Races, Lands, and Food, a Program of World Subsistence* (New York, 1946).

F. W. Notestein et al., *The Future Population of Europe and the Soviet Union* (Geneva, 1944).

L. Dudley Stamp, *Land for Tomorrow* (Bloomington and New York, 1952).

W. S. Thompson, *Plenty of People* (Lancaster, Penna., 1944).

CHAPTER IV

Economics and International Relations

IF SOME yardstick existed to measure the sum total of international affairs quantitatively, it would almost certainly be found that the greater proportion is economic. The process of international arrangement is political. But the summation of the underlying economic motives, of the actual economic content of relations among states, and of the economic element of power in interstate relations would, we suggest, exceed any other category in a quantitative measurement. Such measurement is in fact impossible, and hence the foregoing may be questioned. We do not intend to imply that international affairs are determined by the economic element but rather to stress that international politics are largely concerned with and conditioned by economic factors. Thus there is little chance of understanding international affairs without comprehending their economic aspects.

The role of economics was not always so important and may conceivably not continue indefinitely. Nineteenth-century international economics had a substantially lighter impact on international politics. During the current century, and particularly the last two decades, states have taken an increasing responsibility for internal economic matters (unemployment, standard of living, availability of critical materials, and so forth). This change has increased regulation in the international economic field inasmuch as external economic matters affect the economy of almost every state. A managed internal economy leads inevitably to management of external economic affairs. The gold standard, that traditional thermostat of international economies, no longer operates. And, perhaps more important than any other single element of change, states have increasingly used economic means and measures to further political and security objectives regardless of their soundness from the standpoint of a strict economic analysis. A major concern in the field of international economics is whether problems which are basically economic in nature will be evaluated more by political norms or by a greater degree of economic objectivity.

THE ECONOMIC NEEDS OF NATIONS

Whatever the forms of economic systems that exist within states—whether capitalist, socialist, fascist, or communist, and whether primitive or advanced —the rudimentary needs of states bear considerable resemblance.

Basic Requirements. The most basic economic needs of states are adequate supplies of foodstuffs and productive materials, particularly minerals. As societies become industrialized their mineral requirements rise. The United States, in spite of its rich endowment of natural resources, finds its demands for raw materials in excess of its own supplies. To satisfy economic and security requirements it now seeks a continual flow of over seventy raw materials from abroad.[1]

Heavily populated and highly industrialized countries such as England, Switzerland, and Japan must constantly obtain foodstuffs as well as raw materials from other parts of the world to sustain their populations and keep their industries at full employment. States with predominantly agricultural economies and standards of living above the subsistence level, such as Denmark, Australia, and Argentina, must increase their production of foodstuffs which are exported in order to pay for imports of manufactured goods demanded by consumers. Sometimes analysis of national interest leads predominantly agricultural states to develop particular industries that can, if the need arises, be converted to defense or war, even though the cost is high and the relative productive efficiency low compared with the heavily industrialized countries. Industrial, agricultural, and "balanced" states seek foreign outlets for their products in order to obtain foreign exchange with which to purchase commodities they desire from abroad. The importance of this trade is clearer when seen as a proportion of a nation's production than when given in monetary terms. Since World War II United States exports have been about 4 to 5 per cent of national production, imports somewhat less. But the Netherlands has exported about 40 per cent of its production in exchange for necessary imports (see chart).

The movement of goods, people, and services raises a problem of communications and transportation across boundaries, through foreign territories, and on the high seas. In 1951, for example, the ocean shipping costs of moving the world's goods were about 6 billion dollars. Today electric power is transmitted across many boundaries, and the flow of many rivers is of joint interest to states. The Nile, for instance, rises in Ethiopia and Kenya, yet is the life-

[1] During World War II iron ore and coal were the only two major minerals the United States did not have to import to satisfy war production requirements. Necessity required the importation of sixty-five varieties of minerals. On raw-material situations see *President's Materials Policy Commission Report* (Washington, 1952).

blood of Egypt. The Indus is vital to both India and Pakistan. Boundary crossing arrangements for economic resources are a primary and increasing concern of governments.

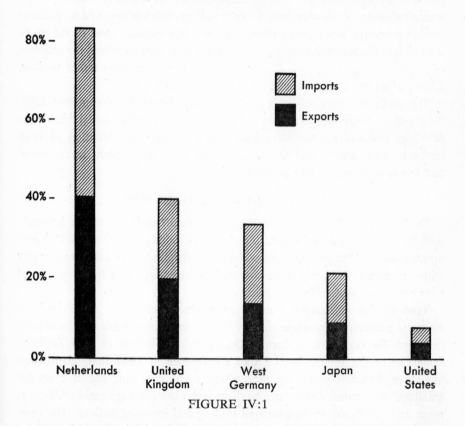

FIGURE IV:1

Political Consequences. The international economic problems outlined above have to be solved by projection of the power of the state concerned, that is, by imperialism, or by international political agreements some of which are so well established that they are part of international law.

Certainly the successive waves of colonialism and imperialism throughout history cannot be explained entirely, or even perhaps primarily, by reference to economics. But the economic factor was often a material contributing cause. Germany, in the late nineteenth century, claimed a need for colonies as a source of raw materials. Mussolini's Italy, as late as the 1930's, embarked on imperialistic adventures in Ethiopia, pleading a need for raw materials and an outlet for Italian overpopulation. Turning to the factor of transportation, the United States interest in the "freedom of the seas" doctrine was basically economic. British acquisition of the Suez Canal shares in 1875 and the development of the British position in the Middle East may be called imperialism motivated partly by economic interests.[2] Some may charge the United States' political arrangements for, and development of, the Panama Canal to economic reasons.[3] The new communist imperialism, which is imposed by political control measures, has a major economic base. It eliminates most of the problems of boundaries within the communist orbit and tends to reduce the problem of exchange of goods. But it does so on an authoritarian basis rather than on a basis of mutual economic advantage and political equality.

The traditional imperialism is dying or dead. Outside the communist orbit, the economic relationships of states must be arranged by individual free enterprise, by political negotiation among states, or by a combination of both methods. The recent trend has been toward more government arrangement and less dependence on free enterprise.

INTERDEPENDENCE AND RIVALRY

States are dependent on one another economically and yet compete intensely with one another in foreign trade. This is the paradox of the international economic situation. Put another way, when Great Britain cannot compete strongly with our country for Latin American trade we are very likely to be concerned over her economic health and stability.

Transmission of Prosperity and Depression. Fluctuations in the business cycle are transmitted from one country to another through trade and fiscal relationships. Sir Walter Nash, former Deputy Prime Minister of New Zealand, remarked at the International Labor Conference in 1944 that "depression anywhere threatens prosperity everywhere." The economic life of even the small and semi-isolated states can be disturbed if there is large-scale unemployment and depression in the principal trading and investing nations. The one-product states (the Middle East with its oil, Bolivia with its tin, Chile with its copper) are particularly sensitive to the ups and downs of world economic conditions. So also are those states which have an economy dependent on major exports and imports. In 1953, for instance, British experts estimated that a 1 per cent drop in United States production would occasion a 5 per cent drop in United States imports of British goods. The slight United States reces-

---

2 See Halford L. Hoskins, *British Routes to India* (Philadelphia, 1928).

3 See Miles P. Duval, *From Cadiz to Cathay* (Stanford, 1947); *idem, And the Mountains Will Move* (Stanford, 1947); N. J. Padelford, *The Panama Canal in Peace and War* (New York, 1942).

sion in 1948–1949 caused a 30 per cent drop in international trade with the NATO area alone. The possibility that domestic employment and local welfare may suffer as a consequence of economic conditions abroad, forces each state to decide whether or not to try to insulate itself against the effects of economic fluctuations abroad by regulating trade and foreign financial affairs.

The concern among economists and statesmen for full employment and a stable or rising standard of living reflects an awareness that high unemployment can be a source of serious internal political developments. For example, it was among the unemployed of Germany in the early 1930's that the Nazis found many of their recruits. Areas of economic depression or unemployment or both are a hunting ground for Communists. It is well-known communist doctrine that the weaknesses of the noncommunist economic systems will bring about their collapse. One of these systems is the free world international economic system. When that system thrives, internal economies tend to prosper. When that system is disrupted, the same internal economies are likely to be depressed and to lag in production, as occurred after World War II.

International Economic Rivalries. The economic interrelationship of states manifests itself in another way. Just as there is competition within countries for scarce commodities, markets, and profits, so in the international scene individuals, industrial concerns, and states compete with one another for scarce materials, markets, and profitable trade.

International rivalry is exhibited in the competition of British, American, German, Japanese, and French business interests for the profitable Latin American markets; in the competition among foreign nationals and states for economic concessions and loans in China during the late nineteenth and early twentieth centuries; in the competition of British, Japanese, and American industries for the trade of India and Southeast Asia; and in the rivalry of European producers and ship operators for the valuable American dollar trade. These contests and relationships form a routine part of international relations, broadly speaking. Ordinarily, the frictions and disputes that arise, if not settled directly by the private parties and interests involved, can be adjusted with the assistance of governments, or through them, without leading to international crises.

With many countries now having socialist or dictatorial forms of government, rivalries tend to be directly between states rather than between individual traders. Individual traders may receive some governmental support but are activated primarily by the profit motive. State trading has become a widespread feature of international commerce. Because of the privileges, immunities, and power which governments can give to their state trading agencies, serious handicaps are sometimes encountered by private enterprise in competing or dealing with state trading. In some parts of the world it has become exceedingly difficult or impossible for private business to trade other than with government agencies and on their terms. The closing door for free enterprise and for the free market is, indeed, one of the gravest issues in international affairs. With the economic health and political stability of many states now completely dependent on international trade, we can expect a continuing government interest and close supervision of this trade.

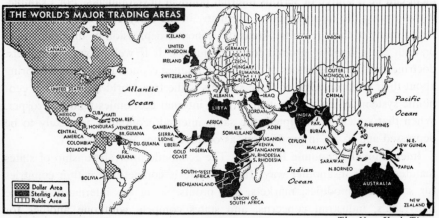

The New York Times

FIGURE IV:2

The Soviet Government, in Eastern Europe, has demonstrated how it is possible to reduce or entirely eliminate competition by other countries. This has been accomplished, in part, through the device of joint state companies. In these arrangements the Soviet Government has usually advanced 51 per cent of the monetary capital required, in the form of rubles. The satellite state is required to make its contribution in the form of tangible assets—transport facilities, factories, mines, and so forth—taking by expropriation or nationalization whatever is necessary to provide the joint company with an absolute controlling position in the industry involved. By refusing foreign operators fuel, warehouse, dockage or transport facilities, and labor, and by creating interminable legal and administrative requirements, foreign interests have been driven out of activity in every country behind the Iron Curtain, thereby eliminating contacts with the West considered dangerous by the Soviet Union.[4]

---

[4] See Cyril E. Black, "Soviet Policy in Eastern Europe," *Annals,* May, 1949; B. Raditsa, "The Sovietization of the Satellites," *ibid.,* Sept., 1950; Harry Schwartz, *Russia's Soviet Economy* (New York, 1950), ch. xiv; D. Tomasic, "The Structure of Soviet Power and Expansion," *Annals,* Sept., 1950. See also W. C. Armstrong, "The Soviet Approach to International Trade," *Pol. Sci. Quar.,* Sept., 1948.

INTERNATIONAL TRADE

The Basis of International Trade. From the early days of foreign trade when, for example, Oriental spices were sought by European merchants for flavoring and for making aged meats more palatable, people have sought many kinds of exotic and foreign goods. However, not until the industrial and technological revolutions provided new and more efficient means of production and transportation, and made states economically interdependent if they wished to raise the standard of living of their people, did international trade become truly global, with vast, complicated arteries of commerce interlacing all continents and major centers of habitation. One of the primary objectives of this trade is to secure a larger variety of goods and services more cheaply than they can be produced domestically. Differences in costs of production and therefore of selling price give impetus to specialization, to international division of labor, and to the most economical use of resources.

A nation which has an absolute advantage in relation to another country in producing certain goods generally finds it beneficial to exchange such commodities for those in which the other country has an absolute production advantage, when conditions of trade and political relationships permit. Thus, the United States, which has an absolute advantage over Brazil in making automobiles (due to know-how and established industry) sends these to Brazil in exchange for coffee, in the production of which Brazil has an absolute advantage. But when a country has no absolute advantage it may have a comparative advantage indicating a flow of trade. Thus if a given quantity of factors of production produce, in the United States, twenty automobiles and ten carloads of textiles and, in England, fifteen automobiles and ten carloads of textiles, it is to the advantage of the United States from the purely economic standpoint to specialize in automobiles and to the advantage of England to specialize in textiles. Both profit from the trade.[5]

Where the costs of production including shipping costs and tariffs are approximately the same in two countries, trade may still take place owing to differences in quality, style, or market appeal. Thus British and French-made automobiles find a market in the United States and Canada, and Japanese silk still finds a sale in the American market even though artificial fibers made by American industry can replace it. A country may import and export the same commodity for various reasons—economic or strategic. Thus, the United States imports Chilean copper while at the same time exporting some of its own production.

[5] See any standard general economics text for a discussion of absolute and comparative advantage.

International trade is a testimony to the unity of the earth's physical resources. National boundaries seldom coincide with ideal or adequate economic regions. Whereas national policies tend to create compartments in the world, international trade as a whole, in times of peace and harmony, tends to compensate for these divisions. In an increasingly industrialized world community, states are becoming more dependent upon international trade to make up their own deficiencies in resources and industry. From this has followed a growing awareness of the need for international cooperation in the maintenance and expansion of trade and in the reduction of restrictions thereto.

Patterns of Trade. There are traditional, but no fixed, patterns of international trade. Commerce is influenced by the economic conditions of the various countries, by natural conditions such as droughts and disasters, by business competition, and by the variations in the friendly relations, tensions, and conflicts among nations. Generally speaking, the most heavily freighted trade routes of the world are between Western Europe and North America, that is, between the countries of highest production and income. Next in order, in time of peace, is usually trade among the countries within Europe, followed by trade between Western European states and Latin America and between Britain and the members of the Commonwealth. Ranking far behind the trade that moves across the Atlantic, both in volume and dollar value, but nevertheless highly important in itself, is the trans-Pacific trade, with Japanese-

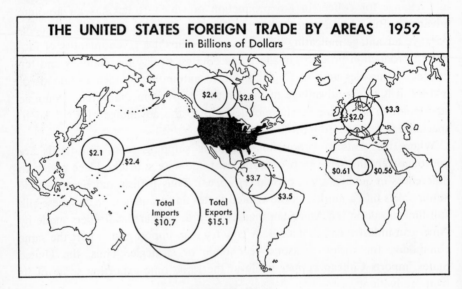

THE UNITED STATES FOREIGN TRADE BY AREAS   1952
in Billions of Dollars

$2.4 $2.8

$3.3

$2.0

$2.1 $2.4

$3.7

$0.61 $0.56

$3.5

Total Imports $10.7   Total Exports $15.1

·FIGURE IV:3 *

*Exports by areas do not include military supplies and so do not add to total.

United States trade normally ranking highest in the past. To a large extent the principal trade patterns tend to flow where easy access to water routes and where economic development afford convenient means of transportation and a desire and need for a large interchange of goods.

Although the USSR, with its rich natural resources and growing industry, good - could gradually come to occupy a prominent place in world trade, its policies and attitudes toward other countries have prevented it thus far from doing so. The exchange of goods for the advancement of the standard of living of its peoples—a fundamental objective behind the trading of most of the rest of the world—is secondary to other considerations. The communist program of rapid collectivization and industrialization leaves few agricultural products and raw materials for exchange with the industrialized countries of the world. From its point of view, international trade is to be used primarily as an instrument, or weapon, for gaining political or imperialist advantage.

MULTILATERAL AND BILATERAL TRADE

Multilateral Trade. Under "normal" international economic and political conditions, most countries have engaged in multilateral trade. That is, they import goods from those countries from which they can obtain the best supply or price, and export to those places where the best markets can be found. When such trading policies and relationships prevail, a country does not arbitrarily limit its purchases in another country or in a particular currency to the exact value of its sales to that country over a particular time period.

For example: United States imports from the Asiatic countries in the past have exceeded American shipments to those countries. On the other hand, United States exports to Britain have been greater than imports from the United Kingdom. In turn, Britain has exported more to Asia than it has imported. British Malaya bought goods in England with dollars earned through sales of rubber and tin to America. Britain in turn was then able to purchase American goods with these dollars. In such a manner multilateral trade relationships develop in which the interests of several parties are served and foreign exchange obligations are cleared. One country is enabled by this method of trading to export to a second more than it imports from that country because it can get repayment through the trade relationships of both parties with a third or fourth state.

In addition to the flow of goods, the sum total of multilateral trade includes other items of expenditure and receipt which help balance international indebtedness. These include such things as the large expenditures of American tourists abroad, the earnings of shipping, rail, and air transport companies, private and intergovernmental loans, and investments and their earnings. These all go to make up an intricate network of relationships beneficial in many ways to a wide circle of individuals and countries. While we discuss problems of foreign exchange later in the chapter, it is here pointed out that multilateralism is only possible with a high degree of freedom of convertibility from one type of currency to another.

Bilateralism. Under some circumstances states choose to pursue trade policies which limit their imports of goods and services from other states to the approximate value of their exports to each of those states separately, or restrict them to specified types or quantities of goods from particular states. In a sense, such bilateral trade is comparable to barter.

Bilateralism has had several plausible objectives. It has been used as a supporting policy for economic nationalism—the attainment of maximum economic self-sufficiency. This was the Nazi program of the 1930's. Combined with control of specific items exported and imported, it is a useful policy for placing political pressures upon other states. Bilateralism is an attractive recourse for states having limited balances of foreign exchange (not enough money in the till to do business). It gives a seemingly greater assurance of maintaining an approximate balance of exports and imports. Its attractiveness must be recognized because it gives protection to the internal economy against fluctuations in the free world market. It was followed by many states after World War II and probably served some useful purpose in getting trade started again. It is, however, a practice hard to lay aside, once adopted.

Bilateralism is bound to act to reduce total world trade in the long run. It discourages specialization and the most economical use of resources. It may have little relationship to the purely economic approach of selling where prices are highest and buying where they are cheapest. Finally, it may bind a state politically to another by leaving it with no other place to sell its products, which it must sell in order to maintain an acceptable standard of living.

Bloc Trading. Complete multilateral trade has not existed since before the Great Depression. It is probably correct to date the beginning of its demise at the outset of World War I. The most common variety of trading arrangement is that of blocs of countries which strive to maintain within the bloc a large proportion (in the case of communist countries, almost all) of their total foreign trade, thereby reducing the effect of economic competition and fluctuations in the remainder of the world. The Commonwealth imperial preference system, instituted in the 1930's, certainly had this objective.

The post-World War II sterling bloc, comprising states with a population of around 800 million, is based on the link to the pound sterling as the international currency. Proceeds of sales in one part of the area, which includes the Commonwealth less Canada, are freely transferable to other parts of the area.

The arrangement has encouraged trade within the bloc which might otherwise have gone elsewhere. As an expedient for providing some insulation against economic fluctuations in the remainder of the world, it must be recognized as directed against the dollar area—which constitutes most of the remainder of the trading world. But, until the sterling area acquires confidence that it can earn dollars to match outgo of dollars it will likely maintain restrictions on complete multilateralism. In the early 1950's the free world was divided generally into a "soft currency" (principally sterling) bloc and a "hard currency" (dollar) bloc. Free convertibility of sterling into dollars and vice versa has always been, and still is, the essential element to any effective multilateralism.

RESTRICTIONS ON TRADE

Restrictions and regulations of one form or another on the flow of trade across national boundaries have been practiced by states since the birth of the national state system. Until late in the eighteenth century international trade was regarded as a means of acquiring national wealth and power and a fit subject for close governmental control. Adam Smith's *Wealth of Nations,* published in 1776, was the principal impetus to the rise of the *laissez-faire* theory that governments should not, in general, regulate or interfere with international trade.

Great Britain, with her great trading advantage due to her long lead in the Industrial Revolution, adopted the *laissez-faire* principles in the mid-eighteenth century and continued the general policy until after World War I.

Rise and Decline of Multilateralism. Led by Britain, world trade during the nineteenth century was, in considerable part, guided by purely economic considerations such as selling in the most profitable market and buying in the cheapest. There were opposing trends, however. There was a strong stream of argument and belief that a state should strive to become self-sufficient in important products and industries. This thesis led logically to the imposition of tariffs and other restrictions for protection of home industries and was always a more attractive thesis to Germany and the United States than the *laissez-faire* concept.

Multilateralism broke down in the 1920's owing to the aftermath effects of World War I and has not been re-established. The disruption of old-established trade relations due to the fragmentation of Central Europe, the United States demand that war debts be paid when United States tariff barriers did not conceivably permit payment, the distortions of trade arising out of German reparations and large uneconomic United States loans to Europe, the consequent acquisition by the United States of most of the world's gold supply—these were some of the reasons for the collapse. The United States tariff of 1930 was the highest in our history. Britain was forced to abandon free trade and the gold standard in 1932. The world was launched into a period of international economic controls and restrictions which were quickly increased by the Nazi use of economic instruments to further German aggressive objectives. Efforts in the international economic field since World War II have reflected a yearning to return to the comparatively untrammeled pre-World War I situation. The efforts have received a great deal of lip service but progress has been slow in putting back into Pandora's box the great array of restrictions perfected and adopted since 1930.

Types of Restrictions. We make no attempt at a complete listing or description of the many and varied types of restriction on international trade. The reader is referred to any recent standard text on international economics for a complete description of restrictive practices. We have mentioned bilateralism and bloc trading on a previous page. There are three other general classifications which should be kept in mind.

1. *Tariffs and Subsidies.* These are respectively taxes on imports and assistance to home producers which enable them to compete with foreign producers. The former policy increases cost to the consumer, the latter is a charge on the taxpayer (and hence ultimately on the consumer in most cases).

2. *Export and Import Quotas.* These may be in quantities of a particular commodity or service. Or they may be in foreign exchange allocated to purchase from a particular country or for purchase of a particular commodity.

3. *Exchange Control.* Until recently, at least, an Englishman desiring to spend a holiday in France, perhaps no farther from his home than Atlantic City is from New York City, was permitted to change no more pounds into francs than would buy a hotel room in Atlantic City for a few days. This is an example of exchange control. The restrictions on obtaining dollars to travel in America were more severe, since England was short of dollars and needed them more for goods than for touring. All major trading countries except the United States and Canada instituted exchange controls after World War II. The individual desiring to do business had to have both the money and a project which his government was willing to license under conditions of rationed foreign exchange.

We list the above three classifications with emphasis that restrictions in all three must be lessened or eliminated if the world is to make effective progress on a return to multilateralism and what is loosely termed "free trade."

FREE TRADE

Arguments for and Against Free Trade. Those who believe in the merits of free trade maintain that unfettered trading promotes greater world productivity—and hence is beneficial—through specialization due to aptitude and the most efficient use of the factors of production. They argue that the greater division of labor which results is advantageous to all, and therefore to the prosperity and well-being of states and peoples separately. They also hold that as the competitive process operates, consumers are benefited through lower prices.[6] These classical arguments were formulated generations ago, before economic interdependence became a fact of international life. Currently, the free trader can point out that no civilized nation can be self-sufficient without expanding control over areas possessing the materials it needs. The alternative is trade.

The advocates of protection maintain that under modern world political conditions, overspecialization exposes a nation to weakness in the struggles of power politics. They argue that diversity of industry is necessary if a nation is to protect itself against aggression; that tariffs and other governmental devices can foster and protect "infant industries" needed for defense purposes from ruinous foreign competition. Some protagonists insist that a tariff, quota system, or subsidy program can prevent extreme specialization of a nation either in the direction of an industrial economy or an agricultural and raw-material producing economy.[7]

Protectionists, particularly business men inclined to identify national interests with their own, often state that tariffs and quotas are needed to "protect" domestic producers and the local market from an influx of "cheap labor" foreign goods. It is also argued that protective restrictions provide a means of insulating the local economy from fluctuations of trade and production abroad. This aspect is discussed further in the subsection below and is probably the major consideration influencing the international trade policies of many states. A socialist-type planned economy such as that envisaged by the British Labor Party is most difficult to manage, and doubly difficult if completely exposed to external economic factors beyond the management's conceivable control.

---

[6] Discussions on the problem of free trade *versus* protection will be found in Sir William H. Beveridge (ed.), *Tariffs: The Case Examined* (London, 1931); C. B. Hoover, *International Trade and Domestic Employment* (New York, 1945); C. P. Kindleberger, *International Economics* (Homewood, Ill., 1953); P. S. Samuelson, "International Factor—Price Equalization Once Again," *Econ. J.,* June, 1949; J. Viner, *Studies in the Theory of International Trade* (New York, 1937). See particularly *Report of the President's Commission on Foreign Economic Policy* (the Randall Report), GPO, 1954.

[7] Adolf Wagner, "Agrarian State vs. Manufacturing State," in F. W. Taussig (ed.), *Selected Readings in International Trade and Tariff Problems* (Boston, 1921).

Finally, it is sometimes said that the existence of restrictive devices provide a state with bargaining tools useful in dealing with other states.[8]

Supporters of free trade reply to the infant industry argument that such businesses, sheltered by protective tariffs, readily incline to remain in their swaddling clothes and become vested interests opposing removal of the protection. In this way high tariffs that may conceivably have some justification in the beginning are continued indefinitely, burdening international commerce and keeping prices unnecessarily high. To the objection to national specialization, free traders answer that specialization is not economically harmful, but on the contrary increases productivity and, through trade, results in a larger social product. Some concede that the use of protective measures against economic fluctuations abroad may not be unreasonable under critical circumstances, although they are opposed to such devices as a general rule.

Foreign Trade and Full Employment. Governments have become "full-employment conscious." In numerous countries a full-employment policy is intimately associated with the existence of the government in power. Hence, whether or not the Keynesian theory of a relationship between foreign trade and national income is accepted,[9] the insurance of full, or at least high, employment is today a vital political issue.[10]

It was demonstrated in 1929–1933 that depression in one part of the world can "spill over" into other countries. When United States imports shrank 77 per cent and American lending virtually dried up, there was a corresponding reduction of foreign purchases from the United States by 70 per cent. Before the depression was relieved, this contractive situation spiraled into a 64 per cent reduction in *all* international trade.[11]

Free Trade Today. It must be noted that, from the practical political and economic standpoint, there are no absolutely pure free traders or absolutely pure protectionists. These matters are, in practice, matters of degree rather than absolutes. The trade of the world is now encumbered with more and a greater variety of restrictions than at almost any time in modern history. And yet there is probably more general agreement that the needed direction of progress is toward freer trade. There are, of course, some countries striving to build more balanced economies, for example, Indonesia and Argentina,

8 For protectionist arguments see J. Grunzel, *Economic Protectionism* (Oxford, 1916); F. W. Taussig, *Some Aspects of the Tariff Question* (Cambridge, 1915), chs. i–iii; *idem, Selected Readings*, chs. x, xvii, xxiii.
9 See Ragnar Nurkse, "Domestic and International Equilibrium," in Seymour Harris (ed.), *The New Economics* (New York, 1947).
10 See William H. Beveridge, *Full Employment in a Free Society* (New York, 1945), especially part VI.
11 Summary from United States Dept. of Commerce, Bureau of Foreign and Domestic Commerce, *The United States in the World Economy* (Washington, 1943).

which give great weight to the "infant industry" argument. But the great and increasing economic interdependence of states is clear if these states are to maximize their standards of living. Even the United States, least interdependent of developed states outside the Soviet bloc, depends on export markets for over 20 per cent of the production of some of its industries (machine tools, cotton, tobacco; in 1951 agricultural exports averaged $1,100 per commercial United States farm). Such exports have to be paid for by imports or United States grants and there are no substitutes in the United States for some of the imports, for instance, the approximately two billion dollars' worth of raw materials imported in 1951.

Obviously no supranational power is going to wave a wand and eliminate trade restrictions. The problem is a continuous one requiring the attention of the most expert, coupled with hard international bargaining.[12]

MOVEMENTS TO REDUCE TRADE BARRIERS

Hull Trade Agreements Program. One of the most notable efforts to reduce world trade restrictions in the post-1929 period was the Reciprocal Trade Agreements program inaugurated by United States Secretary of State Cordell Hull in 1934. Under the terms of the Trade Agreements Act the Congress authorized the President to enter into executive agreements with foreign countries to raise or lower existing United States tariff rates by as much as 50 per cent for nations willing to make reciprocal concessions.[13] This was supported by President Roosevelt on the ground that "a full and permanent domestic recovery depends in part upon a revised and strengthened international trade." [14]

Reciprocal trade agreements, which are good examples of executive agreements consummated within specific dimensions set by Congress, were negotiated bilaterally with some fifty countries between 1934 and 1951. These covered areas involving over three-fifths of the United States export and import trade. Nearly half of the agreements allowed reductions up to 50 per cent in the American tariff rates, and by 1949 Congress had approved further cuts making it possible to grant rates to some countries on some goods as low as 25 per cent of those of the 1930 Smoot-Hawley Tariff Act. Furthermore, the

---

12 Report to the President by the Public Advisory Board for Mutual Security, *A Trade and Tariff Policy in the National Interest*, 1953, summarizes the United States foreign trade situation and effect of proposed lessening of United States restrictions. J. K. Jessup and M. A. Heilperin in "A New Daring Plan to Unshackle Trade and Enrich the Free World," *Life*, Jan, 4, 1954, summarize the world problems and suggest some solutions.

13 Statute at Large No. 48, p. 943.

14 Quoted in P. T. Ellsworth, *The International Economy: Its Structure and Operation* (New York, 1950), p. 546.

agreements carefully provided for unconditional most-favored-nation treatment so that minor supplies from other countries than the major supplier with whom a reciprocal trade agreement was made could also benefit in the reduced import rates within the time period and quotas set. This constituted a valuable contribution to the reduction of the pre-war barriers to trade, considering the height of the 1930 Smoot-Hawley Tariff Act lists and the restrictions in force abroad.

The trade agreements produced benefits in turn for the United States. It was calculated, for instance, that in 1938 and 1939 exports to trade agreement countries increased 63 per cent over the 1934–1935 averages as compared with 32 per cent for non-agreement countries. Imports from the corresponding countries increased by 22 and 12½ per cent, respectively.

The Reciprocal Trade Agreements program had the additional merit of removing tariff-making in the United States from the political arena of Congressional log-rolling and pressure group politics to a rational approach through executive determination subject to public hearing and to revision when and as desirable in the national interest.[15] President Eisenhower, with proponents of high tariffs once again gathering strength, sought to continue the reciprocal trade policy.[16]

Reduction of Barriers through International Organization. The United Nations Charter contains a commitment (Article 55) to further economic cooperation by promoting world trade and the well-being of peoples. This general commitment is found in most of the regional agreements (for example, Organization of American States and North Atlantic Treaty Organization). But general commitments are of little value unless implemented by specific actions, of which there have been several.

The Economic and Social Council of the United Nations[17] has a broad mandate to make studies and recommendations on economic matters. At Havana in 1948, under the leadership of the United States, a charter for an International Trade Organization (ITO) was signed after lengthy negotiation. This charter provided that states subscribing thereto would proceed to mutual

[15] On trade agreements program see Chamber of Commerce of the United States, *Trade Agreements and the American Economy* (Washington, 1950); J. B. Condliffe, *The Commerce of Nations* (New York, 1950); C. B. Hoover, *op. cit.;* J. M. Laticke, *Reciprocal Trade Agreements in the World Economy* (New York, 1948); R. F. Mikesell, *United States Economic Policy and International Relations* (New York, 1952); U. S. Tariff Comm., *Operation of the Trade Agreements Program, June, 1934, to April, 1948,* Rpt. No. 160, 2d ser. (Washington, 1949). On the most-favored-nation clause see R. C. Snyder, *The Most Favored Nation Clause* (New York, 1948).

[16] See Trade Agreements Extension Act of 1953, P. L. 215, 83d Cong., 1st Sess. This provided for a "fundamental review" of United States international trade policy by a Commission on Foreign Economic Policy appointed by President Eisenhower.

[17] See ch. xx.

reduction of trade barriers, sharply limit use of quantitative restrictions (export and import quotas), and accept intensive study by ITO of all aspects of international trade conditions. But the principal trading nations did not ratify the ITO charter.[18]

Twenty-three nations signed a General Agreement on Tariffs and Trade (GATT) at Geneva in 1947 by which the United States principle of reciprocal reductions was applied. GATT provides a forum to thrash out trade disputes. Today GATT agreements cover over half of world trade. The United States has participated within the dimensions set by the Reciprocal Trade Agreements legislation, and by 1953 had extended the reciprocal trade agreements to nearly fifty countries and to cover all United States trade except that with the Soviet bloc.

The effect of reduction of tariffs through United States action and GATT efforts has been in part offset by retention of other restrictions. The United States has not restricted imports quantitatively except for some agricultural products. Other countries, facing the problem of unbalanced trade, have retained quantitative and exchange controls. The only solution to this situation is a restoration of trade balance—one step being a further reduction of United States trade barriers. The alternatives to the retention of the United States restrictions appear to be reduction of foreign purchases from the United States or a program of indefinitely continuing United States foreign loans and grants.

European Economic Cooperation. The Organization for European Economic Cooperation, formed in 1947 to further the Marshall Plan, has provided a forum and mechanism for reducing trade restrictions. The countries participating in the European Recovery Program entered into a European Payments Union (EPU) in 1950 to cushion short-run trade balance disequilibria for the cooperating members having foreign exchange difficulties, in order to facilitate exchange payments so that there might be a larger movement of goods among themselves. The EPU was an expedient in lieu of convertibility, but certainly not a substitute therefor. United States policy has pressed the European states to integrate their several economies further in order to increase their economic and political strength. These suggestions have met, however, with many obstacles springing from nationalistic feelings but even more from the reality that economic adjustments of the magnitude envisaged require time. The most solid advance has been in the European Steel

18 For text of Charter and authoritative commentary see Clair Wilcox, *A Charter for World Trade* (New York, 1949). See also J. C. Campbell, *The United States in World Affairs, 1948–1949* (New York, 1949), pp. 210–220; P. W. Bidwell and W. Diebold, Jr., "The United States and the International Trade Organization," *Internat. Conciliation,* March, 1949.

and Coal Community by which steel, coal, and coke are permitted to move comparatively unrestricted among six countries.[19]

Post-War Trend. The post-World War II trend in trade restrictions has several conflicting elements which make a conclusion difficult. Economic nationalism is still an important policy of a great many states. On the other hand, there has been an unprecedented surge of organized international effort to increase international trade. These conflicting trends are discussed in Chapter VI. Chapters XX and XXI discuss some aspects of economic international organization.

The United States has assumed leadership in reducing and eliminating trade restrictions and has brought pressure to this end through its massive assistance programs, as well as through political means. States are now more competent in appraising and planning their international economic situation. As states have taken more responsibility for full employment and other internal economic and social conditions, there has been an increasing tendency to strive toward maintenance of close control of international economic affairs. International economics has become a subject of both external and internal politics. Institutions such as ITO, GATT, and the International Bank, conceived with the idea that international economics could be generally separated from political affairs have not made as much progress as hoped. The schism in the world extends to economic matters. For reasons which appear political and imperialistic, communism has formed a trading bloc. The situation is further complicated by the fact that a considerable part of United States export trade has been in the form of assistance. Furthermore, the United States has led a movement to use trade as a direct security instrument by curbing East-West trade in "strategic" items.

What can we conclude as to trends? Only, with certainty, that political considerations, both internal and external, and security considerations will continue to bulk large in any program for reduction of trade restrictions.

FINANCING FOREIGN TRADE

In a manner comparable to a business firm making a balance sheet of its income and expenditures, each state has a financial balance in trading operations with other states. This is customarily called its balance of payments.

Balance of Payments. A state's balance of payments covers more than the exact accounting of commodity exports and imports. The so-called "invisible items" in its balance comprise such things as the services of shipping, insur-

---

[19] Agreement establishing EPU in R. Dennett and R. K. Turner (ed.), *Documents on Am. For. Relations,* 1950 (Princeton, 1951), pp. 94–108. See also "European Recovery," *Internat. Conciliation,* Jan., 1949.

ance expenditures and receipts, tourist expenditures and receipts, and interest and principal payments on international indebtedness.

A state's international balance of payments always balances over a period of time. If the total receipts from its exports, services rendered, foreign investments, and other means of return fall short in relation to the value of its imports and expenditures upon all visible and invisible items, an adjustment of its international indebtedness must be made. A temporary disequilibrium is customarily met by a transfer of bullion or currency, or by the procurement of short or long-term loans or grants. When a disequilibrium condition cannot be remedied by any other means, a shift in internal price level reducing market attractiveness, foreign exchange control, arbitrary manipulation of currency values, reduction of imports and expansion of exports (by such methods as quantitative restrictions and "dumping"), or some combination of these measures can result. These moves all have political as well as economic importance in the relations between nations.

If the citizens or government of a country invest funds abroad, the action requires that the value of the funds go abroad in either goods or bullion. When it is said that a state has an "export surplus" this may mean it is making heavy investments, public and private, abroad.

The use of foreign exchange rates provides a medium for translating the currency of one country into that of another at the prevailing market rate. This is essential, both in the payment process and as a means of comparing prices.[20] An unstable and shifting exchange rate adds another hazard for the international trader. The setting of the exchange rate (and the dollar is the principal current standard of measure) has much to do with determining how much, what, and where a country buys and sells.

The Gold Standard. During the nineteenth and early twentieth centuries the currencies of the major trading nations had a gold backing with a gold standard of value against which they were measured and exchanged. The gold standard mechanism of international exchange (that is, free conversion at established rates into gold bullion which might be shipped from one country to another, or transferred into banks for credit) provided a virtual international currency. On the basis of the convertibility of currencies into gold, the free movement of bullion from one country to another to balance international indebtedness, and the relationship of internal price levels to the gold stock of each country, economists erected fine explanations of the operation of international trade and foreign exchange. The "gold mechanism" was the thermostat in an essentially self-regulatory system. But, as Professor Michael Heilperin

---

[20] On the problems of international exchange and methods of payments see George N. Halm. *Monetary Theory* (Philadelphia, 1946).

noted, the gold standard was the monetary standard "of an essentially peaceful world where confidence reigned, trade was reasonably free, and capital movements between countries were regular." [21]

In the 1929–1933 depression the major industrial countries, including the United States and Great Britain and ultimately all states, went "off" the gold standard in order to relieve their domestic fiscal and employment policies from dependence upon rigid exchange rates and external economic situations. Exchange rates were not fixed. In consequence, instabilities and uncertainties developed in international payments and finance Furthermore, to protect themselves insofar as possible from the effects of these fluctuations, states then proceeded to invoke additional protective tariffs and restrictions on the use of foreign exchange. Gold ceased to move freely to balance international payments. The old mechanism through which international payments were cleared and regulated ceased to function.

International Monetary Fund. At the Bretton Woods Conference in 1944 it was agreed that an International Monetary Fund might help to avoid both the rigidities of the gold standard (it being impractical to return to it since the United States had most of the gold) and the uncertainties and paralysis generated by unstable exchange rates and the lack of reserves in central banks. Hence, through international subscription, a working Fund of different national currencies was created which the directors were empowered to use to aid the central banks of member states which found themselves faced with a serious temporary disequilibrium in their balance of payments. Through this means it was hoped that stable exchange rates could be achieved, national exchange control regulations could be reduced, and international trade could rest upon economic rather than political considerations.[22]

Although the Fund has afforded some assistance to a limited number of states, it has not on the whole fulfilled the hopes of its founders. The resources at its disposal were totally insufficient to handle the dollar gap imbalance that arose by 1947. Direct assistance through other means such as the European Recovery Program and the Mutual Security Program became essential. The IMF may be able to assist temporary situations arising from normal trade relationships of countries having stabilized currencies, when these can function freely. But it cannot cope with the enormous exchange imbalances such as

21 Heilperin, *op. cit.* p. 58. See also William Adams Brown, *The Gold Standard Reinterpreted* (New York, 1940); Paul Einzig, *World Finance, 1914–1935* (New York, 1935); H. Feis, *Europe—The World's Banker* (New Haven, 1930); H. B. Killough, *International Trade* (New York, 1938); on the balance of payments generally see J. E. Meade, *The Balance of Payments* (New York, 1951).

22 Final action and related documents of Bretton Woods Conference are in Dept. of State Pub. 2187, Conf. Ser. 55. For commentary see G. N. Halm, *International Monetary Cooperation* (Chapel Hill, 1945); Klaus Knorr, "The Bretton Woods Institutions in Transition," *Internat. Organization,* Feb., 1948.

those arising from requirements after World War II or from a major rearmament program.[23] Nor can it handle a chronic imbalance in world trade such as the "dollar gap" discussed below.

Interrelationship of Imports and Exports. The state with an export surplus must have policies to deal with this surplus unless its citizens, as part of their private enterprise efforts, take steps which manage that surplus. No state or group of states can go on indefinitely with heavy preponderance of goods exports without making grants or loans abroad, or accepting compensatory "invisible" imports, for example, shipping services and upkeep of tourists. Contrariwise, there are limits to the imports, loans, and services a nation can ordinarily agree to receive without having some governmentally arranged program of gaining sufficient foreign exchange or credits with which to pay for these items. Former Secretary of State Acheson pointed out this interdependence when he said, "A big creditor nation that refuses to import can never expect to be paid for its exports." [24]

THE DOLLAR GAP

Prior to World War II, the United States normally had a small excess of commodity exports over imports, but these were adjusted by the expenditures of American tourists abroad, emigrant remittances, payments for foreign shipping services that carried the bulk of United States foreign trade, and foreign investments. A critical international payment situation developed after World War II as a consequence of the destruction, economic derangement, and political changes suffered by the European states and others between 1939 and 1946.

The outstanding characteristic of this situation was the inability of European nations to earn or to borrow dollars to buy essential goods which had to be paid for in dollars. In Chapter IX under the heading of *Economic Consequences of War* we discuss in some detail the reasons for this situation and various assistance programs by which the United States met the dollar gap problem. The problem was made doubly critical by the threat of Moscow-inspired communist elements to seize power in some countries of Western Europe where the economic situation contributed to political instability. The accompanying table and graph illustrate the situation that existed in the postwar years and the amount of foreign assistance extended by the United States.

It was hoped that this assistance, taken together with European self-help

23 C. P. Kindleberger, "Bretton Woods Reappraised," *ibid.*, Feb., 1951; J. B. Condliffe, "International Trade and Economic Nationalism," *Internat. Conciliation*, Dec., 1951; W. M. Scammell, "The International Monetary Fund: An Interim Judgment," *World Affairs*, Oct., 1951.
24 *Department of State Bulletin*, April 28, 1952.

UNITED STATES EXPORTS AND IMPORTS OF GOODS AND SERVICES [25]
(Billions of Dollars)

YEAR	EXPORT OF GOODS	EXPORTS (NET) OF SERVICES	IMPORTS OF GOODS	GAP	US GOVERNMENT [a] GRANTS AND LOANS
1936–1939 (av.)	4.1		3.6	.5	
1946	10.2	2.9	5.1	8.0	5.5
1947	15.1	2.7	6.1	11.7	5.8
1948	13.1	1.8	7.8	7.1	5.2
1949	12.3	1.4	7.0	6.7	5.8
1950	10.6	1.1	9.3	1.4	4.1
1951	15.5	1.2	11.7	5.0	4.2
1952	15.5	.8	11.3	5.0	5.0

[a] Portion of gap not filled by government grants and loans was closed by private donations, private investment, World Bank loans, sale of gold to the US, use of dollar reserves, and International Monetary Fund transactions. It will be noted that in 1950 (prior to Korea and rearmament) the non-US world was building back some gold and dollar reserves.

and cooperation, would help raise the productive capacity of the European states sufficiently to enable them to meet their own domestic needs and at the same time to increase their export trade so that they could stabilize their international payment position, narrowing the annual dollar gap to manageable proportions. It was further hoped that European employment would be kept high so that the threat of communism could be averted and European morale strengthened.

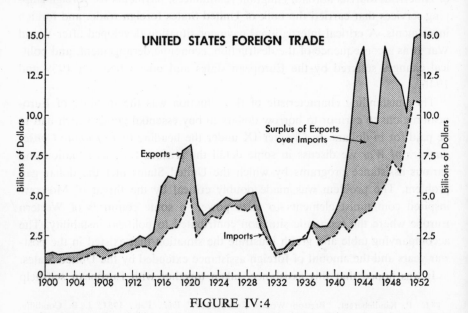

FIGURE IV:4

[25] Figures for the years 1936–1939 are from G. N. Halm and H. Hawkins, *The Foreign Trade Gap;* other figures are from Report to the President by the Public Advisory Board for Mutual Security, *A Trade and Tariff Policy in the National Interest,* 1953.

It was recognized by those responsible for the European Recovery Program that the "dollar gap" would have to be closed sooner or later by American imports of goods and acceptance of services, by an American private foreign investment program, or by both, if the European states were not to depend indefinitely on United States loans and grants. As two authorities on the situation wrote: "The necessity of developing an import surplus is inherent" in the American position as a creditor nation. Otherwise, international trade (unless financed by United States grants and loans) with the United States would drop below the level of United States imports and there would be a continual brake on all international trade.[26]

Economic Effects of Rearmament. Increasing production in Europe showed signs that the dollar gap might be closed early in the 1950's. But an armaments program uses national economic resources otherwise devoted to earning foreign exchange. Moreover, most countries cannot produce all types of modern arms, and certainly cannot produce them rapidly. Furthermore, the outbreak of the Korean War occasioned some disruption of international markets to the disadvantage of European countries. Hence the rearmament started in 1950 was accompanied by a continuation of the dollar gap problem even though the United States, with its Mutual Defense Assistance Program (later merged into the Mutual Security Program) provided the arms which could not be produced indigenously.

Thus, by 1952 much of the nonmilitary foreign aid of the United States was tapering off, and military aid and "defense support" financing were assuming the greatest part of the total foreign aid effort of the United States. To achieve durable security it was becoming obvious that some aspects of the mutual security program would have to be sustained over a considerable stretch of time.[27] But, leaving rearmament aside, there was the troublesome problem of the dollar gap in normal transactions—a gap which could be filled only by expansion of dollar imports or reduction of dollar exports. The latter expedient would gravely affect many United States industries and would move the United States economy toward a recession.

INTERNATIONAL INVESTMENT

The investment and consequent use of savings in the form of capital (factories, equipment, and so on) has been a principal basis of increased human productivity. Capital investment can come from domestic savings or from out-

---

26 Halm and Hawkins, *op. cit.*, p. 7.
27 See *Report to Congress on the Mutual Security Program* for the six months ended June 30, 1953 (Washington, 1953); Senate Com. on Foreign Relations Report No. 403, *op. cit.*; Hearings before the Senate Com. on Foreign Relations on the Mutual Security Act of 1953, 83d Cong., 1st Sess. (Washington, 1953).

side the state concerned. If from outside, it is an international grant or loan between either governments or individuals.

Motives for International Investment. Historically, the principal motive for international investment has been anticipation of a profit. European capital expanded industry and railroads in the United States in the nineteenth century which would have been developed more slowly if left to depend on United States resources alone. European, principally British, capital developed resources and industry during the latter part of the nineteenth and early part of the twentieth centuries in Latin America, the Middle East, and Asia. Britain, for instance, built the textile industry in India that later came to compete with Britain's home industry. United States private capital, entering the arena late, has contributed materially to development of Canada, Latin America, and Middle Eastern oil.

We should also mention international movement of capital due to distrust of, or dissatisfaction with, the indigenous economic situation. This movement of "flight capital" has particularly plagued European economies. The resultant demand for foreign exchange, usually dollars, could obviously gravely unbalance a state's exchange position. Hence the pattern of exchange restrictions established by states usually includes separate provisions covering capital movements.

Undoubtedly the profit motive has at times in the past been combined with imperialistic motives. Russian investments in Chinese Manchuria prior to the Russo-Japanese war, Japanese investments in the same area, German investments in the Balkans and Middle East prior to World War I and in the Middle East and Latin America prior to World War II—these almost certainly had political as well as purely economic motives.

There are well-established practices and laws governing domestic investment. International investment, particularly by private individuals, necessitates some international rules of the game. Here is where major difficulties have arisen, particularly since the disappearance of the gold standard and the development of major problems over convertibility of currency. How is the investor to be assured that he will be able to bring home the profits and payments on his principal to enjoy the fruits of his venture? How sure can he be that, with the socialistic trend apparent in some states, his investment will not be expropriated by a government adopting a program of nationalization? In the nineteenth century, private property and the institution of debt-payment had status close to that of religious institutions, and investors could usually count on effective pressures from their governments (sometimes called imperialism) to assist them when in trouble. But now such pressures are generally limited to diplomatic negotiation, anything stronger being labeled interference in internal affairs. In the nineteenth century the cards were heavily stacked on the side of the foreign investor, and instances of exploitation could easily be proved. Currently the situation seems to be reversed. This condition requires the most serious consideration, since there is a great need for international investment.

Before touching on this need we shall mention two examples of governmental motives for international investment, the Marshall Plan, which was a form of international investment, and the United States Export-Import Bank. The Export-Import bank advances funds to finance industrial developments abroad that may in one way or another further the foreign trade or overseas interests of the United States.[28] In 1952 loans were held in forty-seven countries for such items as construction of power plants and aiding production of scarce materials. Short-term loans are also extended to help finance large exports of American goods such as cotton and tobacco and to protect exporters to countries with frozen currencies. Similar types of financing are offered by government-owned or sponsored institutions in other large countries.

Need for International Development. It should be clear from even the brief preceding discussion that the trend of international investment has moved definitely from the nineteenth century variety of private enterprise for profit, with perhaps a dash of governmental aid sometimes called imperialism, to a considerably different pattern. That new pattern has a large political and security content in many areas of the world.

Three aspects of the new pattern stand out.

First, the United States is the principal holder of capital for export.

Second, there is a generally held thesis that the standard of living in the so-called "underdeveloped" areas must be raised if economic stability and continued prosperity are to be assured in the more industrialized states. When one recognizes that the purchasing power of one American is equal to more than the purchasing power of twenty-five Indians, the trading opportunities with India are seen in better perspective.

Third, there is a definite political and social demand in the areas called "underdeveloped" for improvements requiring capital investment. Recognizing this demand and its implications in the light of the communist threat, there is political concern over ways and means to provide the capital. This capital cannot be provided by domestic savings in the foreseeable future, if only because most of the states concerned lack the industry either to produce the capital in the forms required (machinery and the like) or to make the goods to sell abroad to pay cash for the imports needed. These underdeveloped areas, with a population of about 800 millions, generally have a per capita product of

[28] In 1953 the Export-Import Bank's active credits amounted to more than 3 billion dollars. See Annual Reports of Bank to Congress.

less than one hundred dollars a person. This situation leaves little above the subsistence level to save for capital investment. Some states do not have great difficulties. Oil and other raw materials still attract private investors. Parts of the Middle East, Latin America, and Canada, which is certainly not "underdeveloped," have no difficulty in attracting foreign investment.

The second and third points mentioned are stressed because international economic development is a problem new to international politics. It was hardly discussed before World War II. Now it, rather than such elements of foreign investment as the possible imperialistic taint, is the most significant aspect of international capital movement or lack thereof. Since the consciousness of the need and a desire both exist in most underdeveloped states, and since the capital-owning states are seriously concerned over this need and desire, it might seem that a program should be readily evolved to solve the problem. But the private investor is now cautious as a result of experiences of the 1920's and because of the many trade restrictions. He must usually deal with governments. Many of the governments concerned are not too stable, are highly nationalistic and sometimes socialistic, and are sensitive to the charge of capitalistic exploitation. Some of the development needed is in the nature of long-range investments in roads, railroads, and power installations. The stability of the nineteenth century often made such loans attractive. But there is little comparable assurance that a loan made today will actually be paid in 1985. Having presented some of the adverse considerations, it is still necessary to recognize that a continued United States export surplus must result in a program of grants, loans, or both while the political situation in the underdeveloped areas continues to press hard for foreign capital.

United Nations economists have estimated that a foreign investment flow of up to 20 billion dollars (over ten times the flow in the early 1950's) a year is needed to do an effective job of raising the standards of living of the rest of the world. Anything like this amount would have to come from all the industrialized countries, rather than from the United States alone, and would have to come from private investors as well as public loans. There have been hopeful suggestions that an effective regulation of armaments program would result in release of resources for investment of the magnitude estimated by the United Nations economists and that nations, if freed from the security threat, would be willing to direct a large part of the saved resources to international development.

Cooperative International Development; the International Bank. Representatives of the Allied states meeting at Bretton Woods, New Hampshire, in 1944 at the invitation of the United States, agreed to establish an International Bank for Reconstruction and Development for the purpose of pooling resources for assisting the needy reconstruction and long-term development projects after the war. Working capital for this intergovernmental institution was subscribed by the member states in varying amounts, with voting strength on the Board of Governors being proportioned in accordance with the number of shares subscribed. Additional capital funds were subsequently raised by floating bond issues. Before the European Recovery Program was inaugurated, loans were granted chiefly to restore and increase productivity in the shortest possible time. Since 1948 loans have been granted for more essentially long-range development projects. These have included loans to finance shipbuilding, modernization of woodworking industries, railway and highway construction, hydroelectric development, irrigation projects, purchase of agricultural machinery, land reclamation, mining developments, and other undertakings. Countries which have received loans have included, among others, Belgium, the Netherlands, France, Denmark, Brazil, Chile, Colombia, India, and Turkey.

The Bank, which loaned about 1.7 billion dollars by 1954, is intended to take calculated investment risks to assist worthy projects—both governmental and government-sponsored—which private capital is not prepared to underwrite. The activities of the Bank are guided by an international Board of Directors representing the states subscribing to its stock. In this the United States has the largest voting strength. The Board is assisted by a corps of economists and technical experts who make detailed field investigations of proposals submitted to the Bank. Inevitably the Bank tends to make loans principally on "bankable" risks, that is, those which are considered favorably by private capital. Hence there is a material doubt as to whether it will soon fill the need for long-term development capital for projects which do not give promise of returning the principal in a reasonable number of years. The Bank does not provide funds for rearmament. So long as convertibility of currency is restricted in the world, the problem of repayment (particularly repayment of borrowed dollars) will be complicated by exchange difficulties as well as being dependent on the ability of a state to achieve a favorable balance of international payments at least equal to the amount due on its debt.[29]

"Point Four" Program and Technical Assistance. A new approach to international investment and cooperative economic endeavor was opened with

[29] The Articles of Agreement establishing the Bank will be found in Sen. Doc. No. 123, *A Decade of American Foreign Policy, 1941–1949,* 81st Cong., 1st Sess., pp. 251–311. The literature on the Bank has become voluminous. Among the more generally descriptive treatments see Antonin Basch, "International Bank for Reconstruction and Development, 1944–1949," *Internat. Conciliation,* Nov. 1949; Eugene R. Black, "The International Bank and World Economic Development," *World Affairs,* Oct., 1950: Geo. N. Halm, *International Monetary Cooperation* (Chapel Hill, 1945); C. P. Kindleberger, "Bretton Woods Reappraised," *Internat. Organization,* Feb., 1951; Nathanial Weyl and M. J. Wasserman, "The International Bank," *Am. Ec. Rev.,* March, 1947.

President Truman's Inaugural Address in 1949 when he proposed "a bold new program for making the benefits of our scientific advances and industrial progress available for the improvement and growth of underdeveloped areas." Called "Point Four" because it was the fourth in an enumeration of tenets of policy, this program was envisaged as being primarily technical assistance, a sharing of United States technology, rather than provision of large increments of capital as in the Marshall Plan. This was not, in fact, a new idea. The United States had for some years been conducting a similar program in cooperation with some Latin American states. Essentially a long-range program, the Point Four Program aims to increase productivity and per capita income in the more or less underdeveloped areas through the extension of scientific and technical assistance, and aid in health, sanitary measures, and education to increase productivity and nutrition.[30]

Inspired by the same ideas, the United Nations has undertaken a somewhat similar long-range program of economic development and technical assistance. Economic commissions have been established for Asia, the Far East, and Latin America to study basic economic conditions and needs with a view to recommending measures for their improvement. Missions composed of agronomists, economists, engineers, and public health workers have been assembled to send to countries desiring technical assistance under United Nations auspices.[31]

Experience in operating Point Four quickly revealed that technicians are of doubtful effectiveness without some capital goods—if only to use for demonstration purposes. Put summarily, there is no substitute for capital in an attempt to increase production and raise living standards rapidly.

Colombo Plan. There should also be mentioned the Colombo Plan of the Commonwealth of Nations. This plan for economic development, inaugurated as a result of a Commonwealth Conference held at Colombo in 1950, has as its purpose the initiation of efforts especially for South and South East Asia supplementing the work already being done by the United States Point Four Program and the Technical Assistance Program of the United Nations. The Plan envisaged an outlay by the Commonwealth Countries of over 5 billion dollars, covering a six-year period beginning in 1951. The plan is significant for its encouragement of initiative on the part of the Asian countries themselves and as an illustration of what might be done cooperatively within the

---

30 See J. B. Condliffe and H. H. Hutcheson, *Point Four and the World Economy,* For. Pol. Assoc. Headline Ser. No. 68, March-April, 1948; Annette B. Fox, "President Truman's Fourth Point and the United Nations," *Internat. Conciliation,* June 1949; R. Nurkse, "Some International Aspects of the Problem of Economic Development," *Am. Ec. Rev.,* May, 1952; United States Dept. of State, *Point Four: Cooperative Program for Aid in the Development of Economically Underdeveloped Areas,* Dept. of State Pub. 3719 (Washington, Jan., 1950).

31 See ch. xx below.

Commonwealth with the resources at its disposal. The goals of the plan are to increase the food supply, improve transportation and communication, expand industry, better the means of providing fuel and power, and promote the welfare of the people.[32]

Government vs. Private Investment. A wholly new era of international financing may now be upon us. There is still a large field for private international investment for routine commercial transactions, business expansion, and economic development. But it is apparent that private capital cannot handle problems of the magnitude and political urgency of those which arose after 1945 requiring relief, rehabilitation, economic recovery, increased productivity, rearmament, and large-scale, long-term economic development on projects which may not always be able to provide a profitable or monetary return. Such projects cannot be designed entirely as strictly business transactions because there are objectives additional to those of a business transaction. Politics may at times in the past have been the handmaiden of economics. But in a world struggle such as that taking place in the early 1950's, economics was brought to the service and bidding of politics in many international matters. This reversal of traditional practice as generally understood by most citizens, and the cost thereof, brought warranted questions from United States citizens.

Approached from the private investor's standpoint, there may be some merit in thinking about international investment under three general classifications. Admittedly there is no easy or certain way to categorize a particular project under one of these classifications.

1. The provision of capital for political and security purposes under circumstances where there is little or no guarantee of repayment. The European Recovery Program is an example. Such provision may react to the general economic advantage of the providing state in the long run by expanding world trade. But it is not a project for private investors.

2. Provision of capital for projects which provide low, if any, returns and for which repayment can be made only over a long period. Such provision, if made, is almost certain to have a major political and/or security aspect. There is also the type of risk taken by the United States Export-Import Bank which often includes some political objective. We suggest, with some caution, that capital provided under this classification can usually come from governmental and international lending agencies which, taking into account the political dividends, can sustain the risks without great fear of

---

[32] See *The Colombo Plan for Cooperative Economic Development in South and South East Asia,* Report by the Commonwealth Consultative Committee, CMD, 8080 (London, Sept.-Oct., 1950); John R. E. Carr-Gregg, "The Colombo Plan, A Commonwealth Program for Southeast Asia," *Internat. Conciliation,* Jan., 1951; Wilfred Malenbaum, "The Colombo Plan, New Promise for Asia," *Department of State Bulletin,* Sept. 22, 1952.

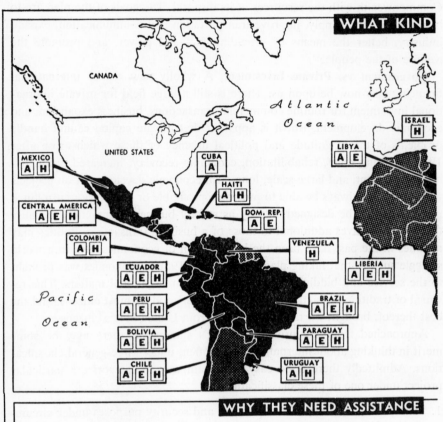

WHAT KIND

CANADA

Atlantic Ocean

ISRAEL
H

UNITED STATES

MEXICO
A H

CUBA
A

HAITI
A H

LIBYA
A E

CENTRAL AMERICA
A E H

DOM. REP.
A E

LIBERIA
A E H

COLOMBIA
A H

VENEZUELA
H

Pacific Ocean

ECUADOR
A E H

PERU
A E H

BRAZIL
A E H

BOLIVIA
A E H

PARAGUAY
A E H

CHILE
A E H

URUGUAY
A H

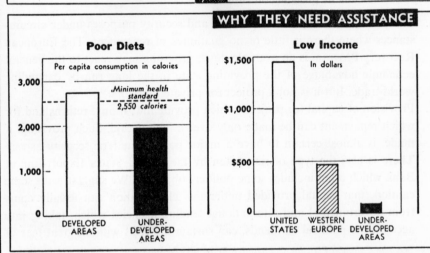

WHY THEY NEED ASSISTANCE

Poor Diets

Per capita consumption in calories

Minimum health standard 2,550 calories

3,000

2,000

1,000

0

DEVELOPED AREAS

UNDER-DEVELOPED AREAS

Low Income

In dollars

$1,500

$1,000

$500

0

UNITED STATES

WESTERN EUROPE

UNDER-DEVELOPED AREAS

FIGURE

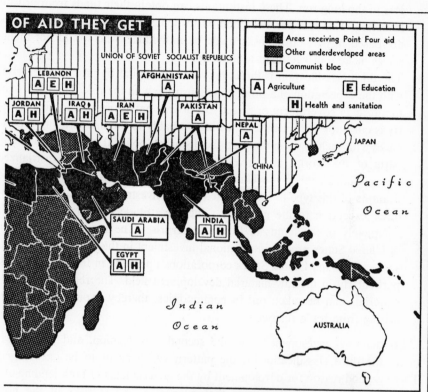

OF AID THEY GET

UNION OF SOVIET SOCIALIST REPUBLICS

Areas receiving Point Four aid
Other underdeveloped areas
Communist bloc

A Agriculture   E Education
H Health and sanitation

LEBANON
A E H

JORDAN
A H

IRAQ
A H

IRAN
A E H

AFGHANISTAN
A

PAKISTAN
A

NEPAL
A

JAPAN

CHINA

Pacific Ocean

SAUDI ARABIA
A

INDIA
A H

EGYPT
A H

Indian Ocean

AUSTRALIA

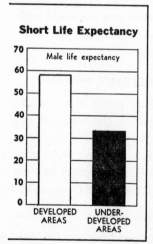

Short Life Expectancy

Male life expectancy

70
60
50
40
30
20
10
0

DEVELOPED AREAS   UNDER-DEVELOPED AREAS

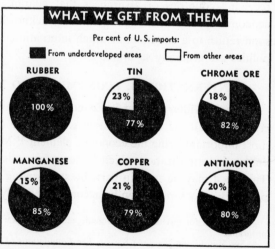

WHAT WE GET FROM THEM

Per cent of U. S. imports:

From underdeveloped areas   From other areas

RUBBER
100%

TIN
23%
77%

CHROME ORE
18%
82%

MANGANESE
15%
85%

COPPER
21%
79%

ANTIMONY
20%
80%

The New York Times

IV:5

loss in the long run. These institutions can obtain their funds from private investors. This is a parallel situation to domestic banking in which loans are based in part on deposits made by individuals who would not themselves make a private loan to industry.

3. The third classification is direct provision of capital by private enterprise, with the expectation of a profit commensurate with the risk. The bank loan to a foreign government or directly to private enterprise in a foreign country is currently not much used, owing probably to the discouraging experiences with such loans in the past, the disturbed political conditions in many parts of the world, and investment opportunities within industrialized states. Bonds sold in the United States by the new Israeli state are one example of this type of loan. United States investments in Canada are another exception to the generally reluctant attitude toward placing funds completely in the hands of foreign enterprise. The predominant pattern of United States private international investment in the post-World War II scene is through United States corporations operating in foreign countries, particularly in the raw-material development field. The returns from raw materials can be taken out in commodities, thereby avoiding difficulties arising from trade restrictions.

International investment under the second classification, and particularly under the third classification, is the pattern which needs to be encouraged. There is good reason for development by the governments of both lending and receiving countries of assurances that guarantee against risks of the non-economic type. This thought admittedly acknowledges that the world will not soon return to a condition in which international economics and international politics are generally separated.

INTERNATIONAL ECONOMICS AND MILITARY POWER [33]

Basis of Military Power is Economic. The military power of a state is derived from all the elements discussed in these opening chapters, one of the most important being the economic element.[34] Military power is very dependent on industrialization which in turn demands raw materials from abroad. This need may be met, in part, by stock-piling for an emergency in time of peace. But stock-piling can be accomplished only if the materials are available

---

[33] See ch. ix for discussion of economic causation of war, reparations, and military assistance programs.

[34] See Harold and Margaret Sprout, *The Foundations of National Power* (rev. ed., Princeton, 1951), and G. A. Lincoln and others, *The Economics of National Security* (2d ed., New York, 1954). The latter includes a discussion of foreign assistance, economic problems of collective security, and economic warfare.

and foreign exchange or credits are available to pay for them. Blockade by sea, by land, or by destruction from the air is a potent threat in the mind of every national security planner. All countries seek to industrialize, some for the objective of improved living standards, some also for increased military strength. The outcome is usually increased interdependence for raw materials and markets and hence continued vulnerability in case of international tension or hostilities. Yet without economic means, principally derived from industrialization, a state has little military power unless assisted by an ally able to provide the industrial production.

Foreign Assistance and Military Power. This close relationship of industry, foreign trade, and military power has been evidenced in the fantastically complicated relationship of United States assistance programs to the internal economic planning of NATO countries and to the NATO program for building armed forces. Armed forces in being, internal industry in each country, the budget of each state, exports and imports, the balance of payments, arms assistance, and assistance other than arms aid—all these items became essential components of the equation of building and maintaining military strength.

War now means a certainty of economic assistance among allies. Oddly enough it was not until the Lend-Lease program of World War II (costing about 40 billion dollars) that the United States placed inanimate resources in the "common pool" of effort and in the same category as American lives in other allied wars. In World War I, for instance, the United States required no balance sheet of effort from the standpoint of casualties, and American troops were placed under high allied command. But repayment of "war loans" was insisted upon. In 1941 it was more clearly understood that modern war is a total national effort for each nation involved. Through the arrangement of Lend-Lease and reverse Lend-Lease (about 7 billion dollars' worth) the main international economic problems were resolved with maximum efficiency.

Economic Warfare. Economic warfare is one of the important techniques of use of force in international affairs. Its objective is the lessening or elimination of the international flow of goods and services to an unfriendly or enemy country. The methods are complicated, ranging from blockade to preclusive buying of supplies in neutral countries which the enemy needs.[35] Economic sanctions, such as those ineffectually imposed on Italy in the Italo-Ethiopian War were economic warfare. So also was the embargo of exports to communist China during the Korean War. Economic sanctions alone are hardly sufficient, however, to restrain an aggressor.

[35] See Paul Einzig, *Economic Warfare* (London, 1941); O. L. Gordon and Royden Dangerfield, *The Hidden Weapon* (New York, 1947).

CONCLUSION

Britain underwrote the heyday of world trade in modern history and profited greatly thereby. That period was characterized by freedom of movement for goods, convertibility of currencies, a considerable flow of international investment, and a high degree of adherence to economic (as opposed to political) considerations. Britain lost this position of leadership in the early 1930's and no longer has the capability to lead. The world has adopted, and become adept in using, a numerous and complicated array of restrictions. Confidence, essential to private international investment, is shaken. The economic instrument is used internationallly for political and security purposes as well as to further economic well-being. Can the people of the world expect a change for the economic better? The answer seems to lie in United States leadership and tariff policy and in Europe. These two areas encompass about 60 per cent of world trade and, together, can determine whether the trend will be back toward the conditions of the British-led golden age or, alternatively, along the road of continued restrictions, imbalances, and crises.

SUGGESTED READINGS

William A. Brown, Jr., and Redvers Opie, *American Foreign Assistance* (Washington, 1953).

J. B. Condliffe, *The Commerce of Nations* (New York, 1950).

Howard S. Ellis, *The Economics of Freedom: The Progress and Future of Aid to Europe* (New York, 1950).

Paul T. Ellsworth, *The International Economy: Its Structure and Operation* (New York, 1950).

G. N. Halm, *International Monetary Cooperation* (Chapel Hill, 1945).

Seymour E. Harris, ed., *Foreign Economic Policy for the United States* (Cambridge, 1948).

Calvin B. Hoover, *International Trade and Domestic Employment* (New York, 1945).

Charles P. Kindleberger, *International Economics* (Homewood, Ill., 1953).

G. A. Lincoln and associates, *Economics of National Security* (rev. ed., New York, 1954).

R. F. Mikesell, *United States Economic Policy and International Relations* (New York, 1952).

Ernest M. Patterson, *An Introduction to World Economics* (New York, 1947).

L. W. Towle, *International Trade and Commercial Policy* (New York, 1947).

John H. Williams, *Economic Stability in a Changing World* (New York, 1953).

CHAPTER V

Psychological Factors in International Relations

THE PRECEDING chapters have discussed some of the geographic factors, population conditions, and economic needs of man which are basic to the policies and actions of all governments and the military and other components of power of all states. These elements are in the area of tangibles. They can be defined and measured, to some extent at least, in specific terms. Relations between states are influenced, however, in no small measure by such intangible elements as the beliefs, prejudices, emotions, and desires which affect the value judgment, behavior, and reactions of men.

RELATIONSHIP OF SOCIOPSYCHOLOGICAL FACTORS TO PUBLIC AFFAIRS

While these social and psychological components of policy can be described, it is difficult to weigh them with any degree of precision for attitudes and reactions are complex in nature. Furthermore, relatively little study has as yet been devoted by social psychologists to the exact bearing of these factors upon international relations.[1]

Influence of Social and Cultural Background. Man's judgment is affected by the scope of his knowledge, his social and cultural background, his emotional susceptibility to particular threats and appeals, his capacity for idealism, and, in general, the conditioning given him by his past and present environment and associations. His beliefs, likes and dislikes, loyalties and dispositions,

---

[1] Among the more useful general studies are Ralph Linton, *The Study of Man* (New York, 1936); T. M. Newcomb, *Social Psychology* (New York, 1950); Otto Klineberg, *Tensions Affecting International Understanding, A Survey of Research* (New York, 1950); Ralph Linton, *The Science of Man in the World Crisis* (New York, 1945); Stuart Chase, *The Proper Study of Mankind* (New York, 1948). For an effort to outline the province of psychological knowledge in relation to international affairs see Gordon W. Allport, "Guidelines for Research in International Cooperation," in T. H. Pear (ed.), *Psychological Factors of War and Peace* (New York, 1950).

are strongly influenced by the traits, outlooks, experiences, and folkways which constitute his cultural, religious, social, and political environment.[2]

Man is not born with certain definite political or ideological inclinations, prejudices, or hatreds. He is not born a "German," an "American," or an "Englishman" in the full meaning of the word. He acquires his political leanings, his attitudes, his antipathies through the cumulative influences of family, neighborhood, church, school, press, law, and the other institutions of his native society. Some countries permit the individual much personal freedom of behavior and belief; others endeavor to limit these or to strait-jacket the individual so that he has little leeway in his attitudes or behavior toward his own state or toward others. The variations in these "cultural alternatives" differentiate the attitudes and conduct of nations and bear closely upon international relations.

Attitudes. Distrust of foreigners and their aims is an age-old characteristic. It is common among peoples who have been, or have believed themselves to have been, the objects of foreign exploitation or aggression. To some degree, however, it is present in all groups of peoples. This "in-group versus out-group" feeling degenerates in its extreme form into xenophobia. In such cases, the objectives, interests, and aspirations of the native population are usually viewed as being gravely endangered by the activities, interests, or aspirations of other groups of a different race or nationality. The Boxer Uprising in China in 1900, the widespread anti-white-man feeling existent in Asia, the anti-Americanism prevalent in certain quarters of Latin America, are instances in point. Basic to such corporate attitudes is the feeling of "we" *versus* "they" which arises with group living and communication.

Aspirations, Objectives, Ideas. The clusters of ideas which people develop concerning political, economic, and cultural institutions, and the moral rationalizations for their actions which we call ideologies, have a psychological foundation and are powerful elements in forming the attitudes and reactions of one group of people toward another. This is readily observable in the conflict between the forces of the free world and of communism in the contemporary era.

The desires of peoples for independence, for a better standard of living, for greater security, can become dynamic motivations in the life of groups and of nations. They can unleash powerful forces as peoples come to believe that they are being denied, because of political, economic, or military conditions, a

---

[2] On influence of cultural factors see especially Ruth Benedict, *Patterns of Culture* (New York, 1934); the same author, "Continuities and Discontinuities in Cultural Conditioning," *Psychiatry*, vol. 1, pp. 161–167; Clyde Kluckhohn, *Mirror to Man* (New York, 1949); Margaret Mead, *Cooperation and Competition among Primitive Peoples* (New York, 1937): the same author, *And Keep Your Powder Dry* (New York, 1942).

rightful measure of what they consider to be due them. If they become convinced that their present status is due to the policies of others, or that the attainment of their objectives is being blocked by the policies or rule of others —as subject peoples are often inclined to feel—they may be led to resort to revolution, economic boycott, or war even though reasoned estimates may show that the goal may as yet be only remotely attainable.

Nationalism. One of the most powerful sociopsychological forces operative in modern world politics is nationalism.[3] The feeling of nationalism springs from the unique cultural and historical background of a given people. It expresses the group's sense of belonging together, of having certain shared values which they desire to preserve.

Nationalism binds together peoples who have common experiences, ties, or values such as a common cultural or linguistic heritage, a common historical experience, or loyalty to the same political group. It represents a body of values which a group holds to be sufficiently unique and valuable to warrant group action and their preservation and transmission to posterity.[4]

When people unite within a spirit of nationalism and a crisis confronts them with a real or imaginary enemy, they become subject to the operation of the intangible forces of group psychology and collective behavior.[5] Many of the manifestations of nationalism are charged with emotion when expressed in terms of economic or political action. Usually the feelings of nationalism tend to emphasize the separateness and differentiation of one group from one or two particular peoples, as for example, Germans *versus* French, Poles *versus* Germans and Russians, Arabs *versus* Jews, and so forth. Nationalism makes it possible to marshal mass enthusiasm for a particular nation-state and against another.[6]

Notwithstanding the compartmentalization and alignment of one nation against another which this feeling tends to evoke, ties of nationality have also positive moral components. Nationalism creates a spirit of group unity. It fires the imagination of people toward action and gives them a love of country. It makes possible the creation of strong social institutions and loyalty to the nation's law. These frames of reference and value systems offer security to the individual and strength to the group.

3 See ch. vi below on "The Force of Nationalism."

4 For general readings in nationalism see E. H. Carr, *Nationalism and After* (New York, 1945); E. M. Earle (ed.), *Nationalism and Internationalism* (New York, 1950); Friedrich Hertz, *Nationality in History and Politics: A Study of the Psychology and Sociology of National Sentiment and Character* (London, 1944); Hans Kohn, *The Idea of Nationalism, a Study of Its Origins and Background* (New York, 1944); Royal Inst. of Intl. Affairs, *Nationalism: A Report* (London, 1939).

5 See Gustave Le Bon, *The Psychology of the Crowd* (London, 1896); R. T. LaPiere, *Collective Behavior* (New York, 1938).

6 See A. de Hegeolus, *Patriotism or Peace* (New York, 1947).

While a strong feeling of nationalism can and has strengthened and unified nations in their ability to withstand vicissitudes and resist aggression, as exemplified by Britain in 1940 and by Turkey in resisting Soviet pressure in 1946, nationalism may, under some circumstances, act so as to weaken a nation in time of crisis or adversity. An appeal to extreme nationalism by emotional leaders may turn a people away from wiser courses of action, or lead to suspicion and unwarranted distrust of others which may prevent a nation from having harmonious or mutually advantageous relations with others having the same interests. Iranian policy on the oil question from 1950 to 1953 under former Premier Mossadegh may be an example.

All these sociopsychological elements are interrelated with one another, together with the specific policies and actions which nations adopt in response to them and in pursuance of their national objectives.

ELEMENTS AFFECTING INTERNATIONAL RELATIONSHIPS

The relationships between states are determined, first, by the objectives which states set for themselves and the bearing which these have on the interests and objectives of other states. Sometimes these relationships are compatible and reconcilable; often they compete and overlap; on occasion they lead to conflict or to war. Secondly, the relationships are affected by the attitudes and feelings which the leading personalities in the government and the people of one country have toward others. These may be influenced by personal experiences, as, for example, the jailing of leaders of independence movements, or by the experiences of the generation from which particular leaders emerge, as in the case of World War I with its losses in life and the disillusionment which followed in the peace. As an example, the attitude of Stalin, and hence of Soviet foreign policy during the period of his rule, toward Turkey was reported to have been deeply conditioned by his native upbringing in Georgia in the atmosphere of a traditional quarrel with Turkey which once controlled the region. Attitudes and feelings may also be influenced by widespread propaganda and misunderstanding. Or they may be conditioned by memory of past experiences, as the French continually remind themselves of the invasions of their country by Germany in 1870, in 1914, and again in 1940. Thirdly, relationships are determined by the policies that governments decide to pursue and by the expositions, sincere or deceptive, that accompany and explain these policies.

The formal labels that are employed in the language of international politics —states, governments, foreign ministers, power politics, competitions for markets, armaments races, peace and war, and so on—tell us little about the human forces that underlie international relationships and are at work within them. Wrapped up in them are "a thousand fragments of personal ambition and patriotism, of secret love and hatred, unconscious purpose and need"—the drives and emotions of group life.

Although international politics are conducted by a relatively small number of statesmen and diplomats, they involve at heart the relationships between large bodies of peoples organized into bodies politic. As such they are affected by the psychology of situations involving large groups.

Subjective Elements in Attitudes. States whose leaders and people feel that their objectives and interests are not being jeopardized or threatened by other states usually find it possible to maintain friendly relations with one another, adjusting their differences and competitions peaceably as they arise. On the other hand, states whose leaders and peoples come to feel that their interests and security are threatened by another state find it more difficult, if not impossible, to reconcile their differences or to settle peaceably disputes which they believe involve their vital interests.

In the past, the feeling of danger or threat to one's security was usually a function of geographical proximity. Thus, for example, there was and still is little danger that Thailand and Brazil could have many political conflicts. On the whole, it can therefore be said that distance made for friendly relations between states, proximity for possible tension. The amazing technological progress in the fields of transportation and communication has, for all practical purposes, annihilated this factor of distance. With jet planes reaching the speed of sound, and with radio-communication linking the whole world, news about actions of one state reaches others almost instantly and evokes immediate countermeasures. Despite their geographical distance, the United States and the Soviet Union view each other as chief rivals and are both apprehensive not only about the intentions but also about the capacity of either to cause havoc to the cities of the other by a surprise attack with nuclear weapons. Clearly, what seemed true in the era of slow-moving land armies does not apply in the age of the radio, the jet plane, and the H-bomb.

Subjective elements are always present, to some degree, in the minds of officials and the public with respect to foreign relations. Perceptions and attitudes—and the responses which are made to them—are influenced by predispositions springing from past experiences, handed down from one generation to the next, or spread by the interplay of group relationships.

The Chinese officials who gave encouragement to the Boxer uprising to expel foreigners from China in 1900 were acting at least partly on a predisposition inherited from the past which held all foreigners to be "devils" and regarded foreign states as tributaries or inferior political entities.

Similarly, many Americans who supported the policies of isolation and neutrality before 1941 did so on the basis of a tradition inherited from their forebears and rationalized in the terms of Washington's Farewell Address of 1796.

The gist of that address was that Europe's conflicts have no interest to America, that America should hold aloof, and that the mere facts of geographical distance from Europe and Asia and the presence of the large oceans conferred security upon this continent. The intricacies of international economic relations, the reality of modern weapons of mass-destruction and of long-range airplanes, and the fact that America had to intervene in the European war in 1917, and was attacked in 1941, illustrate how inapplicable this view is to the world we live in.[7]

The Soviets, in accepting Marxist-Leninist dogma as a basis for judging world events and foreseeing "how and when they must develop in the future," as Stalin asserted,[8] are to this extent guided by subjective judgment founded upon a preconceived picture of what "is bound to happen" regardless of whether it actually is happening. The errors to which this can lead are revealed in their miscalculations of the readiness of Europe for communism in 1919, of the strength and policies of national socialism in Germany,[9] and of the ability of the capitalist states to provide permanently higher standards for workers than the communist states and to give colonial peoples independence.

Persistence and Change in Attitudes. Bodies politic are slow to change their attitudes toward foreign nations or to modify their own national objectives. Each state builds up aspirations and carries with it impressions from the past which become powerful guides, or hindrances, to decision-making in the present. This can be seen in the persistence of French fears and suspicions of Germany expressing themselves in repeated demands for security guarantees and in resistance to granting Germany equal status in European defense arrangements. These persistent attitudes have come down to present-day Frenchmen from the three disastrous invasions by Germany since 1870. The fears of the French are even more comprehensible when the facts of relative population and productive capacity are added to the record of history. French attitudes cannot be expected to change readily save as there may occur material alterations in the balance of power or a basic transformation of the European nation-state system toward a federal form. Other examples from history could be adduced.

Changes can occur, of course, in the attitudes and policies of states, as demonstrated in the remarkable change in American attitudes toward participation in international organizations and in collective security arrangements since 1941, and in the change in attitude toward Germany, Italy, and Japan since

---

[7] Farewell Address in Ruhl Bartlett, *The Record of American Diplomacy* (New York, 1947), pp. 86–88. See Eugene Staley, "The Myth of the Continents," in H. F. Armstrong (ed.) *Foreign Affairs Reader* (New York, 1947), pp. 317–333.

[8] Historicus, "Stalin on Revolution," *Foreign Affairs,* Jan., 1949.

[9] G. W. Millikan, "The Science of Soviet Politics," *ibid.,* April, 1953.

1945. These changes have in effect amounted to a diplomatic revolution.

In most instances, however, the cumulative attitudes held by the peoples and officials of one state toward another exhibit a good measure of continuity. Major alterations occur only over a considerable period of time. When they do occur this is almost always due to some change in the balance of power situation or to some altered perception of the position of national interests. When interests and objectives appear to be endangered by a state that was held to be friendly in the past, attitudes will change. This is illustrated in the case of Soviet-American relations where the suspicion of the Soviet Union, characteristic of American opinion from 1917 to 1941, was briefly suspended during World War II, only to be reverted to when Moscow's actions showed that it had not changed its objectives. The relations between China and the United States before and after the communist victory in 1949 illustrate a similar point. Accommodations, and even cooperative actions, may take place between states that have been suspicious of one another when both are threatened by a common enemy, as happened from 1941 to 1945 when Russia and the Western Powers were both attacked by Germany. But changes in attitudes between states are seldom due to a simple change in people's thinking. Rather, the latter often is the result of real changes in the world situation.

Prejudices and Preferences. Among the psychological elements operative in international affairs are the positive and negative individual and group motivations which arise among peoples. These include preferences and prejudices, name-calling, stereotyping, and the attempt to erect barriers between oneself and nations or groups which are suspected or opposed.

In the same way as individuals prefer certain individuals and are prone to dislike others, so nations, for intangible reasons of history, culture, religion, or sympathy are apt to be more solicitous toward some and more suspicious and cool toward others. Thus the West on the whole was less hostile to weaker Italy than it was to Germany, although both were enemies in World War II. Similarly, the affinity between the United States and Britain, born out of the cultural, linguistic, and family ties of the two peoples, is likely to continue linking the two peoples in triumph or calamity regardless of occasional differences on foreign policy. While the loans and aid extended by the United States to Britain in the difficult post-war years were by no means motivated only by solicitude for a kindred and friendly nation, it would be wrong to disregard this element and to view them only as moves designed to preserve the world's balance of power. The Slavic peoples of Eastern Europe have little love of Russian imperialism or of communist domination, but many of them do have sentiments of kinship with the Russian people which lead them to fear the USSR less than they do German conquest.

Historic memories, symbolic ties, traditions, and an array of other psychological elements make for a climate of emotional predispositions which on occasion can substantially influence foreign policy choices. In an age of democratic influences on the formulation of foreign policy, it is questionable whether any popular government could long resist public pressure when this comes to be focused on an issue of foreign affairs involving popular preferences or prejudices. It is an undoubted fact that foreign policy and popular moods, prejudices and inclinations, are closely interrelated. In the democracies public opinion polls sometimes reveal the persistence of attitudes and the continuance of outmoded conceptions.

Name-Calling and Stereotyping. Name-calling is a frequently observable phenomenon in group relationships as feelings arise. It is observable in the domestic scene when members of a striking union are sometimes called "traitors" for tying up the nation's supply of coal, steel, or some other essential commodity, or when workers passing through a picket line are called "scabs." Name-calling is a common occurrence in conflicts between nations. Russians are called "Bolsheviks" and "Reds," while Soviet newspapers, broadcasters, and diplomats accuse American statesmen of being "warmongers" and "Wall Street imperialists" seeking to enslave others, and that the whole nation is dominated by "capitalist exploiters" seeking to repress an impoverished working class. No one has expressed the role of name-calling more bluntly than the Russian Pan-Slavist, General Fadeev, when he wrote: "Names have a great significance as regards the masses: they take the place of matured opinions." [10]

Walter Lippmann once ascribed the tendency of members of a group to stereotype members of other national groups to the existence of "pictures in our heads"—that is, to the tendency to make artificial classifications first and then to seek out illustrations irrespective of other traits or exceptions. As Mr. Lippmann observed, people do not, for the most part, first see realities and then define them; rather, they make their descriptions first and then identify them. "We pick out what our culture has already defined for us," he says, "and we tend to perceive that which we have picked out in the form stereotyped for us by our culture." Psychologically speaking, the world is not recognized for what it is, but rather in large part for what we have been taught by our experiences to perceive it to be. "We imagine most things before we experience them." [11]

10 General R. Fadeev, *Opinion on the Eastern Question* (London, 1871), p. 48.
11 See Walter Lippmann, *Public Opinion* (New York, 1922), pp. 61, 67, 81. See also G. W. Allport, *The Nature of Prejudice* (Cambridge, 1954); J. Barnard, "Conceptualization of Inter-Group Relations," *Social Forces*, March, 1951; W. Buchanan and H. Cantril, *How Nations See Each Other* (Urbana, 1953); D. Katz, "Psychological Barriers to Communication," *Annals*, Mar., 1947; G. Murphy, *In the Minds of Men* (New York, 1953); A. H. Leighton, *Human Relations in a Changing World* (New York, 1949), ch. 6; Frederick C. Barghoorn, *The Soviet Image of the United States* (New York, 1950).

The Place of Language. In international relations, as in interpersonal relations, language holds a vital place in group associations. It provides not only a means of communication, but helps distinguish one group from another. It affects the psychological impressions and reactions of peoples, and is likely to strengthen "in-group" versus "out-group" concepts. When a foreign language is not easily understood, it is not always easy for ideas and points of view to be fully communicated between peoples. This does not necessarily prevent them from enjoying amicable relations, as evidenced by the long period of friendly intercourse between the Chinese and the Americans, and between Sweden and England. Likewise, the possession of a common language, or of readily understood languages, is no guarantee of permanently peaceful relations, as witness the War of 1812 between Britain and the United States, the Civil War in the United States, the long succession of conflicts among the European states, and the wars between the Spanish-speaking Latin American states.

There is some logic behind the idea of a common language as a step toward international understanding and peace. But on the whole, suspicions and conflicts arise among nations not so much because of differences in language—which after all can be bridged—as because of competitions, conflicts of interests and objectives, and suspicions of motives. Misunderstandings are due primarily to the emotional feelings that are aroused in different countries, and then expressed by language, and to the justifications and approval which one culture gives to a certain action whereas another denies it. A common language among nations might conceivably help in building up common sets of values. It might facilitate a more general exchange of ideas and impressions, but it could not be expected to prevent the occurrence of differences and conflicts. These arise between people who speak the same language and understand one another completely. Furthermore, there are governments which seek to insulate their people so that they may not be free to know the truth about world affairs apart from what their rulers say.[12]

IDEOLOGY AND POLITICS

The ideas men hold about their religion and about their economic, social, and political institutions are the prime movers of their actions. Men will strive unstintingly for the attainment of their ideals. For their protection and advancement in competition with rival ideas they will make even the supreme sacrifice of life itself. Ideas and ideals, despite Marxian emphasis on economic determinism, are the fountainhead of civilization, the soul of progress in national and international life. They are also at the root of conflict and war.

---

[12] On the effects of language see S. I. Hayakawa, *Language in Thought and Action* (New York, 1949).

Nature of Ideology. What do we mean when we speak of ideology? An ideology may be defined as a cluster of interrelated, though not necessarily logically interdependent, ideas. As the term is generally used, it refers to ideas about government, economics, society, history, or life itself.

There are some who have sought to maintain that ideas are principally the by-product of material forces. But history shows that men's beliefs are not the result of biological or material determinism alone. Mind does function separately from matter, although it may be strongly influenced by it and by environment. Concepts of the nature and ideal of political relationships are conceivable apart from a particular economic structure even though they may function in actuality in close conjunction with it.

Ideologies often originate "as consciously advocated or dogmatically asserted social, political or religious slogans or battle cries," and through "usage and preachment gradually become the characteristic beliefs or dogmas of a particular group, party, or nationality." [13] We shall use the term *ideology* to signify a body of ideas having a popular appeal and referring to the social-political-economic order.

Function in the Nation-State. An ideology accepted within a state—whether it be democracy, socialism, communism, Shintoism, or some other—serves certain useful functions in the body politic which have a bearing upon foreign relations. In the first place, it constitutes a medium of communication within the state, providing a common set of values and a rallying standard around which individuals and groups may be drawn together. Secondly, once an ideology has been accepted by the group as a whole it acts as a cohesive force providing a basis for rationalizing and upholding the social, economic, and political institutions of the society.[14] In a free society an ideology firmly believed in by the people can become an energizer of individual and collective action inspiring men to effort and to sacrifice. In a sense, nationalism itself is such an ideology. In a totalitarian society the propagation of an ideology may aid the regime in power in fastening its grip upon the country or in presenting some appearance of philosophical basis for its deeds, as did fascism in Italy and nazism in Germany. Thirdly, ideology offers a means by which popular distinction may be drawn between those who belong "within" the group and are friendly to it and those who are "outside" the group and therefore alien to it.

A nation that is ideologically divided within itself is vulnerable to foreign propaganda and unable to mobilize the full strength of its capabilities. The

13 R. C. Snyder and H. H. Wilson, *Roots of Political Behavior* (New York, 1949), pp. 506–516 has a useful analysis of the nature of ideology.
14 See M. B. Ogle, *Public Opinion and Political Dynamics* (Boston, 1950), chs. 5–8; D. H. Munro, "The Concept of Myth," *The Sociological Rev.*, vol. XLIII (1950), sec. 6.

annals of history are replete with instances of peoples who have suffered defeat when they had failed to achieve or had lost their ideological unity. This was demonstrated in recent times in the vulnerability of pre-war France to Nazi propaganda and so-called fifth column activities and in the inability of France to project effectively all the elements of its national capability when attacked by Germany in 1940. Likewise, it may be recalled that the Chinese lacked ideological unity at the time of the communist victory in 1949.

The National Ethos. It may, and in fact does, frequently occur that a nation is not wholly agreed within itself upon the tenets of political ideology. Thus, present-day England is about evenly divided between the ideas of the Liberal-Conservative tradition and the socialist precepts of the Labor party. Similarly, Belgium, France, Germany, Japan, Sweden, and others have their internal ideological splits and groupings. Yet in these cases ideological divergencies do not create a climate of violent conflict. The explanation of the absence of violent civil strife in such countries lies in the existence, in most of these countries, of what may be called the national ethos—a traditional way of going about things and of resolving public problems, the "way of life" of the nation. While the Socialist is anxious in each case to dislodge the government in power if it is not of his party, he does not do so through the use of conspiratorial, unconstitutional, or untraditional means. Such restraint and tolerance are also due to the fact that democracies do not demand the "total political mobilization" of their citizenry in time of peace. They recognize the right of the individual to his own political views, and value the right to differences in political thinking and action. There is an area of values and things shared in common among all of the people which exceeds that on which groups within the nation disagree; and these shared values are considered to be more important than partisan differences.

When partisanship seizes a group with such fervor that it regards the attainment of its desires as being more vital than respect for the traditional ways of handling political differences or to be desired regardless of whether the employment of means to its ends violate the law, the national constitutional principles, or the national "way of life," civil strife, revolution, and violence occur as in the Spanish Civil War in 1937–1938.

It is the breakdown of common identification with the ethos that separates communist groups out of every nation to which they belong. They are not satisfied to be merely one other political party within a common over-all society. They negate and deny the fundamental tenets of existent society and seek to undermine both the institutions and the ethos of society through the creation of revolutionary situations which may be manipulated by coercive means so as to lead to the overthrow of established institutions and the creation of their own exclusive structure. This is one of the reasons why they are so dangerous in the political life of democratic societies and why governments in the free world have reacted vigorously against them.

While some people may disagree on what it means to be a Democrat or a Republican, and upon some facets of ideology, there is a large area of agreement about those ideas, principles, and procedures which compose the "American way of life." Such things as respect for and attachment to the Constitution, respect for the rights of the political party out of office, the rule of law, the rule of the majority with consideration for minorities, freedom of the press, freedom of speech and of assembly, the freedom to derive profit and respect from one's own work, the liberty to move wherever one will and to engage in whatever occupation one desires, the freedom to belong to the church of one's choice—all these and many others compose an admittedly hard-to-define but very real and highly successful American ethos. These are the things which Americans value above party differences. They are the common ground, the "bundle of ideas," the great things which Americans believe in, prize, and will fight to defend. Coupled with the high standard of living which has resulted from the practice of these standards in a country blessed with rich resources, this ethos makes for general allegiance to the American system of government and for a high degree of national morale and cohesion.

Ideology in World Politics. Ideology plays a variety of roles in international affairs. Let us notice a few of them.

1. ADVANCEMENT OF NATIONS' INTERESTS. In the first place, ideological principles may be used by a state, or group of states, to advance national interests through justifying or disguising their policies and deeds in the struggle for power.[15] European imperialism was sometimes justified on the ground that the Western nations had a civilizing and cultural mission to undertake.[16] Americans in the mid-nineteenth century felt impelled by a sense of "manifest destiny" to spread republican principles and institutions as well as to gain territorial holdings and influence abroad.[17] In contemporary times the Soviets have employed their Marxist-Leninist ideology to mask and to further their imperialist ventures in Europe and Asia. By propagating communist doctrine abroad, organizing local parties, training and infiltrating agitators and subversive agents, and taking advantage of local political crises, the Kremlin has been able to extend its power from Czechoslovakia to China and to spread its influence in other quarters of Europe and Asia. In many places this has

---

15 W. Brown, "Psychology of Ideological Conflict," *Fortnightly*, Nov., 1950; Hans Morgenthau, *Politics Among Nations* (2d ed., New York, 1954), pp. 80–87.

16 Parker T. Moon, *Imperialism and World Politics* (New York, 1926), chs. 3–5.

17 On popular conceptions underlying American expansion see T. A. Bailey, *The Man in the Street* (New York, 1948).

occurred with the help of the Red Army, but not everywhere. China and Czechoslovakia are cases in point.

2. IDEOLOGY AS AN INTERNATIONAL LINK. Ideology may figure in international politics also by linking together peoples of different nationalities. The Christian, Moslem, and Buddhist religions, with adherents in many lands, provide something of both a spiritual and an ideological tie between peoples in various countries. At times these common religious associations form a bond strong enough to influence national positions. American sympathy toward China in its struggle with Japan in the 1930's and 1940's was, in some measure at least, influenced by the links of Christian missionary activity in China and a feeling among Americans that the Chinese were moving toward acceptance of Christian and democratic ideals. In this case sentimental and political factors were a more influential agent in determining American attitudes than trade and finance. For United States trade with Japan prior to 1941 much exceeded that with China; and investments in Japan were stable, whereas in China they were precarious.

Another instance in which adherence to a common faith has affected political alignments has been the case of the League of Arab States. All of the states participating in this alliance are attached to Islam and drawn together in their concerted opposition to Zionism.

European socialist leaders in the late nineteenth and early twentieth centuries attempted to give the principles of socialism an internationally cohesive effect. But disunity within the socialist ranks and fragmentation of the movement in response to national appeals have left this ideology with relatively little strength as a unifying international force. It is conceivable, however, that in a Western European political community—should such a body be formed—socialism might become a significant political factor.

In a similar fashion, but with the distinct difference of having the power of the Kremlin behind them, the principles of Marxism and Leninism have been advanced as a bond of world communism from which Moscow has fought deviation from its own interpretations.[18]

The importance of ideology in international politics is further evidenced by the fact that the principles embodied in the Atlantic Charter, together with the "fundamental freedoms" proclaimed by President Roosevelt, formed the framework around which the Grand Alliance was assembled in World War II and whose spirit did much to help in the final defeat of the Axis Powers. Likewise, the broad affirmations of "Principles and Purposes" contained in the Preamble and Chapter I of the United Nations Charter form a fundamental

[18] See C. L. Sulzberger, "Heresy, The Bogy of the Kremlin," in N. J. Padelford (ed.), *Cont Int. Rels. Readings*, 1949–1950, pp. 62–66.

basis upon which sixty nations have found it possible to join in membership of this world organization. The Bogota Charter establishing the Organization of American States likewise contains a body of "Principles" constituting a platform upon which the twenty-one Republics have agreed to be associated. And the Preamble to the North Atlantic Treaty states that the parties to this collective defense arrangement "are determined to safeguard the freedom, common heritage and civilization of their peoples, founded on the principles of democracy, individual liberty and the rule of law." From these illustrations it is clear that bodies of ideas play an important part in forming a link upon which sovereign states find it possible to agree upon measures of international cooperation and association.

3. IDEOLOGY AS A SOURCE OF CONFLICT. It is obvious from the circumstances of international politics that ideology operates also as a source of conflict among nations. The bitter clash which the world has witnessed between the Machiavellian ideology of communism on the one hand, and the principles of freedom, truth, democracy, and decency on the other, has been the central feature of international relations in the post-war world.

The contemporary conflict emphasizes a fact which history has attested many times before—namely, that struggles between rival systems of ideas held by organized and determined bodies of people not only permeate and affect the life of society as a whole but become one of the principal sources of conflict among nations as well. One can recall a succession of ideological conflicts which have studded the pathway of civilization: the Biblical conflicts between those believing in Jehovah and those believing in other gods; the conflicts between Christianity and the Roman imperial idea and between Christianity and Mohammedanism; the conformists and nonconformists within the Christian faith during the wars of religion in the seventeenth century; the struggles between the forces of autocracy and privilege epitomized by the "ancient regime" of France, and later between the powers of the Holy Alliance and those espousing the ideals of liberty and equality stemming from the French and American Revolutions. The existing struggle between democratic liberalism and totalitarianism is of a similar nature. So long as men think, have will power to pursue and champion their ideas, and attach values to them, conflicts of ideology are bound to be a part of the social process and of international politics.

The Struggle for Men's Minds. In the present world conflict between the forces of freedom and democracy and those of communism and totalitarianism, the basic objective or target of the struggle is the minds of men everywhere—in Europe, in Asia, and elsewhere. To win this struggle the free nations must have sufficient unity and strength to prevent noncommunist lands from being overrun by Red military forces or from being subverted by native communist "fifth columns." In addition the forces of freedom must also give men ideals by which to live, aspirations for which to strive, and point out a way, as well as supply some of the means, by which men may find promise in their time of alleviation from suffering and want. Above all, they must find ways of communicating these ideas to others.[19]

The concepts of freedom, independence, equality, justice, and respect for the rights of others inherent in American idealism are capable of inspiring subject peoples with a goal worthy of attainment. They hold within them a realistic basis upon which underprivileged people may work toward higher standards of living. They also hold in them a revolutionary power against tyranny and reaction. Effectively harnessed and wisely advanced, these ideas can become the most powerful political force in the world.[20]

Upon the outcome of the clash of ideas now under way will depend in large measure the kind of civilization in which mankind will live in the decades to come. If this conflict is won by the free peoples, it will be because men believe sufficiently in the principles of their ideology to live by them, to struggle to see that they are applied, and, if need be, to sacrifice their own lives for their furtherance.

Paradoxes of Group Action. It is an observable fact that social and political groups not infrequently engage in concerted action which is at variance with the tenets of the ideology which they profess. Nations adhering to principles of the equality of man and to political self-determination have sought colonies and sometimes opposed granting self-government and independence to dependent peoples. Advocates of collective security have been seen to abandon exposed allies or weak neighbors in times of crisis, as Ethiopia discovered in 1936 and Czechoslovakia in 1938.[21] Communist regimes talking loudly about the "emancipation" of workers maintain slave labor camps and prohibit collective bargaining.

This paradox of opposites may be explained in part by the ambivalence of emotions and desires which operates within man as well as within society. It may be attributed in part to the fact that the human mind possesses a power to disguise the purposes of its own thoughts and actions. But above all it is due to the fact that states act in self-interest as the interpretation of that interest changes from time to time. The paradox, therefore, inheres in the conflict among policies, or in the discrepancy between general policy statements and the cost of a specific action.

19 See F. S. Dunn, *War and the Minds of Men* (New York, 1950).
20 W. O. Douglas, "America's Power of Ideals," *Social Research,* Sept., 1952.
21 In this respect the Korean experience of 1950–1953 represents a notable exception in the history of collective security.

In some instances governments have appeared to adopt policies which contradict or disregard their ideology in order to confound and mislead opponents while they seek to attain their own ends. Communist doctrine and practice apparently allow for such techniques.

Ideology and the Future of International Relations. Owing to its many ramifications in international life, ideology, as Joseph C. Harsch has pointed out, will pose a tremendous "obstacle to any effort of statesmen to negotiate settlements of the power struggle of the mid-twentieth century." For "it is today, and probably will be for a century at least, impossible for Westerners to have confidence in any person or country which even has gone through the experience of communism. It probably will be just as difficult for Communists to achieve confidence in any person or country which has not passed through a Communist revolution"—or which, like Tito of Yugoslavia, has defected or been liberated by Western influence.[22] On the other hand, it may be objected that few Americans and Englishmen would have held it conceivable in 1945 that a few years afterward they would have friendly relations with Germany, Italy, and Japan—and that, in fact, all of them would be *de facto* allies in the struggle to stem the post-war expansion of the Soviet Union. Thus, the prior statement seems to need modification in the sense that, if the objective political situation so requires, the availability of mass media of communication can considerably shorten, though not completely obviate, the length of the period needed by democratic peoples for reorientation.

Ideological struggles such as that between communism and democracy, affecting every phase of life, are bound to be long-continued. Arrangements of one kind or another may be arrived at between rival states with respect to economic and technical matters. Where these do not immediately cut across vital competitive interests the chief parties may find it possible to act harmoniously on some questions of international politics. When threats arise endangering the security of both of them, such as Hitlerism in the 1940's, a limited concert of action, though not of ideological rapprochement, may take place as it did during World War II. But to expect that "all questions" between them can be "settled" by negotiation is a delusion.

A general "settlement" between two great ideological blocs, in the customary sense of the term, presupposes a degree of trust that each side is willing to enter into an accord on a *bona fide* basis without employing it for political advantage against the other. Such a settlement, to be effective in the present world struggle, would have to assume a readiness on the part of the Communists to give up their goal of overthrowing noncommunist regimes and

22 Joseph C. Harsch, "The Affairs of Nations—Problems of a Settlement," *The Christian Science Monitor*, June 10, 1953.

of holding national communist governments subservient to Moscow. Conversely, it would have to imply readiness on the part of the West to cease seeking the liberation of the communist satellites from Moscow's control. At the present moment in history, neither of these seems very probable.

There are areas of politics, especially those concerning the rivalry of ideologies, political friendship, and security, in which there can be no negotiation and settlement in the sense of arriving at a lasting compromise or a binding limitation. The fundamental ideas which men believe in with firm conviction, such as questions dealing with the way of life—whether in the realm of political institutions or of religion—cannot be "settled" by diplomatic arrangement. Their relationships must work themselves out through the course of history.[23]

PROPAGANDA AS A PSYCHOLOGICAL FACTOR

In the struggle between ideological forces propaganda often plays a prominent role. It can be seen today in the outpourings of propaganda from Moscow and its satellites in behalf of the communist philosophy and in their attacks upon the policies of the Western Powers. In return the nations of the West themselves have been forced to engage in a "campaign of truth" to defend their principles and beliefs. Because of the correlation between propaganda and attitudes it may be seen that propaganda is among the psychological factors affecting the relationship of nations. This raises the question: What is propaganda? Why is it such a present factor in international politics today?

Nature and Objectives of Propaganda. Propaganda may be defined as a systematic attempt to influence the attitudes and actions of individuals and groups by means of words and other symbols. It is a scheme or device for spreading a particular doctrine, system, or set of ideas. It has as its purpose the guiding of individual and group action by directing attention, intensifying attitudes favorable to its aims, reversing obstructive attitudes, winning the indifferent to its side, and neutralizing or frightening the uncontrollable.

Propaganda activities of one sort or another have been carried on for a very long time. Evidences of it could be found in ancient Sparta, in the early history of the Roman Catholic Church, and as part of a campaign instigated by Napoleon during his wars. Actually, however, its use in international politics was sporadic prior to the rise of modern journalism and the development of mass communication.

Large-scale use of propaganda as an instrument of national policy made its appearance during World War I as belligerents attempted to strengthen opin-

23 Professor F. S. C. Northrup's *The Meeting of East and West* (New York, 1946) and his *The Taming of the Nations* (New York, 1952) provide a philosophical exploration of the areas and means of accommodation between rival cultural systems. See also Arnold Toynbee's *Study of History* (abridgment by D. C. Somervell, New York, 1947).

ion at home, to demoralize their enemies, and to win the support of neutrals. During and since World War II the use of propaganda has been greatly amplified.

Propaganda activities by states have in general two foci. In the first place, they seek to promote national unity and morale within the state. In the second place, they seek to gain and maintain friends abroad, to counteract foreign propaganda, and to deter and weaken opponents and enemies.

Significance of Propaganda Activities. The relative effectiveness of the propaganda and information activities of states is not easily determined. This is because the effectiveness of any propaganda depends upon several things. It must be adapted to the attitudes, conditions, and aspirations of the peoples to whom it is directed. It requires skill in timing, sequence, and emphasis. Propaganda must rest upon some elements of truth or apparent facts. Depending upon its nature, an effective propaganda must create interest, evoke questions, stimulate sympathies, and fire determination. Propaganda can succeed only if it supports the hopes animating those to whom it is directed, if it understands the role it is asked to perform within the nation's foreign policy process, and if it manages to keep the trust of its audiences.

So extensive have become the curbs placed upon information-gathering activities and freedom of the press in many countries, that discussions have taken place within the United Nations looking toward a convention to assure freedom of information. Although the principle of freedom of information has been acknowledged, a majority of nations have signified that they are in favor of restricting the gathering and dissemination of information. This has led Americans to fear that censorship and other national restrictions "may obtain legal or moral sanction" through majority action upon a United Nations declaration or convention.[24]

We shall elaborate further upon propaganda as an instrument of national policy in the conduct of international affairs in Chapter XVII below.

THE MORAL FACTOR IN INTERNATIONAL POLITICS

Few aspects of international relations are fraught with more difficulty than the question whether states have moral obligations toward one another, and if so, what these obligations are. Yet it is generally appreciated that moral ideas are profoundly significant within the international scene.[25]

---

[24] Carroll Binder, "Freedom of Information and the United Nations," *International Organization,* May, 1952; John B. Whitton, "The U. N. Conference on Freedom of Information and the Movement against International Propaganda," *Am. J. Int. Law,* Jan., 1949.

[25] See Reinhold Niebuhr, *Moral Man and Immoral Society* (New York, 1932); J. Elliot Ross, *Christian Ethics* (New York, 1948); A. Robertson, *Morals in World History* (London, 1945); W. Stace, "Have Nations Any Morals?" *Atlantic Monthly,* Nov., 1945; T. Weldon, *States and Morals* (New York, 1947); Arnold Wolfers, "Statesmanship and Moral Choice," *World Politics,* Jan., 1949.

There are writers who deny with Hegel that states have any moral obligations at all and assert that only individuals are capable of moral or immoral behavior. For them the Machiavellian conception of the nonmoral character of politics is a correct statement about the nature of relations among states.[26] This school of thought is generally designated as that of "the Realists." Other writers have held that morality is a universal principle applicable not only to relations between individuals, but also to those between states. These writers maintain that there are moral laws just as there are mechanical or hygienic laws. This school of thought is often spoken of as "the Utopian." [27] The Christian and all other major religions agree that the foundations of social life and the guide of all governments must be and is moral law.

What is Morality? The word *morality* implies a set of approved social notions about what should and should not be done. These ideas derive from customs, tradition, and the thinking of man about himself and his relations with others and with the supernatural forces of the universe. They vary among civilizations, from nation to nation, and in some respects even within the same nation.

Social scientists are generally inclined to the view that man acquires his systems of values and his moral inclinations from observing, learning, and adopting the general moral choices and beliefs of the society into which he is born and in which he lives. In this view there is no single morality pervading all mankind. Native human nature is capable of adopting the moral code of Americans or Frenchmen or Japanese or of the Arabic peoples. Morality in this view is pluralistic. Environmental influences are powerful factors in determining the moral orientations of peoples generally.

A different view is held by some theologians and philosophers and by jurists of the "natural law" school. For them morality is an all-pervading principle of the universe, a body of broad principles and truth, inherent in the rule of God, of Nature, or, to use a phrase from the American Declaration of Independence, of "Nature's God," permeating human action everywhere. The universe is viewed as essentially a moral sphere in which men and states cannot but act in conformity with its postulates, or become transgressors of a divine or natural moral order. Hugo Grotius, the "Father of International Law," gave expression to this in the Prologemena to his famous treatise on *The Law of War and Peace* first published in 1625, when he remarked that there is a "natural morality," not man-made, "written in the hearts of men" and capable

26 See James Burnham, *The Machiavellians* (New York, 1943).
27 Herbert Butterfield, "The Scientific versus the Moralistic Approach in International Affairs," *Internat. Affairs*, Oct., 1951; John Herz, *Political Realism and Political Idealism* (Chicago, 1951); Hans Rommen, "Realism and Utopianism in World Affairs," *Rev. of Politics*, April, 1944; Ross, *op. cit.*

of serving as the basis for world justice. From this Grotius went on to develop his system of the "law of nations" which he believed combined principles of right conduct and agreement among men of good will from different lands.

Two Levels of Morality. It is generally accepted that within a nation men must not do certain things without risking social censure and punishment. The view that man has no obligations whatsoever toward other men and that his only duty is to promote his own selfish good is accepted by few people. Such a view would hark back to Hobbes' theory that in original nature there existed "a war of all men against all men," and would tend to justify a continuous Darwinian struggle for "the survival of the fittest." [28]

A casual examination of society reveals that while people do compete with one another and are, on the whole, mainly concerned with the improvement of their own positions, this competition for prestige and benefits is carried on within an atmosphere of generally recognized moral and legal rules, and that society through its authorized functionaries takes punitive action when these rules are transgressed. This atmosphere within nations is based on a feeling of community between people of the same nationality, on the broad similarity of ethical standards of behavior acquired in the families, schools, churches, and other social institutions of the country, and on the existence of laws and sanctions which, if violated, are known to entail punishment. Men thus behave "morally" toward their fellow citizens because, on one hand, they recognize common moral norms acquired during their maturation and education, and, on the other hand, because the law of their land and its executors make violation of these norms unrewarding.

Another state of affairs characterizes the international scene. The international society, in the legal sense, functions through the governments and the agents of some seventy sovereign states. Great and sincere men have held with Woodrow Wilson that "the same standards of conduct and of responsibility for wrong shall be observed among nations and their governments that are observed among the individual citizens of civilized states." [29] Still, the political realist would have to admit that as yet there is no pronounced feeling of coherence and unity among states, no identical universal morality which they recognize, and no law and sanctions independent of the unpredictable dispositions of the stronger powers to enforce them effectively. The record of modern history shows that states have increasingly agreed in their conduct toward one another to follow certain rules and principles which find concrete expression in treaties, international customs, international comity, and international law.

---

[28] Thomas Hobbes, *Leviathan*, ch. 13. See Max Stirner, *The Ego and His Own* (New York, 1915).
[29] Address of President to Congress on Declaration of War, April, 1917.

Moral Restraints in the Behavior of States. Compared with ancient times and the Middle Ages, states no longer after a victorious war exterminate the mass of their opponents or sell them into slavery, as occurred in Carthage and elsewhere. Also, most states no longer forcibly assimilate their religious or national minorities. The world was outraged when the Nazis employed their concentration camps to gas and burn masses of prisoners whose only "crime" was that they happened to be born of Jewish lineage, and it supported the bringing of those responsible to trial and punishment at Nuremberg for "crimes against humanity" and against the laws of war. The humanitarian impact of the last two centuries has tended to place certain acts of government—which states otherwise could engage in owing to the volume of power which they possess—morally "out of bounds."

The numerous conventions which have been concluded to avoid infliction of unnecessary suffering and death in time of war provide further evidence that states are not impervious to moral restraints on their freedom of action. Noncombatants are, if possible, distinguished from the armed forces and are not supposed to be purposely attacked or injured. Although modern weapons of mass destruction and the nature of total war itself make such a distinction increasingly impractical, the fact that belligerents feel constrained to justify, during the bombardment of a city, injuries to the civilian population by emphasizing the presence of militarily significant targets, indicates that they do not wish to be viewed as openly defying all moral principles.

These considerations have found legal formulation in the Hague Conventions of 1899 and 1907 on the "Laws and Customs of War on Land," the Geneva Conventions of 1864, 1906, and 1929 on the treatment of the sick and wounded and of prisoners of war, and the provisions for the International Red Cross. With certain exceptions these have on the whole been observed. In addition one may mention the treaties for the humanization of warfare such as those prohibiting the use of asphyxiating gases, requiring submarines to conform to the rules of naval warfare with respect to sinking passenger vessels, the Genocide Convention forbidding racial extermination, and the proposed agreement to prohibit the use of nuclear weapons once international control has been established.

Similarly there might be mentioned the conventions to prohibit the sale of alcohol and arms in Africa (1878, 1919), the abolition of the slave trade, the efforts made under the League of Nations and the United Nations to curb the traffic in narcotic drugs, and the attempts to end the white slave traffic.

One might also mention the growth and observance of International Law, which we shall note in some detail in Chapter XIX. Such matters as the duty to respect treaty obligations, to provide equal protection to citizens of foreign states, to make reparation for damages, and many other principles of the law have a foundation in morality as well as a legal obligation.

Although the vast programs of relief, recovery, and economic development following World War II have unquestionably been motivated by considerations of enlightened self-interest, they have also displayed tacit recognition of the principle that those with means should assist those in need. In a sense this represents an extension of the principle of the good neighbor who respects the rights and responds to the needs of others because he respects himself. In similar manner there might also be mentioned the movement for assuring human rights and freedoms.

It cannot be said that moral considerations have been the only reasons for the conclusion of these arrangements. Considerations of mutual self-interest were involved in each case. The service of enlightened national self-interest is the first and governing obligation resting upon states and their governments.[30] Nevertheless, it would be wrong to disregard or to minimize the moral motivations underlying their actions. For governments, being composed of individuals, are likely to reflect, at least at times, the urge of individuals for moral reason and moral rectitude. And states recognize that there is value both internally and in international politics in taking positions that are morally upright and enlightened.

The strongest evidence that morality is a real factor in international politics lies in the fact that national leaders continually seek to justify their actions in foreign affairs upon morally acceptable grounds, and are condemned not only by foreigners but by opposition within their own countries where their actions contravene generally accepted principles or fail to appeal to the moral judgments of individuals. As Professor William T. R. Fox has said, "the chief task of the policy maker lies in the reconciliation of the desirable and the possible. Moral principle is *not* irrelevant, but it can provide by itself no sure guide to policy. It is in weighing the risks and the gains—the value losses and the value increments to the self in whose name one is acting, i.e., the nation-state—that judgments about the possible emerge. It is in formulating this judgment that one arrives at a conception of the national interest."[31]

The "Morality" of War. Moralists and social scientists have long pondered whether war itself is a moral institution. Unprovoked aggression and wars of conquest are now almost universally condemned.[32] Even aggressors have sought to blame their opponents for the first attack, and have usually por-

---

30 For an able argument of the national interest obligation see Hans Morgenthau, *In Defense of the National Interest* (New York, 1951).

31 W. T. R. Fox, "The Reconciliation of the Desirable and the Possible," *The American Scholar*, Spring, 1949. See also Robert Osgood, *Ideals and Self-Interest in America's Foreign Relations* (Chicago, 1953); John H. Herz, "Idealist Internationalism and the Security Dilemma," *World Politics*, Jan., 1950.

32 See U. N. Charter Preamble and Articles 1 and 2.

trayed their own actions as being based on self-defense or on the defense of international law and morality. Benito Mussolini in 1936 brazenly sought to gain moral stature for his war upon Ethiopia by declaring that "Ethiopia has succeeded in imposing war upon Italy." The world did not accept this verdict and the League of Nations voted sanctions against the Fascist Government for its action. The Communists attempted to justify the attack on the Republic of Korea by alleging prior aggression by the victim. The United Nations did not accept this stand and a majority of its Members participated, in one way or another, in thwarting aggression. These and other stands reflect a moral revulsion against aggression.

Once peace is broken and methods of total war are unleashed by an aggressor, considerations of self-preservation and reduction of possible casualties naturally lead those who have been attacked to employ such means as are at their disposal for their own defense and for bringing the war to the earliest possible successful termination. There are complicated and delicate questions in this connection in determining whether the use of atomic weapons is justified and under what circumstances.[33] There seems no logical reason for considering destruction in a single package, as in an atomic bomb, any more or less moral than similar destruction and loss of life resulting from the dropping of more conventional bombs from a thousand planes or from the shells of a thousand powerful pieces of artillery. The basic question is how war can be brought to an end with the least loss of human life and values. There is a question whether the use of atomic or hydrogen bombs might lead to the destruction of vital aspects of civilization, or whether the failure to use them, if they are available, might also result in vital losses to civilization. Perhaps, once war occurs, the choice is less a moral one and more of a choice between greater and lesser evils.[34]

To the philosopher or religious man sitting in detached contemplation, the events of war may seem to lack morality. Yet for those who are engaged, whether as civilians or members of the armed forces, wars are usually fought for ends that are believed to be moral. The preservation of the state, the furtherance of its well-being, the aiding of a weak or defenseless people who have been attacked by an aggressor, the defense of liberty, freedom, religion, or a way of life—these are moral ends in society.

[33] On the moral problem of using the first A-bombs see McGeorge Bundy and Henry L. Stimson, *On Active Service in Peace and War* (New York, 1948), ch. 24; James E. Byrnes, *Speaking Frankly* (New York, 1947), ch. 13. See also Reinhold Niebuhr, "Conditions of Our Survival," *Virginia Quar. Rev.*, Oct., 1950. For discussion of factors in total war that point to a weakening of moral limitations see Morgenthau, *op. cit.*, pp. 181–183.

[34] Sir George Thomson, eminent British scientist, states that it may be possible to make hydrogen bombs of "unlimited size and, hence, of unlimited power," and thereby release sufficient radioactive material to "constitute a serious risk of contamination of the whole earth or, at least, of a large proportion of it." Sir George Thomson, "Hydrogen Bombs: The Need for a Policy," *International Affairs*, Oct., 1950, reproduced in Padelford (ed.), *Cont. Int. Rels. Readings*, 1950–1951, pp. 232–238.

With the increasing destructiveness of weapons of mass annihilation it may be hoped that possibly what is moral in the restriction of human loss in numbers will be increasingly found to be in the self-interest of all and that international behavior may approximate the postulates of a more humane ethics than in the past.

Religion and International Politics. It might be supposed that the main support to international peace and morality would come from religion and the churches. This is true to an extent. The Pope, the leaders of the Protestant churches, the Buddhists, and other religious leaders have repeatedly called for peace and for the application of moral principles in international relations.[35] Religious elements, however, have not been sufficiently determined or influential to prevent bloodshed even between nations of the same religion, and where war has occurred, organized religious bodies have usually adopted the cause of the nation in which they were situated. The wars between France and Germany, both Christian nations, the Second Balkan War in 1913 between nations both of which were Slavic and Orthodox, the drawn-out violence between the religiously kindred peoples of China, Korea, and Japan, show that religion has not been able to prevent bloodshed between nations of the same or similar religions, not to speak of nations professing different creeds. Nevertheless, by continually emphasizing moral postulates and by deprecating the use of violence, the principal religious faiths have been and are contributing to the creation of a more humane climate favoring a wider application of moral principles to the conduct of international affairs.

Conclusion. The politics of nations can be guided by moral motivations only to a limited extent so long as each state continues to be the ultimate guarantor of its own existence and so long as the defense of its own national interest is held to be its highest moral duty. Nevertheless, the cumulative influences of religion, law, humanitarianism, enlightened self-interest, and a disposition to define some aspects of international relations in terms of broad principles of universal applicability have in the last 300 years brought not a few conceptions of moral "oughtness" into the realm of international politics. To say that the field of international politics is served only by selfishness, brutality, self-righteousness, and unrestrained appetite for power is not only overly cynical but manifestly unrealistic.[36] Man's moral nature and his aspirations for a better world do exert a strong influence upon the course of international relations in the political, economic, and cultural realms.[37]

35 See Reinhold Niebuhr, *Christianity and Power Politics* (New York, 1940).
36 See Arnold Wolfers, "Statesmanship and Moral Choice," *World Politics,* Jan., 1949.
37 For further treatments of the problem of morality and international affairs see especially E. H. Carr, *Twenty Years' Crisis,* 1919–1939 (London, 1946), pp. 146–169; H. Finer, *America's Destiny* (New York, 1947), pp. 75–95; Morgenthau, *Politics Among Nations,* chs. 13–14; R. B. Perry, *One World in the Making* (New York, 1945).

SOCIOPSYCHOLOGICAL FACTORS IN TENSION SITUATIONS

Conditions of tension are a recurrent feature of international politics as plainly revealed by the long succession of wars that have transpired within the society of states ever since its formation. But war is demonstrative of tensions only at their most extreme and aggravated stage.[38]

Tensions, as a rule, are caused in international relations by the competitions and conflicts among states over ideologies, territories, political influence, power, markets, and raw materials, and by rival national interests and ambitions. They spring from a rising awareness of a rival's actual or supposed intentions, inclinations, and potentialities that are believed to block or conflict with the aspirations of others.

Blocked Responses. Tension conditions can arise in nations, as in individuals, when objectives and desires are thwarted and there appear to be no available alternatives, or only alternatives that seem suicidal. Various reactions are known to occur: the rise of hatred, resort to extreme or violent methods, exploitation of weaker elements in society. It has been suggested that many of the younger generation of German people who turned to nazism did so because it offered an outlet from frustrations suffered from the defeat in 1918, the terms of peace, the inflation of 1923, and the depression in the 1930's. In any event, the pogroms against the Jews, the martial displays of the Nazi party, the rearmament of the nation, and the rousing of public hysteria against foreign nations gave release to any pent-up feelings the Germans may have had.

Thwarted ambitions of subject peoples for self-rule or betterment of their condition can lead to open rebellion, as in the American colonies in the 1770's. Or they may take the form of civil disobedience and passive resistance as in India in the years before independence was granted. The blocked aspirations of peasants or workers for emancipation from oppressive conditions can also produce a fertile seed-bed for revolution as demonstrated in the unrest in Russia from 1904 to 1917.

Probably one of the most important elements in the world situation today is the demand of people in the underdeveloped areas for a better standard of living. Unless this is given tangible encouragement it may result in irrational actions, political upheavals, and war. Recognition of this fact was instru-

---

[38] On tension situations see B. Bettelheim, "Individual and Mass Behavior in Extreme Situations," *J. Abnormal and Soc. Psych.*, vol. 38, pp. 417–452; Hadley Cantril, *The Psychology of Social Movements* (New York, 1941); H. Cantril (ed.), *Tensions That Cause Wars* (Urbana, 1950); G. W. Kisker (ed.), *World Tension: The Psychopathology of International Relations* (New York, 1951); O. Klineberg, *Tensions Affecting International Understanding*, Soc. Sci. Rsch. Council Bul. 62 (New York, 1950); K. Lewin, T. Dumbo, L. Festinger, and P. S. Sears, in J. M. Hunt (ed.) *Personality and the Behavior Disorders* (New York, 1944); N. R. F. Maier, *Frustration: A Study of Behavior Without a Goal* (New York, 1949); M. A. May, *Social Psychology of War and Peace* (London, 1943).

mental in calling forth the American Point Four Program, the Colombo Plan of the Commonwealth of Nations, and the Technical Assistance activity of the United Nations.

Tension Reactions. As tensions rise in the relations among states, numerous popular and national responses may occur. One of these typical responses is the tendency of perceptions to narrow. Each side tends to become increasingly suspicious of the other, focusing attention upon those elements of stereotyped national character and policy of the opposing state or states which reveal an aggressive nature or explain what are believed to be its objectives or ulterior motives. Rumors spread and are sometimes nourished by official propaganda.[39] Talk of possible war gains currency through the press and other means of communication. If the tension is not allayed at this stage by acts of statesmanship in adjusting or settling some of the outstanding differences or conflicts, talk of war becomes easily magnified into feelings of the inevitability of war. Once this is believed and actions become predicated upon its expectation, further impetus is readily added to the tension. As this occurs, a certain amount of what psychologists have called "group reinforcement of hostility" may take place, multiplying suspicions, increasing resistances, and heightening pressures for strong actions.[40] Finally, in such circumstances, one nation's increased efforts to gain security or to protect what it considers to be its rights and interests may increase apprehensions and insecurity in the other leading to mobilization, countermobilization, and war.

These responses and chain reactions can be identified in such tension situations as the Moroccan crises between 1905 and 1911, the Bosnian crisis in 1908, the Balkan Wars in 1912–1913, the events leading up to World War I,[41] the progressive clashes between Japan and the United States from 1931 to 1941, the crisis over Czechoslovakia in 1938, the outbreak of World War II,[42] and the alarm felt in Europe and America after the communist coup in Czechoslovakia in 1948, the Berlin blockade, and the Korean War.

Peaceful Settlement in Crisis Situations. Peaceful settlement of international disputes is not easily achieved when the emotions of nations have become wrought up in tension situations. Statesmen do not always find it easy to resist a powerful public sentiment, or to keep control of it, once passions have become aroused or extreme positions have been taken. This is illustrated

39 See G. W. Allport and L. Postman, *The Psychology of Rumor* (New York, 1947); H. D. Lasswell, "Propaganda and Mass Insecurity," *Psychiatry*, Aug., 1950.

40 T. M. Newcomb, *Social Psychology* (New York, 1950), p. 602. On group behavior see G. LeBon, *supra;* P. F. Lazarsfeld, B. Berelson, and H. Gaudet, *The People's Choice* (New York, 1944).

41 See S. B. Fay, *Origins of the World War* (New York, 1931); B. Schmidt, *The Coming of the War, 1914* (New York, 1930).

42 See C. G. Haines and R. J. S. Hoffman, *The Origins and Background of the Second World War* (New York, 1943); V. M. Dean, *Why Europe Went to War* (New York, 1939).

in the dilemma of former Premier Mossadegh of Iran in the Anglo-Iranian oil dispute. The nation having been aroused to support nationalization of the oil properties, Mossadegh then found that the resultant internal political situation prevented him from making seemingly reasonable arrangements with the British to permit disposal of the oil on the international market. It is also revealed in the difficulties experienced by Yugoslavia and Italy in reaching a mutually agreeable solution of the Trieste situation, and in the long-continued dispute between India and Pakistan over Kashmir and Jammu. When tensions between nations have reached a high pitch, peaceful settlement of disputes may be possible only when leaders feel strong enough to stay or oppose the stream of public opinion, or when good offices, mediation, or conciliation are offered by some third power or group of nations, or when some kind of international compulsion is brought to bear. On the other hand, leaders sometimes deliberately incite public emotion to demand or support war as did Mussolini with respect to Ethiopia in 1935 and as Hitler did in 1938–1939 for use as a means of pressure in diplomatic bargaining for territorial and political concessions from other powers.

Total War. Modern total war is an outgrowth of the circumstances of group living and group relationships in a shrinking world. War is no longer just "a sport of kings." It has become an activity of the whole society and economy of the state involved in it. The conduct of war, too, is affected by factors of group psychology.

War and aggression are complex social phenomena. There is a simpler explanation following the definition by the German, General Clausewitz, that "war is nothing but a continuation of political intercourse with an admixture of other means." This definition no doubt fits some of the so-called limited wars of the past—those of Prussia and Germany, the Crimean War, the Italian conquest of Ethiopia, and perhaps the Korean War. It is a definition implying a choice of war in lieu of other alternatives and is particularly applicable to the case of an aggressor using war as an instrument of national policy as Bismarck did in fashioning modern Germany. Usually, however, wars have been the end result of a long build-up of desires, competitions, frictions, and conflicts, sometimes frustrations, in which both general causes and specific crises have led to a final outbreak. Generally speaking, the causes of war and aggression can be ascribed to fear, ambition, jealousy, rivalry, conflict over the possession of disputed objects, frustrations, religion or ideology, or economic vital interests. The specific causes may rise from a host of situations: seizures of territory, injury of persons, denials of markets and trade, assassination of officials, affronts to honor or refusal of demands, a fear of imminent attack, and so forth.

One sociologist has remarked that in contrast to animals who merely fight, men "first construct towering systems of theology and religion, complex analyses of racial character and class structure, or moralities of group life and virility before they kill one another. Thus they fight for Protestantism, or Mohammedanism, for the emancipation of the world proletariat, or for the salvation of Nordic culture, for nation or for kind." From these theories impulses are rationalized and the use of violence is justified.[43]

Statesmen are generally swayed by emotional considerations to a somewhat lesser degree than the average man in the street in making their decisions on the issues of peace and war. Their judgments, which are of course subjective human judgments, are ordinarily guided more by weighing the considerations of national security, national well-being, the requirements of time and circumstance, and the long-run self-interest of their country. Once the die is cast, however, matters are rationalized for and by the common man in terms of such emotions and ideas as are likely to enlist his wholehearted support.

For the sake of their ideas, their theories, and their emotions—as well as for the protection of their homes and the acquisition of the basic needs of life— men are willing to battle one another and to run the risk of personal and group extinction. In the past at least one side usually anticipated winning some kind of victory by inflicting greater losses upon the enemy or by forcing him to accept its will. The development of nuclear weapons, with their tremendous power of mass destruction, now warns mankind that warfare has reached a point of such potential loss to both sides that a general war can no longer be entered into with any very reliable estimate as to the cost or the outcome.[44]

CASE STUDIES IN PSYCHOLOGY AND POLITICS

Nazi Germany. The activities of the Nazis in pre-war Germany afford a graphic illustration of the connection which can exist between psychology and politics, and effects which can follow from the manipulation of psychological forces.

From 1934 to 1941, through the press, radio, and public gatherings, the German people were indoctrinated with the belief that they were being victimized by other nations, that adequate living space was being denied them, that

43 On the causes of war see Wright, *Study of War,* cited above; M. Ginsberg, "The Causes of War," *Sociological Rev.* April, 1939. See T. H. Pear (ed.), *Psychological Factors of Peace and War* (New York, 1950), for suggestive contributions to understanding and relationships of psychology and war. Also E. F. M. Durbin, *The Politics of Democratic Socialism* (London, 1948), pp. 49–50.

44 In March 1954 the United States exploded a nuclear bomb reported to have had a force equivalent to more than 12,000,000 tons of TNT and to have been capable of complete, or very considerable, destruction over an area of at least 300 square miles. The radioactive "fallout" several hundred miles away was not the least disturbing aspect of this test which was the second reported United States test of this type. The USSR, according to newspaper reports, exploded a thermonuclear weapon before the first United States test.

enemies were waiting to pounce upon them. The repeated vilification of the Czechs, Poles, and others, the persecution of the Jews, and the publicized character assassinations of opponents inevitably resulted in stirring feelings of hatred, vindictiveness, and lust for violence. Party members and occupational groups were placed in uniform. "Labor battalions" were formed. This together with the universal display of flags, the continual parades of armed forces, and the assemblage of scores of thousands in party gatherings to listen to Hitler's inciting oratory punctuated by mass chants for victory ("Sieg Heil") were bound to end in the creation of a martial atmosphere and a certain amount of mass hysteria.[45] All of this made it easier for the Nazi leaders to impose regulation on the economy and upon the liberties of the individual preparatory to Hitler's conquests. Whatever psychological resistance the German people had to a war of aggression was further decreased by an unceasing barrage of purposeful propaganda.

Some psychiatrists may say that Hitler, and other Nazi leaders, were possessed of a form of insanity.[46] Whether they were or not, psychological techniques were employed to diabolical advantage in Germany's foreign relations. A domineering, aggressive spirit was fashioned, ready to support the Nazi plans for power and conquest. By cleverly engineering a series of diplomatic crises when other nations were off guard and known to be unprepared for collective counteraction, a crisis atmosphere was induced through which the leaders were able to force the nation to "close ranks" and to pressure other states into concessions. German might was made to appear invincible. When Britain and France were caught ill-armed, unable to match Germany's burgeoning power, the stage was set for Prime Minister Chamberlain's shortsighted appeasement of Hitler at Munich and the partition of Czechoslovakia. When the war was started, terror and violence were employed without reserve against weaker peoples, as in the "Blitzkriegs" against Poland and the Netherlands intended to strike defeatism and terror into the minds of others. Coupled with all these was a high-pressured campaign of pre-war propaganda and subversion directed at the prospective victim nations by radio, press, the German foreign service, a "fifth column," and other agencies. When war broke out,

[45] A few recordings and films have preserved something of the hysteria generated by these events. The Columbia record album entitled *I Can Hear It Now* edited by Edward R. Murrow contains some recordings of the Nazi gatherings. The United States Army war-time training film *Why We Fight* contains a section depicting Hitler's influence upon the masses in Germany, while the Nazi film *Triumph of the Will* available from the Museum of Modern Art in New York City shows the Nuremberg gatherings in their frenzy.

[46] Konrad Heiden's *Der Fuehrer: Hitler's Rise to Power* (Boston, 1944) is an interesting study of Hitler's behavior. See also F. Gilbert, *Hitler Directs His War* (New York, 1950); K. Lowenstein, *Hitler's Germany* (New York, 1940); F. L. Neumann, *Behemoth: The Struggle and Practice of National Socialism* (New York, 1944). See also G. M. Gilbert, *The Psychology of Dictatorship* (New York, 1950).

psychological warfare was added to this. The history of this time stands as a grim warning of what a dictatorship can do to a nation and to international relationships by harnessing psychology and politics.[47]

Application in Other Circumstances. The foregoing illustration is not intended to imply that totalitarian governments are the only ones which may utilize knowledge of psychological techniques for internal and external effect in achieving their objectives.

President Roosevelt in his "fireside" radio talks in 1940–1941 played upon the attitudes and emotional dispositions of the American people. These intimate "chats" appealed to the American mind and were an effective means of informing the public and uniting the nation in a sense of mission. Similarly, Churchill's epic appeal to the British people after Dunkerque in 1940, saying that he could promise nothing but "blood, sweat and tears" in a lone stand against Nazi aggression, revealed a deft gauging of the mood and impulses of the English-speaking world. The effect upon the morale of the British people at one of the darkest moments in their history was electric. Moreover, his appeal aroused the sympathy and a feeling for a great cause throughout the Empire and in America.[48]

The same emotions of patriotism, nationalism, and self-sacrifice may be stirred within a democratic nation as in a totalitarian society, but the means of expressing them are usually different. Britain and the United States demonstrated during World War II that they could wage psychological warfare quite as effectively against a totalitarian society, under wartime conditions, as a dictatorship could do. In time of peace, however, the moral precepts accepted by democratic peoples, the freedom of the press, the tolerance and cultivation of political dissent, and the preservation of the essentials of an open society place distinct limitations upon the governments of these states in comparison with dictatorships in the use of psychological techniques for the achievement of international political ends.

GAUGING ATTITUDES, OBJECTIVES, AND RESPONSES

Success in the pursuit of national objectives in foreign affairs requires that the statesman gauge as best he can the attitudes, objectives, and responses of other states and shape his policy and tactics accordingly. This is not always easy, for the attitudes and objectives of other states may be misleadingly stated or veiled, and their responses under new circumstances not altogether pre-

---

47 F. L. Schuman's book *Night Over Europe* (New York, 1941) reflects something of the psychological atmosphere surrounding the prelude to war. See also L. P. Lochner (ed.), *The Goebbels Diaries* (New York, 1948).

48 A cross-section study of the American and British Empire press before and after Churchill's speech would afford an interesting exercise in observing psychological response.

dictable. Even when they are fairly apparent there are few devices with which to measure the strength of foreign motives and attitudes with any degree of accuracy or with which to compute precisely the internal political workings or the outward course of action of another state over an extended period of time. A study of opinion polls, where these are permitted, can yield some clues to public "minds" and sentiments, but these have as yet limited value.[49]

The statesman can only study the apparent or ascertainable facts surrounding the attitudes and actions of a foreign nation. He can observe sequences of action, the utterances of officials, the tone of the public press. He can probe, as best available knowledge and skilled training will permit, the implications contained in the frames of references held by foreign nations. He can chart the preferences and predispositions of the rulers and people. From these he can form some estimates. In addition, he must bear in mind that environmental conditions abroad keep changing, that the nuances of personal and political relationships are constantly in a process of flux.

CONCLUSION

These are a few of the ways in which psychological factors affect international relations. We have only scratched the surface of what is an enormous field in urgent need of more scientific study and joint research between political scientists and psychologists. It is essential, nonetheless, that we be aware of these influences, identify them in so far as possible, and take them into account in considering the relations among nations.

Someone has observed that no theory of human society or history based upon a doctrine of rational or conscious purpose can contain the whole truth. To understand why people behave as they do, we must remember the things that they have forgotten, the motives they dare not confess, the springs of action they cannot admit. The ideology of any movement or of any society is only half the story. The other half, and for us the more important half, lies below the surface.

Learning better how to deal with men's responses and how to guide group desires and inclinations into constructive paths has become one of the most urgent tasks of social science and political statesmanship—especially now as mankind advances into the atomic age.

SUGGESTED READINGS

Gordon W. Allport, *The Nature of Prejudice* (Cambridge, 1954).
Ruth Benedict, *Patterns of Culture* (New York, 1934).
W. Buchanan and H. Cantril, *How Nations See Each Other* (Urbana, 1953).

[49] See H. Cantril (ed.), *Pub. Opinion Polls 1935–46* (Princeton, 1951).

Hadley Cantril, *Tensions That Cause Wars* (Urbana, 1950).

George W. Kisker, ed., *World Tension: The Psychopathology of International Relations* (New York, 1951).

Clyde Kluckhohn, *Mirror to Man* (New York, 1949).

Ralph Linton, *The Study of Man* (New York, 1936).

T. M. Newcomb, *Social Psychology* (New York, 1950).

Reinhold Niebuhr, *Christianity and Power Politics* (New York, 1948).

T. H. Pear, ed., *Psychological Factors of Peace and War* (New York, 1950).

Ithiel de S. Pool, *Symbols of Democracy,* Hoover Institute Studies, Series C, No. 4 (Stanford, 1952).

J. E. Ross, *Christian Ethics* (New York, 1948).

CHAPTER VI

The Force of Nationalism

PROBABLY THERE exists in the world today no more powerful single force than nationalism. A dominant factor in European and American affairs during the nineteenth century, a major cause of two World Wars, nationalism has now become a powerful force for change in Asia, the Middle East, and even Africa. In response to nationalism, barriers to the freedom of trade, of migration, and of ideas have sprung up around the world. In the spirit of nationalism, peoples subject to alien rule risk their lives for political independence, and as a result, colonialism and old-fashioned imperialism are now almost gone.

WHAT IS NATIONALISM?

What is this force called nationalism? What are its components; its historical roots? How has it grown? Is it a force for good or for evil? What is its future? Can the excesses of nationalism be curbed by a society of sovereign states? These are some of the urgent questions of international relations. They concern us as individuals, for in contemporary world politics our lives are bound up with our own nation and the spirit of nationalism which pervades it and other nations with which it must deal.[1]

Definition of Nationalism. Nationalism, like any other psychological force, is not easily defined. It contains emotional qualities, even mystical elements, which make definition difficult. In its broader meaning it refers to the "attitude which ascribes national individuality a high place in the hierarchy of values." Simply described, it is the consciousness of belonging together which a group of people have who share, or believe they share, certain common experiences: a common past, a common culture, a common political allegiance, certain common ideals, and, in most cases, a common language.

Hans Kohn, a leading authority on the subject, has described nationalism in

[1] For a general study of nationalism see C. H. J. Hayes, *Essays on Nationalism* (New York, 1926); Karl Deutsch, *Nationalism and Social Communication* (New York, 1953).

these words: "Nationalism is a *state of mind,* permeating the large majority of a people and claiming to permeate all its members; it recognizes the *nation-state* as the ideal form of political organization and the *nationality* as the source of all creative cultural energy and economic well-being. The *supreme loyalty* of man is therefore due to his own nationality, as his own life is supposedly rooted in and made possible by its welfare." [2]

This suggests the nature and the implications of nationalism.

COMPONENTS OF NATIONALITY

Nationalism, as an idea, stems from the concept of nationality. What is a "nationality"? Is it an objective fact or a subjective concept? Is it "natural" and unchanging, or artificially created and fluid, or is it in part both?

Race. It has sometimes been claimed that race is the basis of nationality. Nazi leaders in the years between 1933 and 1945—and before—asserted, for example, that true German nationality rested upon the Aryan race, and by precept and terror set out to exclude Jews and "non-Aryans" from German nationality. With a propagated myth of "superior race" they claimed that the German nation was destined to rule inferior races including the Jewish and Slavic peoples.

Reputable authorities do not accept the racial foundation theory. An international panel of experts recently reported that (1) no large modern national group is, "scientifically speaking, a race," and that (2) there is "no scientific justification for race discrimination." [3] The experts also agreed that the concept of race is hard to define in itself, and that popular use of the term combined with "the myth of race" has led to untold human sorrow.

Human migrations over the centuries have brought about a complex intermingling of races so that the "nationalities" of today are in most instances a composite of many races. [4] They cut across many racial strains. Daniel Defoe epitomized this when he wrote:

> Thus from a mixture of all kinds began
> That heterogeneous thing, an Englishman. [5]

2 Hans Kohn, *The Idea of Nationalism, A Study of Its Origins and Background* (New York, 1944), p. 16. Italics added.

3 *The New York Times,* July 18, 1950. See also Ashley Montague, *Statement on Race* (New York, 1951); Ruth Benedict and Gene Weltfish, *The Races of Mankind* (New York, 1943); Carlton S. Coon, *The Races of Europe* (New York, 1939).

4 Julian Huxley, the noted English biologist says: "Man is unique among species of animals in the degree to which crossing between already differentiated groups and types has taken place. Accordingly, multiple ancestry is at least as important as common ancestry in considering the nature and origins of any group." Quoted in Ruth Benedict, *Race: Science and Politics* (New York, 1940), pp. 45–46. See also C. S. Burr, *America's Race Heritage* (New York, 1922).

5 Daniel Defoe, *The True-Born Englishman* (Cambridge, 1904) p. 246.

This is even more apparent in the United States where the heavy immigration movement made of America a melting pot of many races and American nationality a composite of many strains. It is also observable in the Soviet Union. There are to be found distinctive Russian, Ukrainian, Georgian, Armenian, and many other "races" and nationalities. Yet there also exists a "Soviet nationalism" which seeks to encompass them all.[6]

The differentiations among most nationalities are more the result of social and historical forces than of so-called "racial" differences.[7] As one social psychologist has put it: " 'Race' is the cheap explanation tyros offer for any collective trait that they are too stupid or too lazy to trace to its origin in the physical environment, the social environment, or historical conditions." [8]

Use of the word *race* in connection with nationalism does not offer a true explanation of the complex thing we call nationalism, and it has come to convey false and dangerous concepts.

"National Character." The idea that nationality reflects a certain "national character" has some validity. Exposure to a given geographical environment, to certain historical experiences, and to a definite pattern of social and legal institutions does tend to produce a certain degree of group uniformity. Let a group exist long enough within common political frontiers, and some traits of what may be called national character will emerge which can be distinguished from groups living within other frontiers.

It is also true, however, that individual and group attitudes exist within a nation quite apart from and often differing from the supposedly dominant national characteristics. In this age when the world is at least technically "one world," certain attitudes and characteristics may also transcend national boundaries. Furthermore, attributes of "national character" change with changing historical and intellectual circumstances. "British genius for self-government" is sometimes spoken of as a national characteristic. But this probably is less a product of a peculiar "national character" than of certain historical circumstances. Voltaire, describing the politics of England in his day, drew a picture which today one would take as typical of France rather than of England: "The French are of the opinion that the government of this island is more tempestuous than the sea which surrounds it, which indeed is true." Times and attributes change.

Common Historical Traditions and Memories. The literature of many nationalities expresses a belief that the historical traditions which the peoples

[6] See H. Kohn, *Nationalism in the Soviet Union* (New York, 1932); Maurice Hindus, *Mother Russia* (New York, 1945).

[7] Benedict, *op. cit.*, pp. 80–95.

[8] E. A. Ross, *Social Psychology* (New York, 1919), p. 3. See also J. Barzun, *Race: A Study in Modern Superstition* (New York, 1937); O. C. Cox, *Caste, Mass and Race* (New York, 1948); P. Radin, *The Racial Myth* (New York, 1934).

composing the nationality have experienced have a large share in molding the national traits. The Norse sagas and the Homeric poems embody some of the traditions which have come down to the present-day national outlook of the Norwegian and Greek nationalities. The seafaring, freedom-of-expression, trial-by-jury traditions of the English people have played a part in the formation of English nationality. In the United States the winning of the frontier, the struggle for independence, the equality of opportunity regardless of creed, color, or origin, freedom of speech and of religion, the free enterprise system, and a strong belief in republican institutions are historical traditions that have left an indelible imprint upon the nationality of Americans.

Apart from these general predispositions, nations usually have certain "historical memories," which are perpetuated and cultivated in history books, popular literature and folklore, and in music. These may incline them to be suspicious of some nations and friendly with others. The nationalism of many nations, indeed, leans on the conception of an historic role and ambition. Czech nationalism, for instance, saw its mission not only in preserving the culture and the language of the Czechoslovak people and in perpetuating and if possible recapturing one day the eminence of the Bohemian Kingdom at its peak, but also in blocking a German advance south. Similarly, Polish nationalism has seen as part of its *raison d'être* the prevention of German and Russian dominance of the lands historically inhabited and ruled by peoples of Polish extraction.

Traditions and beliefs are tenacious things. They are passed on from generation to generation, becoming a cohesive force binding together in times of hardship the peoples who share them, and guiding national policy toward certain goals. The historical traditions of the Czech people were so strong that they survived 300 years of alien rule until Czechoslovakia became a state in 1918. When World War I drew to a close, similar traditions of national feeling also welled up to demand creation of a new independent state in Poland which had been partitioned among Austria-Hungary, Prussia, and Russia for more than a century.

Culture. Another reliable characteristic of nationality is a common culture. Most nationalities have some predominant trait, although some, like the United States, have many diverse cultural strands within them. In some nationalities certain kinds of family relationships and social organization are characteristic features. Sometimes nationalities have distinctive modes of artistic expression.

In numerous cases a close connection exists between religion and nationality. Pakistanis, generally speaking, are Moslems, as are most people in the Arab League countries. To be a true Israeli one is expected to be a Jew. In

Japan, Shintoism has been closely identified with Japanese nationalism, so much so that during World War II Christian Japanese generally were suspect by the police as being sympathetic to the Western nations if not actually spies. When India became independent, Indian nationalism had such an affinity to Hinduism that non-Hindu communal groups were regarded by the rank and file as not being true Indian nationals.[9] Moslem Indians who joined to form the state of Pakistan quickly developed a Pakistani nationalism which became closely identified with the Moslem religion. Hindus, on the whole, became regarded as being "out" of the group and alien to its spirit of nationalism.

A particularly cohesive cultural attribute of nationality is language.[10] The rise and decline of nations and their languages often run in close parallel. Ancient Greece, Rome, and Egypt had distinctive languages which in general rose and fell with their fortunes. England as a national entity and English developed together. The revival of Irish nationalism within the last seventy-five years has been linked with demand for the use of Gaelic as the native tongue. When colonies break away from alien rule, nationalistic sentiment often exerts pressure to abandon the language of the former rulers in favor of some one or more native tongues.

Language is a strong force because it is easily passed on from one generation to the next and acts as a bond helping to perpetuate historical memories and traditions. Yet nations do exist without having a common language, as the Canadian and Swiss bear witness. A culture can, moreover, be shared by various nationalities.

Nationalism a Matter of Feeling. It will be seen, then, that there are several components which, under certain circumstances, contribute to a feeling of nationality. Yet none of them necessarily produces a nation. Furthermore, it is possible for a feeling of nationality to exist and to be expressed in nationalistic behavior where the presence of these factors cannot be objectively demonstrated.

Nationality is not necessarily a "natural" phenomenon in the world community. In the China of former times, "Chinese nationalism" was by and large the attribute of a few political groups and of Chinese students. For the masses of the 400 million Chinese, the prime loyalty unit was the family. Love of family and group and love of familiar environment are natural to man. Love of an abstract entity such as "nationality," love of a homeland he may never see in its entirety, and willingness to sacrifice even life for it are feelings created by

[9] See Bernhard Berenson, *Rumor and Reflection* (London, 1952).
[10] Max Boehm, "Nationalism—Theoretical Aspects," *Encyclopedia of the Social Sciences*, vol. XI, p. 235, says: "A people not only transmits the store of all its memories through the vocabulary of its language, but in syntax, word sound and rhythm it finds the most faithful expression of its temperament and general emotional life." See also Ruth Benedict, *Patterns of Culture* (New York, 1934).

intellectual and historical processes. Nationalities are a product of the historical development of modern society.[11] The concept of nationalism, and the nationalist movement in the world today, are essentially creatures of the Western world exported to and being copied by peoples elsewhere.[12]

Nationality is not an objective, unchanging entity. It is primarily a subjective act of will, changing in meaning and practice as the circumstances creating it change. Certain circumstances combine to cause a people to believe it is a nationality and, because it thinks so, it is. As Hans Kohn has said: "Nationality is formed by the decision to form a nationality."[13] Nationalism—as the most powerful driving force in the relations between states in the nineteenth and twentieth centuries—stems from a feeling of nationality. It is something that is acquired, that grows upon people. Some have the feeling of nationality at a given time; others do not. Many forces enter into its origination within the unique environment of each particular society.

SYMBOLS OF NATIONALISM

Nationalism normally has certain symbols which accompany its growth and which play a large part in its perpetuation. They are not found everywhere in exactly the same form or degree. But they are sufficiently common to be generally recognizable accompaniments of nationalism.

The National State. The national state is one of the most universal symbols of nationalism. Many nationalities aspire to establish their own national state, though it may take centuries to achieve this goal, as in the case of the Jewish state of Israel. But the *summum bonum* for most national groups is "self-determination" to set up separate political entities. The fracturing of the Austro-Hungarian and Ottoman empires in 1918 into the small "succession states" in Eastern Europe and the Near East is a classic example of the search of nationalism for the symbol of the national state. To nationalism, the political independence of the national state is a more prized possession than economic well-being or personal security.

National Symbols. With the national state go the national flag and anthem as additional universal symbols of nationality. Each nation seeks a flag and an anthem to form emotional symbols or rallying points for national sentiment. The flag may be green, black and white, or red and blue. Whatever the combination of colors, with or without such added elements as stars, crosses, scimitars, moons, or hammers, a flag is everywhere identified with not only a given portion of the earth's surface but with a particular nation. To that piece

11 Kohn, *op. cit.*, p. 12.
12 See Arnold Toynbee, *The World and the West* (New York, 1953).
13 Kohn, *cit. supra*, p. 15.

of colored cloth men and women will pledge allegiance. When it passes by, they will stand and doff their hats. They will follow it in battle and lay down their lives for the thing which it represents—nationalism. Likewise, the national anthem and the uniforms of the armed forces are symbols of nationalism.

In pre-1945 Germany, the effect of symbolism was marked. The Nazis festooned their cities with flags bearing the swastika. Parades would be accompanied by masses of flags and blaring bands. At the passing of a group of flags the crowds would snap to rigid attention with arms extended in the angular Nazi salute. Often this would be accompanied by impassioned shouts of "Sieg Heil, Sieg Heil"—"Hail Victory, Hail Victory"—as jackbooted troops goose-stepped past.

The "Star-Spangled Banner" and the uniforms of the United States armed forces are symbols of American nationalism. Americans may not be as demonstrative over their nationalism, especially in time of peace, as are some other nationals, but they are as reverent of these symbols as any and prize the meanings and sentiments which they evoke.

Heroes, Shrines, Slogans. Heroes and hero-worship are symbols of nationalism. Each nationality vaunts the exploits, the personality, and the memory of certain great figures in its national history. Consider the roles that Washington, Patrick Henry, Thomas Jefferson, Andrew Jackson, Abraham Lincoln play in our national feelings. They have become symbols of the unique features of our national spirit. So, likewise, are similar figures built up in the folkways of other nationalities. One has but to mention Kosciusko to think of Polish nationalism; Mazzini, Garibaldi, and Cavour remind all of Italian nationalism; Napoleon of French; and Nelson of English national spirit. Remembrance of such personalities and the legends associated with them are vital factors in keeping alive the national sentiments with which they are associated.

There are many other symbols of nationalism. Certain passages of literature; pledges of allegiance; national shrines such as Mount Vernon, the Arc de Triomphe, Westminster Abbey, Lenin's Tomb; slogans such as "Remember the Alamo," "Don't shoot till you see the whites of their eyes," "Liberté, Egalité, Fraternité"—all these are also symbols of various nationalisms.

Emphasis upon symbols tends to rise as dangers threaten a nationality. War brings them to the forefront. In peacetime, an exceptional increase in appeal to symbolism has often pointed toward preparation for war, the symbols being used as a rallying force to enlist popular support and readiness to accept regimentation. This was revealed in Nazi Germany from 1933 to 1939.

DEVELOPMENT OF NATIONALISM

The conditions which produced the nationalism we see about us today have been for the most part the work of several centuries. Let us look at some of these conditions and at the stages through which nationalism has been passing.[14]

Rise of European Nationalism. Nationalism posits, either in fact or as an ideal, a government over a distinct piece of territory. The absolute monarchs of the sixteenth to eighteenth centuries contributed to the rise of nationalism by suppressing feudalism, creating the nation-state system, and consolidating their realms on a secular basis.

This evolution took place at varying rates and times throughout Western Europe. From there it has spread out to the New World, to the Orient, and now to all parts of the globe. This fanning out of the institution of nationalism has been one of the features of modern international relations. The universalization of nationalism is one of the pronounced characteristics of the contemporary world community. Wherever nationalism has gone from the original Western European incubator to be adopted in another part of the world, it has been partly a result of, sometimes paralleled by and closely related to, other economic, social, cultural, and spiritual forces which contributed to it.

Other movements than the rise of absolute monarchs added forces which further spurred the growth of nationalism in Europe. The gradual decrease in the use of Latin as a universal tongue, the breakdown of the medieval system, and the rise of vernacular literature contributed to the differentiation of peoples and stimulated native expression. The individualism and humanism of the Renaissance splintered and secularized the Church society which had united much of medieval Europe. The growth of capitalism and the commercial middle classes assisted the evolution of the national mercantilism of the seventeenth and eighteenth centuries. The social, economic, and political, as well as religious, forces of the Protestant Reformation paved the way for national churches and national rulers. Throughout all these movements a change was occurring from what was "common to mankind to what is peculiar to the nation." [15] This is the essence, the glory, and the potential danger of nationalism.

Popularization of Nationalism. Modern nationalism is essentially a thing of the people. Perhaps the greatest contribution to its evolution into this form

[14] Ramsay Muir, *Nationalism and Internationalism* (London, 1916); E. H. Carr, *Nationalism and After* (New York, 1945); C. J. H. Hayes, *The Historical Evolution of Modern Nationalism* (New York, 1931); E. M. Earle (ed.), *Nationalism and Internationalism* (New York, 1950); L. Hertz, *Nationality in History and Politics* (New York, 1944).

[15] C. J. H. Hayes, "Nationalism—Historical Development," *Encyclopedia of the Social Sciences,* vol. XI.

was the spirit of the French and American revolutions with their emphasis upon popular sovereignty. Through more or less simultaneous revolutions in the Old and the New World the nation was identified with the people rather than with the person or actions of a ruler.

Although separated by only fifty years in time, Frederick the Great of Prussia and George Washington epitomized the change which was occurring. Frederick ruled Prussia not as a nation, but as an estate; Prussia's wars were his disputes with other sovereigns. Washington and Jefferson, on the other hand, were elected leaders of a government resting upon popular consent. The war which Washington led for the American colonies was a popular war. The democracy which Jefferson helped fashion had as its foundation popular sovereignty. In Europe the armies of Napoleon were for the first time a popular army—a *levée en masse*—and they carried with them across Europe the ideals of the French Revolution.

Character of Nineteenth-Century Nationalism. Nineteenth-century nationalism was in considerable part liberal in nature, at least up to 1870, although revolution, civil wars, and turmoil accompanied the birth of many of the new national states during this period. Throughout Europe and South America, nationalities long ruled by alien masters strove to attain national independence and some degree of political democracy. Moreover, once the unification of their nationals in a single state had been achieved, most populaces of the new states wanted peaceful conditions in which to develop their economic, political, and social systems.

In Western Europe and the Americas, nineteenth-century nationalism grew up in a setting of liberal democracy. The rights of man took pre-eminence in many questions over the rights of states. Since the rights of states were regarded only as a derivation of these more fundamental individual rights, there was a tendency to concentrate more upon the activities and interests of individuals than of states. Furthermore, the widespread adoption of liberal institutions created a certain degree of international solidarity.

Liberal nationalism saw the nation as neither exclusive nor aggressive. The natural love of one's own country was to be extended to a love of humanity as a whole. Service to one's own country was a prerequisite for service to mankind. The Italian patriot, Mazzini, expressed this philosophy in these words:

Our Country is our home, the home which God has given us, placing therein a numerous family which we love and are loved by, and with which we have a more intimate and quicker communion of feeling and thought than with others; . . . Our country is our field of labour; the products of our activity must go forth from it for the benefit of the whole earth; but . . . in labouring according to true principles for our Country we are labouring for Humanity.[16]

[16] Quoted in H. Finer, *America's Destiny* (New York, 1947), p. 104.

Another factor in giving to nineteenth-century nationalism a peaceful character was the identity of interest of the middle classes in various countries. The nineteenth-century middle class had, on the whole, ideals and interests that transcended national boundaries. Being in control of the franchise, this group was able to a large extent to direct the policies of many states.

But probably the chief reason for the peaceful character of nineteenth-century nationalism lay in the growth of an economic order based on an expanding economy, belief in a community of interest among trading nations, and in the benefits of free trade. Underlying the theory of a liberal international economic system was the fact of British economic and financial predominance. The open and prosperous British markets, combined with the widespread investment and financial directive activities of the banking and insurance interests in "the City" of London, made possible the expanding production and delicate balancing of this system. Supporting this economic and financial predominance which stretched out over all parts of the world, lay the political pre-eminence of the British Empire and the power of the British Navy. The nineteenth century was characterized by a "Pax Britannica."[17]

The national states of the nineteenth century grew in strength, proclaiming and exercising the rights of political nationalism. But all the while they tacitly accepted English guidance of their economic destinies. "On this supposed separation of political and economic power, and this real blend of freedom and authority, the nineteenth-century order rested."[18]

TWENTIETH-CENTURY NATIONALISM

In the last decades of the nineteenth century signs of a change began to appear. Germany arose as the dominant power on the continent of Europe. Protectionist tariffs, advocated as early as 1841 by Friedrich List, began to be imposed. By 1900 the commercial supremacy of Britain was challenged. After 1914 its naval strength was no longer determinant in world affairs. This meant the end of the nineteenth-century system. A new era and a new form of nationalism were arising.

Socialization of Nations. One of the most significant changes which began to take place in the latter part of the nineteenth century was the assimilation of the lower classes into the political systems of the various nations. Extension of the suffrage and of social benefits to the masses of people had a profound effect upon national policy. The rise of the "social service state" meant not

17 See Albert Imlah, "Pax Britannica," *South Atlantic Quar.*, Jan., 1951; H. Feis, *Europe— The World's Banker* (New Haven, 1930).
18 Carr, *cit. supra*, p. 17.

only that economic conditions had to be protected against the influences of economic conditions and policies elsewhere, but that the masses themselves developed an interest in the power of the state. Hence, national policy increasingly rested on mass support with all the limitations and implications that this involved. Economic nationalism was the corollary of the socialization of nations.[19] State economic planning contributed to tariffs, trade barriers, discriminatory practices, and state trading.

As a result of this development, one of the great safety valves of the nineteenth century for the dispersion of discontent was closed: freedom of migration. The necessity of maintaining full employment, of raising wages, of demonstrating that steps were being taken to improve standards of living for the workers, brought states to close their national borders to free migration of labor after 1919. Some states, like the United States, restricted immigration to prevent an influx of new labor that would be willing to work for less than organized labor. Other states, like Russia, closed their borders to emigration because of shortages of labor at home. One state after another barred its doors to free migration.

Increase in Number of States. Another change which made for the rise of aggressive nationalism was the large increase in the number of national states. In 1871 there were fourteen sovereign states in Europe; in 1914 there were twenty; by 1924 there were twenty-six. The fragmentation process stimulated by Woodrow Wilson's championing the doctrine of "self-determination" at Paris in 1919 was not restricted to Europe. It spread to the Middle East and Asia. Today, more than seventy political units lay claim to being independent national states.

One of the consequences of this political multiplication has been an increase in the number of international conflicts. Frictions increased, and as the disputes between nations mounted, so did the nationalism within nations.[20] Moreover, with the growth in the number of states and the changes which occurred in political alignments and in technology, Great Power war once unloosed has tended to become global war. Adoption of the principle of "collective

[19] Carr points out that this movement subsequently led to the "nationalization of socialism," which previously had been more internationalist than nationalist in outlook. The result was demonstrated in 1914 when, despite the earlier statements of Socialists that they would stand together against war, the Socialist parties everywhere but in Russia flocked to the support of their several nations when war broke out. (Carr, *op. cit.*, p. 20.) See also Ortega y Gasset, *The Revolt of the Masses* (New York, 1932); J. G. Hodgson (ed.), *Economic Nationalism* (New York, 1931).

[20] Felix Morley suggests in his book, *The Foreign Policy of the United States* (New York, 1952), that the potentiality of conflicts between states can be calculated by the formula $X = \dfrac{N(N-1)}{2}$ in which N represents the number of states and X the number of wars that could theoretically be waged by all of them at a given time.

EASTERN EUROPE CONFLICT AREAS

Umea

FINLAND

LAKE LADOGA

Bergen

NORWAY

Oslo

SWEDEN

Stockholm

Helsingfors

Parkalla

Leningrad

Tallinn

ESTONIA

Pskov

North

Baltic Sea

Riga

LATVIA

DENMARK

Copenhagen

LITHUANIA

Kaunas

SOVIET

Sea

EAST PRUSSIA

Minsk

Hamburg

Stettin

WEST POLAND

Posen

RUSSIA

Amsterdam

Bremen

Berlin

Warsaw

Gomel

BELGIUM

Brussels

RUHR

GERMANY

Frankfurt

POLAND

Brest Litovsk

EAST POLAND

Kiev

FRANCE

LUX.

SAAR

RHINELAND

Prague

CZECHOSLOVAKIA

Vistula

TESCHEN

Lwow

Dnieper

Danube

BERCHTESGADEN

Bratislava

BESSARABIA

SWITZER-LAND

AUSTRIA

S.TYROL

Vienna

Budapest

HUNGARY

BUKOVINA

AOSTA

MT. CENIS

Milan

Turin

Po

VENEZIA GIULIA

Trieste

TRANSYLVANIA

ROMANIA

TENDA BRIGA

Genoa

Fiume

Sava

Bucharest

Florence

Zara

Belgrade

Danube

S.DOBRUJA

CORSICA

ITALY

Rome

YUGOSLAVIA

BULGARIA

Sofia

Bosporus

SARDINIA

Naples

Tirana

ALBANIA

MACEDONIA

THRACE

Istanbul

Dardanelles

N.EPIRUS

GREECE

Smyrna

Tunis

Mediterranean

SICILY

Catania

Athens

DODECANESE IS.

Scale of Miles

0   100   200   300   400   500

CRETE

Lenz

The Christian Science Monitor

FIGURE VI:1

security" in a world community made up of a multitude of national states has tended toward collective warfare once a major aggression occurs.[21]

Rise of Popular Press. Beginning with the last years of the nineteenth century another innovation appeared which had a profound effect upon nationalism. This was the popular press. Newspapers were founded whose market was intended to be the less literate. Sensational journalism, oftentimes heavily colored with ultranationalism, was resorted to in order to appeal to the mass reading public.

Wherever it sprang up, the popular press usually catered to the emotions of the masses and followed a policy of emphasizing nationalism. In the nontotalitarian countries this press is privately controlled. Beginning with the founding of the Bolshevik revolution in Russia, and spreading later to Italy, Germany, Japan, and other states having totalitarian regimes, the fascist and communist states have, however, turned government-controlled newspapers into propagandist tools.

It remained for the Nazis to show the world the nadir to which popular journalism could sink. With screaming headlines, blood-dripping stories, utter disregard of truth, calculated deceptions, crude cartoons and photography, the Nazi press was put to work under Joseph Goebbels to whip the German people into a blind hypernationalist war dance.

From the concatenation of these circumstances, "totalitarian nationalism" conjured itself up into the evil genius of the mid-twentieth century.[22]

TOTALITARIAN NATIONALISM IN ACTION

Nazi Germany. Totalitarian nationalism exhibited itself in extreme form in Nazi Germany from 1933 to 1945. Under the Nazis, the rights of man were surrendered to the rights of the state. Humanitarianism was replaced by "étatism." The state became the supreme end in itself. The individual possessed no inherent value; he existed only to serve and to glorify the state. He was declared to derive his existence and his welfare from the state, and his highest duty was, therefore, to obey its dictates unquestioningly.

With this Hegelian philosophy were compounded the worst features of Prussian militarism. Glorification of the organic state was utilized to assert the superiority of the German state as the perfect culmination of the evolving nation-states of history. Ancient mythologies were revived and popularized to support the theory of a superior German race, destined to subject all lesser peoples to its will. The will of an abstract organic state and a mythological

---

[21] See Hans Morgenthau, *Politics Among Nations* (New York, 1950), ch. xxii.
[22] See G. L. Bird and F. E. Merwin, *The Newspaper and Society* (New York, 1942). On the Nazi press see Louis P. Lochner (ed.), *The Goebbels Diaries* (New York, 1948).

German "Volk" was personalized in an absolute leader who was called "Der Führer."

Justifying itself on these doctrines that turned back the clock on the highest values of 2,000 years of Western civilization, Nazi totalitarian nationalism first turned itself to the oppression of minorities at home and then to military aggression abroad. The extermination of the Jews epitomized internal oppression at its cruelest. Anti-Semitism was organized through mass propaganda and took hold of the German people to express itself in mass hatred of a scapegoat for their troubles. External aggression, under the appeal of "Lebensraum" for the superior race which was to unite all "German peoples" in a Greater Reich, proceeded from the seizure of Austria in 1938 to the overthrow of the Czech state and the invasion of Poland in 1939, subsequently to the conquests and enslavement of the Western European and Balkan nations, and finally to the assault upon Russia and the waging of total war in pursuit of world aggrandizement.

Italy and Japan. To an extent Italian and Japanese nationalism during the years from 1930 to 1945 displayed some of the same totalitarian characteristics. In neither case were pogroms conducted aiming at the extermination of an entire minority race within their midst, although brutalities and oppressions did occur in some foreign areas conquered by their armed forces or brought under their control. In both nations the authority of the state over the individual was exalted; personal liberties were restricted through the machinery of secret police and "thought control" techniques. War was glorified by the governments, and in each country militarism was combined with an inflated nationalism to launch the state upon a campaign of aggressive warfare against peaceful nations and peoples for the sake of aggrandizement.[23]

Consequences of World War II. When the Allies accepted the unconditional surrender of the German and Imperial Japanese armed forces in 1945, those leaders found guilty of "crimes against humanity" by the War Crimes Tribunals were executed or imprisoned. The world seemed relieved of the dangers of totalitarian nationalism. Temporarily at least, the extremes of these nationalisms retreated within bounds. By many efforts the Western nations then sought to assist the peoples of Western Germany and Japan to reconstruct the bases of their national life in such a manner that in the future their nations would form a part of the comity of the peacefully inclined nations, and that their nationalism would not again turn in the directions which led to world war.

Time alone can tell whether this assistance, and the moderation shown in

23 See G. A. Borgese, *Goliath* (New York, 1937).

the treaty of peace with Japan, have accomplished such a change. In Western Germany moderate elements represented in the Christian Democratic Union party under the leadership of Konrad Adenauer gained power in 1949 (and retained it in the 1953 elections) to guide the initial destinies of the Federal Republic at Bonn. Adenauer himself declared, however, that a nation like Germany "has a claim to feel along nationalistic lines." Intransigent nationalist positions have been taken by socialist and conservative groups, and on various occasions neo-fascist (that is, former Nazi) elements have appeared and have been reported to be busily engaged in plotting the restoration of nazism in Germany.

Four things seem clear in the emergent German situation: (1) German nationalism must be reckoned with as a force in world politics; (2) it is inevitable that efforts will be made to reunify Germany and that appeals will be made to nationalism in this process both by the liberal elements in Western Germany, by the neo-fascists, and by the Communists of Eastern Germany under the promptings of Moscow; (3) Eastern Germans are continually being indoctrinated by their communist masters with antidemocratic and extremist propaganda, which although it may be unpalatable to many of them in the form of Soviet-dominated rule, as evidenced by the riots in 1953, is nevertheless continuing to condition their minds to totalitarianism and extremism; (4) what happens within Germany will depend in part upon the relations among the Powers themselves and in particular between the two greatest Powers and the German people.[24]

The questions of which way nationalism will turn in Japan and Italy are no less serious. Since 1945 moderate groups, friendly to the Western Powers, have been in control of the governments in both countries. But the parties in power hold no clear-cut margin of popular support, and there are in each state active elements both of authoritarianism and of communism. So long as there are totalitarian movements operating within the society of nations, or bases of poverty or despair prevalent within countries, the possibility will exist that extreme types of nationalism may gain an ascendant hand.[25]

[24] On the German situation see E. Salin, "Social Forces in Germany Today," *Forum,* Jan., 1950; F. M. Hechinger, "The Eagle with the Swastika," *Harper's,* Jan., 1950; F. Neumann, "German Democracy," *International Conciliation,* May, 1950; T. Taylor, "The Struggle for the German Mind," *New Republic,* Jan. 30, 1950; interview with General Guderian, formerly Chief of Staff of the German Army, *U. S. News and World Report,* Sept. 8, 1950; Hans Morgenthau (ed.), *Germany and the Future of Europe* (Chicago, 1951).

[25] See V. La Malfa, "Touch-and-Go in Italy," *Foreign Affairs,* Jan., 1953; N. Kogan, "The Italian Action Party and the Institutional Question," *Western Pol. Quar.,* June, 1953; E. O. Reischauer, *The United States and Japan* (Cambridge, 1950); L. Parrot, "Problems and Prospects of the New Japan," *The New York Times Magazine,* Nov., 1951; W. M. Ball, *Japan: Enemy or Ally?* (New York, 1949); H. K. Smith, *The State of Europe* (New York, 1951), ch. 11, pp. 202–223.

NATIONALISM IN THE SOVIET UNION

When the Bolsheviks emerged victorious from the turmoil of the Russian Revolution, their leaders were fired with a zeal for a cosmopolitan communism. They set as one of their goals an international uprising in which the Workers of the World would unite in overthrowing bourgeois capitalism for the establishment of a universal polity based on the "dictatorship of the proletariat." Nationalism entered into the scheme of things only in so far as it would prove useful to the realization of the internationalist idea. A new system and a new era were to be inaugurated.

Lenin's Nationality Policy. One month after the bolshevik seizure of power in 1917 Lenin issued in the name of the All-Russian Congress of Soviets a "Declaration of the Rights of Working and Exploited People." This proclaimed the equality and sovereignty of the peoples of Russia, their right to self-determination and to secede and form independent states, the abolition of all national privileges and restrictions, and the free development of the national minorities and ethnic groups inhabiting the territory of the Russian Empire.

Lenin's purpose in this announcement was twofold: (1) to destroy the political and cultural structure of the old Czarist Empire as a step toward a regrouping of its peoples in a new political society, and (2) to encourage the world revolution which Communists believed imminent.

Lenin believed that if the subject peoples of the Czarist Empire were given cultural freedom and allowed political self-determination—in other words, if nationalism were allowed to assert itself—and if at the same time the peoples were indoctrinated with communist ideology, the old Empire would voluntarily recrystallize as a great union of Soviet republics. Nor would the process stop there. As the world revolution proceeded—as each proletariat within other nations "settled matters with its own bourgeoisie"—these nations would enter the soviet federation, until all the world was embraced in it. National self-determination, Lenin affirmed, "leads to a free, more fearless and therefore wider and more universal formation of larger governments and unions of governments." [26]

The Theory in Practice. Lenin's theory worked out almost as he had envisioned it, at least in so far as the Russian Empire was concerned. After a period of disintegration, by 1924 all except the Baltic provinces had been reclaimed. The Russian Federated Soviet Republic formed the central unit in the new Union of Soviet Socialist Republics which embraced some 180 nationalities speaking 125 different languages or dialects and practicing as many as forty religions. [27] The other nationalities were grouped into sixteen Union Republics

---

[26] Quoted in Emile Burns, *A Handbook of Marxism* (London, 1935), p. 687.
[27] See Sir John Maynard, *Russia in Flux* (New York, 1948).

and a number of autonomous regions, which are represented in the federal government through the Council of Nationalities.

Early Soviet practice repudiated the old Czarist policies of "Russification." Cultural autonomy was encouraged in each national group. Their various languages were made official for legal, administrative, and educational purposes. Much emphasis was laid on the liberal treatment and equality of all nationalities. But although nationalism was encouraged on the cultural level, on the political level the diverse groups were held together in a closely knit federation and subjected to the dictates of Moscow by means of the Communist party organization and secret police.

Stalin and the National Question. During the period of Stalin's rule, government policy toward nationalism in the Soviet Union underwent considerable modification. Marxist-Leninist internationalism was subordinated to thoroughgoing Soviet socialist nationalism. Beginning in 1929 the original autonomy of the various republics was progressively curtailed. Central commissariats were set up in Moscow for many phases of economic and social life having plenary authority over all nationalities, peoples, and local governments. Stalin attacked some nationalisms when he wrote in 1934: "The deviation toward nationalism reflects the attempts of 'one's own national' bourgeoisie to undermine the Soviet system and restore capitalism." [28]

Emphasizing "socialism in one country" Stalin drove the government and peoples of the USSR to concentration upon domestic economic development, the construction of heavy industry, and the collectivization of farming.

War-time Nationalism. In 1937 the Kremlin announced that the word *fatherland* should be regarded as a fundamental political concept, and that "unlimited faithfulness to the mother country" was in order.[29] A highly nationalist film entitled "We, the Russians" was produced for showing throughout the Soviet Union. Forgotten heroes of Russian history were resurrected— Peter the Great, Alexander Nevsky, Ivan the Terrible, Suvorov, Kutuzov. Memories of battles won under the Czars were dusted off and given to the peoples for their veneration. The study of Russian history was revived in the schools and historical exhibits were widely displayed. In the Red Army the study of Russian was made a major subject for non-Russian-speaking soldiers. Monuments were restored. Great military displays were staged repeatedly. The flag and the uniform were glorified. Even "The Internationale" was replaced as the anthem of the Soviet Union by a hymn more peculiarly Russian. Stalin, in his order to the army when the USSR was attacked by Germany in 1941, said: "Let the courageous image of our great ancestors inspire you in this war." This was an out-and-out appeal to nationalist sentiment. With the exist-

[28] J. Stalin, *Marxism and the National Question* (Eng. trans., New York, 1942), p. 215.
[29] N. S. Timasheff, *The Great Retreat* (New York, 1946), p. 167.

ence of the Soviet state at stake, the gripping force of national sentiment was needed to fire the sacrifice of the people. Marxian dialectics might appeal to Moscow's bureaucrats and propagandists, but something closer to everyday life was needed to arouse the masses of the people. To Stalin nationalism was the answer, and he did not hesitate to employ it.

Reversing the stands taken previously by party and government, Stalin also enlisted the Russian churches in the cause of nationalism. Churches were allowed to reopen. People were permitted to attend services without being spied upon, and religion was brought to the wedding of Soviet nationalism and communism. By expediency the Soviets managed to bring into focus, first against Germany and then after the war against the West in general, the seemingly incompatible elements of religion and Marxism. To be Russian had meant, prior to the Bolshevik Revolution, to be an adherent of the Orthodox Church. The West had been suspected and hated because it was heretical—in Russian eyes—to this faith.[30] With this background it was not impossible for Moscow to lead its people to hate Germany, and then other Western nations, because they were neither orthodox nor communist and opposed to both which were Russian.

During the war groups in the Ukraine and in the Georgian-Cossack regions were reported to have welcomed the German armies and to have refused to go along with Moscow's campaign for a strong Russian nationalism. But the pillage and maltreatment of the captured lands and people by the Nazis soon led to resistance, and from all outward signs Moscow succeeded in building a true national spirit among its people. Maurice Hindus, well-known observer of the Russian scene, was led to remark: "The revival of Russian nationalism is one of the great phenomena of our time. In my judgment nationalism is certain to be the cornerstone of future Russian policy."[31]

Contemporary Scene. Since 1945 nationalism has been further intensified. Daily the people are told they have a great destiny. Struggle for the Soviet fatherland is constantly emphasized. Pride in national achievements of reconstruction and development are vaunted at the same time that sacrifices are demanded and the terrors of the police state imposed upon the people. Alleged menaces of Western "encirclement," "imperialism," and "war-mongering" are trumpeted in press and radio to maintain nationalist fervor.

One of the interesting facets of post-war nationalism has been Moscow's insistence that communist regimes outside the USSR copy its political structure and follow its domestic procedures in collectivization and industrial organiza-

---

30 See V. Riasanovsky, *Russia and the West in the Teaching of the Slavophiles* (Cambridge, 1952).
31 Maurice Hindus, *Mother Russia* (New York, 1945).

tion. The conflict which developed in 1948 between Marshal Tito of Yugo-slavia and the Kremlin over interpretation of Marxism and communist proce-dure revealed that Moscow's nationalist pride of leadership in the development of communism could not tolerate "deviationism" by local communist regimes or interference by Central and Eastern European nationalisms with its own military-political goals in Europe.[32]

Although condemning imperialist practices of others, the Soviet Union has imposed its own domination and institutions upon Estonia, Latvia, Lithuania, Poland, Rumania, Bulgaria, Hungary, Czechoslovakia, and East Germany. In this instance ambition for power has become a stronger urge than the professed revolutionary ideal of respecting small neighbors. For similar reasons Soviet policy has resurrected the expansionist Czarist policies. It can be argued at length as to whether they are engendered by communist doctrine or by a continuation of traditional Russian policy. But the effect is the same and the method and direction of the former logically encompasses the aims of the latter. Possibly this is a case of "the wheel turns, but it is ever the same wheel."

The Nature of Russian Nationalism. How can Russian nationalism be clas-sified? Obviously it is not identifiable with nineteenth-century liberal national-ism. It is akin to twentieth-century totalitarian nationalism in its intensive propagation by government, its emphasis on the state rather than the individual as a supreme value, its territorial aggressiveness, and its militant displays and insistence on unquestioning obedience.

Soviet nationalism, if present-day nationalism in the USSR may be called this, is unique in representing the fusion of an internationalist ideology with nationalist sentiment. Russian nationalism does not directly clash with com-munist ideology. It has taken over that ideology for its own purposes, but has still left the ideology with internationalist features. Communism has been made a Russian thing, and the USSR has been identified with the so-called "classless society" of Marx. In this way the party strategists have schemed to promote Marxist principles with one hand and Muscovite imperialism with the other. Soviet nationalism more and more has become a revival of old Russian nation-alism and imperialism girded about with a mantle of Marxism and Leninism. This Jekyll-Hyde character provides Moscow a means of advancing its own self-interest while disarming opponents and appealing to innocent bystanders.[33]

---

[32] See C. L. Sulzberger, "Heresy—The Great Bogey of the Kremlin," *The New York Times,* Oct. 10, 1948, reproduced in N. J. Padelford (ed.), *Cont. Int. Rels. Readings, 1949–1950,* pp. 62–66; also Roy Macridis, "Stalinism and the Meaning of Titoism," *World Politics,* Jan., 1952.

[33] During World War II communist groups throughout Europe sought forefront positions in the resistance movements, and with the liberation from Nazi occupation promoted the idea of "national front" governments. Wherever they succeeded in gaining power, however, they allied the governments with Moscow and turned countries into Soviet satellites.

NATIONALISM IN POST-WAR WESTERN EUROPE

Contrasting with the hypernationalism exhibited by the totalitarian regimes, nationalist sentiment in the more strident political sense appears to have been losing some ground in the popular mood of Western Europeans since World War II. Although Frenchmen, Norwegians, and the Dutch people are as much concerned with the security, integrity, and independence of their states as ever, and still hold a distrust toward the Germans, security and social and economic problems have acquired a forefront position in their attention. And from the experiences of the war and the magnitude of the reconstruction tasks have emerged a widespread disposition to seek solutions along international rather than purely national lines in so far as this holds forth promise to them.

These attitudes have been displayed in such movements as Benelux—the proposed economic and customs union of Belgium, the Netherlands, and Luxembourg—the Organization for European Economic Cooperation, the Economic Commission for Europe, the European Payments Union, the movement for European Union, the Council of Europe, the European Coal and Steel Community, the Western Union, and the North Atlantic Treaty Organization. An extraordinary degree of international cooperation has been shown in these endeavors. And, although it cannot be said that they have achieved the dreams of idealists, they have contributed to the growth of a new atmosphere of hope within Europe. Moreover, in some instances, alignments of groups and interests have begun to take place along party and functional lines in place of straight national cleavages. We shall review elsewhere details of these movements.[34]

RISING NATIONALISM IN ASIA

Throughout large sections of Asia a new nationalistic spirit is stirring and becoming an increasingly significant factor in world politics. Nationalism, together with communism, is vying for the allegiance of the peoples of Asia.[35] In some parts of Asia nationalism and communism are making common cause against the older order. Elsewhere, and in the over-all picture, they are opposed to each other inasmuch as communism represents an outreaching of Moscow influence and normally results in ultimate subordination of national independence to Kremlin policies, as demonstrated in Eastern Europe and Korea.

[34] See chs. v and xx. See also A. Dorpalen, "New Nationalism in Europe," *Virginia Quar. Rev.*, July, 1944; A. Dorpalen, "European Polity: Biography of an Idea," *J. of Pol.*, Nov., 1948; W. G. Carleton, "The New Nationalism," *Virginia Quar. Rev.*, July, 1950.

[35] W. M. Ball, *Nationalism and Communism in East Asia* (Inst. of Pacific Rels., 1952); W. L. Holland (ed.), *Asian Nationalism and the West* (New York, 1953); H. R. Isaacs (ed.), *New Cycle in Asia* (New York, 1947). On Asian nationalism see J. Nehru, *The Discovery of India* (New York, 1926); B. R. Sen, "Nationalism and the Asian Awakening," *Annals*, July, 1952.

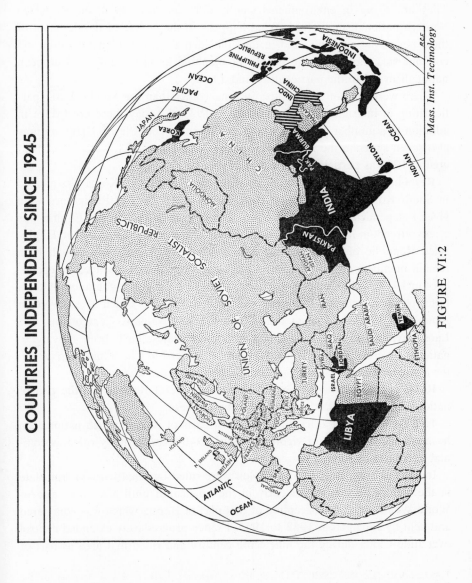

COUNTRIES INDEPENDENT SINCE 1945

Mass. Inst. Technology

FIGURE VI:2

179

These newer nationalisms which represent one phase of a revolution through which Asia is passing, reflect the strivings of more than half the human race. They are rising in environments wholly different from those out of which Western nationalism evolved. What happens in the course of development of these newer nationalisms, and in the coincidental growth of nationalism and communism, may affect the history of mankind as profoundly as European nationalism did in the past century and a half.

There were six political entities in Asia (other than the Middle East) participating in international relations before 1939.[36] Today there are twelve in addition to a number of others recognized by some countries.[37] There are now also seven states in the Asiatic part of the Near East which were not considered in 1939 as participants in world affairs.

Responsive to the urging of nationalism, the Republic of Korea was erected in South Korea after liberation from Japan in 1945. The Philippines were given independent statehood in 1946. The former British Indian Empire was granted freedom in 1947 and divided into two independent states—the Hindu-ruled Republic of India and the Moslem state of Pakistan—although both remain members of the (British) Commonwealth. Burma received independence in 1947, while Ceylon was changed from a colony to a dominion. After a bitter political struggle, Indonesia was accepted by the Dutch as a sovereign republic in 1949. In French Indo-China the Viet-Namese, Cambodians, and Laos, dividing French Indo-China into three states, have been moving to national sovereign status. Under communist leadership China has been asserting a violent nationalist-communist animus against the West.

Reasons for Nationalist Surge. There are several reasons for the rise of nationalism in Asia. Let us identify some of these.

✓ 1. By-product of colonialism. Most parts of Asia in which nationalism has manifested itself most vigorously since 1940 were formerly ruled as colonial territories by foreign powers.

India, Pakistan, Burma, and Ceylon were ruled by Great Britain from late in the eighteenth century or early in the nineteenth until after the close of World War II, with the exception of that part of Burma which was conquered and held by Japan from 1942 to 1945. France progressively extended control over Indo-China during the nineteenth century and ruled that area as part of

---

[36] Japan, China, the USSR, Thailand, India, Afghanistan. India was a Member of the League of Nations and a party to various conventions, although it did not become an independent state until 1947.

[37] Present-day generally recognized states in Asia are: Japan, two Chinas, the USSR, Republic of Korea, Philippine Republic, Indonesia, Thailand, Burma, India, Pakistan, Afghanistan. Political entities recognized by some countries include: Viet-Nam, Cambodia, Laos, Ceylon, Nepal, Bhutan, Mongolian People's Republic. Of these latter political entities, the United States maintains diplomatic relations with Ceylon, Nepal, Laos, Viet-Nam, and Cambodia.

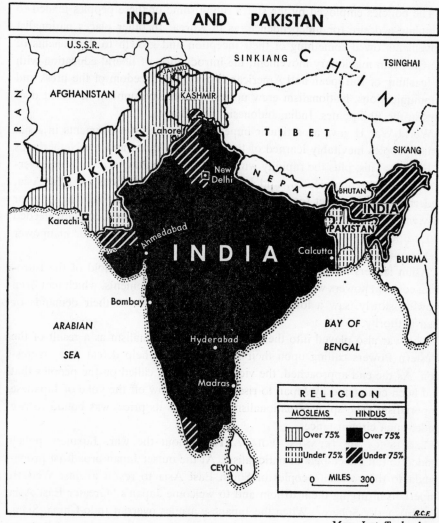

Mass. Inst. Technology

FIGURE VI:3

the French Empire until World War II, when it was occupied by Japan. The Philippines, ruled by Spain from the sixteenth century until 1898, were governed by the United States until its full independence was granted in 1946, excepting also for the interlude of Japanese occupation in World War II. Indonesia was a colony of the Netherlands from the end of the eighteenth century, and was subject also to Japan from 1942 to 1945. Korea was part of the Japanese Empire from 1910.

The policies employed by the states ruling some of these peoples tended to stimulate a desire for independence, as in Korea. In other places nationalist movements owed something of their inception and growth to the benefits of the Christian missionary movement, the introduction of liberal education with its teaching of European and American history, and freedom of the press and communications. Nationalism grew up in such an environment in recent decades in the Philippines, India, Indonesia, and Burma.

World War II gave a particular impetus to nationalist movements in Asia. Asian peoples inevitably learned of the defeat of France and the Netherlands in Europe. This, plus the rapidity with which the Japanese armed forces overran British, French, Dutch, and even American possessions in East Asia, undermined the respect for and the fear of Western rule. Britain, fighting for survival and having to concentrate its power where it was most crucially needed in Europe, North Africa, and the Near East, called upon India for manpower and supplies.

Asian leaders sensed the changing power situation. The hold of the European colonial powers was undermined. Nationalist movements, which had been growing slowly, saw a long-awaited opportunity to assert their demands or their authority.

The war also played into the hands of Asian nationalism as a result of the Western Powers calling upon their Asian wards to help defeat Axis aggression. As the end approached, the victorious powers called on the peoples that had been conquered by Japan to rise and help throw off the yoke of Japanese imperialism. The spirit of nationalism, as well as its price, was bound to rise under such circumstances.

2. EFFECT OF JAPANESE POLICY. Throughout the war, Japanese policy tended to fan the embers of nationalism. At the outset Japan broadcast propaganda to the colonial peoples of South East Asia to revolt against Western imperialism, urging them to join and to welcome Japan's "Greater East Asia Co-Prosperity Sphere." When the Japanese armies overran Indo-China, Siam, Malaya, Burma, the Philippines, and Indonesia, their procedures failed, on the whole, to gain popular support. In Indonesia, in particular, concessions ultimately had to be made to native leaders to prevent sabotage of their military and economic programs. These concessions gave confidence to native elements.

Finally, as the war drew to a close, Japan put two trumps into play. Seeing the handwriting on the wall for their own doom as the allied forces gathered strength close to the heart of Japan itself, the Japanese (1) started propaganda, especially in Indonesia and Indo-China, for local nationalism, and (2) when the day of surrender came, laid down some of their arms to native leaders before Western forces were able to receive them. In this way they contributed to preventing a return in East Asia to the political *status quo ante* of 1939. Moreover, they provided nationalist movements with valuable caches of arms to oppose reinstitution of Western colonial rule.[38] On the whole, it can be said the Japanese policy and tactics during the war gave a fillip to nationalism. Whether the states which have become independent since the war can gain sufficient strength to resist communism or aggression without external protection for a long time is a moot question in the light of events in Indo-China and Korea.

3. SOVIET PROPAGANDA. Moscow has further fanned the flames of nationalism in Asia by widespread propaganda in favor of social revolution and independence from so-called Western imperialism. Wherever possible, within Asia and in the meetings of the United Nations, the Kremlin's diplomats pose as the friends of "oppressed colonial peoples" seeking independence. In abetting the forces of nationalism, Soviet policy has at the same time been seeking its own ulterior objectives of communist seizure of power, as evidenced in China, North Korea, and Indo-China, together with the subsequent drawing of the communist-dominated lands behind its Iron (or "Bamboo") Curtain.

Problems Posed for West. Nationalism and social revolution in Asia pose troublesome problems for the West. The movements are also anticolonial and suspicious of the West. The new nations are inexperienced and generally not stable. Communism poses as the champion of this new nationalism. This raises the question how the Western Powers can oppose communism (with its inherent expansion of Soviet imperialism) without seeming to interfere with or block legitimate nationalist movements, and at the same time promote independence and social reform. For reform is needed to assist Asia's oppressed and underprivileged peoples, not only to attain a decent standard of living but as well to erect bulwarks against native exploitation, the threat of communism, and possible foreign aggression. The problem has presented itself to the United States in another form: How far should the United States go in supporting nationalism in possessions, both Asian and others, of European Powers whose friendship and strength are needed in the over-all struggle against communism?

Prime Minister Nehru of India has stated the issue clearly. He says that Asia's peoples have no love for communism but they will not lend their support to America in a crusade against communism *per se*.[39] General Romulo of the Philippine Republic has given his view that to most of Asia's peoples

---

[38] See ch. viii, pp. 248–249 below.
[39] See interview with Robert Trumbull, "Nehru Talks of the East and West," *The New York Times Magazine,* Aug. 20, 1950.

"democracy," as the West knows it, is an unknown if not opposed concept.[40] The problem the United States has had in its policy toward China, with respect to Indonesia and Indo-China and in enlisting Indian support against communist aggression in Korea and greater Asia, highlights the dilemma produced by the simultaneous rise of Asian nationalism and communist expansion. Concerned for its own security, handicapped by the often conflicting demands of its commitments to European friends and allies, as well as to the cause of independence and justice in Asia, the United States struggles to find a viable policy.

NATURE OF ASIAN NATIONALISM

Resemblance to European Nationalism. There is a superficial resemblance between the nationalisms active in Asia today and their liberal European counterparts of the nineteenth century in the familiar demands for national cultural development and political self-determination. The formation of India and Pakistan from the British Indian Empire, the establishment of the United States of Indonesia out of the Netherlands Indies, and the creation of the Republic of Korea resemble figuratively the upsurge of nationalism in Europe which resulted in the independence of the Balkan states from the Ottoman Empire, the break-up of the Austro-Hungarian Empire into the succession states of Central Europe, and the appearance of independent national states in Poland, Finland, Lithuania, Latvia, and Estonia in 1918.

The protracted disputes over boundaries among the European national states also find a parallel in the struggle between India and Pakistan over Kashmir, and between the Republic of Indonesia and native groups in the East Indies who are opposed to Republican rule.

Differences from European Liberal Nationalism. Fundamental differences cancel out these surface resemblances. The new nationalisms generally do not rest upon strong middle classes, but in most instances upon uneducated, poverty-stricken masses of peasants. In none of the Asian countries experiencing nationalist movements are the concepts of the "rights of man" and fundamental freedoms, embodied in the rationalist philosophy of the late eighteenth century and the Christian religion ingrained in the traditions of Western society, foundational elements of the nationalistic drive.

Although many nationalist leaders in Asia have been educated within the traditions of Western liberalism, they are divided among themselves as to whether this philosophy is appropriate to the conditions existent within Asia. Moreover, they are being forced to act in a situation charged with communist

---

[40] Speech at Harvard University Commencement, *Harvard Alumni Bulletin*, July 8, 1950, pp. 753–754.

pressures and with local moods calling for independence from the West. The combination of these circumstances produces in some countries a desire for a measure of "neutralism" in the struggle between the Western Powers and the Soviet bloc and of nonidentification with such programs as the United States Mutual Security Program. Communist propaganda attempts, moreover, to identify its aims with local traditions and customs and to imply that the Soviet Union has more to offer in its experience than the Western capitalist nations in the solution of the pressing economic and social problems found in the Asian countries. Arguments are not without an appeal to the impoverished and uneducated masses.

The most striking difference between contemporary Asian nationalism and nineteenth-century nationalism is that, for the bulk of the colonial peoples desiring independence, nationalism is identified with anti-imperialism. Once independence is achieved, new concepts are needed to maintain national spirit. Unfortunately, these have not always been found; and there has been some tendency to continue harping upon anti-imperialism and memories of the past to excuse lack of performance under self-rule.[41]

NATIONALISM IN THE NEAR EAST AND IN NORTH AFRICA

As in Asia, developments in the Near East and in North Africa have been characterized since the end of World War I by an increasingly nationalistic emphasis. Seeking, above all, the achievement of formal political independence, the nations of this predominantly Arab region have been, on the whole, successful, and have witnessed as late as January 1, 1952, the grant of complete independence to Libya. With the exception of Tunisia, Algeria, and Morocco, all Arab territories are now independent.

Having achieved external independence, many of these nations, owing to the impact of World War II, have sought to establish greater internal control over their territory and resources, many of which have continued to be controlled by foreign-owned companies or by foreign governments. This tendency has found poignant illustration in the Iranian oil crisis and the Egyptian-British crisis over Suez.

On the whole, the new Near Eastern nationalism tends to assume a rebellious, mass-demonstrative, and internationally precipitous character, although motivated without doubt by high national ideals. It tends to employ methods which, in effect, delay the consummation of mutually agreeable solutions.[42]

41 See N. M. Roy, "Asian Nationalism," *Yale Rev.*, Sept., 1952.
42 For general information on Near Eastern nationalism see G. Antonius, *The Arab Awakening* (New York, 1939); R. N. Frye, *The Near East and the Great Powers* (Cambridge, Mass., 1951); R. Montague, "Modern Nations and Islam," *Foreign Affairs*, July, 1952; J. Hurewitz, *Middle East Dilemma* (New York, 1953).

Iran. Strategically located at the crossroads of Europe, Asia, and Africa, Iran since 1945 has been rent with urban unrest and a growing nationalist resentment against foreign powers. Fanned by well-focused communist propaganda and by international developments, this trend has grown into a proud and defiant hypernationalism which, while gratifying the desire for unrestricted sovereignty, has brought the country to the brink of economic disaster.

The xenophobic character of this Iranian nationalism draws on a series of unpleasant experiences with foreign nations in the recent past. In 1907 Iran was divided into three spheres of influence—Russian in the north, British in the south, and neutral in between. In World War I, its territory became a battleground for Russian, British, and Turkish troops. In World War II, its strategic position led to the occupation of the country by Soviet and Western military contingents. When, at the end of the war, Soviet troops refused to withdraw while setting up in the northern provinces a pro-communist puppet regime, only strong United Nations pressure brought about the withdrawal of the Soviet army in 1946.

The heritage of resentment against foreign interference came to a climax in the Anglo-Iranian oil dispute. The production, refining, and world distribution of Iranian oil has been handled in the past by a company whose controlling stock was acquired by the British government. A treaty with Iran, concluded in 1933, extended the legal concession-rights of the company to 1993. Since 1947, however, a sequence of developments, including Iranian legislation prohibiting the granting of further leases, the demand for higher royalties, and the assassination of an allegedly pro-British Prime Minister, led to nationalization of the oil industry in 1951 and to a drawn-out crisis with Great Britain. As a consequence of this, complete stoppage of Iran's oil production occurred and with it a heavy loss of revenue to the government in Teheran, facing the defiant nationalist Premier Mossadegh with the possibility of complete economic collapse and therewith danger to Iranian independence. This stalemate entered another phase in 1953 with a coup ousting Mossadegh and placing a government friendly to the Shah in power. But the same underlying dangers remained: a weak fiscal and financial system, a weak political system, an emotional people easily turned to mob action, a strong Communist party (Tudeh), and an inexperienced people politically.

Egypt. Egypt has been an independent state since 1922. Not satisfied with this formal achievement of sovereignty, the nationalist Wafd party, until very recently the main political force in Egypt, continued wherever possible an anti-British course. This has found expression principally in disputes over the use of the waters of the Nile, the future of the Sudan, and over the large British military base at the Suez Canal. While the Nile waters problem was solved by compromise in 1929, the political problems of the Sudan and of the Suez base have persisted. After the assumption of power by the popular General Naguib and the forced abdication and exile of King Farouk in 1952, the disputes over the Anglo-Egyptian Condominium in the Sudan led to a crisis and to negotiations which, early in 1953, ended by an agreement to leave the future status of the Sudan up to the Sudanese themselves.

The discovery of a mutually agreeable and equitable solution of the problem of the strategically vital British base at the Suez Canal, guarding not only the Canal and the Empire routes converging on it but also the whole Near Eastern-North African region, involved issues of far greater magnitude. Exploiting the success achieved in the Sudan question and responding to the genuine desires of the Egyptian people, Premier Naguib adopted an ideological program of "liberation" that demanded, regardless of existing treaties, military evacuation by Great Britain of a base involving an investment of over a billion dollars and hardly replaceable.[43]

It is likely that ultimately the Iranian and Egyptian national demands will end in a compromise solution becoming acceptable, with passage of time, to all interested parties. What the West, however, seeks to establish is that *peaceful change* can occur only *by orderly procedures of law,* and not by arbitrary and one-sided abrogations of treaties or by the pressure of inspired mob demonstrations.

Tunisia and Morocco. The defeat of French arms in 1940, the internal instability of France in the first eight years of peace with her need for foreign economic aid, her rebuffs in the Indo-Chinese war, and the successes registered by Arab peoples to the East, led in the latter part of 1952 to nationalist riots and disorders in Tunisia and Morocco. The important aspects of these uprisings were that (1) for the first time they were coordinated in both Tunisia and Morocco, (2) they elicited some favorable response in world public opinion, and (3) the North African nationalists sought to bring their case against France before the United Nations. Timely French policy and political action quieted the situation—at least for the time being. Nevertheless, it can be assumed reasonably that here, too, nationalist forces will continue to press for readjustment of their relationship to France and for a wider degree of national self-government.[44] In 1954 Tunis was granted self-government, becoming responsible for all affairs except military and foreign matters.

[43] See able survey of Egyptian scene by John Badeau in "The Emergence of Modern Egypt," For. Pol. Assoc., *Headline Series,* No. 98, April, 1953. See also "The Anglo-Egyptian Sudan," British Information Services, June, 1951; "Great Britain Approves New Constitution for Sudan Providing Self-Government in Internal Affairs," *The New York Times,* Oct. 23, 1952.

[44] For a statement on United States policy in the Middle East see H. A. Byroade, "U. S. Foreign Policy in the Middle East," in *Department of State Bulletin,* Dec. 15, 1952; W. Polk and W. Butler, "What the Arabs Think," For. Pol. Assoc. *Headline Series,* No. 96; "New U. S. Policy in the Middle East," *Foreign Policy Bulletin,* Aug. 1, 1953.

ECONOMIC NATIONALISM

Economic nationalism has been an active force in the twentieth century. It had its apex in the United States in the notorious Smoot-Hawley tariff of 1930 and in the refusal to enter into international economic arrangements in 1933 directed toward relieving the world-wide effects of the depression. In Nazi Germany it exhibited itself in a policy known as *Autarkie* which aimed at minimizing the dependence of the nation upon foreign trade. Economic nationalism has continued in the post-war period, although the dislocations produced by World War II and the threat of communism have called forth an increased measure of collaboration.

International Economic Cooperation. At the close of World War II there was widespread recognition that economic problems resulting from hostilities would require international cooperation for their alleviation and solution. As a consequence, many nations including the United States, joined in forming and underwriting the United Nations Food and Agriculture Organization, the United Nations Relief and Rehabilitation Organization (UNRRA), the International Bank for Reconstruction and Development, and the International Monetary Fund. These were followed by the establishment of the United Nations European Recovery Program, an Organization for European Economic Cooperation, a European Payments Union, a General Agreement on Trade and Tariffs, and the formation of the European Coal and Steel Community.[45]

Continuance of Economic Nationalism. Notwithstanding this remarkable display of international cooperation there remain many evidences of economic nationalism. This factor is partially responsible for restrictions upon foreign trade, quotas or tariffs imposed upon certain types of imports, regulations fixed upon the convertibility of currency or the use of foreign exchange, and the failure of the effort to establish an International Trade Organization.[46]

The advanced industrial nations of the West are by no means the only ones practicing economic nationalism. The strongest proponents of economic nationalism include some of the so-called underdeveloped countries and nations undergoing industrial growth. The Soviet Union has evidenced an extreme economic nationalism since World War II, having refused to join most of the specialized international agencies, to participate in the European Recovery Program, or to collaborate in any general multilateral reductions in trade and

45 For further discussion of economic activities and organizations see chs. xx and xxi.
46 For discussion of ITO negotiations see Clair Wilcox, *The Charter of the International Trade Organization* (New York, 1947). See also C. A. Hickam and Others, *World Economic Problems* (New York, 1947).

exchange barriers. Economic cooperation in the foreseeable future can probably be achieved only along step-by-step lines rather than through far-reaching, universal schemes. But much has been accomplished since World War II when contrasted with international economic affairs in the decades between the two wars.

NATIONALISM AND INTERNATIONALISM [47]

Nationalism and Conflict. The brutal excesses of Nazi Germany have shown what widespread destruction can result when nationalism becomes an end in itself and combines with modern technology to produce total war. But even where nationalism has not taken such extreme form, elements of dangerous conflict exist.

The humanity of Mazzini's concept of nationalism a century ago is seldom heard today.[48] Some idealists may place service to humanity first in their scale of values. But on the whole, men act on the principle that their highest loyalty is to the nation-state. In times of crisis, even those whose religious and ethical beliefs transcend the nation largely correlate their ideals with the requirements of the national emergency.

There is much that is good in nationalism. It has served a useful purpose in integrating large groups of people into political communities and giving them a sense of belonging. It has enabled states to promote the general welfare for the common man. It has spurred men to sacrifice for the achievement of social gains, and it has provided a basis for nation-wide acceptance of law and order.

When nationalism has become *wholly* an end in itself, however, and has sought to impress extreme and exclusive objects upon others, it has ended, as have some religious faiths and ideologies, in destroying freedom, compromising the general welfare, and producing warfare. At such a point nationalism may destroy human values which it sought to serve.

This danger, plus the fact that nationalism has been a cause of conflict within the international community, has prompted some to ask: What is the alternative?

Limitations of Nationalism. Whatever longing some people may have for "internationalism," there is no higher political entity than the nation-state. The United Nations, whatever its potentialities, is an organization of sovereign states; it is not an entity higher than the states which compose it. It has no provision for nationals of any country who may dislike the rule of their govern-

[47] See E. M. Earle (ed.), *Nationalism and Internationalism* (New York, 1950).
[48] See above, p. 167.

ment becoming "United Nations nationals" with guaranteed civic rights or protection from the police of their state.

Is moderate nationalism the only hope of counteracting totalitarian nationalism? Is there any prospect of its realization in totalitarian-ruled lands short of some major upheaval? Is there any possibility of some international spirit rising to supersede extreme nationalism? These are pertinent questions. But there are few ready answers.

There are positive values in nationalism which no one would wish to give up. Those who believe in the universality of the principles of self-determination of peoples would hardly deny those subject to alien rule the means of achieving independence and material dignity which nationalist movements have conferred upon others.

From the point of view of the individual placing great value on freedom and human liberties, there is a danger that any "internationalism" which attempts to make the world "one" may tend itself to become an absolute and to lose the values it attempts to create. This is revealed in such schemes for world domination as expressed in fascist, nazi, and communist theories. It may also be true of any single system of values, as for example the idea of world government, or conversion of mankind to a single religious and ethical system.

Trial and Error. There is no assurance that internationalism would be a wise or workable replacement of nationalism. "One World," if it is ever realized in the idealistic sense in which that phrase was coined by Wendell Willkie, must come gradually as a result of trial and error. It cannot be produced by force of arms in some great *Pax Romana,* or by the force of an ideology which some nation or group attempts to impose upon all men for all times.

Any guiding principle less than a belief in the oneness of humanity, based on the premise of the supreme value of the individual, is quite capable of leading to further division and conflict. Change, in so far as it occurs, must come about in the minds of men. The single, isolated nation-state cannot give men full security or enable them to attain the highest standards of living. On a small scale and in limited ways this realization begins to force itself upon man's consciousness, as evidenced by the measures for international cooperation which have been taken in recent years.

The Challenge of the Present. The test for the validity of any attempts toward some principle of wider compass than nationalism must be the extent to which it actually advances the well-being and security of each people in its own society and environment, as well as in the world community as a whole, without undermining or destroying the beneficial values which moderate nationalism has in many circumstances been able to convey.

Preserving these values while curbing the excesses of intolerance and hypernationalism, or sublimating them into internationally constructive channels, is one of the grave challenges confronting civilization today. For, as Arnold Toynbee has warned in his *Study of History,* civilization runs the risk of annihilation with the instruments of modern technology in the hands of a parochial or totalitarian nationalism.

SUGGESTED READINGS

Jacques Barzun, *Race: A Study in Modern Superstition* (New York, 1937).
Edward H. Carr, *Nationalism and After* (New York, 1945).
Karl W. Deutsch, *Nationalism and Social Communication* (New York, 1953).
E. M. Earle, ed., *Nationalism and Internationalism* (New York, 1950).
C. J. H. Hayes, *Essays on Nationalism* (New York, 1926).
———. *The Historic Evolution of Modern Nationalism* (New York, 1948).
Frederick Hertz, *Nationality in History and Politics: A Study of the Psychology and Sociology of National Sentiment and Character* (London, 1944).
W. L. Holland, ed., *Asian Nationalism and the West* (New York, 1953).
Hans Kohn, *The Idea of Nationalism, A Study of Its Origins and Background* (New York, 1944).
George Lenczowski, *The Middle East in World Affairs* (Ithaca, 1952).
Royal Institute of International Affairs, *Nationalism: A Report* (London, 1939).
T. C. Young, *Near East Culture and Society* (Princeton, 1952).

CHAPTER VII

The Struggle for Power; Power Politics

IN THE preceding chapters we have noted five fundamental elements affecting international relations: the influence of environment, the world's population, the economic needs of states, psychological factors, and the force of nationalism. We must now consider a sixth factor, the struggle for power in world politics.

POWER IN WORLD POLITICS

At any period in modern history one of the prominent features of international politics has been a struggle for power among states. The central feature of world politics today is the struggle between the Soviet Union and the Western Powers. This is seen and felt in nearly every phase of international affairs. It affects the United Nations. It penetrates world economic conditions. It appears continually in the headlines of the newspapers. There is scarcely a nation or group of people throughout the globe that is not touched in one way or another, directly or indirectly, by the competition and conflict between the Great Powers. Struggles for power are not limited solely to the Great Powers. They occur as well between the lesser powers and small states, as witnessed in the struggles between the Balkan states, the rivalry between India and Pakistan, and the conflict between the Arab states and Israel.

Politics and Power. At whatever level in society politics occurs, it involves competition for positions of influence, social control, and power in the broad sense of the word. The purpose of political action is to serve personal, group, or national ends through political instrumentalities and the gaining of positions or objectives in order to influence or control the behavior of individuals and groups. Because political power is an essential element in the organization and preservation of society, and confers large opportunities and benefits as well as responsibilities upon those in positions of power and authority, the struggle

192

for power has accompanied the course of mankind within states and among them.[1]

Within orderly domestic societies, competition for power and the play of politics take place within a framework of accepted rules and customs, with the right to employ force vested exclusively in the hands of the public authorities. The competition for power among states is, however, subject to few rules or to few universally shared ideas and moral concepts. There are some customs. There is international law, but it does not preclude struggles for power or have the means of preventing them. States have been willing to join in international organizations to "maintain international peace and security," and have on occasions, within alliances or for certain peace-enforcement actions, been agreeable to pooling national units. They have not, however, been prepared to create a single world authority having a monopoly of the right to use armed forces. Consequently, the self-willed threat and use of force play a correspondingly freer and larger role in international politics than in the civil life of national states and domestic communities. This is a cardinal fact in world politics.

Considerations of power, in the broad sense, are virtually always associated, directly or indirectly, with politics among states. Competitions among states for supplies of raw materials, for markets, for political leadership and positions of influence or prestige, for ascendancy in armed strength and a favorable balance of power, as well as for territorial possessions and spheres of influence, are essentially struggles for power.

The Nature of National Power. What is meant when we speak of the *power* of a state? The term implies possession of physical and military strength and capability. But in the broad sense in which the term is employed in speaking of the struggle for power among states in international politics, it involves more than this. National power may be defined as the sum total of the strength and capabilities of a state harnessed and applied to the advancement of its national interests and the attainment of its national objectives.

The power of a state is compounded from many elements which are constantly interacting with one another. We have discussed some of these elements in the preceding chapters. These include such factors as geographical position and the ability to capitalize on environmental circumstances, size, natural resources, population, industrial and economic strength, scientific and technical knowledge, plus ability to apply these to production and to the creation

1 See Franz Neumann, "Approaches to the Study of Political Power," *Pol. Sci. Quar.*, June, 1950; M. A. Ash, "An Analysis of Power with Special Reference to International Politics," *World Politics*, Jan., 1951; Hans Morgenthau, *Politics Among Nations* (New York, 1954); Bertrand Russell, *Power: A Social Analysis* (New York, 1938); Georg Schwarzenberger, *Power Politics* (New York, 1951).

and use of armaments, governmental stability and efficiency, military establishment, and a host of other items. Also included are the more subtle but by no means less important elements of national morale, qualities of social cohesion and unity of action, the role of personalities, political leadership, statecraft, and the good will a country enjoys abroad. The importance of the element of political leadership was shown in the growth and initiative of British power when Winston Churchill succeeded Neville Chamberlain as Prime Minister in 1940. The weakening effect of a lack of firm leadership has been displayed, on the other hand, in the repeated instances of French impotence brought on by the instability of its governments.

THE INSTRUMENTS OF POWER AND POLICY

In the competitions which arise among states for the satisfaction of their self-interest and the attainment of their national objectives, which are the forces producing international politics, these various constituent elements are welded together by government to become the national power of the state. They are projected into international politics to further the interests of states through a variety of instruments and patterns of policy which we shall enumerate in Chapter XVI.

It is customary to categorize power as being "economic" and "military" as well as "political" and "psychological." These categorizations arise because of the ways in which power is manifested by a state. National power can be measured by considering its parts, but even then the most important manifestation—political power—is least measurable.[2]

Appraising the Power of States. Appraising the power of states is a difficult task. The whole power of a state is not equal to the sum of its tangible or physical parts. The factors of statesmanship, moral strength, attitudes, and degree of military readiness, though imponderables, play a large part in determining the strength of states. Furthermore, even if an exact calculus were possible, the absolute answers would be meaningless except as a basis for comparison, for all power is relative.

Consider, for example, the widely varying degrees of power which estimates would show, for such nations as India, Argentina, China, Israel, Yugoslavia, Italy, Iran, and the Soviet Union when viewed from (1) the economic, political, and military aspects separately, (2) the outlook of their immediate neighbors, and (3) the point of view of the United States. In each instance the sum of the power factors pertaining to any given state has a particular and different meaning when viewed in relation to the comparative positions and policies of

2 For a discussion of the manifestations of power see E. H. Carr, *Twenty Years' Crisis, 1919-1939* (London, 1946), ch. 8.

other states near and far, greater and smaller, friendly and opposed, and when considered in the light of the policies and objectives the states concerned are pursuing.

ROLE OF PERSUASION, COERCION, FORCE

In peaceful international relations as in national affairs, reasoning, persuasion, the offering of material benefits, and bargaining with the background presence of force are the principal means by which one state seeks to augment its political power in the international community and to influence other states for purposes advantageous to itself. Power politics under such circumstances are played much as domestic politics by means of a psychological relationship.

Some element of coercive force is nearly always present, in latent or active guise, wherever politics takes place. In the society of states each sovereign state maintains some form of armed establishment for defense or for use, if need be, in augmenting the power of the state to maintain its position and prestige in world affairs, or to enforce its rights, demands, or views upon others. The history of international politics has been studded with wars and almost innumerable instances of resort by states to coercive measures against one another, as we shall note in Chapter IX.

OBJECTIVES IN POWER STRUGGLE

In the arena of domestic politics the objectives which individuals and groups may seek in the struggle for political power are largely defined by tradition, by the nation's constitution, and by its legal system. Comparably sharp and binding definitions are lacking in international politics, save as states agree by treaty, custom, and usage to accept and act upon certain principles and rules. The Charter of the United Nations, now accepted by sixty nations, sets some boundaries for international politics. The Charter of the Organization of American States drawn up at Bogotá in 1948 likewise embodies a set of principles and rules in accordance with which the American Republics have agreed to conduct their relations with one another. Other treaties and agreements establish bounds for power politics among the parties adhering to them.

Aside from such treaties and agreements, and the more indefinite customs and usages of international relations, each state is largely free to pursue such objectives toward other states as it sees fit, although international law has long prescribed that each state should respect the equal rights and privileges of other sovereign states.[3] In political and economic affairs this has not proved to be very restrictive upon the policies and actions of states.

---

[3] See ch. xix below.

Main Types of Objectives. Within the international political scene prevailing at any given time, states, broadly speaking, will pursue one or other of the following general policy directions. They will attempt (1) to preserve the state's relative power position in the world community and to maintain the international *status quo;* (2) to accumulate power in order to better the position of the state within the prevailing power alignment; or (3) to change the existing balance.

The objectives held by states in the international competition for power depend upon the conception which each has of its own interests and ambitions. The policies which are pursued may be within the framework of the existing structure of world power and political relationships or may demand that a state attempt to bring about a radical alteration in that structure as in the case of Napoleon I of France, Imperial and later Nazi Germany, and Soviet Russia.

Influence of Great Power Policies. The world political scene is largely influenced at any given time by the policies and relations of the then Great Powers. Small and middle-power states may at times exercise an important influence in international politics, but by and large the temper of relations between the most powerful states determines the main outlines of international political relationships. If the relations between the Great Powers are harmonious, other states may be free to pursue one set of objectives. If relations between the powers are fraught with conflict and one or more of them is striving to overturn the balance of power, then the objectives and policies of states desiring to preserve the existent political structure of the society of nations are bound to be modified accordingly in order to defend this status.

Influence of Treaty Framework. The pattern of world politics often reflects, for certain periods of time, the results of a major war or revolutionary disturbance. War, indeed, is one of the principal means by which political equilibrium within the international community is readjusted. Thus, the Treaty of Versailles, which ended World War I, together with its Covenant of the League of Nations, set the *milieu* within which power politics occurred between 1920 and 1939, as the arrangements established at the Congress of Vienna in 1815 and immediately thereafter—following the Napoleonic Wars—had a far-reaching influence upon nineteenth-century international relations.[4] Similarly, the *de facto* situation resulting from World War II and the agreements recorded in the Treaties of Peace of 1947 and 1950, and the San Francisco United Nations Charter, have set the framework within which many facets of contemporary power politics are taking place and will continue to do so for some time to come.

4 See below, pp. 201–202.

THE BALANCE OF POWER SYSTEM

If the quest for power is the common denominator of international politics, as indicated in the preceding discussion; if politics in fact means the manipulation of power with a view to achieving specific goals—then it is evident that the long competition of states for power would lead to perpetual tension and open conflict if there were not some limitations upon power politics to reconcile these quests and to help maintain international peace and security. Chief among these self-attempted limitations has been the balance of power system.

Principle of the System. The balance of power concept is based on the assumption and the historical experience that the possession of overwhelming power by one state or group of states is likely to result in subjugation or conquest of weaker states, thereby jeopardizing their security, integrity, and independence. The principle of the balance of power therefore calls for creating a system of counterweights to offset the overly powerful or aggressive-minded as a means of deterring or counteracting threats to peace and security.

The term *balance of power* is used in diplomacy and in common parlance with various meanings, and the precise meaning, in any given instance, must be determined from the context. The following discussion will, it is hoped, provide a guide to these meanings.

The French philosopher Fénelon expressed the underlying motivation of the balance of power principle when he said: "To hinder one's neighbor from becoming too strong is not to do harm; it is to guarantee one's self and one's neighbors from subjugation; in a word, it is to work for liberty, tranquillity, and public safety; because the aggrandizement of one nation beyond a certain limit changes the general system of all nations connected with it." The excessive aggrandizement of one, he added, "may mean the ruin and subjection of all the other neighbors." Hence, he concluded, "attention to the equilibrium between neighboring states is what assures peace for all." [5]

Evolution of System. Applications of the principle, whether formally recognized as such or not, can be traced far back into history. David Hume, in his essay on the balance of power, quotes Polybius' comments upon the aid sent by Hiero of Syracuse to Carthage in its struggle with Rome to the effect that if Carthage were not preserved, the remaining power—Rome—"should be able, without control or opposition, to execute every purpose and undertaking." A force should never be allowed to become so great, added Polybius, "as

---

[5] François Fénelon, *Oeuvres* (Paris, 1835), vol. III, p. 361. See also characterization by Swiss jurist Emmerich Vattel, *The Law of Nations* (Eng. trans., ed. by J. Chitty, Philadelphia, 1854), pp. 135–136, 311–312.

to incapacitate the neighboring states from defending their rights against it." [6]

Rome, the Emperor Charlemagne, and the rulers of the Holy Roman Empire sought to establish domination in Europe rather than a balance of power among sovereign states. But the princes and rulers of the Italian city states and budding national monarchies, from the time of the Renaissance on, employed compacts and alliances to prevent the most powerful political entities from gaining dominion over them all. Machiavelli, in his writings on *The Prince,* expressed the principle of preserving the balance of power when he warned his patron about "a general rule, which never or very rarely fails, that whoever is the cause of another becoming powerful, is ruined himself." It remained to the rulers of the national states who drew up the Peace of Westphalia in 1648 to lay the foundations of the balance of power system as we know it nowadays. For the Peace of Westphalia deliberately sought to erect a counterpoise to the pretensions and power of the Hapsburgs and the Holy Roman Empire. Again, at the Peace of Utrecht in 1713, by a division of the possessions of the Houses of the Hapsburgs and of Bourbon, an effort was made to establish a "European equilibrium" through a balance of power of strong and weak states. Since that time many of the treaties and compacts entered into by the European states have been concluded with the objective of the establishment or maintenance of a balance of power. And during the twentieth century the principle has been amplified to a global one.

Reduced to a simplified context, the balance of power concept may refer to (1) the equation of power among states and (2) use of the principle as a guide to foreign policy.[7]

The Equation of Power. The term *balance of power* has been used, first, to describe the equation and distribution of power existing among states at any given time. Thus, when it is said that "World War II changed the world balance of power," it is meant that, because of the war, the power ratios among the states of the world underwent alteration, with some states emerging with relatively less power, others—especially the United States and the USSR—coming out of the struggle with relatively greater power.[8]

In the equation of power among states, there may of course be either (1) an approximate equilibrium of power between two states or groups of states, or (2) a preponderance of power on one side.

---

[6] David Hume, "Of the Balance of Power," *Essays and Treatises on Several Subjects* (Edinburgh, 1825), vol. I, pp. 331–339. For a general discussion of the principle see Sidney B. Fay, "Balance of Power," in the *Encyclopedia of the Social Sciences.*

[7] See Alfred Vagts, "The Balance of Power—Growth of an Idea," *World Politics,* Dec., 1948; Ernest B. Haas, "The Balance of Power: Prescription, Concept or Propaganda?" *ibid.,* July, 1953.

[8] Hajo Holborn, *The Political Collapse of Europe* (New York, 1951), pp. 189–190, notes that World War II proved that no Western European state could now resist Russia's power.

An approximate equilibrium of power, a sort of system of checks and balances, existed among the European states in the latter part of the nineteenth century, when England, France, Germany, Austria-Hungary, and Russia were more or less equal in strength. From 1907 to 1914 an approximate equilibrium prevailed between the Triple Alliance and the Triple Entente. The creation of a sufficient bloc of power to establish an approximate equilibrium with the Soviet Union, in order to deter it from attacking Western Europe in the post-war years or to defeat it if it should launch a war, was the initial goal of the United States and the Western European powers in forming the North Atlantic Treaty Organization in 1949, and of the United States Mutual Security Program in the early 1950's.

The action of power politics may embrace, on the other hand, the striving by some state or group of states for a definite preponderance of power. This is the sense in which it is often said that a nation or ruler is seeking "a favorable balance of power." Such a "balance" obviously may entail varying degrees of superiority in power, the ultimate being world domination in which one state may be able to subjugate or enslave weaker nations at will and to dominate in the councils of the great.

Guide to Policy. The second general meaning associated with the balance of power concept is that this should be held as a precept of policy making, a goal of statecraft, and that a nation should endeavor to hold in its own hands *the* balance of power among several states. This is the sense in which Cardinal Wolsey (1471–1530) once spoke of "that grand rule, whereby the counsels of England should always be guided, of preserving the balance of power in her hands." [9]

A "Memorandum on British Policy" written in 1907 by Sir Eyre Crowe illustrates the reasoning which underlies the adoption of this guide to policy. After noting the dangers which can arise from the "monetary predominance of a neighboring State at once militarily powerful, economically efficient, and ambitious to extend its frontiers or spread its influence," Sir Eyre observed:

The only check on the abuse of political predominance derived from such a position has always consisted in the opposition of an equally formidable rival, or of a combination of several countries forming leagues in defense. The equilibrium established by such a grouping of forces is technically known as the balance of power, and it has become almost an historical truism to identify England's secular power with the maintenance of this balance by throwing her weight now in this scale and now in that, but ever on the side opposed to the political dictatorship of the strongest single State or group at a given time.

If this view of British policy is correct, the opposition into which England must

[9] Nicholas Mansergh, *The Coming of the First World War* (London, 1949), p. 4.

inevitably be driven to any country aspiring to such a dictatorship assumes almost the form of a law of nature.

Looking to the future of British policy toward the rising and ambitious Germany, Sir Eyre Crowe offered this counsel:

So long as England remains faithful to the general principle of the preservation of the balance of power, her interests would not be served by Germany being reduced to the rank of a weak power, as this might easily lead to a Franco-Russian predominance equally, if not more, formidable to the British Empire.[10]

One can see in the words of this Memorandum the outlines of policy which Britain has followed since 1907—first, in aligning itself against Imperial Germany when this state became too aggressive before and during World War I, then in supporting the resurrection of Germany after 1923 and countering the policies of France and Russia, then once again turning against Germany when Hitler set it on the path of conquest, and after 1945, when Germany had been reduced to complete impotency, aligning itself with the United States to oppose the menace of Soviet imperialism rising from its enormous military power and hegemony over Eastern Europe. In this recent period one can also see Britain lending its support to the rise of a new democratic, free Germany as a measure to introduce an added counterweight to Soviet predominance.

Circumstances can arise in which it becomes impossible for one state to play the role of "balancer" among the Great Powers, either because the policies of one of them pose imminent dangers to the other states and it becomes necessary for all to unite against it, or because there may be such differential in power between two of the Great Powers and all other states that no third party can effectively hold a balance between them. The prevalence of such conditions has prevented Britain, France, or any other country or group of states from acting as "balancer" in the struggle for power which has been taking place between the Soviet Union and the free nations since 1945. But the foreign policies of each of these states appear to be motivated by the search for a balance of power which will give the largest measure of security.

FUNCTIONING OF THE BALANCE OF POWER, 1740–1919

To appreciate the true place which the balance of power system has played in international politics and the extent to which nations have adopted this as a

---

10 The Memorandum will be found in G. P. Gooch and H. Temperley (ed.), *British Documents on the Origins of the War, 1898–1914* (London, 1928), vol. III, pp. 397ff. Crown copyright reserved 1928. Used by permission of the Controller of Her Britannic Majesty's Stationery Office. Felix Morley in *The Foreign Policy of the United States* (New York, 1951), pp. 22–27, contends that insistence upon unconditional surrender in World War II was incompatible with a balance of power system inasmuch as it tended to destroy power elements in the global equation and therefore altered the balance among all states to the disadvantage especially of the free nations.

guide to policy, one must follow at least the broad outlines of the applications of the principle through the period of modern history. For this purpose we may begin somewhat arbitrarily with the ending of the Thirty Years' War by the Treaty of Westphalia in 1648 which undertook to establish something like an equilibrium among the states and power politics of Europe. As the power of France began to rise in the second half of the seventeenth century, European politics entered upon a period of long struggle in which there were repeated wars and shifts in political alignment. Among the earliest coalitions organized to establish a balance of power was that led by William of Orange beginning in the 1680's and lasting through the period ended by the Peace of Utrecht in 1713.

In 1740 Britain and Austria allied themselves against France and Prussia. Sixteen years later Britain became allied in war with Prussia against France and Austria. The existing arrangements proved inadequate in the early part of the Napoleonic Wars and the balance was not redressed until the Grand Coalition of Britain, Austria, Prussia, and Russia was formed by the Treaty of Chaumont in 1814. Such an extensive coalition was required to bring about the defeat of Napoleon in 1814. When he again attempted an imperialist venture in 1815, the formation of the Quadruple Alliance sealed his fate. From this Alliance historians have marked the "beginning of that formal ascendancy of the Great Powers which was to be the characteristic of the nineteenth century." [11]

Shifting Balances in Nineteenth Century. Indicative of the quickness with which power patterns change to meet new international situations, France, against whom Europe had united in 1814 and 1815, was brought into the Great Power directorate in 1818 to form the Concert of Europe and the Quintuple Alliance. Shortly thereafter, however, in 1821, Britain, under Foreign Minister Canning, withdrew from the Concert because of differences with the reactionary Holy Alliance powers (Austria, Prussia, Russia) over intervention in the smaller states of Europe to put down governments established by revolution. From then on Britain pursued a policy of aloofness from European internal disputes save as her interests became directly involved, when she would intervene on one side or the other to maintain an equilibrium favorable to her interests, that is, holding the "balance" in her own hands. This policy was stated by Canning to the House of Commons in these words: "Our duty . . . and our interests equally prescribed to us to persevere in an undeviating path, to preserve our resources entire until the period should arrive, if ever, when we might exercise our only legitimate right to interfere, from being

[11] Ward and Gooch, *The Cambridge History of British Foreign Policy* (Cambridge, 1923), vol. I, pp. 444–445.

called upon to quell the raging floods that threatened to distract the balance of Europe." [12]

As the nineteenth century progressed, the combinations shifted from time to time to meet new threats. In the 1850's, Britain, France, and Sardinia joined with Turkey in the Crimean War to repulse a Russian threat to the Turkish Straits. Austria maintained an uncertain neutrality in this war rather favorable to the allies. Prussia, on the other hand, pursued a "benevolent neutrality" toward Russia. At the Congress of Paris in 1856 all of these states undertook to uphold the settlement which recognized Turkish sovereignty at Constantinople and in the Ottoman provinces of Bulgaria and Rumania. By 1878, however, new arrangements had to be made when Russia again went to war with Turkey, ignominiously defeating it, and Austria-Hungary began to look upon the Balkans as a region for its own expansion.

German Challenge to Balance of Power. The rise of a strong, ambitious Germany further contributed to the change in the equilibrium of Europe and called forth a new power combination. By defeating France in the Franco-Prussian War of 1870–1871, Bismarck isolated France. At the Congress of Berlin in 1878 he played the role of the "honest broker" in apportioning Turkish spoils. He succeeded in reducing Russia's influence in the Balkans and thereby alienating her, while at the same time he was instrumental in handing over Bosnia and Herzegovina to Austria-Hungary and so gaining her friendship. In this way he contrived to keep a balance of power in the Balkan area while at the same time laying the foundation for an alliance between Germany and Austria-Hungary. This was extended in 1882 into the Triple Alliance by the signature of secret treaties with Italy. During this period Bismarck sought to prevent Russia from allying itself with France by means of a Three Emperors' League and a Reinsurance Treaty. Bismarck succeeded, during his ministry in gaining a favorable place for Germany, but those who followed failed to maintain this position. Apprehensive of the rising might in Central Europe and to rescue themselves from the isolation into which each of them had been thrust by Germany's actions, Russia and France entered into a secret protocol in 1891. By 1894 this became the Dual Alliance. Thus on the continent a sort of equipoise was re-established, while Britain continued an aloof but potentially balancing position.

As German ambitions became more apparent after 1900, Britain and France adjusted their differences arising from colonial rivalries and entered into the Entente Cordiale in 1904. This had been preceded by the Anglo-Japanese Alliance in 1902 which allowed Britain to devote more attention to Europe and less to the Far East. The *Entente Cordiale* was ultimately trans-

[12] *Ibid.,* vol. II, pp. 53–54.

formed into the Triple Entente of Britain, France, and Russia in 1907, after British fears of Russian expansionism had been reduced by the defeat which Japan had administered to Russia in the Russo-Japanese War of 1904–1905, and after Britain and Russia had come to an agreement upon respective spheres of influence in the Middle East.

The alignment of Triple Alliance versus Triple Entente established a situation which gave the outward appearance of an approximate two-way equilibrium of powers replacing a balance system of several powers. Actually, however, the situation was a highly dynamic one. German industry forged to the forefront in Europe. The German population became equal to and then surpassed that of France. The new German navy threatened British control of the seas. And the increased fire power of the machine-gun-equipped German army closed the margin of superiority which the larger numbers of the Entente armies had enjoyed.

When the crisis between Austria-Hungary and Serbia arose in the summer of 1914, Austria-Hungary, with the backing of Germany, was so determined to punish Serbian plottings against its power in the Balkans, it was prepared to risk a general war which came after a series of diplomatic blunderings and a chain reaction of mobilization by Russia (to protect the Little Slavs), Germany (to support Austria-Hungary against Russia), and France (to protect itself against Germany and to fulfill its commitment to Russia). The war became general as all the principal states of Europe—with the exception of Switzerland, the Scandinavian countries, and Spain—were tied into the balance system.

The Russian Czar on the eve of the war identified the core of the conflict when he wired the King of England that Austro-Hungarian control over Serbia would "upset the balance of power in the Balkans, which is of such interest to my Empire as well as to those powers who desire the maintenance of the balance of power in Europe . . . I trust your country will not fail to support France and Russia in fighting to maintain the balance of power in Europe." [13]

This appeal of the Russian Czar, and the actions which transpired in the summer of 1914, reveal how the disturbance of a localized equilibrium can produce an effect upon a larger balance of power—in this case the general European balance.

Collapse of the European Balance. Before World War I was over, the line-up on both sides changed. Italy deserted the Triple Alliance to join Britain, France, and Russia. Alarmed by the threat of Germany to the Atlantic community, by the deep thrust into France and the ruthless submarine warfare in the Atlantic, the United States threw its power into the scales against Ger-

[13] *British Documents, cit. supra,* vol. XI, p. 276.

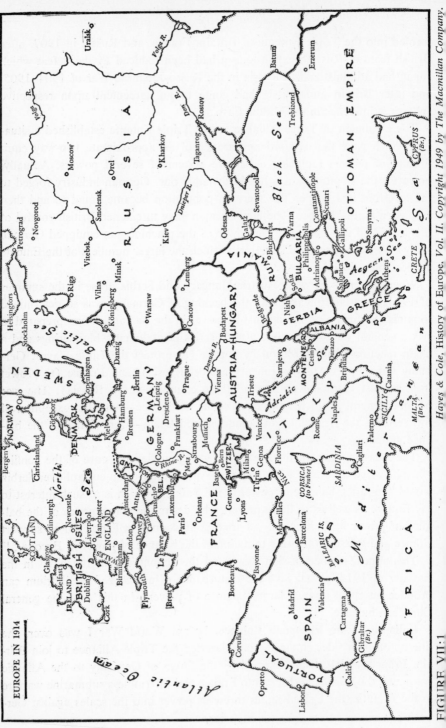

EUROPE IN 1914

FIGURE VII·1   Hayes & Cole, *History of Europe, Vol. II.* Copyright 1949 by The Macmillan Company.

many in April, 1917. Russia made a separate peace with Germany after the November (1917) Revolution, freeing Germany to concentrate upon the Western front. In the spring of 1918 Germany made its supreme bid in France to defeat the Allies but failed. Only by calling on power outside Europe was the Western European Allied coalition saved from defeat. The balance of power system, if it was to continue, would henceforth be a world system. But this fact was not too clearly recognized.

The final days of World War I saw the Central Powers collapse. The Austro-Hungarian Empire disintegrated into six separate states—Austria, Hungary, Czechoslovakia, Poland, Rumania, and Yugoslavia. Arab revolts in the Ottoman Empire weakened that partner and brought about its surrender. Bulgaria capitulated readily. Germany, weakened by losses in battle, by the strangling effects of the Allied blockade, and by unrest at home, surrendered at Compiègnes on November 11, 1918. A new array of power emerged to frame the post-war world.

THE BALANCE OF POWER, 1919–1945

The Versailles System. When the Allied and Associated Powers assembled at Paris in 1919 to draw up the peace treaty, two points of view vied for acceptance as the best means of establishing an acceptable arrangement among the powerful states of the world. France, remembering the defeat of 1870, and the close call the Allies had had in 1914 and in 1918, demanded a settlement that would weaken Germany and prevent her from again menacing European peace. France also wanted Britain and the United States to conclude a permanent treaty of alliance with her that would guarantee her security against any future German attack. President Wilson, on the other hand, wished to establish a general concert of power, to be called a League of Nations, in which all states would participate as conservators of the peace, including eventually even the defeated enemy states. The Versailles Treaty ultimately represented a compromise between these two theories.

Disintegration of the Allied Power. United States failure to ratify the Treaty of Versailles and to enter the League of Nations, or to approve a peace-time alliance with France, at once cut the ground from under the strength of the coalition that had won the war and drawn the terms of peace. From the outset the League was deprived of the power and prestige needed to enforce peace and security. Another pertinent fact was that Russia not only was not a party to the peace arrangements, and no longer allied with the Western Powers, but that its Soviet regime rejected the basic principles of Western democracy and capitalism and set itself upon a course to oppose and overthrow them wherever possible in favor of the creation of a new order of world power centered upon itself. Withdrawal of the last American troops from Germany in 1925 left France and Britain without the symbol of United States support which had enabled them to win the war. Sharp differences between Britain and France over the treatment of reviving Germany, dating from 1922 to 1923, added to the undermining of the former Allied power. Abandoned by its former allies, France resorted to a series of alliances with a number of Eastern European countries in a vain attempt to re-establish the balance of power against Germany which had already entered by the Treaty of Rapallo in 1922 into economic, political, and apparently secret military agreements with Russia.

With France standing alone in Western Europe, fearful of a shadow looming across the Rhine which history had taught her people might one day strike again with relentless fury, and with Germany also fearful of possible French aggression after the Ruhr occupation in 1923 and desirous of an assurance of the *status quo* while recouping her strength, the stage was set by 1925 for the establishment of a temporary equilibrium.

The Locarno Pacts, 1925. After laborious negotiations the Locarno Pacts were signed in 1925. In the Treaty of Mutual Guarantees which formed a part of these, France and Germany covenanted not to attack one another, and Britain and Italy joined in guaranteeing the French-Belgian-German boundary against both French and German aggression. By this pact, France, Belgium, and Germany each received assurances of support in the event of aggression by their historic enemy. Britain reverted to its historic position of balancer of the Western European equilibrium. Germany was admitted to the League of Nations and given a permanent seat in the League Council. Stresemann, the German Minister, by these moves boosted Germany back to the ranks of the Great Powers, placed her in a position where she could agitate effectively for the removal of the Versailles impediments, and set the stage for her assemblage of power which ultimately brought all Europe from the Pyrenees to Stalingrad under Hitler's control. It is significant that in returning to the position of "balancer" Britain refused to make any commitment with regard to the eastern frontier of Germany so that Locarno dealt only with the western boundaries of Germany. France and Britain did conclude compacts with Poland, and honored these to the extent of declaring war upon Germany when Poland was attacked in 1939.

Testing of the League System. The League of Nations concert system was given a crucial test in 1931–1932 when Japan seized Manchuria and reduced it to a puppet state. The League met, debated, wrangled, and finally, long after the event, condemned Japanese action. Japan walked out of the League. The powers agreed not to "recognize" the fruits of its aggression. But Japan held Manchuria while preparing for its next onslaught upon China in 1937. The

Hayes & Cole, History of Europe, *Vol. II. Copyright 1949 by The Macmillan Company.*

FIGURE VII:2

League had not deterred or stopped a great power bent on territorial gain through the use of armed force. Germany, Italy, and Japan, each eager for reasons of its own to change the equation of power, pondered the lesson and shaped its next moves accordingly. France stirred uneasily. Britain stood impotent with the spirit of pacifism pervading its leaders, save Churchill who warned that danger was in the making. The United States, thinking itself secure in isolation and neutrality, assisted in the preparation of the new aggressions by refusing to collaborate with its old allies and by shipping oil, scrap iron, cotton, and machinery to Germany and Japan.

Axis Attempt at World Power. After 1933, the fascist regimes in Italy and Germany began to take advantage of the power vacuum in Europe to establish a power situation favorable to themselves. While arming at home, Hitler continually endeavored to frustrate French attempts to improve its alliances both in Western Europe and in the East, and to prevent a Western rapprochement with Russia. By 1936 the Rome-Berlin-Tokyo Axis was established. This was designed to concert the efforts of the three would-be aggressors in counterbalancing the French alliance system in Europe, in neutralizing the power of the Soviet Union, and in keeping the British Empire and the United States isolated, while their own power ambitions were being satisfied.

From 1936 to 1938 Europe was kept in confusion by Hitler while Mussolini conquered Ethiopia and sought to place Italy in a position (1) to sever the British "life line" through the Mediterranean-Red Sea route and (2) to seize North East Africa. At Munich in 1938 Hitler cowed Britain and France into "appeasement," thereby gaining parts of Czechoslovakia and paving the way to forcible dismemberment of the Republic in 1939. Meanwhile Japan inched its way southward in China toward its "Greater East Asia Co-Prosperity Sphere" with the aid of American imports, diplomatic soothing syrup, and occasional threatening gestures toward the Soviet Union's Far Eastern outposts. Finally, Hitler concluded the pact with the Soviet Union in August, 1939, which made adroit concessions to some of Russia's expansionist desires in the Baltic area and eastern Poland in return for Soviet neutrality while the Nazi hordes descended upon Poland in September, 1939, and then conquered North and Western Europe in 1940.

A new equation of power was thus welded by Hitler, Mussolini, and Tojo, which was in reality an imbalance. The massive sweeps of the Panzer Divisions across Poland, the Low Countries, France, Denmark, Norway, Yugoslavia, Greece, and North Africa demonstrated that, on the continental lands of Eastern and Western Europe and of North Africa, Axis power outranked all opposition. Only upon the seas in 1940 and in the air over Britain was British power superior. In 1941 Hitler temporarily increased the margin of his power by attacking Russia and pressing his armies to the gates of Leningrad and Moscow before winter stalled his forces. Similarly in the Far East, Japan moved southward through Indo-China, Malaya, and Indonesia with neither Asiatic nor the European colonial powers able to restrain it. Within Europe and in East Asia a new order of power was erected superseding that which had prevailed in European and Asiatic politics since 1918. Neither the opposing European nor Asiatic states were able of their own accord to redress the balance of power. To be sure, the accretion of power had been halted at the English Channel and at the portals of Egypt. But further ventures were in the making. At the climax of the German assault upon Moscow the Japanese struck their blow at Pearl Harbor in a move to destroy American naval power in the Pacific, and rapidly extended their conquests in Asia to Singapore, Burma, and eventually the borders of India. And in 1942 the German forces pressed deep into Russia to reach Stalingrad and almost grasp the Soviet oil resources in the Caucasus.

Efforts Required to Break Axis Power. The situation of the Allies appeared dark indeed on the maps of 1942. German might held the continent of Europe from France to the Volga River. It was wreaking havoc with its submarines in the Atlantic. And its forces in Africa were almost at the Suez Canal and the approaches to the Middle East. Japanese power was extended from the Aleutians to Australia and from mid-Pacific to the frontiers of India. This was surely a revolution from the power arrangements envisaged by the peacemakers at Versailles twenty-four years before.

Herculean efforts were necessary to press back this tide of Axis power. Many steps in this slow process had their initiation long before Axis power reached its apogee. But the planning, production, and blows which ultimately broke the Axis Powers were slow in gathering momentum and involved the solution of enormous problems in logistics.

Basically, three steps were required to change the preponderance of Axis power: (1) American, British Commonwealth, and Allied power had to be mobilized, transported to a host of attack points in Africa, Europe, the Middle East, the Pacific and India, and projected with terrific effort; (2) Soviet power had to be realigned, strengthened by internal adjustment, and aided by American production in order to push the Nazi conquerors back into Germany; (3) a new world-wide coalition had to be assembled in order to gather together the necessary resources, bases, and coordinated effort of all kinds to overthrow Axis power.[14]

The story of World War II from Pearl Harbor to V-J Day is the record of

[14] See General George C. Marshall's Biennial Report to the Secretary of War entitled *The Winning of the War in Europe and the Pacific* (Washington, 1945).

HEIGHT AND FALL OF AXIS POWER

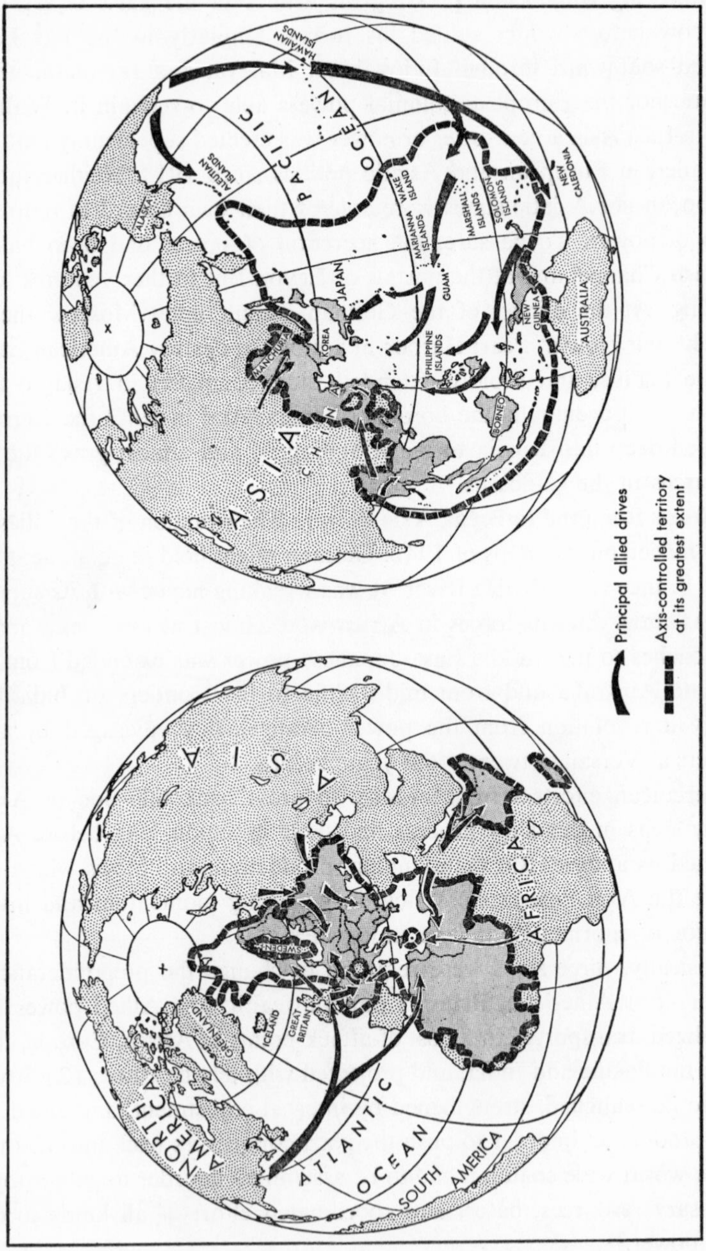

Principal allied drives

Axis-controlled territory
at its greatest extent

FIGURE VII:3

the effort by a host of valiant peoples from many nations to accomplish these objectives. The elimination of the Germans from Africa, the successful invasions of Italy and occupied France, the forced expulsion of the Germans from Russia, Eastern Europe, and the Balkans, the combined Allied-Soviet assault upon metropolitan Germany, the conquest of the Western Pacific, the battering of the Japanese home base, V-E Day, and V-J Day—these were the ultimate fruits of this strategic planning. August 14, 1945, saw the complete collapse of the Axis power; the reduction of Germany and Japan to temporary impotency in world politics.

As the last shot of World War II was fired, an imposing array of forty-seven nations stood allied against the Axis. With this culminating event a new distribution of power was established. The core of this power bloc was formed by the Big Three—the United States, Britain, and the Soviet Union—surrounded by secondary and tertiary powers from every continent. Switzerland, Spain, Ireland, Portugal, Sweden, and Afghanistan stood alone as neutrals or semi-neutrals.

THE BALANCE OF POWER SINCE 1945

Some Basic Assumptions. The system originally envisioned by the victorious powers had two principal aspects. It contemplated reducing the Axis nations to a powerless position for an indefinite period through disarmament, Allied occupation, and "re-education." In the second place, the Allied Powers voiced an intention of continuing to stand together in peace as they had in war, and of designing the United Nations whose organization was agreed upon at San Francisco in the spring of 1945 to help preserve and implement their unity and to maintain international peace and security.

The design for transforming the war-time United Nations coalition into a peace-time structure for preserving the peace was not unlike that of the framers of the peace in 1919. It was intended to create a concert of power which (1) would preserve the power situation won by the war effort and (2) would be a means of maintaining in the future such a state of affairs that world peace and security would be assured, or, if the peace were broken, could be restored. Finally, the new arrangement rested on an assumption that the Great Powers which had borne such a large share of the burden of defeating the Axis would hold together and should have not only special responsibilities in maintaining international peace and security, but to this end permanent seats in the Security Council and the privilege of a veto on any decisions which might involve a possible use of their power.

Could the new system hold together better than the one fashioned in World War I? That was the vital question of 1945. Thoughtful study of the record of history, especially of the period since 1918, would have suggested serious questions as to whether the assumption was valid.

The 1945 Coalition Disintegrates. It is now clear that the 1945 coalition has foundered upon the rocks of international discord. Russia has gone one way, the Western Powers another.[15] A struggle for power between the USSR and the West has been mounting ever since the Yalta Conference, even before hostilities with the Axis were over. Since the explosion of the atomic bomb over Hiroshima a nuclear weapons race has been in progress. Both the United States and the USSR have shaped their military planning toward the possibility of an ultimate fighting war against each other. Animosities reached the point in 1948 in which both sides talked openly about "the cold war." Negotiations for the German and Austrian peace treaties repeatedly stalled because of wrangling between the powers, and the USSR refused to sign the Japanese Treaty of Peace concluded at San Francisco in 1951. Sessions of the United Nations organs have seen the West and the East ranged against each other in bitter contests. On the major issues threatening world peace and security since 1945 the Great Powers have been split. Concerted action by *all* of the Great Powers has seldom been possible.

Historians doubtless will find many reasons for the rapid break-up of the "Grand Alliance." Chief among them, as seen at this close range, are (1) the recurrence of old suspicions; (2) Soviet imperialism in Eastern Europe with its violations of the Yalta accords; (3) rapid withdrawal and demobilization of American forces weakening United States power; (4) rivalry and disagreement over Germany, Austria, Trieste, the Turkish Straits, Iran, Greece, Berlin, China, Korea, Japan, and a host of issues within the United Nations; (5) imposition of the Soviet Iron Curtain; (6) the revival by Moscow of agitation for world revolution together with the attempts of Moscow-guided Communists to seize power in free nations and the discovery in Western states of instances of espionage and subversion; (7) fear of Soviet armed attack in Western Europe and continual propaganda by Moscow against the United States and Britain; (8) fundamental ideological differences; and (9) the lack of any common bond between East and West once the common threat formerly posed by the Axis was removed. With the Soviets adhering to the Marxist-Leninist thesis that Western capitalism is the enemy of their form of society, that a series of violent conflicts must occur between them, and that they must engage in a continual struggle to overthrow noncommunist regimes, it is impossible to see how the war-time unity of the Grand Alliance could have lasted long in the post-war era.

15 See the annual volumes published by the Council on Foreign Relations entitled *The United States in World Affairs,* covering the years from 1945 to the present.

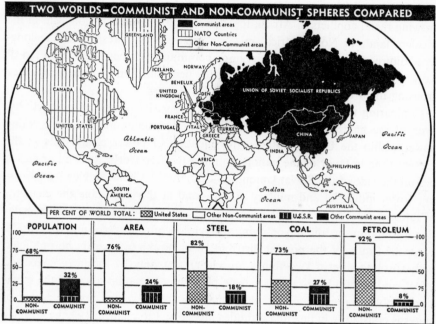

FIGURE VII:4

OUTLOOK FOR FUTURE

Factors in Contemporary Situation. In Germany and Central Europe, in the Middle East, and in Asia a titanic struggle for power is now going on between the forces of communism and of freedom. The future is by no means altogether clear in any of these areas, although in Germany and Japan there were strong manifestations against the communist element in the early 1950's.

In the Middle East and Southeast Asia there is no certainty yet which way the rampant forces of nationalism, so strongly anticolonial and anti-Western at the moment, will ultimately turn. For some time they may seek to adhere to a "neutral" or noninvolvement path in the contest between the West and the Soviet Union, although this may in effect give comfort and aid to the communist cause in Asia. But there is another struggle which may emerge within Asia with the passage of time. This is between an Indian-led bid for the leadership of Asia and a Communist-China attempt to guide the destinies of the vast population of Asia and its outlying islands. It is conceivable that this could become a major contest in the international politics of the second half of the twentieth century.

At the present time Latin America and Africa are, for the most part, associated with the Western nations on the crucial issues of world politics. The growing racial conflicts in Africa, together with the strident nationalism in the Moslem lands of North Africa, raise uncertainties with respect to the long-term future. Moreover, in both regions communist elements are reported at work attempting to lay the groundwork for neutralization of these peoples or arousing them to stand against the Western Powers.

Comparing the total available resources, industrial plant and productivity, over-all mechanized equipment, the numbers of states aligned, and voting power within the United Nations, the equation of power clearly tilts at the present time in favor of the nations forming the free world. In land armies it lies on the side of the Soviet Union and Communist China. In view of the rising Soviet industrial and military power—and at the same time the elements of internal weakness inherent in the Soviet regime—the plottings of international communism, and the on-going struggles in Europe, Asia, and the Middle East, the future of the present distribution of power can hardly be predicted with absolute surety. Two things are clear: (1) only by sacrifice, concerted effort, and careful long-range strategic planning can modification of the equation of power in ways unfavorable to the West be prevented, for the power of states is constantly in flux and attitudes are subject to change; (2) the struggle for power among the states which were allies in World War II has now reached world-wide proportions and new alignments with former enemies are being fashioned. From this struggle for power there can be no drawing back.

Potential Changes in Equation of Power. There has been some tendency for popular opinion to assume that because the United States and the USSR have held such an ascendancy of power over other states since 1945 a condition of permanent bipolarity has been reached. A long time may elapse before any other states attain a productive capacity or a store of nuclear weapons comparable to those which the two greatest powers possess or are capable of developing. But it would be shortsighted to minimize the potentials of Britain, Germany, Canada, and Japan in the foreseeable future, and of India, China, and possibly some other states in the next half century.

Germany staged an extraordinary recovery from World War I in a period of twenty years, and with her limited resources came close to world conquest during the first half of World War II. The energetic, resourceful, and productive people of both Germany and Japan can be counted upon to rebuild the power of their states. They already are hard at it and it will be but a few years before their renewed power and initiative may be able to alter the distribution of power, transforming the present bipolarity into a multipolar constellation. This must be anticipated.

Policy of the Balance of Power Alive Today. The political alignment which has emerged since 1949 with the association of West Germany, Italy, Greece, and Turkey with the North Atlantic Treaty powers, and of Japan and the United States in a mutual security pact—all in opposition to the power drive of the Soviet Union—demonstrates that the policy of the balance of power is still a very living force in the international politics of today.

Considerations to Bear in Mind. We should keep clearly in mind that statesmen guide their nation's external affairs on a basis of their estimate of national self-interest together with their appraisal of internal political feasibility. International tensions lead to the creation and tightening of alliances. A lessening of tension, or of common dangers, is likely to occasion a loosening of alliances and even some crumbling of such arrangements.

Any association with another state, particularly for security objectives, is likely to limit a nation's freedom of action. It is, therefore, continually open to question as to its net worth. When the world becomes superficially more calm, states are inclined to take more liberties in deviation from cooperation with friends on the reasoning that there is no increased risk. Moreover, the play of internal politics—internal public opinion—may force statesmen toward less intimate collaboration with friends.

It seems certain that reasoning along this line activates the Soviet Union in its attempts to weaken NATO, to decrease the unity of the free world in its stand against communism, and to isolate the United States.

TYPES OF BALANCE OF POWER SITUATIONS

Simple vs. Complex Balance. From the preceding brief survey of the functioning of the balance of power it will appear that the "balance" may assume a variety of characteristics. It may at times and in certain areas of the world take the form of a *simple balance* involving only two powers or two groups of states aligned against one another and chiefly concerned with the equation of power between them. At other times, when there are several more or less equalized power centers each operating separately and in competition with the others, it is said that there is a *complex balance* of power. This situation is sometimes likened to a chandelier in which the various parts maintain their relationship to one another and to the whole in a complex but harmonious balancing. There are some writers who believe that there is more assurance of peace in the presence of a complex balance than there is in a situation of bipolarity.[16] This may be true, historically speaking, although there is always

[16] See Morgenthau, *Politics among Nations,* p. 324; DeWitt C. Poole, "Balance of Power," *Life,* Sept. 22, 1947.

the possibility of a multiplicity of wars occurring among the several power blocs unless there is some over-all concert of power to maintain peace and security.

Flexible vs. Rigid. Alignments of power may be flexible or rigid depending upon the relative ease with which governments form and reform their political and military associations. Where combinations of states change from time to time, as varying threats arise and disappear, a flexible balance is said to prevail. When, on the other hand, cleavages become so deep-seated that adjustment does not take place even in the face of a common menace, the balance situation becomes static and rigid. In an age of princely, and mainly intra-European, politics, flexibility was quite possible. The radical shifts which have occurred with respect to Germany and Japan since 1945 among the Western states indicate that even in the circumstances attending contemporary world politics a considerable degree of flexibility may be possible. The history of Western-Soviet relations supports the proposition that a larger degree of rigidity is present in the operation of the balance principle when states are divided by fundamental cleavages on ideology and politics.

Local, Regional, and World-Wide Balances. Finally, it may be observed that the balance of power concept may operate within a continent or among a group of nations forming a geographical or political region, or it may embrace virtually all the states of the world and function on a global basis. Prior to World War I, the balance system, as such, was confined to Europe, although from the seventeenth century on equilibrium was frequently established by adjustments in extra-European holdings or spheres of influence. Since 1917 virtually the entire society of states has become involved in the balance of power system. Today the efforts of the Soviet Union and the United States to marshal the greatest possible power on their side have made the power struggle and the balance structure global in scope.

POLICIES OF THE BALANCE OF POWER

Adherence to the principle of the balance of power system usually rests upon a dual assumption. First, that by cooperation and sometimes alliance with other states a nation may gain a larger measure of security for itself in the face of certain specific threats. Second, that by skillful use of the policy of the balance of power the course of history may be guided and peace and war regulated. In both respects the principle is grounded upon the self-interest of states, and the system functions or fails to function through the foreign policies of the participating states. It is no automatic, self-regulating mechanism apart from the variable policies of states.

Major Policies. The balance system has functioned heretofore through a number of readily identifiable policies. These have included the following: (1) the formation of alliances, counteralliances, and mutual security arrangements; (2) insistence upon compensation, that is, matching any increase in the components of power on one side by some increase on the other—territorial, political, in armaments, or otherwise; (3) intervention in a weak state to prevent rivals gaining control of the country or exclusive possession or use of its strategic resources, as for example, when the United Nations went to the assistance of the Republic of Korea in 1950 to prevent it from being conquered by the communist forces; (4) the establishment of spheres of influence or control in power-weak areas; (5) the creation of buffer zones, sometimes neutralized, as in the case of the Netherlands, Belgium, and Luxembourg, between France and Germany, neutralized from 1830 to 1914; (6) resort to war to defend the *status quo* or to maintain equilibrium of power believed to be favorable, as in the case of the Crimean War to preserve the integrity of Turkey and the Straits, or as in the case of the Triple Entente powers in the European War of 1914–1918.[17]

Postulates of Balance of Power Policy. Considering the balance of power as a mechanism for the limitation of excessive power, such as that amassed by the Napoleons, Hitlers, and Stalins, and its abuse at the expense of states desiring peace and security, six postulates must be borne in mind by those who wish to preserve their independence and territorial integrity.

(1) States must be prepared to shift alignments among themselves in order to establish, maintain, and redress the balance of power as circumstances change.

(2) No state should seek excessive power. The power of a state should not be allowed to become injudiciously weak in a time of relaxation, as was that of the United States immediately after World War II, lest this give encouragement to potential aggressors to expand at the expense of small, exposed nations. Nor, on the other hand, should a nation interested in preserving a balance of power permit its accumulation of power to further policies which threaten its own friends and associates lest this turn them against it.[18]

(3) States must be willing to risk conflict and to go to war if necessary in order to stop any power or group of powers from overrunning others and destroying their independence.

(4) It is also essential, if the balance system is to preserve peace and security and to minimize the risk of war, that states not allied with the principal

[17] For a discussion of policies of the balance of power see Martin Wight, *Power Politics,* "Looking Forward" Pamphlets, No. 8, R.I.I.A. (New York, 1949).

[18] Edmund Burke once remarked with respect to the mounting power of Britain in the nineteenth century, apropos the second postulate: "I dread our own power and ambition. I dread our being too much dreaded . . . sooner or later, this state of things must produce a combination against us which may end in our ruin." *Works* (Boston, 1899), vol. IV, p. 457.

contestants in a crucial situation should align themselves before an outbreak of war with the weaker or threatened grouping in order to redress the balance of power factors and discourage warlike moves by an aggressive power.

(5) War should not result in one state's acquiring so much power that it can do wholly as it pleases regardless of friends or allies. Otherwise, the war will be succeeded not only by a weakening or destruction of the power of the defeated state or states, but also by an additional disturbance of the global equation and lead to a new struggle for power among the victor states.

(6) In view of the constant shifts taking place in the power of states and in international conditions it is important that provision be made for effecting peaceful change.

Lord Palmerston expressed the essence of the balance of power policy when he declared in 1848 that England had no perpetual friends and no natural enemies but eternal interests. And Professor Nicholas Spykman emphasized the same principle when he wrote: "He who plays the balance of power can have no permanent friends. His devotion can be to no specific state but only to balanced power. The ally of today is the enemy of tomorrow." He added, "One of the charms of power politics is that it offers no opportunity to grow weary of one's friends." [19]

EVALUATION OF BALANCE OF POWER AS A PRINCIPLE OF INTERNATIONAL RELATIONS

Claims in Behalf of the Balance System. The balance of power principle has been both praised and condemned. Claims have been made that it has (1) acted to prevent or discourage war, (2) preserved the independence of states and prevented permanent absorption of particular states by great powers, and (3) prevented domination of the world by any one power or group of states and thereby assisted in the maintenance of the multistate system.

These claims can be substantiated, at least in part. It seems reasonably clear from the record of history that adherence to the balance of power principle has prevented, delayed, or discouraged the outbreak of some wars. At the same time it must be acknowledged that it has not prevented all wars; nor has it prevented competitions in armaments or dissolved the fears and suspicions among nations.

The balance system has succeeded since 1648 in preventing the establishment of universal dominion by any one power. It has not, however, been altogether able to forestall temporary domination of a continent or area by one power or coalition. And while it has protected the independence of states gen-

[19] Nicholas J. Spykman, *America's Strategy in World Politics* (New York, 1942), pp. 103–104.

erally, there have been instances in which states have been partitioned in the interest of the balance, as was Poland in the eighteenth and nineteenth centuries and again between 1939 and 1945. Moreover, there have been numerous instances in which weak states have undergone intervention or occupation by others who were pursuing a balance of power policy or seeking to maintain a certain equilibrium.

Criticisms of the Principle. The balance of power principle has not been without its critics. It has sometimes been alleged that instead of being an effective formula for maintaining peace and security, the balance of power policy actually leads to war. This allegation has been made, for instance, with respect to the circumstances leading up to World War I when the European nations were divided among the Triple Alliance and the Triple Entente. Questions have been raised whether the theory of an approximate equilibrium does not really leave all parties without genuine security and hence invite potential aggressors to launch wars in the hope that by striking first they may become so strong that others cannot safely attack them.[20]

The balance principle has been especially criticized by those who reject the idea of power politics. Woodrow Wilson, for example, declared on January 22, 1917: "Mankind is now looking for freedom of life, not for equipoises of power." There must be, he asserted, "not a balance of power, but a community of power; not organized rivalries, but an organized common peace." In the same vein Francis B. Sayre, then Special Assistant to the Secretary of State, said in 1943: "No peace dependent upon the Balance of Power lasts. The Balance of Power theory rests upon the premise of utterly independent nations, owing no obligations of any kind to each other." Under twentieth century conditions, he added, peace "cannot be made secure except through the activity of an organized group, subject to common obligations and restraints. Whatever may be said in its favor under nineteenth century conditions, the Balance of Power theory is, under twentieth century conditions, the sure way to destruction."[21]

This latter view is rejected by Professor DeWitt C. Poole who, from a career experience in international politics, holds that freedom is to be had only in "a world in which power is widely distributed and balanced: a world of a complex balance of power. The most obvious alternative, a world in which power is concentrated at a single point, spells empire and tyranny."[22] One might add that however desirable it may be to have an "organized common

---

[20] See Walter Lippmann, *U.S. Foreign Policy: Shield of the Republic* (Boston, 1943), pp. 106–107.

[21] *Department of State Bulletin*, vol. 8 (1943), p. 510. For a skeptical analysis of the balance system see especially J. S. Shapiro, "That Great Illusion: The Balance of Power," *Social Studies*, Dec., 1942.

[22] DeWitt C. Poole, "Balance of Power," *Life*, Sept. 22, 1947.

peace," this is difficult to achieve in view of the deep-seated historical rivalries and antagonistic ambitions of nations.

Points to Bear in Mind. It would be academic to try to assess the "operability" of the balance of power principle in general terms. One would first have to decide to what extent propitious social, political, or other conditions were present at any given time, and, on the other hand, to what extent skill was exercised by those endeavoring to apply the balance of power policy as a device for maintaining peace. To judge its effectiveness today it furthermore would be necessary to collate past and present conditions and attempt to assess what elements of the past are still operative today, what their relative importance is, and what new elements characterize present conditions and how they affect the establishment and maintenance of an equilibrium.

In evaluating the balance of power principle three things in particular should be kept in mind. In the first place, the "balance" should not be analyzed in terms of "goodness" or "badness," in terms of whether it ought to be or ought not to be. National power exists in fact. Regardless of any moral or ethical considerations relating to the use of power, an equation or distribution of power exists at all times among states. The determination of what will happen in a given power situation lies not in the "balance" itself, but in the attitudes and policies of the parties involved.

In the second place, a balance of power cannot be expected always to operate instantaneously or automatically to preserve the inviolability or territorial integrity of every land or the independence of every political entity. The decisions of sovereign states cannot be controlled absolutely by others, especially when a virile spirit of nationalism is present or when a government becomes determined to pursue an aggressive course in international affairs regardless of possible consequences. Political leaders do arise who are willing to take large risks no matter what the odds may be. The possibility, or even the certainty, that they will be opposed by a coalition having actual or potential overwhelming power will not necessarily dissuade them from following the pathway of imperialism or war.

In the third place, the balance of power principle assumes that the power of different states can be compared. Some of the components of power possessed by two or more states can be compared with a relatively high degree of accuracy and governments do continually make estimates of the strength and weaknesses of others, but there always remain some elements of uncertainty. It is difficult, for example, under the present circumstances of Soviet censorship to compare with any fine degree of accuracy the current resource situation and productivity of the Soviet world with that of the free nations. Moreover, it is difficult to collate present outputs and future capabilities between highly developed and relatively underdeveloped countries. And it is hard to compare meaningfully the attributes of power hinging upon the personal qualities of their leaders.

Altered Circumstances. In considering the functioning of the balance of power as an aspect of power politics in the contemporary era, one must bear in mind the changes which have occurred in the circumstances surrounding international politics since the first decade of the twentieth century.

In the first place, although Europe is still a center of great power, the individual European nations no longer possess the greatest power among the nations. The United States and the Soviet Union have become the holders of decisive power. Their respective positions, interests, and contests, as well as the rise of Japan, China, India and the lesser states of Asia and the Middle East, each with its own power motives, have transferred the locale in which the balance of power principle has operated from Europe to the global scene as a whole. The fulcrum of world power may continue to rest in Europe, but the equation of power and the operation of the balance principle now involve to all intents and purposes the entire political world. States in Asia and in the New World, as well as states in Europe, have adopted the balance of power principle as a guide to their own policies.

In the second place, the industrialization of nations and the determination of peoples of many races and stations to improve their economic and social well-being have introduced both a higher degree of economic interdependence and of competition into the relations of nations. This twofold development has naturally resulted in making the power equation among states more sensitive to changes in the economic and industrial status of nations, thereby necessitating the devotion of increasing attention to the economic factors involved in the balance of power. It has also extended the area of conflict among nations and hence amplified the scope of international politics with which balance of power policies must deal.

In the third place, the disappearance of unclaimed lands and the rise of nationalism in the former colonial lands insisting upon self-determination of their own future have increasingly ruled out the availability of lands which can be readily parceled out to compensate or adjust the balance of power. Consequently, there is less opportunity for the operation of compensatory policies and correspondingly increased basis for international tension.[23]

In the fourth place, the growing spread of extreme nationalism and the susceptibility of people to ideological appeals with the improvements in the techniques of mass communication, make the mechanical shifting of states from one side to another in international politics—which was an indispensable

23 See Walter Webb, *The Great Frontier* (New York, 1952).

part of the classical balance of power system—difficult if not impossible. Shifts can and do take place, as witness what has happened since 1939, but new factors have been introduced which make the self-adjusting feature of the balance mechanism more complex, to say the least.

Finally, Great Power wars are now unlikely to be fought for limited stakes. Their end no longer alters merely boundaries. These wars affect the entire ways of life, economic conditions, and security of whole populations. Moreover, the destructive power of nuclear weapons has now become so great that the principal centers of habitation may be blotted out before the deterrent strength of a coalition or world organization can be brought to bear to stop an aggressor. Consequently, the mathematics of a possible atomic war and the economic cost of a reasonable defense are now introducing new imponderables into the already exceedingly difficult calculus of the equation of power.

OTHER LIMITATIONS ON POWER POLITICS

If these changed conditions of the mid-twentieth century raise questions whether the balance of power system is still a viable means of keeping relations among states within reasonable and peaceful dimensions, the question may be asked what other limitations there are.

Morality and World Opinion. Although the place of morality and world opinion in international politics is difficult to assay with any degree of accuracy, agreements among states and their conduct on numerous occasions reveal the presence—at least at times and among some states—of a moral consciousness and a respect for world opinion, as we have noted in Chapter V.[24] No nation likes to stand condemned before the bar of world opinion. Nations will go to great lengths to avoid this or to refute charges of antimoral conduct.

In the final analysis, however, it must be admitted that self-interest is the guiding force behind the policies of states. If this dictates a course of action contrary to what some regard as standards of international morality, or to expressed world opinion, governments, being agents for executing the national will, are bound to make every effort to follow this.

Morality and world opinion, although influential in the affairs of world politics, lack in themselves, in most instances of a crucial nature, a force sufficiently compelling—apart from other limiting means—to deter a strong power or group of states from proceeding with imperialist designs or acts of aggression against others. They can, nevertheless, serve as valuable complements to other measures aiming also at curbing the abuse of excessive or dangerous power.

[24] See above, pp. 144–150, also E. H. Carr, *Twenty Years' Crisis, 1919–1939* (London, 1946), p. 146.

International Law. The customs, principles, and conventions composing international law lay down certain rules of conduct and principles of responsibility which states have been willing to accept as binding upon themselves. States acknowledge that these principles and rules are proper for adjudication by courts of law and for enforcement by such measures of self-help as states may have available or as may be entrusted to international bodies. States are sensitive to charges of violating international law, and will take steps to avoid being proved guilty, and, if found wrong, will often make reparation and conform even though no power exists to force such action. In these respects, international law functions as a limiting factor upon power politics.

International law, however, has a limited content. And there are unsettled differences of opinion on the interpretation to be given to some of its rules, principles, and customs. Against a determined power, such as that exemplified by the governments of Hitler or Mussolini, international law can exert, before the fact, relatively little dissuasive force upon the accumulation of power dangerous to peace and security or the launching of an aggressive war.[25]

Concert Procedures. A further method which has been employed to effect some limitations upon power politics has been the development and use of concert procedures. During the nineteenth century the Concert of Europe sought to function in such a capacity. We have mentioned in a preceding section some of the operations of the Concert, particularly as they related to curbing the power drives of Russia in the direction of Constantinople and the Turkish Straits.

The League of Nations represented an attempt to provide a more systematic machinery and procedure for concerting the efforts of states from all over the world for the peaceful solution of international disputes and for the maintenance or enforcement of peace. It certainly did not succeed. It proved unable to prevent the amassing of threatening power in Germany, Italy, and Japan. And it was not able to deter or to stop aggressions by these powers when they determined to attack and overrun other countries.

An endeavor was made when the United Nations was founded in 1945 to remedy some of the weaknesses in the League system.[26] It remains to be seen how effective this method of concerting power to oppose dangerous uses of power can be. The tests which have occurred thus far have given no conclusive answer. In the United Nations' most serious trials—the Berlin blockade and the Korean War—the results have been at best mixed, as we shall see in Chapter XX. Furthermore, the operation of the United Nations has been accompanied by Great Power politics directed to the same ends.

25 For a further discussion of the role of law in international politics see ch. xix below.
26 See discussion of the League of Nations and United Nations in ch. xx below.

The record of the League of Nations and of the United Nations thus far shows that the efforts to substitute a universal concert of power for the principle of the balance of power have not guaranteed the hoped-for tangible results in peace and security. A universal association of nations may serve useful purposes in bringing nations together to discuss their common problems and to face the multitude of complex issues of international politics. But a universal association made up of states with widely divergent interests and attitudes likewise affords innumerable opportunities for divisions of opinion to develop which may delay or emasculate necessary action. And it has been shown to be extraordinarily difficult to provide effectively for action against one of the members. A group of nations, on the other hand, jointly sensing a common danger, and united in a special defense arrangement, can prepare in advance a suitable force to counterbalance a threatening power and to oppose *at once* with military force any military action launched against a member of the group.

The joining of the Old World and the New in the Atlantic community by means of the North Atlantic Treaty became an inescapable necessity when the implications of Soviet policy and the limitations of the United Nations made it apparent that only by this means could a sufficient defense be prepared to maintain the independence and the integrity of the Western nations in the kind of world in which we are living.[27]

Both the balance of power policy and the universal concert procedure appear to have useful and necessary roles in international politics.

CAN POWER POLITICS BE ABOLISHED?

Americans and some other peoples have had a penchant for thinking that there is something wrong in the world that leads nations to engage in power politics and conflict. They have at times strongly inclined to the view that these struggles could be avoided if mankind would but use more sense, or that they could be abolished if some particular policy were followed or some ideal political arrangement were adopted.

Former Secretary of State Hull reflected this frame of mind, so strongly espoused by Woodrow Wilson in World War I, when he declared upon returning from the Moscow Conference in the fall of 1943, which established the first agreement among the Big Three on the broad outlines of the post-war United Nations organization: "There will no longer be need for spheres of influence, for alliances, for balance of power or any other of the special arrangements through which in the unhappy past the nations strove to safeguard their security or to promote their interests." [28]

27 See Walter Lippmann, *Isolation and Alliances* (Boston, 1952), pp. 38–39.
28 Dept. of State Press Release No. 484, Nov. 18, 1943.

Mr. Philip Noel-Baker, Minister of State in the British Labour Government, told the House of Commons in 1946 that Britain was "determined to use the institutions of the United Nations to kill power politics." [29]

The difficulty with this conception of the world, that rivalry should not exist among nations and could be stopped by right-minded men, is its very unreality. So long as peoples cherish ambitions to improve their lot, to raise their standards of living, to have their views heard and accepted by others, to increase their prestige and standing, and to gain what they regard as their rightful place in world affairs, rivalries, contests, and struggles for power will be present. The search for power cannot be rooted out of international politics by dismissing or ignoring it.

Professor Spykman once aptly remarked: "A world without struggle would be a world in which life had ceased to exist. An orderly world is not a world in which there is no conflict, but one in which strife and struggle are led into political and legal channels away from the clash of arms; are transferred from the battlefield to the council chamber and the courtroom." [30]

So long as contests for power occur within the realm of international politics, man must concern himself with the equilibrium of power and with devising reasonable and effective checks and balances among the contending forces. This is one of the principal tasks of diplomacy.

A diplomacy fitted to the world "as it is, which is not to expend itself in verbal declarations on the one hand, and on crusades of annihilation on the other, must deal," as Walter Lippmann has observed, "with the balance of power and the determination of spheres of influence." [31]

SUGGESTED READINGS

Edward H. Carr, *Twenty Years' Crisis, 1919–1939* (London, 1940).
William T. R. Fox, *The Super Powers* (New York, 1944).
Hajo Holborn, *The Political Collapse of Europe* (New York, 1951).
H. D. Lasswell and A. Kaplan, *Power and Society* (New Haven, 1950).
Walter Lippmann, *United States Foreign Policy, Shield of the Republic* (Boston, 1943).
———. *Isolation and Alliances* (Boston, 1952).
Niccolo Machiavelli, *The Prince and His Discourses* (New York, 1952).
Hans J. Morgenthau, *Politics Among Nations* (2d ed., New York, 1954).
Georg Schwarzenberger, *Power Politics* (New York, 1951).
Harold and Margaret Sprout, *Foundations of National Power* (2d ed., Princeton, 1951).
Nicholas J. Spykman, *America's Strategy in World Politics* (New York, 1942).
Martin Wight, *Power Politics* (London, 1946).

[29] *House of Commons Debates* (Fifth Series, 1946), vol. 119, p. 1262. See T. McLaurin, *The United Nations and Power Politics* (London, 1951) for a critical review of power politics in the United Nations.
[30] Nicholas J. Spykman, *America's Strategy in World Politics* (New York, 1942), p. 12.
[31] Walter Lippmann, "The Rivalry of Nations," *The Atlantic Monthly*, February, 1948.

CHAPTER VIII

Imperialism

IN THE preceding chapter we observed that power politics is a central feature of international relations, with states generally seeking to gain and secure power as a means of satisfying their wants, advancing their interests, and maintaining their integrity and independence.

One of the common facts of life in the history of international relations has been the repeated attempt of states to acquire domination and jurisdiction over alien territories and peoples—to expand their national domain and to enhance their national power by gaining control or possession of additional lands. Nearly all states, at one time or another, on one pretext or another, have sought added lands from their neighbors. And many have felt the urge to plant colonies or to raise their flags over distant islands and strategically situated or economically valuable lands. When states engage in such a practice, or pursue policies designed to achieve such an end, they are often said to be engaging in imperialism. Because the practice has been so widespread and continuous, imperialism may be placed among the fundamental elements of international relations.

Variable Manifestations. Imperialism is no new phenomenon. It existed in the ancient world. Alexander the Great and the Roman emperors sought to bring the known world of their days under a single empire and law. Beginning in the sixteenth century and extending to the twentieth, imperialism was exhibited in the form of colonialism as Spain, Britain, France, and other European powers vied with one another in claiming and founding colonies in the Americas, Asia, Africa, and Oceania. In the mid-twentieth century, Nazi imperialism harked back in some respects to the Roman idea of a world, or at least European continental *imperium,* seeking to alter the entire balance of power. Imperialism may also manifest itself in attempts to enforce certain political ideas and forms upon men against their will.

Imperialism, like nationalism, is a manifold concept. It may vary in form and emphasis. But it generally has an explicit or implicit core of power motivation.

Loose Usage of Term. The term imperialism is often loosely applied, confusing its essential meaning. Foreign countries are sometimes stigmatized as being "imperialistic" when their policies or actions happen to run counter to national interests or are objected to. Cries of "imperialist capitalist warmongers" have emanated from Moscow or been hurled by Soviet delegates in the United Nations when Western Powers have opposed the Soviet Union. *Imperialism, imperialist,* and *imperialistic* have been made terms of opprobrium for international mud-slinging contests. As a consequence, the term often lacks exact meaning in common parlance.

MEANING OF IMPERIALISM

Imperialism is defined by *Webster's Dictionary* as "the policy, practice, or advocacy of seeking to extend the control, dominion, or empire of a nation."

We shall employ the term here as referring to those situations in which a state acquires foreign holdings, or pursues policies designed to achieve possession, control, or domination of territories belonging to, or chiefly inhabited by, peoples of another race or nationality, whether by colonization, by threat or by use of force without regard to the desires of the inhabitants, or by purchase or cession, for the purpose of enhancing its national power and world position. In defining the term broadly, we pass no judgment upon the political or other considerations that may be involved in imperialist practices. And we recognize that there may be many situations in which there may be differences of opinion whether a given action constitutes a case of imperialism or not.

Aspects of Imperialism. Imperialism, generally speaking, takes one of three forms. (1) It may take the form of an attempt by a state to alter the *status quo* or balance of power within a given area by the extension of its control over neighboring states and territories. Napoleon's effort to establish French hegemony over continental Europe, Russia's historic ambition to control the Balkans, and Japan's effort to establish an empire covering East Asia and the Western Pacific are instances of imperialism in this form. (2) Imperialism may embrace an effort by some state to overthrow the balance of power altogether with a view to establishing world political dominion after the fashion of Rome at its height. Hitler had a self-professed aim of elevating the Third Reich to world ascendency. Communist writers speak in terms of an inevitable conflict between communist and bourgeois states until all political entities are brought within a single state union. (3) The third manifestation of imperialism is the more limited one of extending the control of metropolitan states to overseas territories in order to create or maintain a colonial empire. There are abundant illustrations of this type of imperialism in the colonization of the Americas, Asia, Africa, and the Pacific Islands by the European powers during the past three centuries. In the same category would belong the extension of Russian power across Siberia to the Pacific.

Colonialism and Imperialism. Since one of the principal features of modern imperialism has been the extension of European rule to many other parts of the world through colonialism, there has been a tendency to regard imperialism and colonialism as the same thing. There is some distinction, however.

Colonialism has been described by one authority as an overflow of nationality wherein groups of colonists are sent out to a foreign, and ordinarily more backward, land or go of their own volition to settle and "take up the land," transplanting their civilization and political institutions and retaining the territory for their home country.[1] Imperialism, on the other hand, has been characterized as "something more organized, more military, more self-consciously aggressive."[2] This is not to say that colonialism is not bound up with balance of power considerations also. On the whole, it has borne a close relation to the power balance and served as an element in the power equilibrium, as we shall see presently.

The distinction between imperialism and colonialism, to the extent to which one can be made, must be drawn in teleological terms, that is, in terms of purposes and ends sought. Where rule over foreign territories is sought primarily for the economic, political, or military benefit of the central home land, the action assumes characteristics of imperialism, though it may not always be regarded as such. Where rule is undertaken within a colonial area primarily for the development of the area itself, the action may be said to take on more of the features of colonialism. If force is used to acquire the possession or to keep it politically subordinate, the action is likely to be labeled imperialism by others irrespective of the intent of the initiator. And if the ruling state endeavors to maintain its control in the face of nationalist demands for independence or self-rule, it is almost certain to be charged with imperialist motives and with endeavoring to perpetuate "evils of the colonial system" regardless of the educational, administrative, economic, or public health benefits its administration may have conferred upon the native people.[3] Soviet policy of changing the social and cultural patterns of the non-Russian nationalities of East and Central Asia (a form of the Russification program of the Czars) and of colonizing these areas with Russians may well raise the question whether this is colonialism, imperialism, or nationalism.

---

[1] J. A. Hobson, *Imperialism, A Study* (New York, 1902), pp. 6–8.
[2] E. M. Winslow, *The Pattern of Imperialism* (New York, 1948), pp. 3–4.
[3] For defense of some of the by-products of imperialism see S. W. Brogan, *The Price of Revolution* (New York, 1951); R. Emerson, "Problems of Colonialism," *World Politics*, July, 1949.

MOTIVES OF IMPERIALISM AND COLONIALISM

Why do states strive for dominion over others? Why do they seek colonial possessions? Statesmen and publicists have attributed these endeavors to many different causes. Some have ascribed them to the operation of economic factors, such as the need for sources of raw materials, markets, and profitable opportunities for the investment of capital. Others have laid them to the motivation of political forces, as the furtherance of national security, the advancement of political beliefs, the blocking of enemy states. In still other instances moral, altruistic, and even religious causes have been advanced as reasons why states have sought to extend their rules over other territories and nationalities, as well as justification of their actions.[4]

Assessment of the motives underlying any instance of imperialism is not always easy. Public officials do not always reveal the true motives inspiring their policies and actions. On occasion, they may obscure them, or rationalize them, in other terms. President McKinley, for example, rationalized United States annexation of the Philippines in 1898 as the humanitarian duty of a Christian nation to care for a needy and defenseless people.[5] In reality the United States took the islands for fear that Germany or some other power would do so if the United States did not and thereby jeopardize American interests in the Pacific. So it has often been in other situations.

No one neat formula framed in terms of a single political, economic, or emotional force suffices to explain why nations seek colonies. The answer can be discovered only in the complex of motives and interests of the individuals and groups that make up the state and determine its policies. At times these act from their own particular interests; at other times from what they conceive to be the general interest, or from some combination of the two.

POLITICAL MOTIVES

Political considerations of several kinds have been among the principal motives prompting imperialist ventures.

Increase of National Power. One of the foremost motives of imperialism and colonialism has been the desire of governments to add to the national power of their states. Spain, Britain, and France planted many of their early colonies because of the power and prestige this gave them. Napoleon's imperi-

---

[4] For analysis of various motives and theories see P. T. Moon, *Imperialism and World Politics* (New York, 1926); Winslow, *op. cit.*, chs. 5–8; Klaus Knorr, "Theories of Imperialism," *World Politics*, April, 1952.

[5] See his explanation quoted in T. A. Bailey, *A Diplomatic History of the American People* (3rd ed., New York, 1946), p. 520.

230 Basic Factors Affecting National Policy and International Politics

alist designs, as later those of the German Kaiser and Adolf Hitler, sprang in large part from cravings for domination over others and for outstripping other powers. Even when economic motives may appear on the surface, power reasons may be the real underlying factor, as when Spain was engaged in its frenzied exploitation of the gold and silver of Latin America in order to support the costly wars which its rulers were determined to wage in Europe for thrones and positions.

Colonies or other possessions can swell the power of a state by providing it with strategic raw materials, as for example, tin, rubber, bauxite, tungsten, manganese, kapok, industrial diamonds, asbestos, chrome, uranium, and a host of other natural resources needed in modern industry.

Colonies can also add to a state's political and military strength by giving it an added reservoir of manpower. France, for example, has made extensive use of its Algerian, Moroccan, Senegalese, and other colonial troops not only in connection with its colonial policies, but also in defending France against Germany. Canadians, Anzacs, Indians, and South Africans have played vital roles in the power of "Her Majesty's Government" in world politics, and in the defense of the United Kingdom. The Soviet Union, for its part, has found it profitable to organize and exploit the labor of its satellite states for its defense and schemes of power politics.

National Defense. Conceptions of national defense have often been behind acquisitions of foreign sites. United States acquisitions of bases in the Caribbean, the purchase of the Virgin Islands, and the exercise of influence in Central America from time to time have been determined by the needs of assuring protection to the Panama Canal and the American continent. Similar reasons of state have been behind United States leasing of bases in Bermuda, Newfoundland, Labrador, Greenland, Iceland, and the Azores. Likewise, defense considerations were primary in the acquisition of a strategic trusteeship over the former Japanese mandated islands in the Pacific after World War II.

One can follow the perimeter of the British Empire as it existed before World War II and find various possessions which were acquired for strategic and defensive purposes rather than economic gain. Such holdings would include Gibraltar, Malta, Cyprus, Aden, Singapore, and other sites.

Russia's historic efforts to gain control of the Turkish Straits and of the westward approaches through the Baltic lands had at least a part of their inception in protective rather than in economic motivations. In the same class of motives might be included Germany's acquisition of Helgoland and Japan's former annexation of the Kurile, Ryukyu, Bonin, and Volcano Islands.

Adjustment of the Balance of Power. The acquisition of foreign possessions and spheres of influence has a close relationship to the balance of power and has at times been a key factor in the determination of national policies. French and English competition for colonies in the New World in the eighteenth century, for example, was closely related to the balance of power between the two nations in their struggles for pre-eminence in European and world politics. Germany's drive for colonies at the turn of the twentieth century was a part of her endeavor to catch up with Britain and France in world power. Likewise, Mussolini's efforts to increase Italy's holdings in North and East Africa were a phase of an endeavor to win a more favorable power position.

If one power moves into a politically weak area which lies athwart the communications system of another power, the security conceptions of the latter may lead it to feel that it in turn must make some territorial move for defense and to readjust the balance of power. Thus elements of self-defense and power equilibrium become conspicuous as one expansion is found necessary to counter another. French expansion from west to east across Africa after 1880 had much to do with prompting Britain's effort in the last decade of the nineteenth century to construct a Cape-to-Cairo sphere in East Africa. Likewise, the initiation of German colonization near the turn of the century prompted redoubled imperialism by Britain to safeguard its empire routes and to block what it considered to be the dangerous spread of German power. Nazi imperialism in Eastern Europe from 1938 to 1945 had its repercussion in Soviet imperialism in the same area.

The relationship of the colonial system to the balance of power is also seen in the fact that wars between the Great Powers have often been followed by changes in colonial holdings. In 1919 Germany was stripped of all her colonial possessions which were parceled out as mandates among the victorious states. In 1945 Korea, Manchuria, Southern Sakhalin, the Kurile Islands, Okinawa, Formosa, and the Pacific Islands which had been held under mandate were taken away from Japan. Italy also was forced to give up Libya, the Dodecanese Islands, Eritrea, and Ethiopia, and to accept a ten-year trusteeship of Italian Somaliland in place of full title. The territories taken away from the defeated powers in 1945 were either transferred to one of the victorious Allies, or put under trusteeship, or given independent statehood.

Interests of Official Classes. One other political factor which may enter into the embarkation of a state upon the path of expansion abroad is the influence of public figures. Political leaders, diplomats, civil servants, and military and naval officers, desirous of opportunities for prestige, personal achievement, or promotion, have sometimes been zealous proponents of imperialist actions, using their influence and position to further colonial additions or extensions of national power in the more developed regions.[6]

6 Moon, *op. cit.*, pp. 62–67.

ECONOMIC INTERESTS

Economic interests have been an active factor in motivating colonialism and imperialism. Many illustrations can be found of the activity of business interests in promoting colonialism during its heyday in the eighteenth, nineteenth, and twentieth centuries. British iron, steel, and cotton manufacturing interests, for example, pressed for the opening of colonial markets and then for the exclusion of non-British competitors. Belgian capitalists have held a virtual monopoly in the Belgian Congo, and secured the adoption of policies designed to funnel the products of this wealthy colony into world trade through Belgian hands. As a consequence, Belgian plantation and mine owners have done a fabulous business in diamonds, palm oils, copper, and uranium, and Belgian merchants have been able to reap rich profits by having the trade in these goods directed through their hands and through Belgian ports.

Banking interests have also been active supporters of imperialistic policies in the past. As Professor Parker T. Moon states, speaking principally of a generation or more ago, they have "financial fingers in every industrial pie. . . . Banks underwrite the loans of colonies and backward countries, the capital issues of railways and steamship lines; they extend credit to colonial plantation owners, to importers and exporters, to manufacturers and distributors. . . . The Deutsche Bank was the mainspring of German imperialism in the Near East. The Rothschilds [in England] . . . utilized their political influence to bring about the conquest of Egypt [by England]." He also showed that the National City Bank of New York played an important role in the Caribbean policy of the United States during what he refers to as the period of American imperialist activity there from 1900 to 1935.[7] Parenthetically, the situation is now so changed as to be almost reversed. The United States has had little success since World War II in interesting private enterprise in exporting capital to foreign countries. As a result it has been necessary to call on the taxpayer to provide, in our enlightened self-interest, capital for foreign development in the form of aid programs.

Instances have not been lacking in the past in which gunboats, armed forces, and sometimes annexation have followed traders and investments. And there have been wars in which colonial questions have been major issues. But as we shall see presently, the "old colonialism" is now quite dead. A new concept of responsibility has been developed to take its place.

Economic Theories of Imperialism. Various European writers, particularly Socialists and Communists, have sought to explain imperialism primarily as a

[7] *Ibid.*, pp. 59–61; see also Herbert Feis, *Europe the World's Banker* (New York, 1930).

profit-seeking operation and resting largely or entirely on economic causes.[8]

The English economist, John A. Hobson, laid the foundation for much of the thinking along these lines in his study of *Imperialism* written in 1903. In this he attributed imperialism to the existence of maladjustments in the European capitalist system and suggested that imperialism might be avoided if corrections were made within this system itself. Subsequently, Lenin, the founder of the bolshevik version of Marxism, converted Hobson's thesis to the idea of the contemporary communist doctrine that imperialism is a product of what he called "the monopoly stage of capitalism" in which "the division of the world by the international trusts has begun, and in which the partition of all the territory of the earth by the greatest capitalist countries has been completed." [9]

The Leninist thesis has gained currency by virtue of being officially accepted by the Soviet Government and by all those in the grip of communism. It has been widely propagandized by Moscow and by Communist parties throughout the world. By selecting appropriate examples while ignoring cases which do not fit their theory, Leninist writers claim that the explanation of imperialism is to be found in economic motives. But this has oversimplified a theory into a slogan and ultimately into an absurdity.[10]

Refutation of Leninist Theory. The theory of capitalist determinism maintained by Socialists and Communists does not explain, in the first place, the manifestations of imperialism in ancient times nor where capitalism is not in a stage of overproduction of goods. Spanish, Portuguese, French, and British colonialism in the seventeenth-eighteenth centuries occurred long before capitalism had reached any peak, and quite without regard to economic crises at home.

Secondly, capital movements do not show the existence of an invariable coincidence of surplus capital and imperialist venture. Capital was exported from Europe, for example, during the relatively quiescent period of imperialism in the early nineteenth century, and there was an actual decline of capital export during the scramble for colonies between 1880 and 1905. An examination of instances in which there has been some link between capitalist activity and imperialist expansion reveals that the process is usually the reverse of that argued by the Leninists. Historical investigation has shown that governments nowadays can employ capital to advance their foreign policy objectives more

[8] See writings of Hobson, Winslow, and Knorr cited above. See also L. O'Boyle, "Theories of Socialist Imperialism," *Foreign Affairs*, Jan., 1950.
[9] V. I. Lenin, *Imperialism, the Highest Stage of Capitalism* (Eng. trans., New York, 1933), pp. 80–81.
[10] J. A. Schumpeter, *Capitalism, Socialism, and Democracy* (New York, 1947), p. 51.

readily than capitalists as such can sway governments.[11] Even in the United States the initiative for the so-called "dollar diplomacy" between 1910 and 1930 stemmed largely from Washington, which urged bankers to make loans to facilitate policies which the government wished to pursue in Latin America and the Far East. Similarly, British administrators in the Malay States have long besought investment there rather than the London financial and industrial interests.[12]

In the third place, international trade and investment statistics show that colonial powers have tended to export more capital to the industrially developed areas than to their colonies, and foreign trade among the Great Powers has far outranked their trade with their possessions or with the colonies of others. To paraphrase Professor Langer: "Trade has followed the price list far more than the flag." [13] Moreover, Hobson and more recently the English economist, J. M. Keynes, have shown that from an economic point of view it is not necessary for capitalist states to *possess* foreign markets. Home markets and sources of investment are capable of expansion far beyond present advanced points. Trade and investment can occur without resulting in imperialism or colonialism.[14]

In the fourth place, the economic (single factor) theories of imperialism ignore the political considerations which have motivated many instances of imperialism. Napoleon was hardly trying to conquer Europe or extend his power to Africa and India because of capitalist pleas. Hitler's imperialist plan was certainly more a response to a Nietzschean "will to power" than it was the product of German capitalist influence. Neither Japanese nor United States struggle for control of the small mid-Pacific islands can be laid to economic motives, given the economic status of these islands. Political and security interests provided the main incentives on both sides. The economic theories also overlook the influence which religious and philanthropic motives have played in some extensions of Western rule to colonial lands.

Finally, the Leninist theory of imperialism does not explain the grandiose Soviet imperialist policies themselves. Whatever communist propaganda may say, it is undeniable that the Soviet Government has been pressing for many of the imperialist objectives sought by the Czars, and more as well. Economic considerations no doubt underlie their imperialist policies being pursued in

---

11 E. Staley, *War and the Private Investor* (New York, 1935), p. 55. This verdict is corroborated by other economists.

12 Rupert Emerson, *Malaysia* (New York, 1937), p. 471. Langer says that the British Government several times in the nineteenth century annexed territories principally to prevent their being closed off by rival powers. William L. Langer, *The Diplomacy of Imperialism* (2d ed., New York, 1951), p. 75.

13 Langer, *cit. supra*, pp. 75–76.

14 Hobson, *op. cit.*, p. 88; J. M. Keynes, *The General Theory of Employment, Interest and Money* (New York, 1935), p. 335.

Europe, the Balkans, the Middle East and Asia, in part at least. But their motives also appear to be political in nature: the search for greater power, larger possessions, increased world influence, further security.

The fact that the economic determinist theory breaks down, being too simple to fit all the facts of modern world politics, does not mean that economic factors do not have a part in imperialism. Economic motives admittedly have been influential factors in numerous instances of imperialism, especially of nineteenth-century colonialism. But to be seen in correct proportions they must be viewed in conjunction with the many other motives—political, psychological and other—which have led states to seek to subordinate others to their rule.

OTHER CAUSAL FORCES

Altruism. A motive sometimes emphasized by apologists for colonialism has been altruism. English colonialism was justified by some as "shouldering the white man's burden." This phrase, by the way, was produced by Kipling in referring to the United States annexation of the Philippines. France regarded its colonizing moves as a sort of civilizing mission to bring the benefits of French culture to benighted peoples. And Americans have inclined to stress especially responsibilities for the uplift and advancement of peoples in non-self-governing territories.

Missionary Interests. When the New World first came into the ken of Europeans it presented a field not only for trade but also for the salvation of souls. With the merchants, soldiers, and explorers of France and Spain went forth also a host of Jesuit and Dominican priests zealous for the spiritual conquest of the Indians, at the same time fostering their submission to French or Spanish rule. The mission of Père Marquette to the Indians of the Mississippi Valley is remembered in the annals of the American frontier. Similarly, Protestant leaders in the British Isles were a powerful influence in extending English colonization to North America in the seventeenth century.

In the nineteenth century enthusiasm arose in Europe and America for the spread of the Gospel in Africa, India, and China. Catholic orders in France and Belgium implored the governments of those countries to aid the propagation of the faith by extending the rule of those states in Central Africa. In England the Protestant missionary societies were a vocal impetus to British imperialism. David Livingstone, the famous Scottish missionary to Africa, was said to have "desired with all his heart that British rule might be extended in the Dark Continent, to wipe out slavery, to spread civilization and Christianity." Among the principal advocates of German colonial expansion were members of the German missionary society active in South West Africa.

Reviewing the period, Professor Moon found that "time and again missionaries in some savage land have called upon their mother-country to raise its protecting flag above them. Time and again British missionaries have persuaded a converted chieftain to offer his fealty to the British Crown." [15] Western missionaries played a part in obtaining the extraterritorial rights which were accorded to foreigners in China after 1858. And Germany, as the result of the murder of two missionaries in Shantung Province, seized Tsingtao and forced China to sign a ninety-nine year lease of Kiaochow.[16]

Sense of Destiny. Imperialist ideas have on occasion sprung from feelings of racial superiority. Some of the Nazi officialdom, for example, believed fanatically that Germany had "a mission to rule the inferior races" of Eastern and Central Europe. And numerous German writers during the Nazi era took the position that human progress requires that the "weak races" should accept dominion by superior races; by Germans, in particular.

Some writers have also traced a link between modern imperialism and the Darwinian concepts of social evolution, struggle for survival, and survival of the fittest. These ideas, which gained currency at the close of the nineteenth century, encouraged attitudes of glorification of struggle, race superiority, divine destination. Lord Milner typified this spirit in remarking once: "Alike by the nature of our interests, by the nature of our power, and by certain special qualities in our national character, we seem marked out for the discharge of this particular duty." And Gilbert Murray similarly expressed it when he once observed that every nation felt a certain "whisper from below the threshold" that it was the pick of the nations, generous and just, qualified above others to rule without weakness or cruelty, the excellence of whose rule in backward areas is attested by the writings of explorers, missionaries, public servants, and soldiers, "who all agree that our yoke is a pure blessing to those who bear it." [17]

Popular Support. Nineteenth-century colonialism generally had popular support. People cheered for empire. Awareness of this popular support tended to stimulate exertions in some countries. To what can we attribute this enthusiasm for foreign dominion?

For one thing, nineteenth-century Europe experienced a wave of romanticism at the time colonial expansion was occurring. To factory workers, surrounded by the soot, gloom, and tedium of the average industrial town, accounts of imperialist adventures with tales of strange lands and peoples, heroic exploits and swashbucklers, offered something of an escape from the drab conditions created by the industrial revolution. Because the colonial

---

15 P. T. Moon, *Imperialism and World Politics* (New York, 1926), p. 64.
16 K. S. Latourette, *History of Christian Missions in China* (New York, 1935), p. 489. Kiaochow was seized by Japan in 1915 and returned to China in 1919.
17 Quoted in Langer, *op. cit.*, p. 96.

pioneers were peoples of the same nationality, it was easy to enter into the imperialist activities vicariously.

To read about his country's vast empire, to think about the wealth of Africa and the Orient which his government mastered, gave the city dweller or farm worker a sense of worldliness, a feeling of sharing in great wealth, even though he received little immediate benefit from it. The vagrant could feel himself in a certain sense a millionaire; the London cockney a ruler of bits of red dotted across the globe. Public pride swelled in the thought of the nation owning an empire greater than itself—as was the case of England, France, Belgium, and the Netherlands. Public sentiment warmed in the thought of being master of an "empire on which the sun never sets."

Professor Langer concludes that at the height of nineteenth-century imperialism there was "some room for argument that popular pressure was more important in the growth of imperialism than was the action of the ruling classes." Nurtured by the growth of a popular press and a flood of literature glorifying and epitomizing colonial ventures, of which Kipling was perhaps the arch exemplar, the common folk in England, France, and Germany clamored for imperial excitement—"More chops, bloody ones, with gristle," as one writer phrased it.[18]

The surge of nationalism in Europe which came after the 1870's, which we have noted in the chapter on "Nationalism," also had its part in promoting popular support of imperialism. Even with the lessons of death written large across the homes of Germany by World War I, the German people nevertheless entered into Hitler's imperialist mesmerism with a considerable degree of support.

Summary. Strong economic forces have undoubtedly been behind much of modern imperialism and colonialism. But neither imperialism in general nor colonialism in particular can be wholly explained on economic grounds alone; even less as a sole by-product of advanced capitalism. As we have seen, these extensions of national power have deep psychological, sociological, religious, political, military, intellectual, and personal-rule roots. All of these forces must be taken into account if modern imperialism and colonialism are to be accurately explained. No simple explanation, no dogmatic theory, will suffice.[19] Imperialism, in nearly all its manifestations, is the resultant of the interplay of complex forces. But primarily it is an exemplification of the politics of power.

Professor J. A. Schumpeter, the late Harvard economist, once suggested

[18] *Ibid.*, pp. 80–85.
[19] See A. J. Toynbee, *A Study of History* (abridgment by D. C. Somervell, New York, 1947), p. 190.

that imperialism is "the objectless disposition on the part of a state to unlimited forcible expansion." And he concluded, "It would never have been evolved by the 'inner logic' of capitalism itself," but must be regarded "not only historically, but also sociologically, as a heritage of the autocratic state." [20] A similar conclusion was reached by E. M. Winslow in his study of imperialism in saying that "militarism and imperialism clearly constitute an identical pattern of thought and behavior. . . . They share the same tendency to extend dominion, but whereas imperialism seeks size, militarism seeks strength." [21] And Professor Dennis W. Brogan, British political scientist, notes that discussions of the causes of imperialism have often failed "to see in it an outlet for adventurous, bored, often lazy, often maladjusted people. Imperialism, or militarism, was a way of using, of taming, these people." [22]

EVOLUTION OF MODERN IMPERIALISM

The story of the rise and decline of the leading empires is chronicled in history texts. Historical atlases show the distribution of the world's land spaces at various junctures, and world maps show present-day holdings. These are worthy of study to see how power has waxed and waned. Without attempting to go into details, let us see what have been some of the trends in the evolution of imperialism in modern times.

First Era of Colonialism. The period from the fifteenth to the eighteenth centuries is recognized as the Age of Discovery, when men were exploring the configurations of the globe. With this came the first extension of European power to the Americas, Africa, Asia, and Oceania. This was the time when the newly unified nation-states located on the European seaboard—Portugal, Spain, France, the Netherlands, England—claimed and founded their first colonies. This period reached its climax about the time of the French and American revolutions. For nearly a century thereafter most of the powers were preoccupied with internal developments and with the adjustment of existent holdings rather than with further major overseas accretions. During this time the first independence movements began to show themselves in the colonial world. Led by the separation of the Thirteen Colonies in North America from England, Spain's dominions in Latin America likewise broke away one by one to follow the United States into independence.

Continentalism. Overlapping the recession of the first tide of colonialism came a period of what may be termed *continentalism*. Napoleon I of France launched this phase of empire building with his conquests of Europe reaching

---

[20] J. A. Schumpeter, *Imperialism and Social Classes* (New York, 1951), pp. 7, 128.
[21] Winslow, *op. cit.,* p. 227.
[22] Brogan, *op. cit.,* p. 271.

from Spain to Moscow, and from the North Sea to Egypt. His imperialism did not last long, but it required the energies of a large portion of Europe to destroy his power and return Europe from his "continental system" to the customary balance of power regime.

In the North American continent the United States extended itself during the nineteenth century from the Atlantic to the Pacific and from the Rio Grande to Alaska by means of frontier settlements, pressing the Indians back, purchasing large tracts of territory from France, Spain, and Russia, the war with Mexico, and diplomatic bargaining with England. By and large, this continental westward movement was activated by social, agrarian, commercial, and defense interests rather than by capitalistic search for new markets or centers of investment. Beckoned by the lure of the frontier, by the prospect of free and prosperous land, and by the desire to rid the North American continent of the danger of European power, the American people and their government occupied the continent in response to what the politicians proclaimed to be a "manifest destiny."

During this same time Czarist power spread from European Russia and Poland across Siberia and Central Asia to the western shores of the Pacific.[23] From this East-West axis, Russian continentalism fingered northward along the rivers of Siberia to the Arctic, southward to the borders of Iran and the Himalayas, and, from the beginning of the twentieth century, it repeatedly sought to inch into Manchuria, North Korea, and China.

Second Period of Expansionism. After nearly a century of relative quiescence in colonial expansion, and even some manifestations of anti-imperialism in the Western states,[24] a new struggle for possessions began among the powers from about 1870. This has continued in one form or another until the present time. In this movement the older colonial powers were joined by Germany, Italy, the United States, Japan, and the Soviet Union.

1. COLONIALISM, 1870–1930.[25] The main theatre of European colonialism in this period was Africa and Asia. Africa was dissected and absorbed. The decaying empire of the Ottoman Turks was dismembered. Southeast Asia and the Pacific Islands were partitioned. Concessions were extorted from the moribund Chinese Empire until Secretary of State Hay's appeal to the powers to preserve its "territorial integrity" stemmed this developing policy. Prior to World War I Germany acquired sizable holdings in Africa and the Pacific. Italy made the beginnings of an empire in East and North Africa through

---

23 It must not be forgotten (and it may not be forgotten by the Russians) that Russian rule extended to Alaska and, until stopped by the United States, down the west coast of North America almost to the Golden Gate.

24 Moon, *op. cit.*, pp. 21, 23.

25 For accounts of this period of colonialism see Moon, *op. cit.*, chs. 5–16; W. L. Langer, *cit. supra.*

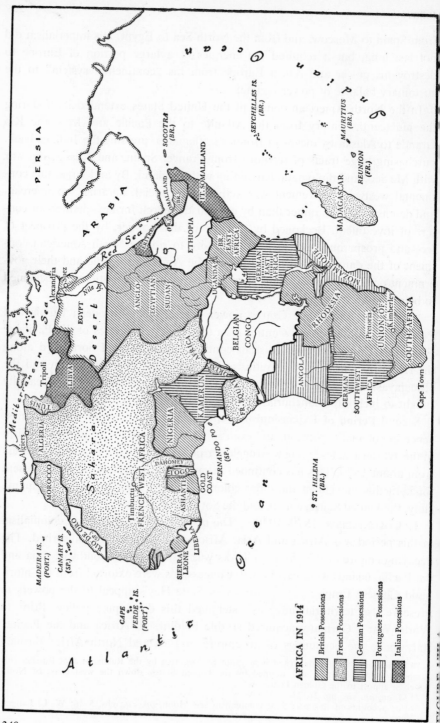

PERSIA

ARABIA

Red Sea

SEYCHELLES IS.
(BR.)

SOCOTRA
(BR.)

MAURITIUS
(BR.)

MADAGASCAR

REUNION
(FR.)

SOMALILAND
(BR.)

IT. SOMALILAND

ETHIOPIA

BR.
EAST
AFRICA

GERMAN
EAST
AFRICA

MOZAMBIQUE

Mediterranean Sea

Suez

Alexandria

ANGLO-
EGYPTIAN
SUDAN

UGANDA

EGYPT

Nile R.

EGYPT

Desert

LIBYA

Tripoli

Tunis

Algiers

MOROCCO

ALGERIA

SINAI

BELGIAN
CONGO

RHODESIA

Pretoria

Kimberley

UNION OF:
SOUTH AFRICA

Cape Town

CONGO

ANGOLA

GERMAN
SOUTHWEST
AFRICA

Sahara

Timbuctu

FRENCH WEST AFRICA

NIGERIA

KAMERUN

FR. EQU.

FERNANDO PO
(SP.)

DAHOMEY

TOGO

GOLD
COAST

ASHANTI

LIBERIA

SIERRA
LEONE

ST. HELENA
(BR.)

MADEIRA IS.
(PORT.)

CANARY IS.
(SP.)

RIO DE ORO

CAPE
VERDE IS.
(PORT.)

Atlantic Ocean

Indian Ocean

AFRICA IN 1914

British Possessions

French Possessions

German Possessions

Portuguese Possessions

Italian Possessions

annexations of Italian Somaliland, Eritrea, Libya, Tripoli, and the Dodecanese Islands. Japan annexed Korea, Formosa, and the islands adjoining its home land. The United States came into possession of a part of Samoa, the Hawaiian Islands, the Philippines, Puerto Rico, the Virgin Islands, and numerous smaller islands and base sites.

With most of the areas likely to be an object of colonization in the hands of imperial powers or independent states, this movement came to an initial halt at the close of World War I. In the peace settlement at the end of this war Germany and Turkey were required to give up their foreign holdings, which were parceled out among the victors in the form of mandates.[26]

2. IMPERIALIST VENTURES, 1930–1945. A second wave of expansion set in during the 1930's, and for a time moved rapidly when the expansionists found they had little to fear from the League of Nations. Japan embarked upon a grandiose scheme of fashioning a Greater East Asia Empire extending from Manchuria and the Chinese mainland to Malaya, Burma, the Philippines, Indonesia, and the South Pacific. Italy conquered Ethiopia in 1936 and vainly attempted to gain Tunisia, Greece, and the littoral of the Eastern Mediterranean.

Perhaps the most ambitious design was that of Hitler's Germany. This aimed at altering the *status quo* in Europe, Africa, and the Middle East and at disrupting the world balance of power. Nazi activities in the Middle and Far East and in Latin America indicated that these regions were also embraced in Berlin's scheming. In his message to the Nazi forces launching their attack upon the West in 1940, Hitler proclaimed that Germany was striving for a power situation that would endure a thousand years. This was to be imperialism on the Roman scale.

The battles of El Alamein, Stalingrad, Guadalcanal, Midway, Normandy, Okinawa, and other famous sites from 1943 to 1945 sounded the knell of these bids for empire. The defeat in World War II lost Italy all its overseas possessions save Italian Somaliland, over which it was given trusteeship for ten years. Japan was stripped of its extraterritorial gains and holdings including Korea, Formosa, the Kurile and Ryukyu Islands, and the Pacific mandates. Germany was reduced to less than its pre-war size.

3. SOVIET IMPERIALISM. Another contemporary imperialistic movement is represented by Soviet communist activities. Since the spring and summer of 1945 Soviet power has extended from the Elbe River in Germany to Manchuria and the Kurile Islands in the Far East. The USSR has taken territories from Rumania, Czechoslovakia, Poland, Germany, Finland, Japan, and China. Additional territories have been sought from Turkey, Norway, Den-

[26] See below, p. 251.

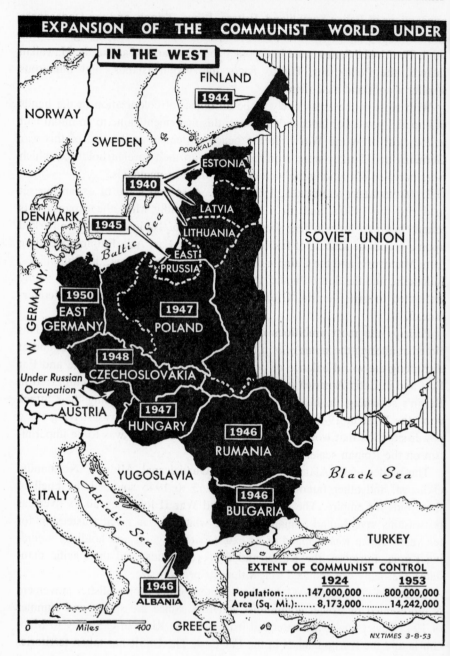

EXPANSION OF THE COMMUNIST WORLD UNDER

IN THE WEST

FINLAND
1944

NORWAY

SWEDEN
PORKKALA

ESTONIA
1940

DENMARK

LATVIA

1945

LITHUANIA

Baltic Sea

EAST PRUSSIA

SOVIET UNION

1950
EAST GERMANY

1947
POLAND

W. GERMANY

1948
CZECHOSLOVAKIA

Under Russian Occupation

AUSTRIA

1947
HUNGARY

1946
RUMANIA

ITALY

YUGOSLAVIA

Black Sea

Adriatic Sea

1946
BULGARIA

TURKEY

EXTENT OF COMMUNIST CONTROL

	1924	1953
Population:	147,000,000	800,000,000
Area (Sq. Mi.):	8,173,000	14,242,000

1946
ALBANIA

0   Miles   400   GREECE

N.Y. TIMES 3-8-53

FIGURE

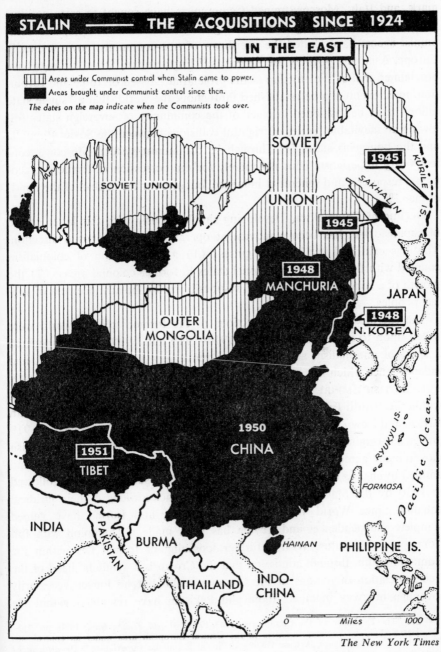

STALIN —— THE ACQUISITIONS SINCE 1924

IN THE EAST

||||| Areas under Communist control when Stalin came to power.

■ Areas brought under Communist control since then.

The dates on the map indicate when the Communists took over.

SOVIET UNION

SOVIET

UNION

1945

KURILE IS.

SAKHALIN

1945

1948
MANCHURIA

JAPAN

1948
N. KOREA

OUTER
MONGOLIA

1950
CHINA

1951
TIBET

RYUKYU IS.

Pacific Ocean

FORMOSA

INDIA

PAKISTAN

BURMA

HAINAN

PHILIPPINE IS.

THAILAND

INDO-
CHINA

0   Miles   1000

The New York Times

VIII:2

mark, and Italy. Moscow-trained Communists have sought to seize political power in lands stretching from the English Channel to Indonesia, and communist agents have plotted the overthrow of non-communist governments in Europe, Asia, and possibly the Americas.[27] Furthermore, Soviet writings have proclaimed that a "dictatorship of the proletariat," based on force and revolution, must eventually be established throughout the world; that a "single state union" must be fashioned in place of the community of sovereign states following an inevitable "series of frightful collisions between the Soviet Republic and the bourgeois states." [28] Through its communist system, Moscow's contemporary imperialism aims not merely for the possession of territories, economic resources, and spheres of influence, but also for the control of the minds of men.[29]

Decline of Colonialism. Developing simultaneously with this latter period of expansionism has been a movement operating in the opposite direction. This has exhibited itself in two guises: (1) a retrogression of colonialism coupled with the rise of new national states in former colonial areas; (2) the growth of a concept of international responsibility for the advancement of subject peoples.

The sacrifices which various sections of the former colonial world were called upon to make in the wars of 1914–1918 and 1939–1945 engendered a spirit of nationalism and produced a movement for self-government and independence which has gained momentum and dispersion since 1918.

1. BRITISH EMPIRE AND COMMONWEALTH. This trend was early manifest within the British Empire when Canada, Australia, India, the Union of South Africa, and New Zealand were admitted to the Paris Peace Conference in 1919 and made original members of the League of Nations. In 1926 the British Government agreed that the Dominions should be coequal with itself and entitled to engage in diplomatic relations with other states. This was followed in 1930 by the Statute of Westminster which acknowledged their juridical equality. Since World War II, India, Pakistan, and Burma have gained complete independence, and Ceylon has been made a Dominion with full Commonwealth status. With a further loosening of formal ties within the Commonwealth, through admission that the Crown is a symbolic head of the free association of nations of the Commonwealth but no longer necessarily sovereign in every member, India and Pakistan have remained within the

---

[27] See "The Evolution of the Cominform, 1947–1950," *World Today*, May, 1950, pp. 213–228. For a study of Soviet procedures in the Central European area under its control, see H. J. Hilton, Jr., "Hungary, A Case History of Soviet Economic Imperialism," *Department of State Bulletin*, Aug. 27, 1951.

[28] J. Stalin, *Problems of Leninism* (Eng. trans., Moscow, 1940), pp. 37, 126, 129, 156, 660. This has been a blueprint of communist policy comparable to Hitler's *Mein Kampf*.

[29] John Foster Dulles, *War or Peace* (New York, 1950), pp. 13–14.

Commonwealth and only Burma has seen fit to withdraw from the circle. Dominion status is contemplated for other units of the Empire, and London has recorded itself as holding self-government as the goal of its colonial policy for all overseas possessions.[30]

Britain has further evidenced its acceptance of the trend of dependent peoples toward independence through terminating its mandates over Iraq in 1932, over Trans-Jordan in 1946, and over Palestine in 1948. It sponsored Iraq into the League of Nations when others doubted its readiness for independent statehood,[31] and it passed to the United Nations responsibility for decision on what should be done in Palestine upon the termination of the mandate in that territory.[32]

2. PHILIPPINE INDEPENDENCE. In 1946 the United States redeemed the pledge made by Congress in 1934 to grant independence to the Philippines even though the war in the Pacific had left a far greater concern for security in that area than had prevailed at any previous time since the islands were acquired in the Spanish-American War. This voluntary grant of independence to a valuable possession was hailed throughout East Asia. The fact that such a great power would support the aspirations of these peoples encouraged independence movements in other lands. Although the circumstances surrounding the grant of independence were not all that some desired by way of economic advantage for the Filipinos, the United States accorded liberal economic assistance to the new state and supported its election to prominent positions in the United Nations.[33]

3. THE FRENCH EMPIRE. At the close of World War II, France was faced with strong nationalist resistance to the continuance of its mandate over Syria and Lebanon, and to the re-establishment of its colonial rule in Indo-China. Early in 1945 it was forced to accord independence to Syria and Lebanon, which became original Members of the United Nations.

In French Indo-China demands for independence by leaders of the Viet Minh movement under the Communist Ho Chi Minh were refused by France.

[30] Accounts of trends within the British Empire and Commonwealth will be found in the quarterly issues of *The Round Table* published in London. Authoritative works on the Commonwealth are H. D. Hall, *The British Commonwealth of Nations* (London, 1920); W. Y. Elliott, *The New British Empire* (New York, 1932); A. B. Keith, *The Dominions as Sovereign States: Their Constitutions and Governments* (London, 1938); F. G. Marcham, *The British Commonwealth: An Experiment in National Self-Government and International Co-operation* (Ithaca, 1944). See articles on recent developments in *Cont. Int. Rels. Readings,* 1949–1950, pp. 126–136. See also British Information Services *Britain's Colonial Policy and Record* (New York, Oct., 1952).

[31] Rupert Emerson, "Iraq: The End of a Mandate," *Foreign Affairs,* Jan., 1933.

[32] L. Larry Leonard, "The United Nations and Palestine," *Internat. Conciliation,* Oct., 1949.

[33] For a review of United States action see Julius W. Pratt, *America's Colonial Experiment* (New York, 1950). On subsequent economic relations see Report to the President by the Economic Survey Mission to the Philippines (Washington, 1950) by a mission under Daniel W. Bell, formerly Under-Secretary of the Treasury.

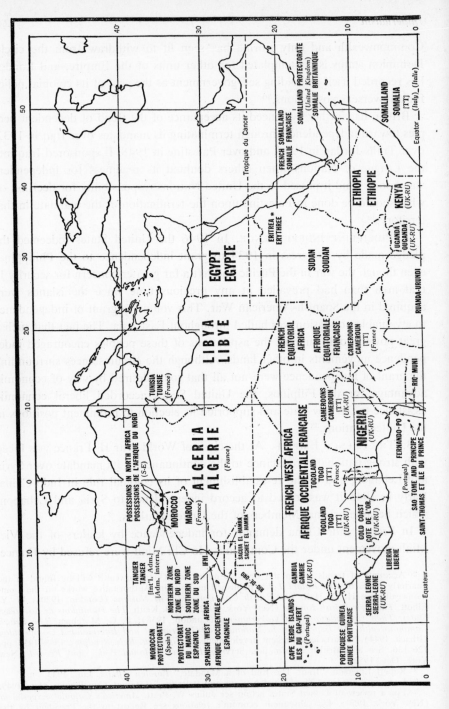

AFRICA TODAY

40

50

Tropique du Cancer

30

SOMALILAND PROTECTORATE
(United Kingdom)
SOMALIE BRITANNIQUE

FRENCH SOMALILAND
SOMALIE FRANÇAISE

SOMALILAND
SOMALIA

(Italy) (Italie)

Equator

ETHIOPIA
ÉTHIOPIE

KENYA
(UK-RU)

ERITREA *
ÉRYTHRÉE

UGANDA
OUGANDA
(UK-RU)

EGYPT
ÉGYPTE

SUDAN
SOUDAN

LIBYA
LIBYE

FRENCH
EQUATORIAL
AFRICA

AFRIQUE
ÉQUATORIALE
FRANÇAISE

CAMEROONS
CAMEROUN
(TT)
(France)

RUANDA-URUNDI

TUNISIA
TUNISIE
(France)

POSSESSIONS IN NORTH AFRICA
POSSESSIONS DE L'AFRIQUE DU NORD
(S-E)

ALGERIA
ALGÉRIE
(France)

MOROCCO
MAROC
(France)

FRENCH WEST AFRICA

AFRIQUE OCCIDENTALE FRANÇAISE

CAMEROONS
CAMEROUN
(TT)
(UK-RU)

NIGERIA
(UK-RU)

RIO MUNI

TOGOLAND
TOGO
(TT)
(France)

FERNANDO-PO
(Portugal)

TANGIER
TANGER
[Int'l. Adm.]
[Adm. intern.]

NORTHERN ZONE
ZONE DU NORD

SOUTHERN ZONE
ZONE DU SUD

IFNI

SAGUIA EL HAMRA
SAGUIET EL HAMRA

TOGOLAND
TOGO
(TT)
(UK-RU)

GOLD COAST
CÔTE DE L'OR
(UK-RU)

SÃO TOMÉ AND PRÍNCIPE
SAINT-THOMAS ET ÎLE DU PRINCE
(Portugal)

MOROCCAN
PROTECTORATE
(Spain)

PROTECTORAT
DU MAROC
ESPAGNOL

SPANISH WEST AFRICA
AFRIQUE OCCIDENTALE
ESPAGNOLE

RIO-DE-ORO

GAMBIA
GAMBIE
(UK-RU)

LIBERIA
LIBÉRIA

CAPE VERDE ISLANDS
ÎLES DU CAP-VERT
(Portugal)

SIERRA LEONE
SIERRE-LÉONE
(UK-RU)

PORTUGUESE GUINEA
GUINÉE PORTUGAISE

Equateur

246

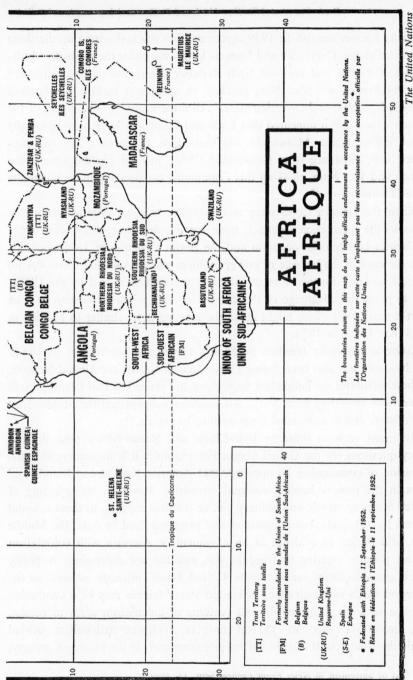

AFRICA
AFRIQUE

The boundaries shown on this map do not imply official endorsement or acceptance by the United Nations.

Les frontières indiquées sur cette carte n'impliquent pas leur reconnaissance ou leur acceptation officielle par l'Organisation des Nations Unies.

FIGURE VIII:3

SEYCHELLES
ILES SEYCHELLES
(UK-RU)

COMORO IS.
ILES COMORES
(France)

RÉUNION
(France)

MAURITIUS
ILE MAURICE
(UK-RU)

ZANZIBAR & PEMBA
(UK-RU)

TANGANYIKA
[TT]
(UK-RU)

NYASALAND
(UK-RU)

MOZAMBIQUE
(Portugal)

MADAGASCAR
(France)

SWAZILAND
(UK-RU)

BELGIAN CONGO
CONGO BELGE

NORTHERN RHODESIA
RHODESIA DU NORD
(UK-RU)

SOUTHERN RHODESIA
RHODESIA DU SUD

BECHUANALAND
(UK-RU)

BASUTOLAND
(UK-RU)

ANGOLA
(Portugal)

SOUTH-WEST
AFRICA
SUD-OUEST
AFRICAIN
[FM]

UNION OF SOUTH AFRICA
UNION SUD-AFRICAINE

ANNOBON·
ANHOBON

SPANISH GUINEA
GUINÉE ESPAGNOLE

·ST. HELENA
SAINTE-HÉLÈNE
(UK-RU)

Tropique du Capricorne

[TT]   Trust Territory
       Territoire sous tutelle

[FM]   Formerly mandated to the Union of South Africa
       Anciennement sous mandat de l'Union Sud-Africain

(B)   Belgium
       Belgique

(UK-RU) United Kingdom
        Royaume-Uni

(S-E) Spain
       Espagne

✦ Federated with Ethiopia 11 September 1952.
   Réunie en fédération à l'Éthiopie le 11 septembre 1952.

247

Guerrilla warfare ensued. In 1949 agreement was reached setting up the three associated states, Cambodia and Laos as kingdoms under the protective jurisdiction of France and the Viet Nam Republic comparatively independent.[34] In 1954 France and Viet Nam reached an agreement making the latter a "fully independent and sovereign state." All three states were members of the French Union and it appeared that Laos and Cambodia were moving rapidly to full independence. Meanwhile, the Viet Minh, Communist led, and supported with assistance from Communist China, pressed warfare against the French and Viet Nam, cloaking this Communist expansion venture under the guise of nationalism.[35]

When the Geneva Conference met in 1954, bringing Asiatic communist states to the international council table for the first time, there were some similarities between the occasion and the Berlin Congress of 1878. But this time the crux of the balance of power problem was in Asia and there was no "honest broker." Furthermore the attitude of communism, led by the USSR, was to press the advantage of the current adverse military situation in Viet Nam toward goals which might make the meeting more similar to Munich in 1938 than Berlin in 1878.

Rising agitation for freedom in Tunisia (given self-government in 1954) and Morocco has also been facing France, and indirectly the United Nations. In these territories the nationalist movements are related to Pan-Islamism with connections extending from North Africa through Egypt and the Middle East to Pakistan, and in attenuated form even to Indonesia.[36]

Situations such as those in Indo-China and North Africa pose difficult policy questions for the United States. For example, it is imperative that the extension of communism be opposed, that America have strong friends and allies in the powers holding colonial territories. However, the granting of United States economic and military aid, or political support, to these colonial powers has, at times, been construed and propagandized in Asia, the Middle East, and Africa as evidence of an alignment of America with colonialism against peoples aspiring to freedom and national self-expression. A policy which can effectively accommodate United States' interests as well as the divergent needs and aspirations of United States' friends may be a continuing problem so long as any of the old patterns of colonialism seem to persist.

4. INDONESIA AND THE DUTCH EMPIRE. Incipient nationalism existed within the Netherlands East Indies Empire from early in the twentieth century.

---

[34] Text of agreement in *News From France*, Sept. 15, 1949.

[35] On the situation in Indo-China see E. L. Katzenbach, Jr., "Indo-China: A Military-Political Appreciation," *World Politics*, Jan., 1952.

[36] H. J. Isaacs, *Africa: New Crisis in the Making*, For. Policy Assoc. Headline Booklet No. 91 (New York, 1952).

It did not become an influential political factor until World War II when the Dutch were faced with, and then overrun by, Japanese conquest. As the war moved toward its climax and the Japanese saw the fate of their imperialist designs being sealed, they encouraged the Indonesian independence movement led by Dr. Soekarno which proclaimed the Indonesian Republic in August, 1945. Dutch aspirations to resume their rule where it had left off were at first blocked by the fact that they had no forces in the Indies to take over and that some Japanese laid down their arms to the Indonesian Republicans. By the time the Dutch were in a position to try to take over from the British who had supervised the Japanese repatriation, the independence movement had gone too far to be stayed.

An agreement signed at Linggadjati in 1946 provided for the creation of a United States of Indonesia within a Netherlands-Indonesian Union. But Dutch use of force against the Indonesian leaders in 1947–1948 brought the United Nations Security Council into the situation. Only after lengthy exercise of good offices and a clear manifestation of world opinion against a renewal of Dutch colonialism, was an agreement reached at The Hague in 1949, recognizing the Republic of the United States of Indonesia as a sovereign independent state and instituting free and equal cooperation between the Dutch and the Indonesians in the Netherlands-Indonesian Union patterned after the principles of the British Commonwealth of Nations. Numerous problems of adjustment of Dutch and Indonesian interests both within the U.S.I. and in foreign affairs remain.

Of primary concern to others is the fact that Indonesian nationalism, in common with that of nationalist movements elsewhere in Asia, has sought to follow a neutral, and even isolationist, course in world politics, thereby raising difficult issues in Indonesian-Dutch relations and in Western-Indonesian affairs generally. This is perhaps a part of the difficulty accompanying the transition of any body of self-conscious people from colonialism to statehood. It has happened before, as exemplified in the relations between the United States and England in the decades following American independence. It is not surprising in a period of tension among the Great Powers that a new nation should try to chart a course according to its own conceptions of national interest—which inevitably vary somewhat from those of the mother country and others. This is one of the issues of effecting a peaceful evolution from imperialism and colonialism to the cooperation of free, equal peoples in a community of states.[37]

[37] On the Indonesian situation generally see Robert Payne, *The Revolt of Asia* (New York, 1947); Charles Wolf, Jr., *The Indonesian Story* (New York, 1948); J. F. Collins, "The United Nations and Indonesia," *Internat. Conciliation,* March, 1950.

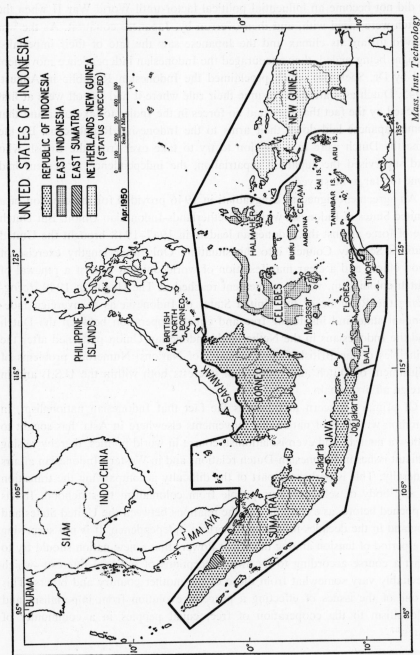

FIGURE VIII:4

Mass. Inst. Technology

5. LIBERALIZATION OF COLONIAL ADMINISTRATION. Along with the decline in colonialism has come a liberalization of administrative policies within many of the colonial preserves still retained by the powers. This includes the adoption of measures to promote social welfare and assist economic advancement. Added emphasis is being placed upon education in many colonies. New social services are being provided. Native councils are being fostered in numerous places, as well as some enlarged opportunities for representation in colonial legislatures and at the seat of the central government.[38]

Contrasting with these trends, the appearance in some parts of Africa of racial strife and struggle over political and civil rights suggests the possibility that there may be serious difficulties ahead in this great continent.[39]

GROWTH OF INTERNATIONAL RESPONSIBILITY

One of the notable stages in the evolution of colonialism has been the emergence of the principle that colonial powers are in some measure responsible to the international community for the way in which they administer dependencies, and that the community has a legitimate concern for the advancement of non-self-governing peoples.

League of Nations Mandate System. The first general beginning in this direction was the incorporation into the Covenant of the League of Nations in 1919 of a principle that the well-being and development of the peoples of the colonial areas taken away from the Central Powers defeated in World War I, "not yet able to stand by themselves under the strenuous conditions of the modern world," should form a "sacred trust of civilization." Selected Allied nations, "who by reason of their resources, their experience or their geographical position can best undertake this responsibility," were entrusted with the tutelage of these territories as "Mandatories on behalf of the League."[40]

1. MANDATE TERRITORIES. Fourteen territories were given mandate status, classified into three groups (A, B, and C) depending upon their relative degree of readiness for independent statehood. A variety of political and strategic motives figured in the decisions of the Supreme Council of the Allied and Associated Powers on the specific assignments.

38 Vernon McKay, "Empires in Transition," *Foreign Policy Reports,* May 1, 1947, surveys significant changes in the principal empires.
39 See H. V. Hodson, "Race Relations in the Commonwealth," *Internat. Affairs,* July, 1950; W. M. Macmillan, "South Africa Today," *African World,* March, 1950; XYZ, "The Significance of South Africa," *J. of Int. Affairs,* vol. VII, no. 2, 1953.
40 For review of the mandate system see H. D. Hall, *Mandates, Dependencies and Trusteeships* (Washington, 1948), chs. 2–16; F. P. Walters, *A History of the League of Nations* (London, 1952), ch. 16, vol. I, pp. 171–173.

TERRITORY	MANDATE CLASS	ADMINISTERING POWER
1. Syria and Lebanon	A	France
2. Palestine and Trans-Jordan	A	Great Britain
3. Iraq	A	Great Britain
4. Togoland ½	B	France
5. Togoland ½	B	Great Britain
6. Cameroons ½	B	France
7. Cameroons ½	B	Great Britain
8. Tanganyika	B	Great Britain
9. Ruanda Urundi	B	Belgium
10. Southwest Africa	C	Union of South Africa
11. Samoa (part)	C	New Zealand
12. Nauru Island	C	British Empire (Australia)
13. German Ids. S. of Equator	C	Australia
14. German Ids. N. of Equator	C	Japan

The mandate system was admittedly a compromise between colonialism and Wilsonian internationalism. It was obtained by President Wilson only after a strenuous negotiation with the countries that wanted to annex the territories. The compromise allowed the victorious states to occupy and administer the territories, but it refused them clear title and required that they administer them according to certain principles and be responsible to the League of Nations for their actions.[41]

2. FEATURES OF SYSTEM. One of the features of the mandate system was that the mandatory powers were required to assume international commitments to guarantee freedom of conscience and religion, prohibition of the slave trade and the traffic in liquor and arms, and nonmilitarization. Forced labor was forbidden, restrictions were placed on the sale of land to foreigners, and the parties were obligated to provide improvements in education and social welfare.

A second feature of the system was that each mandatory was required to submit an annual report on conditions and developments to the League. These were carefully examined by the Permanent Mandates Commission, and in one instance, in Syria and Lebanon in 1925, the administering state was forced to change its governing personnel. The League did not have authority to inspect the territories, but the natives had a right of petition which enabled the League to obtain something of a behind-the-scenes picture of conditions.

During its years of operation the Mandates Commission, which was composed of expert nongovernmental personnel, made several valuable studies of

---

41 The legal status of the mandates was never fully clarified. The defeated states renounced title to the territories to the Principal Allied and Associated Powers which allocated the mandates. The Mandate Agreements were approved by the League of Nations Council. The Mandates Commission ruled in 1924 that the mandatory powers did not possess "any right over any part of the territory . . . other than that resulting from their being entrusted with the administration of the territory." In 1950 the International Court of Justice rendered an advisory opinion that a mandatory could not change the status of a mandated territory without the consent of the United Nations. *International Organization*, Aug., 1950, pp. 476–478.

situations in the mandated territories and was generally regarded as one of the most fruitful bodies of the League.[42]

United Nations Trusteeship System.[43] The San Francisco Conference replaced the mandate system with the United Nations trusteeship system. This made the basic principles of international trusteeship applicable not only to the former mandate territories which remained under trusteeship, but also to some of the territories detached from the defeated states in World War II, and to "any other territories" which states might see fit to place under trusteeship (UN Charter, Chapter XII).

1. OBLIGATIONS. In addition to furthering the economic, social, and educational advancement of the inhabitants of the trust territories, the Charter added that the administering states must promote their "progressive development towards self-government or independence." This is obligatory in *all* trust territories, without distinction as in the different classes of mandates. Although the formula is flexible, the commitment throws a positive responsibility upon the holding states. The United Nations may at any time call for evidence that measures are being taken in the direction of self-government or independence. And it may focus world opinion against any state that may be remiss in its actions. To check on the handling of the trusteeships and on conditions in the trust territories, the United Nations may send inspection missions which the administering states are bound to accept.

2. SECURITY PROVISIONS. Contrary to the mandate system, the United Nations Charter allows the administering powers to fortify and establish bases in the trust territories, to train the natives, and to designate strategic areas in which special defensive precautions may be taken.[44]

Non-Self-Governing Territories. In addition to the trusteeship system proper, the United Nations Charter contains a "Declaration Regarding Non-Self-Governing Territories" which has been called "an international charter of colonial administration." [45] This is a significant extension of the principle and

---

42 On activities of the Commission see in addition to previously mentioned works, D. P. Myers, *Handbook of the League of Nations* (Boston, 1935), pp. 104–119.

43 See ch. xx below for discussion of structure and operation of trusteeship system. For general reference see Leland M. Goodrich and E. Hambro, *Charter of the United Nations, Commentary and Documents* (rev. ed., Boston, 1949), chs. 12–13; Dept. of State, *The United States and Non-Self-Governing Territories* (U.S.–U.N. Information Series No. 18, Washington, 1947); Liu Chieh, "International Trusteeship Visiting Missions," *Internat. Conciliation*, Feb., 1949; Alf Ross, *Constitution of the United Nations* (New York, 1950), pp. 95–98, 178–188; Ernst B. Haas, "The Attempt to Terminate Colonialism: Acceptance of the United Nations Trusteeship System," *International Organization*, Feb., 1953.

44 The Pacific Islands captured from Japan were designated strategic areas when the United States submitted a Trusteeship Agreement for them. Such areas are under the supervision of the Security Council so far as the United Nations functions are concerned.

45 See Ralph J. Bunche, "Trusteeship and Non-Self-Governing Territories in the Charter of the United Nations," *Dept. of State Bulletin*, 8, p. 104; F. W. Riggs, "Wards of the U.N.: Trust and Dependent Areas," *Foreign Policy Reports*, June 1, 1950.

of some of the obligations of international responsibility to dependent territories generally, whatever their title or precise legal status.

By Chapter XI of the Charter, Members of the United Nations having non-
self-governing territories are bound to "recognize the principle that the interests of the inhabitants are paramount, and accept as a sacred trust the
obligation to promote to the utmost, within the system of international peace
and security established by the present Charter, the well-being of the inhabitants of these territories."

1. RESPONSIBILITIES. Members having non-self-governing territories must
insure the political, economic, social, and educational advancement of the
native peoples. They must accord them "just treatment" and protect them
against "abuses." Furthermore, they are committed to develop self-government
in these territories, to take "due account" of the "political aspirations" of their
peoples, and to assist them in the development of "free political institutions."
This undertaking does not specify that policies must be pursued looking
toward an immediate, or even ultimate, grant of independence. Some wanted
such a guarantee written into the San Francisco Charter, but the colonial
powers were not ready to agree to this.

The Members are also required to further peace and security, to cooperate
with one another and with specialized international bodies for constructive
development purposes, and to apply a spirit of good neighborliness to others in
handling the affairs of these territories. Finally, they must regularly transmit
information to the United Nations regarding economic, social, and educational
conditions in the territories. While the United Nations may request information on conditions within non-self-governing territories, and may make recommendations with respect thereto, it has no authority to inspect conditions
within colonies and dependencies or to send missions into them as it may in
the trust territories.

2. POLITICAL ASPECTS. The United States was the first state to transmit
information on non-self-governing territories to the United Nations, and it has
been one of the foremost advocates of vigorous study and action on such
reports by the General Assembly. There is no obligation that the colonial
powers include information in their reports on *political* conditions within the
territories. But there has been steady pressure from various quarters, including
such ideological opposites as the Soviet Union and the United States, that such
information be presented to the United Nations and be discussed. This has
been encouraged by the General Assembly. Such reporting is likely to be a
bone of contention for some time to come, for some colonial powers feel that
other states are interested in this only for purposes of political exploitation and
propaganda.

The General Assembly, the Economic and Social Council, and some of the specialized agencies have taken the obligations and opportunities seriously by exploring ways and means of accelerating economic and social advancement for peoples of the colonial areas.[46]

REGIONAL COOPERATION [47]

Caribbean Commission. Another forward-looking step taken in recent years has been the inauguration of regional commissions to promote international cooperation in furthering the welfare of dependent areas. The first of these was the Anglo-American Caribbean Commission formed in 1942. This was renamed the Caribbean Commission in 1945 when France and The Netherlands joined the other two powers. This Commission has engaged in a series of cooperative studies relating to the possessions of the four countries in the Caribbean area. These have pertained to such diverse matters as labor, agriculture, housing, transportation, health, social conditions, education, production, and marketing. It has also sponsored West Indian Conferences in which native peoples have been represented as well as the governments to debate questions of mutual interest and to make recommendations to the governments.[48]

South Pacific Commission. A similar organization was started in 1947 for the South Pacific. Australia, France, The Netherlands, New Zealand, the United Kingdom, and the United States participate in this commission, whose scope extends to all non-self-governing possessions of these states in the Pacific south of the Equator and east from Netherlands New Guinea. This body, like the Caribbean Commission, has a secretariat, research council, and periodic conferences including representatives of the native peoples, as well as two regular commission meetings each year.[49]

These regional bodies exist primarily to promote the well-being of the peoples living in these non-self-governing territories through international collaboration. Their studies have made contributions not only to the standards of life, but also to the political outlook of the peoples of these territories.

---

[46] See Goodrich and Hambro, *op. cit.*, ch. 11; "International Responsibility for Colonial Peoples," *Internat. Conciliation*, Feb., 1950.

[47] See ch. xxi below.

[48] See C. W. Taussig, "Regionalism in the Caribbean: Six Years of Progress," *Department of State Builetin*, May 30, 1948; Frank Stockdale, "The Work of the Caribbean Commission," *Internat. Affairs*, April, 1947; James Bough, "The Caribbean Commission," *International Organization*, Nov., 1949. See below, ch. xxi.

[49] "Programs for Non-Self-Governing Areas in the Pacific," *Department of State Bulletin*, Jan. 9, 1950; "South Pacific Commission Makes Progress," *ibid.*, July 4, 1949; Annette B. Fox, "International Organization for Colonial Development," *World Politics*, April, 1951.

INTERNATIONAL AID PROGRAMS

Dependent territories have been the beneficiaries, directly or indirectly, of American foreign aid and United Nations Technical Assistance Programs in recent years. Although the European Recovery Program was directed primarily to the assistance of countries in Europe, consideration was given to the problems of dependent territories belonging to the countries participating in this program by the United States Economic Cooperation Administration. Since 1952, assistance has been extended through the Mutual Security and Technical Cooperation Programs.

In the United Nations, the regional commissions of the Economic and Social Council have devoted attention to the conditions in and future of dependent territories. The Economic Commission for Asia and the Far East in particular concerns itself with the problems of countries which were, up to a few years ago, under colonialism. Furthermore, the United Nations' Program for Technical Assistance since 1949 has been of assistance to dependent as well as independent underdeveloped countries.[50]

In these, as in the previously mentioned developments, the international community has been showing an increasing concern for the livelihood and status of the peoples of dependent and non-self-governing areas. This represents a far departure from the concepts of colonialism and imperialism practiced in the past. It is an augury of hope that, step by step, these peoples are coming to make their own contribution to the world community and that the privileged nations are joining in a common effort with the underprivileged peoples to raise the welfare of mankind.

CONTEMPORARY UNITED STATES POLICY

One of the stock Soviet phrases is that the United States is engaging in a gargantuan "imperialism." Georgi M. Malenkov, former Secretary General of the Communist party and now a key figure in the group governing the USSR, charged in 1949 that American policy aims at "converting the whole world into a colony of the American imperialists, of reducing sovereign peoples to the position of slaves."[51] Such a charge, frequently repeated by the Soviet press and radio and by Soviet delegates in the United Nations, merits examination.[52]

Foreign Aid. One of the outstanding features of contemporary international relations has been the unprecedented outpouring of food, coal, machinery,

50 See D. Blelloch, "Technical Assistance: Programmes and Policies," *Internat. Affairs,* Jan., 1952.
51 *The New York Times,* Nov. 7, 1949.
52 See Herbert Feis, "Is the U. S. Imperialist?" *Yale Rev.,* Autumn, 1951.

equipment, dollars, and technical assistance of many kinds in direct and indirect aid programs to needy countries all over the globe by the United States since 1944.

Economic and technical assistance that seeks to relieve suffering, to help peoples that have suffered from war to rebuild their industries and cities along lines of their own choice, and to strengthen their defenses so that they may become stronger, more prosperous, independent nations is hardly synonymous with imperialism or colonialism. United States' aid has not always succeeded in eliminating need of foreign assistance, but it has not sought to keep any of the recipient countries dependent upon the United States, as a policy of imperialism would endeavor to do. Furthermore, the peoples and governments that have benefited from the various assistance programs have on the whole remained free to criticize, to differ with Washington, to refuse to coordinate their economies with others, and to pursue policies conformable to their own national interests, which imperialism would hardly countenance.

Policy toward Dependencies. We have already noted that the United States in 1945–1946 fulfilled its promise of independence to the Philippines. In 1950 constitutional government was voted for Puerto Rico, with all offices chosen by local elections. In 1953 President Eisenhower stated that Puerto Rico could have independence whenever it so desired. Civil rule and local self-government were approved in 1949 in place of naval administration in Guam and the trust territories.[53] In addition to submitting annual reports on all its own possessions, the United States has taken a leading role in urging the United Nations to study political trends in the possessions of all countries, as well as economic, social, and educational conditions. These events hardly resemble imperialism.

Territorial Acquisition. In contrast with some other states, the United States did not claim any territory from enemy powers in either World War I or II. It did take trusteeship over the former Japanese mandated islands in the Pacific (the Marianas, Carolines, and Marshalls) in 1946, but this was unanimously approved by the United Nations and supported by the Soviet Union as "right and proper." Whatever defensive measures may be taken for national security in these islands, the United States has nevertheless undertaken to assist the islands in "progressive development toward self-government or independence as may be appropriate to the particular circumstances of each territory and its peoples." [54] And the United Nations Trusteeship Council has com-

53 R. E. James, "Recent Developments Concerning American Dependencies," in Rupert Emerson and Others, *America's Pacific Dependencies* (New York, 1949), p. 129.
54 Text of Trusteeship Agreement in *Documents on American Foreign Relations*, 1947, p. 394. The same principles apply to the Okinawa trusteeship ordained by the treaty of peace with Japan. See Rupert Emerson, "The United States and Trusteeship in the Pacific," in *America's Pacific Dependencies*, p. 25.

mended the progress made in the islands in education and local government.[55]

Military Bases. It has sometimes been charged that United States acquisition and maintenance of military and air bases in various parts of the world is imperialistic. This overlooks the fact that at the end of World War II the United States gave up scores of bases which it had used for the victory in Europe and the Pacific. While it is true that base rights have been leased in some countries in the interests both of national and collective security, care has been exercised not to interfere with the independence or national policies of the countries in which they are located. The states are free to pursue whatever foreign or domestic policies they see fit, as evidenced by their actions within the United Nations opposing the United States when their national interests so indicate.

Relations with Latin America. United States policy toward Latin America during the first quarter of the twentieth century was frequently criticized as being imperialistic. This was owing to American investment practices, to a series of interventions within some of the Central American and Caribbean countries, and to the protectorate held over Cuba.

Since the proclamation of the "Good Neighbor Policy" in 1933, United States relationships with Latin America have undergone a fundamental change. United States Marines, stationed for years in Haiti and Nicaragua, were withdrawn. The protectorate over Cuba was terminated. Interventions were stopped. As a consequence, when World War II occurred, all the Republics were prepared to declare that any attempt on the integrity, sovereignty, or independence of any American state would be considered an act of aggression against all—a principle solidified in the Pact of Reciprocal Assistance signed at Rio de Janeiro in 1947 by all the Republics.

A milestone in relations between the United States and the Latin American countries was reached in 1948 when a Charter of Organization of the American States was adopted. In this, all signatories agreed to nonintervention in the internal or external affairs of one another, directly or indirectly, "for any reason whatsoever." And they covenanted not to "use or encourage the use of coercive measures of an economic or political character in order to force the sovereign will of another state and obtain from it advantages of any kind." [56] With these steps intervention "died," as Edward G. Miller, United States Assistant Secretary of State, remarked, "a universally unlamented death." [57]

Although there are obvious differences in strength and in world influence among American Republics, the relationships between the states of North and

[55] *United Nations Bulletin,* July 15, 1950, p. 74.
[56] Text of Charter in *Documents on American Foreign Relations,* 1947, p. 534.
[57] *Department of State Bulletin,* May 15, 1950, p. 770.

South America are today characterized by a mutual respect and solidarity that are not very common in international affairs.

CONCLUSION

Strange as it might seem at first thought, the period marked by the two World Wars has witnessed a decrease of imperialism in the traditional sense. Under the influence of the principle of national self-determination proclaimed by Woodrow Wilson, the three decades since Armistice Day in 1918 have seen a large number of former colonial possessions of the Western states gain independence. And for many of the non-self-governing territories remaining under the control and administration of the Western Powers a new day of economic and social advancement, as well as of progress toward self-government, has begun under the influence of the principles of responsibility and trusteeship, enunciated in the League of Nations Covenant and the United Nations Charter.

That imperialism is far from gone as a fundamental factor in international relations is evidenced by the empire-building efforts of fascist Italy, of Nazi Germany, and of Soviet communism. In these contemporary versions, imperialism is closely related to totalitarian political forces and militarism, posing dangers of catastrophic war to the international community as a whole.

Recent events in Morocco, and Indo-China also testify that the aspects of imperialism and colonialism in the older sense of the terms are still alive and that the world still has some problems of adjustment in meeting the newer nationalistic movements and the remaining desires of the colonial nations to retain positions of influence, benefit, and defense which they have prized in the past. Certainly the issues of colonialism and imperialism are still important, if only because of their propaganda appeal to recently dependent peoples. But old-fashioned colonialism is dead in the sense that the term implies further expansion of the Great Powers. And old-fashioned imperialism is practically dead, being replaced by the new imperialism which combines the forces of communism and the old-fashioned nationalistic urge for increased power. The vehicles of the new imperialism are certainly the USSR and probably communist China.

SUGGESTED READINGS

H. Duncan Hall, *Mandates, Dependencies, and Trusteeships* (Washington, 1948).
George E. Haynes, *Africa, Continent of the Future* (New York, 1951).
J. A. Hobson, *Imperialism, A Study* (London, 1938).
William L. Langer, *The Diplomacy of Imperialism, 1878–1902,* 2 vols. (New York, 1935).
Parker T. Moon, *Imperialism and World Politics* (New York, 1926).
Julius W. Pratt, *America's Colonial Experiment* (New York, 1950).
E. M. Winslow, *The Pattern of Imperialism* (New York, 1950).

CHAPTER IX

Conflict and War

VOLTAIRE ONCE complained that history is written primarily as the record of violence, destruction, human suffering, and death. Whether or not one accepts such a grim philosophy, the fact remains that the annals of history and the pages of the daily press are studded with incidents of conflict and violence. Mankind lives in a society charged with disputes and conflict. The recurrent use of armed force by states against one another for the solution of conflicts and the advancement of national interests has been a central feature of international politics since the beginning of the state system.

CONFLICT IN SOCIETY

Violence in Civil Society. In civilized communities only a fraction of the conflicts between individuals end in violence and bloodshed. Likewise, the clashes of group interests are normally adjusted through private arrangement, or by appeal to the institutions of law and justice, or by the processes of politics, without recourse to violence.[1] Force is made a monopoly of the state to be used to preserve order and security. Unauthorized use of violence by individuals and groups is prohibited under constitutional government.

Where control of political power is at stake, factions are sometimes tempted to employ forceful methods to gain office, to attain political ends, or to prevent adversaries from obtaining power. Within liberal, democratic societies, however, the "saber," as Professor V. O. Key remarks, "more often exacts its influence without being drawn."[2] But in some countries riots, revolutions, and civil war are fairly frequent accompaniments of disputes and contests for power in the political process. And in some states totalitarian regimes employ force and terror to compel conformity to governmental dictates and to quell political opposition.

---

1 See L. F. Richardson, "Statistics on Deadly Quarrels," in J. H. Pear (ed.), *Psychological Factors of Peace and War* (New York, 1950).

2 V. O. Key, Jr., *Politics, Parties, and Pressure Groups* (New York, 1948), p. 621.

Recurrent Factors in International Affairs. In the relations among sovereign states, armed force has frequently been an overt instrument. Powerful motivations impel states and political factions to seek satisfaction of their needs and interests. When peaceful means of attainment or persuasion fail to bring satisfaction, the availability of weapons and their effectiveness, if successfully employed, provide an alternative which at times seems attractive to those in charge of the affairs of states, and to political groups striving for power and recognition. At times, the use of armed force appears to hold the only hope for the defense of the body politic and its interests, or for the achievement of political ends. The fact that the community of states, as such, is weakly organized and politically unstable, and that international law recognizes the rights of self-defense and self-help, supports the natural inclination of states to maintain and use instruments of force, if need be, in international affairs.

FREQUENCY OF ARMED CONFLICT

Research has shown that in the period from 1500 to 1940 there were 278 instances of hostilities which amounted to war, or which had important consequences among the members of the community of states. This does not include revolutions, interventions, punitive expeditions, "pacifications," and explorations where force has been used. The addition of these episodes would probably multiply this figure by ten.[3]

In the period from 1820 to 1929, eighty-two wars or "deadly quarrels" have been counted in each of which more than 10,000 people were killed.[4]

Even the United States, which has been regarded as one of the most peaceful states, has been in seven international wars since 1775 in addition to its civil war and many uses of force short of war.

CAUSES OF WAR

Many explanations have been offered for the recurrent use of force in international affairs. Broadly speaking, states and political groups have turned to the use of armed force either (1) to satisfy or to protect political or national interests, or established rights, or (2) to gain or to conserve political power. More specifically, armed force has been employed because it has been found to be an effective or necessary means of (1) establishing or maintaining political independence, (2) acquiring or securing territorial possessions, (3) furthering or safeguarding economic, social, political, or religious institutions

3 Quincy Wright, *A Study of War* (Chicago, 1942), I, Appendix xx; 78 of the 278 wars listed belong in the category of civil war.
4 Richardson, *op. cit.* This author lists another 174 incidents in each of which at least 3,000 were killed.

or ideological concepts, or (4) attaining or protecting international position, power, or prestige.[5]

Explanations from Historical Studies. Reviewing six of the major conflicts since the fall of Rome—namely, the conquests of Islam (622–732), the Crusades (1095–1270), the Hundred Years' War (1339–1453), the Thirty Years' War (1618–1648), the French Revolutionary and Napoleonic Wars (1793–1815) and World War I (1914–1918)—Professor Quincy Wright has reached the following explanations of why states have resorted to war:

Different as were many of the circumstances, each of these six great wars scattered over thirteen hundred years, exhibits idealist, psychological, political, and juridical causes. It appears that in these varying conditions of civilization individuals and masses have been moved to war (1) because of enthusiasm for ideals expressed in the impersonal symbols of a religion, a nation, an empire, or civilization, or humanity, the blessings of which it is thought may be secured or spread by coercion of the recalcitrant; or (2) because of the hope to escape from conditions which they find unsatisfactory, inconvenient, perplexing, unprofitable, intolerable, dangerous, or merely boring. Conditions of this kind have produced unrest and have facilitated the acceptance of ideals and violent methods for achieving them. Governments and organized factions have initiated war (3) because in a particular situation war appeared to them a necessary or convenient means to carry out a foreign policy; to establish, maintain or expand the power of a government, party, or class within the state; to maintain or expand the power of the state in relation to other states; or to reorganize the community of nations; or (4) because incidents have occurred or circumstances have arisen which they thought violated law and impaired rights and for which war was the normal or expected remedy according to the moral standards of the time.[6]

Political Rationale. Professor Wright's description summarizes comprehensively types of conditions which have moved states and politically minded groups to turn to the arbitrament of war. Politically speaking, we may say that states have gone to war because their conceptions of national interests have impelled them to follow such a path. Considerations of right and wrong, of justice and honor, have played a part in the causation of war. So also have nationalism, idealism, religion, fear, and insecurity. But above all, resort to war may be ascribed in many instances to a desire for power, territory, prestige, or position on the part of some state, political leader, or political faction.

Economic Causation. An interpretation of the causes of war widely propagated by the Soviet Government is that of economic determinism and imperial-

5 See L. I. Bernard, *War and Its Causes* (New York, 1944); cf. Wright, "Brief Summary of the Causes of War," *Am. Sociological Rev.*, Aug., 1938; A. L. Goodhart, "International Law and the Causes of War," *Transactions of the Grotius Society*, vol. 28 (1942), pp. 65–82.

6 Quincy Wright, *A Study of War* (Chicago), II, pp. 726–727. Copyright 1942 by the University of Chicago Press. For a sociological view of the factors of war and revolution see P. A. Sorokin, *Society, Culture and Personality* (New York, 1947), pp. 503–514.

ism as set forth in Marxist-Leninist doctrine. The Communists assert that advanced capitalism is bound to seek investments abroad with "surplus capital," from which imperialist wars inevitably result. Both Lenin and Stalin have denied the possibility of lasting peace among capitalist states, and both have insisted that sooner or later violent clashes must occur between capitalist and socialist states.[7] Notwithstanding the fact that the Soviet Union itself has become an imperialist state menacing the peace and security of other peoples, the Marxist-Leninist-Stalinist theories regarding war have gained a wide hearing.

Careful research has established that more often than not financial circles have opposed imperialist ambitions of glory-seeking nationalist statesmen. Jacob Viner writes that "there is overwhelming evidence" that the process "is usually the reverse" of Marxist allegations. "The initiative [for war and imperialistic venture] is taken in the Foreign Offices, not in the counting houses; the bankers, instead of being the prime movers, are the instruments, sometimes willing, often reluctant and insubordinate, of the diplomats." [8]

It can scarcely be denied that economic interests play a significant role in motivating state action. However, it is a gross oversimplification to attempt to rationalize all uses of force by capitalist states by the dogmas of economic determinism and "imperialism." Notwithstanding Moscow's propaganda concerning "Wall Street imperialism" and "Western war-mongers," most major conflicts resulting in international war during the past century have been the result of nationalist pressures, the urgings of power ambitions, and the search for security and increased strength. Economic advantage may accrue to a state through the acquisition of colonies or other territories, but this does not in itself establish that economic determinism was the sole cause of a war which may have ended with some colonial acquisition.[9] Most wars result from the interplay of a complex set of forces. They can seldom be attributed to the operation of one factor alone.

Psychological-Cultural Explanations. Some anthropologists and psychologists have begun to search with the tools of social analysis for explanations of war in terms of human impulses and cultural patterns.

Bronislaw Malinowski, distinguished English anthropologist, attributes war to cultural conditions, rejecting the Freudian concept that it can be explained

7 E. Varga and L. Mendelsohn, *New Data for V. I. Lenin's Imperialism, The Highest Stage of Capitalism* (New York, 1940), pp. 5, 246; Historicus, "Stalin on Revolution," *Foreign Affairs,* Jan., 1949, pp. 1–42, with citations to original Russian sources; Stalin's statement on "Economic Problems of Socialism," *The New York Times,* Oct. 4, 1952.

8 J. Viner, "In Defense of 'Dollar Diplomacy,' " *The New York Times Magazine,* March 23, 1947. This is supported by Lionel Robbins in his *The Economic Causes of War* (London, 1939), and by Eugene Staley in his investigation of *War and the Private Investor* (Chicago, 1935), pp. 55–56.

9 See E. M. Winslow, *The Pattern of Imperialism* (New York, 1948), p. 67.

in terms of some "aggressive instinct." [10] He says: "War undoubtedly is a cultural phenomenon, and its main determinants are artificial, that is, not rooted in human nature. . . . We meet many theories which maintain that war is organically rooted in some inevitable, that is, biological, impulse of man." But, Malinowski maintains, "the simplest analysis of human behaviour shows that aggression is a derived impulse. It arises from the working of one or the other of the basic psychological drives, or else from interference with culturally determined interests, appetites, or desires. When sex, hunger, ambition, or wealth is threatened, aggression occurs." [11]

Clyde Kluckhohn, contemporary anthropologist, also believes that while all the necessary evidence is not in, known facts discount Sigmund Freud's pessimistic analysis based on the theory of so-called instincts of pugnacity and aggressiveness. He says that "the psychological bases in the individual for potential aggression are created by the deprivations incident to socialization." Kluckhohn also observes that the principal psychological basis for modern wars lies in a threat to "the security of individuals or the cohesion of a group." [12] This means that part of the problem of war resides in the insecurities, as well as in the sentiments and desires, of the individuals who direct the destinies of states and peoples.

Glorification of War. Political leaders and regimes have sometimes glorified war and propagated ideas concerning its advantages or inevitability which in themselves become a powerful lever with which to whip up animosities or support for foreign military ventures or aggression.

Thus, Benito Mussolini proclaimed that "Fascism does not believe either in the possibility or usefulness of perpetual peace. . . . Only war carries human energy to the highest tension and prints the seal of nobility on the peoples which have the virtues to confront it." [13] And in response to this doctrine the Fascists succeeded in mobilizing Italian fervor for the conquest of Ethiopia.

Within the Soviet Union the communist leaders have systematically promoted the concept of class war and indoctrinated the people with the idea that the socialist state must strive to bring about revolutionary situations abroad in which the capitalist states will be overthrown in a series of "violent conflicts."

[10] See exchange of letters between Albert Einstein and Sigmund Freud entitled "Why War?" in *Free World*, March–April, 1946.
[11] B. Malinowski, "War—Past, Present and Future," address before American Historical Association, 1940, quoted in J. D. Clarkson and T. C. Cochran, *War as a Social Institution* (New York, 1941), pp. 23–25.
[12] Clyde Kluckhohn, *Mirror for Man, the Relationship of Anthropology to Modern Life* (New York, 1949), pp. 55, 103–104, 136–137, 278–279.
[13] *Popolo d'Italia*, Aug. 4, 1932.

Furthermore, communist followers are also taught that any war "to liberate the people from capitalist slavery" or "to liberate colonies and dependent countries from the yoke of imperialism" is a "just war." [14]

How dangerous such teachings can become in the causation of war needs no emphasis. Their presence in the international community is one of the principal dangers to peace, for it is not easy for others to reach the masses of peoples within totalitarian states being inculcated with such warlike sentiments.

Ignorance as a Cause of War. In recent years there has been a school of thought which holds that lack of understanding of others has been a cause of suspicion and conflict, and if this were remedied peace would prevail. This assumption is expressed in the Preamble to the Constitution of UNESCO in the words: "Since wars begin in the minds of men, it is in the minds of men that the defences of peace must be constructed." Reinhold Niebuhr has pointed out that ignorance may aggravate fear. But it is not true, he says, that "knowledge of each other's ways necessarily allays suspicion and mistrust. Some of the most terrible conflicts in history have occurred between neighbors who knew each other quite well, Germany and France for instance." [15] As a matter of fact, a good case could be made for the thesis that the increased strains and feelings of hostility between the powers in the contemporary period are due in no small measure to their increased knowledge of one another, a knowledge made possible by modern means of communication and research.

Even if it were possible to obtain universal agreement on the principles of justice and conduct, conflict and war would still be possible as states are prompted by their national interests to construe and apply these principles differently.

The Use of the Social Sciences. The confusion which emerges from the complex causation of war and the uncertainty of avoiding war even with a spread of knowledge may be disheartening to some. But for most it is likely to drive home the conclusion suggested by the distinguished social psychologist, Gordon Allport, that an intensified scientific effort toward understanding and dealing with the causes of war is necessary. As he has remarked: "It is entirely possible that social engineering may fail to implement the moral sense of mankind and that mankind may go under. But we shall never know the potential value of social science unless the risk is taken." [16]

---

[14] *History of the Communist Party of the Soviet Union* (Eng. trans., New York, 1939), pp. 167–168.

[15] R. Niebuhr, "Theory and Practice of UNESCO," *International Organization,* Feb., 1950, p. 6.

[16] G. W. Allport, "Guide Lines for Research in International Cooperation," in J. H. Pear, *op. cit.,* p. 143.

FROM "LIMITED" TO "TOTAL" WARFARE

Characteristics of Older Warfare. Prior to modern times the average citizen was relatively little concerned with warfare save when it touched his local community. The Prussian peasant cared little about the success or failure of Frederick the Great in subordinating other German principalities to his crown, or in swelling his prestige through foreign ventures. Wars were on the whole the preoccupation of kings and rulers. They were often the result of dynastic quarrels or disputes over royal domain.

Before the French and American revolutions, armies were generally small professional bodies, often bands of adventurers hired out to the highest bidder. No deep hatred, only a bag of gold, pitted soldiers against soldiers in many combats. War and the profession of arms were often viewed as arts. Adept maneuvering and expert disposal of forces were often the determinative factors, rather than huge expenditures of resources and the ability to sustain many casualties.[17]

War Becomes a Mass Concern. Modern war, by contrast, has become pre-eminently popular warfare. Mass armies are conscripted and hurled at one another.[18] In World War II armed forces in excess of eight million each were put into uniform by Germany, the Soviet Union, and the United States. Women participated in the armed forces of several nations; in the USSR they bore arms at the fighting front on at least some occasions.

The modern "nation in arms" has extinguished the traditional line between soldier and civilian. The staggering demands of mass, mechanized warfare have required that war become the business of every person able to work or fight. Total national effort is now required to supply armed forces in Great Power warfare. Only by mobilizing all sectors of the economy can the infinite necessities of modern warfare and the endless flow of munitions be handled. Only by arousing popular zeal can such exertions be sustained. Moreover, in modern war, hostilities and psychological warfare are being increasingly carried to the home front of the enemy to bring about defeat and demoralization. This seems likely to remain true in the nuclear era with the qualification that effort and losses will shift even more toward the home front.

Influence of Nationalism. We have already noted that one of the powerful social forces of the nineteenth century was nationalism. The rise of modern nationalism out of the turmoil of the French and the American revolutions was responsible in no small degree for the identification of personal and na-

[17] On early interstate warfare see Edward M. Earle (ed.), *Makers of Modern Strategy* (Princeton, 1944), chs. 1–2.
[18] Hoffman Nickerson's book, *The Armed Horde, 1793–1939* (New York, 1940), is an interesting study of the spectacle of mass armies and their operations.

tional interest. It was a justification for the development of popular armies and one cause of the mass character of modern war. And as Edward H. Carr said in the late nineteenth century, "the socialization of the nation, the nationalization of economic policy and the geographical extension of nationalism" combined to produce the totalitarianism of our times—of which one manifestation is "total war." [19]

Influence of Technological Revolution. The technological revolution of the twentieth century, with its precision manufacture, mass production, rapid transportation, and internal combustion engine made mechanized warfare possible. It thereby became the main contributor on the materialistic side to the evolution of modern total warfare. From the applications of science and technology, first to industry and then to weapons, a "new era in warfare was started," as Vannevar Bush has pointed out, as a consequence of which "the world will never be the same again." [20]

With modern equipment and weapons, war has become a struggle of men with machines and technical skill against machines, and of machines against men. With science, invention, and industry mobilized for war, the machines of war have become innumerable and rapidly changing, and the industrial factory has become "a dominant element in the whole paraphernalia of war." The long-range bombers, high-arc guided missiles, rockets, nuclear weapons, automatic-firing guns, homing projectiles, electronic apparatus, ray devices, gases, bacteriological substances, nerve weapons, and other instruments now available are no doubt still but a prelude to what science and technology can devise, and modern industry produce, for mechanized total war between nations.[21]

CHARACTERISTICS OF MODERN WAR

While enlisting the moral and material support of the entire nation for its conduct, "total" war also makes every citizen a potential victim. No person and no property is today theoretically beyond the range of hostilities if a belligerent chooses to extend them.

Increasing Range of Hostilities. In 1900 an armed attack upon a foreign country could affect at any given time only a few miles of territory behind the fighting line. In World War I German "Big Berthas" hurled shells into Paris from a distance of seventy-six miles, and lightly loaded aircraft dropped a few bombs upon London. In World War II fleets of Allied aircraft rained

19 E. H. Carr, *Nationalism and After* (New York and London, 1945).
20 Vannevar Bush, *Modern Arms and Free Men* (New York, 1949), p. 10.
21 On modern weapons see in addition to Bush, Hanson W. Baldwin, *The Price of Power* (New York, 1947); S. T. Possony, *Strategic Air Power for Dynamic Security* (Washington, 1949); John E. Burchard, *Rockets, Guns and Targets* (Boston, 1948); T. Roseburg and E. A. Kabot, "Bacteriological Warfare," *J. of Immunology,* May, 1947; W. F. Ogburn (ed.), *Technology and International Relations* (Chicago, 1949).

1,000-pound bombs all over Europe from bases in England and Africa, and Tokyo was seared night after night by super-fortresses flying missions up to 1,500 miles from bases in Guam. With modern refueling techniques combat forces can operate across the length and breadth of oceans. By 1949 it was possible for long-range bombers, loaded to combat weight, to fly nonstop around the world.

Rising Toll of Civilian Casualties. The terrible bombing inflicted on many large cities during World War II, together with the mass slaughters perpetrated by the Nazis in concentration camps and by harsh handling of civilian populations, raised civilian casualties in that war to unprecedented heights. It is figured that in Poland there were 5,000,000 civilian casualties as against 597,000 military. Civilian casualties in Italy numbered over 700,000; in Japan 670,000; in Germany 500,000; in Greece 400,000. Russian casualty statistics have never been fully revealed. They have been estimated at between 12 to 15 million persons [22] (not counting induced decline in the birth rate during the war), over half of which were civilians.

Mounting Power of Weapons. Phenomenal developments in explosives have made possible property destruction on a scale never before thought possible. It is said that "since 1900 the explosive force of military weapons has increased four million times." [23] In 1900 a single shell from a fourteen-inch mortar could gut a frame house, leaving the walls standing. By World War I, shells had been developed which were capable of demolishing an entire house and inflicting severe damage on surrounding structures. By March, 1945, the "block-buster" had appeared, with explosive force sufficient for one bomb to destroy the better part of a city block. The atom bomb has dwarfed all these records by flattening with one explosion at least a full square mile of urban structures, inflicting damage up to three miles from the point of explosion. Now scientists state that a hydrogen bomb is theoretically possible with explosive power magnifying that of Hiroshima many thousand times. On March 1, 1954 the United States exploded a hydrogen bomb which was the equivalent of more than 12,000,000 tons of TNT and capable of devastating an area 8 miles in diameter and inflicting moderate damage over an area 32 miles in diameter.[24]

"Push-button warfare," the destruction of cities across oceans or continents by ultra-long-range guided missiles, and clashes in interplanetary space may still be in the realm of speculation, or of the future, unable under present conditions to stand the test of "cost analysis" in peacetime. But within the realm

---

[22] *World Almanac,* 1948, p. 552.
[23] *Life,* Jan. 2, 1950, p. 33.
[24] *The New York Times,* April 1, 1954.

VULNERABLE TARGETS FOR ROCKET-FIRING SUBMARINES

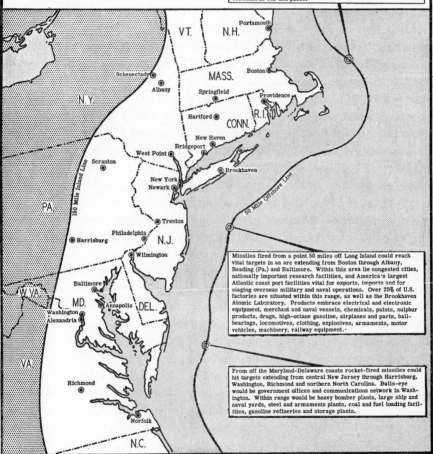

0   50   100   150   200
Miles

Hostile submarines capable of firing rockets or other guided missiles with a range of 200 miles could from surfacing points off the New England coast fire into the important naval, military, industrial and research centers located between Boston, Schenectady and New Haven. In this region are produced critical percentages of U.S. submarines, electrical equipment, precision tools and instruments, locomotives, small arms, plane motors, textiles and other products essential in war and peace.

Missiles fired from a point 50 miles off Long Island could reach vital targets in an arc extending from Boston through Albany, Reading (Pa.) and Baltimore. Within this area lie congested cities, nationally important research facilities, and America's largest Atlantic coast port facilities vital for exports, imports and for staging overseas military and naval operations. Over 25% of U.S. factories are situated within this range, as well as the Brookhaven Atomic Laboratory. Products embrace electrical and electronic equipment, merchant and naval vessels, chemicals, paints, sulphur products, drugs, high-octane gasoline, airplanes and parts, ball-bearings, locomotives, clothing, explosives, armaments, motor vehicles, machinery, railway equipment.·

From off the Maryland-Delaware coasts rocket-fired missiles could hit targets extending from central New Jersey through Harrisburg, Washington, Richmond and northern North Carolina. Bulls-eye would be government offices and communications network in Washington. Within range would be heavy bomber plants, large ship and naval yards, steel and armaments plants, coal and fuel loading facilities, gasoline refineries and storage plants.

Mass. Inst. Technology

FIGURE IX:1

of the possible are (1) tremendous destruction of industrial, urban centers by aerial bombing and short-range guided atomic missiles; (2) large-scale destruction in coastal cities by atomic rockets fired from submarines;[25] (3) infliction of mass casualties by toxic substances and bacterial agents;[26] and (4) increased speed, power, and destructiveness of mechanized weapons. These indicate some of the potentialities of total warfare among nations in the technological era.

Limitation of Rules of Warfare. Between the seventeenth and twentieth centuries elaborate rules for the conduct of war were worked out by international lawyers and military leaders in order to minimize the dangers in taking the field.[27] Learned treatises, such as Grotius' epochal work on *The Laws of War and Peace* (1624), were written setting forth rules and regulations for the governance of armies and hostilities. Limitations were laid upon weapons and procedures, as for example in The Hague Conventions of 1899 and 1907 prohibiting the use of "dum-dum" bullets and the dropping of explosives from balloons. It was generally agreed that civilian lives and property should be spared unless they were in a direct line of fire or being used for military purposes. Unnecessary killings and privation were to be avoided. Merchant ships were to be stopped, boarded, and examined before being fired upon or sunk. In 1925 a protocol was signed and ratified by more than forty states prohibiting use of asphyxiating gases or other poisons.

In the twentieth century many of these limitations have broken down before the national and racial hatreds generated during World Wars I and II, and because of their questionable realism in light of modern military technology. Polite restraints had no place in Hitler's maniacal drives against the nations of Eastern Europe, although gas and bacteriological warfare were not employed. Many old rules seemed beside the point to mass armies fighting desperately for the existence or destruction of entire nations. Not since the religious wars have civilian as well as military personnel been tortured and massacred as they were especially by Germans and Japanese during World War II. Focal cities were bombed mercilessly, and in Eastern Europe civilian populations were

25 The accompanying map suggests some measure of United States vulnerability, assuming the feasibility of firing nuclear warhead rockets from submarines or sneak vessels. Study of a world political and economic map will suggest the comparative vulnerability, or otherwise, of British, German, Chinese, Soviet, and other industrial and urban concentrations.

26 Communist China and the USSR charged in 1952 that the United Nations were employing "germ warfare" in Korea and Manchuria, but opposed impartial international investigation on the spot.

27 The development of rules for the conduct of warfare also represented a reaction to the atrocities practiced during the Wars of Religion in the seventeenth century. The United States has had one of the outstanding codes for the conduct of warfare, drawn up in 1863, entitled *Instructions for the Government of Armies of the United States in the Field*. For present version see United States War Department, *Basic Field Manual*, "Rules of Land Warfare" (Washington, 1940).

deliberately terrorized. In both wars merchant vessels, neutral as well as enemy, were sunk without warning in campaigns of unrestricted submarine warfare. Property was destroyed wherever it was thought to be serving a military purpose. The inhabitants of defeated and occupied territories were pressed by the Germans into slave labor to make munitions and engage in hazardous repair work.

For their "crimes against humanity" and "war crimes," many German and Japanese leaders were tried and punished by International War Crimes Tribunals at the end of World War II.[28] These trials indicated that, even though modern war has become increasingly inhumane and "brutalized" in the weapons and methods employed, the conscience of the civilized world has affirmed that "the man who makes or plans to make aggressive war is a criminal," and that there are brutalities which will not be allowed to go unpunished.[29]

Psychological and Subversive Warfare. Modern war has come to involve much more than military activity by organized armed forces. It includes a large amount of activity designed to cripple production and morale on the "home front." Before hostilities start, as well as after, subversive activity may be attempted. This aims to sow doubt and confusion in the public mind, to undermine confidence in the government, and to enlist cooperation in opposing the government and in sabotaging the war effort if hostilities occur.

The Nazis and the Communists have carried subversive action to the extent of planting "fifth columns" of subversive agents and saboteurs in opposing countries to secure the help of disaffected nationals and sympathizers before their armies strike. The Nazi fifth column was particularly effective in France in 1939–1940 in softening public opinion, sowing confusion and defeatism, and sabotaging communications and the transport of military supplies. Similarly, the Chinese Communists in 1949 sent bands of party agents ahead of their armies behind the lines of the Nationalists to demoralize the public and undermine Kuomintang resistance. The generally liberal laws and attitudes within democratic states make them especially vulnerable to this type of activity. The devising of effective means of countering such activities is one of the primary problems facing democratic, free peoples everywhere.

Guerrilla activities behind the lines of battle have also come to be a significant feature in modern war. In the fighting between Germany and the Soviet

---

28 Text of Charter of International Military Tribunal for Germany subscribed to by twenty-three states in Dept. of State Pub., *Trial of War Criminals, Documents* (Washington, 1945). Judgment in the *Am. J. Int. Law*, vol. 41 (1947), Supplement, p. 172. Documents on Japanese war crimes trials in Dept. of State Pub., *Trial of Japanese War Criminals, Documents* (Washington, 1946).

29 See Henry L. Stimson, "The Nuremberg Trial: Landmark in Law," *Foreign Affairs*, Jan., 1947; Quincy Wright, "The Law of the Nuremberg Trial," *Am. J. Int. Law*, Jan., 1947.

Union in World War II, the Russians left large numbers of trained men behind, as they retreated eastward, to sabotage German communications and transport. The peasantry paid dearly for this as the Germans took retaliatory measures to try to scotch the movement. But throughout the fighting the Soviet authorities kept in touch with the guerrillas who were able to do much useful service. Guerrilla activity also figured in the Korean War.

Propaganda has come to be a prominent institution in modern war. This aims to instill attitudes of fortitude at home, of defeatism among the enemy. News is withheld, colored, editorialized, or falsified for the sake of effect. The wartime broadcasts of "Lord Haw Haw," an English traitor working for the Nazi Government, and of "Tokyo Rose" addressing the American forces in the Pacific were notorious examples. In different forms the Office of War Information, the public relations sections of the armed forces, and the "OSS" broadcast foreign language propaganda in behalf of the United States cause during the war. Radio stations and presses are now one of the foremost adjuncts of war.[30]

Total Defeat. Warfare has also become total in its objectives. The goals of Great Power war today, as evidenced by World War II, have passed beyond the defeat of armies in the field, the exaction of reparations, and the shifting of boundaries. The goals of war today have come to include as well the complete subjugation of the enemy's territory, the destruction and dismantling of his heavy industries and war potential, the reorganization of his government, and the changing of his ideological concepts.

"Unconditional surrender" has been demanded and enforced. In the case of Germany, complete abolition of German government was enforced for four years. In Japan, the Supreme Commander for the Allied Powers exercised virtually complete power, even over the Emperor, until the treaty of peace was signed in 1951. Treaties of peace for the defeated Axis satellite states were drafted by a Council of Foreign Ministers of the victorious Great Powers and, after general reference to a conference of Allied states, were handed to the defeated for acceptance. But the outstanding characteristic of total defeat in World War II was the political and economic, and even social and cultural, changes forced on defeated peoples. The most pronounced of these changes were forced by the Soviet Union, giving cause for sober reflection that in the future the total national way of life of a defeated state may be radically changed. Such changes were part of the real, but not too clearly announced, objectives of World War II. The addition of this type of change to the traditional objectives of war is one of the major changes in the nature of war.

Totality in the "Cold War." Concepts of "totalized" war are likewise

30 See ch. xvi, p. 452, below for further discussion of propaganda.

present in the campaign of communism against the forces of freedom. Communists continually preach the doctrine that capitalist regimes must be completely destroyed throughout the world by revolution, subversion, or violent conflict. And wherever communism has fostered its power, freedom of thought, of enterprise, and of political belief have been ruthlessly wiped out.

Summary. Thus, mankind has moved from limited war to total war; from wars with limited military and political objectives to conflicts having the complete subjugation of other peoples and all their institutions as the end objects of international struggle and war. There have almost always been some rulers and regimes ready to seek complete conquest of their opponents and who did not hesitate to employ the most brutal measures against their foes. Conversely, in the contemporary era, wars that are limited in their methods of conduct do occur. But the features of the two World Wars of the twentieth century and the schemes of Moscow-led international communism evidence marked trends in the direction of war conducted with few limitations and having as its ends not merely a change of policy on the part of the defeated but complete change in his institutions and orientation.

THE RISING COST OF WAR

One of the principal characteristics of modern Great Power war is its enormous costliness, both in direct military expenditures and in subsidiary ways.

Military Costs of Global War. It is estimated that the total direct cost of conducting World War I was 126 billion dollars to the Allied and Associated Powers, and 60 billion dollars to the Central Powers. Property damage was figured at something in the range of 37 billion dollars.

Estimates place the military cost of World War II at over 1,100 billion dollars and property damage at over 230 billion dollars. It is estimated that the total military cost to the chief belligerents was: the United States 330 billion dollars; Germany 272 billion dollars; the USSR 192 billion dollars; the United Kingdom 120 billion dollars; Italy 94 billion dollars; Japan 56 billion dollars.[31]

Attendant Costs. In addition to the military costs there are other attendant "costs." These include the disruption of normal economic production and patterns of world trade; the loss of earning and productive power of those killed or maimed; the drainage of national savings, capital equipment, and resources; a rising burden of national indebtedness; the necessity of providing for displaced persons; a fall in the birth rate and rise in the civilian death rate; and the cost of reconstruction of industry and trade, as well as outlays for veterans' benefits and other claims. These "costs" run into almost incalculable figures; they are shared in one degree or another among all belligerents. And they

[31] *World Almanac 1950,* p. 746.

affect world economy as a whole. States that have suffered severe devastation must in addition face the losses in property and the cost of rebuilding. And if revolution or civil war follows in the train of defeat or victory, as has happened in some countries, the upheaval of political and social life adds another dimensional unit to the gross "cost" of war.

Meeting the Costs of War. Expenditure and indebtedness on the scale required for victory in Great Power war today can be carried by no states, except perhaps the United States and Russia, without external assistance, and by no states without producing severe strains lasting over many years.

War Debts. The Allied powers in Europe were able to succeed in World War I only by procuring large loans from the United States for munitions, food, and other supplies, and by the ultimate intervention of the United States on their side. After the war, Britain, France, and other recipients, with the exception of Finland, found it impossible, economically or politically, to repay most of these debts without new loans or compensatory reparation payments from Germany. High American tariffs made it difficult for these countries to earn sufficient dollars with which to pay. The world-wide economic depression in the 1930's followed by Germany's default on reparations and the rise of a new threat to peace, brought to an end all efforts to secure repayment.[32]

Lend-Lease. United States lend-lease aid eased the financial problem of many Allied states in World War II. This act, passed in March, 1941, was based on the dual premise that Allied states resisting aggression were contributing to the defense of the United States, and that the United States by virtue of its abundant economy and fortunate position should act as the "arsenal of democracy" by supplying at its own expense a sizable part of the war-material needs of the Allies. Aid exceeding 49 billion dollars was extended to others under this act during the war; and reverse lend-lease of over 7 billion dollars was received as part of the Allied war effort.

The Lend-Lease Agreements postponed final settlement until the end of hostilities. They provided that the terms and conditions of payment should be such "as not to burden commerce between the two countries, but to promote mutually advantageous economic relations between them and the betterment of world-wide economic relations." [33]

Consumption of Irreplaceable Resources. Total war accelerates the drain upon the nonrenewable natural resources of the world. Military demands for

---

[32] On war debts history see H. G. Moulton and L. Pasvolsky, *War Debts and World Prosperity* (Washington, 1932); for the French viewpoint see L. Dubois, *War Debts and Reparations* (Paris, 1929).

[33] Text of Lend-Lease Act is in Public Law 11, 77th Cong., 1st Sess., March 11, 1941. Master Lend-Lease Agreement with United Kingdom is in United States Dept. of State Pub. 1790, Executive Agreement Series 241. Story of lend-lease administration is in E. R. Stettinius, Jr., *Lend-Lease, Weapon for Victory* (New York, 1944).

weapons, munitions, equipment, transportation, and the host of items needed to sustain an "all-out" war effort necessitates the production of vastly increased quantities of minerals in every belligerent country. Where normal domestic sources cannot be stretched enough to suffice, marginal deposits are pressed into production and supplies are sought from overseas sources almost without regard to cost.

Some measure of the depletion which this entails is indicated from World War II consumption of irreplaceable resources by the United States—a story which has its counterpart in the British Empire, Germany, Japan, and the Soviet Union. Between 1940 and 1945 United States consumption of copper, iron ore, lead, zinc, manganese, molybdenum, coal, and fluorspar doubled. Consumption of chromium, a commodity which had to be obtained almost entirely overseas, tripled. The production of domestic bauxite for aluminum rose from 375,300 tons to 7,000,000 tons.[34] After both World War I and World War II the peace-time consumption of nonrenewable resources quickly reached the level of war-time consumption, indicating that war merely accelerates the development of increasing difficulties in the raw-material field.

In 1948 the president of one of America's largest steel companies startlingly revealed that, with the 340 million tons of high-grade iron ore taken from the Minnesota mines in World War II, less than fifteen years' supply remained for normal consumption, and that no more wars could ever be fought off Superior's high-grade ores. Now the United States must go to Liberia, Venezuela, and Canada for ore, and turn to beneficiation of low-grade ore.[35] The strategic implications of this in terms of the problem of obtaining adequate supplies of iron ore from across long, exposed sea routes in time of emergency are readily apparent. How dangerous this is appears from the fact that in the first seven months after Pearl Harbor 22 per cent of the ore fleet bringing bauxite from northern South America was sunk by enemy submarines.

ECONOMIC CONSEQUENCES OF WAR

Relief and Rehabilitation. Great Power war has become costly not only in its conduct and property damage, but also in terms of its economic sequel. For many belligerents there are immediate problems of relief for peoples displaced by the events of war, and of repair and reconstruction of the physical damage wrought by hostilities. Industries must be converted back to peace-time uses. Tools and all manner of equipment overworked during the war must be replaced to maintain or raise productivity. Seeds and fertilizers must be pro-

[34] President's Materials Policy Commission Report, *Resources for Freedom*, vol. 1 (Washington, 1952), p. 22.
[35] See T. W. Lippert, "Cerro Bolivar—Saga of an Iron Ore Crisis Averted," *Mining Engineering*, Feb., 1950.

cured to meet new demands for food. Raw materials must be acquired to recommence production of goods both for home consumption and for export in order to earn foreign exchange. Financial structures that have been weakened by the urgent demands of war must be strengthened for the tasks of reconversion to peace-time living.

Finding the means for meeting these needs at the end of an exhausting war has become a problem whose gravity is second only to that of war itself. For it has become apparent that if the basic requirements are not quickly and adequately cared for, economic depression and political instability may occur, or even civil strife and revolution may follow.

Situations after World Wars I and II. Relief missions, loans, and the use of governmental reserves were employed to assist the transition from war to peace after World War I. A more critical problem prevailed in 1945. The destruction and devastation were more widespread. There were greater numbers of displaced persons to be provided for. Governments had been forced during World War II to draw more heavily upon their reserve assets and foreign investments. In the case of Britain, the Netherlands, and Japan, changes in overseas empires reduced the resources formerly derivable from these sources. And in certain colonial areas, notably Malaya and Indo-China which were in themselves important suppliers of basic raw materials, costly fighting against communist guerrillas added other economic burdens. Complicating matters further, a serious world food crisis developed in 1945–1946 as a result of drought and crop failures. So disastrous was the situation that President Truman said in February, 1946, "More people face starvation . . . today than in any war year and perhaps more than in all the war years combined." Achieving the fruits of victory involves more than winning battles.

National and international efforts were mobilized to cope with the colossal problems of relief and rehabilitation. Outstanding among the international endeavors were the activities of the United Nations Relief and Rehabilitation Administration (UNRRA), the provision of civilian supplies by the United States military authorities in the occupied areas, the outpouring of private charity, and the arrangement of a series of intergovernmental loans of an essentially "stop-gap" nature.

United States Contributions. As the nation having the largest available credit and surplus at the end of World War II, the United States had to assume the main burden of such assistance. United States Government contributions to UNRRA amounted to 2.5 billion dollars. Food and civilian goods distributed overseas by the American armed forces in 1945–1946 were valued at more than 1.25 billion dollars. Clothing drives in the United States supplied clothing for between 25 and 50 million people overseas. Through lend-lease,

UNRRA, the military, and private channels, vast, but still insufficient, quantities of food were shipped abroad.

In addition to these relief measures, totaling about 6 billion dollars' worth in grants during the period from mid-1945 to April, 1948, the United States during the same time extended loans and credits to foreign governments to the extent of 8.5 billion dollars.[36] It also made a large subscription to the International Bank for Reconstruction and Development, and supported the United Nations Food and Agriculture Organization (FAO) which sought to mobilize world food resources for bringing relief to starving millions.

A number of factors forced the United States to reconsider foreign aid measures in 1946–1947. In the first place, there were evidences of inefficiency in UNRRA, and certain governments were attempting to use UNRRA aid primarily to further their political rule. Secondly, numerous countries requesting large loans raised the prospect of an awkward "line-up" at the Treasury door unless there were some coherent over-all plan. Thirdly, Soviet imperialism and the expansion of international communism indicated the time had come when the United States should take political considerations into account in extending further foreign assistance. Secretary of State Byrnes signaled the new policy line in November, 1946: "It is our position that whatever the United States does in the way of relief should be done by the United States unilaterally. We want to give aid as the United States and not as a member of an international organization." [37]

Aid to Greece and Turkey. In the spring of 1947 critical situations developed in Greece and Turkey. Civil war, assisted by Russia's communist satellites in the Balkans, threatened to overthrow the Greek government. In Turkey resistance to Soviet pressure for bases in the Straits and territory in the east threatened to bankrupt the country. For over a century these strategically located countries had been supported in one way or another by Britain against Russian imperialism. But in February, 1947, London notified Washington that with its grave financial conditions at home, and the problems within its shrinking empire, it would no longer be able to assist Greece and Turkey. Realizing the gravity of the situation, President Truman appealed to the Congress for funds to aid "free peoples" resisting external aggression or "attempted subjugation" by minority groups aiming to overthrow free institutions.[38]

---

[36] Brown and Opie, *American Foreign Assistance*, Brookings Institution, Washington, D. C., and the annual volumes of *The United States in World Affairs*, Council on Foreign Relations, New York, are the two best general references for foreign assistance matters.

[37] *The New York Times*, Nov. 29, 1946.

[38] Message of March 12, 1947, *The New York Times*, March 13, 1947. Commentary on policy in *The United States in World Affairs* (New York, 1948), pp. 474–480 of 1945–47 edition and ch. 2 of 1947–48 edition.

With economic and military aid from the United States under the so-called Truman Doctrine, Greece was rescued and the Turkish economy was strengthened.

European Recovery Program. With critical economic conditions still facing most of the European countries as UNRRA approached a close, Secretary of State Marshall initiated in June, 1947, one of America's most statesman-like acts—the European Recovery Program.

The Foreign Assistance Act of 1948, passed by the American Congress, as well as the speedy action of the European nations in drawing up a program of their needs and a plan for European economic recovery, gave reality to Marshall's proposals. The former, adopted with strong bipartisan support, was a landmark in the history of American foreign policy. The Economic Cooperation Administration created by it undertook, in collaboration with other states, perhaps the most far-reaching program of cooperative economic assistance ever inaugurated in peace-time.[39] Between 1948 and 1952 more than 11 billion dollars, mostly in grants, were expended to assist friendly peoples in Europe, the Middle East, and Asia to establish their economies

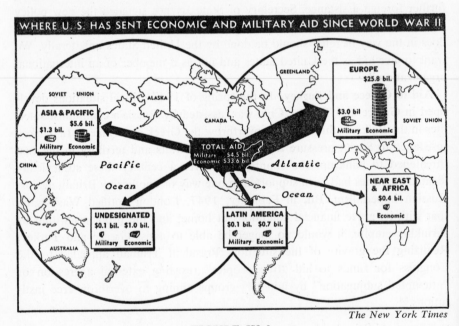

The New York Times

FIGURE IX:2

39 Assistance was given to certain countries in the Middle East and Asia, as well as to Europe. The sixteen "Marshall Plan" countries of Europe created an Organization for European Economic Cooperation in 1948 to take steps for long-range European economic integration as well as to cooperate in the allocation of Marshall aid.

upon a stable, prosperous basis so that there might be hope in place of despair, as well as the possibility of full employment, rising production, alleviation of want and disease, and strength to resist external or internal threats.[40]

Mutual Defense Assistance. The Soviet blockade of Berlin in 1948–1949, coupled with the sweep of communist armies through China in 1949 and the communist attack upon the Republic of Korea in 1950, gave rise to widespread fear that the Red armies might launch an aggressive war upon the disarmed nations of Western Europe and Asia still struggling for recovery from the last war. The North Atlantic Treaty signed in April, 1949, provided for continuous self-help and mutual aid. Conditions abroad quickly made it apparent that many of the nations receiving ECA help could not attain full economic recovery and at the same time undertake major rearmament.

To meet this new danger, at a time when the economic and political devastation of World War II had not yet been fully repaired, the United States Congress took another important step in passing the Mutual Defense Assistance Act of 1949 which granted arms aid to certain friendly countries—principally those of NATO. This provided for "additional measures of support based upon the principle of continuous and effective self-help and mutual aid." [41] For this added burden the United States appropriated 2.4 billion dollars in 1950–1951, and additional increments in later years, reaching a total of about 15 billion dollars by mid-1953.[42]

Further Assistance. The continuing dependence of other countries upon the United States for extensive assistance raises the question how long such aid must be continued. In addressing the Congress on March 6, 1952, President Truman could say only that no one could "give an answer in terms of a specific month and year." The most that could be vouchsafed was the hope that the continuing assistance would "hasten the day" when these nations can "sustain their own programs of defense and economic progress."

The task of recovering from one world war had become merged with the problem of averting another, with the need to help those who had suffered defeat in the last war and those who were endeavoring to maintain newly won independence against communist imperialism. In the larger framework of the world struggle for a balance of power, the outlook for the free world was that of shouldering a heavy burden for years to come.

---

[40] For a review of ECA accomplishments see Gordon Gray, *Report to the President on Foreign Economic Policies, Nov. 10, 1950,* and annual volumes of *The United States in World Affairs.* See also ch. iv above.

[41] Public Law 329, 81st Cong.

[42] For description of Mutual Defense Assistance Program see annual volumes of *The United States in World Affairs;* House Foreign Affairs Committee, 82nd Cong., 2d Sess., *Mutual Security Program for Fiscal Year 1952: Basic Data Supplied by Executive Branch* (Washington, 1952, and later fiscal years).

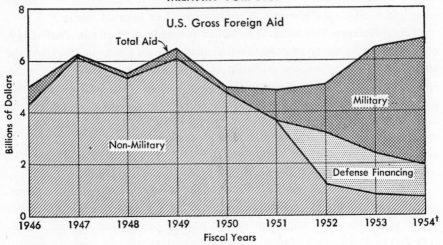

† Estimate for the Mutual Security Program only.

Foreign Operations Admin.

FIGURE IX:3

REPARATIONS AND OTHER OBLIGATIONS ON DEFEATED STATES

Whatever the cost of war to the victors, the burden for defeated states has often been increased by the loss of territory and the payment of reparations.

Reparations have not automatically followed all wars. In wars ending without the surrender of either side, they cannot be demanded.[43] Victorious powers, for political reasons or because of a recognition of the economic realities, have not always demanded reparations in monetary terms.[44] Belligerents have generally, however, demanded reparations or some territorial alterations, or both, when an enemy is brought to surrender. Reparations were required in some fifteen wars between 1815 and 1914.[45]

Terms for the Defeated after World War I. Heavy exactions were laid upon Germany and the other Central Powers following World War I. Their colonial possessions were divided among the victorious powers as mandates. Extensive cessions of territory were required in the name of national self-determination or security. Germany in addition was required to hand over

[43] In the Russo–Japanese War of 1904–1905 and in the Balkan Wars of 1912–1913, for example, cessions of territory took place but no reparations were paid.

[44] Following World War II the United States took the trusteeship of Japan's mandated islands, but did not demand reparations from either Italy or Japan. The friendship of these states was felt to be more important than monetary reparations. See statement of Assistant Secretary of State Thorp, Sept. 11, 1946, on Italian reparations in *A Decade of American Foreign Policy*, pp. 969–971.

[45] Peace Handbook, No. 158, *Indemnities* (London, 1918).

large amounts of raw materials and capital goods to the Allied powers in compensation for materials destroyed or damaged by her armies. And she was assessed reparations to the amount of 132 billion gold marks.[46]

Collection of the monetary reparations imposed upon Germany, however, proved to be a difficult, if not impossible, problem. German ingenuity in delaying and evading payments led to repeated differences among the victors. Catastrophic inflation in the mid-1920's undermined her capacity to pay. Payments made in currency quickly raised problems of conversion, and efforts to win exchange through foreign-trade drives aroused protectionist opposition abroad. Reparation payments also became associated with the question of Allied repayment of war debts to the United States. A succession of "plans" sought to conserve some payments, but in the end Hitler's denunciation of the Versailles Treaty left the Allied powers with but a small fraction of the original assessment.[47]

Terms for the Defeated after World War II. Heavy obligations were imposed upon the states which had started World War II and their satellites. All the defeated states had some territories taken away from them. Possibly the most notable detachments were (1) the Petsamo nickel mine area taken by Russia from Finland, (2) the rich agricultural lands in East Prussia seized by Russia and Poland, (3) the Saar industrial basin incorporated in an economic union with France, and (4) Southern Sakhalin, Korea, Formosa, and the Pacific Islands, all of some economic as well as strategic significance, taken from Japan.[48]

Italian, Satellite, and Japanese Reparations. Reparations and other material compensation from Italy and the Axis satellite states were insisted upon by the Soviet Union and others.[49] In the Japanese peace treaty signed at San Francisco in 1951 an obligation was laid upon Japan to negotiate reparation payments to whatever states demanded them, but much to the objection of the Philippines, Indonesia, and other states that had suffered heavily from Japan, no figure was fixed nor any mechanism established to insure payment.[50]

German Reparations. At the Yalta Big Three meeting in 1945 it was agreed that Germany should be made to pay reparations for the "losses caused

[46] See terms of Treaty of Versailles and other treaties of peace. Also *Report on Work of the Reparation Commission from 1920–1922* (London, 1922).
[47] On reparations see C. Dawes, *A Journal of Reparations* (London, 1939); J. Keynes, *A Revision of the Treaty* (New York, 1922); D. Myers, *The Reparation Settlement* (Boston, 1929).
[48] See ch. ii on international boundaries.
[49] Terms in United States Dept. of State Pub. 2743, *Treaties of Peace with Italy, Bulgaria, Hungary, Rumania, and Finland* (Washington, 1947).
[50] Text of treaty in *Am. J. Int. Law*, July, 1952, Official Doc. Supplement. For comment see Robert G. Menzies, "The Pacific Settlement Seen from Australia," *Foreign Affairs*, Jan., 1952; M. S. Farley, "San Francisco and After," *Far Eastern Survey*, Sept. 26, 1951.

by it" to the Allied states. These, it was agreed, should take the form of (1) removals of industrial and capital equipment for the purpose of "destroying the war potential of Germany," (2) annual deliveries of goods from current production for a period of years, and (3) the use of German labor. More specific provisions relating to removals, controls, and the break-up of larger industrial combines were decided upon in the Big Three Conference at Potsdam, but the reparations from production and from German labor were eliminated.[51]

Virtually a free hand was given to the USSR to remove from East Germany whatever capital equipment it saw fit. This the Soviets did on a large scale in 1945–1946.[52] As a result of the post-war conflict between the Soviet Union and the Western Powers, however, reparation exactions, in the form of industrial equipment from Germany, particularly from the Western Zones, never reached the scale contemplated in 1945. Deliveries from the West Zones ceased in 1948–1949 as the Berlin blockade, the "cold war," and the growing realizations that reductions in German productivity continued the drain on the United States for aid all made the inapplicability of the policy apparent. According to the Inter-Allied Reparations Agency, it was estimated that by 1951 the nineteen participant states would have received the equivalent of 517 million dollars from Germany in German external assets, shipping, industrial equipment, captured supplies, and deliveries from the East Zone.[53] There are no comparable figures on Soviet removals from the East Zone. It can only be surmised that the amount was large.[54]

The Reparations Dilemma. The experience of 1920–1936 suggests that the attempt to extract large monetary reparations after a costly Great Power war inevitably leads to major problems of international exchange and foreign trade. On the other hand, extensive removals of industrial equipment, such as those tried in Germany from 1945 to 1948, are capable of affecting the world balance of power and of having direct effect upon the standard of living and self-sustaining ability of the former enemy peoples.

Given the fluidity of world political and economic relationships and the changing outlooks and competing interests of nations, there is obviously no fixed solution to the problem of procuring just compensation for losses caused

51 Texts of Yalta and Potsdam agreements in *The New York Times*, March 25, 1947. Russian proposals for a 20-billion dollar reparation bill were not acted on.
52 On the basis of "The Plan for Reparations and the Level of Post-War German Economy," drawn up by the Powers in March, 1946, it was estimated that the Inter-Allied Reparations Agency, representing nineteen states not including the USSR, would have for distribution to others about 1,800 German industrial plants.
53 Report of the Secretary-General, Inter-Allied Reparations Agency (Brussels, 1950).
54 On the reparation problem see Lucius D. Clay, *Decision in Germany* (New York, 1950), ch. 17; Campbell, *The United States in World Affairs, 1945–1947, 1948, 1949.*

by an aggressor. Those who have been victimized are entitled to recompense. But within the bounds of the possible, each state must pursue such a course as its own interests and evaluation of the overall world political situation lead it to from time to time. The one conclusion which does stand out from the experience after two World Wars is that the world economy and world politics are so closely interrelated that efforts to obtain very heavy reparations from any power after a war can produce additional serious economic and political repercussions.

SOCIAL AND POLITICAL CONSEQUENCES OF WAR

War produces social and political consequences of far-reaching import: political and social changes in the structure and internal political life of states, the growth of nationalism and the rise of new states, alterations in the world balance of power, or some combination of all of these.

Sequel to World War I. One of the dramatic results of World War I was the revolution in Russia which overthrew Czarism and paved the way for the Soviet regime with its Marxist-Leninist doctrines of world revolution. The latter not only brought into existence a different political system and a new set of economic and social values within Russia, but laid the base for the growth of a power center which at the end of World War II altered the European and world balance of power.

Another political consequence of World War I was the break-up of the Austro-Hungarian Empire into the states of Czechoslovakia, Rumania, Yugoslavia, Poland, Austria, and Hungary. This was in part a response to the nationalist sentiments which were intensified by the war and supported by President Wilson's espousal of the doctrine of national self-determination. In defeated Germany the Hohenzollern Empire was supplanted by the Weimar Republic. The weaknesses of the Republic, in the face of the strains of postwar adjustment and the economic crisis of the 1930's, helped to make possible the rise of nazism which in turn was a major determinant of World War II.

Political Changes after 1945 in Asia. World War II likewise brought in its train political changes of a major order. Japan was reduced from a continental oceanic empire to the small insular state it had been before 1900. The Philippine people were given independence by the United States. Nationalism burst forth in Southeast Asia to lead to the creation of the Indonesian Republic terminating three centuries of Dutch rule. In Indo-China it sought independence from France or at least autonomous rule, and led to decimating guerrilla warfare by communist elements supported from communist China.

India, Burma, and Ceylon ceased to be British colonies. The Indian subcontinent was torn by communal strife between Hindus and Moslems and divided into India and Pakistan.[55] In China the war contributed to the situation which resulted in the communist victory of 1949. The mainland of China was thus removed from the company of states friendly to the West and aligned instead with the Soviet bloc. The Nationalist Government which withdrew to Formosa continued, however, to represent free China in the United Nations and in relations with the majority of free world nations. In other parts of Asia and in the Moslem world the war gave impetus to nationalist forces seeking self-expression.

Political Changes in Europe. Fundamental political changes also followed the war in Europe. Under pressure from the Soviet Union, the states of Central and Eastern Europe lost their pre-war independence and their political ties with France and Britain and became satellites of Russia under communist dictatorships. An "Iron Curtain" cutting free communication between Eastern and Western Europe was created by the USSR. Germany was severed into two parts, one drawn into the Soviet orbit, the other associated with the West. And the USSR sought to weld all of Europe east of the Elbe into a Soviet preserve. A further sequel to the war was the rise of communist activity which sought to disrupt the political equilibrium of Italy, Greece, and France in order to seize power in these countries and take them into the communist camp. These consequences brought forward the spectre which had haunted the geographer, Sir Halford Mackinder, of one power ruling East Europe and Asia and from this "heartland" base threatening the security of the entire "World Island" of Eurasia and later the world.[56]

Alteration in Balance of Power. Most important among the political consequences stemming from World War II was the alteration in the world balance of power. Before the war there were seven powers that might be called Great Powers—Britain, France, Germany, Italy, Japan, the Soviet Union, and the United States. World politics revolved about the adjustment of power relationships and activities of these states and the smaller powers associated with them. In 1945 it could be said that there were only two super powers—the Soviet Union and the United States. A large gap separated the power of these two states from that of Britain, France, and China. An even larger gulf now distinguished these two giant powers from Germany, Italy, and Japan.

Since 1945 one of the prominent features of world politics has been the bipolarization of power that has taken place about these two leading states. The most impelling fact of international relations has been the sweeping influ-

---

[55] Both states and Ceylon remained within the British Commonwealth of Nations. The latter was modified, however, in order to accommodate the Republic of India. The term *British* was dropped from the title, and the Crown remained only a "symbol" of free association.

[56] See ch. ii.

ence which the competing and antithetical policies and objectives of these two powers have come to have for world peace and security. Until some "third force" of comparable power is erected in Europe or Asia, the destiny of nations must largely hinge upon the course of the relationships between these two titans.

PSYCHOLOGICAL CONSEQUENCES OF PAST WAR

We have already noted in Chapter V some of the psychological factors which bear upon national action and international relationships. Among the influences which condition attitudes and stimulate actions and responses are the memories of past wars and apprehension for present and future security. From the experiences of the past grow suspicions, enmities, and fears toward other nations. From these in turn stem responses of resistance, opposition, tension, and in some cases aggression.[57]

Although our knowledge of the operation of psychology in international relations is far from complete, it appears that the chief psychological consequence of the presence of war and conflict in the community of states is a deep concern for national security in nearly all states. This has been increased as technology has multiplied the destructiveness of war and facilitated mass communication. In succeeding chapters we shall examine some of the causes of insecurity and the policies pursued by states in quest of security.

IS THE NATURE OF WAR CHANGING?

Since the close of World War II in 1945, the world has been almost continuously in a situation described as "cold war," with periods of limited "tepid" or "hot" war in Greece, Israel, Indo-China, and Korea. This historical record gives rise to the thought that the clear boundary line between "war" and "peace" has blurred for an indefinite period into the future. This, by the way, is consistent with communist doctrine, which considers military action as merely one aspect of continuous conflict. Military force is now almost always present, and almost always important, in a conflict among states. Because the power, destructiveness, and consumption of resources of military force is now limited only by the sum total of human and material resources, we have many kinds of war varying from strictly limited to unlimited. It is necessary to draw heavily on the imagination to envisage the nature of a future unlimited war involving the use of nuclear weapons. Since there is a wide range of possible types of war, international politics becomes more than ever important in military matters since it is through political action that the "limited" or "unlimited" nature is determined.

[57] See ch. v, especially p. 153, on the effects of war and tension on the minds of men.

Factors Changing the Nature of War. It is worth-while to stress the three factors (there may be others equally important) which seem to be changing the traditional nature of war:

1. Modern war is allied war. This situation tends to limit the freedom of action of individual states in preparing their national security programs. For allies have a definitely limiting effect on policy freedom.
2. Military technology and techniques now cause war to affect large populations directly across a wide span of social, political, and economic institutions.
3. Individuals are now more aware of the institutional changes in a way of life which war may bring; groups and leaders have techniques for turning the disturbances of war to their advantage.

War and Society. The effect of the changed nature of war on society, both upon the individual and upon the nation-states, has not yet received the full attention which it deserves. A few of the changes that can be identified, and which are worthy of contemplation, are these:

1. In 1914, and, for some peoples even as late as 1939, populations went to war with enthusiasm. Except perhaps in Oriental countries, and this exception is worth noting, recent attitudes are those stemming from a grim realization of the probable cost.
2. Major war now almost certainly changes a society materially, even with victory, as witnessed in the change which occurred in Britain following World War II. Defeat may bring extinction.
3. The nature of modern war makes a high state of readiness mandatory at the outbreak. This means a high continuing military cost so long as military force is present as an element in international politics.
4. No small nation, or group of small nations, can now stand alone if major war occurs.
5. Military force, once unleashed, overflows tremendous areas because of its speed, range, and destructive power. Barriers of mountains, seas, deserts, and rivers have much less military—and hence political—significance than formerly.
6. Neutrality has become more difficult to maintain; for some nations it is virtually or altogether impossible.
7. Modern arms are too costly for many nations, and can be manufactured, in all needed types, by only a few.
8. The consciousness of the great destructive power of modern war has generated a great deal of individual and group effort toward war prevention.

Distinction Between War and Military Force as Instruments of Policy.
Clemenceau, the French statesman of World War I, once remarked that war is
too important to be left to generals. By his silence on a related point, he perhaps indicated a belief that it was then still a feasible and safe instrument of
policy for statesmen. It now seems that war is so dangerous as to be an unsafe
instrument for statesmen. Even a small, carefully planned, "limited" war can
become pandemic with catastrophic results to the world. This is not to say
that we will not have more wars. But the increased uncertainties and hazards
of the overt use of military force may now decrease the probability of wars
while at the same time increasing the importance of great political acumen in
use of military force as a background instrument of policy in international
affairs.

For centuries men have sought ways of limiting or even of eliminating war.
The history of this effort is in large part the history of the struggle for security
through national endeavor, through diplomacy, and through the establishment
of international law and organization. By means of armaments, alliances, balances of power, peace organizations, treaties of guaranty, and even antiwar
pacts, men have repeatedly striven to discourage war or bring it within limits.[58]
These efforts will be discussed in the chapters which follow in Parts IV and V
below.

With the spectacle of cataclysmic destruction impending, it is obvious that
one of man's most pressing requirements today is to "wage peace" hard
enough so that states will not find it necessary or profitable to unloose another
great war. Until the removal of threats to the peace is assured, however, no
state can afford to shape its national policy on any basis other than the possibility that it may be called upon to defend by force, if need be, its territories,
its interests, or its way of life and the values which are its heritage.

SUGGESTED READINGS

H. W. Baldwin, *The Price of Power* (New York, 1947).

Bernard Brodie, *The Absolute Weapon: Atomic Power and World Order* (New
York, 1946).

Vannevar Bush, *Modern Arms and Free Men* (New York, 1949).

J. D. Clarkson and T. C. Cochrane (eds.), *War as a Social Institution: The Historian's Perspective* (New York, 1941).

Karl von Clausewitz, *On War* (New York, 1943).

Charles Dawes, *A Journal of Reparations* (London, 1939).

John Foster Dulles, *War or Peace?* (New York, 1950).

Edward M. Earle, *Makers of Modern Strategy* (Princeton, 1944).

Lionel Gelber, *Reprieve From War: A Manual for Realists* (New York, 1950).

[58] See S. J. Hemleben, *Plans for World Peace through Six Centuries* (Chicago, 1945).

G. A. Lincoln and associates, *Economics of National Security* (New York, 1954).

William F. Ogburn (ed.), *Technology and International Relations* (Chicago, 1949).

Gordon B. Turner (ed.), *A History of Military Affairs in Western Society Since the Eigtheenth Century* (New York, 1953).

Alfred Vagts, *A History of Militarism* (New York, 1937).

J. W. Wheeler-Bennett, *The Pipe Dream of Peace: The Story of the Collapse of Disarmament* (New York, 1935).

Quincy Wright, *A Study of War,* 2 vols. (Chicago, 1942).

CHAPTER X

The Problem of National Security

THE INTERACTION in world politics of the basic factors which we have been discussing in the preceding chapters takes on tangible form for most states in the very practical, and often pressing problem, of national security— a basic concern of every state. This is readily evidenced by the facts that most nations maintain large and costly defense establishments, that states have repeatedly sought alliances and coalitions in order to attain a favorable balance of power, and that increasing emphasis is being placed upon collective security and the establishment of an effective system of international peace and security. It is fair to say that the search for security comprises or affects the greater part of international relations. In view of this situation we shall here set forth briefly the aspects of the problem of national security which will be a major consideration in a large part of the remaining portion of this book. Some of the aspects of the problem will be analyzed in greater detail in succeeding chapters.[1]

THE MEANING OF SECURITY

What is it that nations wish to possess when they speak of seeking "national security"? There is no one formula defining what security means, or has meant, to all governments and people under all types of situations. "Security" can mean different things to different people. Like the term *national interest,* it is susceptible to a variety of meanings and applications covering a wide range of conceptions, values, ambitions, and goals. To some it may mean primarily the maintenance of the *status quo.* To others "security" may be attainable only through territorial expansion, the acquisition of an empire, or the subjugation of other nations and people.

Professor Arnold Wolfers has suggested that security "points to some degree of protection of values previously acquired." Quoting Walter Lippmann, Wolfers says, "A nation is secure to the extent to which it is not in danger of having to sacrifice core values, if it wishes to avoid war, and is able,

[1] See especially chs. xviii and xx–xxii.

if challenged, to maintain them by victory in such a war. What this definition implies is that security rises and falls with the ability of a nation to deter an attack, or to defeat it." [2]

The Element of Feelings and Attitudes. The preceding definition is a useful but somewhat mechanical one. We believe that one of the basic elements of security is a *feeling* of security on the part of the national society and its responsible officials. Security undeniably is closely tied to the ability of a nation to deter an attack or to defend itself successfully if attacked. However, the sense of security or insecurity fluctuates with the concern which a people and their government feel as to the likelihood of another nation attacking them or being able to conquer them. A feeling of insecurity is likely to arise, no matter how strong a state may be, if that state feels that a foreign power has embarked upon a program of expansion which may sooner or later harbor aggressive designs upon it or against friendly states. The effects of popular feelings of security or insecurity are, of course, particularly important in democratic countries where public opinion plays a large role in determining national policies and actions.

The degree of security, or insecurity, which governments and people feel at any given time can vary from a feeling of reasonable security to an intense feeling of insecurity or danger of losing independence or territorial integrity. These feelings, moreover, can change quickly regardless of the actual facts of the security situation. In 1950, for example, the United States suddenly quadrupled its security effort, measured in dollars, and intensified its participation in alliances, although no measurable change had occurred in the security threat. The North Korean aggression, significant as it was in the Far East and as further symptom of the total East-West conflict, merely alerted Americans to a danger which in fact was already existent. The degree of security which a nation feels depends upon a number of external and internal circumstances.

A country in an exposed position near a state having expansionist objectives has reason to be more fearful for its security than one located a long distance away, possibly across ocean spaces. If a state is isolated from friendly states, has few defenses, or is easily approachable by an enemy—as was Australia in 1941 by Japan across a chain of "stepping stone" island bases—it will understandably feel considerable insecurity. Even a Great Power can feel relatively insecure if its manpower, resources, productivity, or social unity do not match those of an historic or potential enemy, as has been the case of France with respect to Germany since 1918.

2 Arnold Wolfers, " 'National Security' as an Ambiguous Symbol," *Pol. Sci. Quar.,* Dec., 1952.

Domestic factors also have a bearing upon the sense of security of nations. A country with a weak internal order, with poor communications, with a heterogeneous population having few cohesive elements, or whose people have little feeling of loyalty to their government, has reason to feel less secure than a state that is well coordinated and whose people enthusiastically support the policies of their government. Least secure of all, perhaps, is a country with a large subversive element within its borders or one which is torn by civil strife. Until such a country can re-establish internal order it is a prey to aggression unless allies or friends will stand guard for it.

The attitudes of some people, including small nations, may appear to have little emotion about their security, even though they live in close proximity to great military powers as in the case of Switzerland and Finland. Familiarity with "living dangerously," an element of fatalism, faith in their own ability to resist an aggressor, or hope that others will come to their defense in time of emergency may contribute to their outlook. Or a people may be so wrapped up in their own domestic affairs or national development that they fail to be fully aware of the existence or magnitude of threats to peace and security posed by others.

Fundamental Objectives. In essence, we may say that in searching for security a nation is endeavoring to procure a certain position in international affairs which is satisfying to its interests and outlook.

Fundamentally, the idea of national security implies three things. These are: (1) preserving the national life, independence, and territorial integrity of the state free from outside interference; (2) enjoying a certain cultural and material standard of the nation's own choice and making; and (3) maintaining the national position in world affairs, this being both a means to the satisfaction of the other ends and an end in itself.

Jules Cambon, for many years French Ambassador to Washington, summed up the meaning of security in these words: "Security," he said, means "more indeed than the maintenance of a people's homeland, or even of their territories beyond these seas. It means the maintenance of the world's respect for them, the maintenance of their economic interest, everything, in a word, which goes to make up the grandeur, the life itself, of the nation." [3]

Security for the nation, as for the individual, embodies not only "freedom from fear," in the words of the Atlantic Charter, but also the desire of a nation to go about its national business and life in whatever way it chooses, to pursue its own interests by its own methods. Peace is a "core value" to most peoples; so much so that maintenance of international peace has become the stated

[3] Jules Cambon, "The Permanent Bases of French Foreign Policy," *Foreign Affairs*, Jan., 1930.

objective of the nations that have adhered to the United Nations Charter. To some few nations bent upon increasing their power and position in the world, the purport of security may imply gaining a position in which the nation will be able to force others—by means of diplomacy, economic action, subversion, or the threat or use of armed force—to act in accord with its will, whether that implies political alignment, cession of territory, or the granting of special concessions.

As Professor Wolfers has observed, security is a value "of which a nation can have more or less and which it can aspire to have in greater or lesser measure." [4]

Relative Values. The governments and peoples of different states place "security" at various levels in their scales of values. Some place security at the very top and are willing to subordinate other considerations and values to the acquisition of the greatest possible degree of security. When war threatens or breaks out, nations readily rank security and defense foremost, although situations occasionally arise when peoples are not ready to sacrifice sufficiently to maintain their independence or territorial integrity. Hitler, Mussolini, and the war lords of Japan were prepared to force their peoples to sacrifice all other values to prepare for wars of conquest.

Some peoples place security midway in their scales, being willing to make substantial efforts to maintain national and collective self-defense, but refusing to sacrifice their standards of living, social welfare, economic prosperity, or individual liberties beyond a minimum or modest point. The American people adopted such a minimum position in the 1930's when they failed to prepare adequately against the Axis powers. The European states participating in NATO indicated that this was their disposition with respect to arming against the USSR in 1952–1953.

Some peoples have placed "peace at any price" at the top of their scale of values. Prime Minister Neville Chamberlain indicated as much in his readiness to appease Adolf Hitler at Berchtesgaden and Godesberg in 1938–1939.

There is no fixed position for security in the galaxy of values held by nations. Each must decide for itself from time to time how it will range its "values." Moreover, there are no inflexible norms by which the value or place of security is determined. Attitudes, domestic political factors, traditions, and ideologies all play a part in determining these values.

SOME SOURCES OF INSECURITY

In addition to the intangible feeling of security or insecurity and the several factors of placement with respect to an expanding power, the relative popula-

4 Wolfers, *op. cit.,* p. 484.

tion situation, and the degree of national unity which one state has in com-parison with others, there are some other elements which enter into the determination of the relative security of states.

Exposed or Vulnerable Position. We have mentioned in the chapter on geography the bearing which a nation's store of natural resources has upon its national strength and weakness. Countries having insufficient supplies of raw materials and having to import the bulk of their needs from abroad over exposed sea lanes or foreign land communications, such as England, Greece, or Japan, are bound to feel insecure when potential enemies build up armaments which threaten their lines of communications or sources of supply. Winston Churchill's memoirs tell how anxiously the British Government watched the figures of merchant marine losses at the hands of German U-boats in 1941–1943. During World War II news commentators often referred to Germany's central position in Europe with interior lines of communication running out to all Europe as being an exceptionally strong one. But Germany's position is one of strength only if some of the surrounding lands are friendly or can be maintained under its domination. Otherwise she is subject to attack from two or more sides as the Allies proved in 1944–1945.

The effects of geographic factors on national security are continually changing. Deserted space, once an adequate protection, may become a feasible avenue of attack, as the air space over the Arctic may be today. The margin of security once given by the surrounding presence of oceanic space to nations such as Britain, Japan, and the United States is now being rapidly lessened.

The United States, striving to "contain" Soviet imperialism, has reasons for feeling insecure as it is confronted with the Soviet Union's large and tightly disciplined population, its backlog of untapped resources, and its advantageous geopolitical position facilitating thrusts over contiguous land areas into Europe, the Middle East, and Asia. American insecurity is not so much fear of invasion by hostile armies, although air and submarine attacks have become increasingly feasible and could become exceedingly dangerous to the United States if atomic weapons were employed against it. The principal concern for security is that Soviet forces could overrun friendly nations overseas on the far sides of the Atlantic and the Pacific (as China has already been overrun by Communists allied with Moscow) and the sources of important raw materials and markets. From this situation there could result a critical alteration in the world balance of power with America ultimately becoming an isolated island lacking insufficient resources and means. It is the task of statesmen to weigh such possibilities.

Differential in Population. In the chapter on population we pointed out the relevance of demographic factors to the well-being and security of nations.

The insecurity of nations with a population less than that of possible enemies is clearly illustrated in the cases of some of the small European states. Belgium with a population of 8 million, set between Germany and France, or Norway or Finland in the shadow of the Soviet Union's 200 million, or Poland situated between the much larger populations of Germany and the Soviet Union, have no security except through guarantees by others and participation in mutual security arrangements. France is acutely aware that the power of a revived, united, and hostile Germany, with a population greater by half than that of metropolitan France, can be held away from its land only as the strength of others can be brought to the support of France.

Fear of War. One of the most universal sources of insecurity is fear of war and its consequences. The history of many countries contains a background with instances of invasion and struggle. Some European states have been invaded so many times their peoples have built up conceptions of certain other states as traditional or historic enemies. This is the case of France and of the Slavic countries with respect to Germany, and vice versa. Any alteration in the balance of power to the advantage of a former enemy is likely to raise feelings of insecurity and fan smoldering suspicions into consuming fears. Evil motives are easily read into the statements and behavior of the opposing country, whether they are present in fact or not. Denials may only magnify suspicions and heighten the sense of insecurity. From this situation there arise new demands for security, for alliances, and for aid. The history of Franco-German affairs in the period between the two World Wars affords an example of this source of insecurity at work in the relations between two nations.

A second aspect of this source of insecurity is the fear of what will happen if another world war occurs. Although the Korean War has given evidence that a "limited war" can still occur for an extended period, international relations in this century have tended to indicate that local wars lead to general wars. Total war lurks in the background of world politics, and with it the dangers of terrible devastation through the employment of weapons of mass destruction including guided missiles and nuclear instruments. To the fears of losses in life and property are added the prospects of regimentation of whole populations and the awareness that if total war starts there is no definable limit to its extent. Technological advances render it possible to step up destruction to the point where the extinction of all human life may be possible at some time in the measurable future.[5] Professor Einstein is authority for saying that "general annihilation beckons" if atomic and nuclear weapons are employed in a total

[5] See Sir George Thomson, "Hydrogen Bombs: The Need for a Policy," reproduced in Padelford (ed.), *Cont. Int. Rels. Readings, 1950–1951,* pp. 232–238. See also Hanson W. Baldwin, "What Kind of Defense in the Atomic Age," *The New York Times Magazine,* May 17, 1953; also *New York Times,* April 1, 1954.

war. In total wars subjugation in the form of "unconditional surrender" of entire nations may be sought. Moreover, in the wake of war stalks revolution with its unforeseeable results.

It is with such dangers in mind that European and Asian governments have viewed with alarm the clash of Soviet objectives with the mounting resistance of the free world led by the United States. Some have reluctantly come to realize that their voices have little influence in moderating the action of Moscow, save as they may associate themselves with the United States.

Ideological Conflict. Closely related to other sources of insecurity today is the presence of the ideological struggle between communism and the free society. In spite of some Soviet pronouncements that Western and Soviet social structures may coexist peacefully, Leninist-Stalinist doctrine impresses upon all who are subject to communist rule that a series of "violent conflicts" must ensue between the communist and capitalist states and that ultimately communism will conquer. People on the far side of the Iron Curtain indoctrinated with such ideas are bound to become distrustful and fearful. The promotion of a popular sense of insecurity has, moreover, been made an official undertaking in communist states through propaganda and the rigors of a police regime. And the communist regimes, maintaining their grip through a reign of terror and the promotion of a popular sense of insecurity, themselves become the victims of a feeling of insecurity.[6]

Communist subversive and revolutionary activities within other countries have added to the feeling of insecurity in those lands both for their national security as such and for the integrity of their established political and social structures. Statements by communist leaders in Italy and France, for instance, that they would "welcome" the Red Army if war occurs have given added support to this fear.[7] From the vicious circle set in operation by the ideological conflict introduced by Moscow-inspired communism it is practically impossible for states separated by ideological barriers to disengage themselves save by the intervention of some external force bringing a more immediate threat to each.

Social Uncertainties. The impact of the industrial and social revolutions upon peoples of hitherto economically underdeveloped or colonial lands is an added factor productive of a sense of insecurity in some countries. Feelings of insecurity are aroused as ancient cultural and social patterns are disrupted with the movement of masses of people into crowded cities, factories, and mining centers, and as the livelihood of such peoples becomes geared to a monetary economy subject to fluctuations in business and politics. Combined with rising

---

[6] See George Kennan, "The Sources of Soviet Conduct," *Foreign Affairs Reader,* p. 470.
[7] *The New York Times,* Feb. 27, 1947, p. E3. See R. C. Snyder, "Security against Subversive Activities," *Proceedings Acad. Pol. Sci.,* May, 1951.

and sometimes extreme nationalism, these feelings of insecurity and uncertainty can easily be exploited by reckless politicians casting blame for domestic maladjustments upon foreign powers or former colonial rulers, thereby adding to international tensions and insecurity.

In summary we may say that the sources of feelings of national insecurity in today's world are manifold and complex. Many elements both of a domestic and an international nature, both of actual circumstance and of outlook, interact with one another in producing sentiments of strength, weakness, power, vulnerability. The degree of security that a state's leaders and people feel depends upon judgments based sometimes upon reason, sometimes on emotion, sometimes on both. Further contributions to security take second place behind other values at some point determined by the political calculus made within each state, even though the continued existence of these other values is itself dependent on sustained security. This is seemingly a paradoxical situation, but perhaps a fortunate one since absolute security for one state or group of states may mean insecurity—or nearly that—for another state or group of states.

MEASURING SECURITY

Whatever may be the position and location of a state, its government must continually probe and evaluate its security situation with reference to other states. This implies examining all factors, external and internal, which bear upon the relations of the state with others. It requires a weighing of the capabilities of the state to meet and counter whatever opposition may exist or arise to its policies. And, in particular, it necessitates an attempt to ascertain accurately the nature and extent of any threats, actual or imminent, to its territory, independence, or what it regards as its vital interests.

Measurement of these things is difficult because nations differ in their estimates of and reactions to dangers. Some feel the potential dangers of a given situation more keenly than others, as illustrated in the attitudes of Europeans and Americans to the extent of the Soviet threat following World War II. Moreover, nations are faced with different degrees and types of threats; some lay great stress on immediate conditions, while others appraise their situation more in terms of the long-run factors involved.[8]

It is theoretically possible for each government to appraise the total power which might be brought against it by other nations to force their will upon it. On this basis a government can examine the capabilities of its own state in relation to others and arrive at some estimate of its security status. There is

[8] See Arnold Wolfers, "The Pole of Power and the Pole of Indifference," *World Politics,* Oct., 1951.

unfortunately no reliable calculus for setting up and solving this equation. If there were, it would be used by aggressors also, and both Napoleon and Hitler would have taken other courses of action at critical times.

An appraisal must, nevertheless, be continuously under way by the statesmen of every country if the state is to guard its independence and its vital interests. This appraisal must look far into the future as well as examine the present. Such an appraisal must take its start from a basis of objective judgments concerning the source of possible military attacks or other aggressive measures, such as economic pressures or the seizure of strategic positions, by foreign states.

The leaders of each state, in trying to arrive at a sound analysis of the nation's security position, must continuously appraise the motives and policies of other nations, as well as their actions. They must seek to determine to what extent their motives and deeds are friendly or otherwise. They must evaluate the policies of others to determine whether, and to what extent, they are likely to be harmful to the national security and interests.

This appraisal may lead to changes in attitude and position as circumstances alter. Canada, for example, once had some fear of annexation by the United States, and perhaps had some reason therefor, even as the United States early in its national history feared invasion from Canada. Now Canada does not include the United States in its estimate of possible aggressors. The estimates of the United States concerning the dangers from the USSR and China have changed materially since 1945. And equally important with the appraisal of opponents and possible enemies is the appraisal of those who may be friends, allies, and neutrals in the future.

Difficulty in Appraising Future Policies of Others. It is seldom easy to forecast with accuracy the path other nations will take under all circumstances. Each faces international relations from its own point of view and is guided by what its self-interest dictates at the moment.

How difficult it is to appraise the course some nations will take can be demonstrated from Italy's actions since 1914. At that time Italy was a member of the Triple Alliance. In 1915 it defected from Germany and Austria-Hungary to the Allies. After 1935 it turned against the Western Powers, joined the Rome-Berlin Axis, and fought with the Nazis in World War II until 1944, when it again became associated with the Allies. What course will Italy take in the future? What path will Germany take in world affairs, say, ten years hence? Which way will the Arab states turn in political and military affairs? What policies will India be likely to pursue in the face of various possible contingencies which may arise among the Great Powers? These are vital questions bearing upon the security of many states. Policy makers must continually weigh and re-examine them in the search for national and collective security. In estimating the future positions and capabilities of other states, a large measure of subjective judgment must enter into the evaluation of known facts and intelligence reports.

We have discussed the measurement of security situations by reason. But peoples at large rarely have available all the information upon which statesmen make their judgments. The public feeling about security is more likely to be a state of mind determined by attitudes, emotions, suspicions, and previous national experience. The attitude of many Frenchmen toward Germany, for instance, is not based solely on reason. Preconceptions of race, religion, and national destiny often figure in the formation of popular sentiments with regard to the policies and actions of other nations, and therefore with respect to their own national security position. So likewise may knowledge or misinformation of the potentialities of nuclear weapons affect natural attitudes and politics.

RELATIVITY OF SECURITY

The appraisals which statesmen and people make with respect to security have to recognize that security is relative in at least two ways: first, it is relative in that there is no absolute security, and secondly, it is relative to the security of other states. Except world dominion be established over all states, to which of course self-respecting and freedom-loving peoples will not willingly submit, no state can expect to have absolute security. It can gain only a variable, relative degree of security. This may be satisfactory at times. At other times it may be quite unsatisfactory as when a power arises which cannot be matched or curbed no matter how strenuous the effort to build up national or collective defenses. This being a world of sovereign states in which none are wholly self-sufficient, each state is dependent upon the strength and cooperation of other friendly states. Gaining the necessary cooperation and support from other states, in peace as well as in time of crisis, is the most essential task of the statesman and of diplomacy both for large and small states.

GUIDE LINES FOR PROBLEM ANALYSIS

There is a natural tendency for people to seek simple, even sloganized formulae for the solutions of security problems in view of their often baffling nature. Thus isolation, sometimes called "splendid isolation," the balance of power, outlawry of war, neutrality, and other security policies can all be made superficially appealing by methods of presentation. In the early 1950's, for example, any policy which was "tough" toward the USSR and seemed relatively inexpensive was appealing to the United States public. In some Near

Eastern and Asiatic countries any policy which appeared or could be said to be "neutral" in the conflict between the Great Powers, or to favor "noninvolvement" in their struggle, was thought to be advantageous irrespective of the long-run implications or consequences. Unfortunately, all historical policies, while each has had some record of success, have experienced failures in spite of the confidence once placed in them.

There being no formula for absolute security, we may ask what guide lines there may be for thinking on the problem of national security. There seem to us to be three considerations which must be kept in mind. The first of these is the fact that at the present time and for some time to come international relations must function within a bipolarized world balance of power. The security or insecurity of most states is in the final analysis largely dependent upon the United States and the Soviet Union.[9] The present bipolar condition may be expected to change with time as Germany and Japan arise once more as Great Powers, and as nations such as India, China, and others grow in economic and political strength. The bipolar situation coupled with the realities of nuclear weapons, presents, however, a great paradox. Nuclear power is a major, and perhaps determinant, factor in supporting the security of the noncommunist states. Its elimination would greatly increase the hazard of aggression being committed against them unless very burdensome defense programs were undertaken. On the other hand, the enormous destruction which would occur in an atomic war must make every knowledgeable person recoil from the possibility. Even national values are likely to be insecure in such a war. The hazards of nuclear war make it urgent that policies be considered which are directed to assuring that tensions between the possessors of nuclear power do not rise to the point where the use of these weapons becomes inevitable. This means that while maintaining an adequate defense force and basing foreign policy upon enlightened self-interest, judicious and constructive use should be made of all instruments of policy and reasonable consideration be given to the needs and aspirations of others.[10]

A second guide line to be kept in mind is that the time has passed when nations can attain a reasonable measure of security through their own defense efforts alone or through policies of isolation or neutrality. The conditions of modern society have made it necessary for all nations, large and small, to think in terms of regional and collective self-defense and cooperation. It is for this reason that such arrangements as the Inter-American Defense Pact, the North

[9] On the evolution and consequences of the bipolar situation see W. T. R. Fox, *The Super Powers* (New York, 1944); also Hans J. Morgenthau, *Politics Among Nations* (2d ed., New York, 1954), pp. 324–327.

[10] See George Kennan, *American Diplomacy, 1900–1950* (Chicago, 1951), pp. 129–154. See also Wolfers, *cit. supra*, 497.

Atlantic Treaty Organization, and the United Nations have come to assume a leading place in the policies and actions of nations. We shall discuss these instrumentalities in Chapters XX and XXI below.

In the third place it is important to bear in mind that some equilibrium must be struck between a nation's objectives and its power. Walter Lippmann has said that for security a nation must keep "its purposes within its means and its means equal to its purposes, its commitments related to its resources and its resources adequate to its commitments." [11] The proper balancing of strength and commitments is indeed complicated in a system or systems of collective security arrangements. No one can foretell with certainty the combination of circumstances which may arise to test the arrangement or necessitate the initiation of collective measures. Taking the United States as an example, the most adverse combination of circumstances would undoubtedly find the nation deficient in resources and preparations. But a less adverse combination might not. As another example, consider the case of Norway, or for that matter almost any other NATO country. The balancing of power and the commitment "to consider an attack against one as an attack against all" is very much a function of the size and timing of outside aid in case of hostilities—and hence beyond the certain control of the state concerned.

CONCLUSION

For the immediate future, security or the lack thereof will be a matter of policies of governments and the programs providing the power to carry out these policies.[12] There is no one solution applicable to the security problem of every nation under existent circumstances of international politics short of the elimination of war and aggression. "The road to genuine security," once remarked General Eisenhower, "is to work for peace, applying ourselves fully in the effort, using all the resources of our minds and skills and talents, exercising the maximum patience in negotiation without the least compromise of principle. But it is a long-term program. Conflicting ideologies and traditional attitudes, developed over centuries, cannot be reconciled within a few short years."

SUGGESTED READINGS

Hamilton Fish Armstrong, *The Calculated Risk* (New York, 1947).
Hanson W. Baldwin, *The Price of Power* (New York, 1948).
Bernard F. Brodie, *The Absolute Weapon: Atomic Power and World Order* (New York, 1946).

11 Walter Lippmann, *U. S. Foreign Policy: Shield of the Republic* (Boston, 1943), ch. 3.
12 Ch. xviii contains a discussion of specific security policies.

George W. Kennan, *American Diplomacy, 1900–1950* (Chicago, 1951).

William L. Langer and S. E. Gleason, *The Challenge to Isolation, 1937–1940* (New York, 1952).

Walter Lippmann, *United States Foreign Policy: Shield of the Republic* (Boston, 1943).

———. *The Cold War* (New York, 1947).

———. *Isolation and Alliances* (Boston, 1952).

J. T. Shotwell and M. Salvin, *Lessons in Security and Disarmament* (New York, 1949).

Louis Smith, *American Democracy and Military Power* (Chicago, 1951).

Harold and Margaret Sprout (eds.), *Foundations of National Power* (Princeton, 1951).

Nicholas J. Spykman, *America's Strategy in World Politics* (New York, 1942).

Robert Strausz-Hupé, *The Balance of Tomorrow* (New York, 1945).

PART III

The Shaping of
National Policy

CHAPTER XI

The Nature of Foreign Policy

UP TO this point we have considered some of the ways in which factors of geography, economics, psychology, the search for power, the presence of conflict, and the nature of the community of states affect international relationships. We have seen how they affect the positions, the attitudes, and the activities of states, and form the nucleus around which international politics revolves.

THE ROLE OF FOREIGN POLICY

Within the framework provided by these fundamental factors, as well as within the limits of its own political system, the government of each state formulates and pursues its foreign policy. This policy sets objectives in foreign relations, and marks out steps to be taken toward their realization.

The formulation and pursuit of a chosen foreign policy is essential for each independent state in a community of sovereign states. It is indispensable to the promotion of national security and the maintenance of the position of the state in world affairs. It is necessary for the procurement of critical raw materials and other goods from abroad, for obtaining of favorable markets for its export trade, for the facilitation of international communications, for the maintenance of its international prestige, and for the development of friendly relations with other states.

WHAT IS FOREIGN POLICY?

When the President of the United States says, "The foreign policy of the United States" is to "respect the sovereign rights of other states," to "seek no territorial expansion," to "refuse to recognize any government imposed on any nation by the force of any foreign power," and so forth, the question arises: What is meant by the term *foreign policy*?

Definition: A policy is simply defined as "a settled or definite course or method adopted and followed by a government, institution, body, or individual." [1] It is also described as a "wise stratagem or device" for attaining given objectives.

Policy has also been defined as the "general principles by which a government is guided in its management of public affairs." [2] But more precisely we may say that policy embraces both principles *and* specific courses of action for achieving certain objectives. Foreign policy consists of the courses of action which a state undertakes in pursuance of national objectives beyond the limits of its own jurisdiction. [3]

The foreign policy of a state is something more than a mere collection of the several specific *policies* which it pursues with respect to individual countries. Taken as a whole, a state's foreign policy comprises (1) a general assessment of the state's economic, military, and international position with relation to other states—neighbors, rivals, allies; (2) an appraisal of its capabilities in advising, bold action, caution, self-reliance, isolation, economic ties, or military or political alignments with others; (3) the broad principles of conduct which the state holds and its government advocates with respect to international affairs; (4) specific objectives and national interests which the state seeks for itself in foreign relations and for the course of world affairs generally; and (5) the strategies, commitments, and tactics which are undertaken for the realization of its objectives and interests. Sometimes the more detailed and specific elements of policy are referred to, and thought of, as "programs," for example, the Mutual Security Program, implementing "policy." We will not attempt to make any distinction between policy and program.

Domestic and Foreign Policy. A distinction is sometimes made in the press and in public speech between foreign policy and domestic policy as if the two were quite separate. Such a distinction can be misleading. For the policy which a state pursues in international affairs is at all times closely connected with domestic politics. Domestic politics constitutes the climate in which the major facets of every foreign policy, especially in the democracies, are conceived and determined. Those who formulate and administer foreign policy are a part of the same political mechanism which deals with domestic political problems. Like all other officers of government they are subject to domestic political forces. It could be said, indeed, that by and large a state's foreign policy is the extension of its domestic political concerns to its dealings with the world beyond its borders. Foreign policy and domestic policy cannot be separated into mutually exclusive compartments. [4] Both are parts of *national*

---

[1] *Webster's New International Dictionary* (2d ed., Springfield, Mass., 1949).
[2] Black's *Law Dictionary* (3rd ed., St. Paul, 1933).
[3] See C. B. Marshall, "The Nature of Foreign Policy," *Department of State Bulletin*, March 17, 1952.
[4] See p. 321.

policy, that is, the sum total of the course of action which a state adopts for purposes of furthering its interests and objectives at home and abroad.

ROOTS OF FOREIGN POLICY

The foreign policy of a country is compounded out of many factors and forces. Some of these are permanent, some temporary. Some are obvious, others obscure. All interact upon one another.

Fundamentally, foreign policy has its roots in the unique historical background, political institutions, traditions, economic needs, power factors, aspirations, peculiar geographic circumstances, and basic sets of values held by each state. These condition the attitudes and thinking of those who formulate and administer policy as well as of the general public. Policy formulators and the public are inextricably linked together. A policy can be selected and carried toward realization, whether in a democracy or in a dictatorship, only if it remains within at least the limits of toleration by the public. Needless to say, the limits are less confined in dictatorships or states with an inarticulate or underdeveloped public opinion than in such highly public-centered states as the United States, Great Britain, or France. Day-to-day policy decisions, from which a substantial part of a state's foreign policy is composed, represent in large measure responses to the operation of political and economic forces at home and abroad.

Traditions, Institutions, Beliefs. Elihu Root, one of America's most eminent statesmen, observed that "thousands of years of differing usages under different conditions forming different customs and special traditions have given to each separate race its own body of preconceived ideas, its own ways of looking at life and human conduct, its own views of what is natural and proper and desirable. These prepossessions play the chief part in determining thought and action . . ." [5]

Jules Cambon, former French Ambassador to Washington, substantiated this when he declared that "aimless and contradictory as appear the happenings in the history of each nation, one nevertheless is able to discern, when one surveys them as a whole and in their proper sequence, that they are not disobedient to certain laws." [6]

The traditions of the American frontier, American democratic institutions, the long experience with the free enterprise system, the constitutional division of responsibility between the President and the Congress on matters of foreign affairs, the traditional policies of neutrality, isolation, and freedom of the seas,

---

[5] Elihu Root, "A Requisite for the Success of Popular Diplomacy," *Foreign Affairs,* Oct., 1922.
[6] J. Cambon, "The Permanent Bases of French Foreign Policy," *ibid.,* Jan., 1930.

suspicion of the military, the championing of human rights and of independence of small nations, the American political philosophy of civil rights, of individual freedoms, and of limited form of government—all these and many other values, customs, ideas, experiences, and "ways of looking at life" exercise a profound effect upon policy makers in Washington and upon the public mind when questions of foreign policy are being decided.

Consciously thought of or not, such experiences and beliefs are in the back of American minds whenever we approach the problem of what kind of policy should be adopted toward the advances of totalitarian states, toward the expropriation of rights or properties in some foreign country, or toward the attempt of some colonial people to gain independence. In a similar way, the traditions, institutional practices, political ideals, and historical background of other nations condition their policies toward the United States and other countries.

National Interests and Objectives. From these underlying traditions, beliefs, experiences, institutions, and circumstances there spring in each country conceptions of national interest and national objectives. These become the bedrock upon which policy is founded and the framework for action and decision.

This was appreciated by the "Founding Fathers" of this country. Alexander Hamilton in his "Pacificus" articles wrote as follows:

It may be affirmed as a general principle, that the predominant motive of good offices from one nation to another, is the interest or advantage of the nation which performs them . . . An individual may, on numerous occasions, meritoriously indulge the emotions of generosity and benevolence, not only without an eye to, but even at the expense of, his own interest. But a government can rarely, if at all, be justifiable in pursuing a similar course . . .

It is not here meant to recommend a policy absolutely selfish or interested in nations; but to show, that a policy regulated by their own interest, as far as justice and good faith permit, is, and ought to be, their prevailing one; and that either to ascribe to them a different principle of action, or to deduce, from the supposition of it, arguments for a self-denying and self-sacrificing gratitude on the part of a nation, which may have received from another good offices, is to misrepresent or misconceive what usually are, and ought to be, the springs of national conduct.[7]

Statements of a similar nature may be found in the annals of foreign affairs. None have expressed the role of national interest more succinctly than the former Secretary of State, Charles Evans Hughes, when he said: "Foreign policies are not built upon abstractions. They are the result of practical conceptions of national interest arising from some immediate exigency or standing out vividly in historical perspective." Admiral Alfred T. Mahan wrote in much

[7] J. C. Hamilton (ed.), *The Works of Alexander Hamilton* (New York, 1851), "Pacificus," no. IV.

the same way. "Self-interest," he declared, "is not only a legitimate, but a fundamental cause for national policy; . . . it is vain to expect governments to act continuously *on any other ground than national interest.* They have no right to do so, being agents and not principals." [8]

More recently the United States Department of State declared that "policies are the courses of action taken by a nation in the interests of the welfare of its people. The roots of a democratic nation's policies lie in the values cherished by its people . . . It is the job of the Government, as the agent of the people, to promote these national interests." [9]

Comparable statements can be found emanating from other states as well. For example, the Soviet Government newspaper *Izvestia* not long ago declared: "The Soviet Union will . . . base her policy exclusively on her own interests."

THE NATURE OF NATIONAL INTERESTS

Definition of Concept. The concept of national interest is not easily defined, for it has been used in many connections.[10] In general it may be said that the national interest of a country is what its governmental leaders and in large degree also what its people consider at any time to be vital to their national independence, way of life, territorial security, and economic welfare. They are those outlooks, convictions, positions, and goals which are held to be sufficiently important to the existence, growth, security, and well-being of a nation to have the weight of the state thrown behind their advancement and protection.

Crystallization of Interest. In a democracy conceptions of national interest become articulated through many institutions and in many ways. The press, public expressions of sentiment, the Congress or Parliament, churches, labor unions, business organizations, and others all have a hand in crystallizing the national interest. In an authoritarian state the interests are determined directly by those who hold and exercise the real power of the state.

What are declared to be national interests often represent in a democracy combinations of general and special or local interests. Sometimes the conceptions of national interest held by different groups of people run in divergent directions. In the period from 1939 to December 7, 1941, for example, many

---

[8] Charles A. Beard, *The Idea of National Interest* (New York, 1934), p. 1. See also Hans J. Morgenthau, *In Defense of the National Interest* (New York, 1951); H. J. Morgenthau and W. T. R. Fox, "National Interest and Moral Principles in Foreign Policy," *The American Scholar,* Spring, 1949.

[9] United States Dept. of State Pub. 4466, *Our Foreign Policy, 1952* (Washington, 1952).

[10] Charles Beard concluded at the end of his study that it is not possible to give a precise definition, so variable have been the interpretations and so often has it been associated with the activities of special-interest groups.

people in the United States firmly believed that the national interest dictated a policy of isolation and neutrality. Some of these organized a movement known as "America First." Still others, while not proposing active military intervention, maintained that it was in the national interest to give assistance to the European democracies and China. Some of these presented their case actively through organizational means. After Pearl Harbor the entire country united in support of the war effort. In a comparable manner, some manufacturing and agricultural groups in many states have asserted that a protectionist policy is in the national interest. On the other hand, consumer groups, exporters, and those concerned over the relationship between international trade and the strength of the free world have equally insisted that the nation's interests are best served by a policy of freer trade.

Securing agreement upon what is the national interest is one of the major problems of domestic politics, especially in a democracy, when elements of the public are strongly divided. Agreement upon the national interest is urgently necessary in the basic matters relating to independence, security, and world position. For unless a nation knows what its interests and objectives are, and prepares itself suitably by policy and action to safeguard them, its course in foreign affairs will be determined by accident and force. A clear understanding of what is the national interest, and what its implications are in terms of policy and action, is essential if a state is to hold the initiative in world politics.

Permanence and Change in Interests. The basic interests of states have a strong element of persistence remaining the same over long periods of time. But the means by which interests are expressed and the methods which are employed to further them vary in response to changing circumstances, new senses of values, technological inventions, and evolving national aspirations.

Great Britain has demonstrated that, with its insular position and small geographical size, located just off the continent of Europe, its fundamental national interests include not only control of the seas but the maintenance of a balance of power in Europe sufficient to prevent any power from dominating the continent. From the seventeenth to the twentieth centuries Britain maintained the most powerful navy in the Atlantic and allied or associated itself with various European states, including Russia at times, to hold in its hands the European balance of power. Today, because of the changed circumstances of power in the world, the interests of the United Kingdom are served by the United States having the preponderance of naval power in the Atlantic, the Pacific, and the Mediterranean. Britain is aware that a favorable balance on the Continent can be held only through the existence of the North Atlantic

Treaty Organization which brings together the Western European states and the United States in a comprehensive resistance to the threat of Soviet aggression which no one European state, or combination of states, is sufficient to hold in balance.

In a similar manner United States policy with respect to the maintenance of the integrity of the American hemisphere, as manifest in the Monroe Doctrine, has been adhered to for more than 125 years. On the other hand, American policy with respect to threats to peace and security has changed five times since 1914. From 1914 to 1917 a policy of neutrality was followed. This gave way to association with the Allied powers in Europe in the war against Imperial Germany. In 1920 the United States reverted to a policy of isolation and neutrality, refusing to join the League or ally itself with its former partners. When the aggressions of Hitler and the Japanese attack upon Pearl Harbor and the Philippines in 1941 brought war to the United States, this policy was abandoned for intervention in the war against the Axis powers and Japan. Finally, in 1945 the United States chose to accept membership in the collective security system of the United Nations, and beginning in 1947 took the historic step of negotiating and adhering to a series of long-term mutual assistance pacts including the Inter-American Pact signed at Rio de Janeiro, the North Atlantic Treaty, a security pact with Japan, and the so-called "Anzus" treaty with Australia and New Zealand.

Conceptions of national interest are bound to be affected by changes in world political, economic, technological, military, and even ideological conditions. In a dynamic society, with power elements and the political endeavors of many sovereign states in a process of constant flux, those responsible for the foreign policy of a state must continually review the interests of their country. They must adapt not only their tactics but at times their basic conceptions of interest and policy to alterations in the world situation. A chosen foreign policy, in this sense, thus always carries with it the proviso "until further notice" and the assumption that conditions will remain substantially the same. With the occurrence of basic changes in the pattern that influenced the selection of a policy, the latter must be readjusted. Otherwise it would tend to meet, counteract, and apply to a situation no longer existent. This, in a foreign policy, could be disastrous.

Role of Ideals and Principles. Statesmen sometimes proclaim that their national policies embrace broad moral principles and seek idealistic objectives. President Woodrow Wilson, for instance, once declared: "It is a very perilous thing to determine the foreign policy of a nation in the terms of material interest. . . . We dare not turn from the principle that morality and not expediency is the thing that must guide us. . . . We have no selfish ends to serve. . . . We are but one of the champions of the rights of mankind." [11]

President Truman stated in 1945 that "the foreign policy of the United States is firmly based on fundamental principles of righteousness and justice." [12] And in his Message to the Congress calling for aid to Greece and Turkey he said:

> One of the primary objectives of the foreign policy of the United States is the creation of conditions in which we and other nations will be able to work out a way of life free from coercion. . . . it must be the policy of the United States to support free peoples who are resisting attempted subjugation by armed minorities or by outside pressure. . . . We must assist free peoples to work out their own destinies in their own way.[13]

Another school of thought holds that it is wrong for a state to base its policy upon moral principles. Such writers maintain that the assertion of such principles can only be a pretense, misleading others, and that only as the state rests its policy upon interests defined in terms of materiel and power can it succeed in international affairs. Otherwise it will be led into foreign crusades, endless commitments, and wars with unlimited objectives.[14]

The policies of states unquestionably are influenced by specific political, material, and power interests (and dangers). Yet governments do, on occasion, take positions—sometimes of an intransigent nature—that moral rights and justice entitle their countries to certain rights, territories, or concessions. The world has witnessed this in recent years in the positions taken by Premier Mossadegh of Iran on the matter of the Anglo-Iranian oil properties, by Egypt on the British bases in the Suez Canal Zone, and by President Rhee of Korea in 1953 on the truce terms in the Korean War. Once popular support is aroused for such stands a moral limitation is interposed to easy compromise.

A pragmatic analysis of international relations also shows that states do subscribe on occasion to broad declarations of principles of conduct. Such principles are set forth in the United Nations Charter (Chapter I), in the Constitution of the Food and Agriculture Organization, and in the Charter of the Organization of American States, to take but three illustrations. To each of these historic compacts many states have adhered. Moreover, governments

[11] Mobile, Ala., speech, Oct. 27, 1913.
[12] Navy Day speech, Oct. 27, 1945.
[13] *The New York Times*, March 13, 1947. The state papers of other distinguished American statesmen such as Elihu Root, Henry Cabot Lodge, Sr., Charles E. Hughes, Henry Stimson, and particularly Cordell Hull contain expressions of ideals and moral principles. See also Frank Tannenbaum, "The American Tradition in Foreign Relations," *Foreign Affairs*, Oct., 1951.
[14] See Morgenthau, as cited in footnote 8 above. *Idem*, "Another 'Great Debate'; The National Interest of the United States," *Am. Pol. Sci. Rev.*, Dec., 1952.

do at times seek solutions at international gatherings that are in the interest of many states.

Why do states do this? In the first place, under the conditions of modern politics even the largest states must secure the support of other states, both for security and for the attainment of their political and economic goals. To do this without resort to coercion a state must persuade others that its interests are identified with theirs, that all are seeking a common goal, and that a high purpose motivates its policy.[15] In the second place, through acceptance and observance of agreed principles a basis is laid upon which relationships between states may be conducted, differences may be composed, and national interests reconciled on some ground other than the argument of power alone.[16] In the third place, considerations of morality and of agreed principles can play a part along with other considerations in forming value judgments of what is in the national interest, in "reconciling the desirable and the possible." [17]

Granting that national interests cannot be measured against abstractions, or rest solely upon juridical and moral concepts,[18] principles and ideals can be in the enlightened self-interest of a state *if* realistically conceived, properly related to political and material interests, and interpreted and applied in a practical manner.[19]

IMPORTANCE OF IDENTIFYING INTERESTS

Interests of Home Country. Policy makers need to have a clear understanding of the national interests of their country if they are to enjoy public support at home and if their policies are to be successful abroad. This is not always easy to achieve in a democracy where many groups enjoy the privilege of asserting their partisan views and special interests, or where there are numerous different racial and national backgrounds among the people. Neither is it easy in a political system where the policy-making responsibility is divided between the legislative and executive branches of the government and where it is possible for one political party to be in control of the legislature and another of the executive, as in the United States. Uncertainty or disagreement over the national interest can stall the policy-making machinery, lead to costly delays in policy action, place those in charge of the conduct of foreign affairs

15 See Thomas I. Cook and Malcolm Moos, "Foreign Policy: The Realism of Idealism," *Am. Pol. Sci. Rev.*, June, 1952; "The American Idea of International Interest," *ibid.*, March, 1953. It is noteworthy that both the United States and the Soviet Union appeal to conceptions of ideals and principles in their struggle for the minds of men throughout the world, albeit the conceptions are diametrically opposed.

16 John Price, *Foreign Affairs and the Public* (Oxford, 1946).

17 W. T. R. Fox, "The Reconciliation of the Desirable and the Possible," *The American Scholar*, Spring, 1949.

18 See George F. Kennan, "The National Interest of the United States," *For. Serv. Jour.*, Nov., 1951.

19 See A. H. Feller, "In Defense of International Law and Morality," *Annals*, July, 1952.

in a dangerous political position at home, or even result in steps being taken abroad which may have to be subsequently abandoned.

President Wilson thought in 1919 that he was acting in the national interest when he followed up American participation in World War I with signature of the Covenant of the League of Nations and the Treaty of Versailles. The refusal of the Senate to ratify these instruments or to consent in later years to United States membership in the League or in the Permanent Court of International Justice revealed not only that Wilson made a costly miscalculation, but that the controlling political power in the country believed its national interest lay in the direction of isolation and unilateral action. The acrimonious controversies which prevailed in the United States from 1937 to 1941 over neutrality, the arms embargo, the destroyer-naval base deal with Britain, military service, and lend-lease stemmed from lack of agreement within the country upon the national interest and objectives. The government was uncertain how far it could go in any direction without encountering strong opposition within the country and having to risk retreat as it did in not following up with deeds the President's "quarantine" speech of 1937.

In the British Government with its tradition of Cabinet responsibility to the House of Commons, as well as the two-party system, cleavages cannot occur between the legislative and executive arms as they do in the United States. But there still may be difficulty in identifying the national interest as in the years 1936–1939 in dealing with Nazi Germany and the European situation. In France and other continental countries employing the parliamentary system but with a multitude of parties and with a less clearly defined principle of cabinet responsibility, the government may have its hands tied for weeks or months at a time—as has been the case in France—because of lack of agreement over the interests of the country and the methods which should be followed to implement them.

Interests of Other States. It is also important for the policy maker to understand, in so far as possible, the interests and objectives of other states. This applies to the interests both of states that are friendly and those that are antagonistic. This is where intelligence work and expert analysis based on intimate knowledge of conditions and trends of thought in other countries are important in the making of policy and the conduct of foreign affairs. For unless the policy maker is aware of the moves and countermoves that may be made by other states, his own policy rests upon treacherous ground, and he may find that his policy is brought to nought.

These are some of the situations that may occur between states regarding their national interests: (1) The interests of various states may closely approximate one another, or even be identical in certain respects as when resisting a common enemy. Where interests are this close, cordial relations are possible. (2) The interests may be mutually compatible but not necessarily identical or overlapping. In this case also it is possible to frame policy on the assumption of long-term friendly relations. (3) The interests of two or more states may compete but not be antagonistic or entirely exclusive. This is the case of British and French interests in Europe, in which amicable, cooperative relations are possible in most realms. (4) Interests may be parallel or identical in some aspects of mutual concern and clearly opposed in others. In this case the preponderant type of interest may either lead to a compromise solution of the existing difficulties, or keep these difficulties in abeyance, or—if the preponderant interests are in areas of common opposition—a reduction of cooperation even in areas of identical interest may occur. (5) Interests may be irrevocably and intensively opposed, as were German on the one hand and British and French on the other hand from 1933 to 1945, in which case disputes, clashes, and conflict—peaceful or otherwise—ensue. Within these bounds there are many variants in the relationship between the interests of various states.

Many have criticized the Western statesmen who were responsible for making the Yalta Agreements with the Soviet Union in 1945 with reference to Eastern Europe and the Far East for not adequately weighing the implications of the objectives of the USSR. Viewed impartially it seems correct to say that the Yalta terms, in themselves, did represent a realistic weighing of the compelling national interests of the West and of the USSR. What were not adequately foreseen and guarded against were Stalin's complete perversion and violation of the spirit and intent of the terms and the inability of a demobilized West to prevent the violations. This agreement may have reflected a failure to take seriously the sustained and revolutionary objectives of the Moscow Government. Had these things been more fully appreciated by the policy makers, the agreements might not have been signed—although a case can be made that the agreements were principally a recognition of power realities. If these things had been more fully appreciated by the public, Americans might have grasped more clearly than they did at the moment the dangers of a hasty withdrawal of most American forces from Europe and the almost total demobilization of effective United States military power.

It was desirable to have an accord between the Great Powers as the end of the war approached in Europe and the Far East, if an advantageous one could be reached. Soviet forces were in occupation of Eastern and much of Central Europe at the time and the United States was faced by the possibility of a prolonged war in the Far East.[20] Realizing that the Soviet Union would probably enter the Japanese war in time to gain thereby, the problem was reduced to one of arranging the best timing to further United States' interests. Had the Soviet Government kept the pledges made at Yalta, a basis for a post-war settlement in Europe and the Far East would have been provided. Many of the suggestions which have been made of what should have been done at Yalta ignore the war situation in February, 1945, and the effect of the United States and Western disarmament in 1945–1946.[21]

With the record of controversies, broken agreements, and imperialist expansion before them, Western Foreign Offices have devoted themselves to much painstaking study of the objectives of the USSR, and have become more cautious about entering into agreements for the sake of accord. Likewise, through the North Atlantic Treaty Organization and other channels, the Western Powers have been examining more intensively and critically than ever before their several national interests with respect to peace and mutual security.

Sacrifice of National Interests. Alexander Hamilton in the quotation given earlier noted that, although individuals may at times sacrifice their own interests in behalf of generosity to others, "a government can rarely, if at all, be justifiable in pursuing a similar course." This is a view held by states in the contemporary era. Instances do happen when states are forced to "sacrifice" their national interests, as when they have been defeated in war or when the odds against the attainment of their objectives have become overwhelming. A case in point was Czechoslovakia in 1938 when President Benes, faced with British pressure and a declaration by its French ally that France would not help Czechoslovakia if it fought, decided not to oppose German annexation demands for the Sudetenland and thus sought to preserve at least the lives of people and cities—if not political independence—and the peace of Europe.

Ordinarily a state will make every effort to advance and to defend what it conceives to be its national interests even to the point of the use of force and resort to war. Because national interests and objectives are vital to the life of

20 It may be of historical interest to note that on Feb. 28, 1945, the late James V. Forrestal, then Secretary of the Navy, recorded in his Diary that General MacArthur in 1945 "expressed the view that the help of the Chinese would be negligible. He felt that we should secure the commitment of the Russians to active and vigorous prosecution of a campaign against the Japanese in Manchukuo of such proportions as to pin down a very large proportion of the Japanese army . . . He expressed doubt that the use of anything less than sixty divisions by the Russians would be sufficient." Walter Millis (ed.), *The Forrestal Diaries* (New York, 1951), p. 31.

21 For other views on Yalta see W. C. Bullitt, "How We Won the War and Lost the Peace," *Life,* Aug. 30, Sept. 6, 1948; testimony of W. Averell Harriman in *Hearings before the Com. on Armed Services and the Com. on Foreign Relations, U. S. Senate,* 82d Cong., 1st Sess., Part V, Appendix, Aug. 17, 1951. Walter Lippmann's *U.S. Foreign Policy: Shield of the Republic* (Boston, 1943) contains a clear-sighted prognosis of the bases of possible accord and tension between the United States and the USSR.

each state, questions of national power and of military strategy become closely identified with national policy and action. Judging when some national interests may be sacrificed is one of the most delicate of all tasks in statecraft. It touches the most sensitive nerves of the body politic. For this reason it is not surprising that governments "fall" or statesmen are forced to resign when they are faced with concessions or defeat in the promotion and realization of the national interests.

FORMULATION OF POLICY

There are numerous procedures by which foreign policy is formulated. Variations exist among the different political systems by virtue of different constitutional provisions and customs. We shall trace some of these in the succeeding three chapters. Irrespective of the constitutional or administrative details of the policy-forming mechanism, there are certain generalizations derived from the ways in which foreign policy is "made."

A foreign policy may be carefully and systematically worked out, taking into account the various contingencies that may arise in the pursuit of national objectives. Alternative courses of action may be considered and planned in advance to enable the government to meet anticipated difficulties. Broad principles may be enunciated, followed by application and interpretation as events necessitate. On the other hand, a policy may be arrived at by a sequence of decisions taken on a day-to-day basis dealing with emergent situations. These may follow some general principle, written or unwritten; or the action taken may be purely opportunistic. Variants and combinations of these methods can be found on every hand.

Deliberate Evolution. United States policy making during World War II regarding the establishment of the United Nations illustrated a policy laboriously worked out in advance.

Starting early in the war a group of officers in the Department of State, with the assistance of a committee of advisers drawn from public life and the collaboration of a bipartisan group of Senators and Congressmen, carefully studied various alternative courses of action which the United States might take at the close of the war, together with the contingencies which might have to be met both at home and abroad. From these deliberations evolved a series of "position papers" and draft proposals for the use of negotiators, approved by the Secretary of State and the President. The positions taken by the United States at Dumbarton Oaks, San Francisco, and other conferences, which played a large part in establishing the United Nations and its affiliated agencies in the form that actually emerged, were the ultimate fruits of this program. The care with which this effort was conducted was also largely responsible for the overwhelming vote of 89 to 2 by which the United States Senate consented to the ratification of the United Nations Charter.

As another example, under the leadership of President Eisenhower the National Security Council, with its working staff drawn from the departments of the members, became a top-level agency for formulating foreign policy.

In Britain a substantial portion of the time of the Cabinet is regularly devoted to the consideration and integration of foreign policy. In the USSR it is supposed that one of the principal tasks of the Presidium of the Central Committee of the Communist party (formerly the Politbureau) is long-range policy planning and direction.

Enunciation of Principles. Some statesmen lay considerable store upon formulating policy by first drafting and announcing broad statements of policy principles and then developing policy by making decisions on the application and interpretation of the principles as concrete situations arise. This was essentially the way in which the Monroe Doctrine policy has developed. Former Secretary of State Cordell Hull (1933–1944) was a strong believer in the idea that to have a foreign policy one must first state a series of broad assumptions and principles. He frowned upon the idea that policy should evolve from a series of acts taken without first fixing a set of principles.

Improvisation. At the other extreme of policy formulation may be improvisation, "playing by ear," as it is called in the trade. Such a procedure may have to be resorted to when adequate information is lacking on the intentions of an aggressive state, or when moves have to be taken hastily without time for consultation and deliberate planning. A state ill-prepared militarily and politically divided at home can readily be put in this position by a clever aggressor, as Hitler repeatedly demonstrated with Britain and France between 1936 and 1939. Having inadequate means to stop Nazi aggression, lacking the will to do so by force if necessary, and being governed by divided counsels, the Western democracies could only improvise belated measures in response to the series of "week-end" crises Hitler engineered to overthrow the Versailles peace terms and gain control in Central Europe.

Day-to-Day Decision. In the routine conduct of foreign relations many policy decisions must be made from day to day. These are called forth by the flood of telegrams and dispatches received each day by a Foreign Office from its embassies and consulates scattered over the world, by the requests and proposals of foreign governments, and by the demands of nationals at home and abroad.

Some of the decisions taken in response to these moves and pressures require merely the application of already existent principles and broad policy lines to new situations. In some instances such developments have been anticipated in advance, and action can usually be taken fairly quickly and without resort to more than routine official clearance. Where novel or unexpected developments occur, more exhaustive consideration may be required to discover whether such a situation is covered by existing policy, or whether some new policy guides must be set up and applied.

Year in and out the foreign policies of most states are comprised of combinations of (1) declarations or assumptions of basic principles which are applied as circumstances require; (2) both generalized and specific long-range policies applicable to particular phases of international relations and toward certain countries; (3) specific policies of definite time duration, to be reviewed or supplanted at the end of a given period or when certain circumstances have changed; and (4) actions taken from day to day in response to domestic and foreign conditions.

"Muddling Along." There are times when the only course a state can follow is to "wait and see." This is not necessarily an indication of unpreparedness or indolence on the part of officials charged with the conduct of affairs. Neither is it necessarily representative of a policy of opportunism and expediency which some governments have been known to pursue.

British policy has sometimes been criticized for "muddling along," without following fixed objectives or planned procedures. So, for example, Lord Salisbury once defined the policy of Great Britain as "to float downstream, occasionally putting out a boat-hook to avoid collisions." There are occasions when a government is confronted with a situation in which it lacks adequate information on the objectives of another party, or of the consequences of any move it is free to take at that time. Situations can arise in which a government must "play for time" while waiting for public opinion at home to solidify or for political tempests to calm, or while consulting upon a joint course of action with other powers. Likewise, a government may have to "muddle along" while it prepares to meet a threat of force.

Risk in Policy Making. In dealing with secretive totalitarian regimes such as those of Nazi Germany and the Soviet Union, which have systematically endeavored to cut off sources of information about themselves, other governments must depend materially on information and analysis of intelligence agencies. Anne O'Hare McCormick writing in *The New York Times* commented that "never in history was it so difficult to base policy on facts. . . . The secrecy that envelops half the world, the power of absolute Governments to act without reference to the popular will, and to explain their actions without reference to the truth—this is what reduces the conduct of foreign affairs to something like a guessing contest." [22] This situation obviously poses haz-

[22] *The New York Times,* Nov. 27, 1950.

ards and makes statesmen cautious. When the objectives or capabilities, or both, of other powers are not clearly known the situation is difficult. Any policy, meeting opposition from another power, runs some risk of failure or at least of compromise. An incorrect "estimate of the situation" may precipitate consequences that would not otherwise occur, or it may aggravate the very trouble which the policy maker is seeking to avoid. Under such conditions hesitation, or even temporization, may appear to be the most prudent course. Alternatively, a foreign government determined to press its own policy or to seize the initiative in world politics must go forward fully prepared to accept even the ultimate consequences—war—if the opposing states so choose.

POLICY GOALS

The ends which states seek in their foreign policies naturally vary from country to country, depending upon background, location, needs, political inclinations, national interests, and power factors.

Basic Aims. There are four common denominators among the multitude of aims of states. These can be identified as (1) national security, (2) economic advancement, (3) safeguarding or augmenting national power in relation to other states, and (4) international prestige.

These four objectives can be identified separately, but they are closely intertwined. It can be argued that the latter two are often subordinate to the first two, being means rather than ends. At times a state may make some temporary sacrifice of one objective in order to further national progress toward another objective. Hitler, for instance, placed an increase in Germany's power above the advancement of her economic welfare from 1933 to 1945—"guns before butter" was the slogan. The Soviet regime has since its beginning sacrificed the short-term economic welfare of its people in order to build up heavy industry, great military power, and world position. The United States, on the other hand, during the years from 1920 to 1940 had as its objective economic prosperity regardless of national security. From 1945 until at least 1953 the United Kingdom enforced a policy of economic "austerity" at home, cutting down its imports of consumer goods while forcing a large percentage of its national product into the export trade in order to achieve the related objectives of preserving a sound economic position and national security.

It is sometimes suggested that peace is or should be regarded as the supreme objective of national policy. Desirable as peace may be at most times, there are circumstances in which it may be disastrous to the values and to the independence of a state to remain at peace. A state which places peace as its supreme objective can be lulled into a false sense of security. It gives initiative in foreign relationships to any state that is willing to risk the abandonment of peace for the advancement of its own selfish interests and objectives, or is determined to enlarge its territory or enhance its power through aggression. Pacificism can blind a people to the realities of power politics and lead to uncertainty as to what should be the national course when actually confronted with aggression and armed conflict. This was humiliatingly discovered by the British people in 1938–1939 after years of pacifist thinking when Prime Minister Neville Chamberlain's "peace-in-our-time" appeasement of Adolf Hitler failed to deter the Nazi Fuehrer from attacking Poland and then descending disastrously upon France, Britain, and the small Western European states.

Actions to Further Objectives. In pressing toward its objectives a state may adopt strong positive policies and tactics toward other states. In such a category may be placed the foreign-aid policies of the United States in the period since 1945, designed to help the peoples of the "free world" to rebuild their economies, to sustain employment, and to strengthen their will and military capability to resist communist aggression.

Contrariwise, some policy actions may be essentially negative in their intent to prevent certain things being done that would adversely affect their national interests. The Hay Open-Door Doctrine and territorial integrity of China policies were intended to forestall the partition of China and the closure of its markets to free competition in order to further the United States objectives of peace, security, and economic opportunity in the Far East.

Nations bent on increasing their territorial domain and world power, as Germany and Japan before World War II and the Soviet Union today, naturally tend to pursue dynamic and exploitive policies. States seeking above all to maintain a *status quo,* on the other hand, are likely to adopt conservative policies and procedures.

DOMESTIC POLITICS AND FOREIGN POLICY

It is a patent fact, though often lost sight of by the public, that there is a close connection between domestic politics and foreign policy. National policy —whether it be viewed in its domestic or its international aspects—is the outcome of the conflicts and compromise between the various politically active groups within each country.

Domestic politics may force a government to follow a course of action that will sacrifice international interests, or to alter the policy the country has been pursuing in foreign affairs. Those charged with the making and conduct of foreign policy in any democratic country must constantly keep a weather eye cocked on the domestic political scene, for domestic politics, indeed, is the environment in which foreign policy is conditioned.

In order to get a given policy accepted within the United States, as for instance the Marshall Plan or the North Atlantic Treaty, domestic interests may have to be placated. Concessions may have to be accepted such as a stipulation that 50 per cent of the goods sent abroad under the assistance program should go in American vessels.

Admitting the fact that the national policy of a state has both internal and external manifestations, the conclusion follows that domestic politics have implications both within and without the country.

Domestic Policy and Foreign Relations. Many issues in domestic American politics have far-reaching concern abroad. A few illustrations will make this point clear.

The tariff used to be considered a purely domestic issue. Any evil effects were passed off as the business of the countries who felt them. Many Americans were satisfied that tariffs were beneficial to the country. Historians are convinced, however, that the high United States tariffs of the 1920's, topped off by the Smoot-Hawley Tariff of 1930, had much to do with bringing on the world-wide economic depression, which in turn advanced the rise of the fascist dictatorships.

The decision by President Roosevelt in 1933 to devalue the dollar was taken with the domestic price situation in mind. But that decision led in turn to the wrecking of the World Monetary Conference when the President refused to join in a plan to stabilize currencies.

The removal of price controls within the United States in 1946 was in itself a domestic policy, dictated by domestic politics and generally applauded within the country. Yet the rise in prices which soon followed contributed to increasing the "dollar gap" in American foreign trade and hence to the necessity for loaning and granting billions of dollars to other nations to help stabilize their economies, to assist them to continue purchasing needed goods from the United States (without which employment might have dropped seriously within the United States), and to prevent their becoming prey to communism.

In 1949 a slight business recession in the United States affected the foreign exchange position of Britain and other Western European countries, and was one of the factors causing currency devaluation by some of these states in order to adjust the exchange situation and to stimulate foreign purchases of their goods.

One other illustration of the relationship between the workings of domestic politics and foreign affairs may be taken from the American military position after the war. Domestic politics forced hasty demobilization of the American armed forces after the cessation of hostilities. This, however, soon compromised the effectiveness of the diplomatic arm of the government in negotiations with the Soviet Union. Rapid withdrawal of American forces from Europe, before a peace settlement had been concluded, may have encouraged the Soviet Union to think it would soon have the Continent militarily to itself; that it could proceed with impunity to extend its influence and its power at will, especially through Eastern and Central Europe. The pressures within United States domestic politics completely ignored the facts that (1) the Soviet Union was not disarming correspondingly, (2) disarmament under prevailing circumstances would jeopardize the chances of obtaining the kind of peace Americans wanted, and (3) the Soviet Union had already given evidence in the wartime negotiations that it was impressed and influenced only by considerations of relative power.

Domestic political forces continued to press the United States Government in the direction of economy and reduction of its armed forces until the attack upon Korea in June, 1950, notwithstanding that from 1946 it was apparent that there were grave and basic differences between the United States and the Soviet Union, and that Soviet imperialism was on the march in Europe and in Asia. While no one can be sure, since the Soviet leaders do not divulge their reasoning, a case can be made that American domestic policy encouraged Moscow to believe it could "safely" promote aggression in Greece, Berlin, China, and Korea and further communist activities in other countries. It seems reasonably certain that part of the tremendous outlay by the United States after 1948 under the European Recovery Program, the Mutual Defense Assistance Program, plus rearmament and the Korean War were a part of the price paid for the kind of policies the United States pursued from 1945 to 1947. But on the other hand, it can be argued that the United States would not have undertaken the costly continuous program of military readiness and of responsibility in world affairs unless shocked out of its traditional attitudes by Soviet actions between 1945 and 1953.

Influence upon Policy-Making Personnel. The national officers who determine foreign policy at the highest level are nominated, elected, appointed, or chosen in nearly every country with respect to domestic rather than international affairs.

Domestic issues almost inevitably predominate behind the scenes in the selection of presidential candidates in the United States. Being selected at conventions made up of representatives of local party groups, the choice is usually determined by the support which a candidate can command among state and local party leaders. These men and women are primarily concerned with domestic political considerations: by the votes a candidate can win; by the chances of winning the election and therefore of gaining office; and by the ability of a candidate to influence the Congress. A candidate's knowledge of foreign affairs and his aptitude for leadership in this field are only one of the many concerns in the minds of those who fill the milling convention halls. Fortunately, there is some evidence that the more responsible party leaders now appreciate the fact that these qualities are of major importance in the office of the Presidency.

In Britain the Prime Minister is always selected from the House of Commons. He is therefore strictly a party man, one who has won and held a position in the hurly-burly of domestic politics. In most countries with the Parliamentary system, prime ministers are ordinarily chosen from the leaders of political parties. These men normally attain their positions of party leadership as a result of long and successful service which often includes experience with foreign affairs. In the selection of Winston Churchill in Britain in the dark days of 1940, when Prime Minister Chamberlain resigned, the nation turned to a man who was as much a past master in domestic politics as he was an expert in foreign affairs.

Even in states with dictatorial regimes, domestic politics exercises a large influence upon the foreign-policy maker, although he may be in a much stronger position to control and direct these forces. History contains many illustrations of dictators who have plunged their countries into foreign ventures either to divert attention from internal domestic conditions or to strengthen their own power at home.

Pressure on Legislators. What is true of the heads of state and their immediate subordinates is of course even more applicable in the case of the rank and file of national legislative bodies. Congressmen and Members of Parliament of every country are under constant pressure of domestic politics in all the actions of these bodies having to do with foreign affairs, whether it be in the passage of legislation, the approval of treaties, or action on appropriations for the conduct of foreign relations.

Politics and the Foreign Ministry. Secretaries of State, or Foreign Ministers as they are usually designated in countries other than the United States, are likewise continually under the influence of domestic politics. In selecting this officer, who often ranks next to the head of the government in democratic countries, a man must be picked who has either actual or potential political influence himself. When he is not a political "figure" to begin with, he often ends up being one unless he happens to hold office under a President or Premier who assumes personal direction of foreign policy himself, or when a condition of exceptional harmony prevails and he is not called upon to exercise notable leadership.

Political Pressures. The pressures of domestic politics can become very heavy upon Secretaries of State and Foreign Ministers. They may force a change or adjustment of policy, or even compel resignation from office. Former Secretary of State Acheson, who found himself caught in the toils of domestic politics, once remarked that the business of having to straddle between the exigencies of domestic politics and the requirements of international relations helped explain why "diplomats become dipsomaniacs."

The influences of domestic politics which can be applied directly to the chiefs of state, to Foreign Ministers, and to the members of national legislative bodies with regard to foreign policy may be transmitted, directly or indirectly, to the foreign policy and the foreign relations of a state. This does not always or necessarily follow. A strong President, Premier, or Secretary of State may succeed in standing off even highly organized pressure if he has a firm grip upon his party and commands a clear majority in the Congress or Parliament, or enjoys wide popular support for his policies. But it is not easy for policy makers to resist where pressures are powerfully organized and emotional appeals are broadcast to the public. This is a part of the problem of conducting a responsible foreign policy in a democracy.

The exposure of the policy maker and administrator to domestic political pressures is particularly acute in countries like France, where the presence of many political parties in Parliament usually results in government by coalitions. The foreign policy of such a country is especially at the mercy of political quicksands, for the policy maker may at any time find the support of one of the coalition elements withdrawn and the government forced to resign. Moreover, the country may find itself, as France has on several occasions, without a government and a Foreign Minister at some important juncture in international affairs, or with a government which has at best a temporary lease of life or mere "caretaker" standing. In such circumstances the policy maker must indeed be agile in placating opposition and finding policy lines which successfully compromise the divergent views of many elements.

INFLUENCE OF PUBLIC OPINION

Public opinion is an important factor in the national policy and strategy of countries with democratic institutions. In the United States and in the Commonwealth countries, in particular, where the public is well informed on matters of foreign affairs, where there are articulate means for its views to be pressed upon policy makers, and where it is able through freedom of speech and of the press to bring powerful influences to bear upon those in government, careful attention must be paid to the attitudes and susceptibilities of the people and the press.

Public opinion can set limits upon the freedom of choice and freedom of action of the Executive, as was demonstrated by the strength of isolationist and pacifist sentiment in the United States during the 1930's. A democratic government can go only as far as public opinion will tolerate. It can move only as fast in applying its own concepts of policy action as it can carry public opinion with it. This means that the policy maker must devote thought and effort to informing public opinion, as well as assaying it, through the press, radio, and other media of communication. To ignore public opinion in a democracy is to court dangerous opposition and even risk of being forced to repudiate steps taken without regard to it.

IMPACT OF WORLD SITUATION

It must be apparent from what has been said in the preceding chapters on the influence of the various fundamental factors affecting the positions and actions of states, as well as from what we can note from the daily press, that the policies of states are also conditioned and affected by the realities of the world situation. Alterations in the structure and balance of world political power, the rise or disappearance of aggressive forces, changes in the economic position of states, new applications of technology to industry and to military science, the growth of powerful social forces, together with many other facets of human activity exert an impact upon the work of the foreign policy maker.

A set of policies may be prudent for a Denmark or a Norway, or for that matter a Britain or a United States, to follow when there is a condition of general peace in a power equilibrium having numerous more or less coequal Great Powers, none of which harbors aggressive designs upon others. But such policies require reconsideration when the whole balance of world power is jeopardized by totalitarian imperialism, or altered by the development of thermonuclear weapons and supersonic flight, or modified by shifts in economic strength.

The problem for the policy maker is to identify the nature of the constantly changing world situation as it bears upon the interests and objectives of his country and to determine what steps can be taken in the light of both international and domestic elements. Reliable intelligence of what is in the making abroad is required, along with an acute perception of the nation's capabilities and what is politically feasible.

THE TASK OF THE POLICY MAKER

The task of the policy maker is exceedingly complex. Foreign policy makers are anything but free agents. Let us summarize. In the first place, the field of decision is hedged about by limitations imposed by the principles, values, and objectives which the nation holds. These have a bearing upon both the ends sought by foreign policy and the means adopted for its conduct. Obviously, the policy maker will not ordinarily select policies or actions which will destroy the basic values cherished by the state.

In the second place, there are, as we have seen, many political and private forces that operate upon those who formulate and administer foreign policy. There are expectations and obligations which condition the decisions they reach, responsibilities which cannot be evaded, and constitutional arrangements within which they operate. The policy maker is to an extent subject to what might be called his "market." His policy and his strategy reflect what he believes he can obtain by way of necessary support, and are the outcome of compromises which he is forced to accept.

Foreign policy, in the third place, deals with matters which by and large lie beyond the sole control of the initiating state. The policy maker must deal with other sovereign states which ordinarily enter into only such agreements and concessions as accord with their own conceptions of national interest. Hence, negotiation and adjustment must be the normal milieu of the conduct of foreign policy. Only when the nation is prepared to resort to the open use of force as an instrument of national policy and is successful in its employment, or can reduce another entity to a subordinate political condition, can it impose its will and policy unilaterally upon another.

In the fourth place, relationships between states are generally governed by power politics and the relative degree of power which a state has in comparison with other states.

Finally, policy must be made and pursued in the light of the known or anticipated policies of other states and of the multitude of constantly changing economic, social, technological, and political developments transpiring throughout the world. These provide a kaleidoscope of intermingling, interacting forces. Effective statesmanship depends upon forming an accurate estimate of the totality of these forces, ascertaining their meaning for the state, and fashioning suitable measures for coping with them.

The task of forming and conducting foreign policy involves a perception of all these elements. They cannot be separated into wholly distinct categories. They are constantly overlapping. They must be dealt with concurrently, yet each must be kept within proper perspective and balance. Contradictions and dilemmas arise among which choices must be made to procure the maximum satisfaction of all aims concurrently. Power must be used with as much wisdom as possible to attain the ends desired while maintaining the friendship and respect of others. The problems of political relationships in a power-guided world cannot be eliminated. They must be lived with and managed to the best of the capability of each state. As one who has been close to the planning of foreign policy has concluded: "Only in the light of ultimate purposes can one know how to proceed problem by problem in this field." [23]

THE BALANCE SHEET OF FOREIGN POLICY

In the politics of states, especially of the Great Powers, there can be "a grim accounting," as Walter Lippmann has said, "if the budget of foreign relations is insolvent." A state must always have power commensurate to the goals which it seeks if it is to attain them and to safeguard its security. Otherwise, it may be faced with an "insolvency" which can mean, in Mr. Lippmann's words, that "preventable wars are not prevented, that unavoidable wars are fought without being adequately prepared for, and that settlements are made which are the prelude to a new cycle of unprevented wars, unprepared wars, and unworkable settlements." [24] The logic of this proposition can be tested in examining the relations of the Great Powers during the past century and a half and nowhere better than in the years since 1930.

"A nation's intentions and its power interact on each other. What we seek," as one acquainted with policy making has observed, "is in part determined by what we can do. What we can do is determined in part by what we are after.

"Furthermore, our own aims and power acting as functions of each other are in an interactive relation with adversary intentions and capabilities, which also relate to each other as interdependent variables." [25]

To recognize one's own capabilities and limitations, as well as those of others, to adapt objectives to the means available, and to maintain the available means in a condition of sufficient readiness to meet the demands which may be made upon them under the existent time and circumstances, while at the same time setting the nation's course toward the goals held high by its people, is the essence of attaining a viable balance in foreign affairs.

SUGGESTED READINGS

Charles A. Beard, *The Idea of National Interest* (New York, 1934).
Carl J. Friedrich, *Foreign Policy in the Making* (New York, 1938).
George F. Kennan, *American Diplomacy, 1900–1950* (Chicago, 1951).
Kurt London, *How Foreign Policy is Made* (2d ed., New York, 1950).
Lester Markel and Others, *Public Opinion and Foreign Policy* (New York, 1949).
J. L. McCamy, *The Administration of American Foreign Policy* (New York, 1950).
Hans J. Morgenthau, *In Defense of the National Interest* (New York, 1951).
Robert E. Osgood, *Ideals and Self-Interest in America's Foreign Relations* (Chicago, 1953).
John Price, *Foreign Affairs and the Public* (Oxford, 1946).

[23] C. B. Marshall, "The Nature of Foreign Policy," *Department of State Bulletin*, March 17, 1952.

[24] W. Lippmann, *U.S. Foreign Policy: Shield of the Republic* (Boston, 1943), p. 84.
[25] Marshall, *cit. supra.*

CHAPTER XII

The Formulation of United States
Foreign Policy

AMERICAN FOREIGN POLICY, like that of almost every other state, is a flow through time of decisions and actions. These vary from great policy milestones such as the Monroe Doctrine and the post-World War II Collective Security Program to minor implementing actions such as the return to Mexico of battle flags captured in the Mexican War. This flow of decisions and actions has a method and direction determined by the basic institutions of the United States and by the principal objectives of the nation—national security and well-being as defined and interpreted at a particular time.

POLICY MAKING A COMPLEX PROCESS

Policy making is complex for two main reasons: (1) the number of agencies of government and of political institutions involved and (2) the substantive nature of present-day foreign affairs. As to the first, we must take account of factors extending from the Constitution of the United States through Congress and the executive agencies to the possible effects of small interest groups. As to the latter, policy is now generally much more than a statement of principle or intent. It requires the support of men, money, materials, resources, and actions. Men are stationed overseas, in and out of uniform. Huge sums are appropriated to support foreign policy. A policy normally has to be backed by a program of action and hence the dimensions of policy are, in part, set by capabilities to provide a supporting program. Logically the implementors of policy (for example, Congress through the appropriations process, and the armed forces through their mission of managing military power) share in being architects of policy.

Policy implementation is often a highly operational matter involving both provision of legislation and means by Congress and also coordination among the executive departments. Hence policy formulation requires coordination and participation among many government agencies and interest groups within the body politic. For if means and support are not assured for a policy, that policy has little or no significance.

Policy formulation and implementation must take place within the structure of government established by the Founding Fathers of the Republic. Our heritage from them, defined in the Constitution and its interpretations, places great emphasis on separation of the executive and legislative power. This is in marked contrast to the parliamentary system which fuses the leadership for law making and law executing in the same individuals. Our system is one of checks and balances so that the legislature and the executive brake, and sometimes stalemate, each other. The powers of our federal government, moreover, are limited compared to those of the United Kingdom, for instance, as many powers rest in the states. There is, however, no question that the national government has complete power in the area of foreign affairs.

THE PRESIDENT AND FOREIGN POLICY

Sole Organ of Foreign Relations. The President is, as was acknowledged in Congress in 1800 by John Marshall (later Chief Justice), "the sole organ of the nation in its external relations, and its sole representative with foreign nations."[1] The degree to which presidents have accepted this opportunity has varied with individuals. Presidents such as Polk, Wilson, and the two Roosevelts have exercised their powers extensively. Others have assumed the role more of instrument rather than of initiator.

Although judicial interpretations of the President's powers have varied, history has generally supported the view of Alexander Hamilton that the President has "all powers which the facts of international intercourse may at any time make convenient, applicable, and which the Constitution does not vest elsewhere in clear terms."[2]

Communication with Foreign Governments. One of the principal features of the President's power is his monopoly of the right to communicate with foreign governments. Through his power of appointment of ambassadors, ministers, and other representatives, and through his right of receiving foreign ambassadors and ministers, the President can deal directly with foreign governments.

Right of Recognition. The right to send and to receive diplomatic repre-

---

[1] *Annals,* 6th Cong., col. 613 (1936). Reiterated in the case of *U. S.* v. *Curtiss-Wright,* 299 U. S., 319. See Quincy Wright's *The Control of American Foreign Relations* (New York, 1922) for a general analysis of the foreign relations power.

[2] Quoted in E. S. Corwin, *The President's Office and Powers* (3rd ed., New York, 1948), pp. 210–211. For other studies of the President's powers see Louis Brounlow, *The President and the Presidency* (Chicago, 1953); E. P. Herring, *Presidential Leadership* (New York, 1940); H. J. Laski, *The American Presidency* (New York, 1940).

sentatives from other governments and states, and to refrain from sending or receiving, gives the President the power to recognize or to withhold recognition of foreign states and governments. This can have important consequences abroad. In 1915, for example, President Wilson helped to hasten the downfall of the Huerta Government in Mexico by refusing to accord recognition. Some foreign governments (for example, the United Kingdom) consider recognition as a formal acknowledgment of a factual situation concerning the government in firm control of a state. The United States, however, has used recognition as a political instrument, giving or withholding it as the interest of the United States has seemed to warrant.[3]

Through the power to negotiate and conclude treaties and other international agreements, the President is enabled to exercise initiative in foreign policy; for, as the Supreme Court has recognized, this power extends "to all proper subjects of negotiation between this Government and other nations."[4] In executing treaties and agreements the President may employ such means as appear to him necessary, including the sending of troops abroad to protect citizens or national interests. As members of the Senate have conceded: "In the international field, the President has the duty to carry out not only the letter but the spirit of the Nation's treaties."[5]

United States treaty making normally involves five steps: (1) negotiation and signature, which are usually accomplished by the Secretary of State or his representatives; (2) consent of two-thirds of the Senate; (3) ratification of the treaty by the President, that is, formal acceptance; (4) exchange of ratification with other countries concerned; (5) proclamation by the President stating the contents of the treaty and announcing its ratification. A treaty is generally considered to be legally binding on individuals only after proclamation. The United States entered into over 1,400 treaties (sometimes called "pacts," "agreements," "protocols," or other names) between 1778 and 1945, over a thousand being concluded in this century.

When President Washington abandoned his initial attempt to make treaties with the advice as well as the consent of the Senate, the role of the latter in treaty making became, for the most part, that of consent or rejection of a

---

[3] On United States recognition policies see G. H. Hackworth, *Digest of International Law* (Washington, 1940), I, ch. 3; C. C. Hyde, *International Law Chiefly as Interpreted and Applied by the United States* (rev. ed., Boston, 1945), I, secs. 35–46. See also H. Lauterpacht, *Recognition in International Law* (Cambridge, 1947).

[4] *Holmes* v. *Jennison*, 14 Peters, 540, 569 (1840). See also *Missouri* v. *Holland*, 252 U. S. 416 (1920) where the Court affirmed that while laws must be "made in pursuance of the Constitution," treaties could be made more broadly "under the authority of the United States."

[5] *Powers of the President to Send the Armed Forces Outside the United States*, Committee Print, 82nd Cong., 1st Sess., Senate Coms. on Foreign Relations and Armed Services, Feb. 28, 1951, pp. 11–13. For discussion of evolution of the treaty power see E. S. Corwin, *National Supremacy* (New York, 1913).

signed agreement. In recent years, however, the employment of bipartisan consultation between the Secretary of State and members of both parties in the Congress with respect to United Nations affairs, treaties of peace, foreign aid, the North Atlantic Treaty Organization, and some other matters has restored some of the relationships between the Executive and the Senate originally provided for in Article II, Section 2, of the Constitution. The extensive use which has been made in late years of executive agreements not requiring consent by two-thirds of the Senate, in lieu of treaties, has led to allegations, however, that the originally intended role of the Senate in foreign affairs has been compromised. Serious objections have been raised in Congress which we shall note presently.

Executive Agreements. An executive agreement is an arrangement entered into with a foreign government without the formal consent of the Senate. It seems only reasonable to accept that some such agreements have been entered into, in lieu of treaties, in order to avoid the normally time-consuming treaty procedure or because of doubt of obtaining a two-thirds vote.

Within the category of executive agreements have fallen some of the most important agreements in United States history. For example, the annexation of Texas was consummated by means of an agreement having only the blessing of a joint resolution of Congress. But the greater proportion by far of executive agreements have involved no major issues of policy and have been undertaken as being the most, and often only, feasible way of handling international arrangements. These agreements are used to cover routine administrative matters, arrangements of a temporary type, those requiring secrecy (a matter of particular concern in war and in strategic arrangements with allies), and for occasions requiring expeditious action. The increase in both their use and their importance is directly traceable to the operational and substantive nature of foreign affairs in the contemporary period. The Senate can and should debate adherence to a United Nations Charter. But should it debate standardization of the pitch of screw threads or the leasing of land for an air base?

Professor Plischke sums up the realities of the situation by stating: "To deny the agreement-making authority to the President therefore would hamstring him to the point of rendering his conduct of foreign relations well-nigh impossible." This statement might have been open to some argument in the early days of the Republic, but can hardly be contested in these times of multiple and intricate economic and collective security arrangements with "agreements" sometimes averaging several per day.

There is no difference, on the international scene, between a treaty to which the United States is a party and an executive agreement. The difference, internal to the United States, is, broadly speaking, a juridical one. A treaty, being legislated by Congress, can controvert existing law. On the other hand, the President in making executive agreements must remain within the bounds of law and enacted policy (for example, the Reciprocal Trade Act and the North Atlantic Treaty) insofar as agreements affect domestic matters, and also for reasons of practical politics inasmuch as Congress may deny the President essential appropriations or other legislative authorization to make executive agreements effective.

The rate of conclusion of executive agreements has exceeded that of treaty making since the end of the nineteenth century. Between 1889 and 1939, for example, 917 executive agreements were concluded as compared with 799 treaties; 279 are said to have been entered into during World War II. Since the commencement of the cold war and the beginning of the present collective security period the number has jumped enormously. Secretary Dulles estimated in early 1953 that some 10,000 such agreements had been entered into in relation to the North Atlantic Treaty alone.[6] United States foreign policy is now no longer a unilateral matter of an aloof "take it or leave it" attitude. It is a cooperative, collective security policy requiring numerous agreements for any acceptable degree of success.

President as Commander-in-Chief. One of the most important powers given to the President by the Constitution is that of Commander-in-Chief of the armed forces of the nation. Although Congress has the constitutional authority to raise and support the armed forces, to make rules for their governance, and to declare war, the President's powers to command and dispose of the armed forces are virtually unlimited.

Indicative of the scope of the President's authority is the fact that since the Constitution was adopted there have been "at least 125 incidents in which the President, without Congressional authorization, and in the absence of a declaration of war, has ordered the Armed Forces to take action or maintain positions abroad."[7]

Some measure of the breadth of the Presidential initiative in a nonwar emergency is revealed by the steps taken by President Roosevelt from 1939 to 1941. The President (1) concentrated the bulk of the United States fleet in the Pacific as a warning to Japan; (2) concluded (August, 1940) the Ogdensburg Agreement setting up a permanent Joint Board of Defense with Canada

6 On the use of executive agreements see especially Wallace McClure, *International Executive Agreements* (New York, 1941); Elmer Plischke, *Conduct of American Diplomacy* (New York, 1950); Quincy Wright, "The United States and International Agreements," *Am. J. Int. Law,* July, 1944; E. M. Borchard, "Treaties and Executive Agreements," *Am. Pol. Sci. Rev.,* Aug., 1946; B. V. Cohen, "Evolving Rule of Congress in Foreign Affairs," *Proceedings Am. Phil. Soc.,* vol. 92, no. 4 (1948).

7 *Powers of the President, cit. supra,* p. 2. See also Report of House Com. on Foreign Affairs, *Background Information on the Use of U.S. Armed Forces in Foreign Countries,* House Report 127, 82nd Cong., 1st Sess., containing specific listings.

to consider the defense of North America; (3) signed the Atlantic Charter of war aims with Prime Minister Churchill; (4) exchanged fifty over-age destroyers with Britain for base rights in Britain's North American possessions; (5) sent United States forces to Iceland to prevent German occupation of that strategic outpost of the American hemisphere; (6) ordered American merchant vessels to be given naval escort in both the Atlantic and the Pacific; (7) started construction in England and Northern Ireland of facilities for the reception of American forces; and (8) directed, as of August, 1941, that American naval vessels fire at sight upon German submarines approaching convoyed shipping.

The President's enormous task as coordinator-in-chief of foreign policy formulation and implementation is discussed later in this chapter.

THE DEPARTMENT OF STATE

The Department of State which surrounds the Secretary of State exists to provide the Secretary and the President with the necessary information and assistance for the efficient conduct of foreign relations. This Department has grown from an office comprising a Secretary, four clerks, and a part-time translator in the days of the first Secretary, Thomas Jefferson, to a vast organization with a recent peak of some 7,000 employees in Washington and more than 11,000 Foreign Service employees (about 1,500 being officers in the Foreign Service) stationed in approximately 290 missions and consulates abroad.[8]

The Secretary of State. The Secretary of State is the chief advisor to the President on foreign policy matters. He is also the President's chief helper in dealing with Congress on foreign policy matters and in coordinating the planning and execution of foreign policy operations by the executive branch of our government. The Secretary should be the chief molder, other than the President, of public opinion on foreign policy matters. He is charged with administration of the State Department and is the individual to whom our emissaries abroad look for routine guidance as well as with whom foreign ambassadors routinely conduct any important business.

Principal Assistants of the Secretary. There are today two Under-Secretaries of State, one handling diplomatic matters and intragovernmental liaison, the other handling administration. Ranking next below these officers are a group of Assistant Secretaries, varying in number from time to time, who head

---

[8] On the history of the Department see especially Graham H. Stuart's authentic work entitled *The Department of State: A History of Its Organization, Procedure and Personnel* (New York, 1943). See also J. L. McCamy, *The Administration of American Foreign Affairs* (New York, 1950). For biographies of past Secretaries of State see S. F. Bemis (ed.), *The American Secretaries of State and Their Diplomacy,* 10 vols. (New York, 1927–1929).

DEPARTMENT OF STATE

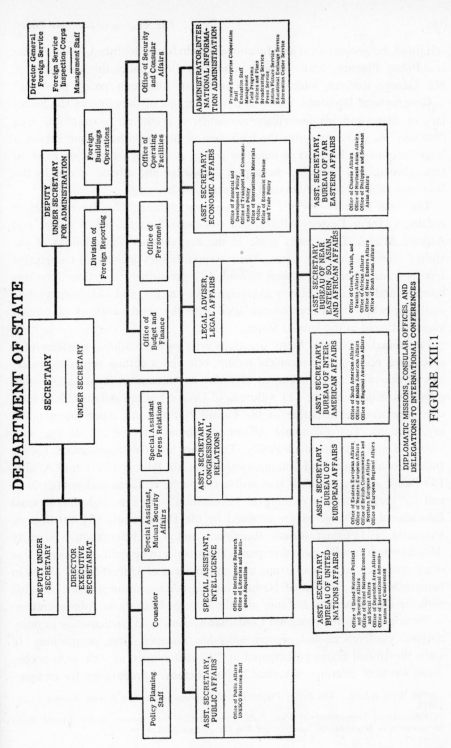

DIPLOMATIC MISSIONS, CONSULAR OFFICES, AND
DELEGATIONS TO INTERNATIONAL CONFERENCES

FIGURE XII:1

335

336 The Shaping of National Policy

certain of the geographical and functional subdivisions described below. There is a Policy Planning Staff, formed initially in 1947 under the leadership of Mr. George Kennan, which is responsible for long-term policy planning.[9]

Geographical Divisions. Below the top echelons of the office of the Secretary of State and his immediate assistants, a group of geographical area "bureaus" or divisions forms the backbone of the Department and carries a large share of the business of initiating policy, reviewing information received from abroad, and providing the expert knowledge and advice needed by the Secretary of State for the conduct of foreign affairs.

The area bureaus include (1) European Affairs, (2) Inter-American Affairs, (3) Far Eastern Affairs, and (4) Near Eastern, South Asian, and African Affairs. These units guide in the first instance the relations of the United States with other states. Their responsibilities include (1) analyzing reports from American missions abroad, (2) preparing instructions for these missions and notes for delivery to foreign governments, and (3) dealing informally or below the ambassadorial level with the representatives of foreign states stationed in the United States.

Functional Divisions. Many questions arise in international relations of a specialized economic or technical nature, oftentimes cutting across the interests of several states. Functional divisions or bureaus exist to handle such questions. Examples are: (1) a Bureau of United Nations Affairs, which handles American participation in the United Nations and other international organizations; (2) Economic Affairs, which includes offices dealing with Financial and Development Policy, Transport and Communications Policy, International Trade, and International Materials Policy; (3) Legal Affairs; (4) Public Affairs, which is responsible for public relations and publications, and for such functions relating to information programs and international Educational Exchange as are retained by the Department; (5) Intelligence Research; (6) Congressional Relations; and (7) International Security Affairs, which handles policy responsibilities concerning military assistance to other countries, exports of arms, and employment of United States forces in conjunction with the United Nations mutual defense arrangements, working with the Department of Defense and the Foreign Operations Administration.

Participation in International Conferences. American participation in international conferences and organizations has assumed large proportions. In 1950 the United States participated in 291 conferences, as well as in a continual round of meetings of United Nations organs.[10] Preparation for and par-

---

[9] See Ware Adams, "The Policy Planning Staff," *American Foreign Service Journal* (Sept., 1947).

[10] An annual Department of State Publication entitled *Participation of the United States Government in International Conferences* lists the gatherings each year.

ticipation in these meetings place heavy demands upon the Department's personnel. To care for the multitude of details encompassed in sending delegations to these gatherings and providing them with adequate staffing and facilities requires an extended effort by an International Conferences Office.

The Department in Operation. It is impossible to describe in a few words the operation of an organization as large as the Department of State.[11] The consideration of questions requiring policy decision starts at many levels and is pursued in an intricate variety of ways. Action may be precipitated by an ambassador of some foreign country calling upon the Secretary of State for the views of the United States upon a given matter. It may be initiated by some officer of the Department thinking that the United States should take a certain line of action, or by another department asking for policy guidance. It may be occasioned by a report of some development abroad from one of our Foreign Service officers or ambassadors.

Wherever policy action begins, the matter is in general referred to the appropriate geographical or functional "desk" or "desks" for study. There possible alternative lines of action are considered. The matter is discussed with other units in the Department which may have some knowledge or interest therein, and in some instances with experts outside the Department. After agreement has been reached on the principles involved, a note, memorandum, or telegram is drafted. This must then be "cleared" with the necessary Assistant Secretaries and the Under-Secretary before it is passed through the office of the Secretary for signature, authorization, or issuance.

The Foreign Service. The Foreign Service provides a major portion of "eyes and ears" and operating organization of the United States abroad which is strongly supplemented in the modern day, however, by personnel from the Defense Department, Foreign Operations Administration, and other government agencies. It is composed of career officers selected by competitive examination, ambassadors and ministers appointed by the President, together with clerical and staff employees. In recent years the Service has numbered over 11,000 persons of whom about 1,500 are career Foreign Service Officers.

The functions of the overseas missions staffed by the Foreign Service are essentially threefold. *First,* they are expected to gather, interpret, and transmit to Washington a continual flow of information on events, personalities, and trends abroad, thus affording a sound basis upon which the government can frame and correlate policy and action. *Second,* they represent the United States abroad, to protect its interests, and to cultivate friendly relations with the

---

[11] See Bertram Hulen, *Inside the Department of State* (New York, 1939); McCamy, *cit. supra;* The Brookings Institution, *The Governmental Mechanism for the Conduct of United States Foreign Relations* (Washington, 1949).

countries with whom diplomatic relationships are established. *Third,* they carry out the policy of the United States in accordance with instructions from Washington.

Some of the more experienced Foreign Service officers come to have a considerable influence upon policy making itself. This they can do through their knowledge of conditions abroad, dispatches which they send to Washington, actions which they may take at their posts, and through their presence in the Department under the rotation system. A strong-minded ambassador can wield a good deal of influence within the Department when he is a political or respected (or both) figure reporting personally to the President. Final decisions on policy, and the issuance of instructions for its execution, must in principle always rest with Washington. For only at the nerve center can policy toward a given country or situation be evaluated in terms of the nation's total interests and commitments.[12]

ROLE OF OTHER DEPARTMENTS AND AGENCIES

The Departments of Defense, Treasury, Commerce, Agriculture, Labor, and such executive agencies as the United States Information Agency, the Civil Aeronautics Board, the Foreign Operations Administration, the Federal Communications Commission, and the Maritime Commission, to mention but a few, are also directly concerned with particular phases of America's relationships with other nations. The Hoover Commission reported in 1948 that "of 50 major departments and agencies in the executive branch, at least 46 are drawn into foreign affairs to a greater or lesser extent." The interests and policies of these other departments and agencies, each acting within the framework of its own responsibilities, flow into the over-all process of forming and conducting American policy toward the rest of the world.[13] These departments and agencies are very much in the picture due to the totality of United States interests in foreign affairs and the operational functions which have to be performed in order to make policies effective. The State Department is the coordinator and leader in this intricate process of policy formulation and execution.

Department of Defense. National security is currently the basic objective of

12 The best accounts of the Foreign Service are in J. R. Childs, *American Foreign Service* (New York, 1948); G. H. Stuart, *American Diplomatic and Consular Practice* (New York, 1936); and United States Dept. of State, *Foreign Service of the United States: General Information and Pertinent Laws and Regulations* (Washington, 1947, pub. no. 2745). Childs' book contains a description of a typical day in an embassy abroad (pp. 88–90). For further discussion of the functions and activities of diplomats see ch. xvii below.

13 See Brookings Institution, *Governmental Mechanism,* pp. 18–32; McCamy, *op. cit.,* chs. v, x–xiii; and Hoover Commission Report on Organization of the Executive Branch of the Government, *Task Force Report on Foreign Affairs* (Washington, 1949) for analyses of participation of other departments.

foreign policy. The responsibility for planning and preparing defense, while not a monopoly of the Department of Defense, is its primary mission. Hence most important foreign policy matters are of interest and concern to the Department of Defense which reasonably has a voice in determining both the military posture of the country and also the commitments and arrangements pertaining to security matters which it makes in foreign affairs. The numerous and variegated relationships of the Departments of State and Defense are occasioned in considerable part by two conditions new to United States experience: (1) the Department of Defense is deeply involved in implementation of foreign policy through such programs as arms aid; and (2) the United States has forces stationed in many foreign countries and is allied to approximately forty states, thereby occasioning continual political-military consultation and negotiation with these states.

Within the Department of Defense, experts in each of the Service Departments (Army, Navy, and Air Force) continually study America's responsibilities and interests in the various parts of the world. They watch military developments abroad and draw plans to meet situations which may arise. Many hundreds of individuals in Washington and thousands abroad are engaged in staff work and administration affecting, and affected by, foreign countries. The Secretary of Defense and Joint Chiefs of Staff are the source of advice on military aspects of foreign policy matters. The Secretary of Defense is a member of the National Security Council. He and the Chairman of the Joint Chiefs of Staff have direct and constant access to the President, and are thus in a position to influence his thinking and decisions on questions of policy and conduct of foreign affairs pertaining to security.

Given the differing, but related, backgrounds and duties of the Departments of State and Defense, differences in viewpoint occasionally emerge between them on matters of policy and action. These are usually adjusted through informal contacts and discussions. Where they become hardened as departmental positions, the National Security Council provides a forum for consideration and advice to the President.[14]

Other Departments and Agencies. Among the other departments which have some concern with foreign relations, the Treasury Department is actively interested in policies which relate to credit, currency, international exchange arrangements, and foreign economic commitments. Because of its concern over taxes and federal expenditure, it tends to have a material impact on foreign policy indirectly by often favoring lower expenditures for foreign assistance in support of United States armed forces and for other programs labeled "national security." The creation of the International Bank for Reconstruction

14 See below, p. 343.

and Development and the International Monetary Fund resulted in large part from planning done in the Treasury Department. Officials of this Department represent the United States in the governing bodies of these organizations. The Department of Justice is responsible for administering the immigration laws and thus is intimately concerned with policy questions bearing on immigration, refugees, and displaced persons. The Postmaster-General has charge of negotiating international postal conventions and represents the United States at meetings of the Universal Postal Union. The Department of the Interior, along with the Office of Defense Mobilization, is concerned with the resources and raw-material position of the United States. Both have an interest in policies relating to the acquisition and use of strategic and critical resources.

In view of the fact that there are large areas of the world with inadequate supplies of foodstuffs, the wise use of America's surplus and the promotion of increased world productivity call for participation of the Department of Agriculture in determining certain features of America's foreign relations. The Secretary of Agriculture, or his deputy, represents the United States in the United Nations Food and Agriculture Organization. Experts of the Department of Agriculture also take an active part in Technical Assistance programs in underdeveloped areas overseas.

The Department of Commerce has an interest in foreign policy through its responsibility for promoting foreign commerce. The Secretary of Commerce sits on a number of interdepartmental committees dealing with foreign economic policy. His Department has taken an active part in evolving the details of the Point Four Technical Assistance programs and in developing agreements on international air transport. The Department of Labor participates in United States representation at the International Labor Organization and is concerned with questions which arise within the United Nations Economic and Social Council. The Department of Health, Education and Welfare participates in the World Health Organization and in the United Nations Educational, Scientific and Cultural Organization.

In addition to the Departments, many of the agencies, commissions, and regulatory boards which have been established by Congress likewise have some association with international affairs, as indicated by the accompanying chart.

In view of the large number of departments, agencies, and other bodies concerned with foreign affairs, it is little wonder that the process of formulating national policy has become a complex one. The activities and interests of this multiplicity of bureaucracies inevitably create serious problems of coordination within the executive arm of the government as a whole.

AGENCIES INVOLVED IN FOREIGN AFFAIRS

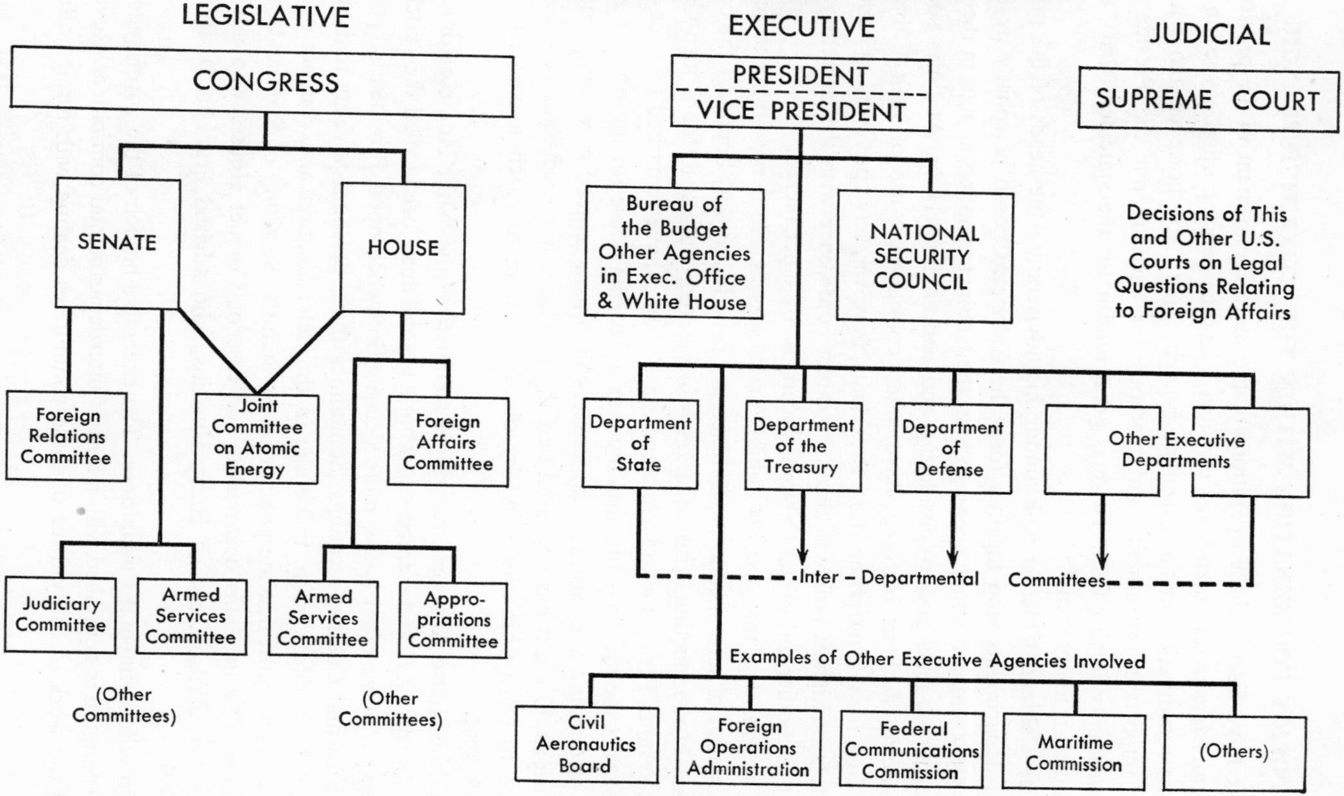

FIGURE XII:2

POLICY COORDINATION WITHIN THE EXECUTIVE BRANCH

We have discussed the operations of the State Department in the previous section. Measured in man-hours of effort it has the major portion of the job of policy coordination in the executive branch. There are, however, other and very important instruments and methods for carrying out the President's responsibility in this field. There is good reason for the statement that "the President is many men."

The Cabinet. Chief in rank among his advisers are the heads of the principal departments who together form the Cabinet. Chosen personally by the President and with ready access to him, the Cabinet members should in theory form a high-level policy-considering and coordinating body. At times some Presidents, such as Harding, have made considerable use of their Cabinet meetings for this purpose. Many Presidents, however, have preferred to handle matters of highest policy decision by direct conference with the Secretary of State and other individual Cabinet officers, or by other means.

The President may use his Cabinet as he sees fit. He is not bound to refer any matter of substance to the Cabinet, nor is he in any way bound by the consensus of the meeting. This situation is in marked contrast to the British Cabinet system. Persons who have served in Cabinets have remarked that for the most part the meetings function more as a clearing house for information and for reconciling administrative differences than as a center for reaching policy decisions. Often it has appeared that the President has used Cabinet sessions more to clarify his own mind by discussion than to reach a consensus of agreement.

White House Advisers. Individual members of the White House entourage, "brain trusters," and members of what has sometimes been called the "kitchen cabinet," have often had a more decisive influence upon Presidential policy than formal Cabinet meetings. Sometimes these personal advisers and aides become, in effect, more influential in the determination and conduct of the highest and most delicate policy matters than the Secretary of State and other Cabinet officers. This occurred in the case of Colonel House, who advised Woodrow Wilson, and of Harry Hopkins, who advised Franklin D. Roosevelt.[15]

Interdepartmental Committees. The executive branch of the government in Washington is enmeshed with a host of interdepartmental committees. Reviewing the work of thirty-three of these committees dealing with foreign affairs,

---

[15] See Charles Seymour, *The Intimate Papers of Colonel House* (Boston, 1926); Robert Sherwood, *Roosevelt and Hopkins* (New York, 1949). See also G. A. Graham, "The Presidency and the Executive Office of the President," *J. of Pol.*, Nov., 1950.

the Hoover Commission found the machinery cumbersome, time-consuming, and inclined to spawn a myriad of subcommittees.[16] Officials in Washington regard this, however, as an essential part of the mechanics of policy making in a government which proceeds on the assumption that it is desirable to have many minds focus on national problems. No matter how loudly officials bemoan the time spent in committee meetings, the general sentiment is that the prevailing system does achieve at least the essentials of coordination.

Bureau of the Budget. Another instrument within the Executive Office of the President for furthering coordination is the Bureau of the Budget. Being in the Office of the President, the Director of the Budget is close to the President and thus able to exert great influence upon the various departments and agencies in the direction of correlating policy. It is charged with responsibility for improving administrative organization and practice throughout the government. But perhaps the most important avenue of influence is through advice on the annual budget which determines the resources available for implementation of policies—and hence the feasibility and efficacy of these policies.[17]

The National Security Council. The National Security Council, established by the National Security Act of 1947, is becoming increasingly significant as a coordinating agency.[18] The Council is composed of the President, the Vice-President, the Secretary of State, the Secretary of Defense, the Administrator of the Office of Defense Mobilization, the Administrator of the Foreign Operations Administration, and such other persons as the President may designate. This latter category has included the Secretary of the Treasury. The Secretaries of the Army, Navy, and Air Force, the Chairman of the Joint Chiefs of Staff, the Director of the Central Intelligence Agency, and the Director of the Bureau of the Budget are often present at the meetings.

The Council's role, by law, is to advise the President on decisions which require top-level action "with respect to the integration of domestic, foreign and military policies relating to national security." Thus, the Council is a national policy-planning cabinet for security matters which include most of the important foreign affairs. It brings together, for the benefit of the President, the different points of view on foreign relations, national defense, intelligence, economics, strategy, and resources as they converge upon the creation and implementation of national policy, and it is intended to be a means of resolving controverted positions.

The contribution of the Council is primarily dependent on the pleasure of

16 *Task Force Report on Foreign Affairs,* appendix V, "Interdepartmental Committee Structure for Foreign Affairs." The thirty-three committees examined were found to proliferate into 130 subsidiary committees. See also J. L. McCamy, *The Administration of American Foreign Affairs* (New York, 1950), chs. v–vi.

17 See Bureau of the Budget, *The United States at War* (Washington, 1946), esp. ch. 12.

18 Public Law 253, 80th Cong., 1st Sess., amended in 1949.

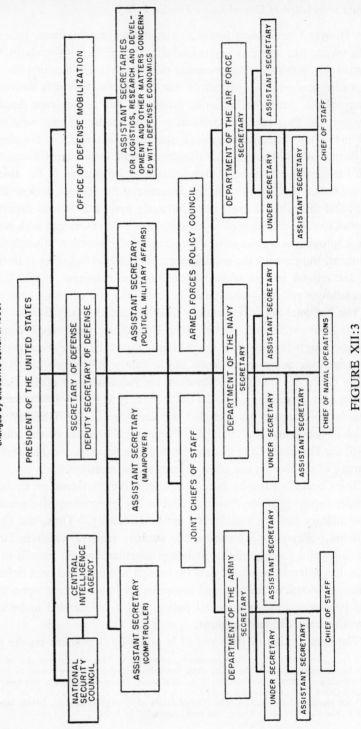

ORGANIZATION FOR NATIONAL SECURITY

(As set forth in the National Security Act of 1947, as amended 1949, and further changed by executive action in 1953)

PRESIDENT OF THE UNITED STATES

NATIONAL SECURITY COUNCIL

CENTRAL INTELLIGENCE AGENCY

SECRETARY OF DEFENSE
DEPUTY SECRETARY OF DEFENSE

OFFICE OF DEFENSE MOBILIZATION

ASSISTANT SECRETARY (COMPTROLLER)

ASSISTANT SECRETARY (MANPOWER)

ASSISTANT SECRETARY (POLITICAL MILITARY AFFAIRS)

ASSISTANT SECRETARIES FOR LOGISTICS, RESEARCH AND DEVELOPMENT AND OTHER MATTERS CONCERNED WITH DEFENSE ECONOMICS

JOINT CHIEFS OF STAFF

ARMED FORCES POLICY COUNCIL

DEPARTMENT OF THE ARMY
SECRETARY

DEPARTMENT OF THE NAVY
SECRETARY

DEPARTMENT OF THE AIR FORCE
SECRETARY

UNDER SECRETARY

ASSISTANT SECRETARY

ASSISTANT SECRETARY

CHIEF OF STAFF

UNDER SECRETARY

ASSISTANT SECRETARY

ASSISTANT SECRETARY

CHIEF OF NAVAL OPERATIONS

UNDER SECRETARY

ASSISTANT SECRETARY

ASSISTANT SECRETARY

CHIEF OF STAFF

FIGURE XII:3

344

the President as to how he uses it. Under some Presidents it may have limitations, including a tendency, as Vannevar Bush has observed, "to become a meeting place of departments for compromise, rather than of chiefs of departments for momentous deliberation." But it can draft policy after thorough study and act as a coordinating organ, and has done so under President Eisenhower. Policy making in such an agency is very dependent on the competence of the staff which analyzes the problems and prepares the recommendations. The National Security Council has a talented staff drawn from the agencies and departments of its members. It has at times played an outstanding part in policy decision. One of the keys to successful operation is insistence by the President that the Council be regarded as *the* top-level policy-making and correlation center, and that he preside over it regularly. President Eisenhower has done much to strengthen the Council in this respect.[19]

The President as Coordinator-in-Chief. The President holds in his own hands ultimate responsibility for attaining unity on policy and implementing action within the Executive.

One of the problems which sometimes confront policy makers below the presidential office is that plans made on the basis of expert technical judgment may be overruled by the White House for political considerations. This, however, is the prerogative of the President as Chief Executive and as leader of his party. Such decisions may sadden high officials and departmental experts. But this situation is inherent in the American political tradition and within the bounds of the Constitution. The President, in carrying out his coordination responsibility, has problems extending far beyond the complications within the executive branch. He and his advisers must take Congress, the need for public support, and even his responsibilities as leader of his party into account.

ROLE OF CONGRESS IN POLICY MAKING

The change in the pattern of our foreign relations during the past few decades, and particularly since World War II, has greatly increased the interest and role of Congress. The Congressmen are very close to the people in their constituencies. Foreign affairs have ceased to be far removed from our daily lives. They now impinge directly on every family in terms of the draft, heavier taxes, perhaps some controls on the domestic economy, newspaper and radio accounts arousing concern over our country's security, and other items of

19 See Vannevar Bush, "Organization for Strength," address at Tufts College Centennial. *Tufts Alumni Review*, Centennial Issue, 1952; S. W. Souers, "Policy Formulation for National Security," *Am. Pol. Sci. Rev.*, June, 1949; H. P. Kirkpatrick, "The National Security Council," *American Perspective*, Feb., 1949; G. C. Lee, "The Organization for National Security," reprinted in Padelford, *Cont. Inter. Rels. Readings* 1949–1950, pp. 261–270: J. S. Lay, "The National Security Council's Role in the U.S. Security and Peace Program," *World Affairs*, July, 1952.

interest to a large proportion of the voting population. Since foreign policy issues are now of general public interest, there is publicity and political capital in supporting or opposing particular policies. Hence Congress, formerly often apathetic in the field of foreign policy, now demands complete information and an influential voice.

Constitutional Status. The breadth of Congressional interest in foreign policy making is indicated by the fact that at least two-thirds of the enumerated powers of Congress set forth in Article I, Section 8, of the Constitution are concerned in whole or in part with foreign relations.[20] The importance of Congress' place in determining the character of America's foreign relations is further emphasized by the fact that in a session of Congress nearly half of the bills introduced may have direct or indirect implications for foreign policy.[21] The drastic change, as between pre-World War II and post-World War II, in United States foreign policy methods and techniques, with the great increase of actions and cost, has made the appropriations and authorizing powers of Congress more important in the foreign policy field than the treaty-making power. As a concomitant, the power and position of the House, with its primacy in appropriation matters, now approaches that of the Senate. When a policy requires authorizing legislation, or appropriations, or both, Congress has a very effective check thereon.

Appropriations. The "power of the purse" is one of the principal means by which the Congress may influence national policy. It may be true that "Congress has never refused to make available funds which the President has committed the United States to spend in international agreements."[22] But the President is unlikely to make commitments he does not think Congress will finance. In debating appropriations, and in using such tactics as delay, criticism, or the attachment of "rider" clauses, the Congress can embarrass the Administration. By specifying the exact amounts which may be expended for given activities, Congress can circumscribe or attempt to enlarge the operations of any agency. This it has frequently done with regard to appropriations for the Department of State, the Voice of America, the foreign aid programs, and the Defense Department.

Congressional committees hold annual hearings on the proposed budgets of each department at which ranking officers must explain the operations of their

20 Article I, Section 8, and Article II, Section 2, of the Constitution should be read in full. For a general study of Congress' role see R. A. Dahl, *Congress and Foreign Policy* (New York, 1950). See also Sept., 1953, issue of *Annals* on Congress and foreign relations.

21 In the 81st Cong., of 10,627 bills introduced in the 1st Sess., 5,120 had some relationship to foreign policy. The State Department reported its views on as many as 657 of these bills. H. H. Smith, "Reorganization—Senate Style," *American Foreign Service Journal*, June, 1950.

22 B. Bolles, *Who Makes Our Foreign Policy*, Foreign Policy Assoc. Headline Booklet 62 (New York, 1947), p. 45.

divisions and offices. Appropriations or authorizations may be held up until a department has satisfied Congress that a policy to which it objects will be modified or directed along the lines it favors.

Policy Areas of Special Congressional Interest. The Congress is jealous of its power to impose taxes, duties, and imposts. It controls policies on exports and imports closely and in so doing has a tremendous effect on our foreign relations, since much of the remainder of the free world is affected by United States trade policies.[23] True, the Reciprocal Trade Agreements have been executive agreements, but they have been agreements drawn within dimensions carefully laid down in legislation.

Another area of policy requiring legislation prior to executive action is the matter of foreign loans from our government. The price to be paid for gold and silver bullion is another. The commerce power is still another area of deep Congressional interest exemplified by the Embargo and Non-Intercourse Acts of the Napoleonic Wars, the Neutrality Acts of the 1930's, and the subsidies to the merchant marine. Immigration is another area in which the Executive must function within boundaries closely defined by Congress.

Congress and Executive Agreements. The institution of the executive agreement became an issue in internal United States politics in 1952 with the introduction before the Senate by Senator Bricker of the much discussed Bricker Constitutional Amendment designed, according to its proponents, to prevent executive abuse of the agreement-making power and to protect the domain of power reserved to the States. The chief arguments of the proponents of this move turned on the dangers to individual American citizens of some drafts of arrangements particularly relating to human rights being prepared in the United Nations.

The Bricker Amendment proposed to augment Congressional power over executive agreements by allowing the Congress to "regulate all executive and other agreements with any foreign power or international organization," and raised a possibility of requiring additional legislation by Congress, and even by the 48 States, to execute certain aspects of foreign policy.

Opponents of the Bricker Amendment feared that the restrictive provisions contained in the proposal might be so operated as gravely to weaken the position of the Chief Executive in dealing with foreign affairs at a time when the United States is facing a most difficult period of foreign relations. A minority of the members of the Senate Judiciary Committee warned in their report on the Bricker Amendment that with such an amendment in the Constitution,

---

[23] For comparison of the various tariffs see C. Taussig, *The Tariff in American History* (7th ed., New York, 1923); A. Isaacs, *International Trade, Tariff and Commercial Policies* (Chicago, 1948).

"Congress could regulate the conduct of affairs down to the last detail." Secretary of State Dulles, with the backing of President Eisenhower, stated that "the Executive cannot surrender the freedom of action which is necessary for its operations in the foreign relations field." [24] President Eisenhower himself strongly opposed the amendment, which, in 1954, was defeated in the Senate by one vote. The vote indicated, however, that strong sentiment continued for some constitutional change.

Power Regarding Armed Forces. The Constitution gives Congress the mandate to raise and support the armed forces of the United States. The combination of this power with the control of appropriations enables the Congress to determine the size, character, and strength of the armed forces, thereby giving Congress a major element of responsibility for determining whether a security policy will be a "paper" policy or have the means to make it truly effective. Although the extent of the right of the President to order the armed services to duty overseas without prior Congressional approval is debatable, it is certain that he must obtain adequate funds from Congress to maintain them abroad. Congress at the end of the World Wars I and II exerted such pressure on the Executive to bring American forces home that the United States world position and foreign policy were seriously jeopardized.

War Powers. Among the most vital prerogatives of Congress are its powers relating to war. As the repository of the authority to declare war, coupled with its powers concerning the armed forces and the maintenance of the "common defense and general welfare," Congress possesses broad discretion with respect to the most critical aspects of foreign policy.

In declaring war, Congress has in practice followed the lead of the President when he has requested that such a declaration be made. Once a state of war has been declared to exist, it has generally supported the requests of the President for legislation relating to the conduct of the war and the mobilization of the nation.[25] In periods of international crisis preceding an attack upon the United States or a declaration of war, Congress has at times sought to fix national policy independently of the Executive, and even to tie his hands, as in the enaction of the Neutrality Acts of 1935, 1937, and 1939.[26]

24 Text of the Bricker and Knowland Amendments will be found in the *Congressional Record,* 83d Cong., 1st Sess., Aug. 1, 1953. See Majority and Minority Reports of Senate Judiciary Committee on "Constitutional Amendment Relative to Treaties and Executive Agreements," Sen. Rpt. No. 412, 83rd Cong., 1st Sess., June 15, 1953. For general discussions see Arthur H. Dean, "The Bricker Amendment and Authority over Foreign Affairs," *Foreign Affairs,* Oct., 1953; also A. E. Sutherland, Jr., "Restricting the Treaty Power," *Harvard Law Rev.,* June, 1952.

25 See S. E. Baldwin, "The Share of the President of the United States in a Declaration of War," *Am. J. Int. Law,* Jan., 1918. See also H. White, "Executive Responsibility to Congress via Concurrent Resolution," *Am. Pol. Sci. Rev.,* Oct., 1942.

26 Texts in *Peace and War: United States Foreign Policy, 1931–1941* (Washington, 1943), pp. 266–271, 313–314, 355–365, 494–506.

Finally, under its power "to promote the progress of science," Congress may provide funds for scientific research either for peaceful or military purposes. It may also, under a combination of this authorization and its war powers, lay down basic law concerning the development of atomic energy as it did in the Atomic Energy Act of 1946.[27]

Taking the Congressional powers as they have been developed in practice, it may be concluded that "as foreign and domestic policies tend more and more to become intertwined, the impact of Congressional legislative power on foreign relations increases." [28]

SPECIAL POWERS OF THE SENATE [29]

Advice and Consent to Treaties. The constitutional arrangement which divides the treaty-making function between the President and the Senate by requiring that all treaties must have the advice and consent of the Senate with "two-thirds of the Senators present" concurring, is one of the unique features of the United States Constitution. Senate treatment of treaties [30] once led Secretary of State Hay to remark: "A treaty entering the Senate is like a bull going into the arena. No one can say just how or when the final blow will fall. But one thing is certain—it never will leave the arena alive." [31] The historical record of the Senate is not quite so dire on the whole as Secretary Hay's observation would imply.[32] When it wishes to do so, the Senate can act on treaties with dispatch. The United Nations Charter, for example, signed at San Francisco on June 26, 1945, was submitted to the Senate, considered in Committee, subjected to hearings, and ratified by the Senate on July 28, 1945, by a vote of 89 to 2. Similarly, the North Atlantic Treaty, signed on April 4, 1949, was given sixteen days of public hearings plus intensive study by the Foreign Relations Committee, and consented to by the Senate on July 21, 1949, by a vote of 82 to 13.[33]

Effect of Two-Thirds Rule. The two-thirds rule, coupled with the quorum rule, in effect, would allow seventeen Senators, in an extreme case, to block the necessary two-thirds majority if only a bare quorum of forty-nine were pres-

27 Public Law No. 585, 79th Cong., July 20, 1946.
28 Brookings Institution, *Governmental Mechanism*, p. 44.
29 See Sen. E. D. Thomas, "The Senate's Role in Foreign Policy," *World Affairs Interpreter,* Winter, 1947.
30 K. Colegrove, *The American Senate and World Peace* (New York, 1944), pp. 1, 15; W. S. Holt, *Treaties Defeated by the Senate* (Baltimore, 1933). For a different view see R. J. Dangerfield, *In Defense of the Senate: A Study in Treaty-Making* (Norman, Okla., 1933).
31 W. R. Thayer, *Life and Letters of John Hay* (Boston, 1920). vol. II, p. 393.
32 For analysis of results of Executive—Congressional cooperation see D. S. Cheever and H. F. Haviland, *American Foreign Policy and the Separation of Powers* (Cambridge, 1952), chs. 9–11.
33 See H. L. Hoskins, *The Atlantic Pact* (Washington, 1949); R. H. Heindell, R. V. Kalijarvi, and F. O. Wilcox, "The North Atlantic Treaty in the United States Senate," *Am. J. Int. Law,* Oct., 1949, pp. 633–665.

ent. Such a minority may be able to block a treaty signed by a President having a clear mandate from a majority of the nation's electorate.

In some instances local or private interests have succeeded in exploiting the two-thirds requirement to hold up treaties adverse to their particular views and not of general interest to any large group. Some obstruction has sprung from aspirations to seek political gain by embarrassing the President or Secretary of State. Republican leaders determined to discredit Woodrow Wilson and to defeat the Democratic party in the 1920 elections made common cause with the sincere isolationist sentiments of some Senators to defeat the Versailles Treaty and the Covenant of the League of Nations.[34] Proposals have been made that the Constitution be amended to make possible approval of treaties by a simple majority of the Senate, or by a simple majority of both Houses of Congress, but these have not aroused wide enthusiasm.

Approval of Appointments. There is one other respect in which the Senate enjoys special powers bearing upon foreign relations. This is its power, under Article II, Section 2, of the Constitution, to review and approve presidential appointments of ambassadors, ministers, and consuls. Many appointments to the lower ranks of the Foreign Service are approved without difficulty. The Senate, however, scrutinizes top nominations closely and has occasionally refused confirmation. In this way it can express approval or disapproval of presidential policies and make itself to an extent a partner in policy making.

PLACE OF CONGRESSIONAL COMMITTEES IN POLICY FORMULATION

One of the distinctive features of the American political system is the active role which committees of Congress and their chairmen have come to hold in the fashioning of national policy. Among the standing committees having the most direct concern with foreign affairs are the Senate Foreign Relations Committee, the Armed Forces Committees of both Houses, the Appropriations Committee of the House, the Senate Judiciary Committee, the House Committee on Foreign Affairs, and the Joint Committee on Atomic Energy.[35] It must be recognized that this particular type of committee system leads to a piecemeal approach to policy making and to division of responsibility between houses and committees. Thus, for example, a foreign assistance program must be based on authorizing legislation processed separately by the foreign policy committees of each house. The respective appropriations committees then consider the request for implementing funds and can, in so doing, conceivably

---

34 See H. C. Lodge, *The Senate and the League of Nations* (New York, 1925).

35 Accounts of the background of the Senate and House Committees on Foreign Affairs will be found in R. E. Dennison, *The Senate Foreign Relations Committee* (Stanford, 1943), and A. C. F. Westphal, *The House Committee on Foreign Affairs* (New York, 1942).

re-examine the entire policy and change it through addition or subtraction of funds.

Power of Committees. The powerful influence of the Congressional committees stems from the fact that all proposed legislation, appropriations, expenditures, treaties and agreements, proposals for national defense, and presidential nominations are referred to a committee for detailed consideration before being taken up on the floor of either House.

The committees' findings based on hearings and investigations, which call for the appearance and testimony of the most responsible officers of the executive departments and agencies, may be influential in moving public opinion as well as in leading to legislative enactment. If proposals by the executive branch fail to win the sympathy of committee members, or even of the chairman alone, they may be drastically revised, side-tracked, pigeon-holed, or given an adverse report. The committee reports carry much weight in Congress when measures are reported out.

Consultation with Executive. Because of the power which the committees have to grant and to dispose of executive requests and proposals and to guide the enaction of legislation, the President and other executive officers maintain close contacts with the committees and their ranking members. The Secretary of State now often appears before the Senate Foreign Relations Committee before and after attending important conferences. Key members of the Committee are invited to serve on United States delegations to significant international gatherings. Similarly, the Secretary of Defense and the Chairman of the Joint Chiefs of Staff are frequently reported meeting with committees on the Hill. The cultivation of a sense of partnership in the formulation and conduct of policy has come to be recognized as vital in contemporary world conditions.[36]

DIFFICULTIES IN CONGRESSIONAL CONSIDERATION OF FOREIGN AFFAIRS

In considering the relationship of Congress to foreign policy several circumstances must be borne in mind. In the first place, the leading Congressmen, with a heavy load of committee work each session and their political responsibilities, have little time for extensive study of complicated problems of foreign affairs. Secondly, members of the House of Representatives hold office for only two years and consequently have little time to become fully informed before

[36] *The Legislative History of the Committee on Foreign Relations, United States Senate*, published for each Congress, reviews the work of the Committee during the preceding two years. The *History for the 82nd Congress* shows that the Committee held 251 meetings. It spent 123 days in hearings, had a total of 73 treaties and 106 legislative measures before it, and dealt with 1,061 nominations received from the White House. Sen. Doc. 161, 82nd Cong., 2d Sess. (Washington, 1952).

they must turn their attention to re-election. Thirdly, members of Congress are continually under pressure from political forces for action favorable to their interests. This makes it difficult for Congressmen to deal altogether impartially with questions or as their own best judgment may suggest. Finally, in a two-party system with a fairly close balance of power between the parties, the Congressional atmosphere is often charged with partisan contest. Even when the leaders in Congress possess unusual qualities of statesmanship, policy formulated under this condition cannot easily escape political complexion.[37] This assures the country, however, that major issues will be openly debated, that public opinion will be consulted and have an opportunity to register its views, and that alternative courses of action will be considered. Whatever difficulties attend Congressional participation in policy decision, this system provides a method by which public opinion and popularly elected representatives have a major effect on policy making.

URGENCY OF EXECUTIVE-LEGISLATIVE TEAM-WORK

Few major decisions on foreign affairs can be taken without entailing some action by both the Executive and Congress. Yet sustained cooperation between the two branches is difficult, especially in time of peace. One study has, indeed, concluded that "the weakest and most critical link in the process of making United States foreign policy is the relations between the White House and Capitol Hill."[38]

Difficulties Involved. A number of factors contribute to this. In the first place, coordination within the executive arm of the government is often slow and not always complete, as we have already noted. As a result, the executive agencies do not always speak with a single voice in their relations with Congress. In the second place, Congress is heavily burdened with pressures of legislation and public relations, so that the time of many Congressmen for anything approaching continuous joint consideration of policy with the Executive is limited. In the third place, many observers believe that the Congressional mechanism itself is poorly geared for sustained collaboration in view of the difficulty party leaders often have in maintaining party discipline. American Congressmen prize their independence of action and may insist on the right of following the interests of constituents rather than the guidance of their party leaders. In the fourth place, there are deep-seated attitudes of rivalry and suspicion between Congress and the Executive. Members of Congress and the President cannot overlook their own political positions and fortunes.

---

[37] For thoughtful discussions of Congressional handicaps and possible solutions see G. B. Galloway, *Congress at the Crossroads* (New York, 1946); J. M. Burns, *Congress on Trial; The Legislative Process and the Administrative State* (New York, 1949).

[38] Cheever and Haviland, *op. cit.,* p. 1.

Finally, American parties have sometimes regarded questions of foreign affairs as appropriate subjects for the "great game of politics." Parties in power have not hesitated to use the handling of foreign affairs as a means of enhancing their own prestige and power. Conversely, the minority party has regarded it as fair to "play politics" over matters of foreign relations in order to embarrass the Administration. The controversy over adherence to the League of Nations is an outstanding example of partisanship in this respect, but it does not stand alone.

The upshot of these various factors has been that struggles have repeatedly occurred between Congress and the Executive, and between the parties, "for the privilege of directing American foreign policy."

Methods Employed. A variety of procedures have been tried at one time or another in search of a workable degree of understanding and collaboration. These have included: (1) Presidential meetings with the leaders of Congress— on a regular or occasional basis; (2) personal, informal contacts between departmental officers and members of Congress, particularly the members of the major committees; (3) the appearance of executive officers at hearings and in closed committee sessions where there can be informal exchanges of information and opinion (for example, the Secretary of State appeared twenty-two times before the Senate Foreign Relations Committee during the 82nd Congress); (4) the establishment of Congressional subcommittees to maintain close touch with appropriate divisions of the Departments of State and of Defense and other executive agencies;[39] (5) the use of expert staffs on the Senate and House Foreign Relations Committees who enjoy the confidence of the White House and the executive departments as well as of the ranking members of their committees; (6) energetic activity by the Vice-President in a combined liaison and leadership capacity; and (7) bipartisanism, that is, two-party sharing in the formulation of policy.

BIPARTISANISM IN FOREIGN POLICY

Bipartisanism is one of the principal devices employed at times in late years to give increased support and more assured continuity to foreign policy within the structure of our government. This approach has been implemented by taking the leaders of the party in opposition to the President into conference and partnership in the formulation and conduct of some aspects of foreign policy.

War-time and Post-War Practice. This practice was inaugurated by Presi-

[39] The Senate Foreign Relations Committee has subcommittees on United Nations Affairs, Economic and Social Policy Affairs, American Republics Affairs, Public Affairs and State Department Organization, European Affairs, Far Eastern Affairs, and Near Eastern and African Affairs.

dent Roosevelt in 1940 when he induced two eminent Republicans, Henry L. Stimson and Frank Knox, to join his Cabinet as Secretaries of War and Navy to help prepare America against the threat of war. Partisanship was laid aside in the common cause of defending the nation and winning the war. As thought began to turn to the settlement of the war, a biparty Advisory Committee on Post-War Foreign Policy was appointed by the President, and Secretary of State Hull invited a biparty group of Congressmen and Senators to advise with him on the fashioning of United States policy with respect to a world organization.

The device of bipartisanism was continued through Republican as well as Democratic participation in United States delegations to many international gatherings. The fruits included biparty support in Congress for ratification of the United Nations Charter, the Peace Treaties, and the North Atlantic Treaty, and for the implementation of the European Recovery and Mutual Defense Assistance Programs.

Where leaders of the Republican party were not invited to share in the framing of policy, or permitted to claim some credit for its accomplishment, agreements or policy decisions submitted to Congress did not fare so well. An outstanding example of the nonapplication of bipartisanism and its consequences was the China policy from 1944 to 1953 and outspoken Republican condemnation of the handling of China affairs by the Truman Administration. On the other hand, an equally outstanding instance of effective bipartisanism was President Truman's appointment of John Foster Dulles as special adviser on foreign affairs in 1950 with chief responsibility for preparing the American terms for the Treaty of Peace with Japan and negotiating with other powers on this treaty before and after the San Francisco Japanese Peace Conference.[40]

Why, it may be asked, has the bipartisan approach not been applied to all phases of foreign policy? The answer probably is that from the Administration's viewpoint, bipartisanism was employed to prevent the opposition from crippling foreign policy. No more concessions were made than necessary, for each concession meant some limitation of the Administration's freedom of action and some sharing of the dividends of success.

Merits and Criticisms of Bipartisanism. The merits of bipartisanism are that it tends to modify the cleavage placed by the Constitution between the

40 Included in the delegation to the San Francisco United Nations Conference, for example, were Senator Arthur Vandenberg (R., Mich.), formerly an isolationist, Congressman Charles Eaton (R., N.J.), John Foster Dulles, and Governor Harold Stassen of Minnesota. First-hand accounts of the evolution of bipartisanship will be found in Cordell Hull, *The Memoirs of Cordell Hull* (New York, 1948), esp. vol. II; H. L. Stimson and McGeorge Bundy, *On Active Service in Peace and War* (New York, 1948); A. H. Vandenberg, Jr., and J. A. Morris (eds.), *The Private Papers of Senator Vandenberg* (Boston, 1952). See also Cheever and Haviland, *op. cit.*, chs. 10–11.

Executive and Congress, and to provide national unity on crucial issues of world politics.

If American parties were as disciplined as are the British parties in Parliament, a President with a clear majority in Congress could be sure of the necessary support for his policies. But the President is almost invariably confronted with defections or "independents" in his party so that on many occasions he may seek some support from the opposition. President Eisenhower's foreign policy program during his first year of office received at least as much support from the opposition party in Congress as from his own. If the party alignment is closely balanced, or if, as has often been the case, Congress is controlled for half of a Presidential term by the opposite party, the support of some members of the other party is indispensable. Bipartisanship holds the prospect of securing this and thereby providing a consistent foreign policy.

Bipartisan collaboration on foreign policy is not above criticism, however, despite its accomplishments. Extended over any length of time, bipartisanship tends, in the name of national unity, to limit free discussion and free political action. By associating the leaders of both parties in a single policy, less opportunity is left for the "great debates" on issues of foreign policy which have been a part of the American democratic process. The public could conceivably be left in danger of being told but one side—the official point of view—of the situations arising before the country. The government might be allowed to function without being held to task by responsible criticism. Furthermore, extended bipartisanship in time of peace may result in undesirable compromises for the sake of obtaining the consent of diverse elements.[41]

The dangers suggested above seem unlikely, however, to become realities. With the traditionally loose party discipline prevailing in the United States, members of Congress have always spoken out on strongly held views regardless of the stand of their Congressional leaders. The free press and many articulate writers on foreign affairs add further assurance of continual public discussion. There is a grave question, on the other hand, to what extent, in a dangerous world, Americans can afford violently partisan divisions on matters of foreign affairs. For these tend to weaken the confidence of the people in the nation's foreign policy. They tend to bring comfort to enemies. And they create doubts and fissures among friends.

The optimum objective is, of course, a nonpartisan foreign policy having substantial support in both parties even though detailed aspects and methods of implementation may be subjects of controversy. Such a situation gives that assurance of continuity which is important in dealing with other countries and

41 See H. F. Armstrong, "Foreign Policy and Party Politics," *The Atlantic Monthly*, April, 1947.

for attaining national objectives. At the same time, it enables responsibility to be fastened upon the party in power for successful administration.

Other Means of Furthering Collaboration. Various suggestions have been offered of other means of furthering coordination within the government on foreign affairs. These have included such diverse steps as creating a super-Department of Foreign Affairs (including not only diplomatic relations but also foreign assistance, information, and possibly commerce); emphasizing policy making to a larger extent in the President's Cabinet; creating a Cabinet Secretariat; making greater use of Joint Committee proceedings in Congress; permitting Cabinet officers to appear on the floor of Congress to debate policies; creating a bipartisan Executive-Legislative Advisory Committee on Foreign Policy similar to the post-war planning committee in World War II; and possibly adding a ranking majority and minority member of each House to the National Security Council.[42]

For the immediate future the best hope perhaps lies in systematic use by the President of the National Security Council as an effective top-level, policy-formulating body, and in search for a closer *rapport* between the White House and the Secretary of State, on the one hand, and the leadership on Capitol Hill on the other.

POLITICAL PARTIES AND FOREIGN POLICY

The functions of nominating candidates for Congress and the Presidency, and furthering their election campaigns, give the two leading parties, directly and indirectly, a powerful sway over the destinies of the nation's foreign policy and its relations with other countries. There have, in the past, been inclinations and attitudes discernible on certain issues relating to foreign policy and characteristic of a particular party, such as on the tariff and on isolation. One cannot, however, say that the party which has chosen Theodore Roosevelt and Dwight D. Eisenhower as Presidents is necessarily inclined to guide the country toward isolation and neutrality—or even high tariffs. Proceeding from certain general philosophies, the positions of the parties have on the whole, although sometimes with some reluctance and even party schisms, swung with public sentiment. The stands of each party have been basically grounded upon the calculations of their leaders as to what will sway the majority of the voters at election time and be most likely, under existing circumstances, to win public office.

42 Discussions of various suggestions appear in Cheever and Haviland, *op. cit.*, chs. 13–14; G. B. Galloway, *Next Steps in Congressional Reform*, *op. cit.*; L. H. Chamberlain, *The President, Congress, and Legislation* (New York, 1946); A. N. Holcombe, *Our More Perfect Union* (Cambridge, 1950); W. Y. Elliott (Chairman of Study Group), *United States Foreign Policy, Its Organization and Control; Report of a Study Group for the Woodrow Wilson Foundation* (New York, 1952).

Foreign Affairs and Elections. American elections have usually been fought to a larger extent on domestic issues than they have on questions of foreign affairs. But this has not always been the case, and it may be less true in the future than in the past in view of America's changed position in world affairs. Foreign policy has at times become a burning issue in national elections. In the elections of 1792 and 1796 public opinion was sharply divided over relations with Britain and France. In 1812 British interference with American shipping became a critical issue. The annexation of Texas and Oregon were focal points in the Presidential contest of 1844. In 1916 the American position with respect to the European War was the central question in many voters' minds, while in 1920 adherence to the League of Nations became a prominent issue. In 1952 the Truman Administration's handling of the Korean War, the China policy, and policy toward communism were heatedly contested questions.

There are always national, local, economic, political, and personal factors which enter into the final outcome of national election campaigns. Consequently, it is often difficult, if not impossible, to say with exactness what issues have been decisive in the minds of the voters. For this reason an election can hardly be considered a "mandate" on foreign policy.[43] But that it can produce effects touching the nation's foreign relations is beyond question. As a final and perhaps the most important point, a foreign policy stressing cooperation with other nations and collective security can be successful only if it has a considerable degree of continuity. Such a policy is certainly weakened by being a major election issue and may conceivably be suddenly overturned by internal political struggles. Hence it seems only sound to seek for a considerable degree of bipartisanship on foreign policy matters in election campaigns as well as in the functioning of government.

INTEREST GROUPS

In the American political scene there are many groups held together by common interests and having as group objectives furtherance of those interests through political action. Some foreign policy matters are of direct interest only to small groups. But no one should make the mistake of assuming that such groups are not very powerful in the areas of their interest. A small group may be a determinant of policy because it has a tremendous interest in a particular issue or program whereas the mass of the public are uninformed or little concerned. The cynic might quote Yeats, "The best lack all conviction; the worst are filled with passionate intensity." But an analysis will probably show

[43] T. A. Bailey, *The Man in the Street* (New York, 1948), pp. 92–99. See also Bailey, *A Diplomatic History of the American People* (4th ed., New York, 1950); S. F. Bemis, *A Diplomatic History of the United States* (New York, 1936).

that the intellectual leadership on most issues comes from a relatively small group. An example of a small but very effective group interest has been the pressure relative to a tariff on cheese. The pressures related to policy on Palestine and the formation of the state of Israel involved a larger interest group. Group pressures are brought to bear on government departments and on Congress. Some groups maintain lobbyists in Washington and engage in extensive publicity activities.

To some extent certain interest groups act on and through particular departments and form a vague sort of "constituency" to lobby for those departments which execute their interests; for example, farm organizations and the Department of Agriculture, business organizations and the Department of Commerce. The State Department has no "constituency" unless one counts a few academic-type organizations having minor political impact. Perhaps because of this vague, but recognized, political institution of departmental "constituencies," the Department of State has been plagued by the suspicion in some people's minds that it represents foreign interests and hence is suspect.

Groups having some interest in foreign affairs and organized to mobilize and express opinion in Washington cover many facets of American life. Among these may be identified (1) educational organizations such as the Foreign Policy Association and the League of Women Voters; (2) farm groups such as the National Grange, the Farmers' Union, and the Southern cotton and tobacco producers; (3) business interests represented by such organs as the National Association of Manufacturers, the Chamber of Commerce of the United States, and the National Foreign Trade Council, as well as the more specialized groups representing individual industries; (4) the leading labor organizations; (5) ethnic groups representing peoples of foreign birth or extraction; (6) religious bodies, including such national mouthpieces as the National Catholic Welfare Conference, the National Council of Churches of Christ in America, and the National Jewish Welfare Board, together with the various churches and denominational bodies; (7) patriotic societies such as the Daughters of the American Revolution, the American Legion, the Veterans of Foreign Wars, and others; and (8) groups interested in world peace and disarmament such as the American Peace Conference, the National Council for the Prevention of War, and the American Friends Service Committee. The policies advocated and supported by these different interest groups run the gamut of foreign relations and extend from one extreme of possibility to the other.

Through the activities of paid agents in Washington, circularization of the country with literature and pleas, the organization of public opinion polls, use of the press, the direction of campaigns to flood official Washington with letters and telegrams, and the manipulation of the social lobby, the interest groups speak with a myriad of insistent and sometimes very powerful voices to those who are responsible for making and conducting the foreign policy of the United States. They are an active part of the fabric of American life and can and often do play a constructive role in the formulation of policy and the administration of foreign affairs.[44]

PUBLIC OPINION AND FOREIGN POLICY

It is not always easy to identify public opinion on a national scale on matters of foreign policy. Often it is quiescent, consisting of many varying points of view arising from the interplay of local, regional, political, economic, religious, or other influences. But at times mass sentiment can arise to express itself.[45]

For a century and a half after Washington's Farewell Address, the American people were opposed to alliances and determined to "stay out of Europe's quarrels." Popular sentiment early in the nineteenth century supported the limitation of European colonialism in the Western Hemisphere. It demanded war over Cuba in 1898. It insisted upon a hasty reduction of armaments after 1918 and again in 1945. It opposed the use of American armed forces to stop Japanese aggression in Manchuria in 1931 or the Nazi conquest of Poland in 1939. It supported American participation in World War II after the Japanese attack upon Pearl Harbor. It favored resistance to Soviet imperialism and communist aggression after 1947. Difficult as it may be to define, public opinion can make itself felt in one way or another on American foreign relations. Professor Gabriel Almond says: "The function of the public in a democratic policy-making process is to set certain policy criteria in the form of widely held values and expectations," leaving to those who have a positive and informed interest the actual formation of policy.[46]

The Press and Foreign Policy. Second to none in providing the base for public opinion and in giving expression to it are the press, radio, and television. These media give the people the bulk of their information on national and international affairs. Through the handling of news stories, through editorials, and through the columns and broadcasts of "big-name" syndicated columnists and news commentators, the press and radio can focus, crystallize, and project public opinion.

---

[44] For an able analysis of the positions taken by many of these different groups see especially Gabriel A. Almond, *The American People and Foreign Policy* (New York, 1950), ch. 8.

[45] For a systematic analysis of the forces operating on American public opinion see Almond, *op. cit.;* Bailey, *Man in the Street;* L. S. Cottrell and S. Eberhart, *American Opinion on World Affairs in the Atomic Age* (Princeton, 1948); L. Markel and others, *Public Opinion and Foreign Policy* (New York, 1949); J. S. Bruner, "Public Opinion and Policy Making in the United States," *World Politics,* July, 1950.

[46] Almond, *op. cit.,* p. 5.

Newspapers and the radio, like other private enterprise, are in business in this and other free nations for the papers and advertising they can sell, as well as for the public service they render. Catering to differing publics, wide discrepancies naturally result in the amount of attention different papers and news chains devote to foreign affairs, as witness the contrast between, on the one hand, the *New York Times, New York Herald Tribune,* etc., and, on the other hand, the tabloids. Furthermore, the press editorials and news commentators range far apart in their basic attitudes and predispositions, depending upon political leanings, group attachments, and the groups they seek to reach and for which they endeavor to become exponents. Taking the press as a whole, and radio commentators to a somewhat less degree, the generalization may be ventured that they tend more to go along with and to reflect the sentiments of their public than to pioneer new ground in public opinion.[47]

One historian has remarked that "without sound information there can be no sound public opinion, and without sound public opinion there can be no intelligent foreign policy." [48] Part of the problem and program of sound policy formulation is the need for "educating up" the whole level of public understanding of foreign affairs.

Ascertainment of Public Opinion Consensus. The views and sentiments of organized interest groups are made known to the policy maker. But distinguishing the consensus of public opinion is not always easy. Newspaper editorials, the resolutions of public gatherings, public opinion polls, elections, and the correspondence pouring into Washington can indicate trends and cross sections, although each contains but a fragment of the whole and may be actuated by a variety of special or localized interests or intermingled with extraneous issues.[49] Furthermore, if deeply concerned with internal political aspects, the policy maker may be primarily interested in those interest groups which feel so strongly about an issue that they will grant or withhold their votes over that issue. This fact is the principal explanation for the great influence of those interest groups which are, numerically, comparatively small.

A consensus does not consist of an unchanging set of values or objectives. We have only to contrast the isolationist consensus of American public opin-

---

[47] Bailey's *Man in the Street* gives an extensive historical account of the press and public opinion in American foreign policy. See also J. F. Scott, "The Press and Foreign Policy," *J. Mod. Hist.,* vol. III, pp. 627–638.

[48] Bailey, *op. cit.,* p. 304.

[49] See F. H. Russell, "The Function of Public Opinion Analysis in the Formulation of Foreign Policy," *Department of State Bulletin,* March 6, 1949. An able evaluation of the public opinion polls on foreign policy is found in Almond, *op. cit.,* ch. 3. More accurate gauges are needed for the true consensus of public opinion as it becomes crystallized from time to time. This is a task calling for careful application of the most modern research methods and knowledge of the techniques of communications.

ion in the 1930's with the wide (although far from unanimous) acceptance today of United States leadership as a world power. A consensus existed in the thirties that Axis aggression should not be resisted by use of American power other than diplomatic protest; today the consensus favors resistance to communist aggression, whether in Asia or in Europe. Both the existence and the changeability of the consensus, therefore, create a complex situation for the policy maker.

The Executive and Public Opinion. The policy maker is not always on the receiving end of public opinion. Actually, he is in a strategic position to fashion it. The President, the Secretary of State, and the government departments can and do use press conferences, public addresses, statements before Congressional committees, "trial balloon" releases from unidentified sources, and the reports of specially appointed executive commissions, not only to pass information to the public, but also to guide public opinion. In recent years there has been an observable tendency on the part of the Executive to launch major foreign policies, such as the United Nations Charter and the North Atlantic Treaty, with an organized information campaign to insure their adoption. Thus the government not only has the means of gathering public opinion but of channeling it and shaping it. This can be a fact of some relevance in the formulation and conduct of foreign policy.

CONCLUSION

American foreign policy should not be thought of as a series of written and oral pronouncements but rather as the ways by which the nation deals with its international affairs. These ways are determined by a very complex set of political institutions and processes which we have described summarily in this chapter. But the determination, and hence the policies, are essentially democratic; for the American people are, by these institutions and processes, made ultimately responsible for their own welfare and their own survival in an age of peril.

American foreign policy should be viewed as a matter of very complicated dynamics. The operational relationships between Congress and the Executive are at least as important as the constitutional role of either viewed separately. There is a premium on cooperation and coordination, and good administration. Foreign policy formulation and operation are indivisible and mutually interacting. This is now a business requiring experts for leadership. It is difficult for the average citizen, going about his daily affairs, to acquire all the necessary facts and considerations needed in order to reach sound judgments on the complex nature of present-day foreign affairs.

SUGGESTED READINGS

G. A. Almond, *The American People and Foreign Policy* (New York, 1950).

T. A. Bailey, *The Man in the Street* (New York, 1950).

Hollis W. Barber, *Foreign Policies of the United States* (New York, 1953).

Brookings Institution, *Major Problems of United States Foreign Policy 1953–1954* (Washington, 1954).

S. F. Bemis, *A Diplomatic History of the United States* (New York, 1950).

L. H. Chamberlain and R. C. Snyder, *American Foreign Policy* (New York, 1948).

Daniel S. Cheever and H. F. Haviland, *American Foreign Policy and the Separation of Powers* (Cambridge, 1952).

J. R. Childs, *American Foreign Service* (New York, 1948).

Robert A. Dahl, *Congress and Foreign Policy* (New York, 1950).

William Yandell Elliot and others, *United States Foreign Policy: Its Organization and Control* (New York, 1952).

George F. Kennan, *American Diplomacy 1900–1950* (Chicago, 1951).

L. Larry Leonard, *Elements of American Foreign Policy* (New York, 1953).

James L. McCamy, *The Administration of American Foreign Affairs* (New York, 1950).

Dexter Perkins, *The American Approach to Foreign Policy* (Cambridge, 1953).

———. *The Evolution of American Foreign Policy* (New York, 1948).

Elmer Plischke, *Conduct of American Diplomacy* (New York, 1950).

Ithiel de Sola Pool, *Symbols of Democracy,* Hoover Institute Studies, Ser. C, No. 4. (Stanford, 1952).

Graham H. Stuart, *The Department of State: A History of Its Organization, Procedure, and Personnel* (New York, 1949).

R. W. Van Alstyne, *American Diplomacy in Action* (Stanford, 1947).

F. W. Wilcox and T. V. Kalijarvi, *Recent American Foreign Policy* (New York, 1952).

CHAPTER XIII

Policy Making in the
Parliamentary Democracy

WE DESCRIBED in the previous chapter the procedure by which foreign policy is formulated and conducted under the American presidential form of government. This form has been adopted, with local variations, in numerous countries, particularly in the Americas. In most of the countries of Western Europe, in the Commonwealth of Nations, Japan, and the Republic of Indonesia, to mention only a few, a parliamentary form of government exists in which responsibility for policy making is in the hands of a Prime Minister and Cabinet chosen from a Parliament and responsible to it. In this chapter we shall consider the institutional and political framework within which policy is formulated and administered in the "mother of parliamentary democracies," that is, Britain, and in France, a continental country employing the parliamentary system with a multiparty political environment.

EVOLUTION OF POLICY-MAKING AUTHORITY IN BRITAIN

Policy-making power in Britain has gradually shifted from the King, and later the King and a group of councilors, to the leaders of the majority party in the House of Commons acting through a Cabinet which holds itself responsible collectively to the House of Commons. In policy matters the prerogatives of the Monarch have diminished from their original absolute control and direction to that of sometimes expressing views or counsel to the Prime Minister, usually after the Cabinet has reached a policy decision and sometimes after action has been initiated. Custom has established that the Prime Minister and Cabinet do not have to accept the views of the ruler. When expressed, however, they are given respectful attention. The real initiative and control of governmental policy now reside in the Prime Minister and his Cabinet. The Cabinet is composed of the party leader who is invited by the Monarch to form a government, and a group of Ministers chosen by the Prime Minister. The

Cabinet as such is not formally approved by the King (or reigning Queen), although he does swear in each Cabinet officer to the Privy Council.

The Prime Minister and his Cabinet are expected to act as the fountain-head of the policy-making process in Britain. They are expected to introduce and guide through Parliament such legislation as may be necessary to serve the national interests. They are responsible for executing the laws and directing the administrative departments of government. And they are expected to resign as a body if they lose majority support for their policies in Parliament. This arrangement forces the Cabinet members to seek unity on policies and to give them their undivided support once decision has been reached. It enables the Parliament to exercise constant surveillance and constructive criticism of national policy. It also assures unity of purpose between the majority in the legislative branch of government and the executive.

In Britain the system has usually operated with two major parties, one in power, the other in opposition. In many other countries which have copied the British system of government, more than two parties customarily hold blocs of seats in the legislature, with the result that coalition cabinets become necessary. In either situation, the party or combination of parties whose leaders compose what is called the Government generally hold office so long as they enjoy the support of a working majority in Parliament and in national elections.[1]

ROLE OF THE PRIME MINISTER

Over-all Direction. As leader or ranking member of the majority party and head of the Government, the Prime Minister predominates in his Cabinet and has over-all direction of policy making. In this context a Prime Minister must inevitably concern himself with foreign policy.

Some Prime Ministers have taken a large hand in foreign affairs. Lloyd George from 1916 to 1921 did so much on his own initiative that he virtually relegated his Foreign Minister, Lord Curzon, to the stature of an Under-Secretary, and at the same time built up a private secretariat rivaling the Foreign Office staff. Neville Chamberlain, who was Prime Minister from 1937 to 1940, took direction largely into his own hands and relied on advisers other than his Foreign Secretary and the Foreign Office. Lord Vansittart, then Permanent Under-Secretary of State for Foreign Affairs and Chief Diplomatic Adviser to the Prime Minister, made the astounding statement afterward that

[1] Among the best up-to-date writings on the British Government are Ivor Jennings, *The British Constitution* (Cambridge, 1950); and the same author, *Cabinet Government* (2d ed., Cambridge, 1951). See also Hiram M. Stout, *British Government* (New York, 1953); Herman Beukema and associates, *Contemporary Foreign Governments* (3rd ed., New York, 1953), ch. ii. On the tasks of the Cabinet see Herman Finer, "The British Cabinet, the House of Commons and the War," *Pol. Sci. Quar.*, Sept., 1941.

"as Chief Diplomatic Adviser I saw Chamberlain only thrice in three years, and never once alone." [2]

One British authority says that in peace-time, as distinct from war, a Prime Minister "ought not to have a policy" of his own. He should be a chairman with an eye on all, giving advice and suggesting caution when he believes it necessary. He should recommend further consideration before actions are taken, if he deems this wise. He should warn of domestic political difficulties if he sees them involved in a proposed policy or action. But otherwise he should place reliance and responsibility upon his Foreign Secretary.[3] In war-time a Prime Minister may be justified in exercising a more positive role, as Winston Churchill's memoirs relate that he did in World War II.[4]

Resolution of Differences on Policy. It is a part of a Prime Minister's task to resolve differences which may arise between members of his Cabinet on questions of policy. Some of these can be adjusted directly or within the Cabinet. Others he must decide personally.

One of the gravest situations which can confront a government arises when a Prime Minister and a Foreign Secretary take irreconcilable positions on major questions of policy. These can split a Cabinet and lead to the downfall of a government. A threat or tender of resignation by the Foreign Secretary may induce the Prime Minister to modify his stand. But it is his privilege to insist on his course if he so determines and can carry his colleagues with him. In this case he may ask for or accept the Foreign Secretary's resignation and replace him by someone who will preserve a policy in accordance with his beliefs.

Such an instance occurred between Prime Minister Neville Chamberlain and Foreign Secretary Anthony Eden in February, 1938. The Prime Minister was unwilling to pursue a policy of opposition to German and Italian aggression by international sanctions which the Foreign Secretary believed to be essential. When no formula could be found to resolve the difference, Mr. Eden resigned. Thereafter Mr. Chamberlain, with another minister, embarked upon the path of appeasement which led to the ignominious agreements at Munich and Godesberg.[5]

---

2 Lord Vansittart, "The Decline of Diplomacy," *Foreign Affairs*, Jan., 1950, p. 186.

3 Jennings, *British Constitution*, pp. 164, 174–175, 178–179. Prime Minister Baldwin represented the opposite extreme from Lloyd George. At the time of the negotiation of the Locarno Pact in 1925 he is said to have told his Foreign Secretary, Sir Austen Chamberlain, "Well, Austen, do what you think fit and I will support you."

4 Volumes 2–6 of Churchill's memoirs on *The Second World War* cover the period of his war-time premiership: vol. 2, *Their Finest Hour* (Boston, 1949); vol. 3, *The Grand Alliance* (Boston, 1950); vol. 4, *The Hinge of Fate* (Boston, 1950); vol. 5, *Closing the Ring* (Boston, 1951); vol. 6, *Triumph and Tragedy* (Boston, 1953).

5 Churchill, *The Gathering Storm*, ch. 14. For Chamberlain's side of this situation see K. Feiling, *The Life of Neville Chamberlain* (New York, 1946).

High-Level Negotiations. The Prime Minister may at times engage personally in diplomatic negotiations. He may request interviews with foreign diplomats on certain important issues. He may go abroad to hold conversations with the heads of foreign states. He may lead his country's delegations to international conferences or to meetings of the United Nations. The exigencies of war and its settlement often call for high-level negotiations in which the head of the government must participate. Times of crisis always enhance a Prime Minister's part in the conduct of foreign affairs. This was evidenced in World War II by Churchill's personal handling of many of the political and military questions on which he felt the United States should be consulted by his own communications with President Roosevelt, rather than through his Foreign Office.

A Prime Minister who engages in such negotiations is more obliged, however, than a President of the United States to consult with his colleagues in the executive branch of government. At the Atlantic Conference meeting of Churchill and Roosevelt in 1940, for example, Churchill constantly consulted his War Cabinet by radio on the strategic questions and terms of the Atlantic Charter which were being discussed, while Roosevelt, with Under-Secretary of State Welles, General Marshall and other military advisers, Harry Hopkins, and Averell Harriman present, made all decisions on shipboard without referring to Washington.[6]

THE CABINET AND POLICY MAKING

In the parliamentary form of government the focal point in policy decision is the Cabinet. Here the most important decisions on foreign and domestic policy are reached.

Cabinet Composition. Normally all members of a British Cabinet and Ministry are selected by the Prime Minister from the leaders of his own party in Parliament.[7] In time of war or when this party does not have a clear majority in Parliament, the Prime Minister may invite leaders of the opposition to join in forming a National Government. In composing the Cabinet the Prime Minister naturally seeks a team that will work together harmoniously in support of his leadership. At the same time, he must, of course, conciliate the various interests within the party, and he may have to make certain appointments in response to political pressures as do political leaders in other countries.

Since 1911 it has been the practice to draw most of the Cabinet members

---

[6] R. S. Sherwood, *Roosevelt and Hopkins* (New York, 1948), p. 361.

[7] Since the Cabinet has no legal status in Britain, all members are formally appointed Privy Councilors.

from the House of Commons. Three ministerial heads and the Lord Chancellor, however, must be peers. Occasionally a Lord has been appointed Secretary of State for Foreign Affairs. But this practice is not favored since it deprives the House of Commons of the opportunity of obtaining personal answers by the Foreign Secretary to criticisms of foreign policy.[8]

Ministers composing British Cabinets change somewhat from time to time, but the Foreign Secretary is always a member of the Cabinet. Similarly, the Minister of Defense, the Chancellor of the Exchequer, and the President of the Board of Trade, three other departmental heads extensively concerned with foreign affairs, are Cabinet members. The Cabinet may contain fourteen or more other ministers.[9]

GOVERNMENT OF UNITED KINGDOM

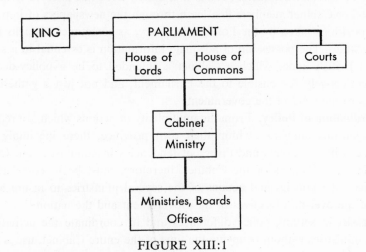

FIGURE XIII:1

Foreign Affairs in the Cabinet. Foreign affairs normally are the first item on the agenda of the Cabinet which meets at least once a week. Sometimes there may be merely a report on the progress of some negotiations or on the international situation. On other occasions the Foreign Secretary may ask for an expression of views from other Cabinet ministers in order to confirm his judgment or to strengthen his hand. Or there may be some development calling

8 Lord Halifax was the last peer to hold the Foreign Secretaryship. He was in office from 1938 to 1940. In this instance Prime Minister Chamberlain assumed personal responsibility for answering questions on foreign affairs in the House of Commons. In 1953, when Anthony Eden was ill, Lord Salisbury was Acting Secretary of State for Foreign Affairs.

9 On the formation of Cabinets see Jennings, *Cabinet Government*, ch. 3; Churchill, *Their Finest Hour*, pp. 8–15. Surrounding the Cabinet are additional ministers without Cabinet rank.

for a major policy decision, as when a critical stand must be taken at a major international conference, when an agreement with serious implications must be negotiated by British representatives, or when some delicate question has been raised in Parliament. It may be possible at one sitting to obtain sufficient clarification of the action which the Government is to take. On the other hand, the question may have to be referred to a Cabinet subcommittee for further study and recommendation or put over to a later meeting, while the members reflect upon it or seek out indications of parliamentary and public sentiment. Any action taken is recorded in a Cabinet minute for the guidance of all concerned.

To keep the Cabinet informed it is customary for the Foreign Secretary to circulate important diplomatic correspondence to his colleagues. The Foreign Office "boxes" always contain a significant part of the after-hours official reading of Cabinet members.[10] Thus a situation does not arise in Britain in which other Cabinet members first learn through the newspapers of important policy positions taken by the Foreign Secretary, as sometimes happens in the United States. The possession of adequate information is essential in a system like the British under which a Cabinet is intended to be a policy-deciding body, collectively responsible to the Parliament, and not just a gathering of advisers to the head of the government.

Coordination of Policy. From the multiplicity of actions which are required by the various ministries within their own province, there inevitably arise differences in viewpoints and divergent tendencies in administration. One of the principal functions of the Cabinet, therefore, must be to correlate and coordinate the policies and actions of the several ministries to insure attainment of the over-all objectives of the Government and the nation.[11]

To assist in settling policy differences and to coordinate the activities of related ministries without ocupying the time of the entire Cabinet, use is made of Cabinet committees which may include ministers not in the Cabinet. The most important standing committees having to do with foreign affairs are the Defense, Legislation, and Policy Committees. The Defense Committee, under the chairmanship of the Prime Minister, and normally attended by the Chiefs of Staff in advisory capacity, is in a sense a committee on national security fulfilling within the British Cabinet the functions which the National Security Council was designed to serve outside of the Cabinet in the United States.

10 Churchill, *The Gathering Storm,* pp. 239, 240; also Jennings, *Constitution,* p. 156. See R. V. Langford, *British Foreign Policy, Its Formulation in Recent Years* (Washington, 1942), chs. 2–3.
11 The work of the Cabinet is assisted by a Cabinet Secretariat, with an Economic Section and Central Statistical Office which provide analysis for the Cabinet, coordinating committees, and departments. See Lord M. P. A. Hankey, *Diplomacy by Conference, Studies in Public Affairs,* 1920–1946 (London, 1947); Jennings, *Cabinet Government,* pp. 223–227.

Inner Cabinet. Prime Ministers sometimes select a few Cabinet ministers to act with them as an inner planning group, especially in war-time, to deal with problems of national security and to see that foreign policy is properly related to war strategy. These inner cabinets usually include the Foreign Minister. They may meet daily, or even twice a day, without formality or the keeping of formal records. In the words of Mr. Churchill, "Such meetings are an essential counterpart to the formal meetings where business is transacted and decisions are recorded for guidance and action. Both processes are indispensable to the handling of the most difficult affairs." Within this close association policy matters can be discussed expeditiously.[12]

Implementation of Cabinet Action. Cabinet decisions may be implemented in a variety of ways. They may be announced to Parliament by the Prime Minister or the Foreign Secretary or issued in a public statement. They may be carried through by the dispatch of instructions to a mission or delegation abroad. They may be expressed in a conversation between the Foreign Secretary and a foreign diplomat, or in a note handed to another government.

Once a policy decision has been reached, all members of the Cabinet assume collective responsibility for the decision. Even while a question is before the Cabinet, it is customary for all to adopt the same position in public. If any member cannot subordinate his own views to the judgment of his colleagues, he must resign, as did Sir Herbert Samuel and other Liberals from Ramsay MacDonald's Coalition Government in 1932 over the Ottawa Empire Preference (trade) Agreements, and as did Aneurin Bevan from Clement Attlee's Cabinet in 1950 over the relative emphasis on social welfare and rearmament.

The Cabinet has the power and the machinery within the administrative departments and Parliament to carry out its plans. Only a lack-of-confidence vote in Parliament can interfere with this decision. Under such circumstances the Government must either resign or ask the King to dissolve Parliament and call a national election on the issue. This latter possibility, taken together with the majority party's other means of control over members, has a disciplinary value in keeping party members in line; for no member desires to incur the hazards and expense of an election, and dissidents, lacking party support, have difficulty in returning to Parliament at the next election.

THE FOREIGN SECRETARY

Relation to Prime Minister, Parliament and Cabinets. British Foreign Secretaries are usually, though not always, ranking lieutenants to the Prime Min-

---

[12] Churchill, *The Gathering Storm,* pp. 418–420, 452; *Their Finest Hour,* pp. 12–15, 18–26; Jennings, *Cabinet Government,* pp. 200–206.

ister in his own political party. Occasionally, an individual is selected from outside of Parliament, but in this case he must stand for election to Parliament at a special by-election. In Governments headed by Mr. Churchill from 1940 onward, Anthony Eden, one of the foremost members of the Conservative party and a member of the House of Commons, was Foreign Secretary. In Prime Minister Attlee's Labor Government, Ernest Bevin, head of the Transport and General Workers' Union, was Foreign Secretary from 1945 to 1949, followed by Herbert Morrison, who had been Deputy Leader of the Labor party and Leader of the House of Commons.

Although the Foreign Secretary frequently occupies a position next in rank to the Prime Minister and carries considerable weight in the Cabinet, he nevertheless conducts affairs, as Mr. Churchill has remarked, "under the continuous scrutiny, if not of the whole Cabinet, at least of its principal members." He must maintain the confidence of the Prime Minister, for the latter has the right to full information on foreign affairs and may take matters into his own hands at any time. Furthermore, support by the Prime Minister is essential to the success of the Foreign Minister's policies. Personal factors can, of course, affect the degree of freedom which a Foreign Secretary may enjoy in the conduct of foreign affairs, such as his public standing, his knowledge of the field, and the relative strength of his personality compared with that of the Prime Minister and his other colleagues.

The Work of the Foreign Secretary. Probably the major difference between the routine of the United States Secretary of State and that of his British counterpart arises from the continuous responsibility of the latter to Parliament and to the Cabinet. The United States Secretary of State generally attends the weekly National Security Council meetings and the Cabinet meetings. But the British Foreign Secretary must, in addition to Cabinet meetings, devote considerable time to Parliament which is regularly in session a good part of each year with meetings five days a week. He must participate in debate, answer questions on foreign policy presented at the question hour, and be present when critical decisions are being taken. As a party figure, he must also appear at important party meetings. Along with all of these responsibilities he must of course be thoroughly informed on both domestic and foreign questions and meet often with the Prime Minister, members of his department, and foreign diplomatic representatives.

THE FOREIGN OFFICE

There is relatively little difference in the general structure and operation of Foreign Offices under the presidential and parliamentary forms of government.

Growth of the British Foreign Office. The British Foreign Office as it exists today was established in 1782. The first Secretary of State for Foreign Affairs was appointed at this time, although previously there had been Secretaries of State to assist the Monarch in conducting foreign affairs. Until the end of the eighteenth century the staff included a Parliamentary and a Permanent Under-Secretary and eleven clerks. From the beginning, the Foreign Office was set apart from other departments in that "its affairs were considered to be in a peculiar degree the special concern of the Cabinet as a whole, and not simply or mainly that of the Foreign Secretary." [13]

The Foreign Office acquired its eminent standing chiefly through the efforts of a distinguished line of Foreign Secretaries in the nineteenth and early twentieth centuries, including Viscount Castlereagh, George Canning, Lord Palmerston, Lord Salisbury, and Sir Edward Grey. Although these Secretaries differed greatly in their approach to politics, they established the doctrine of continuity in the conduct of foreign affairs which has become a distinguishing feature of British foreign policy.[14]

As a result of the growing complexity of international politics and the rising position of Britain in world affairs, Foreign Office work increased enormously, beginning with the last quarter of the nineteenth century. To cope with this changing situation, extensive reorganization took place in 1905–1906, with enlargement of the permanent staff and a termination of patronage in the appointment of members of the Diplomatic Service.[15] Steps were taken to fuse the personnel of the Foreign Office and Diplomatic Service into a single Foreign Service, and to recognize the rising importance of the commercial and consular activities by the appointment of an Assistant Secretary of State for their administration beginning in 1918.[16] In 1943 the Diplomatic and Consular Services were amalgamated into a united Foreign Service. A further broadening of the base of the Foreign Office occurred during and after World War II, in response to the exigencies of the war, the rise of new tasks, and as a result of Labor party criticisms of undue influence of "old school tie" connections in recruiting of personnel.[17]

Political Aides to Foreign Minister. In directing foreign affairs, the Foreign Secretary is closely assisted by two Ministers of State for the Foreign Office and two Parliamentary Under-Secretaries of State, each a member of Parliament and therefore each coming and going with changes of Government. The

---

13 A. W. Ward and G. P. Gooch, *The Cambridge History of British Foreign Policy* (New York, 1923), III, p. 547.

14 *Ibid.*, p. 555.

15 F. T. Ashton-Gwatkin, *The British Foreign Service* (Syracuse, 1950), p. 14; Ward and Gooch, *cit. supra,* p. 616.

16 Ward and Gooch, *op. cit.*, pp. 619–620.

17 See *The Organization of the British Foreign Service,* British Information Services, 10938 (New York, February, 1953).

Ministers of State for the Foreign Office who do not have Cabinet rank devote much of their attention to British participation in the United Nations, other international and regional organizations, and the many international conferences which demand high-level representation. The two Parliamentary Under-Secretaries of State for Foreign Affairs assist the Foreign Secretary in handling matters on the floor of Parliament, answering questions when the Minister is absent, and helping maintain liaison between Parliament and the Foreign Office. These appointees are often persons being "eyed" by their party for higher positions of leadership.[18]

Permanent Under-Secretary. The head of the corps of permanent officials, comprising Her Majesty's Foreign Service—the amalgamation of the Foreign Office, Diplomatic Service, Consular and Commercial-Diplomatic Services—is the Permanent Under-Secretary of State for Foreign Affairs. This career official holds office regardless of changes in Government and is expected to be the Foreign Secretary's principal adviser. He has under his administrative control deputies, assistant secretaries, and some fifty division heads in the Foreign Office. As a career civil servant, who has come up through the ranks of the Foreign Service, he occupies a post which is the prize of all career members of the Foreign Service.

The role of the Permanent Under-Secretary is an indispensable one in the parliamentary system. It is he who gives continuity of leadership to the staff of the Foreign Office, providing a link between changes of Government. He is always at the right hand of a new Foreign Secretary to assist him in mastering the intricacies of foreign relations, to assemble information and documentation for him, and to caution him on a course of action which might depart from historic policies or those which in the opinion of the experts would lead the nation into questionable positions.[19]

Divisions of Foreign Office. Under the direction of the Foreign Secretary and the Permanent Under-Secretary are the various geographical and functional divisions. These may be grouped into four categories: (1) *the geographical area departments* of which there are ten; (2) *functional subject departments,* including offices dealing with Economic Relations, Cultural Relations, Commonwealth Affairs, and United Nations Affairs and Research; (3) *public information,* comprising a series of departments and services taken

---

18 The Foreign Secretary has a Private Parliamentary Secretary who serves as private secretary on matters concerning Parliament, but this individual normally has little to do with policy decisions.

19 On the dignity of the office see Ward and Gooch, *op. cit.,* III, p. 610. The office of Permanent Under-Secretary is not altogether beyond the reach of politics, as demonstrated in 1938 when Prime Minister Chamberlain eased Sir (now Lord) Robert Vansittart out of office because his insistent warnings on the Nazi menace ran counter to Chamberlain's policy of seeking German friendship.

over from the Ministry of Information at the end of World War II, including the British Information Service offices operating in other countries; [20] and (4) *administration,* covering personnel, financial, and service matters.

These departments function much as do their corresponding units in the Department of State in Washington. They are staffed with officers, most of whom have had some experience or service abroad. Their task is to analyze reports from the field, to prepare memoranda, to draft outgoing instructions and dispatches, and to help initiate policy position papers. It can hardly be said that these civil servants formulate top-level policy; but they do play an important part in assembling the necessary materials for arrival at viable estimates of a situation and for intelligent decision on policy questions.

Mention should also be made of the British Foreign Service. This is not unlike the United States Foreign Service, except that it is smaller in size. Foreign Service officers are selected by competitive examinations emphasizing intelligence, practical ability, and psychological suitability. Before being sent abroad, new officers are given preparatory training to familiarize them not only with the foreign country in which they will be posted, but with British economic and social conditions as well. Abroad these officers engage in the same kind of responsibilities as officers of other nations—representation, observing, reporting, cultivating friendly relations, gathering and disseminating information, and engaging in such negotiations as the Foreign Office directs.

Policy Decision. It is the duty of the Permanent Under-Secretary and Assistant Secretaries to place all the necessary facts for policy decision before the Foreign Secretary and the Ministers of State, to call their attention to important facts, ideas, or events, and to recommend upon request, or as their judgment dictates, courses of policy action.

However valid the views and recommendations of the permanent staff may be, the Foreign Secretary, the Ministers of State, and the Parliamentary Under-Secretaries are free to accept or reject them. As members of the Government, theirs is the right of decision on policy so long as it is consonant with Cabinet action. Not only in Britain, however, but in other parliamentary countries as well, a considerable degree of continuity has come to prevail in most aspects of foreign policy. This is due to the presence of an efficient, permanent staff as well as to the fact that a nation's interests and objectives abroad rarely change abruptly, even though the party in power may change.

OTHER MINISTRIES CONCERNED WITH FOREIGN AFFAIRS

Like the government in Washington, any parliamentary government has ministries other than Foreign Affairs with an active concern for international

20 For further details on the British Information Service see ch. xvi below.

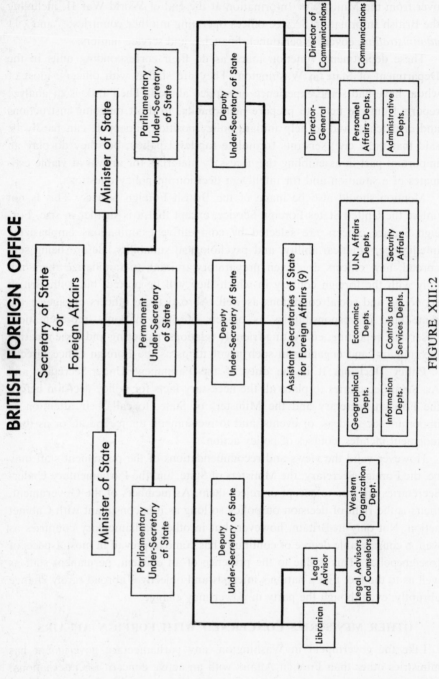

BRITISH FOREIGN OFFICE

Secretary of State for Foreign Affairs

Minister of State

Minister of State

Parliamentary Under-Secretary of State

Parliamentary Under-Secretary of State

Permanent Under-Secretary of State

Deputy Under-Secretary of State

Deputy Under-Secretary of State

Deputy Under-Secretary of State

Director-General

Director of Communications

Communications

Personnel Affairs Depts.

Administrative Depts.

Assistant Secretaries of State for Foreign Affairs (9)

Geographical Depts.

Economics Depts.

U.N. Affairs Depts.

Information Depts.

Controls and Services Depts.

Security Affairs

Western Organization Dept.

Legal Advisor

Legal Advisors and Counselors

Librarian

FIGURE XIII:2

problems. These ministries are substantially the same in all states. In England they include the Ministry of Defense and its component Departments of the Admiralty, War and Air, the Treasury, the Board of Trade which is in charge of foreign commerce, the Office of Commonwealth Relations, and the Ministries for Agriculture, Health, Colonies, and Posts.

Policies proposed by the Ministry of Defense, officially created in 1946, or its component departments often bear upon foreign relations as do those of the Foreign Office upon the defense arrangements of the services. The promotion of commerce by the Board of Trade at once reaches into the political and economic relationships with other countries. The Department of Public Health must be concerned with the status of communicable diseases throughout the world. As in many countries, this Department provides the national representation in the World Health Organization. It is a part of the duty of the Foreign Office to see that the various contacts and activities of other governmental departments which bear upon external relations are properly kept in balance.

Close contacts must exist between the Foreign Secretary and his assistants on the one hand, and the Secretaries of State for Commonwealth Relations and for Colonies, their Parliamentary Under-Secretaries, and the Secretary for Overseas Trade on the other hand. For this purpose consultations, exchanges of information and memoranda, and interdepartmental committee meetings help to clarify overlapping interests and resolve differences among the various departments as they do in other governments. In the final analysis the Cabinet is the ultimate seat for coordination of all interests into a single national policy and governmental decision.

PARTIES AND POLICY

While it is the Cabinet which directs British foreign policy, Parliament has the power to check the Executive if the later exceeds its powers or adopts a policy which the House of Commons believes is inacceptable to the British people. This power of Parliament in turn rests upon a vigorous two-party system, which keeps in close touch with public opinion.[21]

It is somewhat difficult to generalize about the positive influence of the parties upon policy making. Although a party elected to office presumably shapes national policy in accord with the platform upon which it appealed to the electorate, platforms are usually so general when they do mention foreign affairs that they can influence the determination of foreign policy only in the broadest outlines. It is fair to say that the details of policy action are likely

21 Jennings, *Cabinet Government*, p. 32; see also A. L. Lowell, *The Government of England* (New York, 1908), I, chs. 24–25; and general works on comparative government.

to be shaped in large measure by the memoranda and counsel of the experts in the Foreign Office as long as this remains within the limits of toleration set by public opinion. On the other hand, the party leaders in the Government cannot ignore specific commitments written into their party platforms by the rank and file of the party, without imperiling their party unity.

The limitations which events and public responsibility can impose upon a party in power are illustrated in the case of the Labor Government from 1945 to 1951. Before assuming office the Labor leaders thought that their socialist outlook would enable them to put British-Soviet relationships on a more amicable basis than could the Conservative Government. The Government discovered, however, that because of Russian behavior in Eastern Europe and elsewhere there was no alternative to cooperating with the United States in resisting Soviet imperialism. It also found that it was necessary to accept and support rightist governments in Greece and elsewhere as the only reasonable alternative to civil war and communist coups.[22] When a point is reached at which the members of the party in power cannot compose their own differences, and the party becomes split, as did the Laborites over relative emphasis on social security and defense in 1950, the party's hold upon public office may be shaken.

PARLIAMENTARY CONTROL OVER POLICY AND POLICY MAKERS [23]

Contrast with Congress. Parliament in Britain enters into the arena of foreign policy in a somewhat different way from the Congress in Washington. Parliament, like Congress, must pass all necessary laws and enabling acts. It must appropriate funds for governmental operations. But it does not, like the American Congress, have special powers apart from the Executive and enumerated by the Constitution to regulate foreign commerce or immigration. The Cabinet, not Parliament, declares war. Parliament must, however, be called into session, if it is not meeting, to put the armed forces on a war basis and to enact necessary war legislation. Express consent of Parliament is not necessary

22 John Parker, *Labour Marches On* (New York, 1947), ch. 14; also G. D. H. Cole, *A History of the Labour Party from 1914* (London, 1948), ch. 12; Paul Gore-Booth, "The Foreign Policy of the Labour Government," *J. of Pol.*, May, 1950. The election manifesto in 1945 was entitled *Let Us Face the Future* (London, 1945). See also *Cards on the Table, An Interpretation of Labour's Foreign Policy* (London, 1947).

23 Useful references on Parliament are Sir Courtenay Ilbert, *Parliament, Its History, Constitution and Practice* (rev. ed., London, 1948); W. Ivor Jennings, *Parliament* (Cambridge, 1940); Lord Hemingford, *What Parliament Is and Does* (Cambridge, 1947). Brief readable descriptions are contained in K. R. MacKenzie, *The English Parliament* (Penguin Books, 1950); British Information Series, *The British Parliament, A Short Account of Its Constitution, Functions and Procedure* (rev. ed., New York, 1952).

to the ratification of most treaties.[24] Neither is it asked to approve the appointment of individual ambassadors and other envoys.

The chief role of Parliament is to be the source from which the leaders of Government are chosen, and to be the forum within which the Government's policies and actions are to be scrutinized, attacked or defended, and the Government itself supported or overthrown. As a British authority says, "The function of Parliament is not to govern but to criticize."

Government vs. Opposition. A government with a clear majority and a well-disciplined party in Parliament knows that it can have its way on major policies so long as it has the confidence of its party. But well-organized criticism of its policies and administration before the public and the press by the leaders of the Opposition, who have a "Shadow Cabinet" ready to take over the Government, is bound to keep a Government attentive to the task of advancing the national interests and to keeping in tune with public opinion.

Ordinarily a Government supported by a clear majority cannot be defeated by the Opposition on record votes. But persistent challenge by the foremost leaders of the Opposition can reveal weaknesses in policy, blunders in administration, and lack of adequate attention to vital issues, in foreign affairs as well as in domestic matters. The Opposition can also arouse the country to dangers in public policy. It is in this area that the British Parliament plays an outstanding role in conjunction with foreign policy. And it is the essence of the parliamentary system in Britain that criticism and reasoned argument may be able to persuade the Government in power to adjust policies and actions that are shown to be inacceptable to the country.

In time of war, opposition may be withheld publicly in the interests of national security and a concerted war effort, as was the case in both World Wars. At such times it is usual for the Government to keep the Opposition leaders fully informed on matters of defense and foreign affairs. In both World Wars National Governments sooner or later emerged to insure maximum war effort. Otherwise, however, "Her Majesty's loyal Opposition" exists to criticize and challenge the policies of the Government in power and to hold itself ready at all times to assume office if the Government loses the confidence of Parliament.

The Question Hour. Basic to Opposition activity is the "Question Hour" in the House of Commons. During this period, which occurs four times a week,

[24] Treaties involving cessions of territory or expenditures of funds must go to Parliament. In 1924 the Labor Government announced that it would "table" all treaties for a period of days before ratifying. But other Cabinets have not followed this practice. The Cabinet may enter into secret treaties, and has done so in the past, although in recent years there has been a tendency to make formal agreements public. *Ibid.,* pp. 451–452.

members of the Government, including the Foreign Secretary, must answer for their policies on the floor of the House. The questions have as their main purpose "the throwing of a searchlight upon every corner of the public service." Questions may be put to them ranging over the entire spectrum of foreign relations. A typical sheaf of questions may ask for explanations of some aspect of Her Majesty's Government's policy regarding Greece, China, Korea, issues before some organ of the United Nations, United States policy in Southeast Asia, trade across the Iron Curtain, or the failure of Her Majesty's Ambassador in Moscow to protest vigorously against the slurs on Britain in some broadcast or newspaper article.[25]

Questions are frequently aimed at the conduct of foreign relations. But they may be directed at the very heart of Government policies. They may range from matters of highest principle to the smallest detail of Foreign Office administration.

Most questions on foreign affairs are directed to the Foreign Secretary. These must be answered orally or in writing by the Foreign Secretary, the Ministers of State, or the Parliamentary Under-Secretaries if the Foreign Secretary cannot be present. There may be so many questions on a given day, or they may be of such a character, that the Prime Minister or some other minister may answer some of them. The printed questions, which must be handed to the Secretary in advance to allow him and the Ministry time to prepare answers, may be followed by supplementary oral questions if the interrogator can gain the floor. These sometimes are deliberately intended to confuse or trap the Government.

An astute Minister may be able momentarily to parry embarrassing questions. He may plead public interest in refusing to answer questions that would jeopardize negotiations or national security. But if he does not answer well, or stalls unreasonably, he may be subjected to scathing rebuke by the Opposition and to criticism in the press. No Secretary can forget that in answering questions he is speaking to all his countrymen and that sooner or later his foreign policy must be acceptable to both the majority of his own party and of the country as well. Otherwise, his Government will not be returned at the next election.

Debates and Motions. There are many other opportunities for the Opposition to challenge and debate Government policy. The principal occasions are the debate which takes place on the budget, discussions on so-called "Supply Days" when the Opposition can ask for and debate any subject, debates on

---

[25] The lists of questions posted for each period, together with the answers given, are printed in the *Official Reports of the Debates in Parliament,* House of Commons, known as *Hansard's Debates.*

motions for adjournment, and the reply to the "Speech from the Throne." This last is in actuality the official statement of Cabinet policy written by the Prime Minister but read by the Monarch at the opening of Parliament. Debate always takes place on bills when they are given a Second Reading and when they are in Committee.[26] At the latter stage the Opposition may introduce amendments. While many of these fail, reasoned argument can win acceptance for some.

Control over Expenditures. The historic weapon of the Legislature over the Executive in democratic countries has been the "power of the purse." In Britain, as in other countries, appropriations for governmental expenditure, including of course foreign affairs and national defense, must be voted by Parliament.

The British Parliament does not as a rule change the Cabinet's budget materially. It may not add amendments or riders. In theory, Parliament may reject the Government's budget or reduce any item. In practice it seldom does so because of the Government's control over the majority in Parliament and the principle of following party leadership.

In the budget debates the Opposition always has an opportunity to attack the handling of foreign affairs by debating the appropriations for the Foreign Office. A customary tactic is to move a reduction in some salary or proposed item by £100. From this springboard any phase of foreign policy may be questioned or attacked. Although the Government has the votes to block any amendment it does not want, it is a part of the "fair play" of British practice for the Government whips to assist the Opposition in arranging time for debate on items it may wish to criticize. This amicable arrangement "behind the Speaker's chair" is made on the principle that similar treatment will be accorded to the party in power when it has to move into Opposition. When time has run out for debate, the "whips are put on" and a vote is taken on the proposal. Should the Government be beaten on a motion to reduce a proposed expenditure for foreign affairs, this would be regarded as a vote of censure leading to immediate cries for resignation of the Government.

Committee Activity. The House of Commons has no functional standing committees comparable to the Senate Foreign Relations Committee, the House Foreign Affairs Committee, or the Committees on the Armed Services, which play a large part in the control exercised by the Congress over United States foreign affairs. The principal committee is the Committee of the Whole House on Supply in which debate occurs on appropriations and expenditures. Select

26 Any Member of Parliament may introduce a bill bearing upon foreign relations upon which a debate may take place. But this stands little chance of passage unless it is supported by the Government, for Parliament traditionally looks to the Executive for necessary bills on such a subject.

Committees, or Joint Committees with the House of Lords, may be set up to deal with special questions. But on the whole the British Parliament does not employ committees to conduct hearings and investigations on the executive program in the manner constantly resorted to in Washington. Where special inquiries are felt desirable, Parliament may induce the Government to establish an interdepartmental committee or a royal commission whose findings and recommendations may become quite influential.

Limitations on Control. Given a clear majority and fair play discipline in the House of Commons, the British Cabinet possesses considerable freedom from internal interference in its conduct of foreign affairs. General belief in strong party discipline and the two-party system tends to limit the control that Parliament exercises over the policy makers. The power of the Executive is also enhanced, as mentioned previously, by the right of the Prime Minister to ask the Monarch to dissolve Parliament for a national election if there is opposition to Cabinet policies or if he believes that an election would strengthen the Government's hand on controversial issues. No majority Government has had to resign merely because of an adverse vote in the Commons since 1885. But the fact remains that if a Government loses its majority on a sufficiently important issue, it must resign or call for a dissolution.

Compared to the United States Congress, the influence of the British Parliament on the Government is weak in the field of foreign affairs. Ordinarily the influence can be exerted outwardly only during question time or in a debate on foreign affairs. The latter normally occurs only three or four times a year and for one or two days' duration. There are no prolonged "Great Debates" such as those which took place within the United States Congress on the sending of troops to Europe in 1950 and on Far Eastern policy after the withdrawal of General MacArthur in 1951. Without a committee on foreign affairs it is not possible even for the ranking members of the Commons to investigate and debate high-policy issues with a thoroughness comparable to the United States Senate Committee on Foreign Relations. Correspondingly, the opportunity for exerting pressure upon the Government is less.

The House of Lords. Since the House of Lords has been shorn of most of its power with respect to legislation and appropriations, its work is lighter than that of the Commons, attendance is usually small, and the time allowances for debate are more liberal. As a result, and because many of its members have had careers in government service, discussions on foreign affairs in the House of Lords are sometimes notable. Through personal associations with the leaders of party and Government, some Peers can be influential in policy decisions.[27] Moreover, there is always the possibility that the House of Com-

---

[27] See p. 366 above regarding Peers in the Cabinet and Foreign Ministry.

mons will accept amendments on some bills. On the whole, however, such influence as the House of Lords can today bring to bear upon the formulation and conduct of foreign policy depends to a large extent upon whether the party affiliation of its more active members coincides with that of the Government at the time. Not surprisingly, most Peers are Conservatives, although the recent Labor Government secured the appointment of some distinguished supporters to the Peerage.

THE CROWN

We have considered in the preceding pages the decisive power now held by Cabinet and Parliament in policy making within the United Kingdom. But neither the Crown which is the institutional Monarch, nor the person of the Monarch, who reigns but does not rule, can be overlooked. For the institution of the Crown is in theory the source of all the powers of government. And the Queen still has important functions to fulfill in the total process of public affairs.

The Monarch as a Symbol. Under the British Constitution the Monarch is the head of the British state. To the Queen all British subjects owe allegiance. The Queen is also accepted as the head and the unifying symbol of the Commonwealth of Nations.[28] But even more importantly, all government is conducted in the name of the Crown.[29]

Prerogatives of the Monarch. In accordance with constitutional practice, the Monarch names as Prime Minister the leader of the majority party, or, on the advice of party leaders, the person best able to form a government.[30] Other ministers are appointed on the Prime Minister's nomination.[31] Parliament is summoned and dissolved by the Monarch on the advice of the Prime Minister. As the head of state, the Monarch receives the credentials of the heads of other states. With the advice and consent of the Cabinet, or upon its request, the Monarch may pay state visits to other countries, as did King George VI to France in 1938 and to Canada and the United States in 1939, and Queen Elizabeth to many states in 1953–1954. The Monarch may engage in official conversations with the heads of foreign states or their envoys in the presence

[28] Although India is a member of the Commonwealth, being a republic it does not accept the Queen as its reigning or ruling head. See p. 386 below for further discussion of the Commonwealth.

[29] See R. V. Langford, *British Foreign Policy, Its Formulation in Recent Years* (Washington, 1942), ch. 1.

[30] Coalition and minority Governments have been fairly numerous since 1895, so that the Monarch's power of choice has occasionally been more than empty formality.

[31] A story appeared in the press some time ago that in 1945 the King suggested to Mr. Attlee the appointment of Mr. Bevin as Foreign Secretary in place of another proposed nominee. The Labor Prime Minister publicly denied the event, for he could not admit that he had not taken full responsibility for his list.

of the Prime Minister. But "the power to initiate or to obstruct a foreign policy" has long since passed beyond the reach of the Monarch to the Cabinet, in conformity with the long-time accepted concept of limited constitutional monarchy.[32]

The British Monarch has a right to be kept informed of foreign policy, and is sent the important diplomatic and state papers. The Queen is notified of the Cabinet agenda, of policy decisions taken by the Cabinet, of executive orders issued under the imprint of the Privy Council, of reports of the Chiefs of Staff Committee, and of acts pending and passed by Parliament—to which royal assent is given—but usually after Cabinet decision has been reached. Thus, in a sense, it may be said that the Queen "is better informed than the average Cabinet Minister on matters which are brought before the Cabinet." [33]

The British Monarch has "the right to be consulted, the right to encourage, and the right to warn," as Walter Bagehot once remarked. A Cabinet with a parliamentary majority would be in a position to precipitate a serious political crisis by resigning, if a Monarch ever took the unlikely course of being obstinate. Of this Britain's Monarchs are quite aware. But it is also quite true that the views of the ruler, who is after all the symbolic ruler of all the British people and who is above party strife, deserve and are given the most respectful attention when vouchsafed to the Prime Minister.

Actions in the Name of the Crown. Every statute passed by Parliament is enacted "by the Queen's most Excellent Majesty, by and with the advice and consent" of Parliament and by authority of the same. Executive orders are issued "by the Crown" through the Executive Committee of the Privy Council. The "Speech from the Throne" opening each session of Parliament sets forth the Cabinet's policy for that session, but it is read by Her Majesty. British armed forces are in the service of the Crown and act in its name. Foreign relations are conducted in the name of the Crown. Treaties are concluded in the name of the Crown. War is declared in its name and by its authority. All these actions are in fact decided by the Prime Minister and the Cabinet. The authority of the Crown, however, as the embodiment of British sovereignty is given to them.[34]

Thus, it can be seen that the Sovereign as a person, and the "bundle of executive powers" formerly exercised by the Monarch but now held in the Crown as a symbol and institution, occupy an important place in the process of British policy decision and action.

[32] Ward and Gooch, *The Cambridge History of British Foreign Policy* (New York, 1923), III, p. 615.
[33] Jennings, *Cabinet Government*, p. 327.
[34] On treaty making see Robert B. Stewart, *Treaty Relations of the British Commonwealth of Nations* (New York, 1939).

PUBLIC OPINION AND FOREIGN POLICY

Sensitivity to Public Opinion. Although British Governments are on the whole remarkably sensitive to public opinion, this does not mean that governmental policy is always in complete accord with popular sentiment or that a Cabinet may not remain in office for some time in the face of popular criticism.

In 1935 the Conservative party ran for election on a pledge to "do all in our power to uphold the Covenant and to maintain and increase the efficiency of the League." Yet the Government was no sooner in power than it undertook to avert the adoption of vigorous sanctions against Italy's aggression in Ethiopia and became party to an arrangement acceding to policies aiming to keep Mussolini friendly. When Foreign Secretary Sir Samuel Hoare entered into the ill-famed Hoare-Laval (France) accord to settle the Italo-Ethiopian war by giving Mussolini control of two-thirds of Ethiopia after his attack upon that country, a storm of protest swept the British Isles. So violent was this outburst that the Government was forced to repudiate the agreement. Sir Samuel Hoare resigned, stating that "it is essential for the Foreign Secretary, more than any other Minister in the country, to have behind him the general approval of his fellow-countrymen," and since he did not have it he should withdraw. Rather than resigning *en masse,* however, the remainder of the Cabinet continued in office. So strong was the Cabinet's control over its large majority in Parliament that the episode did not change the principal line of the Baldwin Government's policy of seeking to prevent League action against Italy which might lead to military sanctions or war. However, public opinion had clearly forced the Government to change its open stand on appeasing the aggressor.[35]

A Government with a strong following may at times evade expression of public opinion on certain foreign-policy issues. From 1933 to 1935 Prime Minister Stanley Baldwin refused to make rearmament an election issue even though the Cabinet was aware of the significance of what Hitler was starting to do in Germany. This was done because Baldwin believed that the Conservative Government would be defeated if it went to the country on an adequate armaments issue in view of the pacifist sentiment in England at that time.[36]

It is not always easy for British public opinion to be effective on questions of foreign affairs owing to the complexity of international politics. Moreover, public sentiment itself is seldom altogether clear and united. Nevertheless, it is an important fact in helping British opinion to become articulate that most people read one of about half a dozen major dailies with nation-wide circula-

---

35 See *House of Commons Debates,* vol. 307, 5th ser., pp. 2012, 2030–2031.
36 Jennings, *British Constitution,* p. 203. Light is thrown on Chamberlain's belief that defense should be made an election issue in Feiling's *Life of Neville Chamberlain, op. cit.*

tion. If the electorate is not satisfied with the Government's foreign policy, it does not hesitate to make its sentiment vocal through the press and correspondence with members of Parliament. This may precipitate a change. On the other hand, if the Government has a powerful grip upon Parliament, the only recourse may be to vote the Government out at the next national election, which may occur as much as five years after the last. In the last fifty years public opinion has reversed many policies.

CONCLUSION ON POLICY MAKING WITHIN BRITAIN

United vs. Divided Responsibility. The outstanding characteristic of the British mechanism for policy making is the single line of power and responsibility for initiation, execution, and control which runs from party leadership through Parliament to the Cabinet and back to Parliament in a system of popular representative government. In the words of Bagehot, "The Cabinet is a combining committee—a *hyphen* which joins, a *buckle* which fastens, the legislative part of the state to the executive part of the state." [37]

Not only is there an inseparable tie between Parliament and the Executive, but all policy-making power is centered in a group of officers of state who can be held accountable at any time if their policy does not meet with the approval of the elected representatives of the people. On the whole, the Cabinet is able to control Commons in most policy matters. The British Prime Minister has at his call tremendous powers. But the House of Commons can turn upon a Government and force it to change its policy. A deadlock does not go on for years over policy as it can between the Congress and the Executive in Washington. The British system thus avoids one of the difficulties which can encumber policy making and policy control in a political system which enforces separation of powers and division of responsibility between separately elected executive and legislative branches of government.

The Importance of Attitudes and Party Discipline. The smooth operation of the British system, which distinguishes it from parliamentary government in some states of Europe, does not spring merely from the organic structure of British government. It results in part from the vigorous two-party relationship which ordinarily prevails in the United Kingdom and which provides a majority single-party government as well as offering the electorate a clear choice of alternatives. It is due also to the sophisticated sense of public trusteeship which those attaining Cabinet position have held. It is the product of a spirit of tolerance and fair play which is an outlook of mind rather than the consequence of any institutional arrangement. It is also the result of a strong attitude of respect for law and order.

[37] *The English Constitution* (Boston, 1873), p. 79.

These factors have kept party controversy within bounds. But perhaps above all, the effectiveness of parliamentary government in Britain has been due to strong party discipline, which on the whole has succeeded in insisting that members follow party leadership and policy decisions.[38]

Agreement on Fundamentals. General agreement among the British people on many of the fundamentals of foreign policy has also contributed to a substantial degree of continuity in British foreign policy through successive Cabinets and party alignments. English people generally are aware of the need for keeping the sea lanes open for the importation of food and raw materials required to make up the great deficiencies within the British Isles. They recognize the necessity of policies that will secure world markets for Britain's industrial products. Public sentiment is conscious of the need for adequate defense of the narrow space separating Britain from the Continent, and for defending the approaches to the Channel in Western Europe against any aggressor who would establish hegemony over the Continent and the approaches to the Empire routes. The British people generally also attach importance to partnership with America, and currently to the North Atlantic Treaty Organization. With an Empire and Commonwealth scattered around the globe and dependent in part upon Britain for protection, and at the same time vital for Britain's economic livelihood and defense, there is broad support for policies toward Europe which allow Britain sufficient leeway to meet its obligations toward the Empire and Commonwealth.

There have been differences in the degree of support given in the past to international organization, as between the Labor and Conservative parties toward the League of Nations from 1924 to 1940. But throughout the public there has been general conviction that Britain not only should be a Member of the United Nations, as previously of the League, but that it should pursue a strong and active policy within the organization. Likewise, there have been variations in attitudes on the relationships which Britain should have with certain states. Conservatives and Laborites have differed on relations with the Soviet regime. But the responsible leaders of both parties have opposed Soviet moves threatening strategic areas vital to the protection of Britain's world-wide position and interests.

Since World War II there has been awareness of Britain's diminished power and vulnerable economic position. Reluctantly, public opinion has acknowledged the need for foreign economic assistance where formerly Britain had been the "banker of the world." At the same time there is no doubt that all shades of public opinion have yearned for economic and financial independence, regardless of practical necessities.

[38] See Jennings, *Cabinet Government,* ch. 15; also his *Parliament,* chs. 5–6.

Notwithstanding some differences, there has been a large measure of continuity in British foreign policy, as successive Governments have adapted their own party views to the broad pattern of historic British policy.[39] This has been supported by a measure of agreement that party differences should "end at the water's edge" and by consultation between the leaders of Government and of Opposition when international crises demand a united front from the nation. In such situations the attitudes of tolerance, mutual respect, and fair play which have characterized British parliamentary government have produced a national strength in foreign affairs.

FORMULATION OF POLICY IN THE BRITISH COMMONWEALTH

No discussion of British foreign policy would be complete without some reference to the Commonwealth of Nations. For British policy places considerable emphasis upon maintaining and strengthening the ties with the Commonwealth countries. Concerted action by the Commonwealth countries can be and often is an important factor in international politics.

Composition of the Commonwealth. The Commonwealth of Nations is a unique concert of independent states, all formerly parts of the British Empire. It is not a glorified empire but "a free association" of states held together by common bonds and interests.

The membership of the Commonwealth today comprises the United Kingdom, Australia, Canada, Ceylon, India, Pakistan, New Zealand, and the Union of South Africa. Ireland was a member of the Commonwealth but ceased to act in concert with the group in 1939. Burma became independent in 1947 and chose not to remain in the Commonwealth. Plans are under way for British Malaya and for the Rhodesias in Africa to become members of the Commonwealth. In composition the Commonwealth is not static but evolutionary.

Relationships of Members. The basic relationships of the Commonwealth states to one another have been determined by a series of agreements, understandings, laws, and usages. The members of the Commonwealth are legally "equal in status" and "in no way subordinate to one another in any aspect of their domestic or external affairs." [40] None of the members of the Commonwealth is obligated to follow United Kingdom policy in world politics, although all mutually recognize the Queen (or King) as "the head" of the Common-

---

[39] See Paul Gore-Booth, *A History of the Labour Party from 1914* (London, 1948), pp. 371–382; L. D. Epstein, "The British Labor Left and U. S. Foreign Policy," *Am. Pol. Sci. Rev.*, Dec., 1951.

[40] Declaration adopted at 1926 Imperial Conference. The Statute of Westminster passed in 1931 embodied in British law the principles established by this declaration. See Stewart, *op. cit.*, pp. 28–42; also W. Y. Elliott, *The New British Empire* (New York, 1932); Heather Harvey, *Consultation and Cooperation in the Commonwealth* (Oxford, 1952).

wealth, and all are "freely associated" by bonds of tradition and historic kin-ship, by an interest in mutual defense, and by economic links.[41]

All the present members, except India which is a republic, accept the Queen as Queen of their land and "owe a common allegiance to the Crown." Except for India, all have a Governor-General who represents the Crown in their land. At the Conference of Commonwealth Premiers in 1949, following the attainment of independence by India, Pakistan, and Burma, and India's deci-sion to become a Republic with a President as head of the state, it was agreed that the Commonwealth could be maintained and adapted even though the ties binding India and other members are not identical. All, however, accept "the King as the symbol of the free association of its independent member nations and as such the Head of the Commonwealth." Accordingly, the governments of all the Commonwealth countries declared that "they remain united as free and equal members of the Commonwealth of Nations, freely cooperating in the pursuit of peace, liberty and progress." [42]

Such a recognition of the adaptability of the Commonwealth reveals the solidarity which can be created within this association of states by enlightened cooperation and diplomacy.[43]

Policy Formation. Concerted policy within the Commonwealth of Nations is formulated by a loosely organized system of conferences and consultations. The Prime Ministers of the member nations meet irregularly in Common-wealth Conferences. At these conferences matters of common interest, par-ticularly in the fields of trade, defense, and international organization, are discussed. Views are exchanged and lines of action agreed upon. But these gath-erings have no power to bind Commonwealth members. The Government of each Commonwealth state decides for itself whether and to what extent to accept these policy agreements.

Prime Ministers' conferences are supplemented by frequent exchanges among various Prime Ministers on regional or special questions and by confer-ences at the technical level. Additional policy agreements are arrived at by continual interchange of information among the governments. They are also assisted by frequent meetings between the High Commissioners representing each of the member states in the other states, and in London between these Commissioners and the Secretary of State for Commonwealth Relations. The

---

41 The measure of change that has taken place is indicated by the fact that in 1914 Britain declared war for each of the dominions; in 1939 each acted for itself, on its own volition.

42 Text of Declaration adopted in London, April 27, 1949, in *External Affairs*, Ottawa, May, 1949, p. 13.

43 Asked why India remained within the Commonwealth after the long struggle for independ-ence, Prime Minister Nehru replied: "We join the Commonwealth obviously because we think it is beneficial to us and to other causes in the world that we wish to advance." It may be noted that Nehru attended in person the coronation of Queen Elizabeth II.

development of common and complementary policies is further promoted by participation of representatives in the Imperial Defense Committee in London, and attendance by officers of the armed services at the British staff colleges and Imperial Defense College.

So far as logical policy-making and implementation machinery goes, the Commonwealth defies the rules of organization. It has no formally established Commonwealth organs as such, other than the Prime Ministers' conferences, and no Secretariat to carry through between conferences.

In essence, policy making in the Commonwealth is the product of continuous consultation on many levels among the governments of the member states. When a concerted policy effort is made by the members of the Commonwealth, this association can be a potent factor in world politics.[44]

COMPARATIVE PROCEDURE IN OTHER EUROPEAN PARLIAMENTARY DEMOCRACIES

The parliamentary form of government has been adopted in most Western European countries. Although the external forms have been copied, there are, as would be expected, numerous adaptations to meet local traditions and circumstances. A contrasting feature found in most of the continental countries, from Scandinavia to Italy, is the presence of an active multiparty situation in which instead of a single party in office and a single party in opposition, both Government and Opposition usually contain several competing parties. France is an outstanding example, having had a multiplicity of political parties holding seats in both the lower and upper houses of Parliament during the Third and Fourth Republics. But the same has been true, in varying degrees, in Belgium, the Netherlands, Germany, Italy, and the Scandinavian states.[45]

Coalition Governments. One of the frequent consequences of a multiparty situation is that no one political party is able to command an absolute majority in Parliament. As a result, Governments are often coalition affairs in which two or more parties combine to form the ministry. A Cabinet composed of leaders of several parties is continually subject to the strains of political competition. These may bring about the downfall of a Cabinet on almost any issue

[44] Useful works on the Commonwealth include W. K. Hancock, *A Survey of British Commonwealth Affairs*, 2 vols. (Oxford, 1937, 1942); W. I. Jennings, *The British Commonwealth of Nations* (New York, 1948); N. Mansergh, *The Commonwealth and the Nations* (London, 1948); J. A. R. Marriott, *The Evolution of the British Empire and Commonwealth* (London, 1938); H. M. Stationery Office, *Origins and Purpose: A Handbook on the Commonwealth of Nations* (London, 1949); J. Simmons, *From Empire to Commonwealth* (London, 1949). The quarterly review, *Round Table*, is devoted to articles and documents on current developments relating to the Commonwealth.

[45] Information on current party alignments may be found in the annual volumes of W. P. Mallory (ed.), *Political Handbook of the World* (New York); the *Statesman's Yearbook* (London); and *The World Almanac* (New York).

and at any time, rendering a Government impotent at some critical juncture in domestic or international affairs.

Coalition Governments are almost inevitably less stable than Cabinets composed of a single majority party where the two-party system prevails. France, for example, had seventeen ministries between November, 1945, and December, 1952, having an average life of four months, while Britain had only two.

Political Extremism. The competitions and conflicts among many parties make long-range foreign-policy planning difficult. Furthermore, swings to the left or right in national elections can produce significant changes in national policy if entirely different combinations of parties are empowered to take over the Government, as in Germany when the Nazis with Adolf Hitler replaced the Social Democratic coalition in 1933. The so-called "popular front" Governments, coalitions of the left which were formed in some European countries after liberation from the Nazis in 1944–1945, are a case in point. The Communist parties in France, Italy, Hungary, and Czechoslovakia attempted to use these coalitions to acquire key posts in order to seize full power in time of crisis. Their objectives were realized by the communist coups in Hungary and Czechoslovakia in 1947 and 1948. In France and Italy, the more moderate elements, with economic and psychological assistance from abroad, were able to prevent such action.

Parties that always remain minorities never having to assume complete responsibility for governing the nation, or guiding its foreign relations, can easily fall into irresponsible attitudes. Factional groups may resort to high-pressure tactics to impel a Government into extravagant or uncompromising stands on foreign issues to the ultimate detriment of the nation. Although the multiparty system is, of course, not the only cause of political extremism, it can and does contribute to it. Rational policy decisions cannot be taken where parliamentary proceedings are kept in an uproar or where intolerance leads to the suppression of freedom of criticism and democratic opposition.

One of the unfortunate results that follow from a situation in which no one party ever has a clear majority and parties are tempted to adopt uncompromising positions is that it may become exceedingly difficult at times to form a Government. This has occurred in France at a time when a Big Three conference was urgently needed and scheduled. Even when the National Assembly does finally accept a candidate, he may have to make his policy declaration so vague as to be almost meaningless. Situations can arise in which a Government is little more than a "caretaker" until the political situation clarifies sufficiently to permit formation of another ministry.

The rise of dictatorships cannot be attributed solely to the existence of multiparty conditions. But in some cases such conditions have formed a part of the seed-bed in which dictatorship has been nurtured.

Continuity of Policy. The maintenance of continuity in the foreign policy of states having a multiparty Parliament is a difficult task when party conflicts bring about frequent changes in ministries. There are factors present in most countries, however, which alleviate these tendencies toward instability.

If successive Governments are formed by similar coalitions of center parties, for example, changes in policy from one ministry to another may not be great. Portfolios may be shuffled and the basis of cooperation modified by new bargaining, but the same individuals, or at least representatives of the same groups, will appear in succeeding ministries. In the seventeen ministries formed in France from 1945 to 1952, for example, three men held the Ministry of Foreign Affairs—Georges Bidault, Léon Blum, and Robert Schuman. Between 1925 and 1933 there were extended periods when Aristide Briand was Foreign Minister throughout several Cabinets.

The existence of a strong corps of permanent civil servants in the Foreign Office and other ministries contributes to continuity in foreign affairs. Ministers who are basically politicians must rely heavily upon these experts. Some measure of their stature in France is indicated by the fact that the heads of the various divisions in the Foreign Office have had from ten to twenty years' experience in that department.

Finally, popular agreement upon certain basic national interests which transcend politics limits the variations in policy which would otherwise result from party differences. With the exception of the extreme interests represented by communist or neo-fascist elements, parties are not likely to be divided on the basic questions of independence, territorial integrity, and national defense. Even when these factors are taken into account, however, the formulation of foreign policy in a country having a multiparty Parliament, where no one party has a clear majority, does suffer a measure of uncertainty due to the instability of coalition groupings, the shifting of voting which accompanies the competition for power within Parliament, and the relatively short life of ministries.

Comparison of Parliamentary Control in France. The provisions for parliamentary control over foreign-policy formulation in France are especially interesting, since French Cabinets have been particularly subject to the stresses of multiparty Government. In addition, they are limited by an unusual degree of parliamentary control. Under the Constitution of the Fourth Republic, the individual invited by the President to form a Cabinet (the Council of Ministers) must first appear before the National Assembly (lower house) for a vote of confidence on his general policies. This insures parliamentary supervision of the broad outlines of Government policy at an early stage.

When the Premier has won a vote of confidence, he must then try to form a ministry which, under present political conditions, is a coalition. This slate in turn must be submitted to the Assembly for approval. As a result, the Assembly may, after approving a Premier, postpone or prevent effective government action by rejecting his ministry. While this requirement may give the Assembly more direct control over the Cabinet than is possible in Britain, it can cause or prolong a governmental crisis and open the door to agitation by extremist groups.

Finally, the principle that ministers may be held individually as well as collectively responsible for their policies—which is followed in France and some other continental states—tends to provide somewhat greater parliamentary control over a Cabinet than is the case in Britain. On major issues, however, the Cabinet is ordinarily held collectively responsible. Foreign-policy questions are usually so important that an adverse vote upon them will precipitate a general Cabinet crisis.

Conclusion. In the multiparty states the formulation and conduct of foreign policy are especially sensitive to fluctuations in the domestic political barometer. This policy is likely to undergo gyrations at more frequent intervals than is normally the case in a two-party situation where one party usually has a working majority in Parliament for from four to six years—the intervals between national elections.

The saving feature in most multiparty states is that there is generally accord based on broad foundational principles of national policy among the supporters of the various political elements which normally come and go in the successive ministries. In France there may be sharp differences among the various centrist parties on details of domestic and foreign policy, but there is general accord on the principle that France should cooperate with the Western nations in NATO and in the United Nations, and that Germany should be prevented from becoming a military menace to Western Europe. In Italy, likewise, there are great differences between extreme left and right on Italian relations with Russia and the West, but most moderate elements have been in accord on the principle that Italy should seek to regain Trieste and should maintain close associations with the NATO powers. In Sweden the socialist elements which have controlled the Government have differed from other parties on the question of neutrality versus alignment with the NATO powers, but all save the Communists are in accord on a policy of vigorous resistance to Russian encroachments. Multiparty conditions further complicate the operation of parliamentary democracy. But on the whole the formulation and conduct of policy proceed along lines generally similar to those we have noted in Britain.

SUGGESTED READINGS

F. T. Ashton-Gwatkin, *The British Foreign Service* (Syracuse, 1950).

Walter Bagehot, *The English Constitution* (London, 1925).

Herman Beukema and associates, *Contemporary Foreign Governments* (3d ed., New York, 1953).

P. W. Buck and J. W. Masland, *The Governments of Foreign Powers* (rev. ed., New York, 1950).

Sir Winston Churchill, *The Second World War* (Boston, 1949–1953), vols. 2–6.

Edward M. Earle (ed.), *Modern France, Problems of the Third and Fourth Republics* (Princeton, 1951).

J. E. Howard, *Parliament and Foreign Policy in France* (London, 1948).

Sir Ivor Jennings, *Cabinet Government* (2d ed., Cambridge, 1951).

———. *The British Commonwealth of Nations* (New York, 1948).

R. V. Langford, *British Foreign Policy* (Washington, 1942).

Nicholas Mansergh, *The Commonwealth and the Nations* (London, 1948).

F. A. Ogg and R. Zink, *Modern Foreign Governments* (New York, 1951).

S. K. Padover, *French Institutions: Values and Politics.* Hoover Institute Studies, Ser. E, No. 2 (Stanford, 1954).

F. H. Soward, *The Changing Commonwealth* (Toronto, 1950).

H. M. Stout, *British Government* (New York, 1953).

CHAPTER XIV

The Bases and Formation of Soviet Foreign Policy

FEW ASPECTS of international affairs arouse more concern throughout the world than the foreign policy of the Soviet Union. While Russian policies have long been a disturbing element in international politics, they have seldom before appeared to threaten the political independence and security of so many states as they do at present.

Soviet policy is often baffling because of the veil of secrecy and the recourse to deceptive moves with which the Soviet leaders constantly shroud their thinking and action. Policy is not made in an environment of publicity such as attends government in the Western democracies. Nor is it subject to constant harassment by public debate and criticism in the press, the legislature, and among the people. Foreign Minister Vyacheslav Molotov once remarked that the Soviet Union need not be studied since "everybody who can read and write can understand it." To most people, however, Winston Churchill's famous characterization of it as "a riddle, wrapped in mystery and enclosed within an enigma," more nearly describes the general feeling about Soviet policy. The difficulty of obtaining accurate information about Soviet affairs is another contributory factor. For as Paul Winterton, Moscow correspondent of the *London News Chronicle,* has remarked: "There are no experts on the Soviet Union; there are only varying degrees of ignorance."

BASIC APPROACHES

Soviet foreign policy, like that of other states, is a composite of numerous underlying factors. Certain features of the Russian environment exercise an influence upon behavior and outlook. Political traditions and historical experiences, differing from those of the West, condition policy thinking. The attitudes, personalities, and relationships of the Soviet leaders play an important part. Finally, the ideological concepts of Marxism-Leninism-Stalinism, which

393

are accepted and propagated by the Soviet Government and the Communist party, contribute their specific share to Soviet policy direction and formation.

ENVIRONMENTAL FACTORS

Geophysical Features. The most elemental geophysical factor in the case of the USSR is that it is a country of tremendous land space extending from Eastern Europe to the Pacific Ocean, a distance of 4,500 miles, and from the Arctic Ocean to the Himalaya Mountains and the borders of the Middle East and South Asia. All told, the Soviet empire comprises more than eight million square miles. Much of this land is still frontier territory especially in Siberia and Central Asia.

One of the prominent features connected with this vast land mass is the great plain which extends from the borders of Poland to Central Asia, inter- rupted only by the narrow spine of the Ural Mountains. Actually this is an eastward extension of the great North European plain which begins at the English Channel. Although the frozen Arctic shields most of the Soviet north- land from hostile sea power—though perhaps not from transpolar air power— and the mountain masses guard its southern borders, the flat and open plains of the Western flank have for more than three centuries provided avenues of invasion for the armies of Poland, Sweden, Turkey, France, and Germany.

Sitting astride the Eurasian land mass, the USSR occupies one of the most important strategic positions in the Northern Hemisphere. It has direct land connection with interior lines of communication with Central Europe, the Middle East, Central and South Asia, China, and Korea. In the South it is but a short distance from the Mediterranean world and from the subcontinent of India. In the Northwest it shadows Scandinavia and reaches toward the North Sea. In the Northeast its fingers stretch to within sight of Japanese and Ameri- can territory. Its Arctic holdings verge on the polar region. This is the "heart- land" which geopolitical writers have warned might one day be able to domi- nate the "world island" and threaten the globe.[1]

One of the features associated with the geophysical characteristics of the USSR is that although the Soviet domain touches the Arctic and the Pacific Oceans, and also the Baltic and Black Seas, the peoples of the USSR have often been reminded that, in effect, their country is a landlocked state. Nearly all their principal ports are icebound for a part of the year. The exits from most of their ports lie through narrow straits that have historically been com- manded by foreign powers which have not always been friendly.

A further point worthy of note is that nature has supplied the USSR with a large store of natural resources, rivaling or surpassing that of the United

[1] See ch. ii, section on geopolitics.

States. In basic raw materials the country has sufficient supplies to support one of the world's major industrial complexes. Moreover, its agricultural lands, with further development, are capable of sustaining a population well in excess of its present approximately 200 million. Although the USSR has shortages in a few raw materials essential for total war, it has been able to make up some deficiencies by international trade and through extension of communist rule abroad.

Power-Weak Neighbors. One of the notable features associated with the geopolitical position of the USSR is that from the Baltic Sea southeastward and around its Asiatic periphery it is adjoined by alien peoples whose countries have for the most part in the past rated relatively low in the scale of military potential. In modern times the establishment of Japanese power on the Far Eastern mainland after defeating Russia in the Russo-Japanese War in 1905, communist China's recent emergence as a military power, and Turkey's military renaissance, may be considered exceptions. Many of the peoples adjacent to the USSR have been suspicious of Russian imperialism and have at one time or another opposed Russia in world politics. This comparatively power-weak area surrounding the USSR has been a temptation to Russian expansionists. It has also attracted foreign powers for political, economic, or strategic reasons, or for the creation of buffer zones. In this process struggles and tensions have repeatedly arisen between Russia and other powers.

Eastern Orientation. Following in part from its very size and remoteness from Western Europe, with only the most difficult communications between Moscow and the Western capitals until less than a century ago, and separated from the West by the alien peoples and territories of Central and Eastern Europe, the political and cultural life of Russia has developed quite differently from that of Europe. Both physically and culturally, the Russian peoples were cut off from the intellectual and social movements of the Renaissance, the Reformation, the French Revolution, and nineteenth-century liberalism which have fashioned much of the thinking and outlook of the West. In addition, of course, the schism between the Orthodox and the Roman Churches has tended to magnify the separation between East and West.

Effects of Environment. The distances separating Russia from the main streams of other civilizations may explain something of the provincial, self-centered, antiforeign attitudes displayed at various times by the Russians. To most of the inhabitants of the Russian domain, foreign affairs are far removed from the urgencies of daily existence.

It is apparent that in a country of the size and geographical complexity of the USSR, with its ethnically heterogeneous population of some 180 national groups speaking as many as 125 different native languages, unity is not easily achieved.[2] Only by a most vigorous policy can such a dispersed and mixed population be held together and mobilized behind a single national effort. This handicap may explain in part why Russian governments have in the past felt the need to employ autocratic methods, and why much propaganda has been expended by the Soviet Government to convince the Soviet peoples of threats of "capitalist encirclement," "fascist imperialism," and supposed sinister designs by foreign nations to destroy the "socialist state." Some may argue that these conditions give Russia's rulers a feeling that they are "riding a tiger" and account for the police state methods, suspicion, secrecy, and a basic caution in international affairs such as that displayed during the thirties.

On the other hand, the vastness of empire, abundance of resources, size of manpower, and strategic position have at times exercised a reverse effect upon Russian governments. They have given the Russian rulers, Czarist or Soviet, the power and position to follow foreign policies predicated upon strength. At times, when Russia's military strength has existed as latent rather than immediately effective potential, she has courted and suffered disaster. Owing to the industrialization, education, military training, and national regimentation which the Soviet regime has been pressing in recent years, a state of vastly greater national power is now being created. This development may give further encouragement to the Kremlin to try to "lead from strength" in international affairs. It is necessary, however, to bear in mind that the industrialization of the country and the development of agricultural and other resources will absorb a substantial portion of the national effort for some time to come. This development is required if the standard of living within the country is to be raised to a level approximating that projected by the Kremlin.

Its vast area has enabled the Russian state in the past to trade space for time in which to mobilize its strength when attacked by foreign nations. Russia followed this strategy in the Napoleonic campaign and in World Wars I and II. But the devastations suffered in its exposed yet immensely rich Byelo-Russian and Ukrainian lands have undoubtedly been one of the reasons impelling the successive Russian governments to push the existent national boundaries forward at every opportunity. This tendency has also been stimulated by the urge to secure possession of warm-water ports, and to gain, if possible, control of the straits leading from its landlocked harbors to the high seas. It has been further encouraged by the attraction presented by the power-weak lands surrounding Russia's borders, and the desire to prevent other Great Powers from gaining ascendancy in these areas from which they might sometime be able to threaten the Russian home land.

2 On the Soviet population see Frank Lorimer, *The Population of the Soviet Union: History and Prospects* (Geneva, 1946); Edward Crankshaw, *Russia and the Russians* (New York, 1948), pp. 57–90.

RUSSIAN ATTITUDES

In addition to the factors of physical environment, national attitudes of mind have a bearing on a country's foreign policy. Obviously it is not possible to characterize in a few words the qualities of mind of an empire of 200 million people so diverse in composition as the Soviet Union without resorting to meaningless stereotypes. Even the "Soviet man," living within the matrix of a highly regimented society, has many variable qualities. One complex state of mind has been fairly constant, however, among Russian officials. This is a certain ambivalence in attitudes toward the West.

Suspicion of West. On the one hand, suspicion of the West and opposition to many of its policies and social institutions has deep roots in Russian history.[3] These attitudes may be traced in part to the reasons given above with respect to Russia's eastward orientation. Russia's exclusion from the emergent community of states in the fifteenth and early sixteenth centuries, and its later political isolation from 1917 to the 1930's, have contributed to these attitudes. The invasions and interventions from the West, as well as the long struggle for mastery over Eastern Europe and the Middle East, have also left a legacy of suspicion and hostility toward Western Powers.

Attraction to Western Ideas and Methods. On the other hand, Western ideas and methods have intermittently had a strong attraction for Russian intellectuals, and for Soviet as well as Czarist rulers.[4] Peter the Great is known as the first "Westernizer" of Russia. Catherine the Great was influenced by the ideas of the French Enlightenment. In the nineteenth century concepts of the French Revolution, though anathema to the government, attracted members of the intellectual class. The Marxist base of Soviet ideology is of Western origin. Finally, the Soviet Government has endeavored to introduce the techniques of modern large-scale production, heavy industry, and diversified economy which have been uniquely Western in their origin and perfection. "Bourgeois capitalist" ideas are violently rejected and the Russian individual is carefully shielded from their impact. Yet the Kremlin planners strive, with all the methods of the police state at their command, to obtain for the Soviet Union the benefits which Western ideas and institutions have created.

Implications of Basic Factors. Taking its various characteristics into account, it is apparent that the forces of the Russian physical and intellectual environment, the economic and social conditions of the people, and the experiences of history move the Russian leaders to approach international affairs from a viewpoint wholly different from that of the West. It is difficult to

[3] See U. K. Riasanovsky, *Russia and the West in the Teaching of the Slavophiles* (Cambridge, 1952).

[4] See Max M. Laserson, *Russia and the Western World* (New York, 1945).

evaluate the Soviet viewpoint in Western terms. Nevertheless, it must be constantly appraised if the Western states are to cope effectively with the policies of the Soviet Union—both as they affect their own security and as they may be designed to subvert or conquer other parts of the world.

THE POLITICAL SYSTEM

The Tradition of Absolutism. One of the basic factors affecting the determination of Soviet policy is the absolutist nature of the government. This is not new in Russian political life. Government has been autocratic or absolutist in nature throughout a large portion of Russian national history. For generations policies have been made by authorities far removed from the people, in what—from the Western point of view—were strictly nondemocratic ways. Although the period from 1905 to 1914 witnessed some progress toward constitutional government and although the Soviet Government itself promulgated in 1936 a Constitution sprinkled with seemingly democratic concepts, Russian foreign policy has traditionally been determined and shaped by a tightly closed circle of officials in the capital.[5] Since 1919, general policy making—including the guidance and final determination of foreign policy—has been the domain of the Politbureau, supplanted in 1953 by the Presidium.

Pervasive Influences of Communist Party. The dominant political force behind Soviet foreign policy is unquestionably the power of the Communist party leadership. The latter permeates every phase of society in the USSR. It is the controlling agent in the policy-making mechanism. It is the organizing, integrating, and directing force of all aspects of Soviet life.[6]

Economic and social undertakings which in a Western democracy would be based primarily upon private initiative are in Russia planned and governed by the party. Industry and trade are monopolized by the government in accordance with the precepts of Marxism and Leninism. Maintaining its hold over the people by means of a tightly organized and highly disciplined party structure, a large propaganda organization, and a vast secret police force, the Communist party is able to gear the productive activity of the Soviet Union to the goals of the state as determined by the leaders in the Kremlin.[7]

5 See Michael Karpovich, *Imperial Russia,* 1801–1907 (New York, 1932) for an excellent account of the prerevolutionary era. See also Sir Bernard Pares, *Russia* (New York, 1943); B. H. Sumner, *A Short History of Russia* (New York, 1949). The Constitution of the USSR as amended Feb. 25, 1947, was published in English by the Soviet Embassy *Information Bulletin* (Washington, 1947).

6 Merle Fainsod, "Post-War Role of the Communist Party," *Annals,* May, 1949, p. 20.

7 Alex Inkeles says the Soviet Government has "one of the largest and most complex public communications systems in the world," controlled by a "more elaborate and thorough" party apparatus than exists anywhere else. *Public Opinion in Soviet Russia* (Cambridge, 1950), p. 317. For discussion of the Soviet propaganda system see ch. xvi below.

The Soviet Union is a one-party state in which no political opposition is tolerated. The Supreme Soviet is the "Legislature" of the USSR. Executive ministries and a Council of Ministers serve as official agents of executive power. There are courts. But all political institutions are subordinate to party control and leadership. The party Presidium is the central directing body over the party hierarchy, extending from Moscow to the most remote village and over the entire machinery of government. The vital issues relating to the Soviet state are referred to it. It provides a direct interlocking relationship between Soviet policy and diplomacy on the one hand, and the world communist movement on the other. There is no appeal and must be no deviation from its directives.

Everything thus is guided by the party—organizations, large sectors of private life, industry, army, national policy. Far from finding it reprehensible, the Soviet leaders are proud of this system. "The highest expression of the leading role of the Party, here in the Soviet Union . . . ," said Stalin, "is the fact that not a single important political or organizational question is decided by our Soviet and other mass organizations without the guiding directions from the Party." [8] This control is exercised by a party with a formal membership in the USSR of approximately 6 million out of the 200 million inhabitants.[9]

Significance for Policy-Making Process. In the Soviet system, foreign policy can be made and carried out without being affected positively or negatively by private international contacts, by a free expression and exchange of ideas, by citizen participation—save in the most generalized manner in support of the government's views—or by the challenges of a political opposition, which are basic components of the political process in democratic states.

This situation enables the Kremlin to pursue its policy with little fear of internal checks. It permits the formulation and conduct of foreign policy in secret, keeping from the people whatever the leaders see fit and releasing for public consumption statements that cannot be disputed or readily verified at home. This technique makes it possible to mobilize mass opinion at will, to screen the Soviet populace from ideas which the Kremlin abhors, and to withhold from them facts that are not to its liking. The Soviet leaders are in a position of tactical advantage in dealing with most foreign powers, since they can appeal through the press to foreign peoples who can exercise a major influence on their leaders. At the same time, they tend to view the motives of others from preconceptions and interpretations based on influences which they are

8 J. Stalin, *Problems of Leninism* (Eng. trans., 1940), p. 73.
9 There are said to be an additional 900,000 candidates for membership.

not forced to question. Their political environment can lead them into dangerous pitfalls abroad. These elemental facts need to be borne in mind by others
as they are confronted with the Soviet world and must deal with it.

ROOTS OF RUSSIAN FOREIGN POLICY

Soviet foreign policy springs from two basic sources. In the first place, it
reaches back into the historic interests and attitudes of Russia with respect to
the lands and seas near its domain. Secondly, it issues from the Marxist-
Leninist-Stalinist ideology espoused by the Soviet leaders and the Communist
party. Both are present in varying degrees in Soviet policy.

THE UNION OF SOVIET SOCIALIST REPUBLICS

FIGURE XIV:1

Historical Interests. The persistent historical interests of the Russian state,
whether Czarist or Soviet, can be described under two main categories—
namely, those of defense and those of expansive penetration.[10]

Defense against Invasion. The "open" geographic border of Russia in the
West as well as its vulnerability through the approaches of the Black Sea have
impelled generations of Russian statesmen to espouse policies having as their
goal the protection of these boundaries. Mindful of the repeated invasions of
Russian lands, and remembering especially the two German invasions during
the World Wars of the twentieth century and the Polish invasion in 1920,

10 See Julian Towster, "Russia: Persistent Strategic Demands," *Current History*, July, 1951.

Soviet foreign policy has inherited a deep concern for avoiding a repetition of such disasters.

In the Far East, history has provided a comparable lesson and task. The ruinous invasions of the Russian heartland by the Mongols in historic times, the decisive Russian defeat by the Japanese in 1904–1905, and the Japanese conquests of Manchuria and China in the 1930's and 1940's are lessons which make the government in Moscow wary of any accumulation of hostile power on the Far Eastern border.

These essentially defensive considerations springing out of historical experiences have left a deep concern for security in Russian minds. The expansive aspects of Russian and Soviet policy are consistent with, and contribute to alleviating, this concern. Penetration and control or incorporation of bordering areas serve the threefold purpose of improved defense, expansion of Russian power, and communist advance.

Search for Warm-Water Outlets. The "imprisonment" of Russia within its landlocked state, has caused Russian diplomacy from the time of Peter the Great to seek warm-water outlets and ways of establishing Russian control over the Turkish Straits.

These considerations have underlain the persistent pressure upon Turkey in the nineteenth and twentieth centuries. Similar motivations, although there certainly were others, have also been behind Russian efforts to control a large share of the eastern Baltic shores which has now reached its height with the absorption of Estonia, Latvia, and Lithuania and the inclusion of most of the East Prussian littoral in the Soviet Union. Comparable aspirations can be adduced in explanation of the Soviet demands in 1945 for the return of the southern part of Sakhalin Island and the Kurile Islands from Japan, and for rights in the Chinese ports of Dairen and Port Arthur. Soviet interest in Korea has a background of imperialist desire to reach the Tsushima Straits.

At various times, Russian policy has also sought to penetrate oil-rich Iran and to reach toward the Persian Gulf and the Indian Ocean. In this instance it has met determined British resistance.[11]

Actually, the "warm-water outlet" argument is hardly logical in so far as concerns the procurement of a port on the Persian Gulf or Indian Ocean. Ports here would be of little commercial value to the USSR because of the difficult terrain and long hauls between ports in these areas and the heartland. Their accessibility for the importation of critical items from overseas allies in time of war, as demonstrated in the heavy flow of United States lend-lease

11 Professor G. P. Gooch considers this "urge toward warm-water ports" the "key to the foreign policy of Russia throughout the centuries." See G. P. Gooch, *Before the War, Studies in Diplomacy* (London, 1936), vol. 1, p. 28. See also R. J. Kerner, *The Urge for the Sea: The Course of Russian History* (Berkeley, 1942).

goods to Russia via the Persian Gulf and Iran during World War II is another matter. With its own wealth of natural resources, which, properly exploited, make it almost wholly self-dependent in the matter of basic economic needs, the USSR is not dependent upon the possession or use of these ports in time of peace. The argument for gaining them is not entirely logical, therefore, unless interpreted as a part of a long-range general expansion program.

Struggle for Power in Eastern Europe. Russian history has manifested a curious ambivalence with respect to Europe. Placed geographically in part in Europe, Russia has at times been reluctant to be of Europe. On the other hand, considerations of military security, prestige, and ambition have at some times impelled it to expand toward the heart of Europe and into the Balkan peninsula—into the territory inhabited by the Polish, Magyar, Rumanian, and smaller Baltic nations.

At the close of the eighteenth century, the Russian Czar participated with Prussia and Austria in partitioning Poland so that a large part of this country lay within the Russian domain. Although Russia was forced to relinquish these lands, together with the Baltic countries, for two decades after World War I, the Nazi-Soviet pacts of 1939–1940 divided Poland once more between Germany and Russia and permitted the latter to establish its defenses within and control over the Baltic Republics.[12] The Polish state was again re-established in 1945 with its *de facto* control shifted westward as far as the Oder in recompense for eastern lands taken by Moscow, but it was forced to become a satellite subject to strict control by the USSR. The forms of control have changed since the nineteenth century, but the substance of control and its motivation are what they were a hundred years ago—to make Poland a buffer for defense or an advance base for offensive policies against the West.[13]

Hungary and Rumania, holding the approaches to Central and Southeastern Europe, have also long been an object of Russian interests. During the nineteenth century Russian armies repeatedly marched through the territories of Rumania in their attempts to gain Constantinople and the Turkish Straits. The victorious advance of the Red Army into Central and Southeastern Europe in 1944–1945 resulted in Rumania, Hungary, and Czechoslovakia granting cessions of territory to the Soviet Union, and, in a short time, led to the establishment of communist governments and satellization of these states, together with Bulgaria. Albania, although not entered by Soviet forces, also became a com-

---

12 An account of the Nazi-Soviet negotiations will be found in Max Beloff, *The Foreign Policy of Soviet Russia, 1929–1941* (New York, 1949), vol. II, chs. 11–12. See also R. J. Sontag and J. S. Beddie (eds.), *Nazi-Soviet Relations, 1939–1941* (Washington, 1948); D. J. Dallin, *Soviet Russia's Foreign Policy, 1939–1942* (New Haven, 1943).

13 See Philip E. Mosely, "Aspects of Russian Expansionism," *Am. Slavic and East European Rev.*, Oct., 1948. See also M. M. Laserson, *cit. supra.*

munist satellite, and Yugoslavia followed the Moscow line until 1948 when Tito rejected Moscow control.[14]

Although Pan-Slavism—supported assiduously by the Czars in the nineteenth century—may not be an official part of Soviet policy, the underlying political aim of gaining predominant influence and control in Central and Southeastern Europe and the Balkans remains.[15] And Moscow's political ambitions reach toward the Adriatic Sea and the Mediterranean to outflank Greece and Turkey and ultimately force them into the Soviet orbit away from the influence of the West.[16] This goal seemed close at hand following World War II, when Albania and Yugoslavia were made Soviet satellites and communist forces seized large sections of Greece. But the defection of Yugoslavia and the victory of the anticommunist forces in the Greek civil war frustrated the Russian designs.

Interest in the Middle East. The Middle East also has long figured in Russian foreign policy aims. Territorial gains during the nineteenth century in South Central Asia and in the Trans-Caucasus region carried Russia to the borders of Afghanistan and into northern Persia, bringing her into close proximity to lands of vital significance to the British Empire. Suspicions of Russian ambitions in the direction of the Persian Gulf and of India led Britain to counter Russian moves in this area time and again in the nineteenth century. Faced with the rise of a mutual threat from Germany, Britain and Russia in 1907 negotiated a *modus vivendi,* recognizing Russian interests in northern Persia and British interests in the oil-rich south. In World War I and World War II, Russia and England found themselves on the same side and were able to concert their policies in Persia in the face of a common German threat.[17]

The termination of World War II witnessed a reappearance of the old conflict of interests when the USSR failed to withdraw its war-time troops from Northern Iran and sought to promote a communist revolt in Azerbaijan Province. United Nations pressure in the spring of 1946 finally prevailed, and the Soviet Union withdrew its forces. Since then Iran has been a storm center of crises exacerbated by the activities of the Soviet-supported Tudeh Party in Iran.[18] While the fall of the ultranationalistic Premier Mossadegh and the

14 See Y. Gluckstein, *Stalin's Satellites in Europe* (Boston, 1952).

15 For general background see G. Vernadsky, *Political and Diplomatic History of Russia* (Boston, 1936). The Soviet version of Russia's diplomatic history is set forth in V. P. Potemkin (ed.), *Histoire de la diplomatie,* 3 vols. (Paris, 1946–1947).

16 On the history of the Turkish Straits issue see Erik Bruel, *International Straits* (London, 1947), vol. II, pt. 4; J. T. Shotwell and F. Deak, *Turkey at the Straits* (New York, 1940); United States Dept. of State Publication No. 2752, *The Problem of the Turkish Straits* (Washington, 1947).

17 See B. H. Sumner, *Tsardom and Imperialism in the Far East and the Middle East, 1880–1914* (London, 1942); D. J. Dallin, *The Rise of Russia in Asia* (New Haven, 1949).

18 See George Lenczowski, *Russia and the West in Iran, 1918–1948: A Study in Big Power Rivalry* (Ithaca, 1949).

reinstatement of the constitutional rule of the Shah in 1953 momentarily relieved one of the most dangerous political situations, it would be premature to
conclude that Russian interests and aims in Iran, which are economic, political,
and strategic, have been relinquished. History has shown that Russian objectives have qualities both of durability and resiliency, irrespective of internal
changes within Russia, and that the Kremlin policy makers return to them
whenever an opportunity offers easy prospects of successful intervention.

That the Soviets would gain immeasurable advantage—and weaken the
West correspondingly—were they to succeed in establishing control over Iran
with its rich oil resources and its strategic position in the heart of the power-
weak Middle East, or even if they were merely to isolate it from the free
world, is not hard to fathom. A glance at a strategic map of the Middle East
should supply the reasons. Success in Iran would be a springboard for pressures along similar lines in the other strategic lands of this area—Iraq, Kuwait,
Saudi Arabia, Syria, Lebanon, Israel, and Jordan. These in turn could lead to
efforts to establish Soviet hegemony throughout this bridgeland, to encircle the
historic enemy, Turkey, to interrupt the British routes to India and the Orient,
and to reach the doorway to Africa.

Trend to the Far East. Being situated at the heart of the vast Eurasian land
mass, Russia for more than a century has striven for influence and a special
position in Asia and the Far East. Since the 1850's, Russia's rulers have striven
for land, power, and special privilege both in the Far Eastern littoral (that is,
the Far Eastern Provinces, the Kuriles, Kamchatka, Sakhalin, Korea) and in
China (especially Manchuria, Mongolia, Sinkiang).

From 1922 to 1927 the Soviets endeavored to win control of the Kuomintang party in China, and thereby of China itself. These initial efforts failed,
but when the communist armies of Mao-tse-Tung swept over China in 1949,
replacing Chiang Kai-shek with the Peiping communist regime, Soviet influence supplanted all other powers in China. The Soviet role in the recent
Korean War, however camouflaged, and its own and communist China's support of the communist forces in Indo-China, leave little doubt that Soviet
foreign policy aspires to further expansion of the communist revolution and
the power of Moscow in the seething areas of Asia's millions of inhabitants.[19]

Expansion Provided a Power Base. In 1939, the land mass encompassed
by the Soviet border was more than an adequate base for the protection of the
nation's security against anything short of an overwhelming military effort.
Hitlerite Germany and imperial Japan offered the only serious threats. The

19 On Russian policy with respect to the East see Sumner, *op. cit.;* D. J. Dallin, *Soviet Russia
and the Far East* (New Haven, 1948); Hu Shih, "China in Stalin's Grand Strategy," *Foreign
Affairs,* Oct., 1950; G. M. Friters, *Outer Mongolia and Its International Position* (Baltimore,
1950); Pauline Tompkins, *American-Russian Relations in the Far East* (New York, 1949).

subsequent destruction of the military power of those two countries, added to the guarantees spelled out in the Charter of the United Nations, left the USSR with a degree of security never before enjoyed. To the men in the Kremlin, however, the power vacuum left in Europe by Germany's collapse and its counterpart in the Far East provided the opportunities forecast in communist ideology. Expansionism became the order of the day. More, however, than the dictates of communist ideology were followed in the successive thrusts of Soviet communist power since 1945. During this time about 800 million people have been added to communist control. All of these, with some qualification as to China, have come under the close domination of the Kremlin.

The Soviet Union, like the imperialist Czardom, was maintaining a five-century record of expansion into areas of weakness. In so doing, it was in step with historic precedents of expansionism, the record of which shows that such drives are halted only when they encounter equal or greater force. Unless such precedents fail in this case, there is little reason to believe that the satisfaction of any specific Soviet territorial claim, however great, will serve any end other than her attainment of a more advanced base as a prelude to a further drive.

Difficulty Imposed upon Other Nations. It is the realization of these facts by the governments of the Western powers that makes it so difficult for them to enter into negotiations with the USSR for the adjustment of conflicting interests on the basis of merit alone.

Negotiations are rarely successful without some compromise and give-and-take. How to find any negotiating position and not at the same time strengthen the military and ideological potential of Soviet imperialism and world communism has become a serious dilemma for the statesmen of the free world.

Summary. To conclude our analysis of the historic roots of Russian foreign policy it may be noted that:

1. Since the relinquishment of Alaska in 1867, Russian expansion of overt political control has gravitated toward contiguous areas rather than seeking overseas, territorially unconnected lands. This has given it advantages in penetrating such lands and consolidating its rule.

2. The chief instruments of Russian expansionism have been diplomacy, political intrigue, and land armies. Since 1917 the communist apparatus has been an instrument of covert imperialism weakening established governments, urging their support of, and acquiescence to, Moscow, and seeking political control wherever opportunity offers. The great successes have come in the disruption after World War II, and particularly under the shelter of Soviet military occupation.

3. In its strategic moves in the contiguous areas of Europe and Asia, Russia has often been able to rely on friendly or ideologically sympathetic segments

of population in areas intended for domination. In this sense the nineteenth-century solicitude for the Orthodox Christians and the Pan-Slav movement in the Balkans and Central Europe has more recently been supplanted by the bonds of communism.

4. Russian leaders have shown capacity for biding their time for the attainment of long-range goals, waiting for periods of weakness or division among their opponents. They have on numerous occasions withdrawn in the face of concerted foreign opposition rather than assume the risk of a Great Power war against themselves.

5. Owing to the nature of its geographical position astride Europe and Asia and touching the Middle East, Russian policy has displayed a particular tendency to operate in two different territorial regions at a time. Opposition in one area does not necessitate the suspension of all activity, but merely the shifting of it to another theatre using interior lines of communication. The instances of Russia's Far Eastern expansion after its defeat in the Crimean War and the opposition of the powers in 1878, and of its recent successes in the Far East when successfully "contained" in Europe, provide telling examples. In this respect it is worth recalling that Bismarck once urged Russia to turn to the bountiful East in order to deflect its energies from being applied to the Eastern European neighborhood of Germany.[20]

6. Finally, a fact which should not be overlooked is that Russia, Czarist or Soviet, has nearly always had friends in Western Europe who believed that the West was treating the land of the Czars with excessive suspicion and injustice. This has been no less true in more recent times, and has had a bearing upon divisions within the West on policy toward Russian imperialism.

IDEOLOGY AND SOVIET FOREIGN POLICY

Communist Base. The statements of Soviet leaders, the phraseology of the Soviet Constitution, the exclusive and dominating role given to the Communist party, and Moscow's continual propagation of Marxist-Leninist doctrines since the Bolshevik Revolution in 1917 demonstrate that communist ideology occupies a prominent place in the policy, thinking, and action of Moscow. This is further substantiated by Moscow's encouragement and guidance of communist activities abroad and by its insistence that all its satellite countries must adopt communist regimes. It is also borne out in the flood of foreign propaganda which pours from Moscow's press and radio and that of its satellites.

The ideological premises held by the Soviet leaders and propagated by the

20 See Lt.-Cmdr. R. F. Colvile, R.N., "Russia's Foreign Policy—The Lessons of History," *Journal of the Royal United Service Institution*, Aug., 1950.

Communist party apparatus throughout the world are based primarily upon the writings and work of Karl Marx and Friedrich Engels, as expanded and modified by Vladimir Lenin and Joseph Stalin and the ruling clique of the communist hierarchy. There is no need to go into the details of this ideology. Its contents are generally known and it has been criticized in many readily available works.[21] Suffice it to call attention to the fact that its tenets embrace: (1) dialectical materialism; (2) economic determinism regarding the characteristics of society and politics; (3) the doctrine of class struggle with the violent overthrow of bourgeois states in order to establish the dictatorship of the proletariat; (4) the inevitability of conflict between socialism (that is, communism) and capitalism with the ultimate victory of communism; (5) the disintegration of the capitalist system through internal "contradictions," the rise of monopoly capitalism, imperialism, and war between the capitalist states; (6) the inevitability of world revolution modeled after Soviet experience and looking to its leadership; and (7) a belief that war is a prime cause of "revolutionary situations," weakening capitalism, which Communists can exploit and is therefore to be welcomed.

A vital part of the Soviet ideological doctrine is taken up with the strategy and tactics of revolutionary conspiracy for the overthrow of the noncommunist governments. Included in this are theories on the ebb and flow of the revolutionary movement, the exploitation of class differences and social weaknesses, the character of a revolutionary crisis and its manipulation for communist ends.[22]

Conflict vs. Coexistence. On several occasions Soviet leaders have declared that there is no reason why the USSR and the Western states cannot live together in "peaceful coexistence." Although such statements are primarily designed for foreign consumption, they pose a problem to the statesmen of the West. It is by no means certain whether they actually represent the convictions of the Soviet leadership, or whether they are merely tactical propositions designed to beguile the unthinking and gain time to allow the Soviet Union to consolidate its realm, to rearm, and to be ready to seize future opportunities when it might be better prepared to strike effectively at the West. Despite these conciliatory voicings, the idea of conflict, the continual charges of

[21] Doctrinal writings important in Soviet ideology include: Karl Marx and Friedrich Engels, *Communist Manifesto* (1848); V. I. Lenin, *State and Revolution* (1917) and *Imperialism, The Final Stage of Capitalism* (1917); Joseph Stalin and others, *History of the Communist Party of the Soviet Union* (Bolsheviks), (1939); and *Problems of Leninism* (1940). For critical appraisals of the Soviet ideology as it bears upon foreign policy see especially "X" (George Kennan), "The Sources of Soviet Conduct," *Foreign Affairs,* July, 1947; G. H. Bolsover, "Soviet Ideology and Propaganda," *Internat. Affairs,* April, 1948; Historicus, "Stalin on Revolution," *Foreign Affairs,* Jan., 1949.

[22] For an outstanding analysis of the doctrine on the strategy and tactics of revolution see the article by Historicus, cited above, pp. 183–192.

"capitalist encirclement" and of "war-mongering" by the Western Powers, and the imputation of fear of an imminent war have been fostered and continue to be used as justifications for the Soviet dictatorship and the exaction of heavy sacrifices from all within the Soviet orbit.[23] A basic and inescapable concept of international relations embodied in the Soviet ideology is one of continuous conflict.[24] It is little wonder that Western suspicions cannot be set at ease.

Influence of Ideology on Foreign Policy. There is a lack of complete agreement among experts on the degree of influence which the Marxist-Leninist-Stalinist ideology actually exercises upon Soviet foreign policy. Some authorities hold that the exigencies of power politics count more heavily with the Soviet leaders than ideology. Others believe that the ideological precepts exert a strong influence upon policy.[25]

Professor Max Beloff of England points out that, despite the publications which reach us from behind the Iron Curtain, we do not have at our disposal sufficient information to determine with any accuracy the nature and strength of the conflicting interests that without doubt are at work in the Kremlin. These are carefully veiled to the outside world. What we have are at best interpretations and intelligent estimates by outsiders.[26]

1. FACTORS AFFECTING RELATIONSHIP. Despite this situation, several things concerning the relationship of ideology and Soviet foreign policy are reasonably clear.

1. Soviet foreign policy embodies a combination of deep-seated historic territorial interests and Leninist-Stalinist ideological doctrines.
2. Proceeding upon the premise of continuing conflict between itself and the noncommunist world, Moscow follows policies anticipating the possibility of war.
3. Soviet fear for its own national security is closely related to the maintenance of the regime at home and to expansion of the communist system beyond Russia's borders. The ideological doctrine of inevitable conflict substantiates the fear of attack by foreign powers and reinforces the ideological impetus for tactical aggressive actions against others.
4. Communist propaganda and action have been made tools for the advancement and consolidation of Russian national political interests and for the

23 Kennan, *op, cit.,* p. 570; see also Frederick C. Barghoorn, *The Soviet Image of the United States* (New York, 1950).

24 Beloff, *op. cit.,* vol. II, p. 392.

25 See, for example, Barrington Moore, *Soviet Politics—The Dilemma of Power* (Cambridge, 1950), pp. 404–412; and the articles by George Kennan and Historicus, cited above.

26 The Soviet history of diplomacy throws little light on the real place of ideology in Moscow's foreign policy. See Potemkin, *op. cit.*

extension of Soviet control over both the masses at home and revolutionary movements abroad.[27]

5. The absolute power of the party leadership over all political action within the Soviet Union permits the Kremlin to apply or withhold ideological considerations in Soviet foreign policy as it may believe that state or party interests are furthered or hampered.

6. The imposition of communist regimes upon countries surrounding the Soviet Union and the reorientation of their policies to a regimented adherence to Moscow and antagonism to the noncommunist world, demonstrates that communist ideology is a politically influential reality. The goals set forth in this ideology do affect Soviet behavior toward other states.

Former Ambassador Walter B. Smith concluded after his mission to Russia that "the more one studies Soviet statements and policies the more one realizes how fundamental and deep-seated are the basic tenets of Leninism-Stalinism and how antagonistic they are to the aims, desires, and hopes of Western democracy." [28]

The territory and power of the USSR have expanded tremendously since 1939. It remains for future history to determine whether the basic Russian territorial and nationalistic interests will gradually come to guide Soviet policy, or whether the essentially aggressive, expansionist, and imperialistic philosophy of the communist creed will dominate that policy. Or perhaps the two interests will be considered by the Kremlin as indistinguishable from the standpoint of policy execution.

2. JUDGMENT OF EXPERTS. In reconstructing the history of the Bolshevik Revolution from 1917 to 1923, Professor Edward H. Carr of England, who takes a deterministic view of history, is of the opinion that the policy of world revolution, admittedly a logical development of communist doctrine, "was in fact imposed on the regime, not so much by doctrinal orthodoxy, as by the desperate plight of the civil war" of the early days.[29] Reviewing Mr. Carr's third volume, Professor Philip E. Mosely of the Russian Institute at Columbia University, points out that at the same time "even from its first steps in world politics, the Soviet leadership was, first of all, determined to assure its own survival and to control as much territory as it could take and hold." What appears as a conflict between two sets of aims—the one territorial and national, the other ideological and revolutionary—was, at least in the early days, com-

---

[27] See section on Soviet propaganda in ch. xvi below, p. 456.
[28] Walter Bedell Smith, *My Three Years in Moscow* (New York, 1950), p. 308.
[29] See E. H. Carr, *The Bolshevik Revolution, 1917–1923*, 3 vols. (New York, 1950–1953). For an evaluation of Soviet history, sympathetic to the USSR, see F. L. Schuman, *Soviet Politics At Home and Abroad* (New York, 1946).

ments Professor Mosely, "a reflection of kaleidoscopic changes in its often mistaken judgments."

Pursuing his review of Professor Carr's study of the evolution of Soviet policy through its vital formative period, Professor Mosely remarks further:

> Aside from a basic minimum interest in maintaining its control over Russia as the "citadel of world revolution," the Soviet leadership had the aim of gaining territory in order to exert its power more widely and at the same time to intensify its power over whatever territories it could grasp and hold. If this aim could be achieved through the spontaneous uprisings of revolutionary allies within advanced countries, so much the better. If not, then the new Soviet state would have to enlist, control, and discipline its foreign auxiliaries, while simultaneously maneuvering to conciliate potential friends and isolate enemies among the capitalist states.[30]

One cannot but feel that this analysis of the past reflects the path which will be followed in large measure in the future.

Professor Beloff concludes that since 1923 the prime motive of the Moscow regime has been to strengthen its position and power in Russia first and to treat world revolution as secondary. But, he adds, there is solid evidence that the conception of revolution has not been abandoned. "To try to comprehend the Soviet outlook and to dismiss the inevitability of the world proletarian revolution," he believes, "is as idle as to try to comprehend the outlook of medieval man and to dismiss the reality of the Last Judgment."[31]

Which of the two elements will play the upper hand in the years ahead will depend not alone upon the competitions and struggles for power within Russia itself, but also upon the strength, the intelligence, the vision, and the policies pursued by the nations forming a united or a divided free world.

FORMATION OF SOVIET FOREIGN POLICY

The processes and procedures by which foreign policy is formed and controlled in the Soviet Union differ markedly from those of the United States, Great Britain, and other parliamentary democracies. In part, this is a consequence of the absolute and dictatorial system that prevails in Russia; in part, it is because of the unique governmental and political structure of the Soviet state. It is also in part the logical result of the pervasive and all-embracing influence of the Communist party which exercises a complete monopoly of power in the direction and control of almost every aspect of Soviet life.[32]

[30] Philip E. Mosely, "World Revolution and Soviet Policy," *The New York Times Book Review,* Sept. 27, 1953.
[31] Max Beloff, *The Foreign Policy of Soviet Russia 1929–1941* (New York, 1949), vol. II, pp. 391–392.
[32] See Merle Fainsod, "Post-War Role of the Communist Party," *Annals,* May, 1949, p. 20.

THE SOVIET CONSTITUTION AND FOREIGN POLICY

The Soviet Constitution of 1936 which, while amended in several respects since then, is the most recent to have been promulgated, makes explicit the formal governmental structure of the USSR. It does not, as Western constitutions usually do, delimit sharply the specific roles and fields of competence of the various administrative organs, and it does not provide for safeguards against the abuse of governmental power. Nor does it reveal the all-important channels through which policy is formulated and controlled.

What it does do is to legalize the monopolistic power of the Communist party as the trustee of the "dictatorship of the proletariat," to make, in effect, the ruling leadership of the country self-perpetuating, and to place no limit on its all-inclusive and therefore arbitrary powers. Finally, it defines the Soviet Union as "a socialist state of workers and peasants" and its character as a "federal state." [33]

THE USSR AND THE REPUBLICS IN FOREIGN AFFAIRS

Constitutional "Rights" of Republics. While the Constitution gives each Union Republic the "right freely to secede," it circumscribes the powers of the central government in so vague a way that the decentralized federal character of the state is rendered in many respects merely theoretical. Each of the present sixteen Union-Republics has, according to amendments of February, 1944, "the right to enter into direct relations with foreign states and to conclude agreements and exchange representatives with them" as well as the right to have "its own Republican Military formations." [34] These provisions have not found much practical implementation beyond the admission, at Moscow's demand, of the Ukraine and Byelo-Russian Republics to membership in the United Nations.[35] The negotiating usefulness of the "right" given to the Republics seems to have more or less ended (save for relations with Soviet satellites) in 1947 when a British suggestion that the Ukraine and England establish diplomatic relations was brusquely rejected by Moscow.

Power of Central Government. Despite the fact that in 1944 the Commissariats of Defense and of Foreign Affairs, renamed two years later the Ministries of Defense and Foreign Affairs, were officially decentralized,[36] the Central Government in the Kremlin continues to represent the whole of the USSR in

[33] On the Soviet Constitution and functioning of the Soviet governmental mechanism see Merle Fainsod, *How Russia is Ruled* (Cambridge, 1953); Barrington Moore, *cit. supra;* Julian Towster, *Political Power in the U.S.S.R.* (New York, 1948).

[34] Articles 18a and 18b.

[35] For political reasons the United States declined to ask for a matching three votes. See James F. Byrnes, *Speaking Frankly* (New York, 1947), pp. 21–45.

[36] See Merle Fainsod, *op. cit.,* p. 322.

international relations. The Constitution gives it the authority to determine "the general procedure governing the relations of Union Republics with foreign states." And it holds the power to devise, carry out, and control the foreign policy of the realm. The letter of the Constitution and the actuality of Soviet practice are in this and other respects at variance with each other.

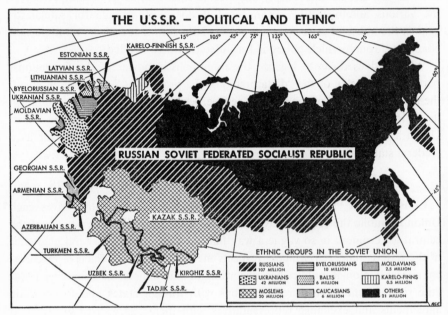

FIGURE XIV:2

The Constitution also assigns to the Union government in Moscow jurisdiction over "questions of war and peace," changes in external boundaries, the actual direction of Soviet armed forces, national security, foreign trade, transport and communications, Soviet citizenship, and the ratification of treaties. Thus, despite the fiction of a substantially decentralized federation, the Soviet Union is—even if the centralizing role played by the Communist party is ignored—in many of its most important aspects, and certainly in the field of foreign relations, a highly centralized state. The perennial display of support given by the Ukraine and Byelo-Russian "delegations" to their older brethren from Moscow at United Nations meetings only attests further to the fictional character of their independent "selfhood."

Party Control. Basic identity of policy toward the outside world is assured above all by the pervasive control exercised by the leaders of the Communist party over the entire governmental machinery throughout the territory of the

USSR. The monopolistic political position of the party is established by Article 126 of the Constitution which provides that the party "is the leading core of all organizations of the working people, both public and state" and by Article 141 which gives the party priority in nominations to all public offices, organizations, and societies. Every sphere and department of government—federal, state, local—is as a consequence directly controlled by the far-flung organization of the Communist party hierarchy. This being so, the latter has today not only full control over the policy-making process, but is also in a position to assure the translation of precepts of party ideology into foreign policy where its leaders—who are also the official leaders of the Soviet government—find it desirable or useful.[37]

THE SUPREME SOVIET AND PRESIDIUM

The 1936 Constitution endeavors to give the Soviet dictatorship the appearance of a popular government by declaring that "all power . . . belongs to the working people of town and country as represented by the Soviets of Working People's Deputies" (Article 3). It also makes the Supreme Soviet "the highest organ of state power in the USSR" (Article 30).

The Supreme Soviet. The Soviet Constitution provides for a bicameral Supreme Soviet, consisting of the Soviet of the Union and the Soviet of Nationalities.[38] It is not a continuously sitting nor, in actuality, a deliberative body. When it meets—biennially—it is asked to pass within the relatively short time of two weeks on such complex questions as the reorganization of the government of the USSR, the Five-Year Plan, the annual budget, foreign policy, and many others. As all seems to be well prearranged, and as the membership of the Supreme Soviet is predominantly recruited from party and governmental ranks, there is seldom time or will for debate; the ready-made decisions, prepared by the leaders, are readily approved. Like the German Reichstag in World War II days, it serves as a rubber stamp to "legalize" decisions made by the high command of the party.

With respect to foreign affairs, the Supreme Soviet hears reports from the Foreign Ministry and applauds them. It approves the budget of the ministry, usually as submitted. It passes resolutions drafted for it in party or government headquarters. As the highest legislative organ of the USSR, it passes laws that are requested by the Council of Ministers and the Presidium and approves the decrees, decisions, and ordinances issued by them between sessions. Among its formal functions is the power to appoint the Council of Ministers, including the Foreign Minister, and the power to declare war. On occasion,

[37] On the role of the party see Fainsod, *op. cit.,* pp. 190–208, 262–290.
[38] See Towster, *op. cit.,* pp. 250–263.

important treaties may be referred to it for ratification, as was the Nazi-Soviet Pact of 1939, the Anglo-Russian Alliance of 1942, and others. Apart from these "legislative" functions, the meetings of the Supreme Soviet provide the government and the party with a forum in which to announce to the Soviet people and to the outside world important policy decisions. In this sense the "Legislature" provides an impressive, even though unreal, background against which offers of peaceful coexistence, affirmations of military strength, announcements of the explosion of atomic and hydrogen bombs, and offers of Big Power Conferences can be made.

CONTROL OF THE GOVERNMENT OF THE USSR

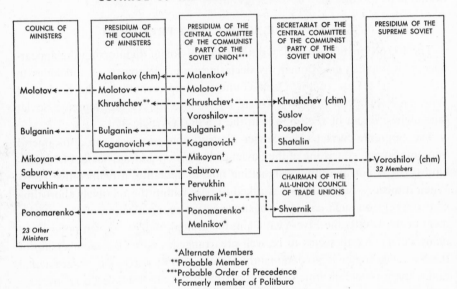

*Alternate Members
**Probable Member
***Probable Order of Precedence
†Formerly member of Politburo

FIGURE XIV:3

The Presidium of the Supreme Soviet. Every four years the Supreme Soviet elects a so-called Presidium which performs, in essence, the role of a standing executive leadership, a "collegial presidency." [39] This Presidium consists of one President, sixteen Vice-Presidents (comprising the Chairmen of the Presidiums of the sixteen Union Republics), a Secretary, and fifteen other members of the Supreme Soviet, most of whom are usually leading functionaries of the Communist party.

The Constitution makes the President of the Presidium the titular head of the Soviet State, a position held by Marshal K. E. Voroshilov at the beginning of the Malenkov regime. Foreign ambassadors present their letters of credence

[39] Fainsod, *op. cit.*, p. 316.

to the President before they are received by the Chairman of the Council of Ministers.[40] All laws passed by the Supreme Soviet must be signed by the President before they become valid.

The Presidium, functioning as the executive leadership of the Supreme Soviet, has extensive powers. It convenes and dissolves the sessions of the Supreme Soviet; appoints or removes Cabinet Ministers, including the Ministers of Foreign Affairs and Defense; proclaims martial law; orders mobilization; and declares war if the Supreme Soviet is not in session. It also ratifies—and denounces—treaties, and appoints or recalls Soviet envoys. It can issue decrees binding as law throughout the USSR. It interprets the laws of the USSR, exercises the right of pardon, and has the power to annul decisions of the Council of Ministers if they do not conform to law. In all these and other functions, the Presidium acts as a kind of "pocket Supreme Soviet" with certain prerogatives and duties.

THE COUNCIL OF MINISTERS

While the Supreme Soviet is the "highest organ of state power," the Council of Ministers is named "the highest executive and administrative organ of state power" (Article 64). It is officially appointed by the Supreme Soviet and remains theoretically accountable to it and its Presidium. It is composed of a Chairman, several Vice-Chairmen, and the Ministers of the executive and administrative departments and bureaus of the Central Government. Prior to March, 1953, there were fifty-one ministries. After Stalin's demise the function of coordinating and directing the Council of Ministers was undertaken by an inner circle, consisting of Chairman Georgi Malenkov; Foreign Minister Molotov; Defense Minister Bulganin; Mikoyan, the Minister of Internal and External Trade; and Kaganovich, who held no specific portfolio.

Powers. These leading men of the Council can be considered for all practical purposes *the* government of the USSR. The Council, with the cooperation of the other ministers, initiates and approves policy directives and departmental policies, and supervises the activities of the individual ministries when a particular problem arises. It may issue decisions and ordinances binding on officials and populace alike. It may appoint deputy ministers and lower officials. The Council of Ministers is a medium for pooling and integrating the concerns of the Ministries of Foreign Affairs, Defense, Internal and Foreign Trade, Defense Industry, State Control, and Internal Affairs. Through the Council the peaks of the governmental and party pyramids intertwine.

---

40 On occasion past presidents have exchanged messages with the heads of other States. See exchange of messages between Presidents Truman and Shvernik, *Department of State Bulletin,* July 16, 1951.

Guidance of Foreign Affairs. The Constitution expressly provides that the Council of Ministers shall exercise "general guidance in the sphere of relations with foreign states" (Article 68). This gives it a broad mandate not only to initiate and participate in the making of foreign policy, but at all times to exercise a guiding and checking hand in the administration of foreign affairs. It appears to enact specific rules and policies. It decides on the recognition of foreign governments. It is reported to examine and approve proposed treaties, and confirms those that do not require formal ratification. It may enter into executive agreements with foreign governments.

Since the Soviet regime operates largely through executive and administrative decrees and orders, rather than on the basis of legislative enactment as do the American and British systems, the Council of Ministers is a most important body. But its significance in policy making and administration derives essentially from the fact that its leading members are also members of the Presidium of the Communist party which is the real seat of power.

THE ROLE OF THE PARTY IN POLICY MAKEUP

The Constitution does not mention the highest Communist party organ which, in terms of wielding and determining the uses of political power, is the supreme body in the USSR. We refer to the Presidium of the Communist party, which after the Nineteenth All-Union Communist Party Congress assumed the functions of the former Politbureau and Orgbureau.[41]

Composition of Party Presidium. Prior to Stalin's death the former Politbureau was enlarged from a membership of fourteen members to twenty-five full and eleven alternate members, comprising the highest ranking figures of the Communist party and Soviet Government. In March, 1953, a reorganization reduced the reconstructed Presidium of the Central Committee of the Communist party to ten full members and four alternates. In this new Presidium the most powerful men were Georgi M. Malenkov, Chairman of the Council of Ministers; V. M. Molotov, Minister of Foreign Affairs; N. S. Khrushchev, First Secretary of the Central Committee of the party; K. E. Voroshilov, Chairman of the Presidium of the Supreme Soviet; N. A. Bulganin, Minister of Defense; and C. M. Kaganovich, first Deputy Chairman of the Council of Ministers.

Functioning. Inasmuch as the deliberations of the Presidium are conducted in the greatest secrecy there is no way of definitely knowing how it functions or influences the operation of the government. It is not known whether the

---

41 On the former Politbureau and Orgbureau see Towster, *op. cit.*, pp. 159–166; Fainsod, *op. cit.*, ch. 10; and G. K. Schueller, *The Politburo,* Hoover Inst. Studies, Ser. B, No. 2 (Stanford, 1951).

discussion of policies leaves room for debate or whether, on the contrary, acquiescence to decisions handed down by a Stalin or his successor is obligatory. The mishaps befalling members of this top level agency create the surmise that disagreements do arise, usually with unfortunate consequences for the objectors. So far as exercising control of the government goes, it may be noted that a large majority of the Presidium members are at the same time leading members of the Council of Ministers.[42] Malenkov is the Chairman of both bodies. Molotov, Bulganin, Kaganovich, Mikoyan, Saburov, Perukhin, and Ponomarenko belong simultaneously to both organs. It is thus evident that even on the purely personal level there exists a close identity between the high commands of the party and the government—which should not be surprising in a system where all state power relies in essence on the power and work of the party.

THE FOREIGN MINISTRY

The Ministry of Foreign Affairs is mentioned in the Constitution as one of the principal administrative and executive organs of the Soviet Government. From what is known of its structure, it is not unlike other Foreign Offices in organization.

The Foreign Minister. The ministry is headed by the Foreign Minister. This official has customarily been a person of high rank in the Soviet hierarchy. In the three and a half decades of the Soviet regime the Ministry has changed hands relatively few times.

For the first twelve years, when the government was consolidating its power and striving for recognition abroad, the Foreign Ministry was headed by Georgi Chicherin, a diplomat of pre-Soviet professional training. From 1930 to 1939 Maxim Litvinoff, an "old revolutionary," was Foreign Minister. His term was noted for success in winning United States recognition and for developing friendly relations with the Western Powers.

From May, 1939, to 1949, Vyacheslav Molotov, one of Stalin's most trusted associates, became Foreign Minister. Mr. Molotov was able to carry foreign affairs directly into the highest councils of state and party; for he was Vice-Chairman of the Council of Ministers and also a ranking member of the Politbureau. During his administration, Soviet foreign policy fluctuated widely between several extremes. From May, 1939, to July, 1941, it was characterized by suspicion of the West and collaboration with Nazi Germany. From July, 1941, to VJ Day in 1945, it sought to obtain all possible aid from Britain and America in the war against Germany while closely guarding Soviet reciprocation. From then until 1949, Soviet foreign policy was characterized by a

42 See Nathan Leites, "Aspects of Politburo Behavior," *World Politics,* July, 1950.

steady growth of aggressive attitudes and hostility toward the West, hardening finally into the cold war.

From 1949 to early 1953, Andrei Vyshinsky was Foreign Minister, moving up from the position of Deputy Foreign Minister. Prior to this he was known as the chief State Prosecutor in the purge trials of 1936–1938. However able, Vyshinsky by no means occupied as influential a position within the Soviet Union as Molotov, as he was not a member of the Presidium or the Polit-bureau. Consequently, his administration did not enjoy the same personal linkage between the conduct of foreign affairs and the formulation of high political policy which existed under Molotov.

With the passing of Stalin in 1953, Molotov again became Foreign Minister, relegating Vyshinsky to the lower post of chief Soviet delegate to the United Nations.

Deputy Foreign Ministers. Immediately below the Foreign Minister are a number of deputies whose functions are in general analogous to those of Under-Secretaries and Assistant Secretaries of State. Among those known in the West who have been holders of these posts are Andrei Gromyko, formerly Ambassador to the United States and Soviet delegate to the United Nations Security Council from 1946 to 1950; Fedor Gusev, formerly Ambassador to London; Jacob Malik, delegate to the United Nations Security Council from 1950 to 1953, formerly Ambassador to Japan and in charge of Eastern affairs; and Valerian Zorin, formerly Ambassador to Czechoslovakia, now representative of the USSR in the United Nations Security Council.

Advisory Groups. Situated within the Foreign Office is a group of advisory specialists. Among those reported in this group at one time or another have been Maxim Litvinoff after retirement from ambassadorship to the United States; Professor Boris Stein, one-time representative at United Nations meetings; Ivan Maisky, war-time Ambassador in London; Professor S. B. Krylov, Soviet judge on the International Court of Justice from 1946 to 1951; and Sergei Golunsky, formerly legal adviser in the Foreign Ministry and subsequently Soviet judge on the International Court.

The background of the majority of Deputy Foreign Ministers and advisers suggests that the Foreign Ministry attaches considerable importance to knowledge of Britain and the United States in the formation and conduct of Soviet foreign policy. This may be deliberate not only because of Soviet ideological conceptions of those two powers as inevitable opponents, but also because only one or two members of the party Presidium are known to have visited these Western states. Hence, a particular need of "experts" within the Foreign Ministry.

Operational Divisions. The lower echelons of the Foreign Office are said to be divided into three main groups, each of which has numerous sections dealing with specific areas and problems.

The first grouping apparently comprises five geographical sections: (1) "Western Europe," including the Scandinavian countries and Poland; (2) Central Europe and the Balkans; (3) "Section West," encompassing Italy, Spain, France, Belgium, the Netherlands, Great Britain, and the Americas; (4) "Section East," including the Near and Middle East; and (5) a second "Section East," dealing with Australasia, China, Japan, and the Philippines.

The second grouping is a "functional division." This contains subdivisions responsible for legal, economic, consular, protocol, and press matters. A third group of divisions seemingly is devoted to administration, handling personnel, training, finance, and so forth. Both of these latter groups apparently correspond to offices bearing similar designations in the Foreign Offices of Western countries, although their methods of operation may differ widely.

The Foreign Service. The Soviet Foreign Service is the overseas arm of the Foreign Ministry, organized under a decree of 1927.[43] Foreign Service officers are reported to be trained in a College of Diplomacy within the Foreign Ministry. Soviet embassies include not only officers of the Foreign Service and the armed services, but also representatives of the state trade monopoly, the Secret Service (MVD), and political agents. In numerous countries Soviet embassies and consulates contain larger staffs than the corresponding offices of other states. Although international law prohibits diplomatic representatives engaging in subversive activities, the Report of the Royal Commission investigating espionage in Canada and other revelations since 1917 indicate that Soviet embassies do on occasion support and shelter espionage, subversion, and propaganda.

ROLES OF MINISTRIES OF FOREIGN TRADE
AND OF ARMED FORCES

Like the noncommunist countries, the Soviet Union uses economic and military measures as instruments of foreign policy. The Ministry of Foreign Trade, long headed by Mikoyan who has also been a party Presidium member, is an important agency in foreign affairs. It conducts all economic intercourse with other states, seeking to gain for the USSR needed raw materials and capital goods either through purchase or through barter arrangements. At the same time Soviet foreign trade has political objectives, to gain an entree for Soviet

43 Text in T. A. Taracouzio, *The Soviet Union and International Law* (New York, 1935), Appendix.

influence, to pave the way for propaganda and revolutionary activities abroad, or to tie the economic and political life of a foreign country to Moscow's bidding as in the case of its satellites.

The Soviet armed forces are the instrument of power which has conditioned and overshadowed a large proportion of the world's international affairs since World War II. They are the instrument which made possible, through occupation, the satellization of Central Europe. Their strength and strategic location are obviously viewed and used, by Soviet leadership, as an effective instrument of power politics.

The role which the armed forces play in the formulation of high policy and in the politics within the Kremlin is by no means wholly clear. There are evidences, however, that the leaders of the armed forces do take a vital part in policy making by virtue of the fact that two members of the party Presidium are Army men—Marshal Voroshilov, who was for many years Minister of Defense and is now President of the Supreme Soviet, and Marshal Bulganin who has succeeded him as Minister of Defense. In addition to being a member of the Presidium, Marshal Bulganin is also a Deputy Premier and one of the inner circle of the Council of Ministers. Through these positions, plus the fact that the Army leaders hold in their hands the instruments of force and raw power upon which the USSR is dependent for its defense and national security, the armed forces can play a decisive role in Soviet policy decisions. That the Army's political importance is recognized is evidenced by the systematic efforts which have been made by the Kremlin to build up their loyalty to the Soviet regime and to guard against their adopting a separate political line. This is attested by the indoctrination continually impressed upon them, by the planting of MVD and party agents in their midst, and by the purges of officers who do not hew closely to the government and party lines. The impressive appearance of Army units in Moscow at the time of the arrest of Beria, head of the secret police, in 1953 indicates that the armed forces may play a critical role in the struggle for power among the Kremlin leaders themselves. Should an extended split occur within the Presidium ranks, the armed forces could play a decisive role not only in domestic matters but in foreign policy as well.[44]

POLICY MAKING IN THE USSR

The foreign policy of the USSR is, as has been pointed out previously, a mixture of Russian national considerations and those initiated and pursued primarily in the service of communist ideology. To be effective, such a policy

[44] See W. W. Rostow, *The Dynamics of Soviet Society* (New York, 1953), pp. 197, 240–241, 255–257; Fainsod, *op. cit.*, pp. 276–277, 395–418; see also dispatch by Drew Middleton, "Soviet Army Role Reported Growing," *The New York Times*, Nov. 21, 1953.

must be based on a high degree of coordination among the Foreign Ministry, the organs of the party in the USSR and abroad, the various other ministries relevant for foreign relations, and, of course, the Soviet intelligence services.

Procedure. While detailed information about the internal working of Soviet foreign policy making is scarce, we have reason to assume that, in routine matters involving no questions of policy change or major decisions, the Foreign Minister and his aides are authorized to issue the necessary instructions and take the requisite steps.

When, however, a situation involves new or serious issues, or brings into question the applicability of prior high-level policy decisions, the matter may be referred to the Chairman of the Council of Ministers or to the Presidium. When questions are submitted to the Presidium it is said that the party Secretariat may prepare memoranda and documentation which then are collated with the recommendations and reasonings of the Foreign Ministry. The decision resulting from the discussion of this is then transmitted to the Foreign Ministry or to any other ministry or instrumentality, according to which the Presidium may wish to entrust the execution of the decision.

The hedging actions of Soviet delegations at various international conferences and the frequent delays which foreign states encounter in receiving replies to notes handed to the Soviet Foreign Minister, his lieutenants, or ambassadors point to the probability that the Foreign Ministry refers a large number of issues to the leadership of the Council of Ministers and to the party Presidium rather than run the risk of incurring disciplinary or corrective action. Such a procedure, naturally, is likely to result not only in delays and protracted negotiations, but also in throwing a heavy burden of work on the Council of Ministers and the Communist party Presidium, as other ministries doubtless follow similar "safe" paths.[45]

MONOLITHIC NATURE OF SOVIET POLICY MAKING

The monopolistic position of the Communist party in Soviet society tends to reduce the room for the adoption of contradictory or competing policies within the government. It is clear, nevertheless, that at times there have been conflicts and powerful rivalries between the party leaders and between the Ministries of Interior, Defense, and Foreign Affairs. The close alignment of the policy-making and executing agencies enables the Soviet Government to act, if need be, rapidly and forcefully.[46]

[45] For an informative series of analyses of negotiations with Soviet diplomatic representatives throwing light on Soviet policy and its formation see R. Dennett and J. E. Johnson (eds.), *Negotiating with the Russians* (Boston, 1951).

[46] Towster says that "complete unity and solidarity in the Party ranks from the lowest rung to the top leadership are considered a basic and absolute prerequisite for the success and survival of Soviet rule." See *Political Power in the U.S.S.R.* (New York, 1948), p. 124.

On the other hand, such a system of policy making cannot but be attended by grave dangers. The absence of political competition and criticisms can permit such policy making to deviate into unrealistic, risky, and inflexible channels. Moreover, its policy makers may become seriously misguided in their analyses of foreign events and national interests. Besides, the fact that staff and line officers are completely dominated from above and must be afraid to incur the displeasure of their masters, makes it unlikely that they will present to their superiors unpalatable facts about the outside world—even if they are able to see them. Thus, it is possible that high foreign policy decisions may in fact be made on the basis of reports sent in with a view to pleasing official policy and doctrine—and not primarily with a view to informing about international realities. The secrecy and exclusiveness with which real goals are devised, and the shrewdness with which sentiments and hatreds are implanted through the vast system of propaganda and terror available to the Kremlin— make the Soviet Union an unpredictable and dangerous factor in world affairs.

Any foreign power, disposing of vast armed forces, unhindered by moral scruples, and free to move aggressively in both the Asian and European theaters, would be grave cause for concern to the rest of the world, as has Russian policy for nearly 200 years. Soviet foreign policy has, in addition, the further dimension: the ideological.

The ideological element, as mentioned above, enters in varying degrees into the formation of Soviet policy. While it cannot be authoritatively stated that the postulate of world revolution dominates every foreign action of the Soviet Union, this postulate certainly is not absent in its policy making. Furthermore, even if official Soviet policy should *prima facie* espouse a more peaceful course than it does now, it still has millions of dedicated communist agents abroad whose conspiratorial activities cannot be ignored.

However one may look at Soviet policy, its doctrinal components and implications cannot be disconnected. As long as this continues, the free world will have to guard not only against the political and territorial ambitions of the USSR, but also against the related world-wide objectives of the Communist party which, at this juncture of history, are fused in the challenge which a powerful and expansionist Soviet Empire presents to the security, institutions, and ways of life of the free and democratic states.

SUGGESTED READINGS

Max Beloff, *The Foreign Policy of Soviet Russia, 1929–1941,* 2 vols. (London, 1947–1949).
———. *Soviet Policy in the Far East, 1944–1951* (New York, 1953).
David J. Dallin, *Soviet Russia and the Far East* (New Haven, 1948).

Raymond Dennett and Joseph E. Johnson (eds.), *Negotiating With the Russians* (Boston, 1951).

Merle Fainsod, *How Russia is Ruled* (Cambridge, 1953).

Louis Fischer, *The Soviets in World Affairs*, 2 vols. (Princeton, 1951).

Waldemar Gurian, ed., *Soviet Imperialism, Its Origins and Tactics* (Notre Dame, 1953).

R. N. C. Hunt, *The Theory and Practice of Communism* (New York, 1952).

Alexander Inkeles, *Public Opinion in Soviet Russia* (Cambridge, 1950).

Sir John Maynard, *Russia in Flux* (New York, 1940).

Barrington Moore, *Soviet Politics—The Dilemma of Power* (Cambridge, 1950).

Sir Bernard Pares, *Russia* (New York, 1943).

Walt W. Rostow, *The Dynamics of Soviet Society* (New York, 1953).

F. L. Schuman, *Soviet Politics at Home and Abroad* (New York, 1946).

Walter Bedell Smith, *My Three Years In Moscow* (New York, 1950).

L. Stevens, *Russian Assignment* (Boston, 1953).

B. H. Sumner, *A Short History of Russia* (New York, 1949).

Pauline Tompkins, *American-Russian Relations in the Far East* (New York, 1949).

CHAPTER XV

Policy Making in Other Powers

THE PRECEDING three chapters have discussed structures and methods of policy making in the United States, in the parliamentary democracies of Britain and France, and in the USSR. These states are normally called "great" when states are categorized as great, middle-sized, and lesser powers. States are also placed in other categories, for example, by areas or by association with the Great Powers. Thus the communist Central European states are bound to the USSR in their foreign policies. The democratic states on the rimland of Europe have a sense of a European community and generally have similar structures and methods of foreign policy making. Their cultures, political institutions, and reactions in foreign affairs are related to each other.

Until the last few decades, international relations were determined almost entirely by the policies of the Great Powers. It is startling to pause and consider that, as late as World War I, the British Foreign Office could speak for a dozen or so peoples that now have their own sovereign states. The European states plus non-European Great Powers composed until recently most of the firmament of international politics. Today, international organization has given many small states a new importance. The growing economic interdependence of the world has likewise emphasized this trend. The global struggle between communism and anticommunism has created a tendency for disputes between even small states to draw other states into the controversies; thereby making the middle and lesser powers more important in international politics. Finally, the increased fear of war and the general recognition that security and well-being depend upon collective effort have magnified the importance of these states.

There are approximately eighty sovereign states in the world. This chapter will endeavor to identify and to analyze, in broad and admittedly sketchy terms, some of the circumstances affecting the formulation of policy in more than half of these states. It may be argued that some of them are not important. But, as one yardstick, the group discussed can constitute a majority vote in the United Nations General Assembly. Their environment is, in most cases, very different from the North American-European environment of policy formulation to which the English-speaking peoples are accustomed by their own experience, education, and public press. Most of these states are economically or technically underdeveloped. Individual productivity is low, they are agricultural rather than industrial, birth and death rates are high. The peoples and governments are relatively inexperienced in foreign affairs and often in handling their internal political affairs. Generally, international affairs are a concern to only a very limited portion of the population of a particular state —the few people with higher education, individuals engaged in foreign economic relations, and government officials. Hence personalities and small interest groups are more likely to be determinant in the international relations of the states considered in this chapter.

In the pages which follow we shall discuss the setting from which states in Latin America, the Middle East, and Asia view world affairs and some of the conditions guiding their policy making. In dealing in generalities, as we must, we are of course aware that there are exceptions. We must, therefore, caution against dogmatic assumptions or rushing to conclusions without carefully examining the unique situation of each country.

POLICY MAKING IN LATIN AMERICA

The twenty republics of Latin America have an estimated population of 173 million people—approximately the same as that of the United States and Canada combined.[1] A large percentage of these are engaged in agriculture and live where illiteracy and disease are high. Their lands and soils are of a fertility which, with more up-to-date equipment, farming techniques, and conservation measures, could yield substantially higher crops and national incomes. At the present time most Latin American countries produce exportable surpluses in meat, grain, or tropical food products. Their exports of tin, copper, tungsten, petroleum, and other strategic and critical raw materials fill an important place in the supply needs of the free nations. With incipient but rapidly accelerating industrialization in several of these states and with a continuation of the high population growth which characterizes all of these nations except Argentina,[2] the Latin American countries are bound to play an increasingly important and independent role in world affairs.

Economic Factors. Under the Spanish Crown the tradition of awarding large land grants to individuals was established. This practice was continued

[1] Robert C. Cook, "Latin America: Area of Population Explosion," in *Population Bulletin*, Vol. IX, No. 6, Oct., 1953, p. 65.
[2] *Ibid.*, p. 67.

after the revolution of the early nineteenth century and has affected the pattern of land ownership up to this day. While more than two-thirds of the Latin American people are employed in agriculture, the system of land tenure has concentrated ownership of much of the best land in many areas in the hands of a small group, relegating the mass of the Indian farms into small, often mountainous, plots. In Chile, which is an extreme case, 570 land-owners control almost two-thirds of all privately owned land.[3] With variations in degree, this condition prevails in many other Latin American states. The economic situation is further complicated by the tendency of large land-owners to specialize in the production of a few cash crops resulting in a "one-crop" economy which is highly susceptible to the demands and pressures of foreign markets. In other cases a mineral product can and does produce a "one-crop" effect on a nation's economy with pronounced economic instability resulting from relatively slight international economic fluctuations. Great dependence upon foreign markets makes a state highly susceptible to foreign political as well as economic pressures.

Indigenous capital is seldom available in sufficient quantity to undertake large-scale exploitation of mineral resources. Large influxes of foreign capital are essential if resource potentialities are to be realized. Some 95 per cent of Chile's copper production in 1945, for example, was produced in American-owned mines.[4] Approximately 87 per cent of the crude oil produced in Venezuela in the same year was controlled by American, British, and Dutch corporations.[5] Such a condition may create strained relations between investors and the national government unless intelligent restraint is exercised by all parties concerned. A further complication results from the fact that a few states have an inordinately high economic dependency upon the export of one or two mineral products. Notable cases in point are those of Venezuela in which petroleum represents about nine-tenths of her total export value and Bolivia in which tin supplies approximately three-quarters of her international exchange.[6]

Dependency also accrues from the relatively narrow manufacturing base within the continent. Lack of sufficient native capital has compelled the countries in most instances to seek foreign investment.[7] Only in the relatively industrialized states—Brazil,[8] Mexico, Argentina, and Chile—do domestic products

---

3 S. G. Hanson, *Economic Development in Latin America* (Washington, 1951), p. 61.
4 See George Wythe, *Industry in Latin America* (New York, 1945), p. 220.
5 Hanson, *op. cit.*, p. 287.
6 Renner, Durand, White, and Gibson, *World Economic Geography* (New York, 1953), p. 459.
7 The United States Department of Commerce estimated that North American direct investments in Latin America in 1950 amounted to $4.7 billion in some 2,000 enterprises controlled by United States companies. *The New York Times*, Oct. 18, 1953.
8 George Wythe, *Industry in Latin America* (New York, 1949), p. 149.

or manufactured goods constitute more than 20 per cent of the national income.[9] The dearth of coal is a particularly limiting factor. Industrial development is further hampered by the rural decentralization of much of the Latin American population. Failure to develop the interiors extensively has slowed the growth of an expanding market in most states.

LATIN AMERICA

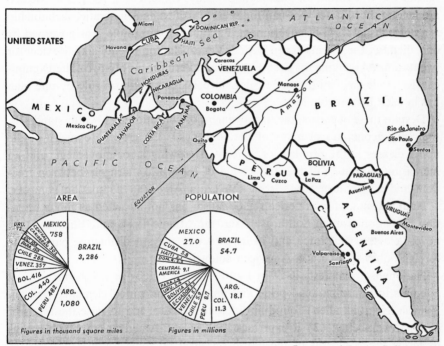

Courtesy of Foreign Policy Assoc.

FIGURE XV:1

Government in Latin America. Aspirants for political power are often tempted to resort to extreme methods to gain control of government. Organizing successful revolts offers to ambitious persons the prospect of lucrative governmental and army positions. The recurring *coups d'état,* however, have had, with few exceptions, little effect on the bases of power. Nor have they introduced major changes in the economic and social conditions of their countries. For the most part, they have led to reshuffling of governing personnel who seek to control or exploit the existent situation. In other words, there have

[9] *United Nations Economic Survey of Latin America, 1948* (New York, 1949), p. 2.

been many successful revolts but few revolutions such as occurred in Mexico beginning in 1910.[10]

While Anglo-Saxon peoples differentiate between "government" as an institution and the persons who compose it at any time, some segments of the population in Latin American countries tend to think of government in personal terms expressing a fondness for *el caudillo*—the leader. The constitutional governmental structure in Latin American states is, however, modeled after that of the United States. Although Uruguay, Chile, Costa Rica, and Mexico are among those states that can today be classified as democratic, dictatorship is a not unusual form of government. Paraguay, for example, was governed by one dictator for twenty-seven years, Venezuela for twenty-six, Mexico for twenty-four, Argentina for twenty-three, and Peru for twenty-two. The Dominican Republic has had the same ruler since 1930. Long-term rule by one man has in itself bred revolution.

Despite these elements, the improvement of education and health standards, the rising economies of many of the countries,[11] the growing concern of the upper classes in the problem of poverty, a growing labor movement, and an increasing awareness of the implication of the world's struggle between freedom and communism are stirring the Latin American population complex.

Nationalism. Latin American nationalism has not attracted as much attention as nationalism in Southeast Asia, the Middle East, and Europe. It is, nevertheless, a vital force and in its own way plays a distinctive part in the foreign policy of all Latin American countries.

Nationalism manifests itself in Latin America chiefly in two forms: (1) it attempts to infuse national pride and unity into the varied elements (Indian, Spanish, Negroid, alien) found in different republics and to raise the levels of national well-being; (2) it expresses itself in anti-Americanism which has as its target the "Colossus of the North," viewed by some Latin Americans as the rich, capitalist, Anglo-Saxon democracy—the United States.[12]

The roots of anti-Americanism stem from (1) historic experiences of some Latin American countries with United States intervention; (2) a mixture of fear and envy over the prosperity and power of the northern neighbor and their economic dependence upon it; (3) resentment over the inroads of an alleged low-level, nationalistic "gringo culture" (aggressive and often coarse

[10] See Frank Tannenbaum, *Mexico—The Struggle for Peace and Bread* (New York, 1950), pp. 49–80, for a treatment of Mexico's revolution. For a general discussion of the Latin American situation, see G. Arciniegas, *The State of Latin America* (New York, 1953). See also Austin F. MacDonald, *Latin American Politics and Government* (New York, 1950).

[11] Nelson A. Rockefeller stated on Oct. 14, 1953, that the economy of Latin America increased by 2½ per cent per year from 1946 through 1952. *The New York Times,* Oct. 15, 1953.

[12] See "Anti-US Sentiment Seen Rising in South America," *The New York Times,* May 10, 1953.

business practices by United States concerns in the early twentieth century and, more lately, comic books, cheap advertising, gadgets) into the aristocratic patterns of native civilizations; and (4) a belief, accentuated by communist propaganda, that the United States is bolstering local dictatorships opposed to popular rule.[13]

The United States has endeavored to counteract such attitudes by gestures of friendship, economic assistance, political cooperation, and the Good Neighbor policy. A sense of genuine partnership as pledged in repeated Pan-American pronouncements has been slow to develop, however, save in time of crises, because of the cultural, economic, and political differentials which exist between the United States and Latin American ways of life.

Latin America in World Affairs. Notwithstanding that Latin America is physically located somewhat distantly from the principal focal points of world conflict today, it is far from isolated. It is inextricably tied to the world situation and international politics.[14]

Although most of the Latin American republics are heavily dependent upon the United States as a market for their goods, as their prime source of manufactured articles and investment capital, and for hemispheric security, all place a high value upon their political independence of United States foreign policy. They are particularly desirous of achieving inter-American unity by means of political association among sovereign equals. Like most other countries, they want to earn United States dollars rather than receive economic aid; hence, their concern with trade restrictions in the United States.[15] While the Latin American states normally stand with the United States on issues arising within the United Nations, their occasional support of issues opposed by the United States illustrates their political independence from their northern neighbor.

United States respect for this proud spirit of independence and equality and its willingness since the special Inter-American Conference in Buenos Aires in 1936 to abide by the principle of "nonintervention" in the internal and external affairs of Latin American states have been important factors in winning Latin American cooperation on major international issues. The complementary need of the United States for Latin American goods and for the friendship and cooperation of these people in matters of hemispheric defense and on world issues, make the partnership a matter not merely of choice but of enlightened self-interest for all parties.

13 See "Latin American Dictatorships and the United States," *Foreign Policy Report,* Dec. 1, 1949.

14 See address by John C. Dreier, former United States Representative to the Council of the Organization of American States, April 18, 1951, in *Department of State Bulletin,* April 30, 1951.

15 View presented by Mr. Delfin Enrique Paez, Consul General of Venezuela in New York, in a speech before the Spanish Club at the United States Military Academy at West Point, New York, on Oct. 31, 1953.

Cultural ties with Spain have encouraged the rise of a Spanish-sponsored movement termed *Hispanidad*—a movement which has emphasized the cultural relationship of all Spanish-speaking peoples and seeks to promote their closer cooperation. Some governments in Latin America have responded to this by pressing for acceptance of the Franco regime in the United Nations and by their attempts to regularize Spain's diplomatic relations with the rest of the Western world. These pressures may have played some minor part in the decision of the United States to shift its position with reference to the Franco regime in 1953 in the signing of an agreement for the development and use of Spanish bases.

Latin America has inevitably been involved in the struggles of modern world politics. Before and during World War II a considerable strata of population, especially in Argentina and Chile, supported Fascist Italy and Nazi Germany and constituted a grave concern to the war effort of the Allied powers. Since 1945, political currents have taken a somewhat different turn. The continued dictatorial rule in many countries combined with a rising sensitivity to social injustices and clever propaganda by communist elements have brought threat of communism, despite the fact that Communist parties are outlawed in many of the states. The nature of this turn has been sharply revealed by the tolerance of Communists displayed by governing authorities in Guatemala and by the attempted communist coup in British Guiana. The Foreign Ministers of the American states formally recorded their concern in 1951 when they agreed that steps should be taken to counter the threat. They stressed the importance of a more effective exercise of representative democracy and of the need for reviewing existing laws and regulations for the prevention of sabotage and other subversive acts.[16]

Aside from the numerically small educated class—the Church, the students, and to an extent the city populaces—the vast bulk of the native peoples throughout Latin America have no knowledge of foreign affairs and no real interest in international politics. While interest in local politics is frequently pronounced, *Conservative, Liberal,* etc. labels often have little exact meaning. The average Latin American has not been noted for adopting doctrinaire attitudes toward political movements.

In most of the countries communication systems are relatively poor. Newspapers, the radio, and the activities of political parties are for the most part confined to the cities and towns. In some countries where dictatorships are in power, opposition parties have been outlawed or prevented from functioning openly. Hence, those who formulate and administer foreign policy of these states may be speaking only for a minority of the politically articulate people.

16 See resolution adopted by Foreign Ministers at Washington meeting, April, 1951.

Within the government, the educated classes, and the foreign trading circles of most of the Latin American countries, there are close cultural ties and identifications of political and economic interests with France, Spain, Italy, England, and in some cases Germany. Many of the intelligentsia have received a part of their education in Europe and feel a sense of closer cultural attachment to Europe than to the United States. If for no other reason than a desire for an association which offsets dependence upon the United States, Latin Americans maintain these cultural, political, and trade connections. These affect to varying degrees, and at different times, their warmth or coolness toward inter-American relations. Apart from commercial air service, much of Latin America has better transportation and communication with Europe than with North America. All these factors, working separately and with subtle interconnection, exert an influence upon the formulation, conduct, and nature of foreign policy in Latin America.

Each Latin American state possesses a distinct culture, tradition, and independent nationality of which it is justly proud. Failure of the United States to recognize this and to conduct its relations with the other American states within this framework inevitably weakens the drive for inter-American solidarity which has become a cornerstone of United States foreign policy.

THE NEAR AND MIDDLE EAST

The area conventionally called the Near and Middle East stretches from the eastern borders of Algeria and Tunisia to the western borders of Afghanistan and Pakistan. This covers some 2,600,000 square miles and is inhabited by about 80,000,000 people. Islamic culture is nearly universal, the only outstanding exception being the Hebrew culture of Israel. Christians are politically important only in Lebanon. Except for Turkey, Israel, and Iran, the language is principally a variety of Arabic.

Geographically, the Middle East consists principally of desert and arid regions. The most fertile regions are the Nile and Tigris-Euphrates valleys, the Levantine coast, and the Anatolian plateau. Possibly 80 per cent of the population in this large region gain their livelihood from agriculture, the greater part of which is conducted in a primitive manner. There are still remnants of feudal land ownership, notably in Iran where the Shah has undertaken a personal campaign to eliminate it. Individual productivity is usually low. The greater part of the population enjoy little more than the bare minimum required for subsistence.

Religious Focal Point. Three great world religions, Judaism, Christianity, and Islam all trace their origins to the Middle East. As the center of the Moslem religion and of Moslem settlement, the Middle Eastern peoples maintain

kinship with the Moslem populations stretching from French North Africa in
the west through Afghanistan and Pakistan to Indonesia in the East. Only the
Moslems found in Albania, the Soviet Union, and China are totally isolated
from their religious brethren in the Middle East. The Jews regard Palestine as
their religious and cultural home land and long dreamed of the Zionist state
now established in Israel. As the birthplace of Christianity, Christians every-

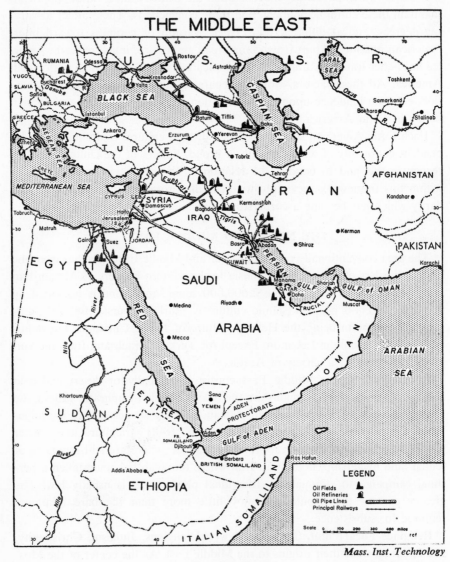

Mass. Inst. Technology

FIGURE XV:2

where—whether Catholic, Orthodox, Protestant, or members of various Middle Eastern sects—look to Bethlehem, Judea, Nazareth, and the holy places in Jerusalem with common emotions.

Strategic Factors. Historically, the Middle East has been a coveted prize among nations. Liberation of the Holy Land from the Moslems was a goal of the European Crusaders in the Middle Ages. Trade with the Levantine states was eagerly sought by the Venetians and Genoese and other Mediterranean traders of the Renaissance and post-Renaissance years. From early in the nineteenth century the Middle Eastern bridge lands, with their routes leading from the West to the Orient and from Russia to India and the Indian Ocean area, became a center of contest between the British, the Ottoman Turks, and the Russians. In the late nineteenth and early twentieth centuries, the Middle East witnessed a struggle for power and influence among Britain, France, Germany, Italy, and Russia. As late as 1940, the USSR declared that the area toward the Persian Gulf and Indian Ocean was the center of its territorial aspirations.[17] A glance at the map will show that a break through the southern rimland of Asia here would establish a very favorable position to roll up that rimland in both directions, encircle Turkey, and, in doing so, achieve the age-old objective of control of the Turkish Straits.

In World War II, British and German-Italian troops fought bitterly in North Africa for the control of the gate to the Middle East. In 1951, General Dwight D. Eisenhower observed that so far as the sheer value of territory is concerned, there is no more strategically important area. That area links three continents; its control means control of the principal air and water routes between Europe and the East; it contains over half the known petroleum reserves of the world.

The Great Powers, following World War II, have continued to recognize that the Middle East occupies a position of tremendous importance in world politics. The United States and Britain supported Turkish resistance to Soviet demands for bases at the Straits in 1946–1947. The United States has provided major economic and military assistance to both Greece and Turkey and will almost certainly have to continue some military assistance if they are to maintain strong military postures. Both these states have become members of the North Atlantic Treaty Organization. The United States exerted continual efforts to help find an amicable solution of the disputes between Iran and Britain over oil and between Egypt and Britain over the British base in the Suez area and the defense of the Suez Canal. Any disturbance in the area arouses the immediate concern of both the United States and Britain.

The leaders of the Middle East appreciate the strategic importance of their

---

[17] See Department of State Pub. 3023, *Nazi-Soviet Relations, 1939–1941* (Washington, 1948), pp. 257*ff.*

area and the consequent bargaining position which this gives them. The situation from the Arab point of view was stated with frankness by Mr. A. K. Hassouna, Secretary-General of the Arab League, in a speech in 1953. "We of the Arab world, while also aware of the threat of communism to our way of life, are nevertheless more immediately and directly concerned about the threat of further Zionist aggression." He asked if the United States bases and facilities in the Middle East are really important to Western security, and if the United States is "really vitally interested in the petroleum and other material resources of the Arab states." [18]

The Factor of Oil. The Middle East contains, according to recent estimates, about 54 per cent of the free world's proven oil reserves. These Middle Eastern fields produce about 75 per cent of the oil needs of Europe and most of those of Africa and South and Southeast Asia.[19] Before the oil resources of Iran were nationalized in 1951, about 50 per cent of the proven Middle Eastern oil resources were controlled by two British companies, 42 per cent by five American companies, and the remainder by a French company.

These rich pools of oil, so vital to the economies of the West, are located in countries which are weak and underdeveloped economically, administratively, and defense-wise. The governments and national economies of Iran, Kuwait, Saudi Arabia, and Iraq have come to depend heavily upon the income from their oil. Measured in percentage of cost, the total profits are huge, since cost of production is low and the oil is sold at the world price set principally by costs of oil production in the United States and Venezuela. The Middle Eastern states have, however, been completely dependent on foreign capital, technology, and marketing to develop this resource. The large profits involved provide wide dimensions for bargaining between companies and governments. The British Government has a particular interest, since profits of its companies contribute foreign exchange—an economic requirement in which Britain has usually been deficient since World War II.

The Middle Eastern states have gained in various ways, and in various degrees, from their oil. The foreign companies have made efforts to provide improved housing, sanitation, health, and educational facilities. Seventy-five per cent of Iraq's oil revenues go to the Iraq Development Board for development of the economy. Kuwait, which may come to have the highest per capita income of any state in the world, is investing oil revenues in such improvements as communications, schools, hospitals, and harbor facilities. Parenthetically, the foreign affairs of this sheikdom are handled by the British, thus far without much complaint, perhaps because little Kuwait is sandwiched between Iran and Saudi Arabia.

18 *The New York Times,* Nov. 15, 1953.   19 See discussion of world petroleum in ch. ii.

The oil revenues of Saudi Arabia have been treated more as the property of its absolute monarch. Those of Iran were derived from a long-standing contract which provided for a royalty rate much below that being paid by American companies. This situation, coupled with a long-standing Iranian feeling that resources were being exploited without adequate recompense, led to nationalization in 1951. This in turn produced a deadlocked negotiating situation with Britain which stopped all Iranian oil sales inasmuch as Britain controlled the marketing facilities for the Iranian oil. In addition, it was not too difficult in this situation for other Middle Eastern oil fields, notably those in Kuwait and Saudi Arabia, to supply oil in quantities equivalent to the losses from Iran. Thus the finances of the Iranian government were struck a near-mortal blow. Iran could look for financial relief only to the Soviet Union or to negotiated settlement of its oil dispute. The fall of the Mossadegh government and a quick grant of aid from the United States in 1953 made the latter choice a practical possibility. The oil industry and oil royalties ("oil diplomacy") are inescapable factors in the foreign affairs of many of the Middle Eastern countries.

Not the least of the factors is the undoubted interest of the Soviet Union in both the oil and the strategic location of the Middle East. All Soviet production statistics are open to question. But even if an estimate of 1,500,000 barrels of Soviet (including satellites) petroleum a day is materially in error it still indicates that a Soviet policy maker would have reason to be interested in the 2,000,000 barrels a day produced in the Middle East plus the capability for cheap and rapid expansion of production.

Nationalism. The peoples of the Middle East are, in general, highly nationalistic. The reasons for, and the intensity of, this nationalism vary from country to country. Turkey has a strong, confident nationalism which is moderate and has little trace of anti-Westernism. Rather, the Turks think of themselves as a European people. The other states are young, and have a strong element of religious feeling about their nationalism. Several have an anti-Western, particularly anti-British, bias. The Arab states, which include all except Israel, Turkey, Iran, and perhaps the emerging state in the Sudan, are strongly anti-Israel. They also lack friendliness toward Turkey because of their one-time dominance by the Ottoman Empire.

Some Political Features. Most Middle Eastern countries have adopted the forms of parliamentary government. Turkey and Israel have developed stable working democracies. In other states internal politics tend to be volatile. Extreme poverty, together with religious fanaticism, political inexperience, and some realization of the possibilities for social and economic improvement, are a fruitful ground for demagogic, and even fanatical, leaders. A middle class is generally small, and there are relatively few educated people. The masses are readily excited by appeal to nationalist issues, which are often connected with religious issues. The forms of democracy are often turned into "mobocracy," or to some pattern of "strong-man" government.

It may perhaps be argued that the "strong man" is a useful, and sometimes necessary, step on the road to responsible democratic government. Turkey followed this road under Kemal Ataturk, who introduced modern and respectable educational and administrative systems, laying a basis for a stable, reasonably democratic political regime. Syria and Egypt have turned to "strong-man" rule in their political evolution. Several states (Saudi Arabia, Yemen, Kuwait) have not been other than absolute monarchies. In Jordan a Parliament shares legislative power with the King. There is little tradition of party responsibility and little experience with party and parliamentary government even in states having this form of political organization. Lebanon, with its one-house Parliament having seats distributed along religious lines, is probably an exception.

The conduct of foreign affairs in many Middle Eastern states is largely a personalized matter. Contrary to the situation in Western states, there is a lack of highly trained administrative and executive personnel. Dealings are centered much more on the Head of State, Premier, or Foreign Minister, and the personal views of these individuals usually bulk larger, proportionately, than in older governments.

The Middle East in World Affairs. We have stressed the importance of the Middle East because of its oil and its strategic position. Except for Turkey, the Middle Eastern area is, for all practical purposes, defenseless against external attack unless supported by an outside power. It lacks an economic production capable of supporting material military power, as well as military technology. Yet its strategic position astride the communication lines between Europe and Asia makes it of tremendous importance for the anticommunist nations.

The peoples of the Middle East, with the exception of Turkey, are not primarily concerned in their external affairs with the conditions outlined in the preceding paragraph. Rightly or wrongly, other factors bulk large in their minds, particularly the Arab feeling about Israel. Secretary of State Dulles remarked on returning from a trip through the Middle East that "the Arabs are more fearful of Zionism than of Communism" and "the Israeli fear that ultimately the Arabs may try to push them into the sea." Responding to extreme nationalist sentiments, political leaders in Iran ousted the British from their oil holdings. In Egypt, the British have been forced to give up most of the privileges they once enjoyed in their Suez Canal Zone base. There is a strong cohesive force arising through the Islamic religion and anticolonialism which has brought the Arab states and some Asiatic states into a loose "Arab-Asian" bloc in the United Nations. No one of the Arab states has sufficient power in its own possession materially to affect world affairs. Yet as a bloc, with the Arab League as the main formal unifying organization, the Islamic states of the Middle East have made themselves a significant political force in international politics. We will discuss the Arab League at some length in Chapter XXI in connection with regionalism and will there comment on the divisive forces which exist in this area.

We leave this compressed discussion of the Middle East with three points. First, the formation of the new state of Israel gave rise to a problem which should have been short-lived—the creation of over three quarters of a million Arab refugees—but which has lingered on unresolved as a fester in international relations. Most of these refugees were fanatically determined to return to their home land and have resisted absorption in neighboring Arab states, which had little capability to absorb them under the best of circumstances. Second, the governments of the Arab states which warred with Israel face a particularly difficult problem in establishing normal peaceful relationships. The strong nationalistic and religious feelings of their peoples make accommodations with Israel a hazard to the existence of any government undertaking them.

Third, and this is a long-term matter, the Middle East is an "underdeveloped area" lacking resources except for its oil. Even the potential agricultural resources are limited by the climate and lack of water. The people are increasingly acquiring aspirations for social and economic advancement. An increase in production, as well as some redistribution of production, is necessary to satisfy these aspirations. Elimination of feudal land tenure does not necessarily increase production. Major changes in economic practices and in living conditions are necessary and may involve political upheavals. These aspirations become internal political issues. One requirement for their realization is capital investment. Most of this capital must come from external sources, through oil royalties, grants, loans, or private subscriptions such as provided to Israel through Zionism. Hence the provision of capital, both in the form of technical assistance and in actual industrial investment, is bound to be one of the major problems of Middle Eastern international affairs during this era. Its availability, or lack thereof, can affect policy making and political conditions in many of the countries of this region.

THE ENVIRONMENT OF POLICY MAKING IN ASIA

Not so many years ago, Asia was calm, static, and, except for Japan, the political entities therein occupied a secondary position in international politics.

Today Asia is one of the most turbulent and changing areas of the world. The direction and character of that change are major elements of international affairs.

The area under discussion stretches from Pakistan to Korea on the mainland of Asia, and from Ceylon and Indonesia to Japan in the parallel chain of island states. It includes fourteen states.[20] In terms of race, religion, culture, degree of industrialization, historic background, and political and ideological orientation, these states represent a vastly diverse set of situations. On the other hand, large parts of the area are confronted at the present time with essentially similar problems and animated by similar resentments and aspirations. Both the common denominators and the differences among these states are significant in comprehending the environment of policy making in this part of the world.

The Germination of Nationalism. All the societies of the Far East are old societies which can look proudly back upon the cultural and spiritual achievements of their past. Yet, at the time of the outbreak of World War I, only China, Japan, and Siam (Thailand) were politically independent and sovereign states.[21] The rest of the area was controlled, in varying degrees, by the powers of the West, with Korea and Formosa controlled by Japan. Great Britain controlled and sought to develop India, Burma, Ceylon, Malaya, and Hong-Kong; France, Indo-China; Holland, the East Indies; and the United States, the Philippine Islands.

There are reasons to criticize the past administration of some of these areas by some colonial powers. Yet (1) the areas became colonies because they were weak, and not vice versa; (2) the imperial era imported into the areas some of the proudest achievements of European culture (law, social and national consciousness, efficient public administration, sanitation, education, industry, and so on); (3) the West helped to create the politically conscious intelligentsia that then formed the leadership of the successful native movements for self-government; and (4) the spirit of nationalism, the main force toward self-government, was imported from the West. In brief, despite the many complaints against colonialism, it was the presence of these powers more than anything else that taught and induced the nations of this area to *want* national independence and that transmitted to them the arts and techniques by which to rule and to improve their societies. Asia's present political emancipation is the result both of its resentment of its colonial rulers and of the successful

20 We do not count Australia and New Zealand in the region. Political entities in the area include Afghanistan, Pakistan, India, Nepal, Ceylon, Burma, Thailand, the Federation of Malaya, Indo-China (Viet Nam, Laos, Cambodia), Communist China, Korea, Japan, the Philippine Republic, Nationalist China (Formosa), and Indonesia.
21 Korea was formally annexed to Japan in 1910.

imitation of those being resented. As Salvador de Madariaga wisely observes: "You may at the same time hate and imitate, in fact very often imitating leads to hating and hating to imitating." [22]

The eclipse of imperialism and the emancipation of Asia were heralded and accelerated by the victory in 1905 of modern industrialized Japan over Czarist Russia, the liberal Chinese Revolution of 1911, the Russian Revolution of 1917, the pronouncement and widespread acceptance of President Wilson's "self-determination of nations," the symbolism of Gandhi's activities in India, the defiant and aggressive military expansion of Japan during the period from 1931 to 1942, and the encouragement given by the anticolonial policy of the United States. It received its crowning impetus, however, from the event of World War II.

The Effect of World War II. World War II was the first truly global war fought with great intensity in both Europe and Asia. The outcome included (1) a temporarily weakened Japan and China, (2) an exhausted Europe, (3) a victorious USSR which was strategically located to exploit that victory, and (4) a very much strengthened United States. These facts had a decisive effect upon further developments in the Orient.

The initial grave defeats of the Western Allies by the Asian Japanese, all the way from Guam to Burma, caused an unredeemable loss of respect and prestige for the Western Powers held previously to be invincible. The accompanying Japanese propaganda for the creation of an anti-white, exclusively Asian "Co-Prosperity Sphere," as well as the irritations and pressures of war-focused colonial policies, contributed to a tremendous upsurge of Asian nationalism. India's contribution to the Allied war effort increased the force of pressure for her own movement toward full statehood. China, partly because of her status as an equal ally, was released from the old restrictions imposed on her sovereignty by various extraterritorial treaties. In Burma, Indonesia, and Indo-China, the local people acquired some taste of local self-government, and, in the latter two, were left with some Japanese arms. Korea was promised freedom by the Cairo Declaration of 1943. Thus it was not surprising that a return to the pre-war *status quo* was out of the question.

Following the war the Philippines (1946),[23] India (1947), Pakistan (1947), Burma (1948), Ceylon (1948), and Indonesia (1949) were granted political independence. Korea remained divided owing to the conflict between communism and the free world. The Korean Republic came into being in 1949 as a generally recognized sovereign state and was accepted as such by

---

[22] S. de Madariaga, *The Theory and Practice of International Relations* (Philadelphia, 1937), p. 39.

[23] The United States had promised the Filipinos independence as early as 1934 and had then set the year 1946 as target date.

Japan in the peace treaty of 1952. Malaya was given a federal constitution in 1948 and has made advances toward self-government. Similarly, the three Indo-Chinese states—Viet Nam, Laos, and Cambodia—threatened by the growing assault of rebels supported from communist China, were promised "independence within the French Union" by France in 1953. For all practical purposes, the aftermath of World War II liquidated the colonial Asian empires of the West and resulted in the new states almost immediately becoming significant factors in international politics.

The Emergence of Communist China. While the rest of Asia was transforming itself toward political independence, the civil war in China between the communist armies and the Nationalist Government was coming to a disastrous close. For a complexity of reasons, the communist forces succeeded in 1949 in ejecting the nationalist authorities to the island of Formosa and of assuming effective control over mainland China.[24] Communist China first supported, and later openly joined, the aggression against South Korea which had called forth the first United Nations military action in aid of a victim state. It also gave material assistance to the Ho Chih Minh (communist) forces in Indo-China.

The fact that the heartland of Asia is now controlled by two communist states, the USSR and China, has exerted an impact on political developments in the adjoining rimlands. Communist elements in the newly independent states have gained strength from the presence of an Oriental communist state of considerable power. Furthermore, the large émigré Chinese minorities, with their traditional family ties to the home land, in Southeast Asia and the outlying islands, are a source of potential communist strength.

The emergence of communist China creates two great questions: (1) Will China be and remain subservient to Moscow? (2) Will Chinese power, either overtly or through communism, overflow the Orient? One point seems clear. Communist China is not just another satellite state of the USSR in the sense of the Eastern European countries. The ties include mutual interests as well as ideology. The relationship is that of two members of a partnership, one of which (communist China) does not have adequate freedom to permit breaking the partnership now. But communist China is in the position of a sovereign state negotiating with the Kremlin. And there are many overlapping interests, which may become conflicts, along the thousands of miles of common border and in the areas of Asia marked for communist penetration. As to the sobering possibilities of Chinese power, these may concern the other Oriental states to an extent causing them to resist communism because of its Chinese connection.

[24] See H. Feis, *The China Tangle* (New York, 1953).

Demographic and Economic Problems. Asia (excluding the Soviet Union and the Middle East) has a population of close to 1,200 million people which constitutes more than 50 per cent of the world's total population. Moreover, it is this part of the world which contains the highest concentrations of population.[25] Such a heavy density of settlement can be supported, with a standard of living above subsistence, only by industrialized and developed urban systems of the type characterizing Western Europe. With the sole exception of Japan, however, such systems are nonexistent in Asia. Most of its economies are overwhelmingly and primitively agricultural. The standard of living in the entire region is very low. The average yearly per capita income of India and Pakistan is about $55. This condition is not unrepresentative of other states of this underdeveloped, overpopulated, rural, and on occasion starving area.[26]

In addition to the low productivity of agriculture, several of the Far Eastern economies are characterized by a heavy dependence on foreign markets (Malayan rubber and tin, Ceylonese rubber and tea, Indonesian oil, and so forth). This dependence makes such countries vulnerable to fluctuations in international markets. Only Japan, and in somewhat smaller measure, India, have important industrial sectors in their economics. Being conscious of the beneficial effects of technological advances and of industrialization, many are striving to undertake such programs. All of them, however, except Japan and India, are handicapped by a general lack of native investment capital and technical know-how. Most of them, with the exception of communist China, have in one way or another turned to the United States, Great Britain, the International Bank, or to private foreign sources for grants or loans of capital funds for assistance in their development programs. In these efforts, and in their urgent endeavors to modernize their agriculture, the United States Point Four Program, the Commonwealth Colombo Plan, the United Nations Technical Assistance Program, and private programs such as those of the Ford and Rockefeller Foundations have performed a valuable and important service, particularly in the provision of technical know-how.

In the long view, however, it is not likely that these countries will succeed in permanently raising their standards of welfare unless they can achieve a slackening of their rapid population growth. Land reform, gradual industrialization, the production of more food and consumer goods, and wider international exchange of goods are also needed in varying degrees in different countries but are generally secondary, in the long run, to the population problem.

[25] Japan had in 1949 about 233 persons per square kilometer; South Korea, 216; Ceylon, 111; India, 109. Compare with this Canada, 1; Argentina and Brazil 6; the United States, 19.
[26] Only the yearly per capita income of Japan ($100) and Ceylon ($67) is substantially higher. See *National and Per Capita Incomes, Seventy Countries—1949,* Statistical Papers, Series E, no. 1, United Nations (New York, Oct., 1950).

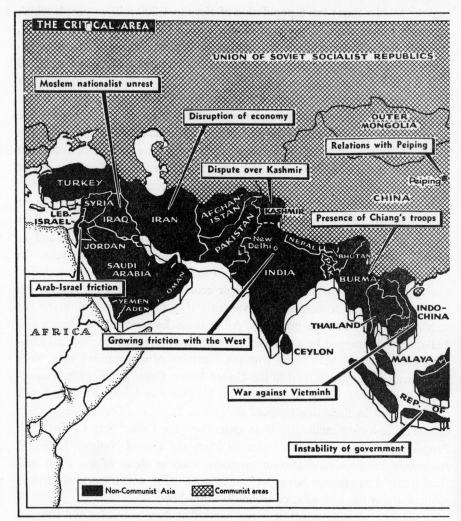

THE CRITICAL AREA

UNION OF SOVIET SOCIALIST REPUBLICS

Moslem nationalist unrest

Disruption of economy

OUTER MONGOLIA

Relations with Peiping

Dispute over Kashmir

Peiping

CHINA

TURKEY

SYRIA
LEB.
ISRAEL   IRAQ   IRAN   AFGHAN-ISTAN   KASHMIR

Presence of Chiang's troops

JORDAN   New Delhi   NEPAL

PAKISTAN   BHUTAN

SAUDI ARABIA   OMAN   INDIA   BURMA

Arab-Israel friction

YEMEN
ADEN   INDO-CHINA

AFRICA   THAILAND

Growing friction with the West

CEYLON   MALAYA

War against Vietminh   REP. OF

Instability of government

■ Non-Communist Asia   ▨ Communist areas

FIGURE

Racial, Religious, and Psychological Problems. The people inhabiting the Far East vary in race (yellow, red-brown, white), religion (Buddhists, Hindus, Moslems, Christians, Shintoists), and political ideology (from the extreme of communism on the left to the extreme of conservative feudalism on the right). Such diversity, of course, makes for difficulties. While the biological element of race differences may not be of great importance, the cultural connotations attached to it create problems between, for example, the Malayan and Bur-

AND RESOURCES

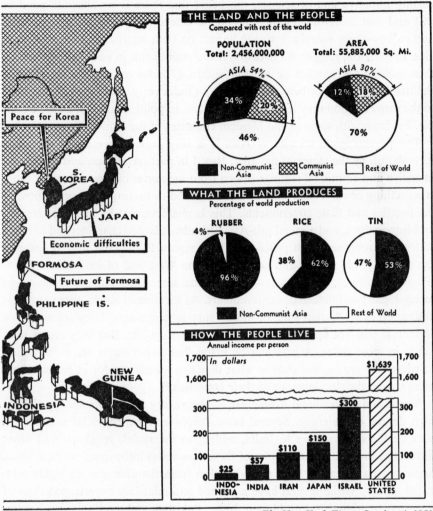

THE LAND AND THE PEOPLE
Compared with rest of the world

POPULATION
Total: 2,456,000,000

ASIA 54%

34% 20%

46%

AREA
Total: 55,885,000 Sq. Mi.

ASIA 30%

12% 18%

70%

■ Non-Communist Asia   ▨ Communist Asia   □ Rest of World

WHAT THE LAND PRODUCES
Percentage of world production

RUBBER   RICE   TIN

4%
96%

38% 62%

47% 53%

■ Non-Communist Asia   □ Rest of World

HOW THE PEOPLE LIVE
Annual income per person

In dollars

$25 — INDONESIA
$57 — INDIA
$110 — IRAN
$150 — JAPAN
$300 — ISRAEL
$1,639 — UNITED STATES

Peace for Korea

S. KOREA

JAPAN

Economic difficulties

FORMOSA

Future of Formosa

PHILIPPINE IS.

NEW GUINEA

INDONESIA

The New York Times, October 4, 1953

XV:3

mese on one hand, and the large Chinese minorities in their countries on the other. Even peoples of close racial linkage, for example, the Japanese and Koreans, are hostile to each other for historical reasons.

Religion plays a most important role in Asian life. For most of the peoples it defines an entire way of life (Hinduism, Mohammedanism, Confucianism) including the values and emphases of social, and therefore also political, activity. Such religion-bound facts as beliefs about caste, the role of women in social life, the other-worldly focus of national philosophy, the disparagement of earthly initiative and of science, the belief that there is no absolute good or evil and that therefore nothing should be categorically sought or embraced, and so on—these exercise a strong impact on both internal and external policies. In addition, religion on occasion is the main factor in nationalistic feeling, thus making for conflict or tension within (Hindus versus Moslems inside Pakistan and India) or between two states (India versus Pakistan). Adherence to the same religion may lead, to some extent, to political affinity, as for example, Pakistan with some of the Moslem countries of the Middle East.

The psychological climate of Asia is a very important element of policy formulation by the states in the area. Based in part on religion and in part on intensive and emotional feelings drawn from memories of recent history, there is something of an "Asian state of mind" shared in varying degrees by most of the peoples and their governments. This is characterized by anti-Westernism, anti-imperialism, and a racial pro-Asia attitude. It is also characterized in some states by strong neutralist proclivities with regard to the cold war. It suspects the sincerity, objectives, and activities of the West and of its missionaries—religious, cultural, or political—while at the same time seeking to adopt its technological and industrial achievements. As mentioned above, these attitudes adding up to an "Asian state of mind" vary among states. They are strong in Indonesia and not apparent in the Philippine Republic. But they are at least latent in most states. A case can be made that Asian states are more united in what they are against than in what they are specifically for in international affairs, save the development of their countries.[27]

Social and Educational Problems. Almost every state is handicapped by a high degree of illiteracy. Several have deeply entrenched social institutions, such as the caste system in India, adding to the racial, religious, and other difficulties in welding the peoples of these new states into strong political units. Some have a spread in level of civilization from the aborigine to highly educated groups. While several have a trained and relatively experienced class of government administrators (Japan, India, Pakistan, and the Philippine Republic), others (Indonesia, the Indo-Chinese states, and Korea) are deficient in this type of individual. Except for Japan and, to a lesser extent, China, they lack technical experts. Such a situation makes difficult the transformation of the forms of democracy into the real practice of democracy.

Political. Under the impact of Western political thought, many of the new Asian states have adopted representative forms of government. India, Pakistan, and Ceylon have chosen to remain associated with the British Commonwealth

27 See L. Menon, "You Are Guilty," and Chester Bowles, "We're Both Guilty," in *World*, Nov., 1953, pp. 11–17.

and, in the first two instances, have chosen the republican and federative form. The Philippines, Indonesia, Burma, and Korea are republics, while Thailand, the three Indo-Chinese states, and Japan continue the monarchial form of governments with, however, some democratic institutions. Most of these countries are faced with grave internal political problems in addition to those of a socio-economic nature. Indo-China, the Philippine Republic, Indonesia, and Burma have been plagued by armed dissident groups connected with communism. We have mentioned the lack of qualified personnel. Parties in the new states tend to be centered on personalities rather than on policies and issues. Budgets (with the exception of Pakistan) have tended to be unbalanced. All Asian noncommunist nations, in their present stage of development, desperately need and want peace and it is therefore logical that they should guard against doing anything that, in the view of their leaders, makes war more probable.

Asia in World Affairs. The Asian states, post-World War II, became important components of the political world. India, Pakistan, Burma, the Philippines, Thailand, and Indonesia are members of the United Nations, as is nationalist China. As such, they have sometimes voted with countries of the Middle East as an "Arab-Asian" bloc and thus influenced appreciably the proceedings of the United Nations. Moreover, this bloc has been consistently pressing against racial discrimination (in South Africa) and against alleged imperialism of the old-fashioned type (in Tunis and Morocco), as well as calling for disarmament and a political rather than a military solution of Asian problems. With respect to the manner of solving these problems, however, the states of Asia are not in accord. The South Korean, Japanese, Philippine, nationalist Chinese, Thailand, and Pakistan governments have generally sided with Western views, and the Indian, Burmese, and Indonesian governments have tended to take an "Asian" stand which recommends recognition of communist China and peaceful cooperation with it.

The peoples of these Asian states are an important weight in the scales of the world power balance. Should a large bloc of the 530 million people in Burma, Ceylon, India, Indonesia, Nepal, and Pakistan be engulfed in the communist camp, the danger to the survival of Western civilization would increase enormously. Thus for reasons of the most immediate self-interest, the West must cultivate the friendship, or at least the neutrality, of these new nations. The representatives of these peoples, particularly those of India, desire to be respected as spokesmen for the people and the problems of Asia. Their pride must be respected. They must be dealt with as sovereign equals, and be assisted, for strategic and political as well as humanitarian reasons, in preserving their independence, and in strengthening their social and economic fabric.

SUGGESTED READINGS

LATIN AMERICA

German Arciniegas, *The State of Latin America* (New York, 1953).

W. C. Gordon, *The Economy of Latin America* (New York, 1950).

M. Jorrin, *Government in Latin America* (New York, 1953).

Austin F. MacDonald, *Latin American Politics and Government* (New York, 1950).

THE MIDDLE EAST

R. N. Frye (ed.), *The Near East and the Great Powers* (Cambridge, 1951).

J. C. Hurewitz, *Middle East Dilemmas* (New York, 1953).

George Lenczowski, *The Middle East in World Affairs* (Ithaca, 1952).

E. A. Speiser, *The United States and the Near East* (Cambridge, 1950).

T. C. Young (ed.), *Near East Culture and Society* (Princeton, 1952).

ASIA

W. Norman Brown, *United States and India and Pakistan* (Cambridge, 1953).

K. Davis, *The Population of India and Pakistan* (Princeton, 1951).

C. DuBois, *Social Forces in Far East Asia* (Minneapolis, 1949).

F. Hailey, *Half of One World* (New York, 1950).

L. A. Khan, *Pakistan: The Heart of Asia* (Cambridge, 1950).

Werner Levi, *Free India in Asia* (Minneapolis, 1953).

J. F. Muehl, *Interview With India* (New York, 1950).

P. C. North, *Moscow and the Chinese Communists* (Stanford, 1953).

R. S. Rau, *East of Home* (New York, 1950).

E. O. Reischauer, *The United States and Japan* (Cambridge, 1950).

C. Wolfe, *The Indonesian Story* (New York, 1948).

PART IV

The Projection of National Policy into International Politics

PART IV

The Projection of National
Policy into International Politics

CHAPTER XVI

Instruments and Patterns of Foreign Policy

WE HAVE seen in the preceding chapters that a variety of political, social, psychological, economic, and other fundamental factors enter into the continuous process of formulation and conduct of foreign policy. Governments conduct their policies within patterns, often quite clearly discernible, as for example a "balance of power" policy or a "collective security" policy. They seek to implement their policies by using those "instruments" of foreign policy which nature, their socio-economic systems, their political and moral values, their own strength, and the maturity of their diplomacy make available. Conversely, the policies and the patterns of policy which states pursue are in part a resultant of the instruments available and must be reasonably consistent therewith. A policy, for example, of opposing the desires of a powerful state which appears possibly willing to use force is hardly consistent with a lack of available military power.

The instruments of foreign policy can be distinguished as political, psychological—including the moral element—economic, and military. They are interrelated and mutually supporting. It is difficult to envisage a situation in which any one is employed to the exclusion of all others. These instruments also make up the components of national power. The wisdom of a nation's representatives in using these instruments determines the success or failure of its policies in international affairs.

THE POLITICAL INSTRUMENT

The normal relationships between states are essentially political in nature. They are conducted by representatives of governments and have to do with the pursuit of national policies, the satisfaction of national interests and objectives, and, where possible, the adjustment of differences between states.

The political instruments of statecraft are the principal determining means by which states normally seek to serve their interests in international affairs in time of peace. By the political instrument we mean the methods of representation, negotiation, inducement, manipulation, arrangement, and agreement. These methods cannot be separated from the means (economic, psychological, military) which often determine their success or failure.

The political instrument is the ultimate implementing instrument of national policy in international affairs, even though at times the economic or military instruments may be brought to the forefront and may predominate.

As an example, following World War II it became apparent that the states of Western Europe were in need of large-scale economic and financial assistance if their economies were to be restored and stabilized. The European Recovery Program was the chosen instrument for the achievement of a broad policy objective. Although the means employed for the achievement of the objectives sought by the United States and the participating states were primarily economic in nature (the European Recovery Program), the objectives were in considerable part political, and the necessary relationships among the states were worked out by means of diplomacy. Likewise, when military action takes place between states, the objectives of this action can be ultimately secured only through the establishment of some kind of political arrangement between the parties concerned. This may be unilaterally dictated by a victorious power imposing the terms of peace upon the defeated. Or it may result from the negotiation of a peace settlement between the belligerents. In the final analysis, the political leadership of the state determines when and for what purposes armed force shall be used and when and on what basis peaceful relationships shall be restored.

Even when the relationships between states are quite inactive or are broken, the political instrument remains a most important factor. The leadership in each state continues to make estimates, to undertake actions which will influence the political decisions of the leadership of other states, and generally to work toward future political arrangements to its liking.

We shall discuss in the next Chapter some of the methods through which the political instrument is most frequently employed. Generally speaking, the art of its employment is called diplomacy. As we use this term we mean the application and administration of foreign policy at all levels and dealing with all subjects, political, economic, and military.[1] Those who wield the political instrument nowadays and who are its spokesmen embrace many kinds of official representatives. The regular members of a state's Foreign Service, and of the so-called diplomatic corps, comprise today but a part of the total personnel appointed by states to engage in one form or another of international relations. Those citizens who are representatives at meetings of technical and specialized

---

[1] Professor Hans Morgenthau refers to diplomacy in a similar manner as describing "the formation and execution of foreign policy on all levels, the highest as well as the subordinate." *Politics Among Nations* (2d ed., New York, 1954), p. 128.

international organizations and agencies, who speak for states at negotiations relating to economic or mutual defense assistance, who are members of delegations or missions to defense organizations and international committees, and even those on international staffs are involved in diplomacy. Such individuals, along with the traditionally accredited ambassadors, ministers, and personnel in other diplomatic ranks, are engaged in handling the political instrument of foreign policy. The men (and women) who carry on the complex business of states in international politics now have little similarity to the stereotype diplomat in morning coat, spats, and monocle. Rather, they are often overworked individuals, usually skilled in many technical matters as well as being charged with the delicate tasks of traditional diplomacy.

PSYCHOLOGICAL INSTRUMENT

Appeal to moral principles and to psychological forces may be made a significant instrument in the hands of governments for the furtherance of national interests and objectives. This we shall call the psychological instrument of policy. A sharp line of demarcation cannot always be drawn between the psychological and the political instruments of policy, for the effective functioning of the one is dependent upon correlation with the other. Indeed, the psychological instrument is most effectively employed when it is utilized in close conjunction with all other instruments of policy.

Most people believe in the application of moral principles as a guide to relationships between individuals. There is a human tendency to believe that states should adhere to a similar set of principles. This view is particularly held among peoples sharing the Judaist-Christian traditions and beliefs. An assurance of adherence to principle and morality gives a larger guarantee of continuity in policy—a characteristic which each nation seeks in the policies with its friends. It forms a basis upon which nations can cooperate with one another. Trust, good faith, and friendship are important factors in international affairs. Hence, nations direct the psychological instrument toward establishing a belief that they are friendly and can be trusted, and that their conduct is moral and based upon principle.

Prestige has always been a major factor in international affairs. It is in part a product of the power and actions of a state. But it is in part psychological. Each state desires to have prestige in the minds of others. This carries with it influence, standing, and political power. These can be exceedingly helpful in the furtherance of a nation's policies. Statesmen are also concerned that their people feel that their country has prestige. An insult or arbitrary action to a nation or its nationals, injuring its prestige, can become a serious matter leading to much friction, especially if internal feelings are aroused. A state cannot be expected to accept proposals which damage its prestige materially. One of the main tasks of a nation's diplomats, accordingly, is to devise formulas for pressing their country's policies in such a way that they are politically accept- able to the statesmen of other nations from the standpoint of prestige.

Information and Propaganda Programs. The democratization and socializa- tion of nations have brought with them in modern times the development and use of extensive public information and propaganda programs on the part of governments. Governments have become conscious of the need for "an in- formed public" at home, and of the need to inform and influence public opinion abroad. With the increasing importance of the public, and of large national armed forces, as well as the close relationship of domestic politics and foreign relations, foreign policies can be conducted only within the leeway of public toleration and support, even within the totalitarian countries.[2] With modern means of rapid communication and mass circulation of news and ideas, use of the press, radio, and television have come to occupy an important place in relation to international politics. Public gatherings of the United Nations have come to afford useful means of broadcasting views and opinions to widespread audiences. Modern technology, together with open diplomacy and an increased understanding of the operation of psychological forces, have thus made propaganda a powerful tool in the hands of statecraft.[3] Use of this psychological instrument may be illustrated from the programs and activities of Britain, the United States, and the USSR.

British Information Service. It is generally not appreciated, at least on the Western side of the Atlantic, that in overseas information activity Britain has occupied one of the forefront positions. First steps to organize an extensive information program—other than the more or less temporary propaganda system set up during World War I—were taken in 1934 when Fascist and Nazi activities began to threaten British interests abroad. At this time a British Council was created to further cultural relations with other countries, the News Department of the Foreign Office was enlarged, and overseas broadcasting by the British Broadcasting Company was inaugurated. During World War II information and propaganda activities assumed a substantial place in the British war activities.[4]

2 See R. C. Tucker, "Malenkov, Too, Must Weigh Public Opinion," *The New York Times Magazine,* Jan. 3, 1954.

3 For general references on propaganda, see B. L. Smith, H. D. Lasswell, and R. D. Casey, *Propaganda, Communication and Public Opinion* (Princeton, 1946); Lyman Bryson, *The Com- munication of Ideas* (New York, 1948); L. W. Doub, *Propaganda* (New York, 1935); D. Lerner, *Sykewar: Psychological Warfare Against Germany* (New York, 1949); P. M. Linebarger, *Psy- chological Warfare* (Washington, 1948); L. J. Margolin, *Paper Bullets* (New York, 1946). See also R. L. Brecker, "The New Arm of Diplomacy," *Foreign Service J.,* Aug., 1951; E. H. Carr, "Propaganda and Power," *Yale Rev.,* Autumn, 1952.

4 For a first hand account of the British war-time system see Sir Robert Bruce Lockhart, *Comes the Reckoning* (London, 1947). See also Ladislas Farago, "British Propaganda—The In- side Story," *United Nations World,* Oct., 1948.

British overseas publicity in peace-time is basically utilitarian, devoted to the propagation of faith in Britain, its aims and achievements. It endeavors to influence opinion by presentation of facts and views as seen by London.

A Cabinet committee determines the general lines of British information policies. Operating under the directives of this committee the Foreign Office guides most of the overseas publicity. Aside from its own News Department and Far Eastern Broadcasting Service, it also exercises considerable influence over the nominally independent British Council and the overseas broadcasts of the BBC.

In addition to the routine program, the British are also known to have employed covert propaganda. Activities along this line have included such procedures as the purchase of foreign newspapers, the use of special news services, the operation of secret or clandestine radio stations, and the spreading of reports and rumors. These methods were used with considerable effectiveness during World War II against the Axis powers and to help shape opinion in some neutral lands. They may have some application under the conditions of the cold war.[5]

United States Program. From the end of World War I until 1939 the United States Government had no organized foreign propaganda or general public information program. The Office of War Information, incorporating the "Voice of America," was established in World War II. This functioned both at home and overseas to support the national policy in the war effort. It cooperated with the Allied armies in psychological warfare and gave encouragement, along with the Office of Strategic Services, to underground movements in countries occupied by the enemy. In addition to the OWI, an Office of Coordinator of Inter-American Affairs carried on a correlated information program especially fitted to the interests of the United States in Latin America. The Office of War Information was abolished at the end of hostilities and its functions, greatly reduced in scope, were transferred to the Department of State.[6]

Information and Education Exchange Act. Events abroad in 1948 awakened Americans to the need for a clearly defined program to cope with the mounting Soviet propaganda against the United States. Congress accordingly enacted foundations of a comprehensive program of information and cultural relations attuned to the nation's foreign policy. This was referred to by President Truman as the "Campaign of Truth."

[5] A résumé of the British propaganda program is contained in Staff Study No. 2, "The Information Program of Great Britain," in the Special Committee Report to the Senate Committee on Foreign Relations, *Overseas Information Program of the United States*, Sen. Report No. 406, 83rd Cong., 1st Sess., June 15, 1953. See also T O. Beachcraft, *British Broadcasting* (London, 1946).

[6] See Wallace Carroll, *Persuade or Perish* (Boston, 1948) for a description of the United States war-time effort.

The purpose of the program is defined as being to promote mutual understanding between the people of the United States and other countries, and to correct misunderstandings about the United States abroad. The USIE Program recognizes that there are many approaches to life; that freedom depends upon the right to differ and upon a free flow of truth and ideas. Until 1953 the United States information program was administered within the Department of State. At that time a separate agency was established known as the United States Information Administration having responsibility for the conduct of all parts of the program excepting the exchange of persons which remained under the administration of the Department of State.[7]

Activities. Approximately 9,470 persons were engaged in USIE work in 1952 with a total of 194 Information Service missions functioning in eighty-five foreign countries. Reductions were made in 1953 as a result both of Congressional economy moves and of public controversy about the loyalty of some employees and the nature of some of the activities carried on by the program.

1. RADIO. Probably the best known feature of the program is the Voice of America. In 1952–1953 this was broadcasting daily to overseas listeners more than one hundred separate programs in forty-six languages from a large battery of transmitters and relay stations located in the United States, in foreign countries, and on ships at sea. The fact that the Soviet Union and its satellites have at times devoted hundreds of transmitters to jamming the American broadcasts in order to interfere with their reception behind the Iron Curtain attests their realization that the American message is capable of exerting a powerful appeal and impact.

2. FILMS AND PUBLICATIONS. Documentary and educational films of many kinds are prepared for showing in foreign countries. These are made available in as many as forty-two languages for showing not only in regular theatres but also in rural villages through the use of special display trucks known as "mobile units." It has been estimated that as many as sixteen million people a month have witnessed these films which carry, directly or indirectly, some message or appreciation of the way of life prized and believed in by Americans. In addition a daily *Wireless Bulletin* with news of official actions and statements is sent to some seventy United States missions for translation and distribution to the local press and government officials.

3. INFORMATION CENTERS. Information libraries and reading rooms are

7 Public Law 402, 80th Cong. For descriptions of program see Edward W. Barrett, *Truth Is Our Weapon* (New York, 1953); *The Objectives of the United States Information Program*, Sen. Doc., 143, 82d Cong., 2d Sess., June 9, 1952; United States Department of State Pub. 4939, *The International Information Administration Program* (Washington, 1953). See also R. Block, "Propaganda as an Instrument of Foreign Policy," *Department of State Bulletin*, June 19, 1950; R. L. Brecker, "Truth as a Weapon of the Free World," *Annals*, Nov., 1951; Wilson Compton, "Crusade of Ideas," *Department of State Bulletin*, Sept. 8, 1952.

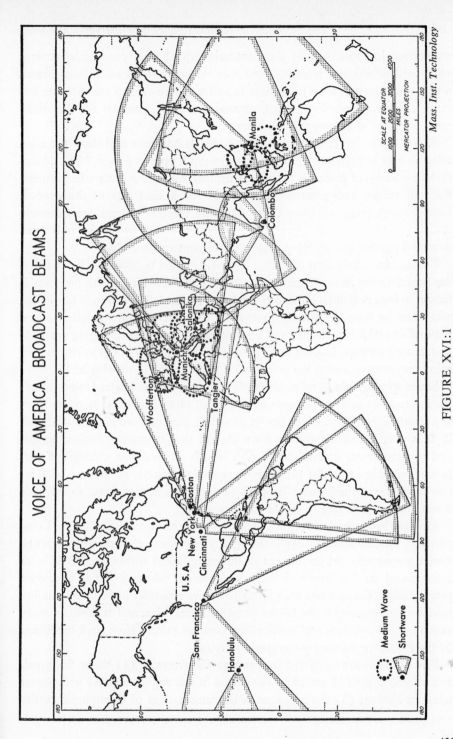

VOICE OF AMERICA BROADCAST BEAMS

Manila

Colombo

Salonika

Munich

Wooffer[ton]

Tangier

Boston

New York

U.S.A. Cincinnati

San Francisco

Honolulu

Medium Wave

Shortwave

SCALE AT EQUATOR
1000   2000   3000   4000
0   MILES
MERCATOR PROJECTION

Mass. Inst. Technology

FIGURE XVI:1

455

maintained in approximately sixty countries with books, periodicals, government publications, and reference materials. As many as twelve million persons a year are known to have used these facilities. These centers are used for lectures, exhibits, discussion groups, extension courses, concerts for American music, and, in some cases, English classes.

4. EXCHANGE OF LEADERS AND SCHOLARS. It has been said that "the most effective way to exchange knowledge is to wrap it up in a person." The educational exchange of students, teachers, scientists, and other leaders in business, the professions, and government is considered a vital part of the over-all United States program. Over thirty thousand foreign students are currently studying in American colleges and universities, and between six and seven thousand persons are studying under government sponsorship.

Evaluation. Evaluation of such a diverse program is difficult. The fact that the Soviet Union has exhibited concern over the activities of the program is reason to believe that its objectives are being realized. The program has added what may be called a "fourth dimension" to United States foreign relations in providing additional avenues of understanding, and in encouraging cooperation, among peoples. It is not to be viewed as an end in itself, but as one among many programs geared to the propagation of American ideals abroad.[8]

Soviet Propaganda. The propaganda campaign of the Soviet Union dwarfs the information and propaganda efforts of all other countries. It pours forth in a multiplicity of forms. The Soviet press and literature are impregnated with it. It is overtly and insidiously sown abroad by Communist parties, agents, and procommunist instrumentalities. Through all available channels Soviet propaganda aims to enlist people by any means possible in support of Moscow's policies to undermine people's faith in the free nations, to advance world communism, and to divide its opponents.

Moscow Propaganda Machine. The *Agitprop* section of the Central Committee of the Communist party is the agency principally charged with directing Soviet propaganda. At the bottom of the party ladder within the USSR is an agent called the "agitator" or "conversationalist" whose job it is to spread propaganda at the common man level. There are reputedly more than a million paid workers engaged in the Soviet propaganda machine, and at times as many as ten million agitators and political workers are said to have been mobilized by the USSR for internal propaganda activity.

Five channels are employed for propaganda overseas: (1) the radio, press, and printed page; (2) personnel connected in one way or another with Soviet missions abroad; (3) the propaganda instrumentalities of Communist parties

8 See report of Senate Special Committee, Sen. Report No. 406, *op. cit.*

in foreign states; (4) communist-controlled international bodies such as the World Federation of Trade Unions, the World Congress of Peace Partisans (which disseminated the so-called Stockholm Peace Petition), and the Cominform; and (5) the United Nations forum. All these are employed both overtly and covertly to spread the Moscow "line," and to undermine confidence in the intentions and motivations of foreign states.

The Soviet Union makes extensive use of high-powered radio transmitters, beaming its programs in many languages to all the major continental areas. It also funnels out vast amounts of printed material, together with information supplied by the official news agency Tass and the leading newspapers, *Izvestia* and *Pravda*. Printed matter is supplemented by Soviet films.

Soviet propaganda attempts to present the features of the USSR, its society, and its aims and objectives in as favorable a light as possible to others. It also endeavors to further what the government conceives to be its interests at any given time. But it also deliberately attacks the policies, institutions, societies, and leaders of other states and sows distrust among nations. And by manipulation of so-called "peace offensives," disarmament proposals, and reports of vast scientific, technical, and social efforts for peaceful pursuits—which may or may not be true but which cannot be verified by the outside world—Soviet propaganda seeks to exert a powerful appeal upon impressionable persons desiring peace and economic or social change.

Use of Communist Apparatus. The far-flung apparatus of international communism has been turned into a tool for the dissemination of propaganda favorable to the interests of Moscow. By being able to utilize native Communist party members, communist-front organizations, and whole segments of populations dissatisfied with existing conditions in their own societies, Moscow is able to use a whole range of native amplifiers sensitive to local issues. Through these channels insidious propaganda is made within foreign countries, directed at undermining their will to oppose Soviet policies and encouraging movements looking toward the violent overthrow of free institutions. Exceptional vigilance, careful counterintelligence, and firm determination are necessary to fight such propaganda effectively.[9]

Propaganda Activity of Other States. Propaganda activity is by no means limited to the Great Powers. Many states, large and small, maintain active

[9] For studies of Soviet propaganda see F. C. Barghoorn, *The Soviet Image of the U.S.: A Study in Distortion* (New York, 1950); Alex Inkeles, *Public Opinion in Soviet Russia: A Study of Mass Persuasion* (Cambridge, 1951); H. D. Lasswell, "The Strategy of Soviet Propaganda," *Proceedings of Acad. Pol. Sci.,* Jan., 1951; A. M. G. Little, "The Soviet Propaganda Machine," *Department of State Bulletin,* Sept. 3, 1951; "The Soviet Propaganda Program—A Preliminary Study," Staff Study No. 3 in Senate Report No. 406, *op. cit.* An examination of the files of the *Current Digest of the Soviet Press* will afford illustrations of Soviet propaganda themes.

information and propaganda services. Before the last war, Germany, Italy, and Japan, engaged in widespread propaganda activities.[10] Some of the Latin American Republics, the Arab-Asian nations, and communist China, to mention but a few, are notable for their use of propaganda in international politics today.

Effectiveness. The relative effectiveness of the propaganda and information activities of states is not easily determined. As we have indicated in Chapter V, its effectiveness is conditional upon many interwoven factors involving timing, sequence, emphasis, and surrounding conditions.[11]

The Nazi regime did much to mobilize the support of the German people behind Hitler, making his demands the more effective as foreign statesmen appraised the temper of his people and the likelihood that, if refused, he could not turn back but would choose war. In more recent times, former Premier Mossadegh of Iran, in permitting and even perhaps organizing mob action in his country, endeavored to impress the world with Iranian resolution in the oil controversy with Britain. In thus committing themselves to riding a tiger, the leaders of both of these countries left themselves few, if any, alternatives other than the most dangerous actions if their programs did not succeed. It has been suggested that the Soviet leaders have deliberately stressed internal propaganda concerning the danger of attack from abroad in order to further acceptance by the people of the strict controls exercised within the USSR by the regime.

Propaganda does not substitute for an intelligent and purposeful foreign policy or for diplomacy to carry out national policy. Propaganda can only support them, can make their success more probable if deftly conducted, and can make more difficult the efforts of opposing forces to frustrate their objectives. As a part of the psychological instrument of policy, propaganda cannot be viewed in isolation from other instruments or from the contents of policy. It must be consistent with actions in the long run, otherwise it may be met with the answer that "your actions speak so loud I cannot hear your words," unless, of course, it is possible to conceal the action realities from those to whom the propaganda is directed. There is a correlation between propaganda and power in the most serious contests of international politics; unless propaganda is presented against a backdrop of strength and determination it usually has little effect.

The interrelationship between the psychological and other instruments of policy can be illustrated in the difficulties over a decision on the Trieste issue

---

[10] See Hans Speier, *German Radio Propaganda* (New York, 1945); H. L. Childs and J. B. Whitton, *Propaganda by Shortwave* (Princeton, 1943).

[11] See p. 144.

in 1953. After the United States and Britain had announced their decision to turn Trieste over to the Italians—following protracted efforts ever since 1945 to bring about a satisfactory solution of this problem—Marshal Tito of Yugoslavia used normal diplomatic channels to protest vigorously against this decision. Through governmental leadership, and partly by spontaneous action, a series of popular demonstrations occurred within Yugoslavia evidencing popular displeasure—thereby strengthening the government's stand through exertion of a psychological effect on other states and their leaders. Yugoslavia at the same time employed the military instrument, moving military forces toward the Trieste area in order to induce some further psychological impact on the United States, Britain, and Italy. Notwithstanding the circulation of rumors that the troops might seize the area if the Italians were allowed to take over the city, the objective clearly was an adjustment or reversal of a political decision. In addition, considerations of prestige were very much at stake.

As long as international competitions and disputes remain, states are likely to employ the psychological instrument, in its various forms and methods, as a means of furthering their policy objectives in international politics.

THE ECONOMIC INSTRUMENT

The objectives of most states, save those bent upon foreign conquest or the stirring up of revolutionary conditions abroad, can normally be encompassed within the broad headings of national security and welfare. As states have come to realize that their territorial integrity and political independence can best be secured by mutual or collective defense efforts, so they have also come to recognize that they are generally economically interdependent. Hence, international relations have become largely concerned with economic matters. The need for, and the provision of, economic resources has come to provide the tangible content of much of the give-and-take of modern diplomatic negotiations.

Virtually every state, no matter how dependent it may be upon the importation of certain vital materials, holds some economic cards in international bargaining. These may be in the form of raw materials, foodstuffs, or manufactured goods desired by others. They may be in the form of markets which others wish to penetrate for the sale of their goods or the investment of capital. Or again, the economic cards may take the form of barriers to trade whose lowering would benefit the commerce of others. Some states hold many and high cards with which they can exercise tremendous leverage upon others. These economic assets, their regulation and use, we shall define as the economic instrument of policy. National economic power is now, if wisely used, power in international politics.

Some Economic Tools and Techniques.[12] One set of techniques for using the economic instrument can be classified under the heading of trade and financial controls. Many of these have been known from the Middle Ages or before. They include tariffs, export and import quotas, subsidies to shipping and to domestic production, exchange rates, currency quotas, barter arrangements, rights of transit for goods going to another country, and similar arrangements. The possibilities in use and adjustment of these techniques give a state important negotiating cards. But, even more important, some states are so dependent on others that the dependent state must gear major portions of its foreign policy to assure continued friendly economic arrangements. Lest we overstress this point, it is worth noting that psychological, military, and political reasons will usually be considered overriding if they clash with the economic relationships. Thus the leadership of Iran, pushed on by internal political pressure, chose to nationalize the oil industry even though that leadership probably realized that the repercussions would certainly involve great economic difficulties.

Loans, both public and private, and grants-in-aid are another technique for applying the economic instrument. Historically their use has ranged from straight business-like propositions, as were British private loans in the United States during the last century, to economic penetration for imperialistic purposes. Any such arrangement, regardless of the purpose, requires accompanying political arrangements. The enormous program of international loans and grants supported by the United States since 1945 has had multiple objectives. At least four stand out: (1) rehabilitation and recovery, believed necessary for a revival of world trade and maintenance of a healthy United States economy; (2) rehabilitation and recovery, to promote and maintain political stability abroad—an important factor in assuring a peaceful world; (3) economic aid and technical assistance for the development of underdeveloped areas, for the same reasons. (4) As the need for military power to oppose the threat of Soviet aggression became crystal clear, assistance was provided to economies of friendly states lacking the economic capacity to support the military strength thought desirable. The reasoning leading to these programs illustrates the inextricable interrelationship of the four principal instruments of policy mentioned at the beginning of this chapter.

Economic Measures as an Instrument of Coercion. Since economic matters are so important internationally, can economic measures be used by a state or group of states to force another to a particular course of action? There are certainly always some elements of compulsion available to each party involved in the normal international arrangement concerning economic matters. Even if

12 See ch. iv and "Economic Consequences of War" in ch. ix.

a state has freedom, from the purely economic standpoint, to adopt a course of action gravely damaging another state, it may not choose to do so because of the adverse political, or even military, effects.

We do not, in the question posed above, refer to this sort of situation. Nor do we refer to a type of situation such as the hard bargaining of the United States with Bolivia in the early 1950's over the price of tin. Bolivia's main industry is tin mining. Her foreign exchange is derived principally from tin. The United States wanted tin for its national defense stock pile. But when Bolivia raised the price, the United States ceased to buy. When Bolivia consequently got into serious economic difficulties, the price came down.

We refer, in the question posed, to coercion of an aggressor or of a nation violating an international agreement or failing to accept a decision of an international organ such as the United Nations. Space does not permit a complete examination of this point. But both historical precedent and reasoned analysis indicate that, while the economic instrument can bring serious pressure, it cannot guarantee results. The Embargo and Non-Intercourse Acts of the United States prior to the War of 1812, Napoleon's continental system, the League sanctions against Italy, the United Nations' ban on trade in "strategic" goods with China during the Korean War, the *de facto* blockade of oil exports from Iran—none of these measures wholly achieved the desired objective. If a nation is determined to persevere in its course, it appears that there is a necessity for calling on one or more of the other instruments of policy to attain a solution and arrange its acceptance.

THE MILITARY INSTRUMENT

What Is the Military Instrument? Military power in being, plus military potential, constitutes the military instrument of foreign policy. The willingness to use it forms a part of the political instrument. The outward form of military power is seen in combat units and their weapons—divisions, air wings, combatant ships, guns, bombs, and so on. But this is only the visible portion of the iceberg to which military power may be compared. These combatant units must be produced by, and supported by, the normally unseen six-sevenths of the iceberg. This portion includes the base and depots and training areas, the inventories of supplies, the munitions factories and ports and communication lines, the industry and raw materials, the human resources, the use that is made of natural assets of position and landform, and, knitting all these things together well or badly, the governmental organization and the awareness and will of the people.

Timing is all-important in appraising the quality and capability of the military instrument. Military potentialities may have little effect on international events if other nations appraise that they cannot be brought to bear on a given situation in time to affect the decision.

Use of the Military Instrument in War. When the relations between states reach the point of hostilities, the military instrument becomes the principal cutting edge of foreign policy. Other instruments must be coordinated for the service of its minimum requirements, otherwise disaster may ensue. Even in a limited war such as Korea, the successful achievement of any acceptable political solution turned on achieving a certain degree of military success. While it can be argued that, in a nuclear age, there may be acceptable substitutes for complete victory, for that victory may be Pyrrhic, it cannot conceivably be argued that defeat is acceptable.

The military instrument in war sets up a situation permitting the political instrument to become dominant once more. But the political instrument, like the psychological and economic instruments, must continue to be active during hostilities, especially in relation to allies and neutrals. In past wars intermittent but continuing contacts have often been kept with an enemy—usually through the good offices of neutrals. There is reason for this; for, unless the objective is absolute, unconditional surrender, hostilities must be brought to an end through political action, and contacts via the political arm may hasten the conclusion of a war. Moreover, political facts and considerations need to be kept in mind in making military decisions and choices during hostilities.

Deterrent and Supporting Function. The concept of military force as a power for peace and stability is somewhat new to general American thinking. It is not new to those familiar with the balance of power principle, and particularly to the British who in the past have endeavored to maintain peace in Europe by holding the balance of power. The counterargument that armaments bring wars is certainly worthy of examination. But serious examination seems to show that, historically, many if not most wars can be ascribed to inadequate military power in the possession of some nation tempting an expansionist state to the overt use of military power.

The most important function of the military instrument in the hands of nonexpansionist states in times short of war is as a force to deter other states from resorting to the use of violence to achieve their objectives or to settle international differences.

Theoretically, the force needed to deter aggression and to maintain international peace and security could be placed under some form of supranational control. But governments and peoples are exceedingly jealous of the command and control of armed forces drawn from their respective states. They are equally concerned about large physical power beyond their influence and control. No supranational political mechanism of a global nature has yet been devised which satisfies states to the extent of making them willing to pass on to it their armed forces and the responsibility for their own national defense. Part of the difficulty lies in the complexity and the heavy cost of raising and supporting armed forces. The central point of the matter, however, is the responsibility for defense inherent in the sovereign power of a state. While this responsibility can be carried out through a wide variety of programs—unilateral armament, alliances, collective security arrangements of various sorts, even neutrality—a state cannot shift this responsibility to another state, national or supranational.

Most of the military power in the world is not actively in use at any one time as a deterrent to the outbreak of hostilities or as a threat of such an outbreak. It serves rather as a background element against which each state formulates and executes its policy. In the absence of this tangible power, the statesman's voice at the negotiating table may be halting and unsure. His proposals and his stands on issues must be trimmed to the realities of his country's capabilities.

We have had in late years an instructive illustration of the relative importance of this instrument. In the demobilization following World War II, the United States allowed its military power to fall below the level of its international political objectives, with a result that it did not attain all of those objectives. To contain the Soviet menace and to re-establish positions of strength from which negotiations could take place, the European Recovery Program, NATO, rearmament, and the inauguration of the Mutual Security Program became necessary to sustain and support the political arm.

Psychological Aspects of Military Instrument. There is an important psychological aspect in military power. Until tested in actual hostilities, its strength and efficacy are what statesmen and peoples think its capabilities to be. Such estimates may vary widely from reality, but they, and not the reality, condition the formulation and execution of policy. History is filled with errors in this respect, as for example Hitler's estimate prior to attacking Russia that the United States lacked the military power to affect the war's outcome, the pre-World War II faith of the French in the invulnerability of the Maginot Line, the communist error of estimate on both the Berlin blockade and Korea. There are many other examples. The military instrument is predictable in its operation only within wide dimensions. Broadly speaking, peoples and statesmen have faith in the military power to which they are historically accustomed and which protects them, as they think, from what they fear most.

Use Short of War. We should not leave this subject without mentioning that armed services have been widely used as an active instrument of policy in nonwar periods. The use of forces for intervention in disturbed areas to protect life and property is well known historically. Armed forces are also sometimes employed to make a show of strength or determination to indicate the seriousness with which an issue is viewed. Observation patrols, rescue and disaster relief missions, military missions, pacific blockades, participation in policing or occupation forces or military missions—these are some of the many functions performed by armed services in aiding, supporting, or executing national policies and international agreements. Military, air, and naval forces are also sent on "good-will" visits to foreign countries to strengthen friendship and add to national prestige. This latter effect is not illogical, being a matter of increasing confidence in the strength of a friend.

Concerted Action Requires Use of All Instruments. Finally, we must note that rapid changes which can take place in the relationships of states, and which have occurred in recent years in the realm of national security, require a careful integration of all instruments of policy. This is nowhere better revealed than in the complex relationships and actions of a coalition security arrangement, such as NATO, which illustrates why the concept of "diplomacy" must today be viewed in a broad rather than a narrow technical sense.

PATTERNS OF POLICY

In the employment of the various instruments of policy, certain general patterns of policy action emerge as states seek to further their interests and attain their national objectives. Obviously, there are many combinations of policy action which any individual state or group of states may employ and which are utilized by the states of the world from time to time. One must make an extensive study of diplomatic history and of the foreign policies of the principal states to observe the manifold details of these policy patterns.

Types of Patterns. No set of mutually exclusive categories for patterns of policy is practicable. But guided by the basic objectives of policy it is possible to distinguish certain groupings. In seeking to promote its economic welfare, a state may lean to free trade, to protectionism, to international collaboration, or even to some forms of economic union with others having mutual interests. A state may follow policy patterns of imperialism, colonialism, satellization, respect for the rights of free peoples, support of political aspirations of dependent peoples, or some combination of these patterns. For security a state may seek a balance of power, it may decide to join in collective procedures with others; it may seek security through international order and the rule of law; it may pursue a policy of isolation; or it may follow a combination of two or more of these approaches which are not mutually inconsistent. Then there are patterns of policy execution which might be called techniques. A state may prefer bilateral or multilateral dealings. It may prefer to handle each specific relationship as a separate problem or alternately to enter into long-term treaties defining dimensions within which detailed relationships such as disputes will be handled.

In general, any adopted pattern of policy is the best way to further a particular state's interest as seen by its leadership. There is merit in consistency and continuity. In fact, these characteristics of policy are patterns in themselves. Generally a state makes no attempt to conceal its policy patterns. Thus, Britain, for the entire period since Napoleon, has made no attempt to conceal the fact that its policy sought friendly states on the continental shore of the North Sea. A state bent upon territorial expansion or promotion of subversion or revolution abroad may, on the other hand, logically strive to conceal its patterns of policy, even to representing them publicly as something entirely different from their true method and direction.

A complete discussion of patterns of policy, with historical illustrations, would fill a bookshelf. A brief summary of some of the observable patterns may, nevertheless, be helpful.

Patterns to Facilitate Conduct of International Relations. Practically all states adhere to the following patterns to some extent:

1. The recognition of states and the exchange of diplomatic and consular officers.
2. The conclusion of treaties of friendship, commerce, copyright, navigation, and so on with other states, thereby facilitating solution of detailed problems falling within the terms of the treaties.
3. Adherence to international conventions and protocols, and participation in international agencies such as the International Postal Union.
4. Support of international law, thereby decreasing the obscurities over the ways nations will act in any given set of circumstances.

Patterns Concerned with Method of Conducting International Relations. Strange as it may seem, there have been fairly wide differences in methods of conducting international affairs. Some states prefer to operate extensively on a multilateral basis within international organizations of various sorts. Others are cool to multilateralizing certain problems because such action may force them to take a position on a matter on which they might otherwise have remained neutral, or which they would prefer not to have raised and taken out of their hands. Other states, again, prefer bilateral relationships because their bargaining or negotiating position is stronger in such a situation. Thus, on the one hand, one might expect Britain to prefer bilateral security arrangements with the United States instead of participation in the NATO Council, while Finland, on the other hand, might well prefer to discuss international issues within the United Nations rather than directly with the USSR, although circumstances preclude this.

Under the heading of policy of patterns concerned with methods of conducting international relations we can distinguish the following:

1. Bilateralism and multilateralism as discussed above.
2. Special arrangements for the settlement of disputes.
3. The establishment of regional organizations and arrangements.
4. Support of the United Nations and specific policies as to what matters should, and should not, be handled by the United Nations.

Patterns Concerned Primarily with Welfare.[13] Traditionally the policies which fall into these patterns have been primarily economic. But they also include policies having to do with social welfare, for example, the narcotics and white slave trade and cultural matters. These patterns include:

1. Policies relating to international trade, whether free trade or protectionist, whether bloc trading or worldwide, whether discriminatory or adhering to most-favored nation principles, and so on.
2. Policies having to do with economic development and with the flow of capital. Thus a nation's policies on the nationalization of industries and on sending earnings abroad may vitally affect its international relations.
3. Policies concerned with the search for markets and for raw-material sources.
4. The degree of economic self-sufficiency for which a state strives, as compared with dependence upon international trade. The policies followed in this respect have a close relationship to those falling in the next category.

Patterns Concerned Primarily with Security.[14] In matters relating to security, each state must make two basic decisions. Shall it base its pattern of security policy primarily on (1) isolation or collective security or upon (2) world organization or a balance of power? The following patterns are not, in some cases, inconsistent with either choice:

1. The maintenance of a military posture commensurate with the state's policies, objectives, commitments, and its position and economic means.
2. Coalitions and regional arrangements for mutual security.
3. Economic and political support of allies.
4. The Concert of Great Powers concept which might have become effective after World War II but for the schism between Russia and the West.

---

13 See ch. iv.
14 See ch. xviii on policies for national security, ch. vii on power politics, and ch. xxi on regional arrangements for discussions of some of these patterns.

5. The acquisition of bases or base privileges in strategic locations about the world.
6. Neutrality, a policy practiced successfully for over a century by Sweden and Switzerland.
7. Intervention, a pattern of policy which may also fall within the expansionist patterns listed below.
8. The attainment of satisfactory boundaries and the elimination of boundary quarrels.
9. War.

Patterns of Policy Having Expansionist and Revolutionary Objectives. The over-all pattern of Nazi policy was one of eventual world domination. Communist policy has the same doctrinaire objective. For this reason almost every policy of the USSR deserves careful examination to ascertain its intentions and real objectives. Among the patterns of expansionism may be found the following:

1. Imperialism and colonialism, now practically gone in their older forms, and replaced by a new imperialism with an ideological drive, ideological ties, and subversive techniques including "satellization."
2. Economic and cultural penetration.
3. Conquest (attempted in Korea) and the threat of force: age-old and continuing patterns for expansion. No one has yet appraised, with any surety, the possibilities of using the threat of force in our nuclear age.
4. Propaganda and other programs designed to split the unity of opposing allies.

PATTERNS OF POLICY CONFLICT AND ALSO INTEGRATE

Some of the patterns of policy which we have listed are complementary and consistent with one another. Some of them conflict. That two or more patterns seem to be inconsistent or conflict does not necessarily mean that a nation will not use both of them as its national interests and objectives dictate. Governments generally regard it as being proper to support regional organization and world organization at one and the same time, or to participate in the activities of the United Nations and at the same time to strive outside the world organization to fashion a favorable balance of power and to maintain and strengthen their own national defense forces.

The degree of emphasis which a state gives to a particular combination of policies is the important consideration in judging the general nature and objectives of its foreign policy. Top-level national strategic planning determines for each state how the various instruments shall be employed—in what patterns

—in pursuing the objectives of over-all national policy. Each instrument, when properly correlated with the others, becomes in itself an adjunct for attaining the national objectives.

Some people may feel that the patterns of policy when viewed as a whole are like a maze or labyrinth. The clue to them lies in the vital importance to each nation of its security and welfare. Hence, every nation retains in its panoply of active and latent policies as many courses of action and instruments of policy as possible. Each is loath to give up any of them except in return for a program of proven or greater effectiveness. Because of this, changes in the patterns of policy of a particular nation are generally slow and evolutionary rather than abrupt or revolutionary.

SUGGESTED READINGS

E. Barrett, *Truth Is Our Weapon* (New York, 1953).

Edward H. Carr, *Propaganda in International Relations* (New York, 1939).

W. Carroll, *Persuade or Perish* (Boston, 1948).

A. E. Hindmarsh, *Force in Peace* (Cambridge, 1933).

Daniel Lerner (ed.), *Propaganda in War and Crisis* (New York, 1951).

P. M. Linebarger, *Psychological Warfare* (Washington, 1948).

Niccolò Machiavelli, *The Prince and the Discourses* (Modern Library, 1952).

L. Markel, *Public Opinion and Foreign Policy* (New York, 1949).

R. F. Mikesell, *United States Economic Policy and International Relations* (New York, 1952).

J. U. Nef, *War and Human Progress* (Cambridge, 1950).

N. D. Palmer and H. C. Perkins, *International Relations* (Boston, 1953).

R. E. Summers, *America's Weapons of Psychological Warfare* (New York, 1951).

CHAPTER XVII

The Conduct of Foreign Affairs

NATIONAL POLICY is projected into international politics using the various instruments of policy described in the previous chapter. If we use a broad definition of diplomacy such as that given in the preceding chapter, the concept of "diplomacy" will include the use and management of each of the instruments mentioned in their connection with external affairs.

In former times contacts between governments were relatively limited in number, and the terms *diplomacy* and *diplomat* were generally used to describe external political contacts and arrangements entered into by the heads of states and their top level ministers or by professional diplomats.

CHANGING NATURE OF DIPLOMACY

Such a limited concept had a considerable validity until a few decades ago. Contacts between governments were relatively limited in number. They could usually be arranged by statements of broad principle and general agreement and were handled by a few individuals on a high level under instructions from the Heads of State or Foreign Ministers.

The great increase in quantity which has taken place in the relationships among states in modern times and particularly their expansion into military, economic, and technical fields has inevitably brought many governmental departments directly into the international relations field. Personnel drawn from many departments of government accordingly now engage in numerous contacts and negotiations with their opposite numbers in other states and international organizations. It would, for instance, be ridiculous to suggest that because they are not in the Foreign Services of their countries the Secretaries of Defense of the NATO countries are not engaged in "diplomacy" when they conduct negotiations on behalf of their governments at NATO Council meetings.

The projection of national policy into international politics requires "execution of policy on all levels." [1] This extends through many ranges of relationships in peace and war. There is of course some dividing line—a level at which individuals and their activities are best described as "technical" and "advisory," but we see no point in striving to define that line here. Foreign Offices do, as a usual practice, keep a general supervision and exercise general coordination, even over the most technical economic and military international discussions, in order to assure consistency with other policies concerning which the experts may have no knowledge.

DESCRIPTION OF DIPLOMACY

Historical Development of Diplomacy. The term *diplomacy* arose from the practice of providing a national representative with a diploma or letter of credence giving the bearer's official status and requesting that consideration and treatment be given him as an envoy of a sovereign ruler or a sovereign political entity.

Diplomatic representation goes back to the beginning of recorded history. The ancient Greeks are said to have sent ambassadors to adjust relations among their city states. The Papacy developed, in the Middle Ages, its system of legates, nuncios, and papal missions. Machiavelli's writings in *The Prince* indicate that the Italian city states of the early Renaissance had developed diplomacy to a high art. The concept of permanent representation was adopted by the young nation-states of Western Europe from the Italian city states and is now almost universally followed.[2] It involves the maintenance of a permanent embassy or legation at or near the seat of government of each sovereign state.

A large proportion of the routine activities of one state affecting the government of another are channeled through, or under the general political supervision of, the respective embassies. These permanent and routine arrangements for the conduct of international relations on a bilateral basis have, in this century, been supplemented by an increasing number of contacts through special missions. The activities of Colonel House and Harry Hopkins are examples in United States diplomatic history with their meetings with foreign Premiers and Heads of State. In addition there has been a rising tide of multilateral diplomacy by international conference and within the framework of permanent international organizations.

Purposes of Diplomacy. Broadly speaking, the purposes of diplomatic

1 See footnote 1, ch. XVI.
2 On the evolution of diplomacy see D. J. Hill, *A History of European Diplomacy*, 3 vols. (London, 1921); Ragnar Numelin, *The Beginnings of Diplomacy* (New York, 1951); E. Satow, *A Guide to Diplomatic Practice*, vol. I, (London, 1922).

intercourse in time of peace include the following objects: First, to exchange information between governments. Secondly, to develop personal relationships and a climate of opinion, both in the minds of individual statesmen and of the people of the state to which a diplomat is accredited, which further friendship and the reaching of agreements on specific problems. Thirdly, to assist the adjustment and settlement of disputes. In a sense, diplomacy may not inadvertently be characterized as the art of "winning friends and influencing people."

In the case of states aiming at territorial or political expansion at the expense of others, diplomacy may at times be employed in such a way as to mask or conceal the true purposes of the aggressive power. This may include the giving of assurances that a particular country has no further territorial claims, of signing nonaggression pacts, and of engaging in drawn-out diplomatic negotiations while waiting for a propitious moment at which to strike. The diplomatic record of Nazi Germany and of the Soviet Union in the late 1930's and 1940's provides illustrations of this fact.

Contacts are carried on by written "notes" and verbally. Techniques include the presentation of reasoned arguments and appeals to friendship. They also include expressions of concern, warnings, and threats. In the case of some countries the practice of deception is included in the techniques of diplomacy. Diplomacy now involves an increasing flow of agreements which often require a great deal of informal consultation, argument, and technical analysis prior to the formal, and often ceremonial, acquiescence by the parties concerned. Timing is an important aspect of diplomacy. There are right and wrong times for making proposals, for accepting them, and for making them public.

Diplomacy, being conducted among sovereign states, involves negotiation, bargaining, adjustment, and concession. It is standard practice for a state to have a series of positions from "maximum" to "minimum," planned as a preliminary to negotiation on a particular problem—great or small. The discussion, written or verbal or both, then may lead toward a meeting of minds on an acceptable basis, but sometimes still one of "equal dissatisfaction" to all concerned. There are types of diplomacy which are conducted with a view to placing the other party at a disadvantage or thwarting the attainment of its objectives.

Harold Nicolson, British diplomat and scholar, has characterized diplomacy in these words: "Diplomacy is not an end but a means; not a purpose, but a method. It seeks by the use of reason, conciliation and the exchange of interests to prevent major conflicts arising between sovereign states. It is the agency through which the foreign policy seeks to attain its purposes by agreement rather than by war." When agreement becomes impossible, he adds, "diplomacy, which is the instrument of peace, becomes inoperative, and foreign policy, the final sanction of which is war, alone becomes operative." [3]

THE CONDUCT OF INTERNATIONAL AFFAIRS— MACHINERY AT HOME

We have already noted in the chapters on the shaping of foreign policy that the Head of State, the Premier, and the Secretary of State for Foreign Affairs, whether in a republic, a limited monarchy, a parliamentary system of government, or a totalitarian state, exercise principal roles in the formulation and execution of foreign policy. In time of tension or war other government officials may have an importance comparable to that of the Foreign Minister. Many other officials and types of governmental agencies are now concerned with these matters. But, as discussed above, they function as a general rule either as personal emissaries of the Head of State or under the political guidance of the Foreign Office. Hence the following discussion will be principally directed to a description of the functioning of Foreign Offices—while recognizing that many "diplomatic" functions may be carried on by personnel of other agencies.

Role of Head of State. In most states the Head of State—whether he be King, President, or Dictator—plays at least a titular role in the conduct of foreign affairs. Ambassadors are customarily accredited by the Head of one state to the Head of another and are received by him personally. The actual participation of the Head of State in the conduct of diplomatic affairs is determined largely by the constitutional provisions and political traditions of the state, the personality and interests of the Head of State, and the circumstances of the times. As pointed out in previous chapters, the Monarch of Great Britain now has little if any more than a ceremonial position plus a mission of generating favorable public opinion in friendly countries; Presidents of the United States have taken widely varying parts in the conduct of foreign affairs.

Prime Ministers. Prime Ministers of parliamentary democracies not infrequently take the guidance of foreign affairs into their own hands and act as the spokesmen or negotiators for their states. In fact they hold the same foreign affairs position in the public mind, foreign and domestic, as does the President of the United States. The ill-fated journeys of Prime Minister Chamberlain to meet with Hitler at Munich and Godesberg are remembered for the "appeasement" which Chamberlain offered in the form of capitulation to Hitler's

---

[3] Harold Nicolson, *The Congress of Vienna* (New York, 1946), pp. 164–165. For an excellent account of diplomacy in the modern era see Gordon A. Craig and Felix Gilbert (eds.), *The Diplomats, 1919–1939* (Princeton, 1953).

demands over Czechoslovakia. We have mentioned Churchill's practice during World War II, which he continued to some extent when his party returned to power in the early fifties. Unlike the United States Presidents, foreign Prime Ministers are quite likely to have had considerable experience in the field of foreign affairs, and, under the parliamentary system, are likely to be questioned by their Legislature as severely as is the Foreign Secretary.

Tasks of Foreign Offices. Notwithstanding the powers which the Heads of States and of governments may exercise, chief responsibility for guiding the day-to-day implementation of a nation's foreign policy normally rests with the Foreign Office (sometimes called the Department of State or Ministry of External Affairs) under the Foreign Minister or Secretary of State or Secretary of External Affairs.

Aside from responsibility for guiding the formulation of foreign policy and supervising the administration of the Foreign Office and the Foreign Service, the Foreign Minister's life is filled with a round of diplomatic conversations, conferences, visits, and meetings. He must ordinarily carry the burden of "top level" conversations and negotiations—a responsibility which may require not only repeated but prolonged absence from his own country.

The complexity and scope of international affairs have increased so much that the Foreign Ministers of all except minor powers must now lean heavily on their assistants for expert knowledge on many problems of foreign relations and delegate large responsibilities to them. The record of United States Secretaries of State in recent years shows that each has concentrated his energies on a limited number of the more important problems, of necessity leaving responsibility for the more routine matters to the State Department staff and associated agencies. Secretary Hull spent much time on the reciprocal trade treaties and later on the development of the United States' position for a post-war international organization. Secretary Stettinius concentrated on the United Nations, Secretary Byrnes on the peace treaties which took him away from Washington for many months, Secretary Marshall on the European Recovery Program and rising cold war, and Secretary Acheson on the cold war, the fashioning of the North Atlantic Treaty Organization and other regional arrangements, and Korea.

Much advice on foreign affairs, particularly on economic, financial, and military matters, comes from other departments. Within the framework of Foreign Office policy guidance, foreign emissaries may and often do deal directly with representatives of the departments primarily competent in these areas. These departments often furnish representation on international missions and to international organizations in the fields of their responsibility. They also furnish advisers and sometimes top-level representation on delegations to conferences. From the United States, for example, representatives of Treasury, Commerce, Defense, and the United States foreign assistance agency have been common at international meetings during the post-World War II period. These officials, in addition to their relationships to their own departments, normally function under the general guidance and sometimes the personal leadership of the Secretary of State, one of his assistants, or an ambassador or minister abroad.

THE CONDUCT OF INTERNATIONAL AFFAIRS—
PERMANENT MACHINERY ABROAD

The Foreign Service is normally the instrument for providing representation abroad. Through the corps of ambassadors, ministers, consuls, and other grades of Foreign Service officers sent by states to represent their interests in recognized countries abroad, the bulk of top-level official business between states is conducted. Because of the newly developed load of cultural and particularly economic and military relations, there are now a large number of officials dealing with one phase or another of international affairs who are not Foreign Service officers but come from other governmental departments. These all have a hand in the administration of foreign policy and the conduct of international relations.

Rank and Status of Missions. The rank of the permanent mission which one state accredits to another is determined primarily by the importance which the larger and more powerful state attaches to the interchange with the other and by the accord which they reach upon the matter. Missions of the highest rank are called Embassies and are headed by an Ambassador with plenipotentiary powers. Next in rank come Legations which are headed by a Minister Plenipotentiary. Thirdly, there are temporary missions which may be headed by a chief with ministerial rank or merely entitled *Chargé d'Affaires*. The designation is customarily a matter of reciprocity. Considerations of prestige often play a part in determining the agreed rank. Small states as well as Great Powers are hosts to embassies. The United States has gradually made almost all its permanent representatives ambassadors, an example of the use of the psychological instrument and of avoiding any hurt feelings due to being placed in other than the upper caste.

On some occasions governments supplement the efforts of their regular permanent diplomatic representatives by sending special emissaries, or officials from their Foreign Offices, to conduct certain phases of negotiations or of their international affairs. Historically this practice antedates the establishment of permanent missions. But it is utilized as occasion warrants. Examples in recent American practice in addition to Colonel House and Harry Hopkins mentioned before, are President Truman's assignment of Averell Harriman as White House envoy on numerous occasions and President Eisenhower's appointment of his brother Milton Eisenhower to make a special survey of Latin America. The selection and employment of special executive agents is the prerogative of the Head of State. The principal value of this device is that it enables a direct personal contact with the heads of other governments and their immediate advisers on specific items of business about which there may be particular concern. One of the obvious difficulties is that the activities of special envoys may easily overlap the competence and functions of the permanent missions.[4]

Diplomatic Immunities. Certain privileges and immunities have for centuries been accorded to diplomatic personnel in order to enable the diplomat to perform his duties in the conduct of international affairs. In some instances these privileges have been established by treaty, but in general they are derived from international custom, law and comity.

The most fundamental of these immunities is the inviolability of the diplomatic person. This dates from the practices of the ancient Greek city states. The diplomat, together with his family and official household, enjoys inviolability of person and immunity from local civil and criminal jurisdiction. His residence and archives are also exempt from local jurisdiction. The inviolability of diplomatic correspondence has long been insisted upon by states. Elaborate precautions are usually taken by means of secret codes, however, to guard the security of communications between a mission and its home government by cable or wireless. Although the principle of inviolability applies to such communications, attempts to discover the contents of diplomatic messages by means of wiretapping, breaking codes, eavesdropping, and other devices have been known to be fairly widespread.

Members of diplomatic missions are customarily given the privilege of entry and exit of the country to which they are accredited without customs examination or the payment of import or export fees. These and other rights and privileges have been evolved through the years to facilitate the smooth working of diplomacy. It is interesting that, if the possession of diplomatic privileges is used as a test as to who is a "diplomat," the United States has a very wide range of diplomats indeed. Clerical personnel for embassies, missions, and the like normally receive many of these privileges.

Qualifications of a Diplomat. One who is in the diplomatic personnel officially representing his state abroad, whatever his rank, has need of special

4 See H. M. Wriston, *Executive Agents in American Foreign Relations* (Baltimore, 1929); Charles Seymour, *The Intimate Papers of Colonel House* (New York, 1926–1928); Robert E. Sherwood, *Roosevelt and Hopkins, An Intimate History* (New York, 1948). For a review of some of the problems connected with foreign service see Chester A. Bowles, "Some Aspects of Foreign Service," *Foreign Service J.*, Aug., 1953.

skills and talents. He is *prima facie* a representative of one sovereign state in the territory of another, even though his position is subordinate. As such he must carry about himself something of the dignity and bearing becoming such a person. He is charged at all times with representing and forwarding his country's interests abroad and with correctly interpreting and portraying its views and objectives. His task calls for keen perception, presence of mind, readiness and thoughtfulness of expression, tact, ability to carry out instructions with a minimum of guidance, firmness, good judgment, and accuracy in reporting and assessing trends.[5]

The Consular Service. The Consular Service, once usually separate from the Diplomatic Service, is now generally incorporated in one combined Foreign Service.

Consular officers are usually stationed in the principal ports and centers of commerce of foreign states with the primary duty of protecting and promoting foreign trade. Although consuls of all ranks are appointed by the national executive of the sending state, they are distinguished from the diplomatic service in that they deal only with local and subordinate officials, while diplomats deal with the national officers of the host country.

Consuls are expected to assist and protect existing trade, to help find new markets, to make trade reports which will be of value to the commercial interests of their home state, to report on local conditions and developments, to promote the observance of treaties of commerce and navigation, to certify documents, and to represent their country locally. Sometimes they are called on to help settle trade disputes between national firms and those of the country in which they are stationed. In ports they have duties with reference to shipping and the issuance of invoices for the shipment of goods to their countries. They are also frequently assigned the function of granting visas to persons planning to visit their country, where such requirements are in force.

1. HISTORICAL BACKGROUND. The consular service has a history that goes back to antiquity. The ancient Greek city states developed the custom of appointing agents from among the citizens of the state or country where they desired to have protection afforded to their citizens or traders. In the early Middle Ages the merchants of the Mediterranean cities chose consuls from among their own numbers to represent them and to exercise jurisdiction over their traders and seafarers in the Moslem countries of the Near East. With the rise of the nation states and institution of permanent diplomatic missions to

5 The Department of State publishes several pamphlets about the United States Foreign Service which may be had on application. See *The U.S. Foreign Service—A Career for Young Americans,* Pub. 4559, April, 1952; *Some Facts About the Foreign Service,* Pub. 3789, April 1, 1950. See also J. Rives Childs, *American Foreign Service* (New York, 1948); and James L. McCamy, *The Administration of American Foreign Affairs* (New York, 1950), chs. viii, ix.

national governments, states began to appoint their own official nationals to represent and care for the trading interests of their citizens abroad.

2. STATUS OF CONSULS. A consul has more limited privileges and immunities than diplomatic representatives to the national governments, and is not usually considered a diplomat in the sense the term is used in the profession. His duties in the past have not been closely identified with the personality of the state or the fulfillment of its political interests. The consul has responsibilities for caring for and protecting the welfare and interests of his own nationals, for example, tourists who get into difficulties. His contribution to the actual execution of foreign policy is, however, principally an economic and commercial one. He is generally exempt from such local restraints as might interfere with the performance of his duties. Consular practice is widely regulated by consular and commercial treaties. These specify the nature of the consular function and form the base upon which consular activities in any given country may be conducted.

An extreme, and rare, instance of violation of the customary treatment of consuls was afforded by the Chinese communist arrest and trial of United States Consul General Angus Ward and his entire American staff in Mukden, Manchuria. Ward was placed under house arrest in November, 1948, on charges of mistreatment of a Chinese servant and held for more than a year. The Consul and members of his staff were then "tried" by communist authorities and given postponed sentences of varying lengths which were commuted to deportation. They were deported on the familiar but undefined ground of constituting a "spy ring." [6]

TRADITIONAL FUNCTIONS OF THE DIPLOMAT

The functions of the diplomat representing a large power have become manifold in face of the complicated relations among nations. In addition to the routine functions and responsibilities of (1) representation, (2) observation and reporting, (3) protection, and (4) negotiation, added duties may arise as a consequence of a nation's participation in regional arrangements, mutual security, or foreign assistance programs.

Representation. The first responsibility of any envoy sent by one country to another, or to an international gathering, is to represent his state and the interests of its government and people. This is the primary purpose of his appointment. Representation implies, in essence, being a symbol and exemplification of his state and government. Discharge of this responsibility generally entails official presence in the territory of the state to which he is sent, or at the conference to which he is appointed a delegate. It usually involves partici-

[6] See *Department of State Bulletin,* Nov. 28, 1949.

pation on behalf of his country at ceremonies and official occasions. Above all, it calls for presenting the views of his government to others with tact, clarity, and persuasion.

When a new ambassador or minister presents his credentials he is almost invariably instructed by his government to say that it is his hope that his mission will promote good relationships between the two states, even though there may be tension and struggle between them.[7] Cultivation of friendship and understanding for his state is one of the principal tasks of the diplomat. This requires patient and sustained effort along many lines. It involves developing friendly personal associations with the leaders of government, business, and other groups, wherever possible.

Former Ambassador Joseph C. Grew described the diplomat's responsibility in these words: "He must be, first and foremost, an interpreter, and this function of interpreting acts both ways. First of all he tries to understand the country which he serves—its conditions, its mentality, its actions, and its underlying motives, and to explain these things clearly to his own Government. And then, contrariwise, he seeks means of making known to the Government and the people of the country to which he is accredited the purposes and hopes and desires of his native land. He is an agent of mutual adjustment between the ideas and forces upon which nations act." [8]

Observation and Reporting. Diplomats are the eyes and ears of their government abroad. Governments must rely in their formation of policy and conduct of foreign affairs upon the observations and reports which flow in day by day from their diplomatic representatives throughout the world. Such information is needed in order to know where the friends of a country are located and where trouble is to be apprehended. It is one of the principal assignments of every mission abroad, and usually of a delegation attending an international gathering, to maintain a continuous stream of reports to the home government on current economic, political, social, and military conditions, developing issues, trends in negotiations, the significance of stands taken by prominent leaders, the attitudes and disposition of responsible officials and important segments of public opinion, the relationships between the foreign country and other states. Gathering this information requires continual study of all channels of information and statistical data. Its evaluation involves the cultivation of an intimate knowledge of national and local conditions and of key personalities. The combined task of gathering and weighing this information calls for the joint efforts of experts in numerous fields.

7 See Graham H. Stuart, *American Diplomatic and Consular Practice* (New York, 1936), pp. 240–241.

8 Joseph C. Grew, *Ten Years in Japan* (New York, 1944), p. 262.

A glance at communications coming in to a Foreign Office almost any day would leave one with the impression that the government is receiving a mass of bits and pieces, fragments of knowledge. Considering what arrives on one day from a given country this is to a certain extent true, although along with the cryptic messages there also come longer reports containing interpretations and evaluations by officers in the field. It is the job of the Foreign Office staff to piece the parts together, to construe the implications of what is taking place abroad for the national interests and for the application of national policy. A conversation reported from one foreign capital may have seemingly little significance in itself, but when put together with views reported from other quarters, or with some obscure action in another part of the world, may take on significance.

Espionage in the formal sense of secret spying is not usually practiced by the diplomatic and consular representatives of most countries. Their information is gathered from legitimate official, private, and public sources. Undercover information-gathering activities are normally undertaken by secret service and intelligence agencies and not by diplomatic missions and consulates. But investigations conducted during and since World War II have revealed that Nazi and Soviet missions, consulates, and information and purchasing agencies have sheltered personnel engaged in espionage and conspiratorial activity.[9]

Protection. A third function of the permanent representatives abroad is to protect the rights and interests of their country and its nationals. This task is performed through representation, negotiation, and securing rights and privileges. The representatives must counsel citizens who may seek advice or help, and seek redress and reclamation when rights have been infringed, wrongs suffered, property damaged, or persons injured. In countries where there are disturbed political conditions, the protective function may become a heavy responsibility. It may bring into question the use of the embassy or legation as a place of refuge or asylum. When war is imminent or taking place, missions must do everything in their power to help their nationals reach places of safety or to return, if possible, to their home land.

---

[9] Pertinent material on this subject will be found in the Canadian Government *Report of the Royal Commission To Investigate the Facts Relating to and the Circumstances Surrounding the Communication, By Public Officials and Other Persons in Positions of Trust, of Secret and Confidential Information to Agents of a Foreign Power* (Ottawa, June 27, 1946); C. E. Black, "Soviet Objectives, Methods, and Results in Eastern Europe," in H. and M. Sprout, *Foundations of National Power* (rev. ed., New York, 1951), pp. 347ff.; United States Senate Committee on the Judiciary, Subcommittee to Investigate the Administration of the Internal Security Act and other Internal Security Laws, Hearings on *Espionage Activities of Personnel Attached to Embassies and Consulates under Soviet Domination in the United States,* 82d Cong., 1st and 2d Sess., July 9, 1951, and Feb. 5 and 7, 1952; *ibid.,* Report on *Interlocking Subversion in Government Departments,* 83rd Cong., 1st Sess., July 30, 1953.

When war exists and diplomatic relations are broken between the belligerents, neutral states are customarily asked to care for the interests of the contesting parties in one another's territory. During both World Wars, Switzerland and Sweden were called upon by several of the belligerents to exercise this protective and mediatorial function.

Negotiation. A fourth function of the diplomatic representative is to act as the intermediary generally used between his own government and that of the country to which he is accredited. This involves transmitting official communications, negotiating intergovernmental agreements, and settling disagreements and misunderstandings which may arise between the countries. In the case of delegates to international conferences, the negotiating function is carried on simultaneously among the many participants.

The discretionary powers of diplomatic envoys in negotiations have been considerably affected by the development of rapid communications which now make it possible for the Head of State or Foreign Minister to direct or personally participate in negotiations. The Ambassador's role in constantly advising his government and making recommendations at all stages of negotiations has by no means decreased but on the contrary increased with the advent of rapid communications.

The task of negotiation may ordinarily involve, between countries on a friendly basis, amicable though strenuous dealings. At times the diplomat may be called upon to deliver notes with which he is not personally in sympathy, but which his instructions leave him no scope to alter or soften. In times of crisis he may be called upon to present demands or to call upon the government to which he is accredited to adopt a course of action that is not palatable to it. Then he must draw upon his knowledge of the two countries and summon all the acumen he can command to enable his government to succeed in its policy.

Between countries engaged in a bitter struggle for power, or between which there is tension, the task of negotiation can be exceedingly difficult and even unpleasant. This was borne out in the relationships between the diplomats of the Western Powers and Hitler and his Foreign Minister von Ribbentrop in 1938–1939. It was dramatically revealed in the Hull-Nomura interview on the day Pearl Harbor was bombed by Japan. And it has repeatedly occurred in the negotiations since the war between the Western Powers and the Soviet Union.

MULTILATERAL DIPLOMACY—DIPLOMACY BY CONFERENCE

Since 1918 an increasingly large segment of the business of international relations has been conducted through the medium of international conferences and the periodic meetings of international organizations. Multilateral or conference diplomacy has not superseded the more traditional methods and functions of diplomacy discussed above. But it has been employed on an ever-increasing scale for the discussion of the more important questions and for those of wide international interest.

Development of Conference System. Conference diplomacy is by no means an innovation of the twentieth century. It dates back to the Peace Conference of Westphalia held from 1642 to 1648. At this historic gathering, France, the Holy Roman Empire, Sweden, the Papal States, Holland, and Spain, plus a number of German Protestant princes, were represented. In 1712 a similar conference was held at Utrecht. In the territorial settlement drawn up at Utrecht, which included the disposition of some colonial holdings, the powers expressly stipulated that the settlement was intended to conserve "equilibrium in Europe." Another general conference was assembled at Aix-la-Chapelle in 1748.

The Congress of Vienna in 1815 initiated a measure of systematization in the conference method. The provisions of the General Act of Vienna that no change should be made in the Vienna settlement without consultation among the signatories became the basis first of the so-called Congress system and then of the Concert of Europe which operated sporadically throughout the following century. Thus for the first time multilateral international gatherings for purposes other than achieving a general peace settlement became an accepted instrument of diplomacy. This resulted in a series of conferences dealing with such major issues of international politics as the Eastern question, the independence of Greece, the limitation of Russian expansion in the Balkans, and the conflicting interests of the powers in Africa. Included among these gatherings were: the Congress of Paris in 1856, the Congress of Berlin in 1878, and subsequent conferences at Berlin in 1884, Brussels in 1890, and Algeciras in 1906. Conferences held at The Hague in 1899 and 1907 to discuss the laws and customs of war and to establish machinery for the pacific settlement of international disputes drew representatives from most of the principal states of the world. The last conference to be held under the European concert system took place in London in 1912 to supervise the terms of peace between the Balkan states at the close of the Second Balkan War.[10]

The League of Nations Conference System. The creation of the League of Nations brought with it a permanent, regularly organized conference system as a facility for diplomacy. It introduced an institutional continuity, which the

[10] The early conferences are described in most historical accounts of this period. Among the many available works may be mentioned the *Cambridge Modern History;* C. H. J. Hayes, *Modern Europe to 1870* (New York, 1953); David Jayne Hill, *A History of European Diplomacy* (London, 1921); A. W. Ward and G. P. Gooch, *The Cambridge History of British Foreign Policy,* 3 vols. (New York, 1923).

Concert system had lacked, through the periodic meetings of the Assembly and Council. In addition, the League provided for a succession of international gatherings on technical matters.[11] The principle of equality of all states, large and small, was applied in these meetings.

"Open Diplomacy." The meetings of the League of Nations Assembly likewise established a forum for practicing the principle of "open diplomacy" as set forth in President Wilson's Fourteen Points speech in 1918.

While Wilson had called for "open covenants openly arrived at" he did not mean to exclude private discussion of delicate matters, but he did insist that agreements, once reached, should be published.[12] Even this is obviously impractical in time of tension or war when publication of an agreement could be damaging because of a disclosure of strategic plans. Furthermore, negotiations requiring freedom of action by all parties, and entailing some compromises and shifts of positions in order to arrive at mutually acceptable conclusions, cannot easily be carried through in the full glare of public meetings. Although the practice of secret diplomacy is considerably less than in former years, evidences of it are readily discernible. Most of the meetings incident to the cold war have been private affairs among diplomats or Heads of State and their advisers. However, the increasing practice of press conferences and news releases during periods of negotiation, and public announcements of their results in many instances, have altered the character of the old secret diplomacy.[13]

United Nations Procedure. The United Nations has built upon and extended the practice of the League of Nations in providing for regular international gatherings and public airing of international issues. If anything, it has carried international debate and maneuvering to the point of "gold-fish bowl diplomacy" with its open meetings, radio, press, and television coverage. Much of the so-called "open diplomacy" thus witnessed by the public is deceptive, however, in the sense that these openly viewable procedures tend to obscure the fact that many of the statements made within the United Nations meetings are the outgrowth of preceding diplomatic conversations conducted privately among the delegations at various mission headquarters or hotels.

The various agencies of the United Nations illustrate the greatest single stride in diplomatic techniques that has been taken, perhaps, since the institution of permanent representation. These agencies have permanent staffs, regularly scheduled meetings, and established procedures. Bilateral diplomacy has

---

11 The international specialized and technical organizations are discussed in ch. xx below.

12 See Saul F. Padover (ed.), *Wilson's Ideals* (Washington, 1942), p. 70; also Elmer Plischke, *Conduct of American Diplomacy* (New York, 1950), p. 23.

13 See Harold Nicolson, "An Open Look at Secret Diplomacy," *The New York Times Magazine*, Sept. 13, 1953.

had well-understood procedures and arrangements for centuries. Now that national security and welfare are recognized as multilateral problems, there is a great need for established organizations and techniques for multilateral diplomacy.

What Constitutes an International Conference? We have discussed bilateral diplomacy at some length on previous pages. There is a tendency to call some bilateral meetings, and almost any meeting of representatives of three or more states, a "conference." The conference may be on the level of Heads of State, as were the most important World War II conferences. Or it may be a meeting of experts to talk about, and perhaps agree upon, standardizing airplane landing procedures.

We suggest that international conferences can be placed in several categories which, while not clearly delineated from one another, are useful ways to think about this important institution of international affairs.

1. Meetings of Heads of State, of their Foreign Ministers, their Economic Ministers, or other ministers having similar responsibilities, to discuss common problems. This has often occurred in recent years between the United States, Britain, and France, and to some extent with Italy and Germany.
2. Meetings of national representatives on a lower level than described above include, for example, such a gathering as the Temporary Council of NATO which in 1951–1952 employed a staff of over 200 military and economic experts as a study group before reporting to the NATO Council at Lisbon in 1952.
3. Formal conferences of the type of the Council of Foreign Ministers of the Big Four Powers which was charged with drafting the post-World War II peace treaties. Meetings of this type normally have the spotlight of world attention turned on them and are often under considerable psychological pressure to produce some results.
4. Routinely scheduled meetings of established international organizations such as the Allied Control Council in Berlin (while it functioned), the United Nations, the Council for Europe, the Organization for European Economic Recovery, NATO, and so forth and the subordinate agencies of these organizations.
5. The continuous staffwork and negotiations within organizations having permanent staffs and representatives accredited thereto from member nations. The United Nations, with its many agencies, OEEC, and NATO are examples.
6. The permanent operating international organizations, of which the European Payments Union, the European Coal and Steel Community, and the

headquarters of NATO commands, operating within certain realistic political dimensions, are mechanisms for conduct of international affairs.

Any one, except possibly the last noted, of the types of conference outlined above, or variation thereof, provides opportunities for discussion, and even agreement, on matters not within the terms of reference of the conference. The settlement of the Berlin blockade problem, for example, was arranged as a result of quiet discussions between the United States and Soviet diplomats during progress of an annual United Nations Assembly meeting in 1949.

Conference Organization, Procedures, and Techniques. While conferences vary in organization and procedure it is possible to make certain generalizations about them. Organization and procedures are, of course, well established in the permanent organizations such as the United Nations and NATO. Where not established they can be a subject for lengthy argument before getting down to discussion of substantive questions.

Each conference, and each meeting within a permanent organization, has an agenda. The inclusion or omission of items may be the subject of lengthy controversy before and at the meetings. Oftentimes these items will be the subject of preliminary informal conversations, sometimes carried on by the permanent diplomatic representative with their respective Foreign Offices, to determine views and possible areas of agreement. Each delegation usually prepares studies and position papers for use during the meetings, often proceeding on the basis of establishing a maximum desirable position, a minimum acceptable position, and various phase lines in between on which the delegate may stand in argument.

Each conference or committee has a chairman who may be the delegate from the host country. The chairmanship may be rotated, or some other method may be used. There is customarily a secretariat for keeping records, distributing papers, and handling administrative matters. In some of the permanent organizations much of the technical analysis and detailed work, particularly of a non-controversial nature, is done by the international staff or in subcommittees. These subcommittees are frequently lower-level negotiating arenas.

An international conference may result in an increase in mutual understanding, an impasse, an agreement to meet again after further study and further exploratory diplomatic conversations, or definite agreements of some sort. Some agreements require no further political action, since they may be made by individuals empowered to commit their governments. If the agreement is a treaty or convention it usually requires formal ratification by governments. Organizations such as the NATO Council and the European Coal and

Steel Community have implementing agencies under their control which may be the vehicles for carrying out some agreements.

An international conference, whether United Nations or other, which convenes to discuss an issue of grave concern to one or more peoples, may, if it fails to achieve some useful action, do more harm than good in international affairs. "Open disagreements openly arrived at" may be as damaging as secret treaties. Hence perhaps one of the more important techniques is that of delaying conferences and keeping items off discussion agendas until quiet diplomatic talks indicate the possible existence of an area of agreement. Alternatively it may be argued in certain cases that disagreements are better than not conferring at all because the issues may then be more clearly defined. Peoples who may have been restive because no talks had been held or who may have been unduly optimistic on the possibilities of an accord may be enabled to see a situation in its true light and become more reconciled to the realities.

Evaluation of the Conference Method. There is no doubt that the international conference is here to stay as an important instrument in international affairs. Governments engage now in literally thousands of multilateral international meetings every year. Logically, the use of the conference method is one of the first steps toward greater unity among sovereign states. If they cannot make progress by the conference method there is little hope of tightened regional arrangements, a United States of Europe, or the reality of other hopes in these general directions.

We have mentioned on preceding pages several difficulties and dangers of the conference method. They include the disillusionment incident to failure of a conference to produce results; the tendency to use conferences as propaganda sounding boards; the unwieldiness of some groupings of nations; the unwillingness of some nations to take a definite stand on issues in which they are not primarily concerned; the tendency to "follow the laggard" in matters requiring mutual contributions or concessions; the limiting effect of the spotlight of public interest on negotiating latitude of delegates; and the limited time high-level delegates can be away from their capitals. These are some of the drawbacks.

But these drawbacks can be made manageable or entirely eliminated by techniques and procedures. Three principal ones, which are related, are: (1) permanent secretariats and established procedures, (2) good staffwork in preparing for conferences and within delegations at conferences, and (3) use of the more traditional methods of diplomacy in preparatory discussions with representatives of other countries and in negotiation during the actual progress of conferences.

This last requirement indicates clearly the mutual dependence of bilateral diplomacy through permanent representation and conference diplomacy. The first is often incapable of handling the multilateral problems and issues—and international matters are increasingly multilateral. The second is incapable of handling, unaided, the magnitude of multilateral problems, since this magnitude includes interests which must be considered and satisfied on a country by country basis. Hence the new diplomacy seems to be a closely integrated combination of conference and bilateral diplomacies.

As a final comment on the use of conference diplomacy, it is probably true that many Americans lean unwarrantedly far toward this method in preference to more traditional diplomatic practice. The method seems superficially more like some of our traditional democratic political institutions, for example, the New England town meeting. But, as we have stressed before, nations are often not comparable to individuals in their political actions. They vary greatly in their power and importance, and in their interest in particular issues. And their representatives are not free agents, but are bound to loyalties and policies at home. Hence the choice among (1) use of the conference method, (2) which conference (for example, United Nations or some other gathering), and (3) bilateral diplomacy needs to be made on a case by case and category by category basis rather than as a matter of principle.[14]

PACIFIC SETTLEMENT OF DISPUTES

Bilateral diplomacy is still the principal means for settling day to day disputes between individual nations. In fact, it is an established practice of international relations that this method shall be tried first, and Article 33 of the United Nations Charter states this explicitly. Such negotiations may involve oral communications or an exchange of notes between diplomatic representatives, or they may include the drafting of a treaty resolving the issues. The settlement of international disputes sometimes necessitates the intervention of third parties, however, especially when vital issues are at stake or national feelings are aroused to a point preventing the continuance of bilateral discussion of the problem.

Good Offices. When a dispute occurs which the parties themselves cannot resolve, a third state may offer its "good offices" to help settle it. The neutral party attempts to bring the disputants together in an effort to reach agreement, but does not itself try to settle it or suggest the terms of settlement. Thus President Theodore Roosevelt, having in mind American interests in the Far East, offered his good offices in 1905 to bring about a settlement of the Russo-Japanese War. Having secured from both parties in advance an agreement to

14 See A. J. P. Taylor, "The Case for a Return to the Old Diplomacy," *The New York Times Magazine,* Jan. 21, 1951.

meet, Roosevelt made a formal offer of good offices. This was accepted by both parties who then, without a formal mediator, negotiated the Treaty of Portsmouth, signed in September, 1905.

Mediation. Another method used for the settlement of disputes is mediation or conciliation. Unlike the party who simply offers its good offices, a mediator attempts to conciliate the differences between the disputants and may propose solutions to this end. His proposals are not, however, binding upon the parties.

Both mediation and good offices were recognized and established as formal procedures by The Hague Convention for the Pacific Settlement of International Disputes, adopted in 1899 and revised in 1907. Both procedures have been employed by the United Nations, as we shall see in Chapter XX.

Commissions of Inquiry. International commissions of inquiry are often appointed to determine the facts of a dispute in order to clear the way for its settlement. This method was used with success, for example, in the Dogger Bank incident, which occurred during the Russo-Japanese War in 1905. The Russian fleet fired upon British fishing vessels in the North Sea. A commission of inquiry was appointed which reported that there were no Japanese war vessels among the fishing vessels, after which Russia paid an indemnity to Britain. Further use of commissions of inquiry can be found in the annals of the League of Nations and more recently in the United Nations. These will be discussed in Chapter XX below.

Arbitration. A fourth method of pacific settlement is arbitration, which is the settlement of international disputes in accordance with agreed rules and procedures, by employment of arbiters chosen by the disputing parties. Unlike the recommendations of mediators or of commissions of inquiry, the parties usually agree in advance to accept and be bound by the decisions of the arbitrators. In contrast with *adjudication* (discussed below) arbitration is carried on by *ad hoc* groups appointed by the parties themselves and emphasizes the finding of an acceptable solution rather than the determination of legal rights and wrongs. Although arbitration is based upon a respect for international law and may follow legal rules, the disputants themselves determine the principles upon which the arbiters shall act. Arbitration may or may not be compulsory, depending upon whether a treaty to that effect exists between the particular disputants to arbitrate the particular kind of dispute which has developed. It has been extensively used by states since ancient times for the settlement of disputes involving legal questions.[15]

The Hague Conference of 1899 contributed to the development of the arbitration procedure by drawing up a convention which established the Per-

15 See John Bassett Moore, *International Adjudications Ancient and Modern*, 6 vols. (New York, 1929–1933).

manent Court of Arbitration at The Hague. This "Court" consists actually of a panel of available jurists, nominated by the signatory states, and a secretariat. A body of rules governing arbitration was drawn up at the same time. While this tribunal has not been used frequently in recent years, it did arbitrate some important cases prior to 1920, among them the North Atlantic Fisheries question between Great Britain and the United States, a Venezuelan debt case involving Britain, Germany, and Italy, and claims problems arising out of the Italo-Turkish War.

Many treaties providing for pacific settlement of disputes by conciliation and arbitration have been concluded, especially during the period between World Wars I and II.

Adjudication. The adoption of the Statute of the Permanent Court of International Justice in 1920 provided still another means of pacific settlement of disputes by a permanent court of impartial judges applying the accepted rules of international law. While the Court was technically not a part of the League of Nations, it functioned more or less as a part of the League peace system. Some of the treaties of peace and treaties for pacific settlement mentioned above designated the Court as the tribunal to which differences on questions of law or interpretation should be submitted. Moreover, the Court was empowered to give "advisory opinions" in questions of law submitted to it by the League of Nations Council.

The International Court of Justice, established as a principal organ of the United Nations in 1945, is in essence the Permanent Court of International Justice with a new name. Although technically a new body, relatively few vital changes were made in the Statute creating it.[16]

USE OF FORCE IN THE CONDUCT OF INTERSTATE AFFAIRS

We have considered in Chapter IX something of the causes and effects of international conflict and war and have, in Chapter XVI, briefly discussed the military instrument of policy. Let us now discuss some of the ways in which nations have used force actively, short of war, as an instrument of policy in external affairs. We repeat here our distinction, made before, between the active use of force and the use of military power in being as a background for formulation and execution of policy. In the following pages we shall discuss some of the ways in which military power has been used as an obvious operating instrument of policy but still short of war. As first steps we shall comment on the question of what constitutes war and on the evolution of international arrangements pertaining to the use of force short of war.

---

[16] See Manley O. Hudson, *The Permanent Court of International Justice, A Treatise, 1920–1942* (New York, 1944). For a discussion of both courts, see ch. xx below.

Problem of Definition. There is obviously obscurity as to the meaning of the term *war*. Otherwise common practice would not exist of qualifying the term by such words as *limited, unlimited, cold, hot, phony, undeclared,* and others. Practically every democratic state has a constitutional method for recognizing a state of war and hence is not legally at war unless it follows the prescribed constitutional procedure. Thus the United States was not at "war" legally during the Korean hostilities even though it was, in magnitude of effort, the fourth greatest war in United States history. It can be argued, supported by specific instances, that war is a matter of intent and that use of armed force and even hostilities do not necessarily constitute war.

It may be that the term *war* is becoming less capable of precise definition, particularly since military hostilities are now so closely integrated with other instruments of conflict and since totalitarian nations, not conditioned in or accepting traditional Western concepts, bulk large in the power equation.

Effect of International Organization. The United Nations Charter and various regional arrangements have added important procedures and concepts relating to the use of force in interstate relations. These arrangements, stemming generally from the League, retain the concept of the right of individual and collective self-defense and stress peaceful settlement of disputes through such methods as arbitration. But, based on the thesis that hostilities anywhere and under any circumstances are likely to be a threat to international peace and security, the United Nations Charter provides for bringing disputes presenting such threats to the Security Council. This can be done either by one of the disputants or by another state. The Rio Pact of the Organization of American States contains similar provisions.

The United Nations Charter and some mutual security pacts provide methods for setting machinery in motion for collective defense in case of an action determined to be an aggression or threat to the peace. The degree of success of these methods has varied from a situation of almost complete paralysis to the rapid action in the United Nations in the case of the North Korean aggression.

We shall discuss briefly, in the following sections, some of the ways in which states have used force short of war.

Show of Force. This method has been used frequently, particularly in the nineteenth century, to demonstrate resolution and that a state could and might resort to further use of force if a situation developed in certain ways. The method has been implemented in ways varying from overt action, such as Commodore Perry's naval visit to Japan in 1853, to actions superficially administrative in their nature, for example, calling up a conscription class ahead of normal schedule.

The movement and stationing of armed forces close to borders which are the subject of tensions is a type of showing of force that is closely related to international politics. This is illustrated in such moves as, for example, the Soviet troop concentration near the eastern borders of Turkey in 1946–1947, Yugoslav and Italian troop movements with reference to Trieste in 1953, the dispatch of an additional United States Marine division to Korea after the armistice signature in 1953, the heavy Soviet concentration in East Germany located in battle jump-off positions, and the United States' program for stationing of armed forces abroad, which might be interpreted, in part, as a show of force. There are no clearly marked dividing lines between the show of force for intimidation, for the maintenance of a strong military posture as a deterrent to aggression, for the traditional military, naval, and now air parades to occasion sober thought in the government of an opponent in a dispute, and for military "good-will" tours.

Pacific Blockade. Another procedure employed by the powers has been the institution of a "pacific blockade." This comprises the blockading of the ports of a state in order to bring it to terms without actually declaring war and establishing belligerency. A notable instance was the blockade instituted by Germany, Italy, and Great Britain against Venezuela in 1902 in order to compel the payment of contract debts. This was only partially successful and led later to general agreement that force should not be used to collect contract debts if the debtor state agreed to arbitrate. This agreement, based upon the Drago Doctrine originally expounded by an Argentine foreign minister, was embodied in a convention adopted at The Hague Conference of 1907. The widely discussed policy of blockade of communist China during the Korean War is another example. A variation actually employed was the patrol of the channel between the mainland and Formosa by American naval forces to prevent hostilities being launched across this stretch of water.

Bombardment. Bombardment of the ports of one state by another has been used most frequently as a means of reprisal for damages or wrongs. A famous instance occurred in 1923 when an Italian fleet bombarded and occupied the Greek island of Corfu as a measure of reprisal when Greece failed to comply with an Italian ultimatum resulting from the murder of Italian officials engaged in delimiting the Greek-Albanian frontier. Subsequently, the case was submitted to the League of Nations and then to a Council of Ambassadors and settled under its auspices.

Use of Troops and Military Occupation. The use of military forces to occupy territory between cessation of hostilities and conclusion of a peace arrangement is well known. Nations have frequently believed that disturbed or chaotic conditions in a foreign land call for the use of military forces to protect their interests or to retaliate for injuries received. Such a step has often been followed by at least temporary military occupation. During the period 1813–1899 the United States, for example, landed forces in other countries to protect the rights of American citizens abroad on at least forty-six occasions.[17]

Reprisals. The reprisal is another use of force as a means of self-help. Dr. Hindmarsh has defined reprisals as "coercive measures taken by one state against another, without belligerent intent, in order to secure redress for, or to prevent recurrence of acts or omissions which under international law constitute international delinquency." [18] This definition is a legal one. There are certainly other reprisals in an area of controversy from the legal standpoint. Dr. Hindmarsh has classified the Italian bombardment of Corfu, mentioned above, as such a measure.

Members of the United Nations are now under a Charter obligation to refer the grievances which they cannot settle peacefully between themselves to the Security Council rather than attempt to redress them by unilateral use of force. Two post-war cases in which this has been done may be mentioned. In 1946 two British mine-sweepers were sunk with considerable loss of life in the Corfu Channel while engaged in mine-sweeping operations. Albania was charged with responsibility for their loss and demand was made upon her for damages. Ultimately the case was referred to the International Court of Justice, which held that Albania should make recompense; a responsibility which it has never discharged, however. In the same year two United States Air Force passenger planes lost over Yugoslav territory between Italy and Austria were shot down with loss of life. The United States demanded explanation and apology for the action and payment of damages, indicating that the case would be referred to the United Nations in the event of noncompliance. Direct diplomatic settlement, including payment of damages to dependents of airmen killed, made further action in this case unnecessary.

Forcible Intervention. Nations have frequently used military force to intervene in the affairs of other states. Until the 1920's, United States interventions in the Caribbean region were not infrequent affairs. This practice was abandoned, however, with the introduction of the Good Neighbor Policy in 1933. And at the Buenos Aires Conference in 1936, a protocol was agreed to, prohibiting intervention by one American state in the affairs of another for any reason whatsoever.

Intervention has continued to be used by states elsewhere, however, sometimes openly, sometimes subtly. Nazi Germany, Fascist Italy, and the USSR intervened in the Spanish Civil War in 1936–1938. The United States gave

[17] See Albert E. Hindmarsh, *Force in Peace* (Cambridge, 1933), p. 75.
[18] Hindmarsh, *op. cit.*, p. 58.

aid to the Greek Government in 1947–1948 under the Truman Doctrine when that country was torn with civil war precipitated by communist-aided guerrilla forces. In 1950 when the Korean War started, President Truman ordered the United States Navy to patrol the Formosa Straits in order to "neutralize" Formosa and discourage the Chinese Communists from attacking this island. In November, 1950, the Peiping regime intervened in the Korean War. The USSR has intervened in the internal affairs of the Eastern European states since 1944, insisting that they adopt its form of government and become its satellites. Collective intervention may develop as an international pattern from precedents worked out in the United Nations experience in the Korean War.

Right of Self-Defense. All of these methods of using force may, of course, be employed for different reasons.

The right of a state to use force in self-defense is recognized, both by traditional law and with limitations, by the United Nations Charter. The pursuit of the Mexican bandit Villa into Mexico by United States forces in 1916 may quite properly be placed in this category. More extreme measures were the British seizure of the Danish fleet in Danish waters in 1807 to prevent its forced surrender to the French and the British sinking of the French fleet at Oran in 1940, after its refusal to join the Allied forces following the fall of France.

Article 51 of the United Nations Charter declares that "nothing in the present Charter shall impair the inherent right of individual or collective self-defense if an armed attack occurs against a Member of the United Nations, until the Security Council has taken the measures necessary to maintain international peace and security . . ." [19]

Summary: Use of Force Short of War Today. There is no change in the former patterns of policy for use of force short of war which may be undertaken by a state. But several new aspects have been added in recent decades. Use of force is more dangerous, that is, more likely to generate an enlarging conflagration. Force, once unleashed, is now harder to limit and control. Moreover, world opinion has grown against the use of force, particularly in a way which can be called "aggression." Hence the adoption of its more overt patterns is less likely. On the other hand, new techniques in the use of force through puppet and satellite states and through support of internal dissension have been devised by the totalitarian powers in the last two decades.

These new aspects just listed, however, are secondary to the factors added by the United Nations Charter and machinery which provide a forum for

---

[19] For interpretation of Article 51 see Leland M. Goodrich and Edvard Hambro, *Charter of the United Nations: Commentary and Documents* (rev. ed., Boston, 1949), pp. 297–308. See also ch. xx below.

disputants, established procedures for seeking peaceful solutions, and recognized methods by which other states may enter the problem on a collective basis. We do not of course suggest that these new factors added by the United Nations are a guarantee against use of force. Even the short history of the United Nations shows otherwise. But they are factors, giving hope for the future, and we will discuss them in more detail in succeeding chapters.

FOUNDATION STONES OF CONDUCT OF INTERNATIONAL RELATIONS

We have now completed two chapters on the conduct of international relations and there is merit in an attempt to summarize foundation elements which condition this day-to-day conduct by practically every state. First, there are the basic objectives, described in light of the self-interest of the particular state as interpreted by its leaders. They are security and welfare—and, for some states, expansion. These objectives are sought through use of the political, economic, military, and psychological instruments of policy in certain patterns. The arts of employment of these instruments, short of war, can be very broadly included under the term *diplomacy*.

There is another foundation element, not mentioned thus far, which is often called "strategic intelligence." Evaluated information concerning other states is an essential to sound decisions by statesmen.[20] Contrary to some popular belief most intelligence is not a matter of spies and filching of documents. It is primarily a matter of noticing, relating, and correctly appraising the many thousands of items of knowledge and information readily available. Secret intelligence does supply an increment—and a very important one—of information needed. Every Great Power and some small ones maintain secret intelligence organizations. The Central Intelligence Agency is the top control and operating intelligence agency of the United States Government, and its importance is indicated by the routine presence of its director at meetings of the National Security Council. We stress again that the main problem of intelligence is evaluation and its relationship to the policies of the government undertaking the evaluation and to the flow of international affairs throughout the world.

We may close this chapter with emphasis that international affairs are conducted as a continuous flow of actions and interactions. Few problems are completely erased. They may be settled but they contribute seeds, and often sturdy seedlings, for a crop of new problems in a continuously dynamic pattern of world affairs.

---

[20] R. Hilsman, Jr., "Intelligence and Policy Making in Foreign Affairs," *World Politics,* Oct. 1952.

SUGGESTED READINGS

Jules M. Cambon, *The Diplomatist* (London, 1931).

J. Rives Childs, *American Foreign Service* (New York, 1948).

Gordon A. Craig and Felix Gilbert (eds.), *The Diplomats, 1919–1939* (Princeton, 1953).

H. J. Morgenthau, *Politics Among Nations* (2d ed., New York, 1954), Chapters 31–32.

Harold Nicolson, *Diplomacy* (New York, 1950).

Ragnar J. Numelin, *The Beginnings of Diplomacy* (New York, 1946).

N. D. Palmer and H. C. Perkins, *International Relations* (Boston, 1953), Chapter 5.

Elmer Plischke, *Conduct of American Diplomacy* (New York, 1950).

I. de S. Pool, *Symbols of Internationalism,* Hoover Institute Studies, Series C, No. 3 (Stanford, 1951).

Don K. Price, *The New Dimension in Diplomacy* (New York, 1951).

W. A. Riddell, *World Security by Conference* (Toronto, 1947).

Graham H. Stuart, *American Diplomatic and Consular Practice* (New York, 1936).

CHAPTER XVIII

Policies for National Security

NATIONAL SECURITY is, and has generally been, the primary objective of relations among states.[1] States do not follow isolationist or neutral or other security policies to the end that they are good in themselves, but only so long as, in the judgment of the peoples and their leaders, such programs best contribute to security. Preservation and increase of the power of a state are, with a few exceptions, the objective of every security policy.

This chapter will discuss briefly the different security policies which a state might choose to follow.

CHARACTERISTICS OF SECURITY POLICIES

Security Policies Are "National" Policies. The government of each state formulates the security policy for its country with its own position, outlook, and interpretation of the international situation uppermost in mind. States do in fact contribute to the security of other states, but only because it is to their own enlightened interest to do so. It is unfortunately also true that, in seeking to further its own security, a state may impair the security of a friendly state.

Small states have, historically, given support and even leadership to international organizations for security and to methods for peaceful settlement of disputes. The reasons for their interest are obvious. But no way has been found to compel assistance through an international organization in case of aggression. The responsibility seems still, *de facto,* that of each state, large or small. It must conduct its affairs in a way which will gain it the assistance, in case of need, of a large state. Now that large states cannot gain adequate assurance of security except through collective action with small states, the policies of even the Great Powers are conditioned by this fact, thus facilitating the national security policies of weaker states.

Security Policies Are Directed Against Others. Security policies are by their very nature drawn up with some other state or group of states in mind. Hence,

[1] See ch. x.

unlike many economic and humanitarian policies, security matters often become very sensitive and difficult to discuss publicly without charging another state with contemplated aggression or imputing bad faith. Statesmen accordingly may say little about the real basis for their fears and proposals.

Security Tends to Be a Long-Range Matter. States rarely experience a material change in their security situation in the short period of a year or two except through the results of war or some major internal *coup d'état*. The wise statesman guards the long-range future against even improbable situations. The enunciation of the Monroe Doctrine was an example of a long-range security policy. So also was the acquisition of Alaska by Seward when he could not possibly foresee the importance of this area to the air defense of the United States.

Conflict of Policies. Some security policies which a state may select are mutually supporting; some may conflict. Thus, isolation and neutrality were once feasible and quite compatible policies for the United States. Neither of these policies, however, is compatible, strictly speaking, with a regional arrangement, or with having strong machinery for the pacific settlement of international disputes, or with a collective security system such as the United Nations. Security policies may conflict in other ways. The desire for a short-term gain in insurance may conflict with concern over the longer-term future. Western European reluctance to revive German military power through a European Defense Community exemplifies this.

Policies May Employ a Variety of Means. National security policies may be pursued through political, economic, moral-psychological, or military means, or through various combinations of them. The Pentagon has no monopoly on the national security responsibility in the executive branch of the United States Government. This is well illustrated by the membership of the National Security Council, and such other persons as the President may choose.[2]

The national security policy of a state will emphasize political measures at one time and, under changed circumstances, may emphasize other types of measures. But all types of policy and policy instrumentalities are interconnected and must work together. They cannot be compartmentalized. The most drastic security policy is war which requires the coordinated use of all types of policy measures mentioned above.

Security Policies Are Concerned with National Power. The policies which a state adopts for security purposes are concerned with its national power relative to a possible opponent or opponents. The objective of security can be furthered by policies which increase the strength of a state, or policies which aim to decrease the strength of possible opponents (some East-West trade

2 See ch. xii, p. 343.

policies of the United States in the early 1950's are examples), or both. A system for the pacific settlement of disputes tends, for instance, to increase the political power of the participants to force settlement of a conflict which, if left unsettled, might eventually threaten the security of states not initially involved. The system may also provide machinery for mobilization by a weak state of appreciable international pressure against a strong state.

It is difficult to achieve a clear differentiation between the struggle for power to preserve the *status quo* and the struggle for power to "secure" something which a state does not possess. When does a security policy become a policy of imperialism and aggression? Hitler's expansionist policies were pressed in the name of security. So are some of the policies of Soviet communism. The answer lies partly in the state's definition of its national interest. If this is defined as including expanded control over peoples and areas outside its borders, its security policies are likely to result in direct and violent conflict with those of other states.

BASIS FOR SELECTION OF SECURITY POLICIES

The security policies of a state are a product of its internal political system as well as of the analysis made of the international situation by its leaders. Traditions, historical precedents, and conditioning experiences of statesmen and people have important effects upon the specific policies chosen for security at any given time. President Roosevelt could not quickly shift the United States from its policy of isolation, even though he may have felt a different policy necessary, as hinted in his 1937 speech suggesting that aggressors should be "quarantined." Swiss leadership would find great difficulty in abandoning its traditional policy of neutrality. Even dictators must take account of domestic opinion in framing their policies. Recognizing these points, we can still identify some basic factors which influence national choice of security policies.

Identification of the Security Problem. The threat to a state's security must be identified and appraised before a reasonable security policy, measured by the yardstick of national self-interest, can be devised.[3] This is not always easy. For the intents of other states or groups of states are a major factor, and these may be presented as being peaceful, friendly, and cooperative although they conceal expansionist or aggressive motives and designs. The forthrightness of the program set forth in Adolf Hitler's *Mein Kampf,* the pre-war program of

[3] For scholarly analyses of United States policy see Samuel F. Bemis, *A Diplomatic History of the United States* (New York, 1936); T. A. Bailey, *A Diplomatic History of the American People* (4th ed., New York, 1950). See also S. F. Bemis, "The Shifting Strategy of American Defense and Diplomacy," *Virginia Quar. Rev.,* Summer, 1948, reproduced in Padelford (ed.). *Cont. Int. Rel. Readings,* 1949–1950, pp. 241–252.

the Japanese leaders to establish an East Asia "Co-Prosperity Sphere" based on the idea of excluding other interests from Asia, and the basic concepts of communism recorded in published literature are exceptions to the usual situation. Historically the ambitions and goals of one state *vis à vis* the territories, interests, and power of others have often been cloaked in obscurity until the aggressively inclined state moves overtly to execute its designs.

The international scene is an ever-changing one. States content with the *status quo* at one time may become dynamic or expansionist at another, as in the case of the shift of policy which took place between the policy of the Weimar Republic in Germany up to 1933 and that of Hitler thereafter. Allies may become neutrals or even opponents, as for instance Japan, Italy, and Turkey shifted from one side to another between the ends of World War I and World War II. Hence, policies must be chosen which have an element of flexibility and adaptability to long-run conditions.

Several types of threats to national security can be identified, and these are not necessarily mutually exclusive. (1) There is the traditional opponent associated with long-term issues. The history of France and Germany, and of Germany and the Slavic nations, exemplifies this. Arab-Jewish relationships may also reflect a consciousness of this type of condition. (2) There is the long-term threat posed by a state or group of states which are not assuredly friendly. The United States felt this from the dynastic colonial powers of Europe in the 1820's when the Monroe Doctrine was enunciated. (3) There is the type of threat which arises for states, particularly the small ones, as a result of or incidental to a conflict between other powers. The occupation of Denmark, Greece, Norway, the Netherlands, and Yugoslavia by the Nazis during World War II, and the delicate position held by Turkey faced with the possibility of both German and Soviet occupation, are cases in point. (4) There is the threat which may arise from a piecemeal lessening of security due to the weakening or engulfment of friendly states, as, for example, through the advance of communism after World War II. (5) There is also the danger to a nation that acceptance of a change in the territorial status by aggression may create a precedent which may be followed by other demands and aggressions as occurred after Prime Minister Chamberlain's appeasement of Hitler at Munich in 1938.

It is a paradoxical fact that while threats emanate from the objectives and actions of foreign states, the security problems of different states still have an essential unity. This is particularly true for *status quo* states, and has led to the thesis that peace is indivisible, that a threat to the territorial integrity or political independence of one state by aggression is a threat to the security of all, and hence that the security threat to each state is of concern to all states.

Geographical Position.[4] Geographical factors have, in the past, had a large influence in determining the nature and direction of the security policies of individual states. The relative geographic position of a state and the existence, or lack thereof, of physical barriers have been vital factors to the policy makers and defenders of every state. Britain's position long indicated one group of policies. Poland, Belgium, and Korea, in zones between the Great Powers, are in an entirely different situation.

It is almost certain that the security aspects of geography have changed materially with the advent of long-range, highly destructive weapons. The sea

AS ATOMIC RACE IS INTENSIFIED — THE STRATEGIC POLAR ROUTES

Major U. S. bases outside the country   Countries associated with Western defense plans   Communist bloc and occupied Austria

The New York Times

FIGURE XVIII:1

[4] See ch. ii.

and other natural barriers no longer give insulation. Even the Arctic is no longer a dependable barrier. Furthermore, this technological change may make some once strategically important areas less critical since military power can overleap them. Finally, security is more than ever an area matter rather than a national matter.

National Capabilities. Capabilities, both those of the state seeking security and its potential opponents, are an important factor in the selection of security policies. The mechanical approach to devising a security program is simple to describe. The capabilities of the potential opponents are appraised. A program is then devised which equals or exceeds the capabilities—economic, political, psychological, military—of the opponent. This may seem simple. It is in fact neither simple nor capable of precise evaluation. Difficult questions are involved such as: Who are the opponents? The answer to this requires, as we have indicated before, a judgment as to intent, both in the immediate and the long run. Who may be expected to be the neutrals and allies in case of conflict, and what are their relative capabilities and their intents? There also arises the question of what standards and what calculus are to be used in estimating the capabilities of one's own state and of actual and potential opponents and allies. In the 1930's for example, Italy had few tangible basic resources except population. Yet Italy became a major threat to Britain, France, and the Allies in the Mediterranean area.

Small and weak nations lack capabilities for aggression or defense (unless as part of a coalition) except against other small nations. Their statesmen, accordingly, must make even more difficult judgments than those of a strong state. For, in a Great Power struggle, the techniques of estimating capabilities are so rough that a small state may not be able to recognize the significance of its contribution to its own and group security. However, when a pressing threat exists, a major state will almost always gladly accept the association of a small state.

Risk Element. The risk element is an important factor in selecting national security policies. There are at least two types of risk which policy makers must weigh: (1) Statesmen may wrongly appraise the nature and timing of the threat and hence choose the wrong policies, as Britain and France underestimated Hitler in the mid-1930's; (2) the policies, even if correctly selected, may be inadequate either because of inadequate implementation or because of failure to shift with a changing situation. Secretary of State Marshall stated at the outset of the European Recovery Program that it was a calculated risk. It did succeed, with costly implementation, in attaining its objectives of European economic recovery and increased political stability. These objectives in themselves proved to be inadequate, however, to provide the military power which became needed in Western Europe to meet the developing Soviet threat. Today security policies depend very much on the efficacy of the programs of execution—which may be both difficult and costly.

Summary. From what has been said in the preceding pages, we may summarize three points concerning security policies:

1. Few security policies have absolute assurance of success. They would not be necessary unless they were against some other state or group of states. It is obvious that opponents will strive to make them partially or wholly unsuccessful.
2. The choice of policies is usually a choice among several possible courses of action—no one of which is completely satisfactory.
3. Statesmen strive to minimize the risk to their countries. One result of this effort is a reluctance to enter into commitments to assist friendly states beyond that limit which urgent considerations of self-interest dictate—the hope being that everything will work out all right without such commitment. Argentina, Ireland, Spain, Sweden, and Turkey (until late in the war) followed this policy in World War II, and Sweden refused to become a party to the North Atlantic Treaty.

The pattern of analysis described above for selecting security policies is admittedly incomplete. We stress the point that statesmen are continually appraising the factors we have mentioned from the standpoint of the enlightened self-interest of their respective countries. With these things in mind we will discuss in the following pages a number of the principal security policies which states may adopt. The categorization is oversimplified, and the reader should bear in mind that states, in fact, choose a group of mutually supporting and overlapping policies.

ESSENTIALLY UNILATERAL POLICIES

Unilateral policies eliminate those elements of risk inherent in policies which are partially dependent on cooperation of other states for success. No state can now achieve a posture enabling it to stand alone against the theoretical maximum force which might be brought against it. But such a calamity may seem remote to leaders of some governments causing them to lean toward admittedly attractive unilateral policies. Moreover, some unilateral policies may be adjusted to support collective security arrangements and balance of power policies.

Isolation. Isolation is a matter of degree. Perhaps the latest historical instance of complete isolation (excepting Tibet) is that of Japan prior to 1854. A practical policy of isolation implies a fortunate geographic position and a self-sufficiency which permits a state to pursue its security objectives without collaborating with other states. This does not mean, however, that the state is not deeply interested in the equation of power politics among its neighbors.

United States isolation was made possible by geography and by the particular combination of powers and power interests of Europe which, after the early 1800's, guaranteed the initially weak United States against attack. The United States policy of isolation was primarily directed toward the affairs of Europe. The United States never pursued a policy of isolation in affairs of the Western Hemisphere. Nor did it with respect to Asia. United States naval forces, for instance, were instrumental in persuading a reluctant Japan to give up the traditional Japanese policy of isolation. United States forces participated in the intervention connected with the Boxer Uprising in China in 1900, and generally the United States continued an active interest in matters pertaining to the Far East. Hence, it appears that "isolation" is and must be defined on a case-by-case basis.

One may say that isolationism is no longer a feasible policy because of the advance of military technology, the economic interdependence of the world, and the unlimited objectives of communism. Certainly this is true for the United States. But for some smaller nations, geographically removed from dangerous neighbors, some degree of isolationism including a short-term policy of "no entangling alliances" or "neutralism" might be feasible. South Africa, India, and Indonesia are states whose leaders appear to consider such a policy reasonable at this time.

Economic Policies and Security.[5] Economic self-sufficiency, sometimes called autarchy when carried to an extreme, is a security policy which is especially attractive to those who would pursue a policy of either isolation or aggression. Subsidies, as, for example, for shipping, and the protective tariff have been widely used. Foreign investment may have security overtones. Unilateral economic policies for security may take the form of embargoing the export of certain items and information. The United States did not follow this policy toward Japan in the late 1930's, although it was urged. But it has followed such a policy particularly with regard to items associated with atomic energy since 1945, and during the period of the "cold war" it cut off shipment of machine tools, machinery, and critical raw materials to the Soviet bloc area.

The new self-sufficiency expedients include stock-piling of raw materials and finished goods, the erection and maintenance of stand-by synthetic plants, and the development of sources of supply in foreign friendly territories not readily subject to attack by a potential enemy. Perhaps the new autarchy is part of a drive for self-sufficiency within alliances rather than within states.

[5] See ch. iv.

Neutrality. The policy of neutrality which appeals particularly to small and relatively weak states and to larger countries remotely situated from areas of conflict or deeply engrossed in their own development, may be justified as a unilateral national security policy under certain circumstances. It may be justified if (1) a state's security will not be gravely impaired regardless of the outcome of a struggle among other states; (2) formal participation in a war would be suicidal or would not significantly affect the outcome; and (3) the issue seems likely to be decided favorably to the neutral country without its active participation.

The trends in economic interdependence, modern military technology, and collective security arrangements provide a dilemma to the state that would preserve its freedom of action to choose neutrality in case of hostilities between other states. If adequate prior arrangements are made for security in case neutrality fails, the state will probably have to make commitments which force it to take a stand on one side of a struggle. If, on the other hand, the state strictly preserves its freedom of action to be neutral, it may be quickly engulfed if neutrality fails, as in the case of German invasion of Belgium, the Netherlands, Denmark, and Norway in 1940. These states joined NATO in 1949, while traditionally neutral Sweden remained aloof and maintained a theoretical freedom of action.

The urge toward neutrality, sometimes reasoned, sometimes emotional, is strong, however, in some states—particularly the young nations on the rimland of Asia. It is still being actively pursued by some states as a security policy.

Unilateral Armament. Reliance upon a policy of unilateral massing of vast armaments is no longer a completely adequate security policy except perhaps for the USSR. This policy which may be combined with isolation and neutrality was once effective for some states. Britain's security was long guaranteed principally by her Navy and her fleet bases. The longing for a similar condition has caused some Americans to look hopefully for a security program dependent primarily on predominant airpower. But the truth is we live in a world in which complete reliance cannot be put upon one weapon or instrumentality or even upon unilateral armament alone. National armament, however, still has its place, for one should not think only in terms of global war but also of "limited" wars and localized aggressions. In any event it is the responsibility of every government to protect its people and the integrity of its lands insofar as possible.

Imperialism.[6] Imperialism has been a policy in the past by which some states have increased their power. The twentieth-century varieties are the most pertinent. Imperialism was the chosen policy of Italy, Germany, and Japan in

6 See ch. viii.

504   *The Projection of National Policy into International Politics*

the 1930's—associated with unilateral armament and drives for economic self-sufficiency. It is a chosen policy of the USSR, which, since 1940, has established direct control over a buffer area extending from Finland to the Black Sea, and across the middle of Asia. In addition, the Soviet Union has achieved strong influence over China; and Moscow, at the end of World War II, regained islands and other territorial rights and privileges in the Far East once possessed by the Czarist governments. This advance of Russian "security" by means of imperialist expansion of its control, dominion, and influence in less than a decade through a combination of political, economic, psychological, and military means is unparalleled in history.

Intervention. Intervention in the internal or external affairs of another state has at times been a supporting program to further imperialism. At times it has been a policy for preserving the *status quo*. It cannot be expected that a state will view with equanimity a shift in the internal affairs of another which impairs the security of the first state.

The nineteenth-century forms of crudely imperialistic intervention may now be replaced by two somewhat more subtle forms: (1) the activities of the Communist party apparatus directed from Moscow and (2) intervention by collective action through the United Nations or a regional arrangement. The engulfment of Czechoslovakia by communism in 1948 and the attempt against Greece in 1948–1949 may be the new pattern of imperialistic intervention. While the thought is admittedly speculative, it seems possible that the condition of a state's internal affairs, if the difficulties involve other states, might be recognized by the United Nations as a "threat to the peace" requiring collective action.[7]

Other Political and Economic Measures Short of War. The unilateral balance of power policy of Britain [8] during the last century now no longer seems applicable, although some states may be able to apply such a policy in their area, as compared to global relations. Propaganda, economic penetration, and subversion may all be used either as unilateral or multilateral security programs in support of national security policy. The Voice of America is a part of the American security program. Economic penetration of a foreign country may be employed to assure needed materials, or to deny supplies of them to a potential enemy, or to influence the internal affairs of another country toward neutrality or friendly support. Or it may become out and out imperialistic. Indigenous Communist parties, with their ties to Moscow, increase Soviet power and hence Soviet security as Moscow views it.

---

7 See ch. viii for description of United Nations action in Indonesian case and ch. xx for action in Korean case and also for discussion of Charter limitations upon United Nations intervention in matters essentially within the domestic jurisdiction of states.

8 See ch. viii above.

The policies of the weak neighbor, the friendly neighbor, and the buffer state, and varying degrees of political control over another state, have existed since the dawn of the state system. The United States Monroe Doctrine and Britain's traditional interest in having the opposite side of the North Sea controlled by small friendly states stem in part from some of these policies. The modern Soviet variation is to control the buffer states by making them serve as satellites subordinate to its will.

The global importance of the hostilities in Korea and in Indo-China in the early 1950's stemmed from the threats which communist efforts to gain mastery of these would pose to Japan and to all Southeast and South Asia, respectively, if these areas fell under hostile communist control.

Force and War. The threat of use of armed force and resort to war are the most drastic instruments of security policy, both unilateral and multilateral. Probably the most outstanding example in United States history of the use of the threat of force was in connection with the ending of the French Maximilian regime in Mexico in 1867. In hindsight, a clear indication of the use of United States force in Korea in case of aggression there would probably have deterred the aggression that took place in 1950.

War means, however, the failure of a major policy of every nation—the policy of peace. For no nation in the modern day, even an aggressor, chooses war if some other program can be found to achieve the objective. But peace is subordinate to the objective of national security. This is not to say that a state will always fight for its security interests even when they are called "vital." If there seems no chance of preserving those interests, even by war, a statesman may feel justified in giving them up to avoid the destruction resulting from hostilities. Britain might have so estimated in 1940 after Dunkirk. But the world is fortunate that Britain chose to continue the war rather than to surrender.

POLICIES OF INTERNATIONAL COOPERATION

There are certain general policies which, while not unilateral, still do not entail the close association of a formal alliance.

Cooperation and Parallel Action. We have, in Chapter VII, discussed the cooperative effort of the European Concert of Powers during the nineteenth century. The post-World War II situation has brought cooperation of the major powers in the Atlantic area on world-wide matters affecting their security, in addition to matters covered by their formal alliances. This parallel and concerted action has extended far beyond the formal contracts of the North Atlantic Treaty.

Cooperation has at times taken the form of parallel action without any formal agreements. Britain and the United States have collaborated thus on many problems—the first major instance probably being in the preservation of the integrity and non-colonization of the American Hemisphere. Certainly the United States and Britain were collaborating closely, without formal arrangement, during the period from the outbreak of World War II in 1939 until Pearl Harbor in 1941. When two or more states have no major conflicts with each other and face the same security threat, continuous consultation, with its normal outcome of mutually supporting actions, may give substantially the same results as an alliance.

International Law. International law is discussed in Chapter XIX and is mentioned here only to comment that some security values can be ascribed thereto. A broken agreement, even a minor act, may serve to clarify the intent of the potential opponent in the minds of the threatened nation's statesmen and of others. The broken agreement or understanding may be a basis for mobilizing the aid of friendly nations. It can perhaps be used as a basis for effective protest which checks the violation of security interests, but the effectiveness of the protest almost certainly depends on the existence of security policies other than adherence to international law alone.

Peaceful Settlement of Disputes. A dispute between two states may be a threat to the security of one or both of them. There may exist a danger of rising tensions, internal political and economic disruption, or even a war not particularly desired by either. For example, the leaders of neither the United States nor Britain wanted to fight over the "54–40 or fight" issue in 1846; hence, they each welcomed a face-saving solution of the matter through negotiation.

Other states than the actual disputants are almost certain to have security interests in major international disputes. Hostilities—even sharp differences short of hostilities—tend to draw states as supporters to each side and may decrease the cooperation of states whose security interests are mutually supporting. This danger was particularly acute during the short period of Israeli-Arab hostilities. It is generally to the security advantage of states wishing to preserve the *status quo* to have disputes settled among friendly nations.

The procedures for the pacific settlement of international disputes—good offices, conciliation, mediation, arbitration, and plebiscites—whether established through bilateral or multilateral treaties, within or outside of some regional or general international organization, are useful and sometimes important tools of security policy. There is value in achieving prior commitments to use such measures in case a dispute occurs. For then, if the dispute becomes so heated that the parties are beyond the point of being able to negotiate, interested third parties may be better able to persuade recourse to arbitration or some other peaceful expedient. This is the essential purpose of the provisions of the United Nations Charter for the peaceful settlement of international disputes.

As a final point, no state will willingly accept the application of one of these measures if the outcome is likely to impair its security situation materially and if it has a modicum of power to oppose effectively the use of such procedures. Thus, it is inconceivable that Turkey in 1947 would have submitted the controversy with the USSR over Soviet bases in the neighborhood of the Dardanelles to any such machinery.

SECURITY THROUGH TREATIES OF AMITY, NONAGGRESSION, AND RENUNCIATION OF WAR

The security of a state can sometimes be furthered by international contracts such as treaties of amity, nonaggression, and renunciation of war and by the conclusion of compacts stated in broad generalizations such as the League of Nations Covenant and the United Nations Charter. Such agreements must of necessity, however, be highly generalized and be drafted in a manner which does not point a finger of distrust at any participating party. And they do not give a basis for specific preparatory actions against a signatory which may be preparing to threaten or to disturb the peace.

Treaties of Amity and Nonaggression Pacts. Most states are accustomed to enter into treaties of amity (that is, friendship) and commerce with other states in time of peace. These normally provide for and regularize diplomatic and consular relations between them and establish the broad basis upon which trade may take place between them. They may also contain provisions for peaceful settlement of disputes. Such treaties provide little tangible assurance of security, however, for they merely formalize for the most part the bases of peaceful relations and can usually be terminated by notice or denunciation.

To provide more specifically for security, treaties on "nonaggression" are sometimes concluded defining aggression and pledging that the parties will not commit aggression against one another. A large number of such treaties were concluded between 1920 and 1939 by European states and by the Soviet Union. Like the treaties of amity and commerce, these did not prevent any state from actually going to war in 1939–1940, nor did prior adherence to the stipulation in the Kellogg-Briand Peace Pact not to "resort to war as an instrument of national policy" prevent World War II. The security value of such agreements seems to depend upon the attitudes and policies of the signatories toward one another rather than upon the written word of the agreements for enforcement.

Treaties guaranteeing the neutrality of a state, as Belgium's neutrality was guaranteed prior to World War I, and treaties of friendship between specific states are among available security policies. The values of all such attempts to gain security through treaty arrangements must be balanced, in the run of international politics, against the hazards. These hazards include the chance that the state marked for aggression may be lulled into an unwarranted sense of security and a condition of internal unpreparedness. Or the existence of the treaty may deter the peacefully inclined state from entering into arrangements with other states to strengthen its security situation. Deciding what steps should be taken in entering into treaty commitments of this general nature is one of the difficult tasks of statecraft in view of the continually changing nature of international relationships.

SECURITY THROUGH REGULATION OF ARMAMENTS

Regulation of armaments must be viewed from the standpoint of the individual state. This policy seeks to increase security through a mutual reduction of the military power of states, but it is only reasonable that each state should try to attain arrangements which reduce the power of a potential enemy more than its own power is decreased.

Possible Methods of Regulation. Regulation may be attempted in at least four ways: (1) multilateral renunciation of the use of a particular weapon or military technique; (2) limiting the armaments of a defeated state by the terms of the treaty of peace; (3) agreements freely entered into by participating states to limit their armaments; and (4) regulation, by munition-producing states, of armaments of a state lacking industry to manufacture its own arms through control of the export of arms and munitions.

1. RENUNCIATION OF USE OF PARTICULAR WEAPONS. Renunciation of the use of a particular weapon or a technique of force is obviously of limited value as a security guarantee. If the weapon is important militarily, every state will strive to produce it and have it ready for use—as both sides had poison gas available during World War II. Since no statesmen can foretell the future clearly, it is part of the responsibility of governments to their countries to prepare against the breaking of agreements by a potential enemy. If two states enter into armed conflict, it is only reasonable to expect that each will use all means available to avoid disastrous defeat. Hence, once conflict begins, the use of a renounced weapon is a matter of strategy for the present and future. The use is not determined by past agreements. Rather than because of moral principles or international agreements, poison gas was not used during World War II principally because of the questionable military gain and because of the hazards from almost certain retaliation. There is no positive assurance that belligerents would refrain from the use of atomic weapons even if all parties

had signed a convention "outlawing" these weapons and prohibiting their use. A state which is willing to disregard its covenants to settle all disputes by peaceful means and to respect the integrity and independence of others is not likely to be restrained from the use of particular weapons when it resorts to aggression if it believes its ends will be served by their use.

2. LIMITING ARMAMENTS OF DEFEATED STATES. The limitation of the armaments of a defeated state seems only a short-term arrangement if that state is allowed to regain full sovereign status. With that status, the state assumes responsibility for its own security. The limitation of German armaments by the Treaty of Versailles was effective until the 1930's, but after Hitler came to power and determined to rearm the nation, the treaty provisions were nullified by unilateral action. The post-World War II peace treaties, excepting that for Japan, limited the armaments of the vanquished. By the early 1950's these provisions were dead or dying except in the case of Finland close under the shadow of the USSR. After both World Wars I and II, it was hoped that the regulation of armaments of defeated states would be quickly followed by some effective international arrangement for guaranteeing a security so adequate that the defeated nations would have no tenable reason for rearming. This hope did not become a reality.

3. REGULATION BY MUTUAL CONSENT. The regulation of armaments by common consent has had some success. The Rush-Bagot Treaty of 1817 by which the United States and Britain provided for mutual disarmament on the Great Lakes is an outstanding instance, but the long-range and rapid movement of modern military destruction now makes similar actions of doubtful value. The Washington Treaty for the Limitation of Naval Armaments in 1922 and two subsequent agreements placed some checks on the naval building race between the wars but produced no universally acceptable formulas for permanent limitation, reduction, or international supervision. Efforts to secure agreement on the limitation of land armaments were less successful. Efforts in the United Nations to arrive at an agreement between the powers on the international control of atomic energy and the limitation or prohibition of the use of atomic weapons failed to bridge Soviet-Western differences in viewpoint.

There are no standards, no yardsticks, which are universally acceptable as measures of military power. Each statesman argues plausibly for reduction or elimination of the weapons his country fears most, and for retention of those which best contribute to his country's security position. Finally, even if agreement were ever reached, each statesman knows that a breakdown of the arrangement can quickly result in tipping the balance of military power dangerously against his country. Hence regulation without enforcement gives only temporary assurance of security.

4. REGULATION THROUGH CONTROL OF EXPORT OF ARMS. The fourth type of regulation concerns states which do not have an industry capable of producing or supporting all types of modern weapons. Among these states there is a *de facto* limitation on the weapons with which one may threaten or attack another. The high cost of arms in resources is such that a limit is in fact placed on the quantity which a state lacking munitions-producing capacity can purchase from abroad. Furthermore, all states control munitions exports. Hence, it is now possible for a limited number of states, principally the larger powers, to exercise a large degree of control over the armaments of smaller states to the extent that they choose to do so. The care exercised in post-World War II years by the United States over munitions exports to Latin American countries and to the Middle East amounted in essence to a regulation of armaments program. The Soviet provision of arms to guerrillas in Greece and to North Korea amounted, on the other hand, to a raising of the level of armaments of weak parties for the purpose of advancing the expansionist objectives of communism.

The Future. What future, if any, is there in the regulation of armaments? The ingenuity of mankind in making weapons and mobilizing military power has now outstripped the economic capabilities of states. We have already stressed the situation of small and nonindustrialized countries. There is also a practical limit for larger states. Only two powers, the United States and the Soviet Union, are at this time capable of possessing a large, well-rounded arsenal of all modern weapons and modern military forces. Only a handful of other states are likely to be able to amass comparable armaments in the foreseeable future. For the present the two Great Powers serve as an arsenal for their respective allies and friends. The international politics of regulation of armaments is, therefore, principally concerned with the policies of these two states at the present time.

SECURITY THROUGH COALITION

One of the most time-honored policies for security is for two or more states having mutual or complementary security problems and interests to enter into an alliance or mutual defense arrangement. The objective of this policy is thereby to increase the total power supporting the security of each participant in contrast to regulation of armaments which strives toward security through reduction of military power.

Treaties of Alliance. The provisions of treaties of alliance have varied from the most general pledges of friendship, as for example the centuries-old treaty between Portugal and Britain which was invoked to give the Allies bases in the Azores during World War II (although Portugal itself did not engage in hostilities or break relations with the Axis), to specific promises of military aid in case one party becomes involved in war. The Triple Alliance among Germany, Austria-Hungary, and Italy of pre-World War I was of the latter variety. The North Atlantic Treaty is a little more indefinite, providing that in case of an attack upon one of the signatories or its vessels, planes, or armed forces in the area described by the treaty, each party will take forthwith "such action as it deems necessary, including the use of armed force."

Because preparations for defense take a long while, the collective action contracted in a modern alliance may be implemented by painstaking and detailed programs. These, as in the case of the North Atlantic Treaty Organization, may extend far beyond a general understanding as to military strategy and include command arrangements, standardization of equipment, signal communications and other technical matters which give substance and strength to the form of collective security.

Even though a state is not a member of an existent alliance, that alliance may significantly affect its security. Switzerland, Sweden, Spain, and even Finland gain from the North Atlantic Pact through increased security in the European area. Thus, in effect, some states may obtain many of the advantages flowing from an alliance without experiencing a member's costs and restrictions on freedom of action.

States that are threatened by aggression have little alternative other than to ally themselves together in mutual self-defense. Generalities on the dangers of alliances have little merit in these circumstances. The Soviet Bloc is a tight alliance system to which communist China has been added. Some states are striving to hold themselves aloof from the friction between Soviet communism and other states. But even those who would be aloof have their security increased by collective action in the free world—insofar as that action prevents war. In case war occurs, the effect of the alliances on security of would-be neutrals has to be appraised on a country-by-country basis. In summary, it appears that the policy of alliances is currently an essential security policy for most states. The United States, once eschewing all permanent alliances, is now the "switching center" for most of those in the free world.

Regional Arrangements. There seems little point in attempting to make a major distinction between an alliance and regional security arrangements under the United Nations, so far as security is concerned, in view of the fact that regional arrangements are in effect a particular type of alliance. There is at least one security characteristic of regional arrangements which is worthy of particular note. The details of agreement usually provide for pacific settlement

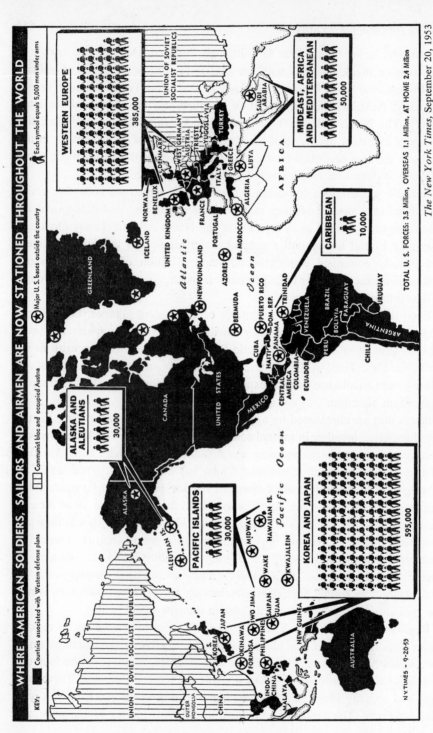

FIGURE XVIII:2

512

of disputes among the parties concerned and also create a concert to restrain aggressive tendencies of a participant in the arrangement. We will discuss regional arrangements further in Chapter XXI.

Economic Cooperation and Assistance. Security may be sought, or implemented, through a policy of economic cooperation and assistance. The United States has utilized many programs (discussed in Chapter IX) along this line since 1947, of which the most notable are the European Recovery Program, the Truman plan of aid to Greece and Turkey, and the Mutual Security Program.

Balance of Power Policy.[9] Regional security problems still exist because some states question the long-range objectives and intent of their neighbors. Within the framework of the global conflict, states are striving to keep at least a local power balance with possible opponents of the future. This is illustrated in the diplomatic maneuvering to effect German rearmament within a European Defense Community and in the politics of the Middle East between the Arab League and Israel. But the conflict between the Soviet Bloc and the free world overshadows, although it does not eliminate, the local security problems. The modern balance of power policies of states operate principally through alliances and regional arrangements and, globally, approximate the "simple balance" described in Chapter VII.

The Soviet Bloc encompasses so much of the power in the globe at the present time that there is, in the immediate future, little chance of a third "balancer" arising to maintain equilibrium in a similar way to Britain's role in nineteenth-century Europe. Ultimately, a revived Germany and Japan in full possession of the exercise of all their rights as sovereign states, together with some other powers in Europe and Asia, may produce a realignment of the scales of power in such a way that the security problem and the balance of power appear somewhat differently from the way they do at the present mid-century. States may then again arrange a "multiple balance" among coalitions.

SECURITY THROUGH SUPPORT OF THE UNITED NATIONS

Support of the United Nations is a security policy of most states. This policy is the application of the universal concert theses of Woodrow Wilson and others, in contrast to the balance of power concept. But the two concepts are not necessarily conflicting from the standpoint of an individual state's search for security. The United Nations was conceived as a world-wide collective security arrangement which would eliminate the need for alliances other than "regional arrangements" to settle local problems. When plans for the world organization were being drawn, many persons visualized it as being an instru-

9 For further discussion of the balance of power see ch. vii.

ment for eliminating, or greatly reducing, the use of most of the policies other than pacific settlement of international disputes and adherence to international law discussed in the preceding pages. Support of the United Nations has great value as a security policy. Public opinion is a security factor and the forum of the United Nations is an important place in which to mobilize world opinion against aggression. Alliances and regional arrangements completed within the terms of the United Nations Charter experience less questioning from peoples and states which have sometimes striven to stand on neutral or middle ground. Moreover, the United Nations machinery for the pacific settlement of international disputes is a useful instrument. Viewed from the standpoint of one of the lesser powers, a United Nations-sponsored security action, as in the Korean case, even if only an assembly recommendation, may be easier to support than an outright Great Power action outside of the international organization. Hence the United Nations may sometimes provide the machinery for concerting the actions of states, outside of the major alliance combinations, which are striving to hold aloof from the conflicts—particularly conflict between the Soviet Bloc and the Western Powers. The United Nations provides another meeting place for diplomacy, particularly when relations are strained. It is not the main instrument for security for which many hoped—without good reason, in hindsight. But its support is a useful security policy today and keeps the future open for possibly greater effectiveness tomorrow.

WEAKNESSES OF COLLECTIVE SECURITY

The term *collective security* is often used indiscriminately to mean both the global security system envisaged by the architects of the United Nations Charter and the system of alliances and cooperation such as NATO, the Inter-American Treaty of Reciprocal Assistance, the ANZUS Pact, and others developed to resist and oppose communism and other threats to international peace and security. The power and cost of modern armaments, coupled with the speed with which an aggression can be successfully accomplished, make collective security the basic national security policy for modern states. States facing immediate aggression must choose between collective security and the "garrison state"—realizing that the latter policy may be inadequate owing to the costs or lack of capabilities. States not immediately threatened by aggression cannot stand idly by while their security position is weakened by the engulfment of a friendly state or land.

There are, however, difficulties and disadvantages to participation in a collective security system. The following are some of these:

1. National sovereignty precludes absolute assurance that pledges will be kept. Security becomes somewhat dependent on the vagaries of internal politics

of another state. Trust becomes a vital element. This is difficult to preserve in a time of crisis and tension, and perhaps equally difficult under the attack of a sustained "peace offensive."

2. Every member of a collective security arrangement has its bargaining position in international affairs affected. A small state, otherwise seemingly insignificant in world affairs, may acquire material leverage in dealing with one of the Great Powers. Compromises, which are distasteful to the stronger parties in the alliance, may be accepted to avoid strains on the alliance.

3. Neutrals, or nonparticipating states with the same security problem as the members of an alliance, may further exploit the *de facto* protection which they gain, at low cost to themselves, by driving hard bargains as a price for their support.

4. Military strategy and preparations have to be adjusted toward the political requirement that each member believes that it has at least as much security as it would if it were to follow a unilateral policy.

5. Armed conflicts, even those which might have remained localized, are likely to lead to general war, especially when there are large power groupings with basically antagonistic objectives.

Other weaknesses can undoubtedly be thought of. None is insurmountable. But dealing with them requires careful diplomacy. Collective security in action is the most complicated form of international relations.

SECURITY POLICIES IN THE FUTURE

If each state's security were merely a matter of considering action in case of atomic war, the problem would be simpler, although no less terrible. History since Hiroshima has demonstrated many hazards to national security in addition to atomic weapons. The capture of free Czechoslovakia by the communist apparatus without use of arms, the wars caused by communist support of internal disturbances in Greece and Indo-China, the communist aggression by armed force in Korea, the confused Israeli-Arab fighting, and the tension between Egypt and Britain over bases in the Suez Canal Zone—these and other instances show the wide variety of possible security problems of the future.

That future may well continue the use, principally within the framework of collective security arrangements, of most of the policies discussed in this chapter. Collective security now provides international contracts which a state can invoke to call into its side of the power balance the major military power of allies. This creates an increased hazard to an aggressor. It may lead an aggressor to seek openings not guarded by such contracts and for softness in internal affairs permitting action similar to that in Greece, Czechoslovakia, and

Indo-China. The answer to the latter policy is preventive action strengthening the internal structure of threatened states. Once an aggression is under way, intervention is an available but traditionally unpopular policy.

The conflicts among smaller states now fall roughly into two categories: (1) those for which the differences and objectives are products of the competing states themselves and (2) those which are in fact a part of the global conflict between communism and anticommunism. A conflict initially in the former category may shift into the second. The anticommunist powers cannot fail to resist further erosion of the free world, and the Soviet Union is certain to support any of its satellites or factions friendly to communism.

There are dangers in looking too hopefully at historical precedents as a basis for passing judgment on security policies in our atomic age. The last decade or two has brought three hitherto unknown conditions to the national security problem.

1. The weapons and techniques of the 1950's now make suicidal the dependence on security policies designed to buy time to mobilize in case an aggression occurs. Readiness is all-important.
2. The concept, supported by the history of the eighteenth and nineteenth centuries, that war is merely a continuation of foreign policy with inclusion of force as an instrument is now inadequate. The use of force, once unleashed, is now difficult to limit. It carries the probability of total destruction of a way of life for the vanquished victim.
3. What is even more important, the costliness and destructiveness of modern war threaten, even for those on the victorious side, many of the fundamental values of life for those believing in freedom of the individual, private enterprise, and higher standards of living.

What, then, are the key security policies for the near future? In the anticommunist world the main policy is that of collective security with particular stress on four facets: (1) building up the unity and strength of the free world; (2) determined opposition to aggression coupled with contesting some areas recently engulfed by communism; (3) creating and maintaining the deterrent force of restraining military power; and (4) preventive policies aiming at the elimination of causes of unrest and at creating stronger interests in peace and rising productivity.

Soviet communism has pursued a policy of imperialism and great military power. So long as that policy maintains its aggressive character and its unlimited objectives of power and conquest, or until the equation of power is changed, no other free world policies will be feasible and acceptable. At that time regulation of armaments and a workable world system of collective security, to which nearly every nation now avows support, will become realistic and a key to the national security policies for all states.

SUGGESTED READINGS

Hanson W. Baldwin, *The Price of Power* (New York, 1948).

William T. R. Fox, *The Super-Powers* (New York, 1944).

———. *United States Policy in a Two-Power World* (New Haven, 1947).

George Kennan, *American Diplomacy, 1900–1950* (Chicago, 1951).

Walter Lippmann, *The Cold War* (New York, 1947).

———. *Isolation and Alliance* (Boston, 1952).

Hans J. Morgenthau, *Politics Among Nations* (rev. ed., New York, 1954).

O. L. Nelson, Jr., *National Security and the General Staff* (Washington, 1946).

R. S. W. Pollard, *The Struggle for Disarmament* (London, 1949).

W. A. Riddell, *World Security by Conference* (Toronto, 1947).

Louis Smith, *American Democracy and Military Power* (Chicago, 1951).

Harold and Margaret Sprout, *Foundations of National Power* (rev. ed., Princeton, 1951).

N. Spykman, *America's Strategy in World Politics* (New York, 1948).

Robert Strausz-Hupé, *The Balance of Tomorrow* (New York, 1945).

Merze Tate, *The United States and Armaments* (Cambridge, 1948).

———. *The Disarmament Illusion* (New York, 1942).

John Wheeler-Bennett, *The Pipe-Dream of Peace: The Story of the Collapse of Disarmament* (New York, 1935).

PART V

Organizing the International Community: The Search for Collective Security

CHAPTER XIX

The Role of Law in International Politics

INTRODUCTION

IN PART II of this book we discussed a number of basic factors affecting national policy and international politics. International law was not included among these factors. This was not an oversight. For, while international law has an important role in international relations, this role, rather than being a basic factor, is derived from the nature of the elements of national power and of the strategies of nations in international politics.

We have already considered many matters which fall partially under the heading of international law. This, stated simply, is the sum total of the rules, principles, customs, and agreements which states accept as having the force of law for the regulation of phases of international relations.[1] Thus, many matters discussed in Chapter XVII on the conduct of foreign relations actually have to do with international law. Moreover, it may be noted that the Preamble of the United Nations Charter sets forth in its opening paragraphs that one of the four main ends for which the United Nations organization has been formed is "to establish conditions under which justice and respect for the obligations arising from treaties and other sources of international law can be maintained."

Confusion Regarding Effectiveness of Law. Confusion and disillusionment concerning international law may easily arise in the minds of thinking citizens. There is a natural tendency to visualize international law as being more or less similar to domestic law with its courts for adjudicating conflicts and its police power for thwarting malefactors and for exacting retribution from them within dimensions set by the law. International law has been unable to solve the problems of conflict, aggression, and war, yet some distinguished, and perhaps

---

[1] For general reading on international law see J. L. Brierly's excellent little volume, *The Law of Nations* (rev. ed., New York, 1949); Edwin D. Dickinson, *Law and Peace* (Philadelphia, 1950); P. C. Jessup, *A Modern Law of Nations* (New York, 1948); Hans Kelsen, *Principles of International Law* (New York, 1952). For detailed study of the substance of contemporary international law see Charles C. Hyde, *International Law, Chiefly as Interpreted and Applied by the United States* (2d rev. ed., Boston, 1945), and L. Oppenheim, *International Law: a Treatise* (7th ed. by H. Lauterpacht, London, 1948–1952).

overidealistic, individuals have talked about international law as if it might soon substitute for armaments, the balance of power, and other security policies. History shows that aggressors are rarely deterred by principles or agreements, and that in reality international law, while being very useful in the routine relations among peaceful nations, has been only a minor element in international politics in thwarting aggression and preventing war.

The limited applicability of international law to the control of aggression and war has caused many people to overlook the essential role which it does play in facilitating normal orderly relations among states. This last function may be compared to such items of our domestic law as the legal requirement that we drive on the right side of the road, pay debts in accordance with agreements, have witnesses to certain types of documents, and other routine legal matters. There is, of course, a sanction connected with domestic law concerning such matters which is lacking in the law of nations. But states will usually adhere to international law on routine matters, if only because such action is generally more convenient.

With the foregoing thoughts as a preface, let us consider the historical foundation of international law and its nature as one of the regulators of international affairs.

Conditions Accompanying Rise of National States. During medieval feudal society, the Holy Roman Empire and the Catholic Church provided some semblance of order in Europe. But the rise of the independent principalities, kingdoms, and city states created a situation which was increasingly anarchical. Each political entity was answerable only to itself and was competing with others for power, territory, and position. Gone was all semblance of political unity. With the coming of the Reformation and Protestantism, the spiritual unity of Europe under one Church and one canon law was dissipated.

The existent intrigue, competition, differences, and struggle for power among the jealous sovereigns must inevitably have led to continual strife and war unless man could find some means by which to restrain aggressive powers and to determine rights and obligations. Extensive conflict did indeed accompany the emergence of the nation-state system. Europe was torn with the Thirty Years' War in the decades preceding the Peace of Westphalia in 1648.[2] And before three-quarters of the ensuing century had passed, it was rent again by the War of the Spanish Succession ending in the Peace of Utrecht in 1713.

THE SEARCH FOR A SYSTEM

The Principle of Equilibrium. We have mentioned in the chapter on power politics that states early came to accept the notion that the most effective way

2 See Leo Gross, "The Peace of Westphalia, 1648–1948," *Am. J. Int. Law*, Jan., 1948.

in which to restrain the overly powerful and to preserve their own existence was to espouse a balance of power system with its process of alignment, re-alignment, armaments, compensation, and mutual assistance. And at each of the historic peace conferences, prior to Versailles, that terminated periods of armed strife, efforts were made to fashion an equilibrium in the hope that this would reduce the possibility of war. Yet a balance of power mechanism clearly did not alone fulfill all of the requirements for an orderly society.

Hence, at the same time the nation-states were developing, men were also searching for means by which international differences might be resolved peacefully and some semblance of law and order brought into the relationship of states. Some believed that these ends could be achieved only through the establishment of some universal dominion, confederation, federation, or parliament of Europe. But rulers and courts were not prepared for such steps. They feared that a loss of independence and sovereignty would end sooner or later in subjection to some alien rule.[3]

Emergence of Concept of Law of Nations. Some philosophers, theologians and jurists began to suggest that nations, like individuals, were subject to principles of law. There gradually emerged from their writings the concept of a law of nations, and a belief that the relations between nations should be conducted in accordance with the precepts of law. With the passage of time, a body of principles, customs, rules, and agreements, growing out of the practice of states and voluntarily accepted by them as having the character and force of law, came to be recognized as forming what we now call international law.[4]

Roots of Law of Nations. It is not altogether surprising that the idea of a law of nations sprang up in the minds of sixteenth and seventeenth-century thinkers in Europe. Western Europeans were conditioned to the idea of an all-embracing law. The heritage and vestiges of Roman law still existed within the Continent from Italy to France and parts of Germany. Not only did the Romans develop the concept of a law universally applicable to their citizens wherever they were, but they also accepted the concept of underlying principles of law based on considerations of good faith and equity, which were a part of the law of each community and governing the relations between nations (known as the *jus gentium*).[5] Roman law was widely studied and applied in the courts.

A second factor contributing to the emergence of a law of nations was the fact that the rulers of Europe generally acknowledged the Christian faith and

---

3 See ch. xx for résumé of early peace plans and evolution of international organization.

4 For the history of international law see Arthur Nussbaum, *A Concise History of the Law of Nations* (New York, 1949).

5 See George Finch, *The Source of Modern International Law* (Carnegie Endowment Monograph No. 1, Washington, 1937), p. 23.

divine ordinance, whether as Catholics or as Protestants. Before the Reformation, all had been members of one communion and subject to canon law which was applicable throughout Christendom. Hence, Europeans were accustomed to the idea of being subject to a law common to all of their societies.

A third factor was the rapid development of European commerce and navigation which needed more orderly and predictable conditions at a time when the political state of Europe was deteriorating into a condition of anarchy. Commercial interests required the presence of some semblance of law and order for profitable venture. This was reflected in the growth of mercantile codes such as the *Consulato del Mare* and the Laws of Wisby at the end of the Middle Ages. In the seventeenth century it was seen in the demands for an assurance of the right of the freedom of the seas.

Fashioning of the Law by Jurists and Philosophers. It was from the concepts of divine canon and Roman law, together with the so-called natural law believed to be applicable to men everywhere, that the postmedieval jurists, theologians, and philosophers reasoned that states—even though sovereign and recognizing no temporal superior—were nevertheless under, and bound by, a common law of nations. Jurists trained in the traditions of the canon law and the Catholic Church stressed the principles deducible from divine and canon law, while at the same time calling attention to practices and customs. Philosophers and jurists adhering to the humanist movement stressed the principles of natural law and "right reasoning"—believed to apply to all men. They also drew upon the Roman law, and especially upon the evidences of custom and practice as borne out by treaties, agreements, the actions of rulers and political bodies, and the writings of scholars and jurists. From these various sources, as well as from the realm of private law, the writers developed the concepts of status, persons, title and jurisdiction, contract, injury, and responsibility for reparation. Political theorists added the doctrine of sovereignty. Practice amplified these with concepts relating to the treatment of ambassadors, the status of consuls, and the sanctity of treaties.[6]

Most celebrated among the writers who laid the foundations of modern international law was Hugo Grotius, a Dutch theologian, lawyer, and diplomat who published in 1625 a treatise entitled *The Law of War and Peace*. Grotius marshaled impressive arguments that the enlightened interest and right reasoning of rulers and states dictated that they should submit—and had done so—to principles and rules of law in their conduct of international affairs. Though many of the precepts which he deduced from the voluminous literature of his

6 See H. Lauterpacht, *Private Law Sources and Analogies of International Law* (London, 1927).

time are not a part of the law today, he nevertheless fashioned the outlines of a system which succeeding generations of jurists and statesmen were able to erect into a living body of law acknowledged and applied by states. Since the seventeenth century, the law has been formalized in treaties, state papers, court decisions, and many learned treatises.[7]

Roscoe Pound has epitomized the origin of the law of nations in these words: "International law was born of juristic speculation and became a reality because that speculation gave men something by which to make and shape international legal institutions and a belief that they could make and shape them effectively."[8]

THE NATURE OF INTERNATIONAL LAW

Law in General. International law cannot be understood without first understanding the nature of law in general. And even when this is clear, it is difficult to understand the law of nations; for we tend to visualize it, erroneously, in the mental framework of our own domestic law. Moreover, most people associate with law the uniformed policeman with his nightstick and revolver, a solemn court before which they can be required to appear for trial, a jail in which offenders can be locked up, and then an electric chair to put to death those found guilty of murder.

Vital as are the elements of adjudication, force, compulsion and punishment, they are by no means the first in order of establishment. Law is first and foremost a psychological and a social device and instrument.[9]

From Custom to Law. When we examine the functioning of any society, one of the first things to become apparent is the early formation of customs and habits. These behavior patterns—things to do and ways to do them—soon become more or less fixed into folkways and mores, either through explicit or implicit agreement. Those which are most useful and necessary to orderly, successful relations are eventually agreed upon as having an obligatory nature and being regarded as law. It is not easy to distinguish in primitive societies when a pattern of conduct changed from a mere custom to a compulsive rule of conduct having an "oughtness" about it. What is certain, however, is that before society made provision for means to compel obedience to law, those who had the strength and will to do so enforced their own rights, exacted

---

[7] Grotius' work has gone through many editions and has been translated into all major languages. An authoritative rendition is that published by the Carnegie Endowment for International Peace, Washington, 1925.

[8] Roscoe Pound, "Philosophical Theory and International Law," *Bibliotheca Visseriana*, vol. 1 (1923), 71*ff*.

[9] See N. S. Timasheff, *An Introduction to the Sociology of Law* (Cambridge, 1939); A. R. Radcliffe-Brown, "Primitive Law," in *Encyclopedia of the Social Sciences*, vol. II, pp. 202–206.

compliance, and imposed punishment by their own means upon those who infringed their rights as they conceived them.[10] Only much later in the process of social evolution is a transition made to centralized enforcement of rights and duties through establishment of a monopoly of force in the hands of the agents of society. It is well to bear this chain of progress in mind, for international politics takes place in a society—that is, the Western state system which is a society without a central supranational government.

Law in Ungoverned Society. The strength and enforceability of law in a society lacking a firm government are obviously quite different from law in a society in which there are powerful organs of government and the people are either accustomed to observing law or can be compelled to do so.

In trying to understand the nature and role of international law in world politics, it may be helpful to think of what the situation was with respect to law in the frontier days of the old West in United States history. Journals and documents of those times reveal that soon after settlements were formed, customs and patterns of conduct developed and laws were passed by the townspeople to regulate the orderly, safe, and convenient uses of things varying from pastures and water supplies to firearms.

The law existed, but with the weak organization of these frontier settlements and the pressing concern of every man for his own livelihood, it was unable to prevent the entrance of lawless elements from the wilderness or cattle trails. These men, some of them merely reckless cowboys and others hardened robbers and killers, were often able to ignore, disobey, or flout the law openly. Nonetheless, the law existed and was supported and obeyed by the law-abiding citizenry. Only after some men became sufficiently concerned over lawlessness, whether as individuals or as duly appointed sheriffs, and were willing to risk their lives to enforce the law did society become governed in the full sense and law take on the full attribute of a rule of conduct laid down by authority and enforced upon the individual by society.

Only at a late stage did law come to have full-fledged government and police forces to legislate and to mete out speedy punishment to those who violated its provisions. When one recalls how long it has taken many national societies to reach this last level, we should not expect a more rapid and perfect development in world affairs where the relations of nations are so filled with a heritage of competitions, fears, struggles, and conflicting interests, and where there are so many different standards and moral codes.[11]

Early Nature of International Law. Although the states newly established

10 See W. G. Sumner, *Folkways* (Boston, 1907).
11 See H. L. Lauterpacht, *The Function of Law in the International Community* (Oxford, 1933).

in the sixteenth century declared themselves independent of any higher political authority, their rulers, nonetheless, came to accept the notion of an international law, as outlined by Grotius and others, as a factor in their relations with one another. Nebulous as some of these rules were, states nevertheless acknowledged their existence, appealed to them in support of their own policies and actions, and invoked them against the actions of others. And by and large, states observed them in spite of the fact that there was no way to enforce them save by the exercise of diplomatic, political, or military pressure against a party alleged to have violated them. Considerations of expediency, convenience, national interest, and moral approbation contributed to their actions in these respects.

Principles and rules concerning both war and peace were comprised within the early international law. The need for it as a guide to conduct was apparently felt to be so strong that even during war, customs and rules were established and followed—just as the lawless ones in the old West often had their code, the rule of the even break—although there was no centralized authority with power to impose obedience or punishment for infraction.

LAW AND FORCE

Law, in the domestic sense, is usually defined as being a rule of conduct promulgated by an authority entitled to make it binding upon a subject. This authority may be a sovereign, a legislature, or a court.

The Binding Force of Law. In a situation such as that prevailing in international politics where the sovereign states composing the society acknowledge no political or judicial authority superior to their own and claim to be legally equal with one another regardless of size or power, it is manifestly impossible to have an international law created and enforced in the manner of other law. This explains why international law in a sense is "a primitive type of law," why its principal source lies in the customs and informal and formal agreements of states, why it is interpreted by them, and why it is as yet exclusively enforced by them according to their own interests and capabilities.

The lack of a central authority or government in the society of states with power to ordain law having compulsory force upon sovereign states has led some to think that international law either is not "true law" or has no binding character. But the fact remains that statesmen declare it to be law and governments assert rights upon the basis of it and make demands upon others for conformity to it.[12] National courts and international tribunals will give effect to the law of nations when it is invoked before them. Governments use the instruments of policy available to them to maintain their rights under the law.

12 See Kelsen, *op. cit.*, pp. 18–89; Gerhart Niemeyer, *Law without Force* (Princeton, 1941).

And such widely accepted agreements as the Charter of the United Nations and the Statute of the International Court of Justice specifically provide for actions and decisions predicated upon the binding force of international law.

This does not mean that the law is always observed. Where the alternative is victory or defeat, considerations of "lawfulness" are likely to be on occasion ignored. Germany's resort to unrestricted submarine warfare in World Wars I and II with the torpedoing of passenger liners and neutral vessels without warning illustrates what can happen. In our own country thousands of people every year are shot or murdered by lawless characters, and some go unpunished. Yet we do not question the existence or effectiveness of the law prohibiting such acts.

Role of Mutual Interest. Here we should emphasize the fundamental truth that a law operative among sovereign states in a climate of power politics depends upon the mutual interest of states. Elements of expediency, mutual convenience, and the possibility or fear of suffering retaliation if there were no rules of law or if they were not observed have all contributed to the motivations of states in supporting the developments of international law and its application to the relations of states.[13]

Sanction of Moral Force. Almost without exception, when states violate international law they refrain from denying its existence. Instead, they find excuses of many kinds, including conflicting precedents of law to support their action. Even in cases of blatant aggression, states have usually striven to make their actions appear "legal." There are few instances of barefaced violation, and most of these have been in connection with the use of force, for example, Germany's treatment in 1914 of its neutrality pledge to Belgium as "a scrap of paper." Where a state infringes on the spirit and intent of an agreement, custom, or principle, it will usually strive to preserve the outward form of adherence to international law; for public opinion, both of other nations' statesmen and of peoples, is an important force often having the effect of a sanction.

When governments have precipitated war without regard to the law or the sanction of public opinion, it has usually been because they are so committed to aggression that they recognize that the public disapprobation incident thereto will be so great that the breaking of one or more treaties will add little if anything to that disapprobation.

Importance of Consensus of Values. It is to be noted that in the eighteenth and nineteenth centuries, when international law was reaching maturity, the parties to the law were for the most part European nations or overseas states

[13] See W. W. Bishop, "Postwar Trends and Developments in International Law from a North American Viewpoint," *Am. Soc. Int. Law Proc.*, 1953.

acting under the influence of Western political ideas. This provided the law with an undergirding of more or less commonly shared values and ideology, even though it lacked an international government to fashion or enforce it. It is obvious that in the present condition of the world, with the clash of ideologies and the many different cultural patterns represented in the society of states, international law lacks such support. This is bound to limit its effectiveness in some realms where crucial differences arise.

Dependence of Law upon Support by Strong Nations. Lacking some powerful nonpartisan agency, such as domestic law enjoys, to enforce submission of disputes to legal and peaceful settlement and to administer certain and swift punishment to those guilty of violations, international law must depend in time of crises upon the support of powerful nations. In the eighteenth and nineteenth centuries British influence and power, which at many points held the balance of power during this time, was placed strongly behind the development and enforcement of international law, which often furthered British self-interest.

With the changes that have occurred in British world power since 1939, the law must now look to an increasing degree to American support and to the combined support of many nations. In this connection it may be observed that the United Nations action in Korea is a first example of a collective use of armed force, following a formal decision by a world body, to uphold the independence of a state against aggression and to enforce respect for international law.

A LAW WITH DIVERSE INTERPRETATIONS

Although the law of nations has been widely accepted and acclaimed, many differences have prevailed over its nature and content.

One school of thought, especially prevalent among writers of the seventeenth and eighteenth centuries, believed that the content of international law could best be ascertained by reference to principles of justice and right reasoning as revealing the "natural law" governing all men.

Since early in the nineteenth century a second school of thought, known as the "positivist," has predominated in juristic thinking and in the viewpoints of Foreign Offices generally. This school holds that the substance of the law is to be derived chiefly from (1) treaties and conventions establishing expressly recognized rules; (2) international custom "as evidence of a general practice accepted as law"; and (3) the decisions and awards of national courts and international tribunals. As further evidence of the law, the writings of the most qualified publicists may be consulted. The Statute of the International Court of Justice expressly authorizes that body to apply these elements as international law, together with the general principles of law recognized by civilized nations.[14]

Differing National Interpretations. There is no one code where the sum of all the rules, principles, customs, and conventions composing international law are inscribed in an officially agreed international document. This is not to imply that there are not many international conventions codifying parts of the law. There are indeed many, including conventions setting forth agreed rules of land warfare, and they are widely accepted.[15] But statesmen and scholars must search the sources mentioned and determine as best they can what "the law" is on any given subject. There is lack of universal agreement among all states on the precise interpretation and permissible applications of principles and rules of international law. There is an "international law as interpreted and applied by the United States," and an international law as interpreted and applied by Great Britain.[16] And so on among states. Being sovereign political entities, each legally the equal of all others, states make their own determination of what "the law" means, what it allows, what it prohibits, and how it is to be applied. Thus, for example, there are numerous views on how far from shore a state may extend its laws and police jurisdiction. Some states claim the limit is three miles from the low-water line. Others hold that the law allows a six or twelve-mile maritime belt, or even more.[17]

Resolving Differing Interpretations. One of the main tasks of diplomacy is that of resolving differences which arise between states over their interpretations of the law and its application to particular situations in their relationships with one another. At times, states may be able to arrive at agreed formulations of the law on specific matters in some declaration or treaty, as for example the Convention on Rights and Duties of States signed by the American Republics at Montevideo in 1933, or the Convention on International Civil Aviation concluded at Chicago in 1944 recognizing that every state "has complete and exclusive sovereignty over the air space above its territory."

States have been willing on many occasions to submit to international arbitration legal claims relating to damages arising from actions alleged to be in

14 See Statute, Article 38.
15 See Manley O. Hudson (ed.), *International Legislation,* 9 vols. (Washington and New York, 1931–1950).
16 See Green H. Hackworth, *A Digest of International Law,* 8 vols. (Washington, 1940–1943); Charles C. Hyde, *International Law Chiefly as Interpreted and Applied in the United States,* 3 vols. (rev. ed., Boston, 1945). For the British interpretation see especially L. F. Oppenheim, *International Law—A Treatise,* vol. I (7th ed., by H. Lauterpacht, London, 1948); H. A. Smith, *Great Britain and the Law of Nations,* 2 vols. (London, 1932). Each government has its own law officers to interpret and advise on the interpretation and application of international law.
17 On maritime jurisdiction see Philip C. Jessup, *The Law of Territorial Waters and Maritime Jurisdiction* (New York, 1927); William E. Masterson, *Jurisdiction in Marginal Seas* (New York, 1929).

violation of international law.[18] In modern times states have been prepared to refer a substantial number of legal or what they regard as justiciable disputes to the International Court of Justice for judicial settlement.[19] But it must be borne in mind that the awards or decisions by international tribunals apply only to the parties to a given case and to the specific issue at stake in a given dispute. Thus, international law, even when interpreted by international tribunals, is lacking in uniformity of interpretation and application.

Codification of International Law. As we have previously indicated, various parts of international law have been embodied in international agreements. Between the two World Wars jurists devoted much attention to the possible codification of additional aspects of the law.[20] Along this same line the Charter of the United Nations directs the General Assembly to initiate studies and make recommendations for "encouraging the progressive development of international law and its codification" (Article 13). An International Law Commission, appointed by the General Assembly, is studying the problems involved in attaining a larger measure of agreement on details of the law and its application.[21]

THE SUBSTANCE OF INTERNATIONAL LAW

The substantive content of international law, manifold as it is, can hardly be described satisfactorily in a brief summary fashion. It is composed of a whole system of rules, each of which, as in all law, has some exceptions, and is subject to different interpretations and applications. It can be fully comprehended only by studying detailed texts and treatises and by examining a great number of leading cases and documents illustrating the rules and their utilization in the many questions comprised within the framework of the law.[22]

In the broadest sense, one may say that international law today is predomi-

[18] On the history of international arbitration see J. B. Moore, *International Adjudications Ancient and Modern*, Modern Ser., vol. I (New York, 1929), "Historical and Legal Notes."

[19] See Manley O. Hudson, *The Permanent Court of International Justice, 1920–1942* (New York, 1943); annual review articles on the present International Court of Justice appearing in the January issues of the *Am. J. Int. Law;* and Oliver J. Lissitzyn, *The International Court of Justice* (New York, 1951). Article 36 of the Statute of the ICJ contains what is known as the "optional clause," permitting states to file declarations accepting in advance the compulsory jurisdiction of the Court for legal disputes. Many states have filed such declarations but often with severely limiting restrictions. Some delegations at the San Francisco Conference in 1945 wished to give the Court broad powers of compulsory jurisdiction, but this was not acceptable to the United States or the Soviet Union.

[20] Attempts made at an international conference of jurists held at The Hague in 1930 to reach agreement on "codifying" three subjects were largely unsuccessful.

[21] See *Survey of International Law in Relation to the Work of Codification of the International Law Commission*, United Nations General Assembly (New York, 1949).

[22] In addition to the works mentioned in footnotes 1 and 10 above, mention may be made of Charles G. Fenwick's textbook entitled *International Law* (3rd ed., New York, 1948). The most generally usable casebook, with extensive editorial notes, is Herbert W. Briggs, *The Law of Nations: Cases, Documents and Notes* (2d ed., New York, 1952).

nantly concerned with the rights and duties of states and with the problems of a legal nature that are bound to arise from their relationships with one another. To give some idea of the substantive nature of the law and the character of its rules, we shall briefly touch on only *some* of the major topics with which the law is concerned.

Establishment of Statehood. Not every political or administrative entity that chooses to call itself a state is regarded as such within the terms of international law. Usually such an entity must (1) possess a definite territory, (2) be inhabited by a politically organized society, (3) have an effective government, and (4) be capable and willing to observe the obligations of international law. In most instances only such units as constitute sovereign political entities, whether they have arisen by evolution or by revolutionary separation from other states, can aspire to recognition by others as states under international law, with all of the rights accorded thereto.[23]

Recognition of States and Governments. Such a new political entity may exist without being recognized. Nevertheless, only after recognition as such by other states does the new unit assume its legally sovereign and independent character in the eyes of the law and is able to enter into international and diplomatic dealings with other nations. Most jurists, therefore, hold that recognition has a declaratory rather than a constitutive effect. Recognition of a new state may be either definite, complete and irrevocable (*de jure,* according to lawyers), or provisional and limited (*de facto,* as the saying goes). Basically, the accordance of recognition means that another state wishes to recognize the competence, legal and political, of the authorities of the new state and desires to deal with it as an equal under international law. Such an act has important effects in international litigations; for in most cases only a recognized state can claim diplomatic immunities and privileges, and only such a state can sue in the courts of the other.

Similar rules attach to unconstitutional changes of governments. A recognized state may undergo violent revolution resulting in the rise of a new government. Other states are under no obligation to recognize this new regime. Each state is free to decide whether (1) it wishes to consider the new ruling group as capable of making binding commitments on behalf of the state it claims to represent, and (2) whether it wishes to enter into political relations with it.

In the matter of recognition, states consult their own interests both as to the

---

[23] On establishment of statehood see the following and further references cited therein: J. L. Brierly, *The Law of Nations* (rev. ed., New York, 1949), pp. 111-122; Briggs, *Cases,* pp. 65-98; Jessup, *op. cit.,* ch. ii. For detailed analysis of the law on this and subsequent topics the reader should consult the appropriate passages in the works by Hackworth, Hyde, and Lauterpacht (Oppenheim) referred to above.

extension of recognition and its timing. They sometimes announce general principles to justify their policies, but few are altogether consistent in following these principles.[24]

Territory in International Law. Territory can be acquired by a state by (1) prescription, (2) accretion, (3) discovery and occupation, (4) cession or purchase, and (5) conquest and annexation.

The territorial jurisdiction of a state extends to its boundaries which, in most cases though not in all, are clearly defined. Its jurisdiction also covers by the same token possessions which it may hold abroad. Within these boundaries a state exercises full jurisdiction. In the airspace above its territories and possessions, and the marginal belt of waters surrounding them, the prevailing view holds that a state has absolute jurisdiction and may exclude or regulate the passage of all aircraft. Permission must be obtained from the state authorities for foreign aircraft to enter or fly over the national jurisdiction. International law has recognized since the seventeenth century the right of each state to exercise jurisdiction over a belt of marginal waters surrounding its territories. The generally accepted distance is three miles from the low-water mark—originally determined by the range of cannon shot—but in some instances states claim a greater distance. International law recognizes, generally speaking, a right of "innocent passage" for merchant vessels of foreign states through this belt of marginal or "territorial waters." National revenue and customs laws can give their local authorities a right to patrol these and sometimes even more extensive areas of water adjoining their coasts in order to prevent smuggling or other violation of the national law.

Where a river forms the boundary between two states, it is generally held that the dividing line will run either along the deepest navigable channel (the *thalweg*), along the middle of the stream, or anywhere else provided by treaty. The high seas do not belong to any state, and thus are regarded by international law as the common property of all in which all have a right to free navigation. War vessels and other public vessels are considered under international law more or less as "floating parts" of their nation's territory and cannot be boarded without permission of their commanding officer by any foreign authorities even if they have been granted permission to pass through the marginal waters of another state or to enter one of its ports. The recent practice of some states in nationalizing their merchant marines and in engaging in state-controlled foreign trading has raised complications in admiralty and international law with respect to exercising jurisdiction over such foreign vessels

[24] On recognition of states and governments see Brierly, *op. cit.*, pp. 122–135; Briggs, *Cases*, ch. ii; Jessup, *op. cit.*, ch. iii; H. Lauterpacht, *Recognition in International Law* (Oxford, 1947).
    On equality of states before law see especially E. D. Dickinson, *Equality of States in International Law* (Cambridge, 1920).

when they are involved in collisions or are within the marginal waters and ports of other states.[25]

Continuity of States and State Succession. Regardless of what government comes to rule a state, the state's international obligations continue. When a new state has emerged by separation from an old one, it need not necessarily be held to be heir to all or even part of the obligations incurred by the old. When, however, the old state has completely disintegrated, then the new units usually exercise some option as to taking over a part of the nationals, duties, and rights of the old state. Contractual obligations of a political nature incurred by a preceding government are usually resisted by succeeding regimes. Neat questions can arise as to whether a given debt is an obligation on behalf of a state.[26]

Jurisdiction over Nationals and Aliens. One of the important matters coming under international law is the conflict of nationality laws. Each state determines for itself, by its own nationality laws, what persons shall be regarded as its nationals and under what conditions. One of the problems which frequently arises in international law is that of reconciling the status of a person who has migrated from one country to another and decides to become a national of the second state. Upon becoming naturalized in his new country of residence, he does not necessarily automatically lose his old citizenship. Some states do not recognize a right of expatriation. Others regulate the matter through bilateral nationality treaties which have not been concluded, however, between all states. Thus, a person may have simultaneously a "dual citizenship." Or a situation may arise in which, by leaving his home land or refusing to return to it, he loses his original citizenship without acquiring another and thus he may become a "stateless" person.

There is no general obligation under international law requiring a state to admit all or any aliens seeking admission into its territory. This is a matter of domestic jurisdiction, save in so far as it may be regulated by intergovernmental agreements or treaties. Once an alien has been permitted to enter a foreign land, however, he comes under the territorial jurisdiction of the host country, unless specific extraterritorial rights have been granted by treaty—as they were in China until the close of World War II. He becomes subject to all its regulations and will be held accountable by it for violations of its laws. He may be arrested and prosecuted. He may be expelled from the country for just reason. In this case the home state of the national has the duty to receive him

25 On territory and jurisdiction on land and sea and over airspace see Brierly, *op. cit.*, pp. 142–194, 223–228; Briggs, *Cases*, chs. iv–v; J. D. Cooper, *The Right to Fly* (New York, 1947); Norman Hill, *Claims to Territory in International Law and Relations* (New York, 1945); W. E. Masterson, *Jurisdiction in Marginal Seas* (New York, 1929).
26 On continuity and state succession see Brierly, *op. cit.*, pp. 135–141; Briggs, *Cases*, ch. iii.

back. Fugitives from justice (but not political refugees) are customarily extradited to a claimant country in accordance with treaty arrangements.

In the absence of special treaties, a state may treat aliens in its territory as it pleases as long as it abides by a minimum international standard which, however, has as yet not been formulated in any certain, exact, and universally accepted fashion. A state has a right to insist that a foreign country treat its nationals as equals before the law and permit them access to its courts for procuring justice. It has a right to protect its own citizens abroad, but it is under no obligation to do so. And within the territory of another state it can act in their behalf only so far as treaty arrangements and comity permit.[27]

Immunities of Diplomats and Consuls. The only aliens not subject to the law of the land in which they reside are foreign diplomats, to a lesser extent consuls, and the members of foreign armed forces. The former represent their states in an official capacity, as we have mentioned in Chapter XVII, and deal with the national authorities of the host country. To facilitate the consummation of their purpose, they enjoy, by usage and by treaty, special privileges and immunities. These immunities guarantee the inviolability of the persons and diplomatic premises, the immunity from prosecution and enforcement of judgment even in cases where local law has been violated, the exemption from the duty to appear as witnesses, and exemption from paying customs duties and local taxes. Consuls deal with the local, not national, authorities, and have certain privileges, as we mentioned in Chapter XVII. But they are not exempt from civil and criminal jurisdiction unless they are registered as members of the diplomatic corps with the Foreign Office of the host country.

The immunities of members of the armed forces of one country present in the territory of another are usually governed by specific intergovernmental agreement.[28]

The United Nations Secretary-General, his assistants, the delegates to the United Nations meetings, and the members of their missions also enjoy immunities and privileges.[29]

State Responsibility. States are subject to a dual kind of responsibility under international law. For "acts of state" they are directly responsible. In cases, however, where there is negligence, or where they refuse a foreign party redress for acts which in the first place were committed by unauthorized per-

---

[27] On nationality and jurisdiction over nationals and aliens, as well as extradition, see Brierly, *op. cit.*, pp. 203–223; Briggs, *Cases*, chs. vii–viii; Jessup, *op. cit.*, ch. iv; E. M. Borchard, *Diplomatic Protection of Citizens Abroad* (New York, 1915).

[28] On diplomatic and other immunities see Brierly, *op. cit.*, pp. 194–203; Briggs, *Cases*, ch. x.

[29] See Charter of the United Nations, Article 105; United Nations–United States Agreement regarding Headquarters of the United Nations, June 26, 1947; and General Convention on the Privileges and Immunities of the United Nations. (Briggs contains the items mentioned.) **Briggs**, *Cases*, pp. 794–801, and following editor's note.

sons or private individuals, they become indirectly responsible. An act will be considered an international delinquency only if it was committed with willful or malicious intent, or with culpable negligence. In general, the law demands that local remedies be exhausted before a claim is litigated before an international tribunal. States are not internationally responsible for legitimate acts done under local law to which, as mentioned above, the resident alien or business firm is at all times subject. Only when an alien has been denied justice or where the state's organs can be shown to have condoned a wrong, does the state incur liability under international law. Usually legitimate claims, when proven before an international tribunal, are followed by payment of reparations, although these need not always be pecuniary.[30] It should be borne in mind that under international law only a state can put forward a claim against another state.

Law of Treaties. The procedures by which states enter into treaty obligations and the question of when and how a treaty comes into force, as well as the obligations which it involves and its length of duration, are partly regulated by the parties and partly by international law. Treaties in general come into force after they have been signed by duly authorized plenipotentiaries and, wherever the constitutions of the parties so demand, following ratification in accordance with the necessary constitutional requirements. The ratifications must be exchanged or deposited according to the specifications of the treaty itself. If a plenipotentiary is forced to sign under personal duress—a circumstance now seldom met with—the law regards the treaty as being invalid. Duress upon the state is another matter, however, and has up to now been regarded as not unlawful. No state has a right to terminate a treaty unilaterally before its fixed term of expiration or otherwise than as provided in its text, unless there have been essential changes in the conditions existing at the time the treaty was concluded. A treaty can, of course, be rescinded, amended, or replaced by another at any time if all the parties so agree. The main rule in this respect goes under a Latin phrase—*pacta sunt servanda.* This means that treaties which are in force are to be observed for the fulfillment of the purposes for which they were concluded. It does not mean that they cannot be changed by agreement. There is a doctrine in international law which goes under the Latin phrase, *rebus sic stantibus,* which does allow a state to nullify or demand mitigation of a treaty commitment if there have been fundamental, vital, or essential changes in the conditions existing at the time the treaty was entered into. But there are usually disputes as to the degree of change which has occurred or is required to justify nullification.

---

30 On international responsibility for damages see Briggs, *Cases,* ch. ix; Jessup, *op. cit.,* ch. v; Borchard, *cit. supra;* M. Whiteman, *Damages in International Law,* 3 vols. (Washington, 1937).

Under international law a treaty prevails over a national law which may conflict with it. This principle can, as might be anticipated, lead at times to political issues within countries. To avoid both domestic and international difficulty, the United States has sought to apply such a construction to its treaties that they are not held to conflict with its domestic laws and vice versa.[31]

There is a whole body of rules concerning the interpretation of treaties. In general, the interpretation seeks to establish the intent of the parties at the time of conclusion of the agreement and to carry out the purpose which the treaty was designed to serve. Jurists are not entirely agreed, however, on all the points of interpretation. The same may be said with respect to the effect of war on treaties. The United States holds that some treaties, due to the nature of their content, become inoperative as a whole with the outbreak of war. Some others regard treaties which do not interfere with the pursuit of war as remaining in effect. Treaties of friendship, alliance, or other political arrangement are dissolved between belligerents.

A treaty may be terminated by (1) mutual consent, (2) the loss of independence of one party, (3) denunciation (if provided for in the treaty or agreed to by the other parties), (4) suspension, and (5) nonrenewal when the period of validity has expired.[32]

Enforcement of Law; Self-Help; Sanctions; War. As mentioned in the introduction to this chapter, there is as yet no central authority for the enforcement of international law, although the United Nations Charter meant to give the Security Council some powers in this direction. Nevertheless, law need not necessarily be enforced by a supranational authority. Individual states can and do act on its behalf.

Traditional international law has distinguished various means of pressure by which observance of international legal rights may be enforced. These means include (1) political or economic pressures, (2) the use of embargoes or pacific blockades, (3) reprisals involving the use of force, (4) the severance of diplomatic and consular relations, and (5) declaration of war. These actions are lawful only when a violation of international law has preceded them. And there are some jurists who hold that the measure of self-help employed must bear some proportion to the gravity of the violation.

Is war legal under international law? For a long time writers sought to distinguish between a "just" and an "unjust" war. But with each side acting as judge in its own case, attempts to apply such judgments became more or less

---

[31] Under the domestic law of the United States a treaty may have the effect of prevailing over an inconsistent prior statute, but a later statute may prevail over an inconsistent previous treaty.

[32] On the law of treaties see Brierly, *op. cit.*, ch. vii; Briggs, *Cases*, ch. xi; Jessup, *op. cit.*, ch. vi; A. D. McNair, *The Law of Treaties* (Oxford, 1938); Payson S. Wild, *Sanctions and Treaty Enforcement* (Cambridge, 1934).

academic. At the present time the tendency is in the direction of considering war as an ultimate sanction or reprisal against an offender who has committed an illegal act.

The Charter of the United Nations obligates all Members, by Article 2, paragraph 4, to "refrain in their international relations from the threat or use of force against the territorial integrity or political independence of any State, or in any other manner inconsistent with the purposes of the United Nations." [33] But it does not prohibit altogether the use of force. It expressly provides for use of force coordinated by the United Nations organization for the maintenance of international peace and security and the enforcement of international law, specifically as applied in the instance of the Korean War. Moreover, Article 51 expressly sanctions the use of national armed force in pursuit of the "inherent right of individual or collective self-defense if an armed attack occurs." And Articles 52–53 envisage the use of force by regional associations at the direction of the Security Council. [34]

Summary. These are some of the provisions that compose the substance of international law. There are, of course, many more. To go into each of the categories with which the law is concerned would take us far afield. It is hoped that the preceding brief sketch may nevertheless provide a sample of the nature of international law and how it works. There are many fascinating problems associated with the functioning of international law, and a study of some of the principal cases which have come before national and international courts relating to the law can be a stimulating and rewarding undertaking.

PRESENT STATUS OF INTERNATIONAL LAW

Law in a Divided World. The political and social environment in which international law functions is obviously quite different today from what it was in the eighteenth and nineteenth centuries when the law was coming to maturity. In the first place, the society of states has now expanded to include many states in the Near and Middle East and in Asia, whose cultural heritage does not include the same legal traditions and political ideas as those of the Western states. As a result, the valuation and interpretations which they place upon the law are bound to be different. Hence, it is more difficult than in the past to obtain general agreement upon a law common to all nations.

More fundamental is the second difference, which is the political and

---

33 Professor Lauterpacht believes that the terminology of the Charter now makes it possible to distinguish again between "just and unjust (or lawful and unlawful) wars—the latter being those waged in breach of the obligations of the Charter." Oppenheim, *op. cit.,* vol. II, p. 223.

34 See ch. xx below on the United Nations and the maintenance of peace and security. On enforcement of international law, self-help, sanctions, and war see Brierly, *op. cit.,* ch. ix; Briggs, *Cases,* ch. xii; A. E. Hindmarsh, *Force in Peace* (Cambridge, 1933); Jessup, *op. cit.,* chs. vii–viii.

ideological division presently existent in the world. The Soviet Union and its communist adherents, while not denying the existence of international law as they choose to interpret it, nevertheless espouse policies which are incompatible with the basic premises upon which international law as we know it is based.

The Soviet Government has repeatedly taken diplomatic refuge in the principles of sovereignty, extension of jurisdiction, and diplomatic and consular privileges and immunities for the protection and advancement of its interests and objectives.[35] But its Marxist-Leninist dogma denounces the principles of justice, reason, and custom generally accepted by other states as underlying international law. And it leads an avowed war upon the basic values of independence, integrity, and respect for the rights of others represented in customary international law. It alleges that Western interpretations and applications of international law are a "bourgeois product" designed to be a tool of capitalism for the exploitation of oppressed classes and the destruction of socialist states.[36] Its rejection of the basic values of the law, as understood by others, including respect for rights and obligations, for justice, and for self-limitation of political objectives, makes it difficult for law to function in many areas of relationship with Moscow and its satellites.[37] At the same time, so long as the Soviets coexist with noncommunist states, they must apply certain rules of international law as a matter of convenience. Otherwise, even diplomatic relations would become impossible.

Areas in Which Law Does Operate. Notwithstanding the difficulties and limitations imposed upon international law, and making full allowance for the fact that it can be, and on occasion is, violated, it is not to be assumed that international law is a dead letter. On the contrary, among the great majority of states of the world, international law is accepted today as a vehicle for facilitating normal, peaceful intercourse.

As a body of agreed rules, principles, customs, and arrangements, which states continue to regard as having binding force, international law fulfills an indispensable role of providing a frame of reference against which actions may be judged and upon the basis of which differences may be settled. Without this latter function, there could be no orderly relations, either economic or political, between nations. If disputes are to be adjusted on their "merits," this must be done on some basis other than a contest of power. The majority of states are willing to do this, on many issues, on a basis of respect for the

[35] See T. A. Taracouzio, *The Soviet Union and International Law* (New York, 1935).
[36] Soviet views on the law are set forth in A. Vyshinsky, *The Law of the Soviet State* (New York, 1948). See also R. Schlesinger, *Soviet Legal Theory* (New York, 1945); J. N. Hazard, "The Soviet Concept of International Law," *Am. Soc. Int. Law Proc.,* 1939; M. Chakste, "Soviet Concepts of the State, International Law, and Sovereignty," *Am. J. Int. Law,* July, 1949.
[37] See H. A. Smith, *The Crisis in the Law of Nations* (London, 1947).

principles of law. This is witnessed by the fact that the bulk of all disputes between states are settled peacefully by means of diplomacy or utilization of the machinery of international organization.

The fact that sixty nations have adhered to the Charter of the United Nations, with its commitment to adjust or settle disputes or situations endangering peace "in conformity with the principles of justice and international law," testifies to their acknowledgment of the reality of law and its rightful place in the handling of international affairs.[38] As we have seen in the preceding section, the law does operate in the daily relations of most states of the world on a wide range of substantive matters.

The law is, on the whole, observed. Its violations, sensational as they may be, are relatively few considering the total number of contacts and issues occurring at all times between states. A government which places first value upon conquest or unlimited aggrandizement of power is not likely to be deterred by international law, if it has sufficient power to impose its policies upon weaker states and its own interpretations of right and wrong as well. The enforcement of international law is admittedly precarious. The equation of power between disputing states can and sometimes does enter into both violation and enforcement since there is no established agreement making enforcement a collective obligation upon the society of states as a whole.

Law can assist in the peaceful settlement of disputes when states are prepared to handle their international relations in this fashion. It cannot guarantee peace. Only the political determination of states and their people can do that. Law can prescribe and uphold, through such institutions as may be available, standards of conduct deemed "to be necessary or conducive to the preservation and advancement of the community."[39] But it remains to the political arm of the national governments to decide the extent to which these shall be enforced. And sovereignty can frustrate international cooperation for the application and enforcement of international law.

In the final analysis, when international law has proven to be ineffective in modern times, it has not been the law that is at fault so much as it is the unwillingness or inability of states to use it in a situation where political ambitions demand the attainment of objectives that cannot be squared with observance of the law.

The International Court and International Law. The establishment of the Permanent Court of International Justice in 1920, and its continuance in the

38 See Herbert W. Briggs, "New Dimensions in International Law," *Am. Pol. Sci. Rev.*, Sept., 1952; Myers McDougal, "Law and Power," *Am. J. Int. Law*, Jan., 1952.
39 Oliver J. Lissitzyn, *The International Court of Justice* (New York, 1951), p. 6.

form of the present International Court of Justice by virtue of the Charter and Statute adopted at San Francisco in 1945, gave to international law for the first time a permanent, international court competent to decide "any dispute of an international character" which states should agree to submit to it "and all matters specially provided for in treaties and conventions in force." Moreover, the Statute establishing the Court gave it competence—in situations in which states had deposited separate declarations accepting the compulsory jurisdiction of the Court—to decide any or all classes of legal disputes concerning "any question of international law," the existence of any fact which if established would constitute a breach of international obligation, and the nature and extent of reparation to be made therefor.[40] We shall discuss in a subsequent chapter the organization and operation of the Court.

The existence of the Court has contributed to the peaceful settlement of a substantial number of cases involving legal questions as well as some disputes of a political nature. It may be admitted that in "the total picture of the international relations of the last thirty years the contribution of the Court to peace through the settlement of disputes does not loom large." The major conflicts between states that have led to war have not been referred to the Court. And many of the lesser conflicts "in which armed force was used or threatened to be used were settled in whole or in part by or with the aid of international organs through political procedures without reference to the Court"—as in the Indonesian case, the Palestine case, the Berlin blockade, and the Korean War.[41]

The availability of the Court has been of no small significance, however, in international relations. It has been used extensively by states, including the larger states of Western Europe. It enjoys prestige and a reputation of impartiality. And it has in at least a few instances aided the relaxation of international tensions. This was notably demonstrated in the crisis arising between Albania and Britain as a result of the blowing up of British naval vessels in the Corfu Channel in 1947. Prior to 1920 a Great Power whose vessels were damaged in such a fashion would have had little hesitation in bombarding a local port or resorting to other forceful measures of reprisal and self-help. In this instance, the matter was taken first to the United Nations Security Council, and upon recommendation by that body—introduced by the United Kingdom—the dispute was referred to the International Court of Justice. In the

[40] The Statute of the original PCIJ will be found as an appendix in M. O. Hudson, *The Permanent Court of International Justice, 1920–1942* (New York, 1943). For provisions relating to the presently existing Court see ch. xiv of the United Nations Charter and the appended Statute of the International Court of Justice.

[41] Lissitzyn, *op. cit.*, p. 98.

calm atmosphere of the Court, the dispute was decided quietly, the popular press ceased to clamor, and the issue was settled without further disturbance, albeit the Albanian Government declined to pay the award indicated.[42]

The reasoning employed by the Court in its judgments and opinions plays a notable part in the literature and cases of international law. Government legal experts continually refer to it. In present-day litigation between nations there is a tendency to appeal to the Court's views as evidence of what the law is in contentious cases. Slowly but firmly the International Court is contributing to the development of international law.

It must be recognized that not all conflicts between states can be settled by juridical methods within the existing framework of international law and politics. States cannot be compelled to go to Court, as can individuals within domestic society. Nor can they, against their will, be made to abide by the decisions of the Court until such time as the international community is prepared to employ collective means for their enforcement.[43] The true significance of the Court lies in the fact of its existence and in the willingness of states to take their disputes to it.

The Problem of Change. One of the serious problems connected with international law, as with any system of law, is that of balancing the maintenance of existing principles and rules with the progressive development of the law consonant with change in society.

Even when a consensus exists, the mechanism of the law has imperfections in that it makes little provision for peacefully changing legal obligations. One of the basic postulates, as we have indicated previously, is respect for law. Respect for the law depends upon a belief that the law will protect the vital interests of all states in changing situations. When the law is so inflexible that it cannot admit desirable changes with facility, respect for the law and inclination to use legal processes diminish.

By virtue of the fact that the law is essentially a conservative force for preserving existing rights and obligations, the law tends to support the *status quo*. Consequently, when the *status quo* is challenged, the law itself will be challenged unless there is a remedy in law. Where there is no remedy, states may be forced either to acquiesce and surrender what they conceive to be national interests or well-being, or they must employ methods of self-help to bring about a change regardless of law.

Within domestic society, remedies are available both through legislation and the judicial process to correct legal inequities within a reasonable period

---

42 *Ibid.,* pp. 78–81 and references cited there.
43 See Lissitzyn, *op. cit.,* p. 71, and references to problem of determining what are "justiciable" disputes; also for consideration of Court action based upon principle of decision *ex aequo et bono.*

of time. In the international scene—lacking the attributes of a central government—means for change are not as readily available. Diplomacy, it is true, is available for the negotiation of change in treaties or other rights and obligations. The International Court of Justice is available for the judicial determination of cases brought to it by the parties. But in each instance, change ultimately depends upon the agreement of the parties rather than upon the interposition of a governmental authority or court, as is the case in domestic society, which can decide the issues in dispute regardless of the will of the parties.

For these reasons international law cannot be expected to function with the simplicity and smoothness of domestic law in a well-integrated society. If states cannot obtain their vital interests by observance of the law, or if they feel that an alteration of the legal obligations binding upon them is being refused upon political grounds, or because others have had the power to impose obligations upon them and will not consider their just demands, they will inevitably resort to other means of obtaining satisfaction.

That change does occur within the framework of established respect for law is evidenced by a number of facts. In the first place, many new states have emerged since 1918 through peaceful means or with the assistance of the world peace machinery. The examples of Iraq, Jordan, Lebanon, Libya, Syria, India, Burma, Indonesia, and Palestine, to mention a few, come readily to mind. Approximately 600 million people, one-fourth of the world's population, gained independence within six years following 1945. In the second place, through the machinery of international conferences and organizations, a large number of multilateral conventions and agreements have been adopted, altered, and replaced. Professor Manley O. Hudson has compiled 670 agreements of this nature signed between 1919 and 1945. This process he has termed *international legislation.* And indeed the international conference technique does fulfill, to a certain extent, this role in bringing about international agreement on changes in the law.[44] In the third place, as a result of the operation of the numerous international specialized agencies and technical organizations, the scope of international law is continually broadening. This is particularly true in matters relating to health, labor, safety conditions, communications and transport, economic and cultural relations, treatment of non-self-governing areas, and mutual security. This process is breaking the rigidities of traditional international law.[45]

[44] See M. O. Hudson, *International Legislation,* 9 vols. (Washington and New York, 1931–1950).

[45] See Briggs, "New Dimensions in International Law," *cit. supra,* p. 693. See also J. E. Harley, "Progress toward Advancement of International Law," *World Affairs Interpreter,* Summer, 1951; J. F. Kunz, "The Swing of the Pendulum: From Overestimation to Underestimation," *Am. J. Int. Law,* vol. 44 (1950), pp. 135–140.

The United Nations and International Law. Finally, it should be noted that the United Nations organization itself is a factor in the progressive development of international law. We have already mentioned previously in this chapter the International Law Commission established under the General Assembly to study and recommend measures for the development and codification of international law. This body has been making an intensive examination of the gaps in the law and of areas in which it may be possible to obtain some larger measure of agreement on the interpretation of the law. In particular, it has been considering such topics as the rights and duties of states, the definition of aggression, the law of treaties, rights, and jurisdiction on the high seas and in territorial waters, nationality, and legal rights with reference to the continental shelf lying off the territory of states.

In the broader sense of providing a forum in which states may debate issues on which they are divided and organs through which they may be encouraged to seek pacific settlement of international disputes, the principal organs of the United Nations—that is, the General Assembly, the Security Council, the Economic and Social Council, the Trusteeship Council, and the International Court of Justice—are serving a useful purpose in furthering the use and the growth of international law. Former Secretary-General Trygve Lie voiced this in his Annual Report for 1950–1951 when he said, "Virtually all important developments in the evolution of international law during the past six years have been closely connected with the United Nations."

CONCLUSION

In viewing the role of international law in modern world affairs, people of the West, particularly British and American, must be watchful lest their ingrained respect for law and their faith in it as a means of solving all manner of domestic and international problems lead them to idealize the capabilities of international law. At the same time, our concern over the struggle for power which is taking place and the dangers which are inherent in the divisions which separate great powers possessing nuclear weapons should not lead us to minimize the law unduly.

International law has rendered a useful service in the past three centuries in providing (1) part of the basis upon which nations may found their foreign policies toward one another, (2) a means for determining international rights and duties, and settling disputes relating thereto, and (3) a foundation upon which the beginnings of an organized society of states could be erected.

Peace and security cannot reasonably be expected to be absolute, since conflict and strife over interests and objectives are constantly present within the world. In establishing international organs to promote the maintenance of peace and security and to further the peaceful settlement of international disputes in "conformity with principles of justice and international law," states have taken a step in the direction of ultimately creating world agencies with power to enforce law and peace—even as the establishment of the first weak agencies of law in the old West led ultimately to public instruments of law and order.

Law enforcement in the realm of world politics cannot be anticipated on a scale comparable with that known in advanced civilizations merely from the creation of "authorities" and "organs." There must first be a strong public support and acceptance of what some have called the imperative character of law.

States, like individuals within domestic societies, must agree upon some basic principles of rights, duties, justice, and orderly settlement of differences before any organization or framework of government can be erected with hope of durability. A substantial measure of agreement has prevailed upon the principles, rules, customs, and agreements forming international law over the past 300 years. And international law has served effectively as a means of determining rights and obligations of states and aiding them in adjusting and resolving a host of differences. But perhaps its most valuable contribution has been that of paving the way for the evolution of a general international organization to maintain peace and security, to further international cooperation, and to promote the general well-being of states.

In this day of a divided world and an international law which has not kept pace with the rapidity of developing international relations, the words of Professor Brierly of Oxford University have a good deal of wisdom: "[although] the problem of world community remains eventually a moral problem, it is also in part a problem of statesmanship, and . . . international society needs institutions through which its members can learn to work together for common social ends." [46]

We shall turn now to consider what steps states have been willing to take to provide instruments of organization for cooperative associations in dealing with the problems of international politics.

SUGGESTED READINGS

J. L. Brierly, *The Law of Nations* (4th ed., Oxford, 1949).
————. *The Outlook for International Law* (Oxford, 1944).
Herbert W. Briggs, *The Law of Nations* (2d ed., New York, 1952).
P. E. Corbett, *Law and Society in the Relations of States* (New York, 1951).
E. D. Dickinson, *Law and Peace* (Philadelphia, 1951).

[46] Brierly, *cit. supra*, pp. 45–46.

C. G. Fenwick, *International Law* (3d ed., New York, 1948).

Philip C. Jessup, *A Modern Law of Nations* (New York, 1948).

G. W. Keeton and G. Schwarzenberger, *Making International Law Work* (2d ed., London, 1946).

Hans Kelsen, *Principles of International Law* (New York, 1952).

Hersch Lauterpacht, *Function of Law in the International Community* (Oxford, 1933).

A. Nussbaum, *A Concise History of International Law* (New York, 1949).

CHAPTER XX

The Politics of International Organization

IN CHAPTER XIX on the role of law we discussed how history has disclosed that aggressors are rarely deterred by principles or agreements, and that although international law is extremely useful in routine relations among peaceful states, its role in attempting to avert aggression and prevent war is a relatively minor one. The law depends upon the disposition of states to observe and enforce it. For those who violate it, there is no sure enforceable punishment. Consequently, these limitations of law have forced nations to seek other means for attaining peace and security in their efforts to resolve the intensifying problems of international relations. Furthermore, the increasingly complex problems of modern society have led governments to favor multilateral cooperation in dealing with some phases of economic, social, and technical matters of mutual concern.

HISTORICAL BACKGROUND

The idea of international organizations can be traced back several centuries.[1] Different as the various proposals and steps may be in detailed content, they have all emanated from the thesis that collective security is the basis for world peace.

The year 1648 marks the beginning of the translation into reality of the dreams concerning international order conceived by philosophers and idealists, and first realized in the concept of the European "equilibrium" and balance of power which was discussed in Chapter VII. Formulated at the Peace of Westphalia, readapted at the Peace Conference at Utrecht in 1713, and again reformulated at the time of the Quadruple Alliance in 1815, this tenuously balanced arrangement paved the way for our modern international organizations.

Subsequent to the withdrawal of Britain from the Congress system established at Vienna in 1815, the powers met intermittently during the nineteenth

[1] See S. J. Hemleben, *Plans for World Peace through Six Centuries* (Chicago, 1943); E. York, *League of Nations, Ancient, Medieval and Modern* (London, 1928).

century as issues arose affecting the peace and security of Europe as a whole.[2] The Concert system, resting upon the idea of Great Power unity, could be successful only so long as the powers were reasonably balanced among themselves, were willing to abide by limited objectives, and so long as no issue divided them to such an extent that negotiation and compromise became altogether impossible.

Neither the Congress nor the Concert system around which much of the diplomatic history of nineteenth-century Europe revolved constituted a collective security system in the full sense of the word. Neither had any permanent organs or authorized powers of enforcement. Irregular consultation contained no sure guarantee of security, for there was nothing to assure states that the powers would meet when peace was threatened or that measures to enforce it would be taken. Nevertheless, the Concert system established the idea of joint responsibility of the Great Powers for the maintenance of some semblance of international order, and this precedent laid the groundwork for the principle of regular periodic meeting of the Assembly and Council of the League of Nations. In addition, the nineteenth-century balance of power concept laid the foundation for the generalized balance of power theory embodied in the collective security principle of the Covenant of the League of Nations.

EXPERIMENTS IN INTERNATIONAL ADMINISTRATION

Increases in trade and communications during the latter half of the nineteenth century resulted in governments' sensing advantages in the establishment of specialized international agencies authorized to engage in limited administrative activities. Thus such bodies as the European Commission for the Danube, the Central Rhine Commission, the Universal Postal Union, the International Red Cross, and many others were formed. By 1911 as many as forty-five organizations of this general nature were in existence.[3]

Most of these agencies provided for periodic conferences on general questions within the province of their framework of reference and for a permanent secretariat or bureau to handle exchanges of information, the gathering of statistics, and the performance of designated administrative functions. These experiments in international cooperation and administration laid a substantial basis of joint activity in the nonpolitical fields upon which a world center for coordinating and furthering economic, technical, social, and humanitarian activities might be erected.[4]

---

2 See W. A. Phillips, *The Confederation of Europe* (New York, 1914).
3 L. S. Wolf, *International Government* (New York, 1916), pp. 221–230.
4 See N. L. Hill, *International Administration* (New York, 1931); D. Mitrany, *The Progress of International Government* (London, 1933); P. Reinsch, *Public International Unions* (Boston, 1911).

THE LEAGUE OF NATIONS

The League of Nations which emerged from the peace conference terminating World War I was built upon the heritage of ideas and experience which had come down from the past, together with the war-time thinking of numerous persons in the United States, Britain, and France.[5] Basically, it rested upon a popular desire "to make future wars impossible."

The Covenant Adopted: America Stays Out. Although the creation of a league of nations was not a major policy of any of the European belligerents, President Wilson made the drafting of the League Covenant the foremost item of the Paris Peace Conference in 1919, and insisted that it be an integral part of the Treaty of Peace. This was ultimately accepted by the other Allied leaders, but the United States Senate rejected Wilson's leadership and the Treaty and Covenant.[6] Deprived of United States participation, the League of Nations was given a body blow at its very beginning. Not only did the United States action undermine the morale and prestige of the organization, it also, more seriously, deprived the League of the power element which had turned the tide of battle in World War I. Without the United States, the balance of power that was to underlie the operation of the League was nonexistent.

The Structure of the League. Although the League failed to prevent World War II, it is well to note its outlines and general features, for the lessons learned in conjunction with the League are important.

Basically, the League of Nations was a voluntary association of states designed to "promote international cooperation and to achieve international peace and security."[7] It was founded on the principle of ultimate universal membership. It never attained this status, however, and before its breakdown in 1939 three of the large powers and several smaller states had withdrawn from membership.

The League had three principal organs: (1) an Assembly in which all states were represented and in which unanimous agreement was necessary for action; (2) a Council originally intended to be composed of the five Great Allied and Associated Powers of World War I plus four members elected by the Assembly, but eventually expanded to a membership of fifteen states owing to political pressures; and (3) an international Secretariat.

The League Assembly had a broad mandate allowing it to consider "any

[5] See Ruhl J. Bartlett, *The League to Enforce Peace* (Chapel Hill, 1945). See also Ruhl J. Bartlett, *The Record of American Diplomacy* (New York, 1947), pp. 452–457, 459–461.

[6] On the drafting of the Covenant see David Hunter Miller, *The Drafting of the Covenant* (New York, 1928); T. Marburg, *Development of the League of Nations Idea*, 2 vols. (New York, 1932); Felix Morley, *The Society of Nations* (Washington, 1932).

[7] For an authoritative account of the League organization and activities see Francis P. Walters, *The History of the League of Nations*, 2 vols. (Oxford, 1952).

circumstances whatever" threatening peace or understanding between nations. Its powers of action were restricted, however, to passing resolutions and recommendations. The powers of the Council to consider and discuss international disputes and threatening situations were concurrent with those of the Assembly. But in addition the Covenant gave it specific powers with respect to enquiry, peaceful settlement of disputes, recommendations for actions by Member states in connection with acts of aggression or threats to independence, and adoption of sanctions to preserve or restore peace and security. In all matters, however, the Council was bound by the unanimity requirement.

In addition to these organs, the Covenant provided for a Permanent Court of International Justice. This institution, which actually was set up by a separate Statute, was empowered to "hear and determine any dispute of an international character which the parties submit thereto." It was also authorized to render "advisory opinions" on legal questions referred to it by the Assembly or Council. With a panel of nine judges this Court rendered distinguished service in acting upon some three score of cases referred to it between 1922 and 1939.[8] The Statute of the PCIJ contained an "Optional Clause" which allowed such states as wished to do so to accept compulsory jurisdiction of certain classes of legal or justiciable disputes by signing a special instrument. Forty-one states adhered to this provision before 1939.

Pacific Settlement of Disputes. The Covenant of the League distinguished between two types of international disputes: (1) those that were essentially legal in nature and (2) those considered to be political in character.

States were urged, but not required, to submit "justiciable," that is, basically legal, disputes to arbitration or to the Permanent Court of International Justice.[9] If a party refused to settle a dispute by these means, the Covenant empowered the League Council to make an enquiry and report on the dispute. If this was unanimous, the parties were urged to accept its recommendations, and the Members were pledged not to go to war against any party that complied therewith. If the Council was unable to agree unanimously upon a report, its Members were left "the right to take such action as they [considered] necessary for the maintenance of right and justice."

In essence, the League procedures for the settlement of international disputes were of a voluntary nature. If a party did not wish to submit a case, or was determined to pursue its own course, there was nothing to prevent it from

8 The definitive treatise on the Court is by Judge Manley O. Hudson, *The Permanent Court of International Justice* (New York, 1943).

9 The difference between a justiciable and nonjusticiable dispute lies not so much in the subject matter as in the attitude of the parties. If the parties are seeking the recognition or satisfaction of legal rights, the dispute is held to be justiciable. Otherwise, it is usually held to be of a nonjusticiable variety. See J. L. Brierly, *The Law of Nations* (4th ed., Oxford, 1949), pp. 262–269.

doing so. On this ground it could truly be said that the Covenant "represented no real challenge to the principle of national sovereignty." [10]

Collective Security. The collective security system of the League of Nations rested fundamentally upon three articles of the Covenant—10, 11, and 16. Article 10 pledged the Members to respect the territorial integrity and political independence of all Members of the League and authorized the Council to advise what measures should be taken if there were a threat or danger of external aggression. Article 11 declared any war or threat of war to be a matter of concern to the whole League, appropriate for consideration by the Council or Assembly. Article 16 provided for the adoption of economic, financial, and possibly military sanctions by Member states if any state resorted to war contrary to the provision relating to the peaceful settlement of disputes, and declared it to be the duty of the Council in such cases to recommend what military, naval, or air forces the Members should contribute for use in protecting "the covenants of the League."

The purport of Article 10 was to deny future acquisitions of title to territory by conquest. But the article left in doubt how far states were obliged to go in supporting by arms a state which was threatened or attacked. President Wilson held that the article contained only a moral obligation, leaving to each state to decide for itself whether an act of aggression had occurred and whether to follow any recommendation by the League. Since, however, the League organs could pass recommendations only if there were unanimity among those present and voting, and any state wishing to block the passage of such a resolution could do so by casting a negative vote, the effectiveness of the article could easily be brought to naught.

Article 16 was invoked by the League of Nations on but one occasion, in the Italo-Ethiopian war against Italy. In this instance, after considerable prior political negotiation among the European powers, the Council did call for the adoption of economic and financial sanctions against Italy. By virtue of the national measures which followed, Italian foreign trade was cut severely. But the embargoes were never extended to the critical item of petroleum, and following Mussolini's threat that closure of the Suez Canal to his troop ships would mean war with Britain and France, the action that might have ended his aggression was never applied.

At least three points stand out from the experiment with sanctions against Italy. First, economic sanctions, even though incomplete, could reduce the trade of an aggressor state. Second, the vacillations of the British Government at this time and political machinations by Pierre Laval of France—war-time collaborator with Nazi Germany—prevented sanctions being carried to the

[10] W. E. Rappard, *The Quest for Peace* (Cambridge, 1940), pp. 114–116.

point where vital pressure might have been applied to Italy. Third, Hitler and Mussolini demonstrated that, by their bold cooperation in aggression and threats, the League system could be overridden and valuable concessions could be wrung from the pacifiers in the process.[11]

Weaknesses in the League Provisions. From the standpoint of achieving the ideal of collective security, the commitments contained in the Covenant were weak, and the powers accorded to the Council and Assembly were limited to the making of recommendations. In addition, even those obligations entailed by ratification of the Covenant were later weakened by a series of interpretative resolutions adopted by the League, which declared that each state should decide for itself whether the Covenant had been violated, whether Article 16 should be applied, and whether any military action should be taken against an offending state. Thus any automatic and compulsory character of Article 16, if any was originally contemplated, was in effect removed and the Council became primarily a coordinating agency with the sole power of moral suasion. The objective of centralized action implicit in the idea of collective security was whittled away.[12] Furthermore, efforts to attain "peaceful change" of outmoded treaty commitments were invariably frustrated.[13]

Security Cases before League. During its nineteen years of active functioning, the League of Nations was called upon to deal with forty-four cases connected in one way or another with the problem of international peace and security. Disputes arose for League consideration from all parts of the globe. Some were minor affairs of misunderstanding. Some were frontier incidents and frictions. Some were controversies over treaty rights, and several were major conflicts.[14]

Of all these disputes and situations involving threats to peace and security and breaches of the peace, the most significant from the point of view of the magnitude of the challenge which they presented to the League collective security system were the Manchurian incident and the Italian conquest of Ethiopia. The implications of the latter we have mentioned above.

11 See E. DeBono, *Anno XIII: The Conquest of an Empire* (London, 1937); A. E. Highley, *The First Sanctions Experiment* (Geneva, 1938); Elizabeth Monroe, *The Mediterranean in Power Politics* (New York, 1938); Pittman B. Potter, *The Wal Wal Arbitration* (Washington, 1938); R.I.I.A., *Survey of International Affairs 1936* (London, 1936), vol. II.

12 An attempt was made to plug some of the loopholes through a Protocol for the Pacific Settlement of Disputes, known as the Geneva Protocol, adopted by the Assembly in 1924, but this was not ratified by any state. See D. H. Miller, *The Geneva Protocol* (New York, 1925); P. J. Noel-Baker, *The Geneva Protocol for the Pacific Settlement of International Disputes* (London, 1925).

13 On peaceful change see F. S. Dunn, *Peaceful Change* (New York, 1937); J. F. Dulles, *War, Peace and Change* (New York, 1938).

14 For discussions of the various situations see Walters, *cit. supra;* J. T. Shotwell and M. Salvin, *Lessons on Security and Disarmament from the History of the League of Nations* (New York, 1949). A résumé of the cases with documentary references will also be found in Denys P. Myers, *Handbook of the League of Nations* (Boston, 1935).

The failure to stop Japanese aggression in Manchuria in 1931 was a major blow from which the League of Nations never fully recovered. It indicated that under certain circumstances a Great Power could commit aggression without suffering any more severe consequences than "nonrecognition" by other League Members. This undermined faith in the League among weak and timid states. The League's failure in this case was due to several factors, two of which were paramount: (1) the powers were not united in their opposition to Japan, and (2) they were not prepared to use force to stop aggression and thus vindicate the League's purposes.[15]

The League and Disarmament. The League of Nations Covenant directed the Council to formulate plans for a reduction in armaments and to advise on ways of removing the "evil effects" of private manufacture of armaments. Although much time and effort were expended in trying to arrive at an acceptable plan for reduction,[16] and a General Conference for the Reduction and Limitation of Armaments was held in 1932–1933 with sixty states represented, the conference eventually ended in failure.[17]

LEAGUE ACTIVITIES IN THE SOCIAL AND ECONOMIC FIELD

The activities of the League were not restricted to the prevention of wars. The framers of the Covenant directed it to assist in correlating and promoting interstate cooperation in certain aspects of labor, economics, and finance, transit and communications, public health, and social welfare matters.

A sampling of the activities of these organizations discloses that the International Labor Organization assisted the improvement of labor conditions and the welfare of workers through bringing together representatives of workers' organizations, employers, and governments.[18] The Economic and Financial Committee of the League handled refugee problems, gave economic assistance to countries whose economies were in danger of collapse following the war, and disseminated statistical information throughout the world.[19] Public health

[15] On the Manchurian crisis see A. W. Griswold, *The Far Eastern Policy of the United States* (New York, 1938); League of Nations, *Report of the Commission of Inquiry* [The Lytton Commission] (Geneva, 1932); Henry L. Stimson, *The Far Eastern Crisis* (New York, 1936); A. J. Toynbee (ed.), *Survey of International Affairs, 1932* (Oxford, 1933); *United States Foreign Relations, 1931*, vol. III (Washington, 1946); W. W. Willoughby, *The Sino-Japanese Controversy and the League of Nations* (Baltimore, 1935).

[16] A treaty of mutual guarantee was signed in 1925 but never ratified, which would have defined "aggressive war," authorized regional defense pacts, allowed the Council to organize sanctions before war started, called on states to earmark forces for international action, and tied the whole to disarmament steps.

[17] On the disarmament problem see especially Shotwell and Salvin, *op. cit.;* M. Tate, *The United States and Armaments* (Cambridge, 1948); J. W. Wheeler-Bennett, *The Pipe Dream of Peace: The Story of the Collapse of Disarmament* (New York, 1935).

[18] See F. G. Wilson, *Labor and the League System* (Stanford, 1934).

[19] See Martin Hill, *The Economic and Financial Organization of the League of Nations* (Washington, 1946).

was promoted by the Health Organization which engaged in dealing with the problems of sanitation, sleeping sickness, malaria, and the like.[20] The League also concerned itself with the problems involved in the slave trade, traffic in women and children, and the control of the traffic in opium and narcotic drugs.

The Mandate System. One of the most significant pioneering steps taken by the League of Nations was the introduction of the Mandate system. Under the guidance of a Permanent Mandates Commission, composed of experts in colonial administration, this sought to promote the well-being and development of the inhabitants of the former colonial territories of Germany and the Ottoman Empire which were assigned to certain Mandatory Powers to be held as "a sacred trust of civilization."

EVALUATION OF LEAGUE EXPERIENCE

Taking the League era as a whole, it is fair to say that this attempt at international organization had to its credit many accomplishments in the economic and social fields. These undoubtedly facilitated international relationships and promoted international cooperation.[21]

Notwithstanding these accomplishments, which in no wise are to be minimized, the real test of the League lay in the fields of peace and security. If the League could not give its Members added security, sooner or later it was bound to fail. This is what happened after Japan, Italy, and Germany had demonstrated that they could employ force, or threats of force, as instruments of national policy with impunity and in disregard of the peace of the society of states. By the time the greatest crisis arose in 1939, statesmen were convinced that the League was not able to give their states the kind of security they needed. Hence, they had already turned to other devices, but too late to prevent war.

FROM LEAGUE TO UNITED NATIONS

The failure of the League of Nations to prevent World War II inevitably raised questions whether in the future the idea of international organization and of collective security should be abandoned as being unworkable, or whether attempts should be made to try again on a revised or new basis. Nations were as determined as ever to guard their national sovereignty and to preserve their integrity and independence. They were determined to have no

20 See *The Aims, Methods and Activity of the League of Nations* (Geneva, 1938), pp. 138–145.
21 Secretariat of the League of Nations, *Ten Years of World Cooperation* (Geneva, 1930), p. 178. For a general review see Viscount Cecil, *A Great Experiment* (Oxford, 1941); Arthur Sweetser, "The Non-Political Achievements of the League of Nations," *Foreign Affairs*, Oct., 1940; Walters, *op. cit.*

part in any world government scheme that might give some state the power, or some personality the opportunity, to dominate international politics and national will. But there were many statesmen and diplomats who were of the opinion that a suitably fashioned and limited international organization could render useful service in promoting international relations and security if it enjoyed (1) the support of all the Great Powers and (2) if there were a reasonable degree of accord among them.[22]

War-time Declarations. In the joint declaration issued by President Roosevelt and Prime Minister Churchill in August, 1941, known as the Atlantic Charter, statesmen affirmed that a "wider and permanent system of general security" must be established which would allow all nations to dwell in safety within their own boundaries and assure men freedom from fear and want. These principles were subsequently accepted as a basis of alliance among all the nations fighting against the Axis Powers through incorporation in the "United Nations Declaration" signed in Washington January 1, 1942.[23] Uncertainty as to the Soviet position on post-war arrangements led Secretary of State Hull to propose that a conference of the Foreign Ministers of Britain, China, the USSR, and the United States be held in the autumn of 1943. At the close of this parley in Moscow a declaration was issued stating their joint recognition of the necessity of establishing a general international organization to maintain peace and security, based on the principle of the sovereign equality of states and open to membership by "all peace-loving states," at the earliest practicable date.[24]

Dumbarton Oaks Proposals. At a conference held in Washington in the summer of 1944 among representatives of the four powers a series of proposals was agreed to which became known as the Dumbarton Oaks Proposals for the Establishment of a General International Organization. These proposals subsequently formed the primary basis for drafting the United Nations Charter at San Francisco. The Dumbarton Oaks Proposals envisaged the establishment of a new international organization to maintain peace and security and to create conditions of stability and well-being necessary to this end rather than a revision and revival of the League of Nations.[25]

Yalta Conference. The conferees at Dumbarton Oaks were unable to agree

[22] A documented account of the government's planning will be found in United States Dept. of State Pub. 3580, *Post-War Foreign Policy Preparation, 1939–1945* (Washington, 1949). On the transition from the League to the United Nations see Leland M. Goodrich, "From League of Nations to United Nations," *Internat. Organization*, Feb., 1947.

[23] Texts of the Atlantic Charter and United Nations Declaration will be found in Sen. Doc. No. 123, *A Decade of American Foreign Policy, Basic Documents, 1941–1949*, 81st Cong., 1st Sess.

[24] Text in *ibid.*, pp. 11–12.

[25] Dumbarton Oaks Proposals will be found in *Department of State Bulletin*, Oct. 8, 1944.

upon voting arrangements in the Security Council, in which primary responsibility for the maintenance of peace and security was to be lodged, and no decision was reached on matters pertaining to trusteeship. Hence, the first of these questions had to be referred to the Heads of States at their meeting at the Yalta Conference in February, 1945. At this meeting President Roosevelt, Prime Minister Churchill, and Marshal Stalin arrived at a compromise formula which then enabled them to agree upon summoning the San Francisco Conference in the spring of 1945 to draw up a Charter for a new organization.[26]

San Francisco Conference. Representatives of forty-six governments assembled at San Francisco on April 25, 1945, to deliberate on plans for a post-war organization. Invitations were presently extended to four other governments to join with them.[27] After two months of intensive discussion and negotiation, held in an unusually favorable atmosphere with the war in Europe coming to a victorious end in the midst of the Conference proceedings, unanimous agreement was obtained upon a charter for the establishment of the United Nations organization.

A host of proposals was filed at San Francisco by the various parties represented there. These were taken into account in the negotiation process. But on the whole the broad outlines of the Charter followed the pattern set forth in the Dumbarton Oaks Proposals primarily agreed to by the Great Powers, save for the addition of a Trusteeship Council and Economic and Social Council, and the insertion of a declaration regarding the treatment of non-self-governing territories.

The Charter Comes into Force. Signed on June 25, 1945, the Charter was immediately submitted to the Senate of the United States, which gave its consent to ratification within the remarkably short time of one month after submission, on July 28, 1945, by the overwhelming vote of 89–2. Other states followed shortly in their ratification, so that the Charter became effective on October 24, 1945. On January 10, 1946, the first meeting of the United Nations General Assembly was convened. Not long thereafter the Members of the League of Nations held a meeting in Geneva to terminate that organization and transfer its assets to the new world organization.

To understand the United Nations organization and its functioning one must be familiar with the provisions of the Charter. For this purpose the reader is referred to the text which will be found in Appendix B.

---

26 Text in *A Decade of American Foreign Policy*, pp. 352–360.

27 All states invited to San Francisco were required to have declared war upon Germany or Japan and to have signed the United Nations Declaration of 1942. Poland was regarded as an initial member of the organization, although it was not represented at San Francisco owing to disagreement over its representation among the Powers.

GUIDING PRINCIPLES UNDERLYING UNITED NATIONS CHARTER

The United Nations must be viewed in the sequence of history. It did not spring full-blown from new ideas. On the contrary, it represented a fresh attempt by statesmen in 1945 to cope with the common problem of insecurity and the need for cooperative arrangements to help resolve problems of international politics as the representatives of states saw them in 1945. The provisions which were framed at San Francisco reflected the fruits of long-continued studies of national interests on the one hand, and of what were thought to be the practical limits of international collaboration on the other hand. It represented a labored effort to reconcile these points of view among fifty nations and to evolve a structure which might stand some possibility of succeeding where the League of Nations had failed.[28] These considerations must be borne in mind in viewing the results of the San Francisco Conference.

The United Nations a Limited Entity. The United Nations, like the League of Nations before it, was designed to be an association of sovereign states with each state retaining all of its rights and powers not expressly restricted by the text of the Charter. The organization was intended to be strictly limited in the powers which it might exercise, having only those prerogatives set forth in the Charter. It was not conceived of as a world government or intended to become in any sense a superstate. It was not meant to replace the functions of any government. It was viewed rather as a supplementary instrumentality, a useful device by which to help channel international politics into peaceful procedures, in so far as possible, and to be a means through which national interests might be furthered.

The statesmen had no thought of creating a world body which would deprive states of their right of national decision. To safeguard national rights, they wrote into the Charter that nothing should authorize the organization to intervene in matters essentially within domestic jurisdiction except in peace enforcement measures, and the only power of decision which they gave to the United Nations binding upon states was the Security Council authority to decide on measures to maintain or restore international peace and security.

Basic Purposes and Principles of United Nations. The United Nations exists, according to the Charter, to serve four basic purposes. These are (1) to maintain peace and security through the peaceful settlement of disputes and the adoption of collective measures; (2) to develop friendly relations and

---

28 Proposals submitted to the Conference in the form of Amendments to the Dumbarton Oaks Proposals will be found in United Nations Conference Documents, Vol. III, entitled *Comments and Proposed Amendments Concerning the Dumbarton Oaks Proposals, Submitted by the Delegations to the United Nations Conference on International Organization,* May 7, 1945.

strengthen peace; (3) to achieve cooperation in solving international economic, social, cultural, and humanitarian problems, including promotion of respect for fundamental freedoms; and (4) to function as a center for harmonizing the actions of nations. Within these broadly stated purposes may be brought virtually every question affecting the relations between states.

A reading of the United Nations Charter will promote an understanding of the ways in which these purposes and principles are woven into the fabric of the United Nations. It will also clarify the bounds of power given to the organization.[29]

ORGANIZATION OF UNITED NATIONS

Membership. The United Nations, like the League, looks in the direction of ultimate membership of all states willing to accept and abide by the Charter. Israel, admitted in 1949, was the sixtieth state to become a member of the organization.

Applicants for membership are admitted by a two-thirds vote of the General Assembly on recommendation of the Security Council, which must first review and pass on all applications. As decisions on recommendations for membership are considered a "substantive matter," these must obtain the unanimous agreement of the permanent members of the Security Council. Disagreement among these Great Powers can stall any application for admission, and has done so in fact in the cases of some twenty states.

No express provision is made in the Charter for withdrawal from membership. It was understood at San Francisco, however, that under "exceptional circumstances" a state might do so, although the organization would have the right to hold it responsible for conformity to the Purposes and Principles of the Charter in common with all non-Member states. A state "persistently" violating the Charter may be suspended or expelled from membership by the General Assembly, on recommendation of the Security Council.[30]

Organs. The United Nations has six principal organs. These are: (1) the General Assembly, (2) the Security Council, (3) the Economic and Social Council, (4) the Trusteeship Council, (5) the International Court of Justice, and (6) an international Secretariat.

Each of the principal organs is empowered to establish subsidiary bodies

29 For a general analysis and commentary on the Charter see especially Leland M. Goodrich and Edvard Hambro, *Charter of the United Nations, Commentary and Documents* (rev. ed., Boston, 1949). See also United Nations Information Service, *Everyman's United Nations* (New York, 1952); Amry Vandenbosh and W. N. Hogan, *The United Nations, Background, Organization, Functions* (New York, 1952).

30 See Yuen-li Liang, "Conditions of Admission of a State to Membership in the United Nations," *Am. J. Int. Law,* April, 1949; Hans Kelsen, "Withdrawal from the United Nations," *Western Pol. Quar.,* March, 1948.

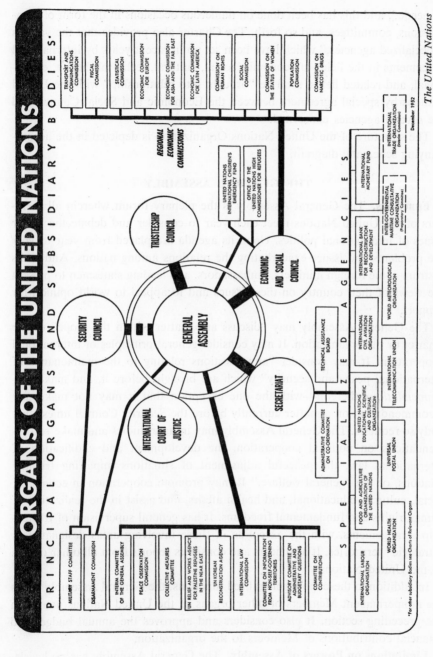

ORGANS OF THE UNITED NATIONS

PRINCIPAL ORGANS AND SUBSIDIARY BODIES*

REGIONAL ECONOMIC COMMISSIONS

- TRANSPORT AND COMMUNICATIONS COMMISSION
- FISCAL COMMISSION
- STATISTICAL COMMISSION
- ECONOMIC COMMISSION FOR EUROPE
- ECONOMIC COMMISSION FOR ASIA AND THE FAR EAST
- ECONOMIC COMMISSION FOR LATIN AMERICA
- COMMISSION ON HUMAN RIGHTS
- SOCIAL COMMISSION
- COMMISSION ON THE STATUS OF WOMEN
- POPULATION COMMISSION
- COMMISSION ON NARCOTIC DRUGS

TRUSTEESHIP COUNCIL

SECURITY COUNCIL

GENERAL ASSEMBLY

ECONOMIC AND SOCIAL COUNCIL

INTERNATIONAL COURT OF JUSTICE

SECRETARIAT

- UNITED NATIONS INTERNATIONAL CHILDREN'S EMERGENCY FUND
- OFFICE OF THE UNITED NATIONS HIGH COMMISSIONER FOR REFUGEES

- MILITARY STAFF COMMITTEE
- DISARMAMENT COMMISSION
- INTERIM COMMITTEE OF THE GENERAL ASSEMBLY
- PEACE OBSERVATION COMMISSION
- COLLECTIVE MEASURES COMMITTEE
- UN RELIEF AND WORKS AGENCY FOR PALESTINE REFUGEES IN THE NEAR EAST
- UN KOREAN RECONSTRUCTION AGENCY
- INTERNATIONAL LAW COMMISSION
- COMMITTEE ON INFORMATION FROM NON-SELF-GOVERNING TERRITORIES
- ADVISORY COMMITTEE ON ADMINISTRATIVE AND BUDGETARY QUESTIONS
- COMMITTEE ON CONTRIBUTIONS

SPECIALIZED AGENCIES

- INTERNATIONAL LABOUR ORGANISATION
- WORLD HEALTH ORGANIZATION
- FOOD AND AGRICULTURE ORGANIZATION OF THE UNITED NATIONS
- UNITED NATIONS EDUCATIONAL, SCIENTIFIC AND CULTURAL ORGANIZATION
- INTERNATIONAL CIVIL AVIATION ORGANIZATION
- WORLD METEOROLOGICAL ORGANIZATION
- INTERNATIONAL BANK FOR RECONSTRUCTION AND DEVELOPMENT
- INTERNATIONAL MONETARY FUND
- UNIVERSAL POSTAL UNION
- INTERNATIONAL TELECOMMUNICATION UNION
- INTER-GOVERNMENTAL MARITIME CONSULTATIVE ORGANIZATION (Preparatory Commission)
- INTERNATIONAL TRADE ORGANIZATION (Interim Commission)

TECHNICAL ASSISTANCE BOARD

ADMINISTRATIVE COMMITTEE ON CO-ORDINATION

December 1952

*For other subsidiary Bodies see Charts of Relevant Organs

The United Nations

FIGURE XX:1

559

as needed, and this has been done on numerous occasions in the form of commissions, committees, and so forth. The Charter also provides that the various "specialized agencies," which have been set up in recent years by international agreements in the fields of economic, social, cultural, technical, health, educational, and related fields, shall be "brought into relationship" with the United Nations by special agreement between the Economic and Social Council and the several agencies concerned.

The structure of the United Nations Organization is depicted in the accompanying schematic diagram.

THE GENERAL ASSEMBLY

Functions. The General Assembly is the plenary forum wherein all members of the United Nations meet each year to consider and debate the major issues of international politics. Upon its agenda are placed from year to year the problems and issues exacerbating the relations among nations. And to its rostrum come foreign ministers, ambassadors, and leading statesmen to present the views of their country on these issues and to appeal to world opinion for support.

The General Assembly may "discuss any matter within the scope" of the Charter or the organization. It may consider general principles of international cooperation. It may consider "any questions relating to the maintenance of international peace and security" which are brought before it, and make *recommendations* thereon—with the one exception that it may not make any recommendation on a matter currently before the Security Council unless that body so requests. The General Assembly may initiate studies and make recommendations on political cooperation, the development and codification of international law, the peaceful adjustment of situations impairing friendly relations, or the "general welfare." It may promote cooperation in economic, social, cultural, educational, and health affairs, and assist in the realization of human rights and fundamental freedoms. It has general supervision of trusteeship arrangements, with the exception of those involving areas designated as "strategic" territories. It also hears and considers reports from all other organs of the United Nations.

In addition to these more generalized functions, the General Assembly elects the nonpermanent Members of other organs of the United Nations named in the preceding section. It also considers and approves the annual budget and financial contributions of Members to the organization.

Limitations on Powers of Assembly. The General Assembly has no legislative authority. It cannot lay down laws binding upon states or individuals. Its recommendations can, however, express a "public opinion of the world" and

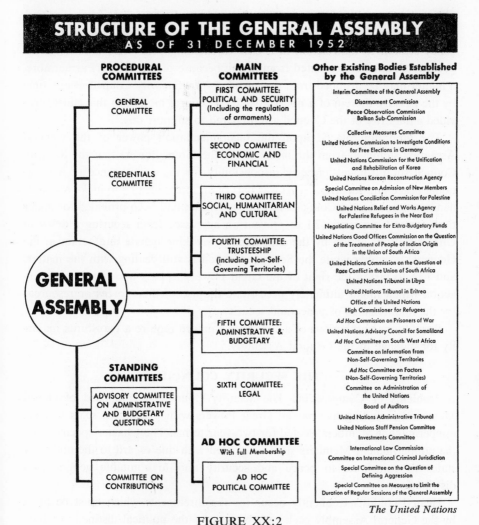

STRUCTURE OF THE GENERAL ASSEMBLY
AS OF 31 DECEMBER 1952

PROCEDURAL COMMITTEES

GENERAL COMMITTEE

CREDENTIALS COMMITTEE

GENERAL ASSEMBLY

STANDING COMMITTEES

ADVISORY COMMITTEE ON ADMINISTRATIVE AND BUDGETARY QUESTIONS

COMMITTEE ON CONTRIBUTIONS

MAIN COMMITTEES

FIRST COMMITTEE: POLITICAL AND SECURITY (Including the regulation of armaments)

SECOND COMMITTEE: ECONOMIC AND FINANCIAL

THIRD COMMITTEE: SOCIAL, HUMANITARIAN AND CULTURAL

FOURTH COMMITTEE: TRUSTEESHIP (including Non-Self-Governing Territories)

FIFTH COMMITTEE: ADMINISTRATIVE & BUDGETARY

SIXTH COMMITTEE: LEGAL

AD HOC COMMITTEE With full Membership

AD HOC POLITICAL COMMITTEE

Other Existing Bodies Established by the General Assembly

Interim Committee of the General Assembly

Disarmament Commission

Peace Observation Commission
Balkan Sub-Commission

Collective Measures Committee

United Nations Commission to Investigate Conditions for Free Elections in Germany

United Nations Commission for the Unification and Rehabilitation of Korea

United Nations Korean Reconstruction Agency

Special Committee on Admission of New Members

United Nations Conciliation Commission for Palestine

United Nations Relief and Works Agency for Palestine Refugees in the Near East

Negotiating Committee for Extra-Budgetary Funds

United Nations Good Offices Commission on the Question of the Treatment of People of Indian Origin in the Union of South Africa

United Nations Commission on the Question of Race Conflict in the Union of South Africa

United Nations Tribunal in Libya

United Nations Tribunal in Eritrea

Office of the United Nations High Commissioner for Refugees

Ad Hoc Commission on Prisoners of War

United Nations Advisory Council for Somaliland

Ad Hoc Committee on South West Africa

Committee on Information from Non-Self-Governing Territories

Ad Hoc Committee on Factors (Non-Self-Governing Territories)

Committee on Administration of the United Nations

Board of Auditors

United Nations Administrative Tribunal

United Nations Staff Pension Committee

Investments Committee

International Law Commission

Committee on International Criminal Jurisdiction

Special Committee on the Question of Defining Aggression

Special Committee on Measures to Limit the Duration of Regular Sessions of the General Assembly

The United Nations

FIGURE XX:2

they carry considerable weight, especially when they have the support of the principal powers.

Although the Charter gives the General Assembly broad power to consider and debate matters within the purview of the United Nations, it places distinct limitations upon its powers of action. For the maximum power given to the General Assembly is that of making "recommendations." And this power is limited, as we have noted, in that Article 12 specifies that it shall not make *any* recommendation on a dispute or situation involving the maintenance of peace and security while the matter is being handled by the Security Council unless the Council so requests. This limitation underwent a *de facto* modification, however, in 1950 when the Assembly resolved that it might meet in emergency session to take action in a case threatening peace and security if the Security Council is prevented from acting because of the veto.[31] Furthermore, a matter may be dropped from the agenda of the Security Council at any time by the passage therein of a non-vetoable procedural motion to this effect, provided a majority of the Council are prepared to support this.

The limitation placed upon the recommendation power of the General Assembly stemmed from the insistence of the Great Powers that the Security Council should have "primary responsibility for the maintenance of international peace and security." This was part of an intention (1) to make a clearer demarcation between Council and Assembly than had been provided for under the League Covenant; (2) to prevent an aggressor from securing a delay in United Nations action by the expedient of invoking debate and action in the General Assembly while the Security Council is still dealing with the matter; and (3) to insure the right of the Great Powers to pass upon or to veto any action which might ultimately necessitate the use of their forces or resources for the maintenance of peace and security.

Resolutions and actions of a substantive nature require a two-thirds majority for passage in the General Assembly.

THE SECURITY COUNCIL

Problems of Composition. The Security Council is composed of eleven Members, including five named Great Powers with permanent seats and six nonpermanent Members elected for two-year terms. The Charter specifies that the nonpermanent Members shall be elected with due regard to the ability of states to contribute to peace and security and to equitable geographical distribution.

Heated contests frequently occur for the three seats which must be filled by the General Assembly each year because of the political distinction which attaches to this election. Active lobbying occurs behind the scenes during each Assembly meeting by states and regional groups eager to obtain a place on the Council. Political factors have on the whole been determinative in the elections rather than a consideration of what a given state can contribute to the maintenance or enforcement of peace and security. Regional· groupings such as the Latin American Republics and the Arab League, and the Commonwealth, have been successful in repeatedly winning election of their members.[32] In

---

[31] See Uniting for Peace Resolution, Nov., 1950. This will be discussed below on p. 580.
[32] See M. Margaret Ball, "Bloc Voting in the General Assembly," *Internat. Organization,* Feb., 1951.

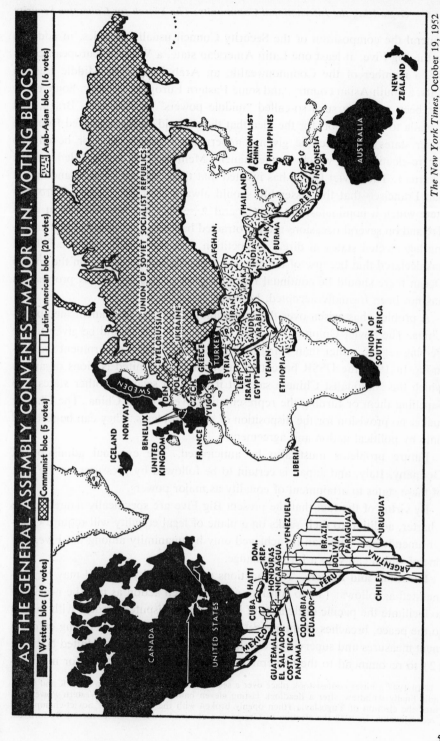

AS THE GENERAL ASSEMBLY CONVENES—MAJOR U.N. VOTING BLOCS

■ Western bloc (19 votes)   ▩ Communist bloc (5 votes)   □ Latin-American bloc (20 votes)   ▤ Arab-Asian bloc (16 votes)

The New York Times, October 19, 1952

FIGURE XX:3

general the composition of the Security Council usually includes, in addition to the Big Five, at least one Latin American state, a Western European country, a member of the Commonwealth, an Arab League or Middle Eastern state, a South Asian country, and some Eastern European country. Some effort has been made by such so-called "middle powers" as Australia, Brazil, and Canada to win support for the idea that they should be distinguished from the lesser states and either be given semipermanent membership or be eligible for re-election (to which nonpermanent Members are not entitled by the Charter). The Soviet Union has insisted that there was an "understanding" at San Francisco that the Assembly should always elect the Eastern European state which it nominates; but the General Assembly has rejected this in practice and on several occasions after protracted balloting and political maneuvering has elected states in direct competition with the Soviet nominee.[33] India has declared that because of the enormous population bordering on the Indian Ocean there should be continual representation of this area. This proposition has not been formally accepted, however.

A problem has arisen over the representation of one permanent member— China. The Soviet Union has insisted that China's seat should be given to the Peiping regime rather than being held by the Nationalist government on Formosa. In 1950 the USSR boycotted meetings in all United Nations organs in which the Nationalist Chinese sat, but it failed to sway the other states into expelling them or turning the representation over to Red China. The Charter makes no provision for the disposition of such problems. They can be resolved only by political action and agreement.

Future problems must also be anticipated. The eventual admission of Germany, Italy, and Japan is certain to be followed by pressures on the part of these states to attainment of equality as major powers.

By virtue of the fact that the present Big Five are specifically named in the Charter, addition to their ranks on a plane of legal equality will require Charter amendment. This can be achieved only by unanimity among the Five, any one of which can veto a formal change.

Functions and Powers. The functions of the Security Council may be enumerated as follows: (1) to consider and take such action as may be necessary to facilitate the pacific settlement of international disputes, to deal with threats to the peace, breaches of the peace, and acts of aggression, including enforcement measures and supervision of military action taken by the United Nations; (2) to recommend to the General Assembly admission of states for member-

---

[33] In 1947 a bitter contest took place over a seat sought by both the Ukranian SSR and India. India finally withdrew after a deadlock lasting eleven ballots. In 1950 the Western Powers secured the election of Yugoslavia (then openly broken with the USSR) over Soviet-championed Czechoslovakia. In 1952 the election of Greece was obtained over Soviet-sponsored Byelorussia.

ship in the United Nations; (3) to recommend expulsion of states for violations of the Charter, or restoration of privileges; (4) to formulate plans for the regulation of armaments; (5) to review the administration of strategic area trusteeship territories; (6) to participate with the General Assembly in the election of judges to the International Court of Justice; (7) to make recommendations or decide upon measures to be taken to give effect to judgments of the International Court in the event a party fails to perform its obligations thereunder; (8) to recommend to the General Assembly the person to be appointed Secretary-General of the United Nations; and (9) to participate in deciding whether a conference to revise the Charter should be held. The Council is obliged, like other organs, to submit annual and special reports to the General Assembly.

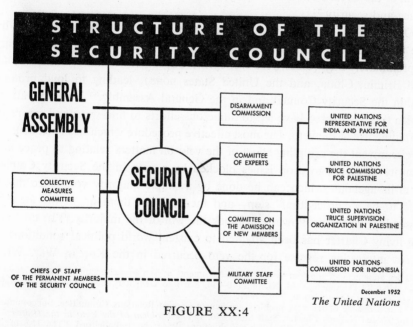

FIGURE XX:4

The powers given to the Security Council are defined in generous terms. The Council can intervene in any international situation or dispute. If it decides there is a threat to peace, breach of the peace, or act of aggression, it may recommend procedures which should be adopted or it can "decide" what measures shall be taken, and this decision the Members of the United Nations have agreed, by Article 25 of the Charter, "to accept and carry out."

Voting and the Veto. Decisions of the Security Council on all matters other than procedural steps require an affirmative vote of seven Members, including the concurring vote of the permanent Members. The sole exception to this is that in decisions relating to pacific settlement "a party to a dispute shall abstain from voting."

The principle underlying this voting arrangement is that Great Power unanimity—in the sense which prevailed during World War II—is essential for the maintenance of international peace and security. Article 27, according to its text, gives to each of the permanent Members a privilege of blocking a decision of any substantive nature by the simple expedient of voting "no" on a resolution before the Security Council. This right was insisted upon by the Powers in order to protect their rights and interests against pressure politics, and to insure a determination of what measures should be taken in any situation which might start a "chain of events" that would in the end require some or all of the Great Powers to employ their armed forces to maintain or enforce peace and security.[34]

Objection has arisen to the way in which the veto has been employed by the Soviet Union to block Security Council action. In the first eight years approximately fifty vetoes were cast by the USSR (while France had cast one, and Britain, China, and the United States none), leading to loud protests within the Security Council and in the General Assembly.[35] The frustrations which this has caused have led to numerous efforts to find ways and means of curtailing use of the veto. The most effective procedure which has been evolved to circumvent the crippling effect of the veto on matters relating to peace and security has been to drop issues blocked by a veto in the Security Council from its agenda—which can be done by a simple majority vote since this is held to be a "procedural" step—and then to take them up in the General Assembly, where no Power can block the will of the majority.[36] In this way the living Charter has been adapted to existent world political conditions.

An interesting reverse for the veto occurred in the Korean War. When

[34] See statement of the four sponsoring governments at San Francisco on procedure, June 7, 1945, UNCIO Documents, vol. XI, pp. 710–714. See also Dwight E. Lee, "The Genesis of the Veto," *Internat. Organization,* Feb., 1947.

[35] For a résumé of the veto problem see Senate Foreign Relations Committee, Subcommittee on the United Nations Charter, Staff Study No. 1, *The Problem of the Veto in the United Nations Security Council,* Feb. 19, 1954 (Washington, 1954); N. J. Padelford, "The Use of the Veto," *Internat. Organization,* June, 1948; L. M. Goodrich and E. Hambro, *Charter of the United Nations, Commentary and Documents* (rev. ed., Boston, 1949), pp. 213–227. For background information on and an appraisal of the Soviet stand on this matter see House Committee on Foreign Affairs, *Background Information on the Soviet Union in International Relations* (Washington, 1950), pp. 33–41; Rupert Emerson and Inis L. Claude, Jr., "The Soviet Union and the United Nations: An Essay in Interpretation," *Internat. Organization,* Feb., 1952.

[36] In 1946 the General Assembly urged powers not to impede the Security Council with the veto. In 1947 it asked the Interim Committee to study the problem and make recommendations. In 1948 the United States proposed that action be taken by a simple vote of any seven members on certain classes of questions. In 1949 the Assembly urged the powers to broaden cooperation and restrain use of the veto. In 1950 it passed the Uniting for Peace Resolution which in effect stated that the General Assembly might exercise some of the functions of the Security Council if in an emergency the latter were blocked by the veto.

hostilities commenced on June 25, 1950, by the North Korean attack upon South Korea, the Soviet Union, having boycotted meetings attended by the Nationalist Chinese, did not attend the sessions of the Security Council on June 25 and 27 which called upon Members to give assistance to the Republic of Korea and invited the President of the United States to designate a Supreme Commander of United Nations forces in Korea. Subsequently, the USSR claimed that the action taken in its absence was "illegal." But the other Members of the United Nations proceeded throughout the war and afterward to act on the principle that the decision was legitimate and binding. This may constitute an important precedent.[37]

Since 1947 a practice of "abstention" from voting has arisen (in the Assembly as well as in the Security Council). Under this practice a state may be present at a voting but abstain from casting any vote if it wishes neither to support a proposed action nor to vote against it, or, in the case of a Great Power in the Security Council, if it wishes to avoid casting a veto. Although abstention would technically seem to amount to "failure to concur" in an "affirmative vote"—and hence, if practiced by one of the five Great Powers in the Security Council, would be sufficient to block a decision according to Charter language—it has not been regarded in practice as constituting a veto.[38]

So long as the veto power remains within the United Nations it is available for use by any one of the Big Five to defend positions which it regards as vital to its national interests when it cannot rally a majority to its stand. There is little likelihood that it will be removed from the Charter, even though it now applies with complete effectiveness only to the election of the Secretary-General and to applications for membership. In agreeing that the General Assembly may exercise many of the functions of the Security Council relating to peace and security if the latter is blocked by the use of the veto, the living Charter has somewhat weakened the arrangement, as originally envisaged, for protecting the Great Powers against being committed to taking military action by a majority vote. An Assembly resolution, however, is permissive and is only a recommendation. It constitutes a basis for cooperation but is not a binding obligation.

[37] See Leland M. Goodrich, "Korea: Collective Measures against Aggression," *Internat. Conciliation,* Oct., 1953.

[38] See Yuen-li Liang, "Abstention and Absence of a Permanent Member in Relation to the Voting Procedure in the Security Council," *Am. J. Int. Law,* Oct., 1950; E. de Arechaga Jiminez, *Voting and the Handling of Disputes in the Security Council,* United Nations Studies No. 3, Carnegie Endowment for Intl. Peace (New York, 1950); Wellington Koo, Jr., *Voting Procedures in International Political Organizations* (New York, 1947); Leo Gross, "The Double Veto and the Four Power Statement on Voting in the Security Council," *Harvard Law Rev.,* Dec., 1953.

PACIFIC SETTLEMENT OF DISPUTES

Pursuant to the fundamental purpose of the United Nations to maintain peace and bring about the adjustment or settlement of international disputes or situations which might lead to a breach of the peace, Articles 33–38 are in a sense the heart of the Charter.

Basic Requirement. The Charter places upon all parties to a dispute, "the continuance of which is likely to endanger international peace and security," an obligation to attempt to settle the dispute, in the first instance, by means of their own choosing. Means suggested for this include negotiation, enquiry, mediation, conciliation, arbitration, judicial settlement, resort to regional arrangements, or "other peaceful means of their own choice."

Role of Security Council

1. DISCUSSION AND PROMOTION OF PEACEFUL SETTLEMENT. The Security Council has a multiple role to play in connection with the pacific settlement of disputes—as the United Nations organ having "primary responsibility" for the maintenance of peace and security. The initiators of the United Nations Charter anticipated that situations and disputes likely to endanger peace normally would be brought to the attention of the Security Council by one of the disputants, by some other Member state, or by the Secretary-General. In this connection the dispute or situation would be aired, statements would be heard from the parties, and they would be urged, formally or otherwise, to settle the dispute among themselves either through negotiation or some other means of peaceful settlement of their own choosing. Problems are continually being brought before the Security Council in this manner.

The role of the Security Council in this respect can be illustrated from one of the first cases which came before this body, the Iranian-Soviet dispute. In January, 1946, the Iranian Government notified the United Nations that the refusal of the USSR to withdraw troops which it had placed in Iran during the war, together with rebellion against the Government of Iran in the province of Azerbaijan which was Russian-occupied, constituted interference in the internal affairs of Iran and had given rise to a situation which "may lead to international friction." Having heard a reply by the USSR that there was no connection between the lawful presence of its troops (in accordance with treaty arrangements) and the Azerbaijan revolt and that negotiations were proceeding between the parties, the Security Council at first merely noted the willingness of the parties to negotiate and asked that it be kept informed on their progress. On March 26, 1946, three weeks having passed since the passage of a deadline date set by a war-time agreement of the Allies for the withdrawal of all troops from Iran (that is, within six months after the end of the war), the Iranian Government charged that Soviet troops were now illegally within its territory, that the USSR was interfering in its internal affairs, and that negotiations had in fact broken down. The Soviet delegate denied Security Council jurisdiction over the case. He insisted that an accord had been reached on troop withdrawal, and demanded complete postponement of a decision for a fortnight. When the Security Council refused to do this, the Soviet delegate left the Council and did not return until the date he had set. Meanwhile it heard the Iranian delegate, and Soviet troops in fact evacuated the country. When the Soviet delegate returned, he contested the proceedings which had occurred. But at the same time the Iranian Government announced its confidence in a pledge given to it by Moscow and it withdrew its complaint. This created a curious situation. Despite Soviet objections, the Council voted to keep the matter on its agenda, although a month later it voted to "adjourn the discussion" subject to recall by any Member.

It cannot be proved that the mere reference of this situation to the Security Council by Iran, and its discussion there, caused the Soviet Union to terminate its occupation or cease interference in the internal affairs of Iran. Nevertheless, during the airing of the Iranian charges, with extensive press coverage, and following the firmness of the Security Council in the face of Russian attempted intimidation, the Soviet Union did withdraw its armed forces and the communist-led rebellion in Azerbaijan collapsed. Consequently, it can be argued that the existence of the Security Council, its hearing of discussion of the issue, and its insistence on retaining the item on its agenda did contribute to peaceful settlement.[39]

2. INVESTIGATION. The Security Council has a broad power to investigate any dispute or situation which might lead to friction in order to determine whether its continuance is likely to endanger peace and security. This is an essential function not only for the determination of facts, and the seriousness of a dispute or situation, but also in order to establish a basis for recommendations.[40]

An illustration of an investigation is afforded by the Security Council appointment of a Commission of Investigation in an early phase of the Greek Civil War. Such a commission was created in December, 1946, to investigate facts regarding alleged border violations occurring in conjunction with civil strife in Greece. The Commission went to the Balkans, where it examined over 250 persons and statements and made over thirty field investigations in Greece and its three northern neighbors. In preparing its report the members

---

[39] For a summary of this case see *Internat. Organization*, Feb., 1947, pp. 74–77. See also George Lenzcowski, *Russia and the West in Iran, 1918–1948* (Ithaca, 1949), ch. xi; Richard W. Van Wagenen, *The Iranian Case, 1946*, Carnegie Endowment for Intl. Peace (New York, 1952).
[40] Goodrich and Hambro, *op. cit.*, p. 247.

of the Commission found themselves sharply divided on the assessment of responsibility. Soviet Bloc members, who comprised a minority, held that reactionary Greek policies were to blame for the situation and that proof was lacking that Albania, Bulgaria, and Yugoslavia—Soviet satellites—were at fault. The majority held that the facts did show that the northern states had refugee camps of Greek guerrillas, that they had been supplied with arms and munitions, and that a separatist movement had been promoted within Macedonia. The majority did acknowledge that internal conditions within Greece could not be ignored as a factor contributory to unrest. But they denied that this relieved Albania, Bulgaria, and Yugoslavia of liability for aiding the guerrillas. The Security Council wrangled for three months following receipt of the Commission Report. Five times Soviet vetoes defeated 9–2 majorities in the Security Council for recommendations relating to settlement of the dispute. Finally, the Greek Civil War, having become wrapped up in the larger issues of Great Power conflict and politics, the majority in exasperation passed a procedural motion dropping the entire question from the Security Council, whereupon it was introduced into the General Assembly for further discussion and recommendation.

In this instance a Security Council Commission of Investigation elucidated the facts involved in a troubled situation endangering peace and security. Owing to division between the permanent Members, the Council, however, was unable to proceed with any recommendation for pacific settlement. The lesson to be learned from this is that the exercise of the veto may render nugatory the power of the Security Council to employ investigation as an effective technique for furthering pacific settlement of disputes or threatening situations. The investigation procedure may, however, be continued by the General Assembly.[41]

3. EXERCISE OF GOOD OFFICES AND CONCILIATION. A third type of procedure which the Security Council may exercise is that of extending good offices and conciliation to disputing parties, either through itself or through some specially created instrumentality, for the furtherance of peaceful settlement. This is well illustrated by Security Council procedure in the Indonesian situation from 1947 to 1949.

In the summer of 1947 Australia and India appealed to the Security Council to consider the hostilities which were occurring in Indonesia between Dutch forces seeking to re-establish Dutch rule in the Indies and those of the Repub-

---

41 See *United Nations Yearbook, 1947–1948,* pp. 74–75, 298–301, 337–352; *ibid., 1948–1949,* pp. 238–256; *The U. N. and the Problem of Greece,* Department of State Publication 2909 (Washington, 1947). See below, p. 574.

lic of Indonesia which had proclaimed its independence in 1945. Putting aside a Dutch objection that the dispute was within "domestic jurisdiction" and therefore not subject to United Nations consideration, the Security Council requested the parties to cease fire, to settle the matter by peaceful means, and to keep it appraised of further developments.

When hostilities persisted, the Council next asked the career consuls of states having such officers in Batavia to form a United Nations Committee of Good Offices to observe conditions in Indonesia with respect to a cease-fire, and to assist the parties in reaching a peaceful agreement on the situation. Under the assistance of this group an agreement for cease-fire and for resumption of negotiations between the Dutch and Indonesians was reached. By December, 1948, these negotiations broke down and the Dutch instituted hostilities—which they termed "police action"—resulting in the capture of a number of Indonesian leaders. Immediate reaction against the Dutch was occasioned by this procedure, both in the Council and in the world press. Release of the prisoners and cessation of hostilities were demanded amid excoriation of Dutch actions. With political pressure being exerted upon them both within the Council and outside, and with the assistance of the United Nations Committee, which was reorganized, strengthened, and renamed the United Nations Commission for Indonesia, the Dutch presently suggested that a conference be held at The Hague to arrange for establishment of Indonesian sovereignty and a United States of Indonesia. This was accepted, and after several months of negotiation in which the United Nations Commission for Indonesia participated directly as a mediating member, agreement was reached at The Hague for the transference of sovereignty to Indonesia and for a Netherlands-Indonesian Union. A Soviet veto cast at the last minute prevented the Security Council from expressing its approval of The Hague agreements, which had already been approved by the General Assembly.

In this instance the Security Council's persistent concern with the difficult Indonesian problem, which had a Western colonial power ranged against the aspirant nationalism of Asia, was unquestionably a contributory element in the ultimate pacific settlement of this issue. The firmness of the United States insistence that any solution must recognize Indonesian independence and that the so-called Dutch police actions would not be tolerated was also a factor. So likewise was a conference of nineteen Asian nations held at New Delhi at the height of the crisis which called for strong action by the Security Council involving enforcement measures if needed. But by no means the least element in the successful outcome was the part played by the United Nations Committee of Good Offices and its successor, the Commission for Indonesia, which painstakingly mediated between the parties, kept bringing them together, and helped them find bases of peaceful adjustment.[42]

4. OTHER PROCEDURES. The Security Council may recommend or adopt other procedures which in its judgment will promote pacific settlement of an international dispute or bring about an alleviation of a dangerous situation. The scope of its action can best be indicated by brief mention of its decisions in several other cases which have come before it. In a dispute between Britain and Albania over the destruction of some British destroyers by mines in the Corfu Channel, the Council recommended that the parties refer the case to the International Court of Justice, which they did. During the fighting in Palestine in 1948, a Truce Commission and a Truce Supervision Organization were appointed, cease-fire orders were issued on several occasions, and Security Council-designated temporary truces established. Finally, a Security Council resolution in November, 1948, directed that these be superseded by an armistice negotiated directly between the parties or through the acting mediator, Dr. Ralph Bunche.[43]

From the foregoing résumé it may be seen that a wide range of procedures is available to the Security Council in its efforts to promote pacific settlement of international disputes. The success or failure of its efforts in any situation is conditioned, however, by a number of variable circumstances. They depend in part upon the degree of willingness of the parties involved to seek a peaceful settlement of the issue at stake. But over and above this the nature of the Council's proceedings is directly related to the political aspects of the situation. Where one of the parties does not find a champion or ally among the permanent Members of the Council, and no division occurs among these powers, Security Council recommendations can carry considerable weight. On the other hand, wherever a dispute or situation becomes involved in Great Power conflict, as many issues have tended to do especially since 1947, the usefulness of the Council is limited. The Security Council may find itself unable to act at all, owing to the use of the veto; or, if it is able to pass a recommendation, this may become fruitless in the continued wrangling among the contestants and their Great Power supporters. The result, as in the Greek Civil War and in the Korean War, may be determined primarily by forces at work outside of or independent of the United Nations. The Security Council, and its efforts in the

---

42 See J. Foster Collins, "The United Nations and Indonesia," *Internat. Conciliation,* March, 1950; Charles Wolf, Jr., *The Indonesian Story* (New York, 1948); *Yearbook of the United Nations, 1948–1949,* pp. 212–237; *ibid., 1950,* pp. 301–304. For a review of United Nations efforts to employ a similar procedure in the Kashmir dispute see Josef Korbel, "The Kashmir Dispute and the U. N.," *Internat. Organization,* May, 1949.

43 For an analysis of the Palestine case see L. Larry Leonard, "The United Nations and Palestine," *Internat. Conciliation,* Oct., 1949. See ch. xix above for further discussion of Corfu Channel case before the International Court of Justice.

direction of pacific settlement, are intimately bound up with power politics and cannot be divorced from them. Where the power factors are favorable to a peaceful solution, this may be obtainable. Where states are irreconcilably opposed and will not reach a settlement regardless of appeals or political pressures, the United Nations can do little.

The General Assembly and Pacific Settlement. The General Assembly has actively concerned itself also with the problems of pacific settlement. As the efforts of the Security Council became increasingly stultified after 1947 as a result of the cold war, the importance of the General Assembly's role has grown correspondingly. One of the most broadly valuable actions taken by the General Assembly in this respect was a comprehensive study of procedures of pacific settlement made in 1948 for the Assembly by its Interim Committee (often called the "Little Assembly") setting out the possible procedures with recommendations for their utilization as occasion may offer.[44]

1. DEBATE AND APPEAL FOR PACIFIC SETTLEMENT. As we mentioned previously, one of the chief functions of the General Assembly is to provide a forum wherein controversial issues may be debated and through which world opinion may be given an opportunity to form behind recommendations to the parties concerned. The agendas of the General Assembly have witnessed a succession of troublesome international problems referred to this body in the hope that some clarification might be obtained through the committee and plenary session debates and through the marshaling of votes or the resolutions which emerge from the political maneuvering at Assembly meetings.

Two samples will illustrate one of the simplest types of moves that the General Assembly may make. In 1946 India charged the Union of South Africa with discriminatory treatment against Indians residing there, with resulting strained relations between the two countries. After debating the problem, the General Assembly called upon the Union of South Africa to adhere to its treaties with India and at the same time it urged both countries to undertake negotiations to settle their differences. Again, in 1951 the Assembly called upon Yugoslavia and the Soviet satellite countries to conduct their relations in accordance with the Charter and to settle their disputes by peaceful means.

This type of appeal, reminding parties of their obligations and urging them to seek composition of their differences, may appear like a fruitless expenditure of time and effort. But the eyes of the world focus upon the General Assembly meetings. A resolution passed by the necessary two-thirds of the Assembly carries political and moral weight. A government whose actions

---

[44] Report of Interim Committee in United Nations Document A/578 (1948); excerpts in *Internat. Organization*, Feb., 1949, pp. 190–202. See D. W. Coster, "The Interim Committee of the General Assembly," *ibid.*, Aug., 1949.

have been aggravating a situation or which has refused to settle a dispute is aware of the implications of criticism implicit in such a resolution, although in some cases it may be quite prepared to risk condemnation for the achievement of its objectives. In such a situation the General Assembly may have to resort to further steps.

2. INVESTIGATION AND GOOD OFFICES. Like the Security Council, the General Assembly may establish investigation or good offices committees to gather information and to assist parties to a solution of their differences if they are so disposed.

In September, 1947, after the Security Council had failed to agree upon steps to cope with guerrilla activity in Greece and the Balkans, the situation was taken up by the General Assembly. This at once established a United Nations Special Committee on the Balkans to investigate border violations and to use its good offices to help the countries concerned to re-establish normal diplomatic relations and cessation of frontier troubles. Although the Committee was not allowed into the territory of the Soviet satellites, it nevertheless rendered useful service. Based upon its recommendations, the General Assembly later adopted a series of resolutions calling upon Albania, Bulgaria, and Yugoslavia to cease aiding the Greek guerrillas and to settle their differences with Greece. Although the Greek Civil War ended in the winter of 1949–1950, the Assembly continued its concern with the problem as reports persisted of threats to the political independence and territorial integrity of Greece. Hence, the Assembly requested the Special Committee to remain in Greece and to assist in a settlement wherever possible. The Assembly in 1951 replaced the Special Committee with a Balkan subcommission of the Peace Observation Commission which had been instituted by an Assembly resolution in November, 1950, directing this body to dispatch observers to any tension spot in the Balkans and to continue the functions of fact-finding and good offices.[45]

The efforts carried on by and on behalf of the General Assembly were distinctly useful in exposing the activities conducted across the Greek frontiers and threatening Greek peace and security. But the suppression of communist guerrilla action was brought about by military action of the Greek Government, aided by the economic and military assistance given to Greece by the United States under the Truman Doctrine and Marshall Plan aid. The rupture between Marshal Tito of Yugoslavia and Moscow and its satellites also contributed to the collapse of the Greek guerrillas.

[45] For résumé of General Assembly action in the Greek case see *Yearbook of the United Nations, 1948–1949* and *1950*; also Factual Summaries in *Internat. Organization* issues of 1948 to 1951.

3. MEDIATION AND CONCILIATION. No more graphic example can be given of some of the problems which may be encountered in seeking to promote pacific settlement of an international dispute than in the General Assembly's attempts to deal with the Palestine problem. For twenty-five years British governments had wrestled with the conflicting interests of Arabs and Jews in the Holy Land, while Palestine was held as a mandate under the League of Nations. In February, 1947, British Foreign Secretary Bevin announced that all British efforts to find an acceptable, peaceful solution had failed. Accordingly, being unwilling to impose a solution upon the Arabs and Jews, the United Kingdom submitted the entire problem to the United Nations, and proposed the convocation of a special session of the General Assembly.

As a first step, after debating the issue and hearing representatives of the Arab and Jewish communities, the Assembly created a United Nations Special Committee on Palestine to make an international investigation of the whole question of Palestine and to report proposals "appropriate for the solution of the problem." After holding over fifty meetings, this Committee brought in two plans: (1) a majority proposal for partition into an Arab state, a Jewish state, and an independent City of Jerusalem; and (2) a minority proposal of a federal state. By a vote of 33 to 13, with 10 abstentions, the General Assembly adopted the Partition Plan and set up a United Nations Palestine Commission to implement its resolution. The Arab League states were unanimously opposed to the decision and stated that they never would accept it.

With violence developing within Palestine during the spring of 1948, the Security Council called for a second special session of the General Assembly. A tentative proposal made at this time for establishing a trusteeship for Palestine when British rule terminated did not meet with support. In place of this proposal the Assembly decided to create a United Nations Mediator to assist in attaining a peaceful transition. Before the final vote was taken on this proposal, a Jewish state of Israel was proclaimed on May 14, the day the mandate was due to expire, and United States *de facto* recognition was announced. As a consequence of the establishment of Israel, Palestine was in fact divided between the state of Israel and the Hashemite Kingdom of Jordan. Notwithstanding this development, the proposed Mediator was duly named by the five Great Powers in the person of Count Bernadotte of Sweden. His function was simply declared to be "to use his good offices with the local and community authorities in Palestine to . . . promote a peaceful adjustment of the future situation of Palestine." Full-scale fighting between the Arab and Israeli armies interspersed with Security Council demands for cease-fire and with temporary truces throughout the remainder of 1948 complicated the Mediator's task. Proposals made by him to the Arabs and Israeli for terms of a political settle-

THE PARTITION OF PALESTINE

LEGEND

🛢 Oil refineries
▭▭▭▭ Oil pipelines
+++++++ Principal railways
──── International boundaries
Jewish State ▨ Arab State

0   50   100
Scale of Miles

RCF

Mass. Inst. Technology

FIGURE XX:5

ment, including modification of the partition plan, were rejected by both sides.

Following the assassination of Count Bernadotte in Jerusalem by a Jewish extremist, and his succession by Dr. Ralph Bunche as acting Mediator, efforts were bent to obtain observance of a truce and then to negotiate an armistice. With the acting Mediator heavily preoccupied with these tasks, the General Assembly in December, 1948, established a United Nations Palestine Conciliation Commission to promote good relations between the parties and to take steps to assist them in achieving a final settlement of all outstanding questions. The acting Mediator was continued in office until the summer of 1949, when armistice agreements were finally concluded between the parties to the previous hostilities.

Repeated efforts were made by the United Nations Palestine Conciliation Commission after the signature of the armistice agreements to improve relations between the Arab states and Israel, but with little success. Efforts by the Trusteeship Council to devise a plan for the internationalization of Jerusalem came to naught. And the General Assembly itself was able to accomplish little during the next few years in the alleviation of the suspicious fears and ill-feeling engendered by the Palestine problem. Its principal contribution was to vote inadequate sums of money for alleviation of the misery of the Arab refugees forced from their homes in Palestine and living under the most deplorable circumstances within the adjoining states.

Thus the Palestine issue in all its complexity illustrates the manifold, and sometimes insoluble, nature of international problems which can be laid on the doorstep of the United Nations. Where the parties to a dispute are irreconcilably opposed to one another, the attainment of "solutions" of their problems by pacific means of conciliation and mediation can at best be a slow, laborious process. Uncertainty, reversals of policy, and disagreement among the larger powers on dealing with the situation are likely to add to the difficulties—as they did in this case.[46]

4. PLEBISCITE AND ELECTIONS. Another type of procedure which the General Assembly has employed for pacific settlement is that of proposing the holding of a plebiscite or election. Thus in 1948 the General Assembly, in conformity with its goal of establishing a united, free, and democratic Korea, recommended the holding of nation-wide elections for a national assembly to constitute a unified state, and for this purpose it established a Temporary Commission on Korea. Although the Commission was denied entry into North Korea, it did supervise elections in South Korea, pronouncing them valid.

---

[46] See footnote 23 above for references on the Palestine problem. See also J. C. Hurewitz, "The United Nations Conciliation Commission for Palestine—Establishment and Definition of Functions," *Internat. Organization*, Nov., 1953.

Owing to North Korean and Soviet opposition, the United Nations was thwarted in its efforts prior to the Korean War to attain its declared objectives.

Settlement of Disputes a Political Matter. Thus it may be seen that a variety of procedures is open to the Security Council and the General Assembly in dealing with disputes and situations calling for pacific settlement measures. The procedure, or combination of procedures, adopted in any given situation referred to the United Nations is determined by the organ before which the dispute or situation is laid in the light of its judgment as to the appropriate course to be followed under the existent circumstances. In reaching this choice the Security Council or General Assembly, as the case may be, is naturally influenced by the political factors which are brought to bear by the parties involved, by their friends and allies, and by the interests of the principal Members. Compromise and expediency are bound to figure in these decisions, and it cannot be expected that what works well in one circumstance will necessarily be successful in another. Willingness on the part of the disputing parties to cooperate in the search for a formula of pacific settlement will be found in some instances. In others intransigence and aggressiveness may defeat efforts of the organization to achieve a just and durable settlement. This is the essence of politics in a society of sovereign states. The organs of the United Nations can do no more than its Members are prepared to agree upon.

THREATS TO PEACE AND ACTS OF AGGRESSION

When a situation arises in which it is charged that there exists a threat to peace and security, a breach of peace or an act of aggression, and the matter is brought to the attention of the United Nations, the Security Council or the General Assembly may be called upon to go farther than to seek pacific settlement. The maintenance or enforcement of peace may be called for, and the provisions of Chapter VII of the Charter invoked. Those who drafted the United Nations Charter intended that in this realm the Security Council should clearly have the primary responsibility for decision and action, and that only exceptionally should the General Assembly take action for the organization. Hence, we shall consider the functions of the Security Council first.

Role of Security Council. Under the Charter the Security Council has the authority and the responsibility to "decide" upon measures needed to maintain and enforce peace, including the use of economic, political, or military measures. And the Member states are bound under Article 25 to "carry out" the "decisions" which it reaches. In this respect a distinction may be drawn between appeals and recommendations on the one hand and formal decisions on the other.

1. DETERMINATION OF BASIS OF ACTION. In determining what steps may be required to deal with a critical situation brought to its attention, the Secu-

rity Council must first ascertain whether in fact a threat to the peace, breach of the peace, or act of aggression does exist. The Charter does not contain precise definitions of these terms. Agreement upon exact, all-inclusive definition has been found to be impossible, there being so many types of situations. Political motives are involved in any action precipitating a question in the Council on this score. And political judgments and interests likewise are involved in any appraisal and decision. Hence, Security Council debates may be protracted and acrimonious on the basic question of whether a threat to peace or aggression does exist even before consideration may begin of the steps which should be taken to deal with a situation. If the Great Powers are divided, and one of them is determined to block Council action by the use of the veto, the Security Council may be delayed indefinitely in taking any effective measures. Had the Soviet Union been present at the Security Council meetings on June 25 and 27, 1950, when it was decided to request that Member states send assistance to the Republic of Korea to repel North Korean aggression, there is no doubt the Security Council would have found itself unable to take action, except to drop the matter from its agenda, thereby making it accessible to General Assembly action. Soviet opposition made it impossible for the Council to continue any action in the Korean case, once the Soviet delegate resumed his seat.

2. PROVISIONAL MEASURES. While the Security Council is considering a threatening situation, it may recommend certain "provisional measures" to maintain or restore peace. Its most frequently employed step in this direction has been to call for a "cease-fire" when hostilities have actually occurred. This was employed in Indonesia in 1947–1948, in the Palestine fighting in 1948, and at the outbreak of the Korean War on June 25, 1950.

3. ENFORCEMENT MEASURES. The Charter (Articles 41–42) allows the Security Council to decide what measures, both of a non-forcible and of a forcible nature, should be employed in order to maintain or to restore international peace and security. These may call for rupture of communications, establishment of embargoes upon certain articles, and complete severance of trade or of diplomatic relations. The Security Council may go farther and call for the institution of a blockade, the sending of armed forces to the aid of a victim of aggression, or "such action by air, sea, or land forces as may be necessary to maintain or restore international peace and security." The Council may, if it sees fit, utilize regional agencies for enforcement action if such are available.

A decision to call for any of these measures involves attempting to stop some party from pursuing a line of action which it has decided to follow for the advancement of what it conceives to be its own interests. In deciding that assistance should be rendered to one party against another, judgment is passed

on the policies of the other. And in initiating restrictive or enforcement measures, it is conceivable that hostilities or war may ensue in which there will be
loss of life and destruction of property. It is not surprising that the governments that sponsored the San Francisco Conference insisted on the right to a
veto on these decisions. The practical question is whether, in a given case, it
is possible to meet the two voting conditions, namely: (a) an affirmative vote
of a majority, and (b) no negative votes from Members with permanent seats.
No sure outcome can be predicted other than that each Member of the Council will decide in accordance with its political interests as it sees them at the
moment under the prevailing circumstances, including the influence of political
factors operating within its own domestic scene.

4. CHARTER PROVISIONS FOR ARMED FORCES. Provisions were written into
the Charter for the making of armed forces available to the United Nations
for use in an emergency and for their unified direction. Owing to world political conditions, the necessary special agreements requisite to this have not been
concluded. And the Security Council's Military Staff Committee has been
unable to proceed even as far as an accord on basic principles of command or
strategic direction.[47] When the North Korean aggression occurred in 1950, the
most that the Security Council could do, therefore, was to recommend—with
the Soviet delegate absent—that Members "furnish such assistance to the
Republic of Korea as may be necessary to repel the armed attack and to
restore international peace and security in the area." This move was taken
after the United States had already ordered its forces to help defend the
Republic. During the ensuing months some twenty-six states made offers of
combat assistance in one form or another which were accepted by the Supreme
Commander. The Soviet Bloc gave aid to the aggressors. With a permanent
Member of the Security Council determined to thwart united action, little if
anything can be accomplished through the Council in the event of future
threats to peace or breaches of the peace. Indeed, if such a Member chooses
to attend the Council sessions, as the USSR did not on June 25 and 27, 1950,
it can block the passage of any United Nations action requiring Members to
"carry out" a "decision" to give assistance to a victim of aggression.

The General Assembly and Collective Security. Awareness of these implications led the United States to propose, and the General Assembly to adopt,
in November, 1950, the so-called Uniting for Peace resolutions by which the
overwhelming majority of the Members of the United Nations resolved that

47 Cf. Articles 43–50. After fifteen months of debate the Military Staff Committee issued a
report in 1947 on "General Principles Governing the Organization of the Armed Forces Made
Available to the Security Council by Member Nations of the United Nations." Text in *Yearbook of the United Nations, 1946–1947*, pp. 424–443. Fundamental differences developed between the USSR and other nations on questions of contributions, supply, command, and strategic planning. The cold war prevented any further efforts in the MSC.

if the Security Council should fail to exercise its responsibilities when a threat to the peace or breach of the peace or act of aggression occurred because of the veto, the General Assembly might be called into emergency session within twenty-four hours in order to make recommendations to Members for collective measures including the use of armed force. By these same resolutions the Assembly established a Peace Observation Commission to observe and report on conditions endangering peace and security, and also a Collective Measures Committee to study and report to the Assembly on methods and resources, including armed forces, which may be available and might be used to maintain or strengthen peace and security. Finally, the resolutions asked all Members to set aside certain elements of their national forces which might be available for use on call by the Security Council or the General Assembly.[48]

These resolutions marked a milestone in the *de facto* alteration of the institutional arrangements within the United Nations organization distinct from that contemplated by the leading powers when the Charter was being drawn up. By the passage of these resolutions the majority of Members signified that they wished to increase the security role of the General Assembly and that they wished it to be able, in effect, to exercise the functions of the Security Council to the point of calling for the supply of armed forces for collective measures if and when that organ is brought to a standstill by the use of the veto.[49]

The United Nations and Korea. No situation in the post-1945 period posed a more crucial test to the peace machinery of the world than the North Korean invasion of South Korea in 1950. The invading army was trained and equipped by the USSR. Its objective was the conquest of all Korea in direct challenge to the United Nations, which since 1947 had been endeavoring to bring about a free, united, democratic Korea by peaceful means. If the United Nations failed to respond to this act of aggression threatening not only Korea but eventually perhaps Japan, the precedent would be written upon the records of history and any future aggressor would certainly be more inclined to dare collective action by the United Nations to enforce peace.

1. BACKGROUND. By a Four Power Agreement of August, 1945, Japanese

---

[48] See Paul H. Douglas, "United to Enforce Peace," *Foreign Affairs,* Oct., 1951; Lester H. Woolsey, "The Uniting for Peace Resolution of the United Nations," *Am. J. Int. Law,* Jan., 1951. Attention should also be drawn to two related resolutions passed in 1950: (1) a Peace through Deeds resolution containing a definition of aggression which includes the fomenting of civil strife as well as armed invasion, and (2) a resolution on the Duties of States in the Event of the Outbreak of Hostilities enumerating steps to be taken to insure utilization of the United Nations machinery and to render a cease-fire effective. For summaries and documentary references see *Internat. Organization,* Feb., 1951, "Factual Summaries—the General Assembly."

[49] See H. Field Haviland, "The Political Role of the General Assembly," United Nations Studies No. 7, Carnegie Endowment for International Peace (New York, 1951).

troops laid down their arms to Soviet forces north of the 38th parallel and to United States forces south of this line. With a political solution to Korea's future lacking, occupation of Korean territory by the forces of these two powers continued until 1949, during which time protracted negotiations had occurred with respect to the creation of an independent, united, and democratic Korea. When these negotiations had become abortive in 1947, the United States referred the issue to the United Nations General Assembly, which recommended the holding of elections throughout the country for the establishment of an all-Korean government, after which foreign forces should be withdrawn. Soviet refusal to admit the United Nations Commission into North Korea resulted in the holding of supervised elections only in the southern half. Following this, the General Assembly recognized the government of President Rhee as the lawful government of Korea. The Soviet Union, nevertheless, supported the establishment in North Korea of a separate regime which it proceeded to recognize as the only lawful government of Korea. The conflict between the Koreans themselves, taken in company with the larger struggle between the Soviet Union and the Western Powers, brought to naught all efforts by the United Nations to unify the twenty million people of the peninsula.

2. INITIAL ACTION. During the night of June 25, 1950, the North Korean Army crossed the 38th parallel and invaded the Republic of Korea, its columns spearheaded by Soviet-built tanks. The Government of the United States and of other free nations recognized an open bid by world communism, under the guidance of Moscow, to conquer by armed force what it had failed to gain through political action. The United States was in a particularly sensitive situation since any faltering on this issue would have raised questions concerning its action in the event of aggression in the European NATO area. Meeting within twenty-four hours at the request of the United States, the Security Council, with the Soviet Union absent, adopted a resolution by a 9–0 vote declaring that the North Korean action constituted a "breach of the peace," and calling upon their forces to withdraw. It also requested the United Nations Commission in Korea to inform it of the situation, and it called upon "all Members to render every assistance to the United Nations in the execution of this resolution and to refrain from giving assistance to the North Korean authorities."

This was quick, decisive action. The measures taken were of a provisional nature, designed to restore peace on a *status quo ante* basis. United Nations prestige rose to a high level, even though collective measures were not specifically requested.

With reports from Korea showing no let-up in the invasion after the Security Council appeal and with frantic appeals for help coming from Seoul, President Truman decided late on June 26 to order United States forces to assist the Republic of Korea and at the same time to institute a patrol off Formosa to "neutralize" it against possible Chinese communist attack.

3. THE UNITED NATIONS CALLS FOR ASSISTANCE. When the Security Council met again on June 27, once more in response to United States request, the President's decision was public knowledge. After hearing a factual report from the Commission in Korea, an appeal from the Korean Government, and an announcement of the action the United States had taken, the Security Council rejected a Yugoslav motion to try mediation and adopted a resolution presented by the United States. This recommended "that the Members of the United Nations furnish such assistance to the Republic of Korea as may be necessary to repel the armed attack and to restore international peace and security in the area." This was adopted by a vote of 7–1, with Egypt and India abstaining because their delegates had not received their instructions in time for the vote.[50] The USSR was again absent.

Despite some criticism that United States action had prejudiced the freedom of decision of the Security Council, and that President Truman's order to neutralize Formosa might easily lead to complications involving others, the sentiment in the United Nations clearly favored backing up the June 25 call for a cease-fire with an appeal for collective measures to save the Republic of Korea.

On July 7, with South Korean resistance rapidly collapsing and communist capture of the entire peninsula looming, the Security Council met once more, again without Soviet presence, and recommended that all forces sent to Korea be placed under the command of the United States. The Council asked the President of the United States to designate a Supreme Commander of all United Nations forces in Korea, which he did in the person of General MacArthur.

Fifty-three Members ultimately signified their approval of the appeal for collective action to stop aggression. During the ensuing year twenty-six states offered assistance of one form or another, and combat units were accepted by the Supreme Commander from sixteen Member states.[51] Contributions of equal size were neither asked for nor expected, and they varied from field hospital units to land, naval, and air forces.

4. ASSEMBLY ACTION: CHINESE INTERVENTION. As the United Nations forces reached the 38th parallel in October, 1950, on their successful counteroffensive, a majority of the General Assembly, which had inherited the problem when the USSR had returned to the Security Council in August, thereby

---

[50] The Indian Government subsequently announced its support of the motion.
[51] See *Yearbook of the United Nations, 1950*, pp. 226–228.

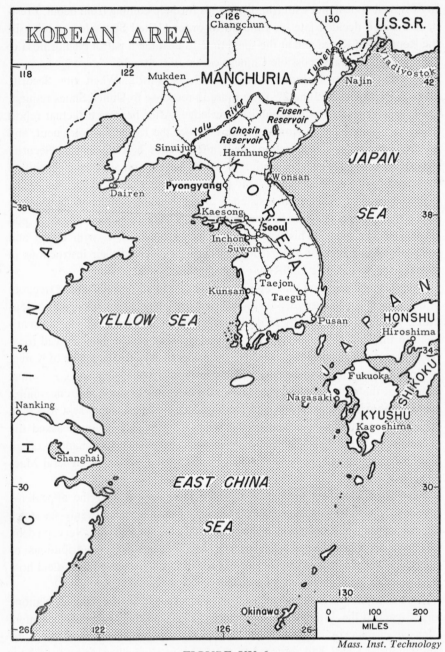

KOREAN AREA

FIGURE XX:6

blocking action, carried a resolution recommending that all appropriate steps be taken to ensure stability throughout Korea, that elections be held to unify the country, and that United Nations forces should not remain save for the achievement of these ends. This was the only United Nations political guidance provided at this particular time. The United Nations forces continued to advance north. On November 26, 1950, a full-scale Chinese communist offensive was mounted against the United Nations forces which were then compelled to retreat with heavy losses to below the 38th parallel before the front could be stabilized.

Efforts of an Arab-Asian group within the General Assembly to obtain a cease-fire agreement from Peiping achieving no success, and American opinion hardening against appeasement, the General Assembly voted on February 1, 1951, its finding that the Peiping Government had engaged in "aggression in Korea." Despite this action, dangerous cleavages opened within the ranks of the United Nations. Burma and India voted with the Soviet Bloc against the resolution. Other members of the Arab-Asian group, with Sweden added, abstained from voting. Further efforts were made between February and May, 1951, by the Good Offices Committee, set up by the Assembly resolution in February, 1951, to bring about a peaceful settlement of the war, but these also failed. When this failure had at length become apparent, and the Chinese refused to agree to any cease-fire or negotiation on acceptable terms, sentiment within the United Nations again coalesced, and the General Assembly on May 18, 1951, voted to call for the imposition of an embargo on the shipment of strategic and war materials to communist China and North Korea.

5. TRUCE NEGOTIATIONS. Virtually a year after the war had begun, Soviet delegate Malik suggested in a radio speech in New York that it might be possible to end the war. Following this speech, truce talks were initiated on July 21, 1951. These dragged on while hostilities continued along a battle line of fixed positions stretching across Korea and straddling the 38th parallel. Finally, on July 27, 1953, a cease-fire and truce agreement was signed at Panmunjom by representatives of the North Korean, Chinese communist, and United Nations commands, bringing hostilities to a close.[52] To a future peace conference the truce negotiators handed the even more difficult problems of a political settlement and ultimate achievement of the United Nations' goal of a free, democratic, unified Korea.

6. APPRAISAL OF UNITED NATIONS ACTION. The Korean War provided a number of lessons, both with respect to collective security measures and the larger aspects of world politics.

In the first place, the United Nations efforts did stop aggression. They did

[52] Texts of the agreements in *The New York Times,* July 27, 1953.

prevent the aggressors from achieving their immediate objective. This marks the first time that forces assembled by an international organization have accomplished such an end. Furthermore, the Communists were faced with an assurance given to the Republic of Korea that collective measures would again be taken if the aggression were renewed.

Secondly, although the United Nations forces did not conclude the fighting on such a basis as to achieve a unified, free, and democratic Korea, they did obtain agreement in the armistice that higher political negotiations would be held to attempt "peaceful settlement of the Korean question." In the midst of the greater conflict between East and West, none can say when agreement upon a united Korea can be attained. But the principle of peaceful settlement was conserved.

Thirdly, by assisting the Republic of Korea and forcing the Communists to engage in a major, protracted battle within Korea, the United Nations delayed and may have upset communist plans for further rapid advance in Asia. Furthermore, by discouraging communist attempts for easy military coups, the collective action in Korea may have reduced the risk of deterioration of the international situation to the point where general war would have been inevitable. For the collective effort increased the strength and working effectiveness of the powers opposing communist imperialism.

Fourthly, the political circumstances surrounding United Nations actions at the various critical stages during the war indicate that those determined to use this machinery must be prepared to improvise, to try various procedures, and at times to exercise restraint and patience for the achievement of commonly acceptable ends. Willingness to make armed forces available merely upon a recommendation rather than a formal "decision," as visualized in the Charter, was essential in a situation in which a conflict between the powers made it impossible to use the machinery as originally intended. Such procedures may not give quite the same degree of assurance as may be afforded by alliances and mutual assistance arrangements. But willingness to cooperate is the heart of any successful endeavor on the part of sovereign states.

Fifthly, the slowness with which the international force was assembled emphasizes the necessity for readiness. South Korea could not have been saved had the United States not rushed large forces of its own to Korea in the opening weeks of the war. If collective measures are to succeed, some forces must be prepared to move quickly and boldly before the opportunity of mounting an effective defense and preparing an offense is lost.

Sixthly, the Korean War demonstrated the indispensability of a supreme command for the international forces. It also revealed that difficulties can arise when policy guides are lacking or unobtainable in time of need for the

Supreme Commander. Had there been a Military Staff Committee functioning, as intended by the framers of the Charter, the needs of the field commander for political guidance might possibly have been better anticipated. On the other hand, the ineffectiveness of committee action might have made the situation even less satisfactory. In the absence of such a functioning agency, diplomacy and improvisation are the only answer.

Seventhly, the devastation which occurred in Korea and the casualties suffered by the United Nations forces—over 139,000 in United States forces alone—show that the cost of resisting aggression may be very high even when collective measures are employed in a "limited war." One cannot count on restoring peace inexpensively through military action merely because collective measures are employed. The brunt of that action will always fall initially on states with ready forces. Nor can nations afford to think that since aggression was made not to pay in the Korean experience there will be no further threats to peace and security. The preservation of peace and security, like liberty, requires eternal vigilance and readiness to act to stop violations whenever and wherever they may occur.

Finally, the political complications which President Rhee caused during the truce negotiations by releasing prisoners of war and later by threatening to carry on the war alone or to recommence hostilities if his wishes were not respected, underline the delicacy and difficulty of proper handling of relations between the nation being defended and those who are rendering it assistance and providing the United Nations forces.

All told, the United Nations action showed in the Korean affair that aggression can be stopped by collective effort handled with the assistance of a general international organization, even when there is conflict among the major powers and some differences among the peace-desiring nations. But the experience also revealed in no uncertain terms that forcing an aggressor to cease armed action can be costly and hazardous and that the solution of the underlying political issues cannot be guaranteed merely by the maintenance or enforcement of peace. The Korean case holds promise, nevertheless, that the United Nations can be made to succeed where the League failed, and that it can serve as a useful instrument in support of national policy.[53]

ECONOMIC AND SOCIAL ACTIVITIES OF THE UNITED NATIONS

Economic and Social Council. The Economic and Social Council (ECOSOC) is the third principal organ of the United Nations. It is composed of

[53] For analyses of the United Nations and the Korean War see Leland M. Goodrich, "Korea: Collective Measures against Aggression," *Internat. Conciliation*, Oct., 1953; Norman J. Padelford, "The United Nations and Korea, a Political Résumé," *Internat. Organization*, Nov., 1951.

eighteen members elected by the General Assembly on a three-year basis.[54]

1. POWERS AND FUNCTIONS. The general purpose of ECOSOC is to bring together within the compass of one organ of the international organization the consideration of questions relating to matters of an economic and social nature that are of mutual interest to many nations and to correlate through this organ the programs of specialized international agencies which have been established to deal with specific aspects of these matters.

The powers of ECOSOC enable it to (1) initiate studies and reports, (2) make recommendations to the General Assembly, to Members, and to the specialized agencies, (3) prepare draft conventions, and (4) call international conferences on matters relative to international economic, social, and humanitarian cooperation. ECOSOC may also (5) enter into agreements with specialized agencies, bringing them into relationship with the United Nations. And it may (6) coordinate their activities and (7) obtain reports from them.

It has been said that ECOSOC is one of the hardest working organs of the United Nations. It frequently has an agenda which requires many months of debate in order to arrive at agreed conclusions and recommendations. Much of its time is taken up with debates, with committee work, with hearing the reports from the specialized agencies and its own numerous subcommissions, and with passing recommendations. It is subordinate to the General Assembly in that it may be called upon by the Assembly to perform additional services. And it must report each year to the Assembly.

2. REGIONAL ECONOMIC COMMISSIONS. To further the study and solution of economic problems of especial concern to states situated in particular regional areas, ECOSOC has established a group of regional economic commissions. These include an Economic Commission for Europe (ECE), an Economic Commission for Asia and the Far East (ECAFE), and an Economic Commission for Latin America (ECLA). These bodies, composed of representatives of states situated in the regions mentioned, together with the United States, meet within the areas concerned. They make surveys and basic studies of economic conditions. They seek to promote trade. ECAFE in particular has attempted to help the underdeveloped countries of South and Southeast Asia to obtain needed technical assistance. For the most part they have made a distinctive and useful contribution to attacking fundamental economic problems.[55]

---

[54] See Herman Finer, *The United Nations Economic and Social Council* (Boston, 1946); A. Vandenbosh and W. N. Hogan, *The United Nations, Background, Organization, Functions* (New York, 1952), chs. 10, 17.

[55] For a concise analysis of the regional commissions see *Everyman's United Nations*, pp. 65–74. The activities of these commissions are summarized in *Internat. Organization*; also in the *Yearbooks of the United Nations*.

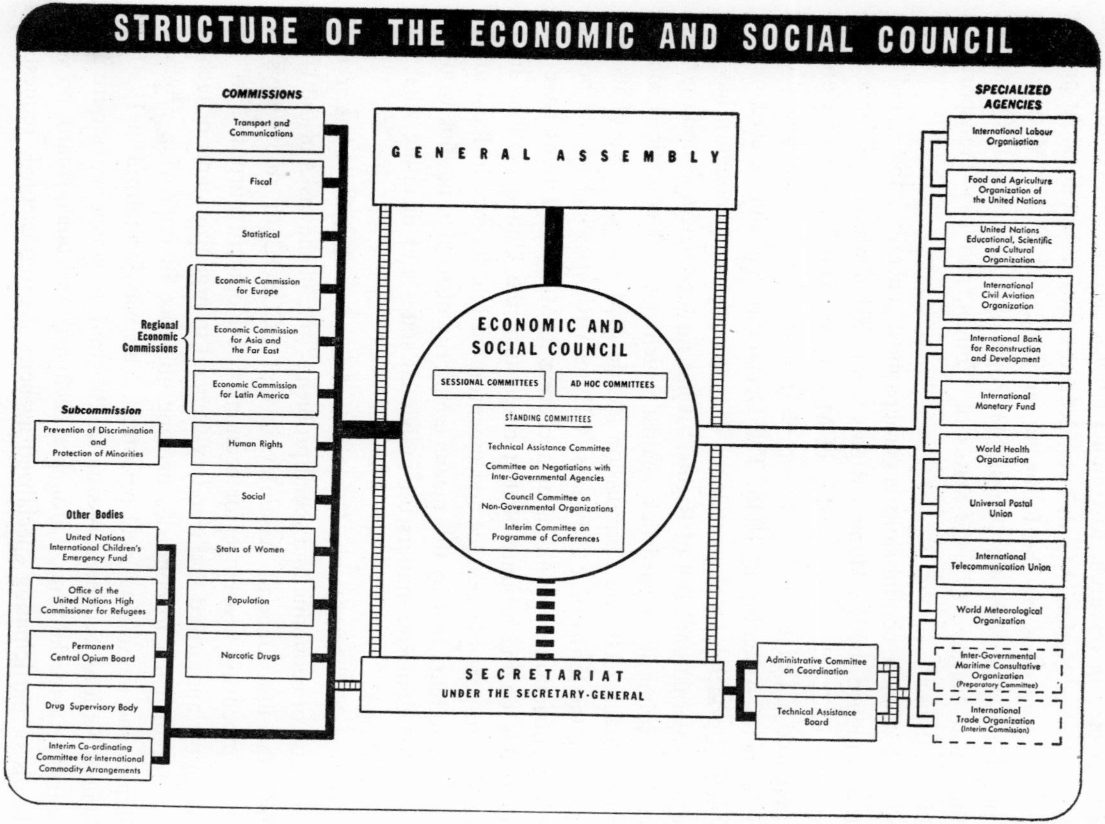

STRUCTURE OF THE ECONOMIC AND SOCIAL COUNCIL

FIGURE XX:7

The United Nations

589

3. FUNCTIONAL COMMISSIONS. A sizable part of the activity taking place under ECOSOC is carried on by nine commissions which have been established to engage in research, to conduct studies and to help coordinate the interests of United Nations Members on defined topics or functions. At present there are commissions on the following subjects: (1) Fiscal Matters, (2) Human Rights, (3) Narcotic Drugs, (4) Population, (5) Social Questions, (6) Statistical Matters, (7) the Status of Women, and (8) Transport and Communications.[56]

The work of these commissions is perhaps most generally known, and to an extent exemplified, by the Human Rights Commission which was for a number of years under the chairmanship of Mrs. F. D. Roosevelt. This Commission prepared a Universal Declaration of Human Rights which was adopted by the General Assembly in 1948. The Declaration contains a statement of fundamental principles and a catalogue of human rights. Although it has been called an "International Bill of Rights," it has no binding force upon governments. It is primarily a yardstick against which national conditions may be compared. Since 1948 the Commission has devoted a large share of its time to discussing the terms of a Covenant of Human Rights which would become a binding obligation upon all states accepting it. Many objections have been raised to this on the grounds that it could turn the United Nations into a device for irresponsible charges and unwarranted interference in local affairs. There are also fears that by this means a majority of foreign nations would be legislating on domestic matters for individual states and dictating what their laws should be.[57]

4. TECHNICAL ASSISTANCE. Conscious of the fact that the Charter made the "solution of economic and social problems" one of the tasks of the United Nations, the first General Assembly invited ECOSOC to study ways and means of procuring assistance for economic development purposes. In 1948 the Assembly authorized the Secretary-General to organize teams of technical experts for dispatch to countries needing guidance in improving productive techniques and in training local personnel. This was formalized in 1950 into the United Nations Technical Assistance Program, to which states were asked to contribute a special fund. Through a Technical Assistance Board, on which the heads of participating specialized agencies are represented, requests for

---

[56] See A. Loveday, "Suggestions for the Reform of the United Nations Economic and Social Machinery," *Internat. Organization*, Aug., 1953.

[57] See H. F. Angus, "The Dangers of Declaring Human Rights," *Canadian J. Econ. and Pol. Sci.*, May, 1951; A. Martin, "The Universal Declaration of Human Rights," *World Affairs*, July, 1949; Charles Malik and Mrs. F. D. Roosevelt, "The Covenant of Human Rights," *United Nations Bulletin*, July 1, 1949; James Simsarian, "Economic, Social, and Cultural Provisions in the Human Rights Covenant," *Department of State Bulletin*, June 25, 1951; Edgar Turlington, "The Human Rights Commission at the Crossroads," *Am. J. Int. Law*, July, 1951.

technical assistance are passed upon and arrangements are made for appropriate teams of experts to be assembled from specialized agencies such as the Food and Agriculture Organization and the World Health Organization. The numbers of requests for assistance in sharing and diffusing agricultural, industrial, sanitation, irrigation, and other techniques and skills have imposed a heavy burden upon the United Nations, taxing not only staffs but also the modest funds of less than twenty million dollars that have been made available by Member states for this activity.

Like the Point Four Program of the United States, the United Nations Technical Assistance Program aims "to help people to help themselves." The acceptance of technical assistance through an international organization rather than directly from the aid program of some large state has an appeal to some of the peoples of the Middle East and Asia who have won their freedom from colonial rule in recent times. The chief problem lies in assembling sufficient funds to underwrite such a program and to support long-range development projects which do not produce a capital return and may therefore fall outside the scope of the International Bank for Reconstruction and Development.[58]

INTERNATIONAL TECHNICAL COOPERATION

Some of the most constructive efforts carried on in conjunction with the United Nations are performed in the field of international technical cooperation by certain Specialized Agencies. These are not to be confused with the Technical Assistance Program, although some of these agencies do participate therein.

The Specialized Agencies. The Specialized Agencies are in effect intergovernmental organizations created by separate international conventions to deal with international problems of a technical or functional nature. Several of the Specialized Agencies are in reality international service bureaus or coordinating agencies dating back to the last part of the nineteenth century or early decades of the present. Of this type are the Universal Postal Union, the International Telecommunications Union, and the International Labor Organization. The others, including the Food and Agriculture Organization (FAO), the International Bank for Reconstruction and Development (IBRD), the International Monetary Fund (IMF), the International Civil Aviation Organization (ICAO), the World Meteorological Organization, the Intergovern-

---

[58] The United Nations is contemplating the establishment of a Special Fund for Economic Development to assist in such projects. On the Technical Assistance Program see Peter and Dorothea Franck, "Implementation of Technical Assistance," *Internat. Conciliation,* Feb., 1951; David Mitrany, "The International Technical Assistance Program," *Proceedings Acad. Pol. Sci.,* Jan., 1953; A. D. K. Owen, "The Technical Assistance Programme of the United Nations," *Pol. Q.,* Oct.–Dec., 1951.

mental Maritime Consultative Organization (Preparatory Committee), the United Nations Educational, Scientific and Cultural Organization (UNESCO), and the World Health Organization (WHO), have their own specific functions and have come into existence since 1943.

Through these so-called Specialized Agencies, several of which have been brought into relationship with the United Nations through special agreements with ECOSOC, matters of common interest are explored and efforts are made to facilitate the conclusion of international agreements that will coordinate and thus promote the interests of all members.[59]

Space does not permit a detailed examination of all the Specialized Agencies. We have already discussed two of the Agencies in the field of financial and economic cooperation—the International Bank for Reconstruction and Development and the International Monetary Fund—in Chapter IV. Accordingly, we will discuss, by way of illustration, social and health agencies in the following sections.

1. SOCIAL WELFARE. Among the Specialized Agencies concerned in one way or another with social welfare, the International Labor Organization is outstanding. We have already mentioned this organization in conjunction with the League of Nations. The ILO has continued unchanged since World War II and has been brought into relationship with the United Nations in such a way that it is assured considerable autonomy of action.

Among its activities have been attempts to promote agreement on minimum wage regulation; the adoption of a Model Code of Safety Regulations in Industrial Establishments; the preparation of similar codes for coal miners, for civil engineering works, and for the chemical and textile industries; aid in settling specific international labor disputes, such as the dispute in 1948 between the International Transport Workers' Federation and certain vessels of Panamanian registry; cooperation in the United Nations Technical Assistance Program in the development of facilities for technical training and international exchange of trainees.

Quiet and unsensational as its everyday work is—a work that seldom makes the headlines—the ILO nevertheless has performed a most valuable service which has contributed to the welfare and just treatment of the working people in many lands.[60]

2. PUBLIC HEALTH. Another example of the Specialized Agencies functioning in relation to the United Nations is afforded by the World Health

59 For an authoritative summary description of these agencies see United Nations Dept. of Public Information, *Handbook of the United Nations and the Specialized Agencies* (Lake Success, 1949). See also Vandenbosh and Hogan, *op. cit.*, ch. 19.

60 See J. Fried, "Relations between the United Nations and the International Labor Organization," *Am. Pol. Sci. Rev.*, Oct., 1947; O. Morse, "Peace on a Basis of Social Justice," *United Nations Bulletin*, Jan. 1, 1950; E. Phelan, "ILO: Record and Prospects," *ibid.*, Jan. 1, 1948.

Organization. Drawing on the years of international cooperation on health problems, a new World Health Organization was established in 1946 to supersede the League Health Organization and other international public health agencies. The aim of this organization is to make an integrated, cooperative attack upon health problems on a world-wide basis. In particular, WHO has focused attention on three general problems: maternal and child health, nutrition, and environmental sanitation. It is also responsible for promoting recreational facilities, better housing and working conditions, and the prevention of accidental injuries. It is also expected to stimulate efforts to eradicate epidemic and endemic diseases, and to foster activities in the field of mental health. Within this field, WHO has concentrated upon three critical diseases: malaria, tuberculosis, and venereal disease. In addition, it has studied improved administrative and social techniques affecting public health and medical care. WHO's budget, like that of every other United Nations agency, is dependent on contributions from Member states.

The World Health Organization has enjoyed virtual universality of membership with some seventy-nine countries participating in it, and many non-self-governing territories having associate membership. At the same time, it has been beset with difficulties. It has suffered from insufficient funds, and like most United Nations efforts it has been affected and restrained by world political tensions.[61]

Coordination. The Charter provides that the Economic and Social Council shall coordinate the plans and activities of all Specialized Agencies brought into relation with the United Nations by acting as a central international clearing-house. This is accomplished chiefly in two ways. The agreements between ECOSOC and the Specialized Agencies generally provide for reciprocal representation. Representatives of ECOSOC participate, without vote, in the meetings of the governing bodies of the Specialized Agencies, and vice versa. In the second place, ECOSOC may propose items for inclusion on the agenda of any Specialized Agency, and vice versa, and each agency must report annually to the United Nations through ECOSOC.[62]

---

[61] See C. E. Allen, "World Health and World Politics," *Internat. Organization,* Feb., 1950; Charles S. Ascher, "Current Problems in the World Health Organization's Program," *Internat. Organization,* Feb., 1953; Dr. Brock-Chisholm, "Barriers to World Health," *Internat. Conciliation,* May, 1953.

[62] See Carnegie Endowment for International Peace, United Nations Studies No. 2, *Coordination of Economic and Social Activities* (New York, 1951).

On ICAO see Virginia Little, "Control of International Air Transport," *Internat. Organization,* Feb., 1949.

On FAO see Horace Belshaw, "The Food and Agriculture Organization of the United Nations," *ibid.,* June, 1947; N. Dodd, "Turning Point in World Food Situation," *United Nations Bulletin,* Jan. 1, 1950.

On UNESCO see C. Ascher, "The Development of UNESCO's Program," *Internat. Organization,* Feb., 1950; R. Niebuhr, "The Theory and Practice of UNESCO," *ibid.,* Feb., 1950; F. C.

Conclusion. It is not easy to assess the record of the United Nations and its affiliated agencies in the fields of economic, social, and technical cooperation. The institutions of international cooperation have been handicapped by the disequilibrium resulting from the last war and from the conflict between the communist and the noncommunist world. The accomplishments of human welfare agencies and of instrumentalities for cooperation in technical matters cannot be judged by any absolute standard. Human needs are diverse and changing, and the manifold problems of international relations impinging upon them are exceedingly complex and difficult to deal with at a time when nationalism is rife in many parts of the world. The task of coordination among the many existent agencies has become increasingly difficult as the numbers of agencies and commissions have grown and as the problems raised before the separate agencies and before the Economic and Social Council itself have multiplied.[63]

No lack of diligence has been exhibited among the delegates and individuals who have worked with these institutions. In spite of acrimonious debates and political maneuvering, a willingness to recognize mutual interests and to work constructively for solutions of many economic and social problems exists in no small measure. The belief of Sir John Boyd-Orr, Nobel Prize winner and former head of FAO, that changing social needs can be met and peace achieved only if all peace-desiring nations "cooperate as equals through the United Nations, on a global scale, to abolish hunger, poverty, disease and bring men into a new era of economic prosperity," points the pathway along which further progress depends.[64] Nevertheless, the outlook is not entirely optimistic. President Hernan Santa Cruz of the Economic and Social Council remarked in 1951 that little appreciable progress has been made in respect to fundamental human rights, but on the contrary, "the area of individual liberty has been reduced, freedom of information is losing ground, forced labor is practiced openly, racial discrimination is increased." [65]

Although the ultimate testing of the United Nations will undoubtedly occur

---

Dunn, *War and the Minds of Men* (New York, 1952); W. H. C. Laves, "UNESCO and the Achievement of Peace," *Pol. Q.* (London), April–June, 1951.

On Inter-Governmental Maritime Consultative Organization see *Yearbook of the United Nations, 1947–1948,* pp. 969–971. ·

On International Refugee Organization (now dissolved) see Rene Ristelhueber, "The IRO," *Internat. Conciliation,* April, 1951.

On International Telecommunications Union see *Yearbook of the United Nations, 1947–1948,* pp. 924–932.

On World Meteorological Organization see *ibid.*

[63] Walter R. Sharp, "The Specialized Agencies and the United Nations, Progress Report I," *Internat. Organization,* Sept., 1947, p. 474.

[64] J. Boyd-Orr, "A Challenge to Civilization," *The Nation,* May 20, 1950.

[65] Report of the Economic and Social Council, Aug. 16, 1950, to Sept. 21, 1951 (Geneva, 1951).

with respect to its ability to maintain peace and security, it does remain true that any achievement which contributes to human welfare, by allaying misery and reducing unrest, is desirable in itself and may contribute in the long run toward an elimination of some of the seeds of strife. In this sense, the arousing of the world's consciousness of the existence of suffering, injustice, and need and the attempt to bring about international cooperation for the alleviation of these problems are useful steps in promoting peace and security. If nations can cooperate for the elimination of disease, for developing backward areas, for improving working conditions, and for facilitating communications because they have realized it is to their advantage to do so, it is conceivable that they may be able to discover bases upon which they will be able to deal peacefully with some of the more difficult problems of international political relationships.

TRUSTEESHIP SYSTEM

One of the salient features of the United Nations is the trusteeship system, successor to the League of Nations mandate system, which applies the principle of "trusteeship" to the administration of certain territories once mandates and to other territories (principally the Pacific islands) separated from the Axis Powers in World War II.

Declaration on Non-Self-Governing Territories. Under the influence of some of the smaller states, Chapter XI was inserted into the United Nations Charter containing a Declaration of Principles with respect to the administration of colonial and dependent areas generally. In accordance with this declaration, Member states recognize that the interests of the inhabitants of these territories must be regarded as paramount; that their well-being must be promoted; that steps are to be taken for their economic, social, educational, and political advancement; and that they are to be assisted in the development of "free political institutions." The United Nations is given no power to enforce this declaration, but the Member states having non-self-governing territories do agree to transmit reports on their administration to the United Nations.[66]

Trusteeship Provisions. For territories which may be placed under trusteeship, in accordance with special agreements entered into by the administering states with the United Nations, certain specific obligations are laid down and oversight of the system as a whole is reposed in the hands of the Trusteeship Council which is one of the principal organs of the United Nations.

[66] See "International Responsibility for Colonial Peoples, the United Nations and Chapter XI of the Charter," *Internat. Conciliation,* Feb., 1950; Department of State Publication 2812, *The United States and Non-Self-Governing Territories* (Washington, 1947); Ernst B. Haas, "The Attempt to Terminate Colonialism: Acceptance of the United Nations Trusteeship System," *Internat. Organization,* Feb., 1953.

1. OBJECTIVES AND OBLIGATIONS. Chapter XII of the Charter ordains certain general objectives which are to be held in view of the administration of territories under trusteeship agreements. These resemble but go farther than the provisions contained in the Declaration of Principles for Non-Self-Governing Territories mentioned above. The general objectives are declared to be: (1) the furtherance of peace and security; (2) advancement of the inhabitants and their "progressive development towards self-government or independence"; (3) encouragement of human rights; and (4) assurance of equal treatment in social, economic, and commercial matters for all Members of the United Nations.

A departure was made from the League mandate system in four important respects. In the first place, trusteeship powers are permitted to fortify and have military establishments in their trust territories. In the second place, the system allows certain areas to be designated "strategic areas," for which special restrictive arrangements may be made for security purposes. For these areas the United Nations functions are placed in the hands of the Security Council instead of in the Trusteeship Council. In the third place, the Trusteeship Council is given authority to provide for periodic visits to trust territories to obtain its own impressions of their administration and progress. In the fourth place, the Trusteeship Council is composed of government representatives rather than of experts on colonial administration, as was the League Mandates Commission.

2. AREAS UNDER TRUSTEESHIP. Although the Charter makes provision for the placement of territories other than the former League mandates and territories detached from former enemy states at the end of World War II under trusteeship, the territories now under trusteeship are limited to these categories as noted on the accompanying chart.[67] Most, but not all, of the League mandates have become trust territories. Lebanon, Syria, and Palestine have become independent states and Members of the United Nations. The Union of South Africa has refused to submit its mandate over Southwest Africa for trusteeship and claimed a right to annex it. This has been contested by other states, and in 1950 the International Court of Justice in an advisory opinion held that the status of such a territory could be changed only by international agreement.[68]

3. TRUSTEESHIP COUNCIL. The Trusteeship Council, which is one of the principal organs of the United Nations, is composed of representatives of all states administering trust areas, together with all permanent Members of the

[67] Texts of sample agreements will be found in *The United States and Non-Self-Governing Territories, cit. supra.* Summaries of their common features are contained in Goodrich and Hambro, *op. cit.,* pp. 448–450. Final text of agreement for United States trusteeship of Pacific Islands and implementation documents in *Decade of American Foreign Policy, cit. supra,* pp. 1031–1036.
[68] See Manley O. Hudson, "The Twenty-Ninth Year of the World Court," *Am. J. Int. Law,* Jan., 1951, pp. 11–19.

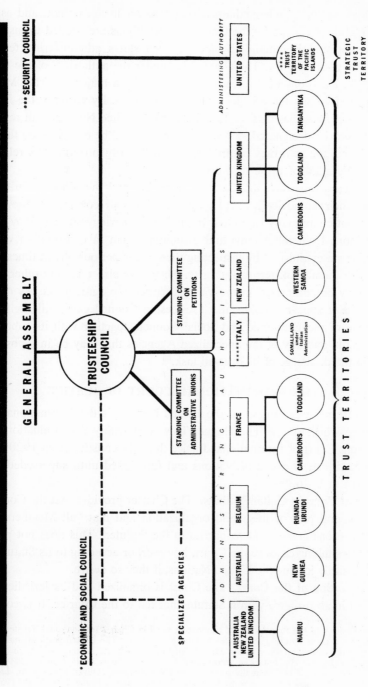

STRUCTURE OF THE INTERNATIONAL TRUSTEESHIP SYSTEM

GENERAL ASSEMBLY

*ECONOMIC AND SOCIAL COUNCIL

SPECIALIZED AGENCIES

***SECURITY COUNCIL

TRUSTEESHIP COUNCIL

STANDING COMMITTEE ON ADMINISTRATIVE UNIONS

STANDING COMMITTEE ON PETITIONS

ADMINISTERING AUTHORITY

UNITED STATES

****TRUST TERRITORY OF THE PACIFIC ISLANDS

STRATEGIC TRUST TERRITORY

ADMINISTERING AUTHORITIES

** AUSTRALIA NEW ZEALAND UNITED KINGDOM

AUSTRALIA

BELGIUM

FRANCE

*****ITALY

NEW ZEALAND

UNITED KINGDOM

NAURU

NEW GUINEA

RUANDA-URUNDI

CAMEROONS

TOGOLAND

SOMALILAND under Italian Administration

WESTERN SAMOA

CAMEROONS

TOGOLAND

TANGANYIKA

TRUST TERRITORIES

The United Nations

FIGURE XX:8

Security Council, whether administering trust territories or not, and as many other Members elected by the General Assembly as are needed to insure that the membership is equally divided between states administering territories and those which do not. The Council is "under the authority" of the General Assembly. Decisions of the Council are made by a majority of the Members present and voting; there is no veto in this Council. By virtue of the fact that the Charter prescribes that the functions of the United Nations with respect to those territories designated as "strategic areas" shall be exercised by the Security Council, the veto may be applied within that organ on matters relating to the consideration of those territories.

The means by which the General Assembly and the Trusteeship Council exercise their authority are: (1) by receiving and considering the reports which must be annually submitted by the administering states; (2) by accepting petitions from inhabitants and examining them in consultation with the governing state; and (3) by inspecting these areas periodically at times agreed upon with the administering authority. They may also take any other actions which may be authorized in the various trusteeship agreements. As occasion may make it appear suitable, the Trusteeship Council can avail itself of the assistance of the Economic and Social Council, together with its subordinate commission, and any of the Specialized Agencies that may be in a position to assist in the discharge of its over-all task.[69]

THE INTERNATIONAL COURT OF JUSTICE

The fifth principal organ of the United Nations is the International Court of Justice which sits at The Hague. This is in reality a continuation of the Permanent Court of International Justice that was constituted in 1920 in conjunction with the League of Nations and functioned until superseded by the new court in 1946.[70]

Place of Court in United Nations. The Charter provides that the Court shall be an integral part of the world organization and that "all Members of the United Nations are *ipso facto* parties to the Statute." This does not preclude other states taking cases to the Court, however, or acceding to its Statute without necessarily joining the United Nations, if they so desire.

Organization of the Court. The Court is organized and its jurisdiction determined in accordance with a Statute annexed to the Charter. It is composed

69 For reviews of the functioning of the system see Liu Cheh, "International Trusteeship System," *Internat. Conciliation,* Feb., 1949; Annette Baker Fox, "The United Nations and Colonial Development," *Internat. Organization,* May, 1950; Vandenbosh and Hogan, *op. cit.,* ch. 11, 18.

70 See Manley O. Hudson, *The Permanent Court of International Justice, 1920–1942: A Treatise* (New York, 1943). On the present Court see especially Oliver J. Lissitzyn, *The International Court of Justice* (Carnegie Endowment for International Peace, New York, 1951); also annual review articles on the Court by former Judge Manley O. Hudson in *Am. J. Int. Law.*

of fifteen judges chosen for nine-year terms by a concurrent election in the Security Council and General Assembly from a list submitted by national groups. Only states may be parties to cases submitted to the Court for adjudication. If a state which is a party to a matter before the Court does not have a judge of its own nationality on the bench, it may choose a judge to sit for it, in order that all sides may be fairly heard and considered. If it so determines, the Court may form special "chambers" to deal with particular types of cases.[71]

Competence of Court. The jurisdiction of the Court "comprises all cases which the parties refer to it and all matters specially provided for in the Charter of the United Nations or in treaties and conventions in force." In addition, the General Assembly and the Security Council, as well as other organs and Specialized Agencies authorized by the Assembly, may request the Court to give an advisory opinion "on any legal question."

At San Francisco there were some strongly expressed opinions in favor of giving the new Court compulsory jurisdiction over all legal disputes of certain kinds. The United States, the Soviet Union, and some other states indicated, however, that they were not ready at that time to take such a step. Therefore, it was provided in Article 36 of the Statute that those states which wished to do so might make a special declaration accepting compulsory jurisdiction in relation to disputes with any other declaring state. Many Members of the United Nations have made declarations recognizing compulsory jurisdiction of the Court with reference to legal disputes. Many of the declarations are so hedged about with reservations that admission of compulsory jurisdiction is strictly limited.[72] The cases which have come before the Court are already numerous, thereby indicating that the Court fills an important place in the international organization of the society of states. Its special contribution is, of course, in the area of furthering pacific settlement of international disputes of a legal nature and in giving opinions which may assist in the extension and development of international law and order.[73]

Codification and Development of International Law. Reference should be made in passing to the not unrelated work being carried on by the International Law Commission established by the General Assembly in 1947. This body of fifteen eminent jurists has been surveying the field of international law with a view to determining necessary topics for study and suitable projects for possible codification. Its studies are essentially of a long-range nature and

[71] Following World War II and the war-crime trials, some steps were taken looking toward the possible creation of an international criminal court. See Yuen-li Liang, "The Establishment of an International Criminal Jurisdiction: First Phase," *Am. J. Int. Law,* Jan., 1952.

[72] At the close of 1952 declarations had been made by thirty-four states.

[73] Summaries of the Court's decisions and opinions will be found in Judge Hudson's annual reviews mentioned above, also in the *International Court of Justice Yearbooks.*

include such matters as the law of treaties, territorial waters, and arbitral procedure. One of its most fruitful contributions has been the formulation of a Draft Declaration of Rights and Duties of States, submitted by the General Assembly to states for approval.[74] Activities of this sort are conducted on the premise that, as the area of agreement among nations on the substance of international law can be enlarged, readiness to submit legal disputes to judicial settlement will also be enhanced, and thus the cause of law and order will be advanced.

SECRETARIAT

The Secretariat is the principal administrative agency of the United Nations. The Secretary-General, the chief administrative official, is chosen by the General Assembly on the recommendation of the Security Council. The staff of the Secretariat is chosen by the Secretary-General under regulations established by the General Assembly. Staffs are assigned to each of the organs of the United Nations. Persons joining the Secretariat are expected to act as international civil servants and are given a status as such.

In the over-all functioning of the world organization, the Secretariat plays an important role, gathering, publishing, and distributing essential factual data and information, preparing special studies on international problems, and servicing the multitude of meetings and conferences held under the auspices of the United Nations. Although the work of the Secretariat attracts few headlines, effective functioning of the United Nations would be quite impossible without its daily services.[75]

THE UNITED NATIONS IN THE CONTINUITY OF HISTORY

The structure which has been reared by the United Nations Charter is an adaptation to the political world of today of ideas and methods of international cooperation which have been in the process of growth and experiment over a long period of time. It is fundamentally in keeping with the ideals of pacific settlement, collective security, and international cooperation in the political, social, economic, and technical fields which underlay the League of Nations. It represents in part an attempt to improve upon the organizational forms and procedures of the League for execution of these ideals. In part, the United

---

[74] See *Survey of International Law in Relation to the Work of Codification of the International Law Commission,* UN General Assembly, International Law Commission (Lake Success, 1949). See *Yearbooks of the United Nations* for reviews of progress.

[75] See S. M. Schwebel, *The Secretary-General of the United Nations: His Political Powers and Practice* (Cambridge, 1952); W. R. Crocker, "Some Notes on the United Nations Secretariat," *Internat. Organization,* Nov., 1950; Bernard Moore, "The Secretariat: Role and Functions," in Clyde Eagleton (ed.), *1949 Annual Review of United Nations Affairs* (New York, 1950), pp. 21–31; Vandenbosh and Hogan, *op. cit.,* ch. 12.

Nations also reflects the vagaries of power politics; it is the embodiment of what states, for reasons of their own choosing, were willing to agree upon when the Charter was drafted and have been willing to apply in practice in the years since 1945. How successful the present model will be depends in large measure upon those who compose and manipulate it. For it must always be borne in mind that, although there is an entity which we call the United Nations, and although this has a legal personality and juridical rights of its own, nevertheless the states that are the Members of the United Nations are its vital element. It is an instrumentality which they have created to supplement other means and instruments of their national policies and to assist them in attaining goals of their own foreign policies. It is the Member states who determine how the organization shall develop and in what ways it shall be employed. What they have created can be changed or abolished, as they may agree. It is they who together will determine to what extent it may become a success or a failure.

The United Nations since its founding has been faced with many complex political, economic, and social problems. It has been sharply divided within its membership since 1947. Obstructive tactics and narrow political interests have impeded its operation. Notwithstanding the impression of vast activity which the casual visitor receives on visiting the United Nations headquarters, many of the eloquent speeches which have been delivered in its meetings and many of the resolutions which have been passed by its organs have been lacking in substantive follow-up. The organization can hardly be said to have become a sure guarantor of peace and security to all states, notwithstanding its action in the Korean War. On the other hand, none of the major powers has withdrawn from membership. States not now Members exhibit a desire to join. In spite of all the heated debates, no state has publicly questioned the foundation principles of the Charter. And the Members continue to display, by and large, a determination to take leading international problems before the organs of the United Nations for discussion and action. It is conceivable that, if international tensions should be relaxed, the United Nations might become even more useful than it has been thus far and it might acquire a greater sense of durable stability.[76]

POSSIBLE AMENDMENT OF CHARTER

The United Nations Charter provides machinery for amendment and review. Amendments may be submitted at any time by any Member state. To become

[76] For a critical evaluation of the United Nations see M. Beer, "The First Seven Years of the United Nations," *Swiss Review of World Affairs*, Nov., 1952. See also Peter Khiss, *The United Nations: How and When It Works*, For. Policy Assoc., *Headline Series No. 88* (New York, 1951).

effective, they must be adopted by a vote of two-thirds of the General Assembly and be ratified by two-thirds of the Members of the United Nations, *including all* the permanent Members of the Security Council. Furthermore, the Charter provides that the Assembly and Council may call at any time for a general review conference. Article 109 specifically states that, if such a conference shall not have been called prior to the tenth annual meeting of the General Assembly (1955–1956), the proposal to convene such a conference shall be put upon the agenda of that Assembly and the conference be held if approved by a majority of the General Assembly and any seven members of the Security Council.

United States Secretary of State Dulles announced in August, 1953, that the United States would press for a review conference in accordance with the Charter provision. And steps have been initiated within the United Nations looking toward the preparation of the necessary background documentation for holding such a gathering.[77]

Hurdles to Formal Amendment. By virtue of the language employed in Article 108 of the Charter, amendments to this instrument, whatever their nature, can become effective only if they are ratified by two-thirds of the organization's Member states, including each of the Big Five (Britain, China, France, the Soviet Union, and the United States). A proposed amendment can fail if any one of these powers fails to ratify it.

With the present lack of accord among the Great Powers, the prospect of achieving any major change in the structure or powers of the United Nations through the amendment process is slight. No amendment has been acted upon thus far, and any change which would alter the delicate balance established within the organization by the San Francisco Conference would be likely to encounter resistance by one or other of the powers. Facing political realities within the United States, it is worthy of serious consideration to what extent the United States Senate may be prepared to approve changes in the Charter— or to reiterate its acceptance of the current Charter without reservations, if given an opportunity to review the matter.

If and when a review conference is held, it is conceivable that proposals will be put forward to abolish or curtail the veto power in the Security Council; to increase the permanent membership of that Council; to increase the powers of the General Assembly; to establish some form of weighted voting; to give the Security Council or the General Assembly or both organs the power to

77 Sen. Doc. No. 87, 83rd Cong., 2d. Sess., entitled *Review of the United Nations Charter: A Collection of Documents,* prepared by the Senate Foreign Relations Committee Subcommittee on the United Nations Charter (Washington, 1954), will be found exceedingly useful in this connection.

recommend terms of settlement of disputes as well as procedures; to increase the compulsory jurisdiction of the International Court of Justice; to broaden the scope of the provisions relating to regional arrangements and individual and collective self-defense; and to reshape the economic and social machinery. International differences are almost certain to be stimulated by any proposal for amendment.

Whatever proposals may be made to change the form or functioning of the United Nations, they will be faced with the fact that presently sensed deficiencies in the United Nations are due, only secondarily, to faulty or unintelligent draftsmanship at San Francisco in 1945. They are due primarily to the unwillingness of some states to assist the existing organization to function to the best of its capability. Few of the possible changes suggested above would be called for if Soviet imperialism and obstructive tactics were to be abandoned. The United Nations was not conceived as being capable of curing major ills among the Great Powers. It was designed on an assumption that the policies of the Great Powers did not look to aggrandizement on their own part and that differences in their policies were reasonably adjustable by peaceful means. So long as this assumption remains unrealized, tinkering with the structure of the United Nations is likely to give no adequate answer to the desire for peace and security in international politics—and might be harmful in its outcome.

Strengthening the United Nations through Usage—the "Living Charter." Under existing circumstances the most practicable course for improving the functioning of the United Nations may be usage and practice within the limits of the Charter as it now stands.

Considerable flexibility has already been introduced into the operation of the United Nations by such practices as (1) not counting abstention from voting in the Security Council as preventing the passage of a resolution, and (2) dropping controversial issues from the Security Council agenda when progress has been blocked by the use of the veto and taking them up at once in the General Assembly. Further change has been accomplished by the passage of the Uniting for Peace resolution in 1950. By this resolution an overwhelming majority of the Members agreed that the Assembly might be called into an emergency session to take up any threat to peace or act of aggression on which action may be blocked by the casting of a veto in the Security Council. By the passage of this resolution these Members also agreed that armed forces might be held available for call by the General Assembly, and they authorized the establishment of the Peace Observation Commission and the Additional Measures Commission. This action signified that over two-thirds of the Members of the General Assembly were in accord on that body's exercising, in time of emergency when the Security Council may be unable to act, a considerable part of the Security Council's responsibility for the maintenance of peace and security.[78]

Further steps which may be available to the Members of the United Nations to increase the over-all effectiveness of the world organization in international politics may include increasing the utilization of the specialized and technical agencies,[79] and further exploration of the possibilities inherent in the Charter provisions relative to regional arrangements and self-defense.[80]

WORLD GOVERNMENT

Some students of international relations have thought that a larger measure of law and order might be brought into international politics by the creation of some form of world government or international federation. The term *world government* is a somewhat ambiguous one and has been used in different ways by different persons. As we shall use it here, the term is understood to refer to the creation of some form of supranational authority having power to bind and coerce states and individuals under a system of law. The conception of world government, or international federation, implies that national sovereignty is merged into and becomes subordinate to a higher authority in at least certain defined fields or respects.[81]

Background. The idea of world government, in modern times, appears to have grown out of a combination of Woodrow Wilson's dramatic appeals for a world order based on reason and organization, the pacifist movement of the 1920's and 1930's with its emphasis on "abolition of war," disarmament and peaceful settlement of disputes, and the failure of the League of Nations to stop aggression. Clarence Streit's book entitled *Union Now,* first published in 1939,[82] contributed to public thinking on this subject. In this volume Streit proposed a union of the North Atlantic democracies in the five fields of (1) government and citizenship, (2) defense, (3) customs, (4) currency and finance, and (5) postal and communication systems. He urged that the "union

---

[78] See Leland M. Goodrich, "Development of the General Assembly," *Internat. Conciliation,* May, 1951, pp. 277–281. See also Salo Engel, "*De Facto* Revision of the Charter of the United Nations," *J. of Pol.,* Feb., 1952.

[79] See David Mitrany, "Functional Approach to World Government," *Internat. Affairs,* July, 1948.

[80] See next chapter.

[81] On world government see Crane Brinton, *From Many One* (Cambridge, 1948); A. C. Ewing, *The Individual, the State and World Government* (New York, 1947); Grenville Clark, *A Plan for Peace* (New York, 1950); G. J. Mangone, *The Idea and Practice of World Government* (New York, 1951); P. McGuire, *Experiment in World Order* (New York, 1948); Oscar Newfang, *World Government* (New York, 1942); F. L. Schuman, *The Commonwealth of Man* (New York, 1952).

[82] C. E. Streit, *Union Now* (New York, 1939). The current edition is entitled *Union Now: A Proposal for an Atlantic Federal Union of the Free* (New York, 1949).

of these few peoples in a great federal republic" be built upon "their common democratic principle of government" in order to safeguard their individual freedom from the threat of totalitarianism.

Approaches to World Government. World government proposals can generally be distinguished as falling into one of two categories: (1) those that would proceed through the development of functional organizations, and (2) those that advocate some form of political federation directly and immediately.

There is a school of thought which believes that as states gain benefits through cooperation in technical international organizations—such as those dealing with public health, transport and communication, fair labor practices, and so forth—they will become prepared to set up international institutions with executive and legislative powers which pull together the established functional relationships under one supranational control and extend this control to political relationships.

Several private groups hold the belief that nations sharing similar political ideals should seek to enter into super-federations based upon the constitutional system of the United States. This approach is illustrated by the ideas of such groups as the United World Federalists, the Committee to Frame a World Constitution, the Culbertson Quota Force Plan group, and the Committee on Atlantic Union. The concept of proceeding by the extension of American federal principles to the unification of groups of nations is present in all the above-mentioned proposals with variations.[83]

Pros and Cons of World Government Idea. Those favoring some move toward world government variously argue that (1) men must take extraordinary steps in the immediate future if extermination in a nuclear war is to be avoided; (2) war cannot be prevented so long as the world is divided into sovereign states free to engage in competitive armaments races and to decide whom and when to attack; (3) the peacefully inclined democracies can survive totalitarian aggression only if they are united; (4) the United Nations is not strong enough or designed for the event of a war among the Great Powers; (5) only world federation or world domination by one power (which is not acceptable to other powers) can prevent the outbreak of another world war.

Those who oppose world federation or government hold that (1) this concept threatens national independence, sovereignty, and civil liberties; (2) world problems cannot be solved by a single organizational device struck off hastily and tying the hands of governments; (3) efforts to redistribute national

---

[83] Cord Meyer, Jr., *Peace and Anarchy* (Boston, 1949), describes the United World Federalists' stand. For information regarding the Committee to Frame a World Constitution, a Draft Constitution may be obtained from the Committee at the University of Chicago. Ely Culbertson's plan is outlined in his book, *Total Peace: What Makes Wars and How to Organize Peace* (Garden City, 1943). Views of the Committee on Atlantic Union are to be found in *Atlantic Union News*, a monthly bulletin, and also in the periodical, *Freedom and Union*.

powers would unleash divisive forces that would be dangerous to peace and security; (4) time is needed to work out sound moves that will have popular support and that will not raise false or illusory hopes; (5) world government could lead to world totalitarianism and dictatorship unless extreme care is taken to provide adequate safeguards; (6) the full possibilities of the United Nations have not yet been exhausted and much can be done if states wish to make it an effective instrumentality; (7) any step that would tend to form a union excluding one of the Great Powers would be a potentially dangerous one, increasing rather than reducing the risk of atomic war; moreover, (8) there is danger of false hopes and panaceas weakening the will of people to undertake the actions which are practicable to maintain peace and security; and (9) the admitted need for better international relations does not necessarily mean that a solution is available, or that world government is a solution.

On balance, it must be said that there is as yet meagre evidence that public opinion in any of the principal states is disposed to restrict or abolish national rule in favor of world government. Few people are prepared to supersede national values that have been built up with the passage of time and common effort with some indefinite cosmic scheme whose ends cannot be seen and which holds within its bounds dangers of imposing an added layer of government of questionable utility.

EVOLUTIONARY PROGRESS ONLY PATHWAY FORWARD

Whatever its present limitations, the United Nations, as an instrumentality supplementing other instruments of national policy in the conduct of international affairs, does cater to a vital need. It is a forum for international discussion and an agency for furthering the maintenance of international peace and security and assisting international cooperation. It provides an additional channel for communication between nations over and above the normal means of traditional diplomatic intercourse. Its pronouncements do carry moral weight, and it has been able to make useful contributions not only in the economic, social, and technical fields, but in international politics as well.

John Foster Dulles has put the case for continuation of the United Nations in these words:

Nothing that is practical or desirable would be attained by destroying or undermining the United Nations or losing faith or hope in it. It is of the utmost importance to preserve an organization, almost any kind of organization, which has in its membership all the Great Powers and representation from both the Communist and non-Communist bloc. The very fact that relations between these blocs are tense, that there are many points of conflict, and that war is possible makes it all the more important to have a place where the tensions can be openly discussed, and where the differences may be fought out with words rather than bombs.[84]

The establishment of some stronger international organization, whatever its form may be, can come about on a permanent basis only upon the growth of shared aims and common values. While it is apparent that these are being evolved among some of the free nations, further progress on a universal basis can be anticipated only as the presently conflicting forces and tensions in the world may be gradually reduced. There is no magical panacea for an instantaneous solution of the complex problems facing the society of nations. Constructive progress in this area can be achieved only by a laborious and time-consuming effort to overcome the problems posed by international dealings and by the very nature of world politics itself. Moreover, there are profound values and deep roots of sentiment wrapped up in the independence and separate nationhood of each state. No one will wish to, or should, sacrifice these.

Testifying before a Senate subcommittee in 1950, the late Dr. Leo Pasvolsky, Special Adviser to the Secretary of State during World War II on the preparation of the United States position on the United Nations, stated: "What matters most in international affairs is not machinery, but attitudes and relationships. These must be conducive. Tinkering with the machinery of international organization will not solve the terrible difficulties with which mankind is faced. Only patience, hard work, ingenuity, moral and physical strength, and the will to use that strength to preserve what free men prize most can solve the dangerous problems of international relations." [85]

This we believe is the soundest guide to policy, thought, and action with respect to international organization and world politics.

SUGGESTED READINGS

Eduardo de Arechaga Jimenez, *Voting and the Handling of Disputes in the Security Council* (New York, 1950).

Crane C. Brinton, *From Many One* (Cambridge, 1948).

Viscount Robert C. Cecil, *A Great Experiment* (London, 1941).

Grenville Clark, *A Plan for Peace* (New York, 1950).

Clyde Eagleton, *International Government* (rev. ed., New York, 1948).

Herman Finer, *The United Nations Economic and Social Council* (Boston, 1946).

D. F. Fleming, *The United States and the League* (New York, 1932).

Leland M. Goodrich and Edvard Hambro, *The United Nations Charter: Commentary and Documents* (rev. ed., Boston, 1949).

[84] John Foster Dulles, *War or Peace* (New York, 1950), p. 204.

[85] Hearings held by a Subcommittee of the Senate Foreign Relations Committee on *Revision of the United Nations Charter*, 81st Cong., 2d Sess. (Washington, Sept., 1950), p. 742. These hearings contain expositions of the positions of all groups advocating at that time some change in the world organization including the various world federalists.

H. Duncan Hall, *Mandates, Dependencies and Trusteeships* (New York, 1948).

H. F. Haviland, *The Political Role of the General Assembly* (New York, 1951).

D. J. Hemleben, *Plans for World Peace Through Six Centuries* (Chicago, 1943).

Norman Hill, *International Organization* (New York, 1952).

Arthur N. Holcombe, *Human Rights in the Modern World* (New York, 1949).

Manley O. Hudson, *The Permanent Court of International Justice, 1920–1942* (New York, 1943).

Hersch Lauterpacht, *International Law and Human Rights* (London, 1950).

L. Larry Leonard, *International Organization* (New York, 1951).

Werner Levi, *Fundamentals of World Organization* (Ann Arbor, 1950).

Oliver J. Lissitzyn, *The International Court of Justice* (New York, 1951).

John McLaurin, *The United Nations and Power Politics* (London, 1951).

Gerard J. Mangone, *The Idea and Practice of World Government* (New York, 1951).

Cord Meyer, *Peace and Anarchy* (Boston, 1949).

Pittman B. Potter, *International Organization* (New York, 1951).

Alf Ross, *Constitution of the United Nations* (New York, 1950).

Frederick L. Schuman, *The Commonwealth of Man* (New York, 1952).

Stephen M. Schwebel, *The Secretary General of the United Nations* (Cambridge, 1952).

Louis B. Sohn, *Cases and Materials on World Law* (Brooklyn, 1950).

Clarence K. Streit, *Union Now* (New York, 1949).

Amry Vandenbosch and W. N. Hogan, *The United Nations: Background, Organization, Functions* (New York, 1952).

F. P. Walters, *A History of the League of Nations*, 2 vols. (London, 1952).

Quincy Wright (ed.), *World Community* (Chicago, 1948).

Sir A. Zimmern, *The League of Nations and the Rule of Law, 1918–1935* (London, 1939).

CHAPTER XXI

Regional Arrangements

THE EXPLANATION for the geographical areas and boundary lines of states must be sought in background such as the history of conquest, geographical barriers once difficult to surmount, nationalism, wars, and in some instances dynastic relationships. Once established, states have not tended to adjust boundaries to changing security, economic, cultural, and social interests by combining to form the larger units which logically seem to be demanded by these changing requirements. One recent trend has been toward fragmentation of political control as empires disintegrated after World War I and colonial dependencies achieved self-rule after World War II. Recent integrating trends have been represented, on the other hand, by the conquest policy of the Axis powers and by Soviet "satellization" and integration using the apparatus of the Communist party.

What tools and techniques of international politics are available to meet the situation in which several nations have long-standing legitimate interests in common? The normal channels of diplomacy may not alone be sufficient to handle complicated requirements such as the defense of an area containing several states. The United Nations is a global organization for furthering mutual interests. But many Members are little concerned with the problems of a distant area unless such problems represent a clear threat to world peace and hence to their own security. Political integration under one sovereignty is theoretically possible. But mutual security, economic or other problems do not necessarily give sufficient cohesion to bind peoples together under one government.

This chapter will discuss regional arrangements—those techniques by which independent states collaborate to achieve regional objectives while still maintaining national sovereignty.

PROBLEM OF DEFINITION

Definition and Scope.[1] A regional arrangement, in international politics, may be described as some form of voluntary agreement or organization established to further joint action by a group of states comprising or having an interest in some geographical area which is either generally recognized as a region or delimited by agreement.

This definition assumes that a "region" comprises more than a single political entity, and it is generally considered that an agreement should include more than two states to be genuinely "regional." The matter of exact size of a region is secondary. The term *region* is a general one and often imprecisely used.[2] The United States and Chile, for example, are considered to be in the same region, while parts, at least, of North Africa are not considered to be in the Western European region.

Regional arrangements may be established for political, security, economic, cultural, or other reasons, or for a combination of two or more of these reasons. Thus the Organization of American States has several types of objectives, and the North Atlantic Treaty mentions mutual economic interests as well as security interests. A state may be a member of several different regional arrangements having the same objective. Thus the United States is a focus for several regional arrangements having security as their primary objective.

It is generally accepted that international agreements for aggressive purposes are not "regional arrangements," at least in the sense in which the term is used in the United Nations Charter. The communist orbit is one vast ideological "region" comprising a considerable portion of the earth's surface and population, and bound together by the apparatus of the Communist party as well as by the traditional type of political arrangements. The voluntary aspect is absent in some associations, but this type of regionalism certainly must be considered in our discussion.

The United Nations and Regional Arrangements. Regional arrangements are specifically recognized in Articles 33 and 52–54 of the United Nations Charter as means for preserving international peace and security and for peaceful settlement of disputes. But, while the term *regional arrangements* is a useful one and the concept important, the situations to which it may apply are so diverse that attempts to formulate a definition in precise legal terms have been rejected at international gatherings.[3] As an example of the obscurity

1 See E. N. van Kleffens, "Regionalism and Regional Pacts," *Am. J. Int. Law,* Oct., 1949.
2 R. Hartshorne, *The Nature of Geography* (Lancaster, Pa., 1939), chs. 9–10.
3 L. Goodrich and E. Hambro, *Charter of the United Nations, Commentary and Documents* (rev. ed., Boston, 1949), pp. 310–311 citing discussions at San Francisco United Nations Conference.

surrounding the term, the North Atlantic Treaty refers to the right of collective self-defense but not to the regional arrangement clause in the United Nations Charter. Yet it is considered, at least popularly, to be a regional arrangement in the generally accepted sense of the term.

THE DYNAMICS OF REGIONALISM

We can distinguish certain definite factors tending toward closer association among states. In discussing these factors we must recognize that the influence of a particular factor, such as geographical propinquity, may have a divisive rather than a cohesive effect on the states concerned. These factors must be considered on a case-by-case basis as applied to groups of nations. No single factor should be considered alone, since the cohesive effect of one, such as geography, may be more than negated by the divisive effect of another. For example, geographically adjacent India and Pakistan are separated by historical antipathies and religious differences.

Geographical Propinquity. We see from a review of modern history, starting arbitrarily about 1500 AD, that there was initially a fairly definite tendency for the peoples of distinctive regions to move in the direction of forming first small political unions and then gradually the larger unions of the nation-states. As mentioned at the opening of the chapter, once the nation-states were formed the progress toward political union in the world tended to stop.

But there are many factors arising from geography which tend toward cohesion of peoples into nation-states and close association of nation-states in the same region. A group of states coexisting in the same subcontinent or similar area of the globe tend to have certain common experiences and outlooks toward the rest of the world. The facts of the geographical distribution of resources and industry lead toward economic interdependence among many states. Increasingly, the problems of security demand close collaboration of neighboring states. Modern weapons and methods of war ignore boundary lines and, if war starts in this day and age, can hardly avoid encroaching on states which might easily have maintained neutrality fifty years ago.

Cultural Affinity. Common racial, cultural, and religious backgrounds can be an influential factor in laying the necessary groundwork for regional cooperation. Ties of race, tongue, and Islamic faith, for example, no doubt facilitated the formation of the League of Arab States in 1945. Likewise, the similarity of the historical, linguistic, cultural, and religious roots of many of the Latin American states has contributed to their disposition to cooperate as a regional bloc.

The long history of conflict among the European states has shown that a common heritage alone is, however, seldom a sufficiently powerful catalyst to produce strong regional unity when states have been torn with suspicions and fears of one another. This is not to say that shared values cannot create or help to create the cohesiveness necessary for an organization's successful functioning. As one statesman has said: "It is a principle of political science that political organizations should not be constructed out of materials of poor cohesive qualities. Where they are so built they are held together only by buttressing, which sometimes requires greater resources than the structure itself." [4]

Desire to Handle Local Differences. A desire by a group of states to handle local or regional questions among themselves without external interference may dispose them to develop regional machinery for consultation or the pacific settlement of disputes. This has been one of the motives underlying the development of the machinery of the Organization of American States for periodic or emergency conferences and for the arbitration and pacific settlement of disputes between American Republics. Before such regional arrangements are likely to acquire much substance in usage, however, some sense of shared objectives and community of interest must develop among governments.

Economic and Political Interests. Economic and political interests are strong driving forces behind movements for regional collaboration. For example, prior to the security element introduced by the appearance of the Nazi menace in the 1930's, United States interest in Pan-Americanism rested chiefly in a hope that this would further trade and investment in Latin America and gradually provide an inter-American political orientation. Many Latin American states were interested in Pan-Americanism for what it would contribute to the enhancement of their political power in relation to the "Colossus of the North" and also in relation to preventing or reducing political pressures or intervention from any other Great Power. Benelux, which is the Belgium-Netherlands-Luxembourg mutual effort to lower trade barriers; the Organization for European Economic Cooperation and its subsidiary organization, the European Payments Union; the European Coal and Steel Community; the Council of Europe—all have economic or political objectives, or both, underlying their formation. But there is a security aspect, implicit or explicit, in almost all regional organizations, since economic strength and political unity contribute to security and support of military power. Conversely, regional arrangements seeming to have security as their primary objective are bound to have major economic aspects and, being associations of sovereign states, will usually be dominated by political considerations except in time of great tension or war.

Security. Fear is one of the primary factors promoting regional association for security purposes. Fear of the rise of a Jewish state contributed to the

[4] Lester B. Pearson, quoted in van Kleffens, *op. cit.*

formation of the Arab League; fear of communist power was the primary impetus toward the Brussels Pact and NATO. The strategy of defense and of aggression may often strain the geographic concept of regionalism. The Rio Pact, the North Atlantic Treaty, and the ANZUS Pact, as examples, span thousands of miles of distance. As mentioned before, a state's security problem is usually a specific matter of fear of a particular aggression—rather than merely a general urge for security. If only the latter, the universal United Nations organization might conceivably fulfill the requirement, and regional security arrangements directed to special needs and against particular states would be weak or nonexistent. A regional arrangement incorporating a potential enemy may, however, give increased security because of the checks placed on any aggression by provisions for pacific settlement of disputes and for sanctions by the entire group of states in case of violation of agreements. The Inter-American System, as an example, encompasses, and may serve as a check upon, several traditional animosities.

The Principle of Enlightened Self-Interest. A regional arrangement is almost certain to place some restriction on the freedom of action of any state participating therein. This aspect is a liability which means that states participate in such arrangements only if there are advantages which outweigh the restrictions. What are the advantages? They include: (1) a mechanism for consultation among states having close mutual interests as compared to the very diverse interests represented in United Nations agencies; (2) a convenient means for carrying on multilateral diplomacy; (3) a method for encouraging and arranging peaceful settlement of disputes without interpolation of outside, and perhaps basically unfriendly, parties into the matter; (4) advancing cultural and political relationships; (5) improving economic cooperation; and (6) increased security. The last two are the strong driving forces for regional organization.

In the following pages, we will examine the regional arrangements in being. This might be done under the headings of political, economic, security, and cultural. But almost every arrangement, when closely examined, incorporates some aspect of two or more of these. Hence we choose a generally geographical approach.

KEY POSITION OF UNITED STATES IN REGIONALISM

Changing from a policy of isolationism to which it adhered as late as 1940, the United States has become the "switching center" for most of the regional arrangements in the free world. There are three main reasons for this: (1) the threat of communism; (2) the nature of the security problem, which makes any combination of free nations critically weak in a stand against communism

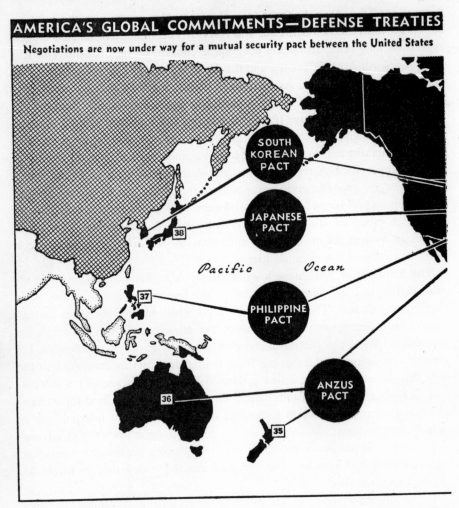

AMERICA'S GLOBAL COMMITMENTS—DEFENSE TREATIES

Negotiations are now under way for a mutual security pact between the United States

SOUTH KOREAN PACT

JAPANESE PACT

PHILIPPINE PACT

ANZUS PACT

Pacific   Ocean

FIGURE

without United States support; and (3) the interdependent world economic situation highlighted by the great dependence on United States economic policy.

United States regional relationships fall roughly into three categories: (1) actual participation in a multilateral arrangement such as the Organization of American States and NATO; (2) active encouragement, support, and even diplomatic and economic pressure toward cooperation and integration, as in the Organization for European Economic Cooperation, the European Coal and Steel Community and others; (3) a network of bilateral arrangements

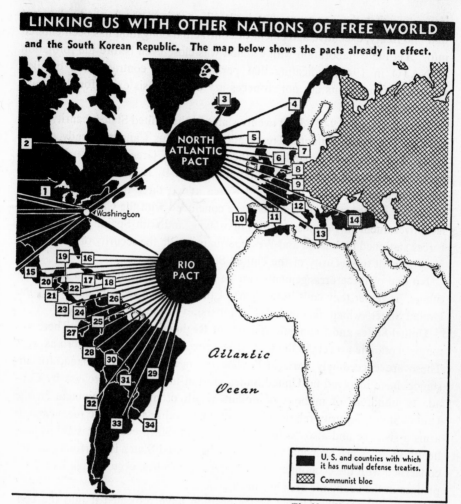

LINKING US WITH OTHER NATIONS OF FREE WORLD

and the South Korean Republic. The map below shows the pacts already in effect.

NORTH ATLANTIC PACT

RIO PACT

Washington

Atlantic Ocean

U. S. and countries with which it has mutual defense treaties.

Communist bloc

XXI:1

The New York Times, July 19, 1953

supplementing the multilateral regional arrangements, for example, with the Philippine Republic, Japan, Spain, Yugoslavia, Formosa, and others.

Regional Arrangements and United States Security. The United States, since 1947, has entered progressively into arrangements which add up to being associated with at least forty states substantially on the basis that an attack against one is an attack against all. First among these post-war arrangements may be listed the joint United States-Canadian announcement in February, 1947, of the continuation of cooperation established by the Permanent Joint Board of Defense set up by the Ogdensburg Agreement of 1940. It is interesting that the announcement in 1947 contained the explicit statement that "no treaty, executive agreement or contractual obligation has been entered into." Yet the collaboration with Canada was close even before the formation of NATO in 1949, indicating that perhaps formal contracts and detailed political arrangements are not so necessary once a basis exists for their easy achievement.

The Rio Pact in 1947 added twenty states to the United States security community. The North Atlantic Treaty added ten (plus Canada already associated). This was later expanded by the inclusion of Greece and Turkey. The pact with Australia and New Zealand added two. Bilateral arrangements with the Philippine Republic, Japan, and Korea added three more. Various types of mutual assistance arrangements were concluded with the Chinese Nationalist Government in Formosa, with Yugoslavia, and with Spain. United States forces stationed in Austria and West Germany made the security of these areas integral with the security of the United States.

No one of these arrangements can be appraised separately from all of the others. Together they constitute a part of the collective security pattern of the United States, which also includes membership in the United Nations.

United States and Economic Aspects of Regional Arrangements. There are major economic aspects to the United States collective security pattern as well. These are exceedingly variegated. The arrangements with Canada, for instance, have involved no United States aid but have meant purchase by Canada of hundreds of millions of dollars worth of military equipment in the United States. Security relationships with many other states have meant major arms assistance and also "defense support" aid. Since economic stability and health in allies are elements of security, the United States is, perforce, deeply concerned with the economic arrangements of its allies, even though its formal pledges in the economic area are most general.

The realities of the United States position have projected it into the economic affairs of regional arrangements in three principal ways:

1. The tangibles of military power are built with economic means. Hence states associated with the United States in a regional arrangement for security have to adjust their planning for support of security in the light of United States external economic policy including any United States assistance.
2. The export-import situation of the members of any regional arrangement having economic objectives, whether the United States is a member or not, is dependent on United States external economic policy and the level of activity of the United States economy.[5]

5 See ch. iv.

3. The United States policy of using trade as a security instrument—"economic warfare" in cold war—is contained in the Mutual Defense Assistance Control Act of 1951. This act provided for termination of United States assistance to any country shipping goods of primary strategic significance behind the Iron Curtain. Since United States assistance has tended to follow United States regional arrangements, this policy, somewhat unilaterally, added a new and positive use of the economic instrument to other instruments of regional arrangements involving United States assistance.

Having emphasized that the United States is an important factor, although not necessarily a formal member, in almost every regional arrangement among the free nations, we will now describe the principal existent arrangements.

REGIONALISM IN THE AMERICAS

We have mentioned on a previous page the community of action in United States-Canadian security matters growing out of the 1940 Ogdensburg Agreement. There are three formal regional arrangements in the Western Hemisphere: the Organization of American States, sometimes called the Inter-American System, the Caribbean Commission, and the Organization of Central American States.

The Organization of American States (OAS). The Inter-American Treaty of Reciprocal Assistance (Rio Pact) of 1947 and the Bogotá Charter of 1948 [6] turned the previously loosely integrated United States-Latin American system into a modern regional arrangement. This system had developed slowly over the past century as Pan-Americanism. There were infrequent Pan-American conferences throughout the nineteenth century and an increasing number of conferences, special gatherings, treaties, and conventions during the first third of the twentieth century. Latin American countries were suspicious of the United States as a result of the tremendous differential in power and because of their fear of imperialism. But after President Roosevelt's announcement of a Good Neighbor Policy in 1933, collaboration improved rapidly. The rising threat of the Axis powers led to agreement on principles of hemisphere defense, and their implementation during World War II set a foundation of association on which to base the Rio Pact and the subsequent Bogotá Charter.

The Rio Reciprocal Assistance Pact. The Rio Pact of 1947 provides for pacific settlement of disputes and defines the security arrangements of the American states. It is a defensive alliance which declares that an armed attack against any "American state" (this includes Canada by implication) is to be

[6] Texts of these two treaties are in Sen. Doc. 123, *A Decade of American Foreign Policy*, 81st Cong., 1st Sess., pp. 421–446.

considered an attack against all of them and each signatory agrees to assist in meeting this attack. The parties agree that in the event of an act of aggression there shall be a Consultative Meeting of Foreign Ministers and the Council of the OAS with power to invoke security and mutual defense measures including the use of armed force. The organization retains a World War II mechanism, the Inter-American Defense Board, and may at any time set up an advisory Defense Committee composed of the Chiefs of Staff of each state.

The "region" covered by the reciprocal assistance pact extends from North Pole to South Pole and from mid-Atlantic to the Aleutians, overlapping the

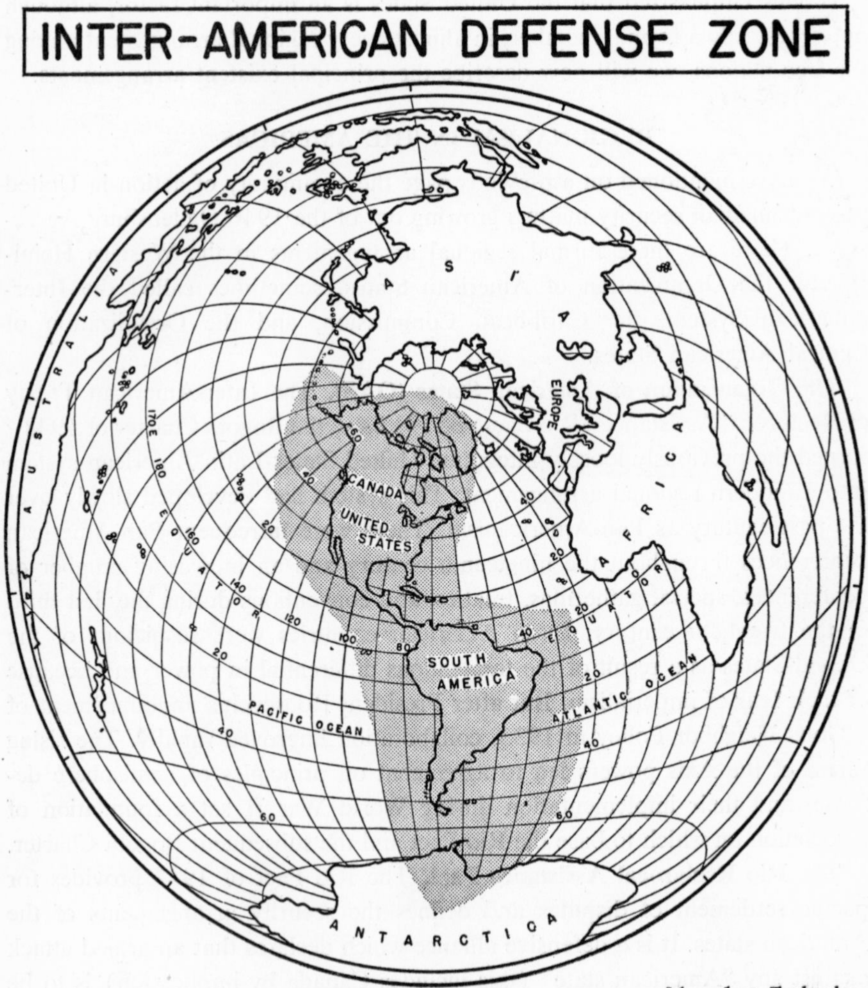

INTER-AMERICAN DEFENSE ZONE

Mass. Inst. Technology

FIGURE XXI:2

NATO area and presumably including Danish Greenland. In view of existent circumstances it is obvious that the brunt of any military action is bound to fall on the United States.

OAS Machinery. The Organization of American States, with headquarters in Washington, D.C., was formally inaugurated by an agreement at the Bogotá Conference in 1948. There is provision for a supreme organ, the Inter-American Conference, meeting every five years. Consultative meetings of Foreign Ministers, mentioned above, deal with threats to peace and security. A Council directs the secretariat which is the former Pan-American Union and supervises the functioning of three subordinate agencies—the Inter-American Economic and Social Council, the Inter-American Council of Jurists, and the Inter-American Cultural Council. There is provision for specialized conferences and agencies to deal with technical matters.

The Council of the OAS is empowered to act in behalf of the Foreign Ministers in event of an aggression until a meeting of the latter can be convened. The Council in 1949 settled a dispute arising from Costa Rican charges of invasion of its territory by Nicaragua. In 1950 the Council settled a dispute arising out of charges by the Dominican Republic that Haiti harbored insurgents planning to overthrow the Dominican Government. In the same year, it also settled a four-country (Dominican Republic, Haiti, Cuba, and Guatemala) dispute growing out of the same type of charges.[7]

The strength of the OAS at any particular time is materially dependent on the degree of political unanimity existent at that time. There are traditional antipathies and discords within it. Argentina, at times, has shown a tendency to pursue a course different from most of the other states. It did not, for instance, declare war on the Axis until 1945. But taking into account the great distances spanned by the arrangement, the differing languages and cultures, and the sometimes unstable and dictatorial governments, the Organization of American States has gotten off to a useful start.[8]

The Caribbean Commission. The United States, Britain, France, and the Netherlands set up a Caribbean Commission in 1946, as was mentioned previously in Chapter VIII. The purpose of this Commission is to promote economic and social cooperation. Its powers are purely consultative and advisory to local territorial administrations. There is a West Indian Conference, composed of delegates representative of island territories, which advises the

---

[7] See E. S. Furniss, Jr., "The Inter-American System and Recent Caribbean Disputes," *Internat. Organization,* Nov., 1950.

[8] A brief exposition of the Inter-American System is given by A. P. Whitaker in "Development of American Regionalism," *Internat. Conciliation,* March, 1951. See also W. Sanders, "The Organization of American States," *Internat. Conciliation,* June, 1948; Alberto Lleras, "The Inter-American System Today," *Annals,* July, 1952; V. Massey, "Canada and the Inter-American System," *Foreign Affairs,* July, 1948.

ORGANIZATION OF AMERICAN STATES

The International Organization of the 21 American Republics established by the Charter signed at the Ninth International Conference of American States, Bogotá, Colombia, 1948.

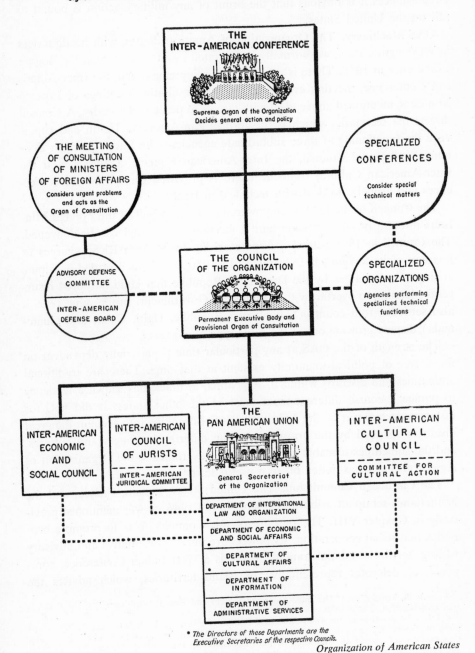

THE INTER-AMERICAN CONFERENCE

Supreme Organ of the Organization
Decides general action and policy

THE MEETING OF CONSULTATION OF MINISTERS OF FOREIGN AFFAIRS

Considers urgent problems and acts as the Organ of Consultation

SPECIALIZED CONFERENCES

Consider special technical matters

ADVISORY DEFENSE COMMITTEE

INTER-AMERICAN DEFENSE BOARD

THE COUNCIL OF THE ORGANIZATION

Permanent Executive Body and Provisional Organ of Consultation

SPECIALIZED ORGANIZATIONS

Agencies performing specialized technical functions

INTER-AMERICAN ECONOMIC AND SOCIAL COUNCIL

INTER-AMERICAN COUNCIL OF JURISTS

INTER-AMERICAN JURIDICAL COMMITTEE

THE PAN AMERICAN UNION

General Secretariat of the Organization

DEPARTMENT OF INTERNATIONAL LAW AND ORGANIZATION

DEPARTMENT OF ECONOMIC AND SOCIAL AFFAIRS

DEPARTMENT OF CULTURAL AFFAIRS

DEPARTMENT OF INFORMATION

DEPARTMENT OF ADMINISTRATIVE SERVICES

INTER-AMERICAN CULTURAL COUNCIL

COMMITTEE FOR CULTURAL ACTION

* The Directors of these Departments are the Executive Secretaries of the respective Councils.

Organization of American States

FIGURE XXI:3

Commission. The two agencies jointly sponsor a program of research for furthering economic and social objectives.[9]

Organization of Central American States. In 1951 the governments of Costa Rica, El Salvador, Guatemala, Honduras, and Nicaragua formed an Organization of Central American States by the "Charter of San Salvador." This subregional arrangement was created for the stated purpose of promoting group action and providing "an instrument for the study and solution of their common problems." [10]

EUROPEAN AND ATLANTIC REGIONAL ARRANGEMENTS

Western Europe has a tangle of overlapping regional arrangements, some of which are formally constituted; others are more informal but nonetheless close. As examples, the Scandinavian countries have long acted generally in concert on many matters, and representatives of central banks have met informally every month (except in war-time) since the early 1930's. It is an arbitrary and inexact categorization to classify the existent arrangements under the headings of politics, economics, and security. All are political in their method of operation and decision. All, except perhaps the Council of Europe, have to take into account each of the three categories of governmental operations. Having this interconnection in mind, we shall note first the arrangements primarily for economic objectives, then those primarily for security objectives, and finally those which are primarily political.

ECONOMIC AND TECHNICAL ASSOCIATIONS

European Regional Arrangements Prior to the Marshall Plan. The conventions relating to the rivers of Europe are among the longest standing international agreements in the world. The Treaty of Paris in 1814 proclaimed the principle of free navigation on international rivers, and the Congress of Vienna provided that navigation on such rivers should be regulated by common consent of the riparian states. A Central Rhine Commission was established in 1831 and has continued with modifications to the present time, now including in addition to the riparian states representatives from Britain, Belgium, and the United States. A European Danube Commission, established in 1856, brought together for nearly a century the European states interested in free

[9] The present Commission was preceded by an Anglo-American Commission inaugurated in 1942. See B. L. Poole, *The Caribbean Commission—Background of Cooperation in the West Indies* (Columbia, S. C., 1951); C. W. Taussig, "A Four Power Program in the Caribbean," *Foreign Affairs*, July, 1946; F. Stockdale, "The Work of the Caribbean Commission," *Internat. Affairs*, April, 1947; J. A. Bough, "The Caribbean Commission," *Internat. Organization*, Nov., 1949. The Caribbean Commission publishes a monthly information bulletin entitled *Caribbean Commission*.

[10] For description, see C. G. Fenwick, "The Organization of Central American States," *Am. J. Int. Law*, July, 1952.

navigation on the lower Danube, while countless International Danube Commissions created after World War II sought to promote navigation and improvements in the fluvial section of the river. The Versailles Treaty also applied the principle of free navigation to the Niemen, Oder, and Elbe Rivers. These freedoms and international cooperation were terminated by the Soviet Union with the descent of the Iron Curtain.[11]

Following World War II a series of provisional international organizations were set up to assist in getting the European economy under way again. They included an Emergency Economic Committee for Europe, a European Central Inland Transport Organization, and a European Coal Organization. These did notable work in getting the wheels of the peace-time economy turning. The Eastern European countries under Soviet control, although invited, did not participate.

Even before the end of World War II the governments of Belgium, the Netherlands, and Luxembourg (Benelux) agreed in 1944 to the principle of setting up a customs and tariff union looking toward complete economic union. Progress, however, has been slow, partly because of conflicting economic policies and partly because the effort has been overshadowed by wider endeavors discussed below.[12]

The Organization for European Economic Cooperation (OEEC). Evolving from a temporary Committee on European Economic Recovery, the participating European states set up the Organization for European Economic Cooperation (OEEC) in 1948 with the initial task of determining the capabilities of its member states and their requirements for United States aid in order to effect recovery.[13] From this beginning there has followed an unprecedented endeavor in the field of economic surveys and economic programing on an international basis.

The OEEC structure consists of a Council representing all participating countries, an Executive Committee of seven members elected by the Council to conduct business when the latter is not in session, and an International Secretariat with a Secretary-General.

The OEEC operates as a cooperative and largely consultative body. American representatives have worked closely with the OEEC but the United States

11 See Osborne Mance, *International River and Canal Transport* (London, 1945); John C. Campbell, "Diplomacy on the Danube," *Foreign Affairs*, Jan., 1949.

12 See J. van der Mensbrugghe, *Les Unions Economiques, Realisations et Perspectives* (Brussels, 1950).

13 See discussion of Marshall Plan aid in chs. iv, ix. For an extensive analysis of OEEC and other arrangements involving United States assistance, see Brown and Opie, *American Foreign Assistance* (Washington, 1953). The participating countries in OEEC are Austria, Belgium, Denmark, France, the Free Territory of Trieste, Germany (Western), Greece, Iceland, Ireland, Luxembourg, the Netherlands, Norway, Portugal, Sweden, Switzerland, Turkey, and the United Kingdom.

is not a member. Its greatest contributions have been in the areas of joint studies, development of uniform procedures and techniques for economic analysis, coordinated planning, and recommendations to participating countries. Its province has not included the internal economies of participating countries but rather trade among these countries and with other portions of the world. Starting in 1949, considerable American pressure developed for the "unification" or "integration" of Europe, using the OEEC as one of the instruments. It was not clear whether this pressure was for organic political integration of the sovereign states, many of them very diverse, or was only for the freeing and integration of intra-European trade—a mid-term objective which might be feasible.

When objectives of European economic cooperation expanded from recovery to include economic support of rearmament, the OEEC and NATO planning were bound to become interrelated. We shall discuss the relationship of these agencies presently in connection with arrangements which are primarily military.

The European Payments Union (EPU). The European Payments Union was set up by the OEEC as an international clearing arrangement for payments among OEEC states. The EPU has made a great contribution to expansion of intra-European trade but was not a substitute for convertibility of currencies. The EPU experience during its first few years also raised a definite question whether the integration of a part of Europe on a regional basis might initially create more economic problems than it solves.[14] Unlike the United States, Western Europe is not a primarily self-sufficient area.

European Coal and Steel Community. The European Coal and Steel Community is an economic regional arrangement having powers of decision lodged in its supranational organization. First proposed by French Foreign Minister Schuman in May, 1950, the "Schuman Plan" called for the creation of one free market under the direction of a supranational authority for the coal and steel industry of France and Germany and other European states joining the plan. A treaty instituting this arrangement was signed in March, 1951, by France, Western Germany, Italy, Belgium, the Netherlands, and Luxembourg —six states having coal and steel industries which are closely interrelated and can be made mutually supporting. The treaty provides for the elimination of customs barriers in the carriage of coal and steel between the adhering states; for the fixing of production quotas, price structures, and marketing operations

---

[14] Brown and Opie, *op. cit.*, p. 294. For further reading on OEEC and EPU see H. S. Ellis, *The Economics of Freedom* (New York, 1950), chs. 9–10; W. Diebold, Jr., *Trade and Payments in Western Europe* (New York, 1952), chs. 3–7, 10–12; J. H. Williams, *Economic Stabilization in a Changing World* (New York, 1953), chs. 4–9; OEEC, *European Economic Cooperation* (Paris, 1951); H. J. B. Lintott, "The Organization for European Economic Cooperation," *Internat. Organization*, May, 1949.

to the end that there may be a mutually advantageous pooling of production and marketing; and for the elimination of conflict over coal and steel among the parties.

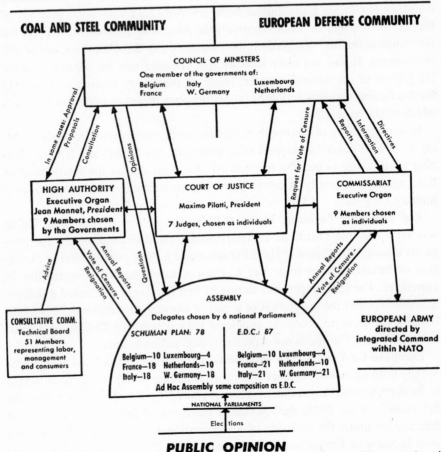

PUBLIC OPINION

FIGURE XXI:4

The ECSC treaty creates a High Authority, with headquarters at Luxembourg City, with supranational powers to enforce provisions of the agreement. Its members are chosen as individuals by the participating governments acting together, and during their tenure are not to receive instructions from or report to any government. The High Authority is responsible to a Common Assembly which is composed of representatives of the participating states on a proportional basis. This Assembly reviews the work of the High Authority annually. It may, by a two-thirds vote, force the resignation of members of the High Authority. There is also an International Court to settle disputes, a Council of Ministers to coordinate the work of the High Authority with the governmental economic policies of member countries, and a Consultative Committee to link the High Authority with employer and employee groups. Under the initial leadership of Jean Monnet, the High Authority pressed through the organizational stages of the plan so that Ruhr coal began moving across the French border to the Lorraine steel mills without the imposition of customs duties on February 10, 1953—a notable day in the annals of European regional economic cooperation.[15]

MILITARY ASSOCIATIONS OF EUROPEAN NATIONS

There are five readily identifiable groupings of European states whose purposes include military objectives. These include, among the free nations, the Brussels Pact of Western Union, NATO, the European Defense Community, and the Turkish-Greek-Yugoslav arrangements. These four are all closely integrated under NATO which is the real coordinating and operating organization for almost all the activities of the free states.[16] The Soviet system of bilateral arrangements with and among the communist states in Europe is in a separate category and will be discussed under "Communist Regionalism."

The four noncommunist arrangements have security as the primary objective. But they also have political and economic aspects. Furthermore, since military strength is founded on pillars which include economic strength, the affairs of these arrangements are inevitably entangled with those of the OEEC, the EPU, and other primarily economic associations of European states.

Western Union. The Brussels Treaty of 1948 linked Britain, France, Belgium, the Netherlands, and Luxembourg in a defensive alliance. This was inspired by the growing tension between the West and the Soviet orbit—specifically by the communist coup in Czechoslovakia in February of 1948.

Following the conclusion of the Western Union Treaty, a resolution introduced into the United States Senate by the late Senator Arthur H. Vandenberg (Senate Resolution 239) called for the "association of the United States, by constitutional process, with such regional and other collective arrangements as are based on continuous and effective self-help and mutual aid, and as affect its national security." The passage of this resolution, in hindsight, was a

15 J. A. McKesson, "The Schuman Plan," *Pol. Sci. J.,* March, 1952; W. N. Parker, "The Schuman Plan—A Preliminary Prediction," *Internat. Organization,* Aug., 1952; "Schuman Plan: Blueprint for Federalism," *The New York Times,* Sept. 14, 1952; F. Sethur, "The Schuman Plan and Ruhr Coal," *Pol. Sci. Quar.,* Dec., 1952.

16 RIIA, *Atlantic Alliance* (New York and London, 1952), contains the documents for the first three of these arrangements and is excellent reference reading for NATO matters.

formal announcement by the United States of relinquishment of its traditional security policy and adoption of a collective security policy. Negotiations led, in April, 1949, to the North Atlantic Treaty. Since then the activities of the North Atlantic Treaty Organization (NATO) have almost completely incorporated those of Western Union—although it is worth noting that the pledge in the latter treaty to act in case a signatory is attacked is more specific than that in the former.[17]

North Atlantic Treaty. The North Atlantic Treaty, signed in Washington in April, 1949, states that its purpose is the security of the North Atlantic area and the territory in Europe and North America of the signatories, including the North Polar region from the tip of Norway to the Bering Straits.[18] The arrangement was extended in late 1951 to include Greece and Turkey. The members have also agreed that French problems in Indo-China are an appropriate matter of concern to the NATO Council.

It may be argued that a region extending from the Aleutians to Kurdistan, with interests in Southeast Asia, surpasses any orthodox conception of a

THE NORTH ATLANTIC TREATY AREA

Area covered by
North Atlantic Treaty

Mass. Inst. Technology

FIGURE XXI:5

17 The Western Union treaty makes provision for economic, social, and cultural collaboration as well as mutual defense.

18 The original signatories were Belgium, Canada, Denmark, France, Iceland, Italy, Luxembourg, the Netherlands, Norway, Portugal, the United Kingdom, and the United States. Text of treaty in Appendix A.

"regional arrangement." But the realities of modern security problems press NATO toward becoming a "grand alliance" in time of tension. The realities include an inextricable relation of economic problems with purely military matters, as for example the allocation of French resources between defense in Europe and combating communism in Indo-China. There is a definite concept of an Atlantic community, and a basis of realities therefor which cannot be ignored (see statement of President Eisenhower below). There is also a definite concept of a European community which is perhaps more clearly delineated and recognized. But the latter is part of the former and the two cannot be treated separately.

Key Provisions. The text of the North Atlantic Treaty is given in Appendix A. The reader is urged to examine this as it sets forth the commitments assumed and the undertakings given. The key articles of the Treaty are Article 3, which provides for "mutual aid and self-help," and Article 5. The latter provides that an armed attack against one signatory in the area covered by the pact will be considered an armed attack against all, and each country will take action as it deems necessary, "including the use of armed force." This wording reserves the legal power of the United States Congress to commit the United States to war. Article 2 pledges the membership to promote stability and well-being and to further economic collaboration. Thus, the over-all objectives of the treaty are, in fact, the same as the stated objectives of the United Nations—security and well-being.

Aside from the fact that this is the first long-term, peace-time security commitment the United States has been willing to enter into with the nations of Europe since the French Alliance of 1778, the unique features of NATO are the machinery, arrangements, and resources which the parties have created in order to achieve its objectives.

NATO Procedure. In setting about the problem of building armed strength jointly on the basis of "self-help and mutual aid," the NATO organization has moved into the realm of the problems facing the executive directorship of a superstate. The combining of United States arms assistance with allied manpower, the stationing of troops on allied soil, the creation of allied military command structures, and the programing of fiscal budgetary and production matters in each state to contribute to the common objective are all involved steps that are quite unprecedented. The only reasonably comparable arrangement was the United States-British arrangement, focused in the Combined Chiefs of Staff, during World War II.

Difficulties are inherent in the very nature of such procedures whenever an effort is made to proceed from generalities and general pledges to effective operational details of increased international unity. The attainment of success in such detailed collaboration clearly requires a considerable amount of mutual trust as each nation learns the secrets and problems of the other nations. Such an operation also depends upon the development of some common reference points and procedures—otherwise collaboration is bound to be slow, if it moves at all, and quarrelsome. The experience of United States-British combined military planning in World War II and of the OEEC economic planning has stood the new organization in good stead.[19]

NATO Organization. At Lisbon in 1952 the NATO Council established a general pattern of NATO programing and adapted the NATO organization thereto as indicated by the accompanying Chart. The NATO Council is permanent and located in Paris. Foreign, Defense, and other ministers of state attend key meetings in addition to each nation's permanent representative. There are two principal permanent staff sections: the International Staff in Paris under the Secretary-General, and the Standing Group (US, UK, and France) in Washington under the Military Committee. The latter is composed of the Chiefs of Staff of all Member nations and, through the Standing Group, commands NATO forces. The Standing Group guides strategic planning, but most of the military planning and policy arrangements are products of the commands which often have complicated and delicate problems to work out with local governments. The International Staff deals principally with political and economic matters, and inevitably finds its affairs intertwined with those of the OEEC and other regional agencies in Europe.

Differing Views on NATO. In leaving this brief, and admittedly inadequate, discussion of NATO it should be realized that NATO has represented different objectives to different states. The United States, which did not commit all its resources to NATO, perhaps saw it principally as a useful instrument for energizing the armed strength of free Europe. Most other Members, committing practically all their military resources to NATO which became the main factor in their security budget and military policies, saw NATO in much more of an international political and economic frame of reference. The difference is one of degree, perhaps not vital, and is evidenced by the judgment expressed by the British authors of the book *Atlantic Alliance:* "Henceforth [from the Lisbon Conference of 1952] it will be the political and economic side of NATO that will set the pace, not the military." [20]

19 For an extended discussion of economic problems of NATO and collective security arrangements in general, see G. A. Lincoln and associates, *Economics of National Security* (New York, 1954).

20 RIIA, *Atlantic Alliance, cit. supra.* For further reading on NATO see H. Kelsen, "Is the North Atlantic Treaty a Regional Arrangement?" *Am. J. Int. Law,* Jan., 1951; R. P. Stebbins, *The U. S. in World Affairs, 1950* (New York, 1951), ch. 6; W. R. Herod, "Strength of the Atlantic Community," *Annals,* July, 1952; *NATO: Its Development and Significance.* United States Dept. of State Pub. 4630 (Washington 1952).

NORTH ATLANTIC TREATY ORGANIZATION

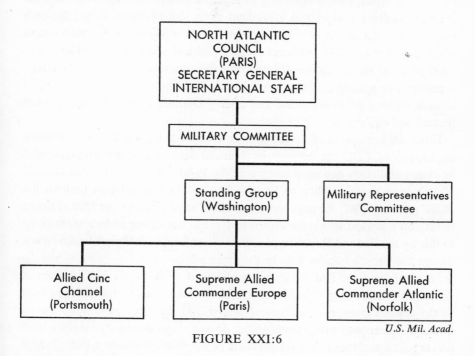

FIGURE XXI:6

European Defense Community. The defense of Western Europe and the creation of an effective deterrent to armed aggression from the East can be assured only by definite support from North America and by the inclusion of Germany in Western defense arrangements. This has involved a fundamental question of how to utilize the resources and strength of the Germans and at the same time how to overcome the traditional, and historically justified, distrust of Germany by France.

The European Defense Communitiy formula, proposed initially by the French and including the same states as the European Coal and Steel Community, provides for a six-member Council of Ministers, a Commissariat of nine members to act as an executive organ, and an Assembly based on that of the Coal and Steel Community which may make suggestions to the Commissariat.[21]

The pledge contained in the EDC treaty is to run for fifty years. It provides, specifically, that an attack against one shall be considered an attack against

[21] Text of the EDC Treaty in C. W. Baier and R. P. Stebbins (eds.), *Documents on American Foreign Relations, 1952* (New York, 1953), pp. 239–248; also in RIAA, *Atlantic Alliance, cit. supra.*

all. The military and closely related arrangements provide for limiting the size of national military units operating as separate commands. They also call for a unified defense budget and agreement as to size of forces raised by each country. But the effect of EDC, except for the addition of German forces which it makes possible, is almost entirely political and economic. The agreement provides that all forces will be under the command of NATO. Militarily it amounts to putting a uniform shoulder insignia on troops of five countries already under NATO command and adding German contingents as they are formed and equipped.

From the standpoint of evolution in international affairs, the most interesting aspects of EDC are perhaps its financial and supervisory arrangements; its close parallelism and association with the ECSC and the associated attitude of Britain, which is willing to be with but not an integral part of both the ECSC and the EDC; the unprecedented effort on the part of the United States to fashion a unified European armed force; and the strong endorsement given to this by the Federal Republic of Germany under Chancellor Adenauer even though the French became cool to the entire affair.

In April 1954 the British Government signed, with the six EDC nations, a convention committing British land and air forces to the continent for as long as the present emergency exists and agreed that these forces may be placed under the European army commander. In the same month President Eisenhower sent a message to the six premiers of the EDC countries which pledged the United States to maintain in Europe a fair share of the forces needed for joint defense of the North Atlantic area, so long as a threat to that area exists. President Eisenhower took this occasion to stress that the United States regarded the North Atlantic Treaty as of indefinite duration, (one of the alleged concerns of EDC Treaty is for 50 years whereas the North Atlantic Treaty is for 20 years). In this message the President indicated a United States view that the European Defense Community is a part of the broader Atlantic community. His message, cited in *The New York Times* of April 17, 1954, read in part:

> These nations (NATO nations) are also seeking to make the Atlantic alliance an enduring association of free peoples, within which all members can concert their efforts toward peace, prosperity and freedom.
>
> The European Defense Community will form an integral part of the Atlantic community and, within this framework, will insure intimate and durable cooperation between the United States forces and the forces of the European Defense Community on the Continent of Europe.

As to the age-old difficulty between France and Germany, it is worthy of note that within seven years after World War II, France achieved a triple military guarantee from Britain (Brussels Pact, NATO, and association of Britain with EDC), and a double pledge from the United States (NATO and association of the United States with EDC). The ghost of Clemenceau, who failed in the same objective after World War I, must nightly pace in jealousy beside his tombstone. Yet France, plagued by a weak internal political structure, had not ratified the EDC in nearly two years after signature of the treaty—an example of the effects of traditional distrusts and historical wrongs as well as of political disunity at home interfering with progress along regional lines. We shall discuss presently the idea of a European political community to supplement the European defense organization.

The Balkan Alliance. In February, 1953, Greece, Yugoslavia, and Turkey, the latter two members of NATO, signed a treaty of friendship and collaboration providing for consultation on matters of common interest including consultations by their military staffs. A permanent secretariat was established to deal with matters of cultural, political, and military cooperation. The interlock with NATO was obvious, taking into account United States mutual aid to Yugoslavia. Some may ask, why should not Yugoslavia have joined NATO? Some of the practical reasons illustrate why regional and world integration is an evolutionary matter. Yugoslavia's Tito was still operating a communist regime, withal a heretical one as far as Moscow was concerned. Hence, membership in NATO might have raised internal problems for him. The quarrel with Italy over Trieste was unsettled, and since entry to NATO is by unanimous agreement, Yugoslavia's entry might have been blocked by Italy.

Regional Security for All Europe. We may well ask, why not have a regional security arrangement for all Europe including the satellite states and the USSR? Such ideas have been mentioned and perhaps the matter should be considered. The USSR proposed, in the spring of 1954, an all-European security agreement and that the USSR adhere to the NATO. The proposals were coldly received. Would such pledges be of more value than the paper written on unless it were implemented by detailed arrangements such as those going forward in NATO? The Locarno Treaty, as an example, proved to be ineffective in 1939. So far as detailed arrangements comparable to NATO go, is there any chance that they would be entered into with communist states? If they proved practicable, would there be the requisite degree of trust and cooperation? If not, is talk of such arrangements a dangerous course lulling tax-ridden peoples into a belief there may be a safe and cheaper way than devised thus far? These are questions which may long be discussed.

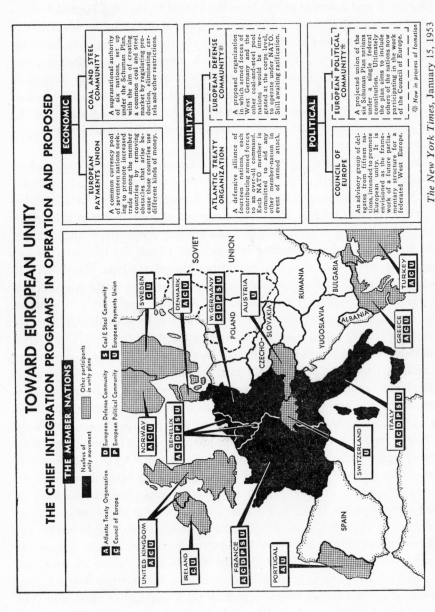

TOWARD EUROPEAN UNITY

THE CHIEF INTEGRATION PROGRAMS IN OPERATION AND PROPOSED

THE MEMBER NATIONS

■ Nucleus of unity movement

▦ Other participants in unity plans

A Atlantic Treaty Organization
C Council of Europe
D European Defense Community
P European Political Community
S Coal & Steel Community
U European Payments Union

ECONOMIC

EUROPEAN PAYMENTS UNION

A common currency pool of seventeen nations seeking to promote increased trade among the member countries by removing obstacles that arise because those countries use different kinds of money.

COAL AND STEEL COMMUNITY

A supranational authority of six nations, set up under the Schuman Plan, with the aim of creating a common coal and steel market by regulating production, eliminating cartels and other restrictions.

MILITARY

ATLANTIC TREATY ORGANIZATION

A defensive alliance of fourteen nations, each contributing armed forces to an over-all command. Each NATO member is committed to aid any other member-nation in event of armed attack.

EUROPEAN DEFENSE COMMUNITY※

A proposed organization in which armed forces of West Germany and the other coal-and-steel pool nations would be integrated at the corps level, to operate under NATO. Still awaiting ratification.

POLITICAL

COUNCIL OF EUROPE

An advisory group of delegates from fifteen nations, intended to promote European unity. It is envisioned as the framework of future parliamentary structure for a federated West Europe.

EUROPEAN POLITICAL COMMUNITY※

A projected union of the six Schuman Plan nations under a single federal constitution. Ultimately the plan aims to include others of the nations now participating in the work of the Council of Europe.

※ Now in process of formation

The New York Times, January 15, 1953

FIGURE XXI:7

MOVEMENT TOWARD EUROPEAN POLITICAL ORGANIZATION

Historic Background. The idea of a united Europe is not a new one.[22] It has been broached time and again since the breakdown of the universal church and empire and the rise of conflicting nation-states. In the seventeenth century Sully's "Great Design" advocated a Christian Republic of Europe. Others after him in the eighteenth and nineteenth centuries proposed various plans for peace that included ideas of organizing Europe. The nineteenth-century Concert of Europe, shattered by World War I,[23] left a tradition leading to new proposals for European union which were advanced in the period following 1918. These were advanced particularly by French statesmen, but achieved no progress against the rising tide of fascism.[24]

A new stimulus was given to the movement toward European regional collaboration and union by the dire economic situation and the specter of Soviet imperialism facing Europe in the aftermath of World War II. A series of privately directed movements merged in 1948 into a single "European Movement" under the joint presidency of four distinguished leaders: Leon Blum of France, Winston Churchill of Britain, Paul-Henri Spaak of Belgium, and Alcide de Gasperi of Italy.

The Council of Europe. The leaders of the European Movement were instrumental in the establishment in 1949 of the Council of Europe.[25] The Statute creating this organization, in which fifteen European states participate, binds the states to promote European unity in order to safeguard the ideals which are their common heritage and to further their economic and social progress.[26]

The Council is composed of (1) a Consultative Assembly which meets at Strasbourg twice a year and (2) a Committee of Ministers meeting ordinarily three times a year. The Assembly is a deliberative body with delegates appointed by, but not instructed by, governments and voting as individuals

22 See Sydney B. Bailey, *United Europe, A Short History of the Idea* (London, 1948).
23 See *The Cambridge Modern History*, vols. X–XI; R. B. Mowat, *The Concert of Europe* (London, 1930); W. A. Philips, *The Confederation of Europe* (London, 1920); H. G. Schenk, *The Aftermath of the Napoleonic Years: The Concert of Europe—An Experiment* (New York, 1948); see also ch. vii above.
24 On background see R. N. Coudenhove-Kalergi, *Pan-Europe* (New York, 1926); E. Herriot, *The United States of Europe* (New York, 1930); W. I. Jennings, *A Federation of Western Europe* (New York, 1940); M. L. Hoffman, "European Integration, 800–1952," *The New York Times Magazine*, March 16, 1952. Briand's Memorandum appears in *Internat. Conciliation*, June, 1930.
25 See R. G. Hawtrey, *Western European Union* (London, 1949); A. Loveday, "The European Movement," *Internat. Organization*, Nov., 1949; H. M. Lange, "European Union: False Hopes and Realities," *Foreign Affairs*, April, 1950; P. H. Spaak, "The Integration of Europe," *ibid.*, Oct., 1950; P. Reynaud, *Unite or Perish* (New York, 1951). John Foster Dulles gave emphatic support to steps in this direction long before becoming United States Secretary of State. See "Europe Must Federate or Perish," in *Vital Speeches*, Feb. 1, 1947.
26 Text in *Am. J. Int. Law,* Off. Doc. Suppl., Oct., 1949.

rather than as national groups. Its debates on the problems of European unity have attracted much attention, and it does provide a European forum and "voice." Moreover, at some Assembly meetings observers have detected the beginnings of a tendency for divisions to occur on lines of group interest (socialist, Catholic, and so on) cutting across nationalities.[27] Lest the movement get out of hand, the governments insisted that the Committee of Ministers, composed of the Foreign Ministers of the member states, have power to initiate or approve the Assembly's agenda, that Assembly recommendations should go to the Committee and not to the governments, and that any discussions of defense matters must take place in the Committee of Ministers. The Assembly may, however, adopt "declarations" expressing its views and aimed at public opinion.

The goal of the architects of the Council of Europe has been said to be the creation of a European Parliament with "limited functions but real powers." The pathway which has been charted toward this end has been the development of a series of functional agencies such as the ECSC and the EDC. In this connection have been discussions with regard to the formation of a European agricultural community. As mentioned before, the United States has given strong support toward increasing Western European political integration.[28]

A European Political Community. There is a live movement, centering in the six members of the ECSC, for the establishment of a European Political Community which would complement and unify the existent bodies, including specifically the Coal and Steel Community and the Defense Community, giving political direction to their more specialized activities. Advocates of the EPC would also have it strive for establishment of a common market among the members, and would seek equilibrium in balance of payments with the remainder of the world and elimination of credit and exchange restrictions. Constitutional drafts for the formation of such an organization have been made by governmental representatives, but many political hurdles remain to be cleared before the idea can be translated into a functioning reality.[29]

The Future of European Political Organization. We should recognize the difficulties and the probabilities on the road to European political union. One of the difficulties in progress on European integration derives from obscurity as to the "Europe" at which the effort is, or should be, directed. There are six

27 W. C. Carleton, "What of the Council of Europe?" *Virginia Quar. Rev.,* April, 1951.

28 President Eisenhower, when Supreme Allied Commander in Europe, declared that "there must be progress toward the unification of Western Europe if the objective of permanent security and peace in the Western world is to be realized." *The New York Times,* Jan. 23, 1952. See also radio address of John Foster Dulles, Jan. 27, 1953.

29 The progress of agreement on the Political Community is set forth in a *News Digest* of the Netherlands Information Service, New York, Dec. 24, 1953.

states in the ECSC, fifteen in the Council of Europe, seventeen in the OEEC, five in the Brussels Pact, and fourteen (including two in North America) in NATO. Relationships to states and other arrangements outside a particular grouping may be materially determinant of relationships within the grouping; for example, France's attitude concerning the EDC is materially conditioned by the relationship of the United Kingdom to EDC and the relationship of the latter to NATO. A political community without Britain increases chance of eventual German dominance, which neither the French nor the smaller states of Western Europe are prepared to accept.

A second factor which should be reckoned with is that the post-World War II advances have been made under the lash of economic necessity and the fear of the USSR. If these pressures are eased, progress may be slow. It is a long jump from the consultative powers of the Council of Europe to any political body exercising any truly sovereign powers. The difficulties over the formation of the EDC indicate that there would almost certainly be greater hesitations with respect to a wider association.

The degree of homogeneity of interests varies widely. Belgium and Luxembourg are thoroughly integrated for all practical purposes, but not so Belgium and the Netherlands. The Scandinavian countries have a subregional community of their own. There is relatively little homogeneity of interests between these countries, however, and the Mediterranean lands. The United Kingdom poses a difficult problem. It is vital to a free continental Europe and continental Europe is important to it. Yet it can be argued that it is not truly a "European" state and that the greater proportion of its interests are in the direction of the Commonwealth and areas outside Europe. The social and cultural structures vary enormously between Sicily and the North Cape. The economic structures and philosophies also vary from state socialism to free enterprise.

With these and other differences and political factors ever present in the minds of European politicians, it may be a long while before Europe is really unified politically—except under the pressing threat of conquest. This being the case, it is conceivable that much of the substance of what might be achieved can be gained through functional regionalism such as the OEEC, NATO, the EDC, and the ECSC.[30] The accomplishments thus far are by no means to be minimized. They stand pre-eminent among regional arrangements.

---

[30] On some of the problems involved see Edgar S. Furniss, Jr., "French Attitudes Toward Western European Unity," *Internat. Organization*, May, 1953. See also Ruth C. Lawson, "European Union or Atlantic Union?" *Current History*, Dec., 1950.

MIDDLE EASTERN REGIONALISM

Our analyses in Chapter XV of factors affecting policy making in the Middle Eastern countries showed that in this region there are niajor elements of both unity and disunity. These conflicts and complexities found there make an appraisal of Middle Eastern regionalism difficult.[31]

Pre-World War II Regional Efforts. Following the break-up of the Ottoman Empire in 1918, the Great Powers, principally Britain, exercised a "regionalizing" influence in the Arab Middle East. The British mandate over Palestine, and political and military arrangements with Egypt, Jordan, Iraq, and the Arab rulers in the Arabian peninsula, contributed materially to political stability. But these arrangements had characteristics of a protectorate, and many of them weakened or disappeared with the rising nationalism engendered by World War II. The Zionist movement for the creation of the state of

ARAB LEAGUE – BALKAN ENTENTE

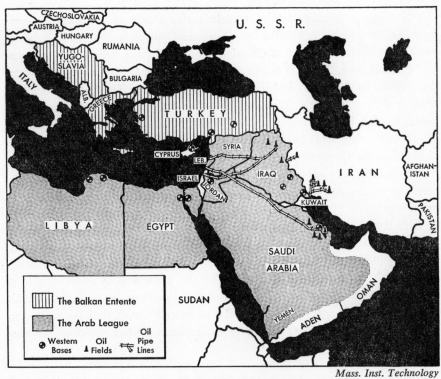

Mass. Inst. Technology

FIGURE XXI:8

31 For a résumé of the problems of the Arab and Near Eastern states see Charles Malik, "The Search for Truth," *Foreign Affairs*, Jan., 1952.

Israel did much to augment this nationalistic feeling and to provide a focus generating unity among the Arab states.

The Arab League. Formed in the spring of 1945, the original members of the Arab League were Egypt, Jordan, Syria, Lebanon, Iraq, Saudi Arabia, and Yemen, to which Libya was added after attaining independence in 1953. The structure and general purposes of the League are somewhat similar to the Organization of American States, with a Council having representatives of all member states meeting periodically to discuss matters of common concern and, by unanimous agreement, to make recommendations to the member governments. The League also has a permanent Secretariat and a number of committees. A Collective Security Pact of April, 1950, defining security aspects of the League and roughly comparable to the Rio Pact, added a Permanent Military Committee reporting to a Council composed of the Ministers of Foreign Affairs and Defense and an Economic Council composed of the economic ministers of the members.

The League agreements provide for advancement of common interests, promotion of collaboration, safeguarding of independence, and pacific settlement of disputes. They provide for cooperation in (1) economic and financial matters, (2) communication matters, (3) cultural affairs, (4) nationality problems, (5) social affairs, and (6) health problems.

The fighting with Israel at the time of the formation of that state and afterward was not a clearly concerted League action. But four of the Arab states took somewhat concerted military action and, while they negotiated separate truces, all Arab states made common cause in refraining from concluding peace treaties with Israel.

The Arab League has shown a considerable degree of unity in dealings with states external to the region. Its members collectively supported Egypt's demands for withdrawal of British troops. It has consistently engaged in bloc voting in the United Nations, a practice giving an importance and prestige which no one of these small states could achieve alone. But the Arab League is weak economically, politically, and militarily. There are dynastic rivalries within its membership. There is dissension over a project for unity and other federation ideas among Iraq, Jordan, and Syria (Greater Syria), jealousy over Egyptian claims to leadership, and schisms between Moslem sects. It may be that the League will long be affected internally by inter-Arab feuds and will have a history of ups and downs and rapid changes.[32]

[32] For discussion of Arab League organization and potentialities see Harry M. Howard in *Proceedings Acad. Pol. Sci.*, Jan., 1952, pp. 101–111. The text of the 1945 Pact will be found in *Am. J. Int. Law,* Oct. 1945, Off. Doc. Suppl. The text of the 1950 Joint Defense and Economic Cooperation Treaty will be found in the *Middle East J.,* Spring, 1952. See also R. C. Doty, "The Arab Talks of Unity But Again Fails to Act," *The New York Times,* Jan. 17, 1954.

Other Regional Ties in the Middle East. Under the leadership of Pakistan, an International Islamic Economic Organization was formed in 1949 with membership consisting of Afghanistan, Egypt, Indonesia, Iran, Iraq, Jordan, Lebanon, Pakistan, Saudi Arabia, Syria, and Turkey. This organization functioned initially through yearly consultative meetings, but has yet had few substantive results. The economic interests of these states are diverse and their geographic dispersion is wide. Religion alone seems hardly adequate as a foundation for economic collaboration. A Middle Eastern United Nations Economic Commission, similar to the Economic Commission of Europe, has been strongly urged, but was blocked initially by the political realities of the Arab-Israeli situation. The Turkish-Pakistan defense association in 1954 brought together the two strongest powers in the area. Located on the western and eastern shoulders of the Middle East, they provide the basis for a possible defense arrangement including the countries between them. There seems no doubt that the Middle East will continue to be moved by strong regional forces. Whether the outcome, however, will be a geographical regionalism, an association founded upon religious ties including states outside the Middle East, such as Pakistan, or some other outcome, is unclear.[33]

SOUTH AND SOUTHEAST ASIA REGIONALISM

Developments in South and Southeast Asia since World War II have been away from, rather than toward, integration. The Indian subcontinent is perhaps a more logical unity from the economic and security standpoints than is the "union" of some Western European countries. Yet this area is divided between India and Pakistan with the latter state split into two widely separated parts. The divisive force is religion which contributes some possibility that Pakistanian associations will in time develop primarily in conjunction with other Moslem countries such as Turkey. It is a fact not to be overlooked that there are more Moslems in Pakistan than in all seven states of the Arab League.

Following around the periphery of Asia from Eastern Pakistan to Indo-China, there are few factors, other than a shared antipathy toward colonialism and a related attitude of neutralism toward the conflict between communism and the West, making for integration. There are many making for division. The economies of most of these countries are not complementary, and the great need of all of them is for development capital which is only available in any appreciable quantity from the Western states. Aside from the Commonwealth Colombo Plan for economic development which we have mentioned in

33 J. C. Hurewitz, "Unity and Disunity in the Middle East," *Internat. Conciliation,* May, 1952; A. G. Huth, "The Problem of Communications," *J. Int. Affairs,* Winter, 1952.

Chapter IV,[34] and the United Nations Economic Commission for the Far East and Asia which includes the states of this area, regional arrangements have as yet to become a force in the political realities of South and Southeast Asia.

PACIFIC REGIONALISM

There are substantial reasons for the lack of many regional associations in the Pacific. In the first place, the region is vast. Secondly, the normal tendency for collaboration of Japanese industry and technology with the less developed areas is checked by memories of World War II and of the record of Japanese imperialism. Thirdly, Indonesia is neutralist, suspiciously nationalist, and still is struggling for a durable political stability. Fourthly, there is no visible leadership toward general cooperation other than that of the United States. And in the fifth place, except for the Republic of Korea and possibly Viet Nam, any cooperation must of necessity stop short of the mainland dominated by the USSR and communist China.

The existent formal arrangements consist of (1) a series of bilateral understandings between the United States, on the one hand, and the Philippine Republic, Formosa, the Korean Republic, and Japan on the other, and (2) two arrangements which can be called "regional": the South Pacific Commission and the ANZUS Pact. As the bilateral agreements which the United States has concluded with the several parties fall outside of the definition of "regional arrangements" as we have accepted the term, we shall not go into them here. Suffice it to say they are, nevertheless, a vital element in the contemporary international politics of the Pacific and Far Eastern regions.

South Pacific Commission. The South Pacific Commission has already been mentioned in Chapter VIII above. The purpose of this regional body, organized after the manner of the Caribbean Commission, is to further the social and economic development and coordination of services within the dependent territories of Australia, New Zealand, Britain, the United States, France, and the Netherlands in the Pacific Ocean south of the Equator (and east from Netherlands New Guinea). Although there are administrative problems in the functioning of a commission spanning such a large area with diversified peoples and social outlook, the South Pacific Commission is nevertheless a useful innovation for assisting development in this "region." [35]

ANZUS Pact. The nearest thing to a regional security arrangement in the collective sense in the Pacific Ocean area is the ANZUS Pact concluded by

[34] See above, p. 120. See also J. R. E. Carr-Gregg, "The Colombo Plan—A Commonwealth Program for Southeast Asia," *Internat. Conciliation,* Jan., 1951.
[35] "The South Pacific Commission, a New Experiment in Regionalism," *The World Today,* Sept., 1950; R. E. James, "The South Pacific Commission," *Pacific Affairs,* June, 1947.

Australia, New Zealand, and the United States in September, 1951. This Pact, like the United States security agreement with the Philippine Republic, paved the way for acceptance, by the countries concerned, of the Japanese Peace Treaty. These agreements gave the three victims of Japanese World War II aggression precise assurance of United States long-term support in case of need. The ANZUS treaty recognizes, for each party, that an armed attack on any of them in the Pacific "would be dangerous to its own peace and safety," and pledges that each will "act to meet the common danger in accordance with its constitutional processes." [36] The qualified wording of the ANZUS treaty contrasts with the more precise commitments for action in the Rio and North Atlantic Treaties. An ANZUS Council composed of the respective Foreign Ministers (or their deputies) meets annually or as often as may be necessary.

The United Kingdom with its possessions and Commonwealth ties in the Pacific has expressed a desire to be associated with the ANZUS Council. The initial reaction of the membership was not favorable, perhaps because such association might bring with it the British problems in Malaya and Hong Kong.

Pacific Pact. There also have been suggestions that the ANZUS arrangement be expanded to a regional arrangement embracing other states in the Pacific and perhaps patterned more closely after the Rio or NATO arrangements.[37] These suggestions were initially resisted by the United States, reportedly because the inclusion of France and Great Britain would place the United States in too close a juxtaposition to colonial problems in the area. Also, there is some question that closer association provides any increased military defensive power in the area. Security, however, is a matter of political and psychological, as well as military, strength. Unity and a "united front" contribute to such strengths. In April, 1954, the situation in the Southeast Asia area having changed, Secretary Dulles initiated, with Britain and France, steps toward a NATO-type regional arrangement in the Southeast Asia area.

Any development of this nature is likely to be even more evolutionary in organization and in acquisition of membership than NATO has been. The most probable initial members are the United States, Great Britain, France, Australia, New Zealand, Viet Nam, Laos, Cambodia, Philippines, and Thailand (10 nations). Such a development would incorporate ANZUS and the United States pact with the Philippines—an interesting parallel to the *de facto* incorporation of Western Union into NATO.

The United States already has defense agreements with Nationalist China

---

36 Text in *Am. J. Int. Law,* Off. Doc. Suppl. July, 1952. This pact also contains a provision, comparable to that in the North Atlantic Treaty, for report to the United Nations Security Council. For commentary on the Tripartite Treaty see R. P. Stebbins, *The United States in World Affairs, 1951* (New York, 1952), pp. 199–201.

37 See B. C. Limb, "The Pacific Pact: Looking Forward or Backward?" *Foreign Affairs,* July, 1951; P. C. Spender, "NATO and Pacific Security," *Annals,* July, 1952; N. D. Harper, "Pacific Security as Seen from Australia," *Internat. Organization,* May, 1953.

(Formosa), the Republic of Korea, and Japan in the northern area of the Western Pacific. These agreements may serve as the basis for another regional arrangement although there is an acute consciousness among all concerned that Japan has been a traditional aggressor of the other two nations.

It may be, however, that regionalism in the Western Pacific will develop in two separate, though related, groupings, linked through United States participation in each.

SOVIET ALLIANCE SYSTEM

A network of alliances has been concluded by the USSR with its satellite countries in Eastern Europe, with Mongolia and communist China, and among the satellite states. These bilateral treaties pledge each party to render all military and other assistance to the other signatory if it is the object of an act of aggression by Germany (in the case of the European countries) or Japan (in the case of Mongolia and communist China), or by any state joined directly or indirectly with either of these powers. In the event of a threat to peace and security, the parties agree to consult. In many of the treaties, the parties undertake to strengthen the ties and collaboration between them.

Although the alliances are directed at Germany and Japan in the first instance, it is apparent that they may be directed at any state the USSR chooses to regard as being associated with either of those powers. Most of the pacts declare that their terms shall be applied in accordance with the "principles" or the "spirit" of the Charter of the United Nations, but none of them provide that actions taken under them shall be reported to the United Nations Security Council or cease when that body has acted to maintain peace and security.[38]

In one sense this network of alliances may be viewed as a regional arrangement in that it embraces a group of nations within the so-called "heartland" area and within one comprehensive geopolitical sphere behind the Iron Curtain. On the other hand, the system differs from the Western regional arrangements, as pointed out above, in that there is no one multilateral instrument or collective regional machinery to tie the whole together. More important, the states have in effect been reduced to subservience to Moscow through the operation of the communist apparatus and the detailed operation of the system. Direction of the system lies to all intents and purposes in the hands of one power—the USSR—except for Soviet-Chinese relationships.[39] Conse-

[38] Texts in "The Soviet Alliance System, 1942–1948," United States Dept. of State, *Documents and State Papers*, July, 1948 (Washington, 1948); Sino-Soviet Pact in *Am. J. Int. Law*, Off. Doc. Suppl., July, 1950. See also "New Links in the Soviet Alliance System, 1948–1949," *Doc. and St. Papers*, March–April, 1949.

[39] See W. W. Kulski, "The Soviet System of Collective Security Compared with the Western System," *Am. J. Int. Law*, July, 1950. The Soviet Union has especially opposed proposals for a political federation of the Danube Basin. See Andrew Gyorgy, *Governments of Danubian Europe* (New York, 1949), ch. 8.

quently, with the exception of the latter arrangement, it seems more correct to categorize the relationship which has been established between the USSR and the other communist states under the heading of the "new imperialism" or of a "sphere of influence" rather than under "regional arrangements."

As to the factor of economic integration, this is obviously very complete. The Soviet Union has used bilateral trade arrangements and the expedient of stock companies in which the Soviet Government holds the majority of stock to make its satellites an adjunct to a self-sufficiency program. The Soviet Union has also made extensive use of arms assistance to European satellites and North Korea, with some to communist China, and has given indications that it may extend its policy implementation to use of resources for industrial development in communist China.

OTHER ARRANGEMENTS WHICH MIGHT BE CALLED REGIONAL

There are many arrangements which have been made by states for establishing a certain regime in a given locality or area which may occur to some as properly classifiable as "regional arrangements." These might include, for example, the multipartite conventions or treaties relating to Spitzbergen, the International Zone of Tangiers, the Turkish Straits, and the Suez Canal, to mention but a few of the areas which have been the subject of some international guarantee or arrangement relating to their governance, use, or disposition. Important as these arrangements may be in the total picture of international politics, they appear to lack the characteristics of "regional arrangements" as defined at the beginning of this chapter or in the generally accepted meaning of the term. The same is true of the (British) Commonwealth of Nations.

REGIONALISM AND WORLD ORGANIZATION

Regionalism and UN Charter. Before concluding this résumé of regional arrangements we must note briefly the connection between regionalism and world organization. In the preceding chapter we mentioned the incorporation of provisions referring to regional arrangements in the United Nations Charter. These provisions not only recognize the legitimacy of regional arrangements that are consistent with the purposes and principles of the United Nations, but also provide for their use in connection with the pacific settlement of disputes (Article 52), and, under some circumstances, for enforcement proceedings (Articles 53–54). These provisions were written into the Charter largely at the prompting of the state members of the Inter-American system and of the Arab League.[40] Speaking toward the close of the San Francisco Conference,

---

[40] See M. Margaret Ball, "The Inter-American System and the United Nations," *London Quar. World Affairs*, April, 1946.

the chairman of the committee which elaborated the article assuring Members the right of self-defense (Article 51) expressly joined actions covered by this article with the provisions respecting regional arrangements when he said: "And the right of self-defense is not limited to the country which is the direct victim of aggression, but extends to those countries which have established solidarity through regional arrangements with the country directly attacked."

The influence of regional sentiment was also apparent in 1945 in the adoption of the principle that the General Assembly shall pay due regard to "equitable geographical distribution" in electing the nonpermanent Members of the Security Council. Since then the same principle has been applied in practice in the selection of Assembly committees and in the election of members of ECOSOC and the Trusteeship Council.

Having these accomplishments in mind, the late Senator Vandenberg of the United States Delegation remarked at the end of the San Francisco gathering:

We have found a sound and practical formula for putting regional organizations into effective gear with the global institution. . . . In my view we have infinitely strengthened the world organization by thus enlisting, with its overall supervision, the dynamic resources of these regional affinities. We do not thus subtract from global unity of the world's peace and security; on the contrary, we weld these regional king-links into the global chain.[41]

Regional Blocs in United Nations Politics. Regional groupings have played an active part in the politics of the world organization. Members of the Inter-American system, the League of Arab States, NATO, the so-called Arab-Asian group, and the Soviet Bloc are known to caucus among themselves on important issues affecting their interests with a view to concerted action within the various organs. Political maneuvering, old-fashioned political "log rolling," and bloc voting can form as real a part of international politics as of domestic. The United Nations proceedings on the whole tend to show that on substantive matters few regional groups are immutable save the Soviet Bloc. Voting alignments tend to form and reform in response to many stimuli, both national and international.

The most important political combination based upon regional lines is that of the Latin American and Arab states. With united effort these twenty-seven states can prevent any substantive issue gaining the necessary two-thirds vote to pass the General Assembly, and with but five additional collaborators they can block any election that does not entail satisfaction of their mutual interests. It is not meant to imply that this combination often works together (a more usual combination is probably that of Arab and Asian states), or that when it

41 UNCIO, *Documents*, vol. XI, p. 53.

does there is complete unison. But bloc voting is a United Nations phenomenon and these states have been an important part of it.[42] With such power in the hands of the small states it is not surprising that the larger powers must engage in assiduous political activity at nearly all United Nations meetings.

CONCLUSION

Scanning the existing regional arrangements, one is struck with the predominance of economic, technical, and mutual defense arrangements as compared with regional political organizations. This may be attributed to the practical needs of cooperation in the modern world in these particular fields in order to attain a satisfactory standard of living and national security. But the retarded development of regional political organizations may also be explained by a combination of suspicions, rivalries, nationalism, and in many cases perhaps a question as to the need or real value of regional mechanisms standing between the national states and the world organization.

Among the various types of regional mechanisms it would be difficult to select any one form which is "best" under a particular set of circumstances. The bases upon which such value judgments may be formed require much more study than has been given to them yet. There is much to be said for the simple consultative Council type employed by the Arab League under present regional conditions in that part of the Middle East. The Caribbean Commission and its West Indian Conference are serving a useful place in their area, but this is no reason why such a structure would necessarily be best in Africa south of the Sahara if a regional movement commences there, or in South Asia. There is a good deal to be said for the sort of effort which is represented in the United Nations Economic Commissions which provide both a coordinated regional approach and sponsorship by the world organization.[43] In a region sensitive to the past history of colonialism the Colombo Plan of regional collaboration by the Commonwealth nations may be able to contribute much in developing local initiative and leadership. In highly vulnerable and politically experienced regions such as the North Atlantic Western Europe, experimentation with the "community" concept and with integrated functional organizations for defense and economic affairs may be justified as being more urgent than in the American hemisphere and in the Pacific at this stage.

Regional arrangements are a response to a mutually shared sense of need among certain states for periodic consultation and concerted approach to given

[42] See ch. xx, p. 588. See also W. R. Crocker, "Voting in the International Institutions," *Australian Outlook*, Sept., 1951; Raymond Dennett, "Politics in the Security Council," *Internat. Organization*, Aug., 1949; E. S. Furniss, "The United States, the Inter-American System and the United Nations," *Pol. Sci. Quar.* Sept., 1950.

[43] In this connection it should be noted that the United Nations Charter has no provisions for limiting the scope of regional economic blocs as it does for regional enforcement measures.

problems or relationships. The present tendency is to strengthen rather than to move away from such groupings. There is, of course, a danger that in creating regional organizations states may intensify already existing conflicts between regions. But if the choice is between survival and conflict as in the case of NATO, the answer seems clear. It is possible for a regional grouping to be so concerned with affairs in its own region that it may oppose the universal United Nations organization, as did the Arab League with regard to the partition of Palestine. But there is no inherent contradiction between universalism and regionalism. Neither is an exclusive principle.[44] In the present imperfect political world, both have a role to play. The weight of the role of one in relation to the other is bound to be determined on a state-by-state and region-by-region basis according to the principle of enlightened self-interest. And the relative weights will shift with the passage of time as nations and groups of nations appraise the degree of effectiveness of action through use of the various patterns of policy, whether regional or universal.

SUGGESTED READINGS

Sydney B. Bailey, *United Europe, A Short History of the Idea* (London, 1948).
S. M. Canyes, *Organization of American States and the United Nations* (Washington, 1949).
Daniel S. Cheever and H. Field Haviland, Jr., *Organizing for Peace* (Boston, 1954).
J. C. Hurewitz, *Middle East Dilemma* (New York, 1953).
George Lenczowski, *The Middle East in World Affairs* (Ithaca, 1952).
OEEC, *European Economic Co-operation* (Paris, 1951).
Pan-American Union, *Organization of American States* (Washington, 1949).
Paul Reynaud, *Unite or Perish* (New York, 1951).
Royal Institute of International Affairs, *Atlantic Alliance* (New York, 1952).

[44] On this subject see Pitman B. Potter, "Universalism versus Regionalism in International Organization," *Am. Pol. Sci. Rev.,* Oct., 1943.

CHAPTER XXII

Crisis and Opportunity

OUR DISCUSSION of international relations in this book has, in large part, been generalized and descriptive of elements which affect the external politics of almost every state. In this last chapter we propose to summarize certain thoughts concerning the realm of international politics—looking at that realm primarily from the view point of our Western civilization which has been dominant in the world for several centuries. That civilization is now being challenged by the rise of Asia, the pressure of a hostile ideology—communism —and the problem of control of massive destructive power.

The United States and the Western world now live not in an instant of peril but in an age of peril. This condition is not a product of tension among nations but of more basic features, some of which cause the tension. It may even be true that real peril increases with decrease in tensions, for the reason that a superficial calm in the world may result in a weakening of unity and effort and thus lead to quick disaster at some future time.

We will attempt to look somewhat into the future concerning the course of international politics—an effort admittedly dangerous for authors who are conscious that the course of international affairs has developed quite differently from the hopes and prophesies voiced by many writers in the recent past.

Responsibility for Citizenship. The task of those responsible for international politics is to preserve the position their nation now holds while at the same time striving to further the interests of that nation in the future. In undertaking this task it is necessary to make some appraisal of that future, to identify the possible alternative courses for furthering national interests, and to select and advance one of these courses. The future is sufficiently uncertain so that wise statecraft dictates that acceptable alternative avenues of policy be kept open in case the selected method fails. The destiny of one's own country is too vital to be put to a gambler's chance, without alternatives, if that chance can be hedged or otherwise reduced.

646

In a democracy all citizens have some responsibility for decision-making in the field of international affairs. Every citizen should therefore think seriously of the future of international affairs and recognize that judgments on present policies based on wrong or questionable premises as to the future endanger his country. "Illiteracy in science and technology is much less dangerous for the citizen of a democracy than illiteracy in history or politics or morality. We can drive an automobile across the George Washington Bridge without knowing much about the scientific principles that govern the motor or the engineering principles that govern the bridge. . . . But in our role as citizens we must have a substantial degree of personal expertness. . . ."[1]

Complications of the Present. Many of the salient features of our current situation have existed before. But it seems safe to assert that they have not before existed in the magnitude and conjunction of the present. The techniques and technology which have produced a rapidly shrinking world have retained the old problems while creating new ones.

These increased complications have come very rapidly, measuring the time of their development against the span of recorded history. Nationalism, viewed worldwide, is now no less important than in prior decades. True, its onward march has eliminated a large part of colonialism and old-fashioned imperialism, once salient features in international politics. Substituted therefor is a confusing multiplicity of new political entities, particularly around the rimland of Asia. While old-fashioned colonialism is largely dead, there is a new form of imperialism in communism. It is not yet altogether clear whether this will develop as traditional Russian imperialism with merely a new ideological cloak. While traditional colonialism and imperialism are dead, their effects still bulk large in international politics because of the memories in newly sovereign states and the tendency to continue identification of the West with colonialism—hence there is some tendency in Asian minds to view both certain Western policies and communism with suspicion.

The world has long had economic problems, but it is only lately that increased economic interdependence has made international affairs extremely and quickly sensitive to economic shifts and disruptions. Technology has raced far ahead of the progress of political science and of the morality of nations.[2] Our competence in "national" economics exceeds that in "international" economics. The lag in the latter is now a brake on achievement of social and

1 C. W. de Kiewiet, "Let's Globalize Our Universities," *Saturday Review*, Sept. 12, 1953.

2 "The rapid progress science now makes, occasions my regretting sometimes that I was born so soon. It is impossible to imagine the height to which may be carried, in a thousand years, the power of man over matter. . . . O that moral science were in as fair a way of improvement, that men would cease to be wolves to one another, and that human beings would at length learn what they now improperly call humanity. . . ." Benjamin Franklin in letter to Joseph Priestley, 1780, contained in *American Heritage*, by Henry and Pannell (New York, 1949).

economic aspirations. A consciousness of the possibility of a better way of life has made large groups of people socially dissatisfied, hence restless for some change in their local conditions.

The two salient features of international affairs overshadowing all others are, first, the pressing problem of security which derives from the great recent technological advances and, second, the conflict between the Communist world and Western civilization.

BASIC FACTORS ARE THE SAME

Elements of Power and Position. The factors described by such broad terms as *geographic, demographic, ethnic, social, psychological,* and *economic* will almost certainly continue to be basic in international relations. We have discussed these at some length in our opening chapters. These are the foundational elements of national power. It is degree of national power that provides the strength or weakness of a nation in its dealings with others. Admittedly a nation may use the foundational elements with wisdom, or, alternatively, may organize and apply them with lack of wisdom. But, in the long run, the strengths and deficiencies in these elements will be very determinant of a nation's policy and position in the world. In the short run the internal political strength and the comparative competence of a nation's statesmanship have appreciable weight in determining the nation's influence and position. We will discuss these two aspects of internal political position and of statesmanship below after a brief reminder that "power politics," like "power" itself, remains as it has been since the dawn of the state system.

The Balance of Power. The balance of power continues to be a basic, and usually an essential, policy of many states. So long as there are interstate suspicions and rivalries there are bound to be consequent efforts by each state or group of states to marshal power on its side. This is an axiom of international politics, even though an increasing proportion of problems come to be resolved by multilateral diplomacy through international conferences and organizations. Even the alignments in the United Nations represent an array of political power although no element of tangible compulsion is introduced.

The world retains its traditional regional balance of power phenomena. Germany, for example, is still a problem and is once again becoming an important element in the appraisals made by statesmen, particularly those of Europe. The Middle East has its fears and internal stresses. The states within the Pacific Ocean area are still concerned about Japan, which is once more becoming an important power and the leading trading and industrial nation in the Western Pacific. There are rivalries and suspicions within Latin America. It is true that post-war international developments have tended to bring many of these potentially opposing states and groupings into common regional arrangements—giving increased assurance that any power struggle will remain on the political plane. Bilateral arrangements, particularly with the United States, have also brought in one or more "third parties" as balancing elements in some regions.

But in addition to the regional balance of power problems there is now a world balance of power problem first clearly apparent at the beginning of World War II. During that war the struggle was between the Axis powers and the United Nations. Now the power struggle is between the communist orbit and most of the states of the free world. While the principal participants (except communist China) on both sides are parties to the United Nations Charter, giving all the mutual guarantees which superficially seem needed to assure mutual confidence, providing there is mutual good faith, yet the world power struggle is with us as a reality.

Nations, National Governments, and Internal Politics. International relations are still predominantly political relations among nation-states. The time has not yet arrived when a nation-state will willingly surrender to a supranational body the power of decision on national "vital interests." While such vital interests may become a subject of consideration by international organizations such as the United Nations, examination will show that by details of arrangements, often procedural and legalistic, states (with the possible exception of the European Coal and Steel Community) have reserved their position so that they have rarely given away any substantial item of sovereign power that they once possessed in fact. Stated perhaps a bit too simply, the politics of regional arrangements is basically still politics among individual nations.

We must be careful to think of international relations as being conducted among governments and by officials who are human beings. Hence they are deeply conditioned by the internal political systems of the participants as well as by the personalities of the statesmen involved. The Constitution of the United States, for example, is a major factor in international affairs. So is the United States system of checks and balances which makes necessary a partially separate program of explanation and discussion to gain support of the United States Congress for a particular foreign policy action—even though the executive branch has already accepted the soundness of the action. Dictatorial states may have fewer complications, but in the long run, the United States way can give equal or greater strength because it can provide that power which Woodrow Wilson described as "the willing cooperation of a free people."

Internal politics must be recognized as a major factor in international affairs. In order to have the privilege of conducting a nation's external affairs, statesmen must "stay elected." Hence the external affairs of a democracy are always conducted with an eye to the next election. No doubt, for instance, Secretary Byrnes' interest in achieving an Italian peace treaty in 1946 was not lessened by the fact that the vote of United States citizens of Italian ancestry would be important in the Congressional election that autumn. Nationalism and the public appeal of internal political opponents castigating a traditional enemy may, for example, gravely limit the freedom of action of statesmen in following their best judgment concerning their country's best interest. And there is no doubt that one state can readily influence the internal affairs of another democratic state by contributing to the success or failure of that state's external policy—and thereby to the prestige, or loss thereof, of the government in power. The statements and actions on the United States internal political scene are studied globally for indications of trends of United States policy. Sometimes they are as significant to foreign statesmen and foreign peoples as the formal statements of United States policy.

Even in undemocratic states internal political considerations may be material factors. For example, the possible damaging effect on a Russian soldier's beliefs by stationing him in close association with Western troops probably contributed to Soviet refusal to assist in the occupation of Japan. Even a dictatorship must pay some attention to the members of the groups and apparatus which maintain it in power and must give some heed to consistency between external and internal policies. And fear of revolution, and even of assassination, may sometimes influence the choice of a course of action by national leaders. Iran's Premier Mossadegh probably· sensed such forces in connection with the impasse into which he led his country during the Anglo-Iranian oil controversy in 1951–1953.

Mechanisms and Techniques. The traditional mechanisms and techniques of international politics are as applicable now, as they were in the days of the ancient Greek city states. One has but to read Thucydides' *History of the Peloponnesian Wars* to realize how timeless are the arts of diplomacy and techniques of alliance and the balance of power. Diplomacy, the statesman's art of using the resources made available to him to the best advantage of his nation, is still the art predominant in international affairs. But its practice is somewhat different from a generation or more ago. Problems of a type which were once bilateral are now multilateral or global, thereby contributing to the great and essential expansion of multilateral diplomacy and international organization. Each state's diplomacy, facilitated by modern communications, is more closely controlled by its Foreign Office. Interrelationships are more complex and detailed, and the diplomat must often be an expert (or the expert a diplomat) in economic, military, or other matters. In a world strained by tensions, the achievement of the diplomat is usually very closely related to the power position of his state.

Negotiation is still the technique through which international business is conducted. But the scope of matters dealt with by negotiation and the number and types of people in the negotiating business have greatly broadened. Consider, for instance, the ramifications of the negotiating process incident to implementation of the United States Mutual Security Program and its system of alliances and regional arrangements. Secretary Dulles, in testimony before a Senate subcommittee, estimated that some 10,000 executive agreements had been entered into in relation to the North Atlantic Treaty alone.[3] This example illustrates the important point that international affairs are now not a matter of limited international contacts between a few individuals dealing principally with generalities, but a business of tremendous operational detail stemming from those relationships usually published as formal agreements phrased in the most general language.

Rise in Importance of Propaganda and International Organization. There are two mechanisms and techniques which, while not new, are expanding in their importance: (1) propaganda and (2) the various ramifications of international organization. The improving technology of communications media (and also more subtle techniques of subversion and black propaganda) now make it more practicable for one state to affect the foreign politics of another through direct appeal to peoples and interest groups within other nations. Also, statesmen may not have as free a hand in foreign dealings because of the public questioning and disapprobation which rapid dissemination of information may bring down upon them at home.

We have discussed international organization at considerable length in preceding chapters. It has greatly increased diplomacy by international conference with its normally wide publicity, making it difficult to work out solutions to delicate and controversial matters. But with the increasing interrelationship in the world, such techniques of multilateral conference and negotiation are essential. The progress toward greater efficiency in multilateral diplomacy is a necessary accompaniment to the gradual transition which seems to be taking place toward increased regional and global cooperation. One of the principal new mechanisms is the formation of permanent multilateral secretariats and staffs (for example, United Nations and OEEC) accompanied by the regularization and standardization of procedures at international meetings, and by the multiplicity of detailed planning and programing actions almost unknown to pre-World War II international affairs. These new aspects of international affairs particularly characterize today's military, economic, and technical arrangements internationally.

International affairs have not developed far along the line of producing

[3] Arthur H. Dean, "The Bricker Amendment and Authority over Foreign Affairs." *Foreign Affairs,* Oct., 1953.

organizations with effective supranational powers. The United Nations and a large number of other political agencies have shown increasing competence in facilitating multilateral diplomacy looking to solution of problems. But we have not reached the stage of world and regional Parliaments.

Objectives of International Relations. The primary objectives of international political action are basically unchanging. They are national security and welfare, with, for some states, expansionism—perhaps excused under the heading of either security or welfare. We deliberately say "national security" rather than "peace" because even the most peacefully inclined peoples will still fight for certain values after other available means of preserving them have proven inadequate. Admittedly there is, and will continue to be, considerable argument as to what constitutes the true values which a nation's statesmen should strive to preserve and improve. Some, for instance, might argue that war may be so damaging to welfare that elements of security should be risked or relinquished in an attempt to prevent it. Others may argue contrariwise. But these types of difficulty do not vitiate the fundamental nature of the two objectives mentioned above.

THE PROBLEM OF ACCELERATING CHANGE

The world has been troubled before with the magnitude of the problems with which international politics dealt. In fact, a continuously troubled world has probably been "normalcy" in modern history except for the long period of the *Pax Britannica* from 1815–1914. Even the latter part of this period was one of tensions and alarms.

We suggest that the unique characteristics of the present and foreseeable future are the rapidity of change, the obscurities of the direction and magnitude of that change, and the difficulties of overcoming mankind's inertia (political, economic, sociopsychological, and military) incident to adjusting peacefully to that accelerating rate of change. "If we could first know where we are, and whither we are tending, we could better judge what to do and how to do it," [4] and we might be less troubled.

The March of Technology. The last decade has seen enormous advances in man's ability to produce, to communicate, and to destroy. National boundaries now often have little relationship to the economic and security realities. They are even less of a barrier to the march of ideas. Technology is not related to competence in the fields of morality and political action.[5] The politically illit-

[4] Abraham Lincoln, June 16, 1859.

[5] "But devotion to science is devotion to science and nothing else. It is an old and exploded view that knowledge is virtue and a more recently exploded view that there is an automatic transfer brought about by study in special fields, that the 'honesty' that a physicist needs (otherwise his physics won't work) somehow leaks into his general attitude to life." D. W. Brogan, *The Price of Revolution,* Harper and Brothers, New York, 1951.

erate can create the destructive weapons and can master and man the mass production process which gives power to a government in its dealings in world affairs. The impact of the quick acquisition of modern technical and industrial developments by the long dormant Arab and Asian peoples is unpredictable —but it is almost certain to mean major changes in world affairs. The nations of the West, with their common denominators in the fields of law, morality, religion, and other values, have long been pre-eminent in world affairs. These common denominators are drawn from a common background of Graeco-Judaic-Roman-Christian traditions and concepts, particularly concerning the position of the individual. But the traditional pre-eminence of the West is now rivaled by nations with other backgrounds and perhaps other values. This is not to prophesy that the golden age of Western civilization is ending. But its unchallenged dominance is ending, and it must set about preserving its existence in the milieu of new forces in the world.

Communications. One of the new forces is the speed and effectiveness of the communication of ideas. Hopes, fears, and threats can now sweep across the globe in a few days. Imagine, for instance, the popular reaction within the United States, and in any other area you choose to speculate about, of a pressing threat of nuclear war. National leaders now have to be wary of statements and policies intended for internal consumption. They may boomerang externally. As a point particularly applicable to the United States, the internal political custom of heated public controversy may not be in the national interest when the subject concerns another nation. Turning to another aspect of communications, the enormous impact of continuous repetition of a selected group of ideas is now a major item in national and international politics. In any conflict short of war the struggle may be decided in the outcome of a contest for the minds of men which only recently became directly vulnerable as a result of modern communications.

The Rise of Asia. Half the population of the world live south and east of a line drawn from Karachi in Western Pakistan to and down the Amur River. The population potential in this area is explosive. Given even elementary sanitation and minimum subsistence, two-thirds of the world's population may live in this area in the next generation. It is conceivable that the revolutionary occurrence of this decade may be not the relationships of the United States and the Soviet Union but the effect of the emergence of India and China in the community of nations.

America's anticolonialism, the communist tactic of attacking old-fashioned and now eclipsed Western imperialism, the Asian adoption of the Western idea of nationalism, and the disruption and opportunities occasioned by World War II have given the world a new and awakened Asia. This once dormant area is no longer willing to let Western power direct its destinies and, because of sensitivity over recent subjection to Western power, may easily be made suspicious of the West. It will be a generation, perhaps several, before the course of Asia is clarified.

The Western world may not understand too well the values and the objectives of Asia. With the differing religious and social tradition will there be continual misunderstanding and conflict with the West? Will differing values placed on the human individual—and different views as to what the individual should honor and value—add an "Asian" problem to the communist problem? [6] Even the clear current difference in Asian and Western economies, the one primarily agricultural, the other primarily industrial, may contribute to differing values and objectives.

Asia is not a unity and the rapid development in this area may include serious intra-Asian conflict. It will be hard for India and China to keep their economic and security interests from clashing. It will be more difficult to avoid intra-Asian friction if Japan returns to a strong position.

Any answers proposed for the questions asked above are highly speculative. But some aspects of the Asian problem stand out fairly clearly. One is the population situation. The other is the facility with which Asians can adopt and utilize advanced technology. Both the manpower resources and the yearning for increased production exist.

The Urge for Better Living Standards. The spread of information about the world has developed a desire for better living standards. Peoples living close to the subsistence level are conscious that something better is possible. Peoples with higher living standards have adopted economic improvement as a primary value. Economic change usually means social change. Both types of change tend to create political change. This change is not necessarily toward communism, but communism finds fruitful soil to till in such situations.

An Age of Revolution? A military revolution involving a change of government or liberation of a subject people is a simple and easily identified affair. But revolutions such as the Renaissance, the Reformation, and the changes in the Western world from 1776 to 1815 were not so easily recognized by the observers in their midst. The world is in the midst of a rapid change which may be called a revolution by historians appraising our struggle from the detached position of 100 years hence.

One of the world's two most powerful states, the Soviet Union, is driven by a revolutionary and materialistic philosophy. This communist revolution strives to move into the crevices created by rapid change in the world. But,

6 C. W. de Kiewiet in "Let's Globalize Our Universities," *Saturday Review,* Sept. 12, 1953, discusses America's backwardness in comprehending the problem of Asia.

quite separately, there seem to be at least three mutually related developments which may, in hindsight, be called "revolutionary." They are (1) the political swing to self-government occurring in Asia and already heralded in Africa, (2) the social-economic changes underway, and (3) the development of international organization and particularly the rapid progress since 1945 in international cooperation on details of economic and security matters. The first two developments are existent beyond a reasonable doubt. Whether the last will really prove so drastic and rapid as to be "revolutionary" is admittedly questionable. But cooperation holds the best hope for meeting successfully the twin problems of economic interdependence and security. The dominant positions of these two related problems are clearly understood by most statesmen and are reflected in the repeated and sincere expressions of desire for trade and peace.

INCREASING ECONOMIC INTERDEPENDENCE

There are certain postulates which are so self-evident that we can accept them with little discussion. Industrialization is necessary for higher living standards. Industrialization brings interdependence of national economies if only for the reason that no nation is self-sufficient in raw materials. Increasing population is made possible by, and usually also brings, both industrialization and interdependence—otherwise the living standard falls toward the subsistence level. It seems safe to forecast that both population and industrialization will increase in the world and hence that the very considerable existent interdependence will increase.

Economic Cooperation Has Not Kept Pace With Interdependence. A case can be made that, except for the United States Foreign Assistance Program, the mechanisms, techniques, and arrangements facilitating economic intercourse in the world have retrogressed since 1914 rather than improved. Exceptions to this statement are the practical elimination of economic barriers between the Soviet Union and Central Europe by measures which contribute somewhat to the exploitation of the satellite states, perhaps the United States Reciprocal Trade Agreements, and some obvious developments in Western Europe. Of these last the Schuman Plan is by far the greatest advance. The OEEC, arising from the United States Economic Assistance Program, has occasioned notable strides forward in the techniques of economic programing on an international basis. But meanwhile increasing world political fragmentation has brought an increase in trade barriers. And the currency and credit arrangements for international exchange have definitely retrogressed since 1914. Again the outstanding innovation is the regional arrangement of the European Payments Union generated out of the United States Mutual Assistance Program—yet this is an inadequate substitute for the convertibility of currency which prevailed before World War I.

The arrangements and political climate for the flow of investment capital certainly have not improved and have in fact deteriorated in some ways since 1914. The sensitive nationalism of new nations, often coupled with socialistic concepts and the precedents of expropriation of foreign-held properties and nationalization of some industries, have made investors in foreign development increasingly cautious. Perhaps more pertinent, World War II left the world with only the United States possessing large amounts of capital which might be exported to further the industrialization of other parts of the world. American investors have had grave doubts as to the adequacy of arrangements for acquiring returns on any such export or of recovering the principal. There has been sufficient opportunity for investment within the United States expanding economy. Hence comparatively little United States capital went abroad in the first years after World War II except in the form of government grants and loans and in private investment in the oil industry. The outstanding exception is investment of United States capital in Canada.

The picture briefly described in the preceding paragraphs and discussed in more detail in Chapter IV has obvious inconsistencies. If the irrevocable trend of the world is one of economic interdependence, due to increasing industrialization, it must be accompanied by arrangements for increasing economic cooperation, free exchange of goods, and a provision of capital where needed. If the means for facilitating and managing this interdependence do not keep pace with the need, the results can be critical and even disastrous.[7]

Underdeveloped Areas.[8] Over half the world measured both in population and in land area can be called "underdeveloped," meaning that capital investment is small, per capita productivity is low, and the standard of living of a large part of the people is at or near the subsistence level. Most of Latin America, Africa, and Asia fall in this category. The economies are primarily agricultural. These areas contain a large portion of the undeveloped raw materials needed to fill the deficiencies of more industrialized states. Hence, at first glance, it appears that the underdeveloped areas and the more highly developed ones should be complementary from an economic standpoint. But the needs for capital do not readily balance with the needs for materials, and the material-producing countries also have ambitions toward industrialization.

The United Nations Charter (Article 55) recognizes that conditions in underdeveloped areas constitute a danger to stability and well-being. It accord-

[7] See *Report of President's Commission on Foreign Economic Policy* (Washington, 1954).

[8] W. A. Brown, Jr., and R. Opie, *American Foreign Assistance* (Washington, 1953), gives clear, concise discussions of underdeveloped areas, economic problems, and many other questions of our interdependent world.

ingly pledges the signatories to promote "higher standards of living, full employment, and conditions of economic and social progress and development." World social and political ferment is most pronounced in underdeveloped areas and it is these areas that have an explosive population potential. The United States interest in the underdeveloped areas is a complicated one and the average citizen is understandably often confused by it. The components of the interest include humanitarianism, expansion of world trade, increase in the supply of raw materials, and combating communism.

The problem of the underdeveloped areas can be broadly stated in two questions: (1) How can industrial and technological progress be furthered so as to yield a productivity keeping pace with social and economic aspirations? (2) How can the relationships of these areas with the more highly industrialized areas of Japan, Western Europe, and North America best be coordinated? The answers have to be worked out in political action within and among states.

Problem Basically Political. Communist doctrine alleges that the economic problem alone will defeat noncommunist civilization and lead to disintegration of the noncommunist economic system and to inevitable war among capitalist countries. There is no doubt that the economic problem is difficult and pressing. Even though capital and technology are provided to underdeveloped areas there is often need for political adjustment within the political entity considered, in addition to the necessary arrangements for movement of capital in order that social and economic aspirations may be achieved. Land reform, which requires internal political action, is an example. Sometimes there may need to be adjustments in local customs and religious practices. Can agricultural production conceivably keep up with the population rise possible if modern sanitation is adopted?

Equally important from the standpoint of the communist prophesies and warning just cited are the problems of markets and provision of raw materials for the industrialized nations. Economic competition often leads to political differences. Reaching for economic objectives can shatter political unity. As an example, few countries outside the communist orbit are likely to go hungry or even accept a lower standard of living in lieu of trade with that orbit, unless there is high tension and a firm belief in danger of immediate aggression.

A closely integrated world economically is bound to be the best world for assuring the economic welfare of the peoples therein. But it is a very dangerous world if it contains possibilities of political tension disrupting this integration, or if it does not develop a better mechanism than at present for guiding and coordinating that integration. The nation that bases its standard of living partially on economic interdependence with other nations becomes inevitably dependent on the foreign economic policies of these other nations and on the economic health of the world as a whole. The very existence of some nations and the standard of living and political strength of many more are now dependent on economic arrangements and relationships beyond the sovereign control of the affected state. It is for these reasons that international economics has come to hold such a cardinal place in international politics. A recession in the United States or a change in its economic policy can cause depression and even financial and political crises in many other states and a depression in Europe would affect prosperity in many parts of the world. There is some tendency to view these facts with reluctance and even to pretend they are not there—or, if there, are not our responsibility. But they are inescapable realities.

THE SECURITY PROBLEM

National security is the predominant consideration of the international policy of most nation-states. In appraising the security problem it is necessary to recognize that each government and each people make their own independent appraisal. Experts on Asia, for instance, have been quick to point out that some Asian leaders and peoples may consider that anything that smacks of the colonialism just discarded is as much of a security threat to them as is communism.

Technology and economic interdependence have rapidly increased the effectiveness of power instruments other than military force. As we have indicated in preceding paragraphs, this increase in potency of such instruments as the psychological and the economic is almost certain to continue. For instance, the power to blockade by political action alone is increasing; witness the Iranian internal difficulties in 1951–1953 directly traceable to inability to sell oil.

But the changed and changing nature of armed force and war is by far the most important aspect of the security problem. We are entering an era when war as an instrument of policy is likely to be generally recognized as too dangerous even for aggressors. Yet armed force as an instrument of policy may determine the survival or eclipse of Western civilization. And while war is not inevitable, there is no assurance that war will not occur.

Armed Force as an Instrument of Policy. It is conceivable that the tensions under which mankind is living today are not just a temporary "phase of history that is going to end tomorrow in a third world war that is just around the corner," but that they will continue, in one form or another, "for a lifetime, or perhaps for several generations or even centuries on end, without being wound up either by a Last Judgment or by a Millennium." [9] We enter this phase of history, about which Professor Toynbee is speculating, with a military situ-

[9] Arnold J. Toynbee, "The Next Step in History," *Look,* Nov. 18, 1952.

ation materially different from prior decades. Hence perhaps the nature of war and the nature of force as an instrument of policy are changing at the same revolutionary rates as are some other elements of international affairs. We mention only three aspects of great change from the recent past: (1) the totality of military requirements, (2) the totality of destructive capabilities, and (3) the importance of readiness.

In the first place, military power now rests on total national mobilization. Techniques have been developed which permit the concentration of a large proportion of national resources, social and psychological as well as economic, demographic, and other, on a military effort. Since there is no absolute security, political decision is necessary to determine what resources will be devoted to security, that is, what "calculated risk" will be taken. This political process is fraught with great difficulties in any nation and with greater difficulties within regional arrangements organized for security purposes.

In the second place, man's technical ingenuity in devising and delivering destruction has now surmounted the barriers which nature once presented to his ability to harm his fellow-men. Distance, space, oceans, mountains, and deserts are now no longer effective blocks to aggression and destructive power. Technology has made it possible to destroy small nations in a few days using only conventional weapons and forces. Any state can be economically and militarily paralysed in a few hours if it experiences, unchecked, the total destructive power which at least the United States and the Soviet Union (perhaps others) now can command or will soon command. The condition of "total destruction facing total destruction" may be perilously near—or upon us. Disparities in technology are not particularly important when both states concerned have enough. Facing the terrors existent in the points that have just been made, it still seems obvious that military force will remain a major factor in world affairs for a long while.

Because of the rapidity with which military force, once unleashed, can achieve objectives unless quickly controlled, military readiness—this third aspect of great change—becomes a factor now much more vital than in any past generation except for those pioneers who lived in constant danger of an Indian raid. Such readiness is expensively measured by any standard, whether that standard be social, economic, or other. This involves problems with which democracies are particularly unfamiliar. It requires a constancy of effort both nationally and on a regional basis which is unprecedented.

The very concept of military power as power for peace used as the background in front of which statesmen work to maintain a world in being and not in fragments is foreign to the basic thinking of most democratic people. United States Secretary of State Dulles, speaking on the art of peace, said:

"Peace requires anticipating what it is that tempts an aggressor and letting him know in advance that, if he does not exercise self-control, he may face a hard fight, perhaps a losing fight." The action of "letting him know" requires both an unequivocal policy position, which was lacking on Britain's part in 1914 and on the part of the United States prior to the Korean aggression, and ready means, which were lacking on the part of Britain and France in 1939 and barely available in the Korean case.

Some Directions of Policy. The nuclear shadow over the world may well make it a superficially calm one. This does not mean it will necessarily be a peaceful world. Prevention of major hostilities is certainly a vital objective. But if avoidance of all risks of hostilities becomes an overriding consideration in world politics, then the security of nations may be eroded successfully by threats and other means short of war. A compromise to alleviate tension can mean dangerous retrogression. A world under the nuclear shadow may, more than ever, be a world of power politics. Forces for conciliation will need to be supported by force or the result may be continual appeasement which in the end could prove fatal.

Obviously the search for an answer to the security problem develops many suggested courses of action, some based on the thesis that because the need exists, there must be a solution thereto just around the corner.

Neutralism is one of the panaceas. The reasons for it vary with individuals and groups of people. For some it is an ostrich-like refusal to recognize the situation, and may be associated with an insistence that less costly means actually exist, if properly used, to alleviate that situation. For some it is a manifestation of fatalism—a feeling that nothing can be done about it, so why attempt to do anything. For some there is hopeful faith that other nations and other peoples will do that which is necessary and adequate. Some nations and governments have internal situations which absorb most of their attention.

During long periods of modern history, security was preserved, sometimes inadequately, by a multiple power balance among nations. But this condition applied almost exclusively to Europe, whereas today the security problem is global. The nature of modern weapons, together with the present combinations of power in the world, do not seem to permit formation, in the near future, of a multiple power balance which would give assurance of peace and stability. Nevertheless, this is a concept which will probably be retained and promoted.

There have been serious suggestions that the security problem be alleviated by multilateral guarantees in which all parties, the feared, the fearing, and the neutral, guarantee to take action against any aggressor—the "Locarno" principle. This is the United Nations concept and is implicit in the Charter. But such an arrangement cannot go far beyond paper promises if it incorporates strong nations which deeply distrust each other. Strategic planning and detailed operational arrangements are needed for timely movement against an aggression. Such arrangements cannot be made by a global organization having within its midst opposing powers and states determined to pursue a neutral course. Nor will one state distrusting another engage in cooperation therewith to an extent to which the action might impair security if the distrust proved warranted. Trust among states is an important element in the security problem. And there is little in history to justify unqualified trust even among traditionally friendly states.

Trust and Regulation of Armaments. If we could move quickly to the millennium, there would perhaps be no armed force in the world. The intervening step is regulation of armaments, and here the prospects are anything but bright. Military power is now based on economic and other types of power. Any nation possessing the basic factors of power can move in a few years to a position of overshadowing dominance unless other powers keep pace. Atomic destruction is now already packaged in small lots as well as in hydrogen bombs. The carrying out of any arrangement on regulation of armaments is dependent upon precision of detailed technical arrangements coupled with a considerable degree of trust in the other states associated in the agreement.

We have a circular problem. The technical aspects of the regulation of armaments may not be solved until trust among nations improves materially. And when trust improves materially regulation may not be such a pressing need. As an example, Canada and the United States once made a regulation-of-armaments agreement pertaining to their common border.[10] But today the trust between these two states is such that the matter of armaments is not a subject for discussion in the sense we are considering it here. It is certain that effective regulation of armaments must be preceded by, and paced by, political actions increasing the degree of trust among nations. From the present outlook this affords a gloomy prospect but not a hopeless one. But certainly the answer does not lie in unilateral disarmament.

The Security Problem of a Democratic State. There are important differences between the security problem of a democratic state and that of a totalitarian state. The government of the democratic state must be sensitive to the will of the people and will attempt to conduct its policies so as to remain in power. The well-being of the individual citizen is a basic objective of practically all democratic states. Security measures are generally viewed as an "economic waste" in that they do not contribute to maintaining and raising the standard of living, even though they do protect that standard from aggres-

10 The Rush-Bagot Treaty of 1817.

sion. Furthermore, associations with other nations for security purposes are often irksome in their details. There is some degree of xenophobia in almost every people, which adds another difficulty to collective security arrangements. For these reasons among others, democracies in their internal affairs and in relations with other nations have the greatest difficulty in maintaining a consistency of security effort. Rather, their security efforts have tended in the past to be a succession of ups and downs. This traditional "up-and-down" policy does not appear applicable to the problem of the present and the future.

The hard truth may be that the security problems of tomorrow's world are sometimes too complicated for even an informed "average" citizen to pass judgment thereon. Yet the democratic process, which is one of the basic values we struggle to preserve, requires that citizens pass such judgments. We are caught in and will continue to live in this dilemma and its nature must be clearly recognized.

COMMUNISM AND INTERNATIONAL RELATIONS OF TOMORROW

Since the awakening of the Western world after World War II to the threat of communism, it has generally been held that the main problem of international affairs is communism both in its aspects of Soviet imperialism and in its threat to the institutions and life of free peoples. Communism has been the source of our principal security problems and of a considerable proportion of world economic problems. It is, however, worth considering that no movement is static and that all movements, even revolutionary ones, change their nature and direction. Furthermore, in focusing on communism we may overlook other problems which contribute to making this an age of peril. One of these may be the rise of Asia discussed above. The apparent emphasis on Asia of the communist drive may reflect a realization of the long-term importance of that area. Another cause for concern, related to the communist threat, may be the ineptitude of nations now called "free" in their effort to collaborate against common dangers. We have reason to be apprehensive of disunity among the free allied nations for communism quickly exploits such differences. Consequently, the pressing problem of the immediate future remains communism.

As suggested above, the communist revolution may change its methods and objectives. But, unless its relative power experiences a major decrease, we are unlikely to know assuredly, in our generation, whether its driving concepts have become any different from those expressed by Lenin: ". . . the existence of the Soviet Republic side by side with the imperialist states for a long time is unthinkable. In the end either one or the other will conquer. And until that end comes, a series of the most terrible collisions between the Soviet

Republic and the bourgeois states is inevitable." [11] The collisions may have started with Greece, Berlin, China, Korea, and others. As "the main aim of the internal policy of the state is the establishment of a Communist society in the USSR, the main task of the foreign policy of the Soviet state according to International Law is the creation of most favorable conditions for the establishment of a Communist society." [12]

No responsible statesman can afford to gamble the future of the United States and Western civilization on a premise that Soviet communism has turned to follow wholeheartedly the principles stated in the United Nations Charter until there is convincing evidence that present policies and ideologies have been abandoned.

What Are the Alternatives of Policy? The alternatives of policy depend initially on the appraisal of the nature of communism. Here opinions differ, not only among groups within states, but also among governments. There is, as previously noted, the question whether this force in the future will be primarily Russian or communist imperialism? It is worthy of consideration that perhaps even the men in the Kremlin do not know. Obviously the initial increment of our policy is one of "containment," because if this force is not at least contained, it may conquer the world. Some may argue that containment is an adequate policy, since forces within the communist orbit will gradually change communism into a condition where it is less lethal. It can be argued that an active containment policy is the only realistic one since, in the foreseeable future, the element of trust will not be existent to make any accommodation practicable, and that quick liberation of communist-dominated areas is not likely to occur short of war.

On the one side of the policy of containment there is a policy of "accommodation"; on the other side is a policy which might be called "liberation." As to the chances for accommodation, one may well ask what assurance there is that Soviet leadership would willingly allow the dynamism of communism to be checked? But even assuming a temporary accommodation, one is impelled to ask what assurance there is that communism, after lulling the world into a state of unreadiness and perhaps bickering disunity, might not suddenly be on the march again? Western statesmen and peoples will not soon forget that since 1939 approximately 600 million people of some fifteen countries have been taken into the Soviet camp. Words are not an adequate guarantee. Communist doctrine sanctions the use of words to beguile. Time-tested actions might bring some degree of trust—but hardly in this decade.

[11] "Stalin on Revolution," by Historicus, *Foreign Affairs*, Jan., 1949.
[12] Quoted from a publication of the Institute of Law of the Academy of Sciences of the USSR in an article by Samson Soloveitchik in University of Kansas *Law Review*, Summer, 1953. Note the indicated Soviet definition of international law.

There is perhaps an in-between policy of "containment-accommodation" under which the United States and the free world will resist any further encroachment, will strengthen the free world, and will negotiate on specific, clearly delineated issues on which it may be to the mutual advantage of the communist orbit and the Western Powers to reach some agreement.

As to the liberation policy, this implies that positive things can be done to draw portions of the communist orbit away from the controls of Moscow. Undoubtedly this action is desirable from the standpoint of the Western world. But the policy, in addition to other difficulties, encounters the fact that statesmen are very conscious of history. Historical differences over the political control of territory have often generated hostilities. Hence, public discussion of the liberation approach contributes to misunderstandings on the part of some nations in the free world, along the line that the proposal might include use of armed force—perhaps unleashing nuclear destruction.

We have no conclusion as to a choice of policy except to suggest that the three concepts we have mentioned—containment, accommodation, liberation —are each oversimplifications, and progress in the future will probably contain elements of all of them.

IS TIME ON OUR SIDE?

Communists have frequently claimed that time is on their side as they look forward to an "inevitable collapse" of their capitalist enemies as a result of class struggle. This Marxist-conceived hope is implemented with both strategy and action.

It would be suicidal for us to rely on a blind optimism that time is on our side simply because we believe our goals to be higher than those of our opponents. Certainly no millennium lies ahead in the foreseeable future. But it may be helpful to review what constructive aspects can be found to encourage if not justify a faith in the future. Without faith, or at least hope, it is impossible to summon the patience to persist in our search, or the wisdom to find the key to our problems.[13]

As a basis for hope, there are indications that time in its long sweep shows rising progress in international relations. With all the enormous complications existing today and discouraging retrogressions, is it not true that more individuals and more states than ever before are at least aware of the problems in international relations and concerned not only by their magnitude but with their solution? The United Nations, imperfect as it may be, is by its very existence, and by the principles of its Charter, a symbol of hope. Aggressions

---

[13] The Psalmist expressed this faith in these words: "I had fainted unless I had believed to see the goodness of the Lord in the land of the living."

are being thwarted and conflicts settled by peaceful means, or at least short of all-out hostilities. International conferences, even though often stalemated, are evidence of man's reach forward toward reasonable solutions of international problems. The quiet, constructive work of United Nations' agencies in such fields as international health, social welfare, economic cooperation, and technical assistance is ground for encouragement. The whole network of governmental and intergovernmental aid, assistance, and relief, whether financial, technical, or otherwise since World War II, is but another evidence of the growth of international cooperation and sense of interdependence.

It is well to remember also that not all relations between nations are political, economic or military in origin. Cultural interchanges, multiplied by improved communications, often create temporary frictions and misunderstandings, but gradually build up areas of mutual appreciation. The oldest international institution in the world is the Christian Church, which with all its divisions and dissensions, has nevertheless been a force for the unity of mankind. From the Christian Church through the centuries have come manifold movements for the betterment of the world, which have pioneered in realms of education, health, social welfare, interracial justice, and even agricultural and economic improvement. Christendom today is a powerful, dynamic force for the meeting of human needs everywhere.

Christian ethics, if not the Church, have inspired such agencies as the International Red Cross and privately supported foundations which sponsor educational, medical, and other charitable work in many parts of the world without either imperialistic or self-gain motives. A strong case can be made that the Christian religion, with its emphasis on the value of the individual, is primarily responsible for the concepts and objectives recorded in the United Nations Charter and announced as basic tenets of foreign policy by practically all free nations, as well as for the great outpouring of relief whenever a disaster or other pressing human need catches the attention of people of good-will.

Explorations in the field of interfaith relationships in the Western world have begun. It is perhaps conceivable, as Arnold Toynbee suggests—and note that he suggests a long time—that two thousand years from now the unity of mankind may be an accomplished fact, and that historians in A. D. 5047 may say that "the importance of this social unification of mankind was not to be found in the field of technics and economics, and not in the field of war and politics, but in the field of religion." [14]

Though all the efforts of past generations have not been enough to establish firm and lasting peace and security, the method and direction of the struggle of many peoples are indicative of the importance and strength of moral and

[14] Arnold J. Toynbee, *Civilization on Trial* (Oxford, 1948), p. 216.

spiritual forces which are inherent in mankind defying permanent suppression. Sir Winston Churchill, in addressing the Mid-Century Convocation at the Massachusetts Institute of Technology said: "Laws, just or unjust, may govern men's actions. Tyrannies may restrain or regulate their words. The machinery of propaganda may pack their minds with falsehood and deny them truth for many generations of time. But the soul of man thus held in a trance or frozen in a long night can be awakened by a spark coming from God knows where, and in a moment the whole structure of lies and oppression is on trial for its life. Peoples in bondage need never despair. Let them hope and trust in the genius of mankind. Science, no doubt, if sufficiently perverted, could exterminate us all, but it is not in the power of material forces, at present or in any period which the youngest here tonight need take into practical account, to alter permanently the main elements in human nature and restrict the infinite variety of forms in which the soul and genius of the human race can and will express itself." [15]

We should recognize the reality of this spiritual force in humanity pressing toward "peace and good-will among men," while also recognizing the necessity for sustained and sometimes costly effort on the part of governments toward the same goals. Success is without question dependent upon the cooperation of the United States and the peace-desiring free nations. The United States, notwithstanding all its strength, is not omnipotent in international affairs. There are forces and movements which will continue their course and cannot be eliminated by United States policy actions alone. But the United States, acting wisely, can be the deciding factor in so influencing these movements as to prevent disaster and to make progress toward a better world. If we accept these propositions and guide ourselves accordingly, time can be made to be on our side.

THE TRUSTEESHIP OF THIS GENERATION

Over thirty years ago one of America's great statesmen, Elihu Root, commented that the United States had become a world power and hence it was necessary that the American people "learn the business" of international affairs. There is a good case for arguing that his injunction was not then adequately heeded. The enjoinder is even more applicable today and was repeated by Adlai Stevenson in September, 1953. "Foreign affairs has been and will be the most important, the most difficult, the most intricate problem for the Administration in Washington and for us as citizens for years to come." The problems presented by international affairs are much more complicated than

15 John E. Burchard (ed.), *Mid-Century: The Social Implications of Scientific Progress* (Cambridge, Mass.), p. 60. Copyright 1950 by the Technology Press.

when Elihu Root appraised their importance. The West no longer dominates the world, and international affairs are global rather than being primarily problems of Western civilization.

The Problem of Leadership. We live in a situation which must seem contradictory to many thinking Americans. Our country is the world's most powerful nation. The welfare and any assurance of continued existence of most states outside the communist orbit have become heavily dependent on the policies and continually increasing strength of the United States. Yet there are constant frictions and differences both with those states which have taken a stand against Soviet communism and those in the obscure area of being "neutral against" communism. We instinctively look for gratitude and understanding from our associates. Also many United States citizens expect unanimous acquiescence to United States policies even though unanimity may be lacking within the United States body politic. We will not be loved because the world considers us very rich. But we may earn respect. We will not be completely trusted because we are very powerful, because we are young in a leadership position, and because trust among nations is always qualified. But we will be followed, providing we exercise a reasonable amount of wisdom, if only because there is no other nation to exercise leadership. That leadership is the new responsibility of the United States in its own self-interest. It is well to bear in mind that every other nation is acting in its own self-interest as its statesmen appraise the situation.

A "DANGEROUS OPPORTUNITY"

Some Americans search for quick and seemingly simple panaceas extending from isolation (sometimes called, in its new form, unilateralism) to world government. Some of the lunatic fringe suggest preventive war. But even a little imagination leads to the conclusion that destruction of the most obvious problem currently bothering us would still leave many problems and probably create enormous new ones. In an age of crisis there are no easy answers to our nation's problems. There is no panacea, and often no certain assurance that the courses selected in world affairs will be successful.

Here is the point at which this age of crisis taps the shoulder of each citizen. The Chinese character for *crisis* contains the two root characters meaning *dangerous* and *opportunity*. There is danger in almost every aspect of international relations today. Yet this very danger is an opportunity, an opportunity not only for statesmen, for leaders in national political and economic concerns, but for individual citizens on whom a democracy rests. It is an opportunity to search for wisdom, to maintain courage in the face of danger, to lead, with faith in the future.

The United States is in the business of international relations to stay, and it behooves responsible citizens to learn the business. While few citizens can become experts on international affairs (and the history of recent years is full of names of experts now discredited), many can have a solid basis of knowledge to assist their thinking. Because responsible citizens vote and influence opinion on the specific, and often costly, national programs which carry out policies it is important that they have this foundation of knowledge to assist them in their judgments.

The authors have prepared this book realizing full well that no book and no library of books can tell all that needs to be said about international politics. They hope and believe that the elements selected for discussion herein will help the reader toward a reasoned understanding and better judgment concerning a world bound to be troubled throughout our generation.

APPENDIX A

North Atlantic Treaty, April 4, 1949

PREAMBLE

The Parties to this Treaty reaffirm their faith in the purposes and principles of the Charter of the United Nations and their desire to live in peace with all peoples and all governments.

They are determined to safeguard the freedom, common heritage and civilization of their peoples, founded on the principles of democracy, individual liberty and the rule of law.

They seek to promote stability and well-being in the North Atlantic area.

They are resolved to unite their efforts for collective defense and for the preservation of peace and security.

They therefore agree to this North Atlantic Treaty:

ARTICLE 1

The Parties undertake, as set forth in the Charter of the United Nations, to settle any international disputes in which they may be involved by peaceful means in such a manner that international peace and security, and justice, are not endangered, and to refrain in their international relations from the threat or use of force in any manner inconsistent with the purposes of the United Nations.

ARTICLE 2

The Parties will contribute toward the further development of peaceful and friendly international relations by strengthening their free institutions, by bringing about a better understanding of the principles upon which these institutions are founded, and by promoting conditions of stability and well-being. They will seek to eliminate conflict in their international economic policies and will encourage economic collaboration between any or all of them.

ARTICLE 3

In order more effectively to achieve the objectives of this Treaty, the Parties, separately and jointly, by means of continuous and effective self-help and mutual aid, will maintain and develop their individual and collective capacity to resist armed attack.

ARTICLE 4

The Parties will consult together whenever, in the opinion of any of them, the territorial integrity, political independence or security of any of the Parties is threatened.

ARTICLE 5

The Parties agree that an armed attack against one or more of them in Europe or North America shall be considered an attack against them all; and consequently they agree that, if such an armed attack occurs, each of them, in exercise of the right of individual or collective self-defense recognized by Article 51 of the Charter of the United Nations, will assist the Party or Parties so attacked by taking forthwith, individually and in concert with the other Parties, such action as it deems necessary, including the use of armed force, to restore and maintain the security of the North Atlantic area.

Any such armed attack and all measures taken as a result thereof shall immediately be reported to the Security Council. Such measures shall be terminated when the Security Council has taken the measures necessary to restore and maintain international peace and security.

ARTICLE 6

For the purpose of Article 5 an armed attack on one or more of the Parties is deemed to include an armed attack on the territory of any of the Parties in Europe or North America, on the Algerian departments of France, on the occupation forces of any Party in Europe, on the islands under the jurisdiction of any Party in the North Atlantic area north of the Tropic of Cancer or on the vessels or aircraft in this area of any of the Parties.

ARTICLE 7

This Treaty does not affect, and shall not be interpreted as affecting, in any way the rights and obligations under the Charter of the Parties which are members of the United Nations, or the primary responsibility of the Security Council for the maintenance of international peace and security.

ARTICLE 8

Each Party declares that none of the international engagements now in force between it and any other of the Parties or any third state is in conflict with the provisions of this Treaty, and undertakes not to enter into any international engagement in conflict with this Treaty.

ARTICLE 9

The Parties hereby establish a council, on which each of them shall be represented, to consider matters concerning the implementation of this Treaty. The council shall be so organized as to be able to meet promptly at any time. The council shall set up such subsidiary bodies as may be necessary; in particular it shall establish immediately a defense committee which shall recommend measures for the implementation of Articles 3 and 5.

ARTICLE 10

The Parties may, by unanimous agreement, invite any other European state in a position to further the principles of this Treaty and to contribute to the security of the North Atlantic area to accede to this Treaty. Any state so invited may become a party to the Treaty by depositing its instrument of accession with the Government of the United States of America. The Government of the United States of America will inform each of the Parties of the deposit of each such instrument of accession.

ARTICLE 11

This Treaty shall be ratified and its provisions carried out by the Parties in accordance with their respective constitutional processes. The instruments of ratification shall be deposited as soon as possible with the Government of the United States of America, which will notify all the other signatories of each deposit. The Treaty shall enter into force between the states which have ratified it as soon as the ratifications of the majority of the signatories, including the ratifications of Belgium, Canada, France, Luxembourg, the Netherlands, the United Kingdom and the United States, have been deposited and shall come into effect with respect to other states on the date of the deposit of their ratifications.

ARTICLE 12

After the Treaty has been in force for ten years, or at any time thereafter, the Parties shall, if any of them so requests, consult together for the purpose of reviewing the Treaty, having regard for the factors then affecting peace and security in the North Atlantic area, including the development of universal as well as regional arrangements under the Charter of the United Nations for the maintenance of international peace and security.

ARTICLE 13

After the Treaty has been in force for twenty years, any Party may cease to be a Party one year after its notice of denunciation has been given to the Government of the United States of America, which will inform the Governments of other Parties of the deposit of each notice of denunciation.

ARTICLE 14

This Treaty, of which the English and French texts are equally authentic, shall be deposited in the archives of the Government of the United States of America. Duly certified copies thereof will be transmitted by that Government to the Governments of the other signatories.

In witness whereof, the undersigned plenipotentiaries have signed this Treaty. Done at Washington, the fourth day of April, 1949.

APPENDIX B

Charter of the United Nations

We the peoples of the United Nations determined

to save succeeding generations from the scourge of war, which twice in our lifetime has brought untold sorrow to mankind, and

to reaffirm faith in fundamental human rights, in the dignity and worth of the human person, in the equal rights of men and women and of nations large and small, and

to establish conditions under which justice and respect for the obligations arising from treaties and other sources of international law can be maintained, and

to promote social progress and better standards of life in larger freedom,

and for these ends

to practice tolerance and live together in peace with one another as good neighbors, and

to unite our strength to maintain international peace and security, and

to ensure, by the acceptance of principles and the institution of methods, that armed force shall not be used, save in the common interest, and

to employ international machinery for the promotion of the economic and social advancement of all peoples,

have resolved to combine our efforts to accomplish these aims.

Accordingly, our respective Governments, through representatives assembled in the city of San Francisco, who have exhibited their full powers found to be in good and due form, have agreed to the present Charter of the United Nations and do hereby establish an international organization to be known as the United Nations.

CHAPTER I Purposes and Principles

Article 1

The Purposes of the United Nations are:

1. To maintain international peace and security, and to that end: to take effective collective measures for the prevention and removal of threats to the peace, and for the suppression of acts of aggression or other breaches of the peace, and to bring

about by peaceful means, and in conformity with the principles of justice and international law, adjustment or settlement of international disputes or situations which might lead to a breach of the peace;

2. To develop friendly relations among nations based on respect for the principle of equal rights and self-determination of peoples, and to take other appropriate measures to strengthen universal peace;

3. To achieve international cooperation in solving international problems of an economic, social, cultural, or humanitarian character, and in promoting and encouraging respect for human rights and for fundamental freedoms for all without distinction as to race, sex, language, or religion; and

4. To be a center for harmonizing the actions of nations in the attainment of these common ends.

Article 2

The Organization and its Members, in pursuit of the Purposes stated in Article 1, shall act in accordance with the following Principles.

1. The Organization is based on the principle of the sovereign equality of all its Members.

2. All Members, in order to ensure to all of them the rights and benefits resulting from membership, shall fulfil in good faith the obligations assumed by them in accordance with the present Charter.

3. All Members shall settle their international disputes by peaceful means in such a manner that international peace and security, and justice, are not endangered.

4. All Members shall refrain in their international relations from the threat or use of force against the territorial integrity or political independence of any state, or in any other manner inconsistent with the Purposes of the United Nations.

5. All Members shall give the United Nations every assistance in any action it takes in accordance with the present Charter, and shall refrain from giving assistance to any state against which the United Nations is taking preventive or enforcement action.

6. The Organization shall ensure that states which are not Members of the United Nations act in accordance with these Principles so far as may be necessary for the maintenance of international peace and security.

7. Nothing contained in the present Charter shall authorize the United Nations to intervene in matters which are essentially within the domestic jurisdiction of any state or shall require the Members to submit such matters to settlement under the present Charter; but this principle shall not prejudice the application of enforcement measures under Chapter VII.

CHAPTER II **Membership**

Article 3

The original Members of the United Nations shall be the states which, having participated in the United Nations Conference on International Organization at San Francisco, or having previously signed the Declaration by United Nations of

January 1, 1942, sign the present Charter and ratify it in accordance with Article 110.

Article 4

1. Membership in the United Nations is open to all other peace-loving states which accept the obligations contained in the present Charter and, in the judgment of the Organization, are able and willing to carry out these obligations.
2. The admission of any such state to membership in the United Nations will be effected by a decision of the General Assembly upon the recommendation of the Security Council.

Article 5

A Member of the United Nations against which preventive or enforcement action has been taken by the Security Council may be suspended from the exercise of the rights and privileges of membership by the General Assembly upon the recommendation of the Security Council. The exercise of these rights and privileges may be restored by the Security Council.

Article 6

A Member of the United Nations which has persistently violated the Principles contained in the present Charter may be expelled from the Organization by the General Assembly upon the recommendation of the Security Council.

CHAPTER III **Organs**

Article 7

1. There are established as the principal organs of the United Nations: a General Assembly, a Security Council, an Economic and Social Council, a Trusteeship Council, an International Court of Justice, and a Secretariat.
2. Such subsidiary organs as may be found necessary may be established in accordance with the present Charter.

Article 8

The United Nations shall place no restrictions on the eligibility of men and women to participate in any capacity and under conditions of equality in its principal and subsidiary organs.

CHAPTER IV **The General Assembly**

COMPOSITION

Article 9

1. The General Assembly shall consist of all the Members of the United Nations.
2. Each Member shall have not more than five representatives in the General Assembly.

FUNCTIONS AND POWERS

Article 10

The General Assembly may discuss any questions or any matters within the scope of the present Charter or relating to the powers and functions of any organs provided for in the present Charter, and except as provided in Article 12, may make recommendations to the Members of the United Nations or to the Security Council or to both on any such questions or matters.

Article 11

1. The General Assembly may consider the general principles of cooperation in the maintenance of international peace and security, including the principles governing disarmament and the regulation of armaments, and may make recommendations with regard to such principles to the Members or to the Security Council or to both.

2. The General Assembly may discuss any questions relating to the maintenance of international peace and security brought before it by any Member of the United Nations, or by the Security Council, or by a state which is not a Member of the United Nations in accordance with Article 35, paragraph 2, and, except as provided in Article 12, may make recommendations with regard to any such questions to the state or states concerned or to the Security Council or to both. Any such question on which action is necessary shall be referred to the Security Council by the General Assembly either before or after discussion.

3. The General Assembly may call the attention of the Security Council to situations which are likely to endanger international peace and security.

4. The powers of the General Assembly set forth in this Article shall not limit the general scope of Article 10.

Article 12

1. While the Security Council is exercising in respect of any dispute or situation the functions assigned to it in the present Charter, the General Assembly shall not make any recommendation with regard to that dispute or situation unless the Security Council so requests.

2. The Secretary-General, with the consent of the Security Council, shall notify the General Assembly at each session of any matters relative to the maintenance of international peace and security which are being dealt with by the Security Council and shall similarly notify the General Assembly, or the Members of the United Nations if the General Assembly is not in session, immediately the Security Council ceases to deal with such matters.

Article 13

1. The General Assembly shall initiate studies and make recommendations for the purpose of:

a. promoting international cooperation in the political field and encouraging the progressive development of international law and its codification;

b. promoting international cooperation in the economic, social, cultural, educational, and health fields, and assisting in the realization of human rights and fundamental freedoms for all without distinction as to race, sex, language, or religion.

2. The further responsibilities, functions, and powers of the General Assembly with respect to matters mentioned in paragraph 1 (b) above are set forth in Chapters IX and X.

Article 14

Subject to the provisions of Article 12, the General Assembly may recommend measures for the peaceful adjustment of any situation, regardless of origin, which it deems likely to impair the general welfare or friendly relations among nations, including situations resulting from a violation of the provisions of the present Charter setting forth the Purposes and Principles of the United Nations.

Article 15

1. The General Assembly shall receive and consider annual and special reports from the Security Council; these reports shall include an account of the measures that the Security Council has decided upon or taken to maintain international peace and security.

2. The General Assembly shall receive and consider reports from the other organs of the United Nations.

Article 16

The General Assembly shall perform such functions with respect to the international trusteeship system as are assigned to it under Chapters XII and XIII, including the approval of the trusteeship agreements for areas not designated as strategic.

Article 17

1. The General Assembly shall consider and approve the budget of the Organization.

2. The expenses of the Organization shall be borne by the Members as apportioned by the General Assembly.

3. The General Assembly shall consider and approve any financial and budgetary arrangements with specialized agencies referred to in Article 57 and shall examine the administrative budgets of such specialized agencies with a view to making recommendations to the agencies concerned.

VOTING

Article 18

1. Each member of the General Assembly shall have one vote.

2. Decisions of the General Assembly on important questions shall be made by a two-thirds majority of the members present and voting. These questions shall include: recommendations with respect to the maintenance of international peace and security, the election of the non-permanent members of the Security Council, the election of the members of the Economic and Social Council, the election of members of the Trusteeship Council in accordance with paragraph 1 (c) of Article 86, the admission of new Members to the United Nations, the suspension of the

rights and privileges of membership, the expulsion of Members, questions relating to the operation of the trusteeship system, and budgetary questions.

3. Decisions on other questions, including the determination of additional categories of questions to be decided by a two-thirds majority, shall be made by a majority of the members present and voting.

Article 19

A Member of the United Nations which is in arrears in the payment of its financial contributions to the Organization shall have no vote in the General Assembly if the amount of its arrears equals or exceeds the amount of the contributions due from it for the preceding two full years. The General Assembly may, nevertheless, permit such a Member to vote if it is satisfied that the failure to pay is due to conditions beyond the control of the Member.

PROCEDURE

Article 20

The General Assembly shall meet in regular annual sessions and in such special sessions as occasion may require. Special sessions shall be convoked by the Secretary-General at the request of the Security Council or of a majority of the Members of the United Nations.

Article 21

The General Assembly shall adopt its own rules of procedure. It shall elect its President for each session.

Article 22

The General Assembly may establish such subsidiary organs as it deems necessary for the performance of its functions.

CHAPTER V **The Security Council**

COMPOSITION

Article 23

1. The Security Council shall consist of eleven Members of the United Nations. The Republic of China, France, the Union of Soviet Socialist Republics, the United Kingdom of Great Britain and Northern Ireland, and the United States of America shall be permanent members of the Security Council. The General Assembly shall elect six other Members of the United Nations to be non-permanent members of the Security Council, due regard being specially paid, in the first instance to the contribution of Members of the United Nations to the maintenance of international peace and security and to the other purposes of the Organization, and also to equitable geographical distribution.

2. The non-permanent members of the Security Council shall be elected for a term of two years. In the first election of the non-permanent members, however,

three shall be chosen for a term of one year. A retiring member shall not be eligible for immediate re-election.

3. Each member of the Security Council shall have one representative.

FUNCTIONS AND POWERS

Article 24

1. In order to ensure prompt and effective action by the United Nations, its Members confer on the Security Council primary responsibility for the maintenance of international peace and security, and agree that in carrying out its duties under this responsibility the Security Council acts on their behalf.

2. In discharging these duties the Security Council shall act in accordance with the Purposes and Principles of the United Nations. The specific powers granted to the Security Council for the discharge of these duties are laid down in Chapters VI, VII, VIII, and XII.

3. The Security Council shall submit annual and, when necessary, special reports to the General Assembly for its consideration.

Article 25

The Members of the United Nations agree to accept and carry out the decisions of the Security Council in accordance with the present Charter.

Article 26

In order to promote the establishment and maintenance of international peace and security with the least diversion for armaments of the world's human and economic resources, the Security Council shall be responsible for formulating, with the assistance of the Military Staff Committee referred to in Article 47, plans to be submitted to the Members of the United Nations for the establishment of a system for the regulation of armaments.

VOTING

Article 27

1. Each member of the Security Council shall have one vote.

2. Decisions of the Security Council on procedural matters shall be made by an affirmative vote of seven members.

3. Decisions of the Security Council on all other matters shall be made by an affirmative vote of seven members including the concurring votes of the permanent members; provided that, in decisions under Chapter VI, and under paragraph 3 of Article 52, a party to a dispute shall abstain from voting.

PROCEDURE

Article 28

1. The Security Council shall be so organized as to be able to function continuously. Each member of the Security Council shall for this purpose be represented at all times at the seat of the Organization.

2. The Security Council shall hold periodic meetings at which each of its members may, if it so desires, be represented by a member of the government or by some other specially designated representative.

3. The Security Council may hold meetings at such places other than the seat of the Organization as in its judgment will best facilitate its work.

Article 29

The Security Council may establish such subsidiary organs as it deems necessary for the performance of its functions.

Article 30

The Security Council shall adopt its own rules of procedure, including the method of selecting its President.

Article 31

Any Member of the United Nations which is not a member of the Security Council may participate, without vote, in the discussion of any question brought before the Security Council whenever the latter considers that the interests of that Member are specially affected.

Article 32

Any Member of the United Nations which is not a member of the Security Council or any state which is not a Member of the United Nations, if it is a party to a dispute under consideration by the Security Council, shall be invited to participate, without vote, in the discussion relating to the dispute. The Security Council shall lay down such conditions as it deems just for the participation of a state which is not a Member of the United Nations.

CHAPTER VI **Pacific Settlement of Disputes**

Article 33

1. The parties to any dispute, the continuance of which is likely to endanger the maintenance of international peace and security, shall, first of all, seek a solution by negotiation, enquiry, mediation, conciliation, arbitration, judicial settlement, resort to regional agencies or arrangements, or other peaceful means of their own choice.

2. The Security Council shall, when it deems necessary, call upon the parties to settle their dispute by such means.

Article 34

The Security Council may investigate any dispute, or any situation which might lead to international friction or give rise to a dispute, in order to determine whether the continuance of the dispute or situation is likely to endanger the maintenance of international peace and security.

Article 35

1. Any Member of the United Nations may bring any dispute, or any situation of the nature referred to in Article 34, to the attention of the Security Council or of the General Assembly.

2. A state which is not a Member of the United Nations may bring to the attention of the Security Council or of the General Assembly any dispute to which it is a party if it accepts in advance, for the purposes of the dispute, the obligations of pacific settlement provided in the present Charter.

3. The proceedings of the General Assembly in respect of matters brought to its attention under this Article will be subject to the provisions of Articles 11 and 12.

Article 36

1. The Security Council may, at any stage of a dispute of the nature referred to in Article 33 or of a situation of like nature, recommend appropriate procedures or methods of adjustment.

2. The Security Council should take into consideration any procedures for the settlement of the dispute which have already been adopted by the parties.

3. In making recommendations under this Article the Security Council should also take into consideration that legal disputes should as a general rule be referred by the parties to the International Court of Justice in accordance with the provisions of the Statute of the Court.

Article 37

1. Should the parties to a dispute of the nature referred to in Article 33 fail to settle it by the means indicated in that Article, they shall refer it to the Security Council.

2. If the Security Council deems that the continuance of the dispute is in fact likely to endanger the maintenance of international peace and security, it shall decide whether to take action under Article 36 or to recommend such terms of settlement as it may consider appropriate.

Article 38

Without prejudice to the provisions of Articles 33 to 37, the Security Council may, if all the parties to any dispute so request, make recommendations to the parties with a view to a pacific settlement of the dispute.

CHAPTER VII **Action With Respect to Threats to the Peace, Breaches of the Peace, and Acts of Aggression**

Article 39

The Security Council shall determine the existence of any threat to the peace, breach of the peace, or act of aggression and shall make recommendations, or decide what measures shall be taken in accordance with Articles 41 and 42, to maintain or restore international peace and security.

Article 40

In order to prevent an aggravation of the situation, the Security Council may, before making the recommendations or deciding upon the measures provided for in Article 39, call upon the parties concerned to comply with such provisional measures as it deems necessary or desirable. Such provisional measures shall be without prejudice to the rights, claims, or position of the parties concerned. The Security Council shall duly take account of failure to comply with such provisional measures.

Article 41

The Security Council may decide what measures not involving the use of armed force are to be employed to give effect to its decisions, and it may call upon the Members of the United Nations to apply such measures. These may include complete or partial interruption of economic relations and of rail, sea, air, postal, telegraphic, radio, and other means of communication, and the severance of diplomatic relations.

Article 42

Should the Security Council consider that measures provided for in Article 41 would be inadequate or have proved to be inadequate, it may take such action by air, sea, or land forces as may be necessary to maintain or restore international peace and security. Such action may include demonstrations, blockade, and other operations by air, sea, or land forces of Members of the United Nations.

Article 43

1. All Members of the United Nations, in order to contribute to the maintenance of international peace and security, undertake to make available to the Security Council, on its call and in accordance with a special agreement or agreements, armed forces, assistance, and facilities, including rights of passage, necessary for the purpose of maintaining international peace and security.

2. Such agreement or agreements shall govern the numbers and types of forces, their degree of readiness and general location, and the nature of the facilities and assistance to be provided.

3. The agreement or agreements shall be negotiated as soon as possible on the initiative of the Security Council. They shall be concluded between the Security Council and Members or between the Security Council and groups of Members and shall be subject to ratification by the signatory states in accordance with their respective constitutional processes.

Article 44

When the Security Council has decided to use force it shall, before calling upon a Member not represented on it to provide armed forces in fulfillment of the obligations assumed under Article 43, invite that Member, if the Member so desires, to participate in the decisions of the Security Council concerning the employment of contingents of that Member's armed forces.

Article 45

In order to enable the United Nations to take urgent military measures, Members shall hold immediately available national air-force contingents for combined international enforcement action. The strength and degree of readiness of these contingents and plans for their combined action shall be determined, within the limits laid down in the special agreement or agreements referred to in Article 43, by the Security Council with the assistance of the Military Staff Committee.

Article 46

Plans for the application of armed force shall be made by the Security Council with the assistance of the Military Staff Committee.

Article 47

1. There shall be established a Military Staff Committee to advise and assist the Security Council on all questions relating to the Security Council's military requirements for the maintenance of international peace and security, the employment and command of forces placed at its disposal, the regulation of armaments, and possible disarmament.

2. The Military Staff Committee shall consist of the Chiefs of Staff of the permanent members of the Security Council or their representatives. Any Member of the United Nations not permanently represented on the Committee shall be invited by the Committee to be associated with it when the efficient discharge of the Committee's responsibilities requires the participation of that Member in its work.

3. The Military Staff Committee shall be responsible under the Security Council for the strategic direction of any armed forces placed at the disposal of the Security Council. Questions relating to the command of such forces shall be worked out subsequently.

4. The Military Staff Committee, with the authorization of the Security Council and after consultation with appropriate regional agencies, may establish regional subcommittees.

Article 48

1. The action required to carry out the decisions of the Security Council for the maintenance of international peace and security shall be taken by all the Members of the United Nations or by some of them, as the Security Council may determine.

2. Such decisions shall be carried out by the Members of the United Nations directly and through their action in the appropriate international agencies of which they are members.

Article 49

The Members of the United Nations shall join in affording mutual assistance in carrying out the measures decided upon by the Security Council.

Article 50

If preventive or enforcement measures against any state are taken by the Security Council, any other state, whether a Member of the United Nations or not, which finds itself confronted with special economic problems arising from the carrying out of those measures shall have the right to consult the Security Council with regard to a solution of those problems.

Article 51

Nothing in the present Charter shall impair the inherent right of individual or collective self-defense if an armed attack occurs against a Member of the United Nations, until the Security Council has taken the measures necessary to maintain international peace and security. Measures taken by Members in the exercise of this right of self-defense shall be immediately reported to the Security Council and shall not in any way affect the authority and responsibility of the Security Council under the present Charter to take at any time such action as it deems necessary in order to maintain or restore international peace and security.

CHAPTER VIII **Regional Arrangements**

Article 52

1. Nothing in the present Charter precludes the existence of regional arrangements or agencies for dealing with such matters relating to the maintenance of international peace and security as are appropriate for regional action, provided that such arrangements or agencies and their activities are consistent with the Purposes and Principles of the United Nations.

2. The Members of the United Nations entering into such arrangements or constituting such agencies shall make every effort to achieve pacific settlement of local disputes through such regional arrangements or by such regional agencies before referring them to the Security Council.

3. The Security Council shall encourage the development of pacific settlement of local disputes through such regional arrangements or by such regional agencies either on the initiative of the states concerned or by reference from the Security Council.

4. This Article in no way impairs the application of Articles 34 and 35.

Article 53

1. The Security Council shall, where appropriate, utilize such regional arrangements or agencies for enforcement action under its authority. But no enforcement action shall be taken under regional arrangements or by regional agencies without the authorization of the Security Council, with the exception of measures against any enemy state, as defined in paragraph 2 of this Article, provided for pursuant to Article 107 or in regional arrangements directed against renewal of aggressive policy on the part of any such state, until such time as the Organization may, on request of the Governments concerned, be charged with the responsibility for preventing further aggression by such a state.

2. The term enemy state as used in paragraph 1 of this Article applies to any state which during the Second World War has been an enemy of any signatory of the present Charter.

Article 54

The Security Council shall at all times be kept fully informed of activities under-taken or in contemplation under regional arrangements or by regional agencies for the maintenance of international peace and security.

CHAPTER IX International Economic and Social Cooperation

Article 55

With a view to the creation of conditions of stability and well-being which are necessary for peaceful and friendly relations among nations based on respect for the principle of equal rights and self-determination of peoples, the United Nations shall promote:

a. higher standards of living, full employment, and conditions of economic and social progress and development;

b. solutions of international economic, social, health, and related problems; and international cultural and educational cooperation; and

c. universal respect for, and observance of, human rights and fundamental free-doms for all without distinction as to race, sex, language, or religion.

Article 56

All Members pledge themselves to take joint and separate action in cooperation with the Organization for the achievement of the purposes set forth in Article 55.

Article 57

1. The various specialized agencies, established by intergovernmental agreement and having wide international responsibilities, as defined in their basic instruments, in economic, social, cultural, educational, health, and related fields, shall be brought into relationship with the United Nations in accordance with the provisions of Article 63.

2. Such agencies thus brought into relationship with the United Nations are hereinafter referred to as specialized agencies.

Article 58

The Organization shall make recommendations for the coordination of the poli-cies and activities of the specialized agencies.

Article 59

The Organization shall, where appropriate, initiate negotiations among the states concerned for the creation of any new specialized agencies required for the accom-plishment of the purposes set forth in Article 55.

Article 60

Responsibility for the discharge of the functions of the Organization set forth in this Chapter shall be vested in the General Assembly and, under the authority of the General Assembly, in the Economic and Social Council, which shall have for this purpose the powers set forth in Chapter X.

CHAPTER X **The Economic and Social Council**

COMPOSITION

Article 61

1. The Economic and Social Council shall consist of eighteen Members of the United Nations elected by the General Assembly.

2. Subject to the provisions of paragraph 3, six members of the Economic and Social Council shall be elected each year for a term of three years. A retiring member shall be eligible for immediate re-election.

3. At the first election, eighteen members of the Economic and Social Council shall be chosen. The term of office of six members so chosen shall expire at the end of one year, and of six other members at the end of two years, in accordance with arrangements made by the General Assembly.

4. Each member of the Economic and Social Council shall have one representative.

FUNCTIONS AND POWERS

Article 62

1. The Economic and Social Council may make or initiate studies and reports with respect to international economic, social, cultural, educational, health, and related matters and may make recommendations with respect to any such matters to the General Assembly, to the Members of the United Nations, and to the specialized agencies concerned.

2. It may make recommendations for the purpose of promoting respect for, and observance of, human rights and fundamental freedoms for all.

3. It may prepare draft conventions for submission to the General Assembly, with respect to matters falling within its competence.

4. It may call, in accordance with the rules prescribed by the United Nations, international conferences on matters falling within its competence.

Article 63

1. The Economic and Social Council may enter into agreements with any of the agencies referred to in Article 57, defining the terms on which the agency concerned shall be brought into relationship with the United Nations. Such agreements shall be subject to approval by the General Assembly.

2. It may coordinate the activities of the specialized agencies through consultation with and recommendations to such agencies and through recommendations to the General Assembly and to the Members of the United Nations.

Article 64

1. The Economic and Social Council may take appropriate steps to obtain regular reports from the specialized agencies. It may make arrangements with the Members of the United Nations and with the specialized agencies to obtain reports

on the steps taken to give effect to its own recommendations and to recommendations on matters falling within its competence made by the General Assembly.

2. It may communicate its observations on these reports to the General Assembly.

Article 65

The Economic and Social Council may furnish information to the Security Council and shall assist the Security Council upon its request.

Article 66

1. The Economic and Social Council shall perform such functions as fall within its competence in connection with the carrying out of the recommendations of the General Assembly.

2. It may, with the approval of the General Assembly, perform services at the request of Members of the United Nations and at the request of specialized agencies.

3. It shall perform such other functions as are specified elsewhere in the present Charter or as may be assigned to it by the General Assembly.

VOTING

Article 67

1. Each member of the Economic and Social Council shall have one vote.

2. Decisions of the Economic and Social Council shall be made by a majority of the members present and voting.

PROCEDURE

Article 68

The Economic and Social Council shall set up commissions in economic and social fields and for the promotion of human rights, and such other commissions as may be required for the performance of its functions.

Article 69

The Economic and Social Council shall invite any Member of the United Nations to participate, without vote, in its deliberations on any matter of particular concern to that Member.

Article 70

The Economic and Social Council may make arrangements for representatives of the specialized agencies to participate, without vote, in its deliberations and in those of the commissions established by it, and for its representatives to participate in the deliberations of the specialized agencies.

Article 71

The Economic and Social Council may make suitable arrangements for consultation with non-governmental organizations which are concerned with matters within its competence. Such arrangements may be made with international organizations and, where appropriate, with national organizations after consultation with the Member of the United Nations concerned.

Article 72

1. The Economic and Social Council shall adopt its own rules of procedure, including the method of selecting its President.

2. The Economic and Social Council shall meet as required in accordance with its rules, which shall include provision for the convening of meetings on the request of a majority of its members.

CHAPTER XI **Declaration Regarding Non-Self-Governing Territories**

Article 73

Members of the United Nations which have or assume responsibilities for the administration of territories whose peoples have not yet attained a full measure of self-government recognize the principle that the interests of the inhabitants of these territories are paramount, and accept as a sacred trust the obligation to promote to the utmost, within the system of international peace and security established by the present Charter, the well-being of the inhabitants of these territories, and, to this end:

a. to ensure, with due respect for the culture of the peoples concerned, their political, economic, social, and educational advancement, their just treatment, and their protection against abuses;

b. to develop self-government, to take due account of the political aspirations of the peoples, and to assist them in the progressive development of their free political institutions, according to the particular circumstances of each territory and its peoples and their varying stages of advancement;

c. to further international peace and security;

d. to promote constructive measures of development, to encourage research, and to cooperate with one another and, when and where appropriate, with specialized international bodies with a view to the practical achievement of the social, economic, and scientific purposes set forth in this Article; and

e. to transmit regularly to the Secretary-General for information purposes, subject to such limitation as security and constitutional considerations may require, statistical and other information of a technical nature relating to economic, social, and educational conditions in the territories for which they are respectively responsible other than those territories to which Chapters XII and XIII apply.

Article 74

Members of the United Nations also agree that their policy in respect of the territories to which this Chapter applies, no less than in respect of their metropolitan areas, must be based on the general principle of good-neighborliness, due account being taken of the interests and well-being of the rest of the world, in social, economic, and commercial matters.

CHAPTER XII **International Trusteeship System**

Article 75

The United Nations shall establish under its authority an international trustee-ship system for the administration and supervision of such territories as may be placed thereunder by subsequent individual agreements. These territories are here-inafter referred to as trust territories.

Article 76

The basic objectives of the trusteeship system, in accordance with the Purposes of the United Nations laid down in Article 1 of the present Charter, shall be:

a. to further international peace and security;

b. to promote the political, economic, social, and educational advancement of the inhabitants of the trust territories, and their progressive development towards self-government or independence as may be appropriate to the particular circum-stances of each territory and its peoples and the freely expressed wishes of the peoples concerned, and as may be provided by the terms of each trusteeship agreement;

c. to encourage respect for human rights and for fundamental freedoms for all without distinction as to race, sex, language, or religion, and to encourage recogni-tion of the interd_pendence of the peoples of the world; and

d. to ensure equal treatment in social, economic, and commercial matters for all Members of the United Nations and their nationals, and also equal treatment for the latter in the administration of justice, without prejudice to the attainment of the foregoing objectives and subject to the provisions of Article 80.

Article 77

1. The trusteeship system shall apply to such territories in the following cate-gories as may be placed thereunder by means of trusteeship agreements:

a. territories now held under mandate;

b. territories which may be detached from enemy states as a result of the Second World War; and

c. territories voluntarily placed under the system by states responsible for their administration.

2. It will be a matter for subsequent agreement as to which territories in the foregoing categories will be brought under the trusteeship system and upon what terms.

Article 78

The trusteeship system shall not apply to territories which have become Mem-bers of the United Nations, relationship among which shall be based on respect for the principle of sovereign equality.

Article 79

The terms of trusteeship for each territory to be placed under the trusteeship system, including any alteration or amendment, shall be agreed upon by the states directly concerned, including the mandatory power in the case of territories held under mandate by a Member of the United Nations, and shall be approved as provided for in Articles 83 and 85.

Article 80

1. Except as may be agreed upon in individual trusteeship agreements, made under Articles 77, 79, and 81, placing each territory under the trusteeship system, and until such agreements have been concluded, nothing in this Chapter shall be construed in or of itself to alter in any manner the rights whatsoever of any states or any peoples or the terms of existing international instruments to which Members of the United Nations may respectively be parties.

2. Paragraph 1 of this Article shall not be interpreted as giving grounds for delay or postponement of the negotiation and conclusion of agreements for placing mandated and other territories under the trusteeship system as provided for in Article 77.

Article 81

The trusteeship agreement shall in each case include the terms under which the trust territory will be administered and designate the authority which will exercise the administration of the trust territory. Such authority, hereinafter called the administering authority, may be one or more states or the Organization itself.

Article 82

There may be designated, in any trusteeship agreement, a strategic area or areas which may include part or all of the trust territory to which the agreement applies, without prejudice to any special agreement or agreements made under Article 43.

Article 83

1. All functions of the United Nations relating to strategic areas, including the approval of the terms of the trusteeship agreements and of their alteration or amendment, shall be exercised by the Security Council.

2. The basic objectives set forth in Article 76 shall be applicable to the people of each strategic area.

3. The Security Council shall, subject to the provisions of the trusteeship agreements and without prejudice to security considerations, avail itself of the assistance of the Trusteeship Council to perform those functions of the United Nations under the trusteeship system relating to political, economic, social, and educational matters in the strategic areas.

Article 84

It shall be the duty of the administering authority to ensure that the trust territory shall play its part in the maintenance of international peace and security. To this end the administering authority may make use of volunteer forces, facilities, and assistance from the trust territory in carrying out the obligations towards the Security Council undertaken in this regard by the administering authority, as well as for local defense and the maintenance of law and order within the trust territory.

Article 85

1. The functions of the United Nations with regard to trusteeship agreements for all areas not designated as strategic, including the approval of the terms of the trusteeship agreements and of their alteration or amendment, shall be exercised by the General Assembly.

2. The Trusteeship Council, operating under the authority of the General Assembly, shall assist the General Assembly in carrying out these functions.

CHAPTER XIII **The Trusteeship Council**

COMPOSITION

Article 86

1. The Trusteeship Council shall consist of the following Members of the United Nations:

a. those Members administering trust territories;

b. such of those Members mentioned by name in Article 23 as are not administering trust territories; and

c. as many other Members elected for three-year terms by the General Assembly as may be necessary to ensure that the total number of members of the Trusteeship Council is equally divided between those Members of the United Nations which administer trust territories and those which do not.

2. Each member of the Trusteeship Council shall designate one specially qualified person to represent it therein.

FUNCTIONS AND POWERS

Article 87

The General Assembly and, under its authority, the Trusteeship Council, in carrying out their functions, may:

a. consider reports submitted by the administering authority;

b. accept petitions and examine them in consultation with the administering authority;

c. provide for periodic visits to the respective trust territories at times agreed upon with the administering authority; and

d. take these and other actions in conformity with the terms of the trusteeship agreements.

Article 88

The Trusteeship Council shall formulate a questionnaire on the political, economic, social, and educational advancement of the inhabitants of each trust territory, and the administering authority for each trust territory within the competence of the General Assembly shall make an annual report to the General Assembly upon the basis of such questionnaire.

VOTING

Article 89

1. Each member of the Trusteeship Council shall have one vote.
2. Decisions of the Trusteeship Council shall be made by a majority of the members present and voting.

PROCEDURE

Article 90

1. The Trusteeship Council shall adopt its own rules of procedure, including the method of selecting its President.
2. The Trusteeship Council shall meet as required in accordance with its rules, which shall include provision for the convening of meetings on the request of a majority of its members.

Article 91

The Trusteeship Council shall, when appropriate, avail itself of the assistance of the Economic and Social Council and of the specialized agencies in regard to matters with which they are respectively concerned.

CHAPTER XIV **The International Court of Justice**

Article 92

The International Court of Justice shall be the principal judicial organ of the United Nations. It shall function in accordance with the annexed Statute, which is based upon the Statute of the Permanent Court of International Justice and forms an integral part of the present Charter.

Article 93

1. All Members of the United Nations are *ipso facto* parties to the Statute of the International Court of Justice.
2. A state which is not a Member of the United Nations may become a party to the Statute of the International Court of Justice on conditions to be determined in each case by the General Assembly upon the recommendation of the Security Council.

Article 94

1. Each Member of the United Nations undertakes to comply with the decision of the International Court of Justice in any case to which it is a party.
2. If any party to a case fails to perform the obligations incumbent upon it under a judgment rendered by the Court, the other party may have recourse to the Security Council, which may, if it deems necessary, make recommendations or decide upon measures to be taken to give effect to the judgment.

Article 95

Nothing in the present Charter shall prevent Members of the United Nations from entrusting the solution of their differences to other tribunals by virtue of agreements already in existence or which may be concluded in the future.

Article 96

1. The General Assembly or the Security Council may request the International Court of Justice to give an advisory opinion on any legal question.

2. Other organs of the United Nations and specialized agencies, which may at any time be so authorized by the General Assembly, may also request advisory opinions of the Court on legal questions arising within the scope of their activities.

CHAPTER XV **The Secretariat**

Article 97

The Secretariat shall comprise a Secretary-General and such staff as the Organization may require. The Secretary-General shall be appointed by the General Assembly upon the recommendation of the Security Council. He shall be the chief administrative officer of the Organization.

Article 98

The Secretary-General shall act in that capacity in all meetings of the General Assembly, of the Security Council, of the Economic and Social Council, and of the Trusteeship Council, and shall perform such other functions as are entrusted to him by these organs. The Secretary-General shall make an annual report to the General Assembly on the work of the Organization.

Article 99

The Secretary-General may bring to the attention of the Security Council any matter which in his opinion may threaten the maintenance of international peace and security.

Article 100

1. In the performance of their duties the Secretary-General and the staff shall not seek or receive instructions from any government or from any other authority external to the Organization. They shall refrain from any action which might reflect on their position as international officials responsible only to the Organization.

2. Each Member of the United Nations undertakes to respect the exclusively international character of the responsibilities of the Secretary-General and the staff and not to seek to influence them in the discharge of their responsibilities.

Article 101

1. The staff shall be appointed by the Secretary-General under regulations established by the General Assembly.

2. Appropriate staffs shall be permanently assigned to the Economic and Social Council, the Trusteeship Council, and, as required, to other organs of the United Nations. These staffs shall form a part of the Secretariat.

3. The paramount consideration in the employment of the staff and in the determination of the conditions of service shall be the necessity of securing the highest standards of efficiency, competence, and integrity. Due regard shall be paid to the importance of recruiting the staff on as wide a geographical basis as possible.

CHAPTER XVI Miscellaneous Provisions

Article 102

1. Every treaty and every international agreement entered into by any Member of the United Nations after the present Charter comes into force shall as soon as possible be registered with the Secretariat and published by it.

2. No party to any such treaty or international agreement which has not been registered in accordance with the provisions of paragraph 1 of this Article may invoke that treaty or agreement before any organ of the United Nations.

Article 103

In the event of a conflict between the obligations of the Members of the United Nations under the present Charter and their obligations under any other international agreement, their obligations under the present Charter shall prevail.

Article 104

The Organization shall enjoy in the territory of each of its Members such legal capacity as may be necessary for the exercise of its functions and the fulfillment of its purposes.

Article 105

1. The Organization shall enjoy in the territory of each of its Members such privileges and immunities as are necessary for the fulfillment of its purposes.

2. Representatives of the Members of the United Nations and officials of the Organization shall similarly enjoy such privileges and immunities as are necessary for the independent exercise of their functions in connection with the Organization.

3. The General Assembly may make recommendations with a view to determining the details of the application of paragraphs 1 and 2 of this Article or may propose conventions to the Members of the United Nations for this purpose.

CHAPTER XVII Transitional Security Arrangements

Article 106

Pending the coming into force of such special agreements referred to in Article 43 as in the opinion of the Security Council enable it to begin the exercise of its responsibilities under Article 42, the parties to the Four-Nation Declaration, signed at Moscow, October 30, 1943, and France, shall, in accordance with the provisions of paragraph 5 of that Declaration, consult with one another and as occasion requires with other Members of the United Nations with a view to such joint action on behalf of the Organization as may be necessary for the purpose of maintaining international peace and security.

Article 107

Nothing in the present Charter shall invalidate or preclude action, in relation to any state which during the Second World War has been an enemy of any signatory to the present Charter, taken or authorized as a result of that war by the Governments having responsibility for such action.

CHAPTER XVIII **Amendments**

Article 108

Amendments to the present Charter shall come into force for all Members of the United Nations when they have been adopted by a vote of two-thirds of the members of the General Assembly and ratified in accordance with their respective constitutional processes by two-thirds of the Members of the United Nations, including all the permanent members of the Security Council.

Article 109

1. A General Conference of the Members of the United Nations for the purpose of reviewing the present Charter may be held at a date and place to be fixed by a two-thirds vote of the members of the General Assembly and by a vote of any seven members of the Security Council. Each Member of the United Nations shall have one vote in the conference.

2. Any alteration of the present Charter recommended by a two-thirds vote of the conference shall take effect when ratified in accordance with their respective constitutional processes by two-thirds of the Members of the United Nations including all the permanent members of the Security Council.

3. If such a conference has not been held before the tenth annual session of the General Assembly following the coming into force of the present Charter, the proposal to call such a conference shall be placed on the agenda of that session of the General Assembly, and the conference shall be held if so decided by a majority vote of the members of the General Assembly and by a vote of any seven members of the Security Council.

CHAPTER XIX **Ratification and Signature**

Article 110

1. The present Charter shall be ratified by the signatory states in accordance with their respective constitutional processes.

2. The ratifications shall be deposited with the Government of the United States of America, which shall notify all the signatory states of each deposit as well as the Secretary-General of the Organization when he has been appointed.

3. The present Charter shall come into force upon the deposit of ratifications by the Republic of China, France, the Union of Soviet Socialist Republics, the United Kingdom of Great Britain and Northern Ireland, and the United States of America, and by a majority of the other signatory states. A protocol of the ratifications deposited shall thereupon be drawn up by the Government of the United States of America which shall communicate copies thereof to all the signatory states.

4. The states signatory to the present Charter which ratify it after it has come into force will become original Members of the United Nations on the date of the deposit of their respective ratifications.

Article 111

The present Charter, of which the Chinese, French, Russian, English, and Spanish texts are equally authentic, shall remain deposited in the archives of the Government of the United States of America. Duly certified copies thereof shall be transmitted by that Government to the Governments of the other signatory states.

IN FAITH WHEREOF the representatives of the Governments of the United Nations have signed the present Charter.

DONE at the city of San Francisco the twenty-sixth day of June, one thousand nine hundred and forty-five.

INDEX

Prepared by George A. Chaffee

THE FOLLOWING abbreviations have been used throughout the index in order to save space:

c.	cited
n.	footnote
U.K.	United Kingdom
U.N.	United Nations
U.S.	United States
U.S.S.R.	Union of Soviet Socialist Republics
W.W.I	World War I
W.W.II	World War II

The agencies here indexed have the following names:

ECE	Economic Commission for Europe
ECOSOC	Economic and Social Council (U.N.)
EDC	European Defense Community
EPU	European Payments Union
FAO	Food and Agriculture Organization (U.N.)
GATT	General Agreement on Trade and Tariffs
ILO	International Labor Organization
IMF	International Monetary Fund
NATO	North Atlantic Treaty Organization
OAS	Organization of American States
OEEC	Organization for European Economic Cooperation
WHO	World Health Organization